RUSKIN AND BRADFORD

RUSKIN AND BRADFORD

AN EXPERIMENT IN VICTORIAN CULTURAL HISTORY

The history of the Victorian Age will never be written. . . It is not by the direct method of a scrupulous narration that the explorer of the past can hope to depict that singular epoch. . . He will attack his subject in unexpected places. . .

— Lytton Strachey
Eminent Victorians, Preface

Malcolm Hardman

Manchester University Press

Published by
Manchester University Press, Oxford Road, Manchester M13 9PL UK
and
51 Washington Street, Dover, New Hampshire 03820, USA

British Library cataloguing in publication data
Hardman, Malcolm
Ruskin and Bradford : an experiment in Victorian cultural history.
1. Ruskin, John—Criticism and interpretation
I. Title
828'.809 PR5264

Library of Congress cataloging in publication data
Hardman, Malcolm
Ruskin and Bradford.
Bibliography: p. 391.
Includes index.
1. Arts and society—England—Bradford
(West Yorkshire)—History—19th century.
2. Ruskin, John, 1819–1900—Contributions in the arts.
I. Title.
NX180.S6H32 1985 700'.1'030942817 85-18760
ISBN 0-7190-1765-3

ISBN 0 7190 1765 3 *cased only*

Typesetting by Koinonia Ltd, Manchester

Printed in Great Britain
by Bell & Bain Ltd, Glasgow

Contents

ILLUSTRATIONS

The illustrations are placed between pages 200 and 201

ACKNOWLEDGEMENTS

This book is published with the aid of subvention from the British Academy, from the Twenty-Seven Foundation, from the University of Warwick, and from the City of Bradford Metropolitan Council. I am deeply grateful to all those who have made this possible. The patience and diplomacy of Lord Briggs, of Theo Redpath, of Jeremy Prynne, of Ronnie Mulryne, chairman of the Warwick University English Department, of Barry Smith and Norman Tilley, of Bradford City Libraries, were particularly encouraging at an early stage of these negotiations. Elvira Wilmot, of the Bradford Local Studies Library, and David James, the District Archivist, have compounded my debt by their kindness and erudition; and I owe much, too, to the staffs of the Bradford Subscription Library, the Bradford Mechanics' Institute Library, the Walworth, Manchester, Bradford, Leeds and Halifax Public Libraries, the British Library, the University Libraries of Manchester, Cambridge, Leeds and Warwick, of the Bradford Industrial Museum and the Bradford Art Galleries. Paul Lawson, Principal Keeper of Art at Bradford, and Caroline Krzesinska, Assistant Keeper, Fine Art, have given advice on local buildings, and a great deal of information on local artists and patrons. Jack Reynolds, Clem Richardson, and Dr F. Happey, of Bradford University, extended to me a measure of the enthusiasm and information they have provided for their own students. I am particularly grateful to John Ayers, of the Civil Engineering Department, Bradford University, not only for his knowledge, but also for his continued moral support; and to John S. Roberts, whose legendary grasp of nineteenth century Bradford has set me right on a number of points. Tony Jowitt, of Leeds University, gave encouragement at a time when that seemed in short supply. To all these and others I am indebted for information and guidance. Any mistakes in the book are my own.

Among Bradfordians whose personal memories have been invaluable, I cannot omit the names of Jenny Symes, Doris Bushell, Jack and Peggy Davies, and Annie Midgeley. Constance Naylor has very kindly made available the diary of her grandfather Henry Fearnside, and David Hebblethwaite has supplied much Bradfordian lore.

For access to John Deakin Heaton's diaries, and for vivid insights into the whole Heaton tribe, I am indebted to Bryan and Dorothy Payne. Maurice Le Blanc Smith has been generous with information about his grandparents Alfred Harris and Harriet Tylor, and has also kindly supplied the photograph of Lunefield. For information about David Binns, and for permission to use one of his flower-drawings, I am indebted to his kinsman Christopher Binns. For the photograph of this, and for other invaluable photographic work – including the print of Cheapside, Bradford – I owe thanks to John Ayers, and the Photographic Department of Bradford University. John Ayers has also allowed me to use H. F. Lockwood's unpublished successful design for Bradford Wool Exchange. Andrew Saint, with the permission of the Royal Academy, has courteously provided a print of their lithograph of R. Norman Shaw's rejected design. Keith Parkinson kindly took the photograph of Parkfield House. Bradford City Art Galleries provided photographs of the Rossetti stained glass panel *Abraham and Isaac*, and of Lobley's *The Dole* and *Little Nell*, and very generously gave permission to publish them. For permission to reproduce illustrations of *Venus Verticordia*, and of Lobley's *The Free Seat*, I am indebted to the Russell-Cotes Art Gallery and Museum, Bournemouth, and to the Birmingham City Museum and Art Gallery, respectively. Kenneth Baker not only provided the photograph of Joseph Gott's memorial to William Sharp, as it formerly existed, but has been meticulous and generous in supplying information and advice. For permission to publish the photograph, and for other courtesies, I am indebted to the Provost of Bradford.

Among much other help, two further names must be mentioned. James Dearden, of the Ruskin Galleries, Bembridge, has kindly allowed me to publish extracts from Ruskin's notebooks, in particular from the juvenile Red Books, which exist in transcript at Bembridge. For access to these and to many other invaluable items from that great collection I am especially indebted. David Alston, of the Ruskin Gallery, Sheffield, has provided most comfortable access to the Tylor Correspondence, and to the twelve unpublished MS letters of Ruskin to Alfred Harris. For permission to publish these, I am indebted to the Master of the Guild of St George.

— M. H.

CHAPTER ONE

A WATER-LILY FOR A PRINCESS

> The utmost that Turner ever allows in his foregrounds is a water-lily or two . . . just enough to lead the eye into the understanding of the rich mystery of his more distant leafage.
>
> —*Modern Painters* Pt VI, Ch. X.9. *Works*, VII, 121

Passionate and exclusive attachment was never Ruskin's way with people. But looking back over his life in *Praeterita*, 'I have had, Heaven be thanked,' he wrote, 'many and true friends, young and old, who have been of boundless help and good to me, – nor I quite helpless to them.' Among those he mentions are two of special interest to his later readers. W. G. Collingwood is one: he later wrote the most popular and accessible biography of Ruskin. The other is Alexander Wedderburn. He was co-editor of the Library Edition of Ruskin's *Works*, which remains the standard edition to this day.

Collingwood was generally dear to him, Ruskin wrote, in the realm of recreation and contemplation; 'because he could sing French songs about the Earthly Paradise'. But Wedderburn endeared himself by his activity; and Ruskin chose to characterise him by recalling a single example of that activity, which occurred sixteen years before, in 1871. 'Alec Wedderburn,' he wrote, endeared himself 'because he could swim into tarns and fetch out water-lilies for me, like a water-spaniel.'[1]

That is a strange detail with which to characterise a friendship. Ruskin's details are always significant, however: sometimes in ways that go beyond his conscious knowledge. This makes him a puzzling writer as well as a suggestive one. The incident of the water-lilies is a conscious clue to relations between Ruskin the man and Alec Wedderburn the Oxford pupil who became his future editor. But it also suggests a clue to a relationship even more fascinating: that between Ruskin 'the finest writer living', as George Eliot characterised him,[2] and another equally important Victorian phenomenon: Bradford, 'the most prosperous place on the face of the earth', as it was characterised by *The Banker's Circular* for June 1850.

In his Library Edition of *Praeterita*, Wedderburn provides a footnote which opens up the significance of these water-lilies:

> What happened was this. Collingwood and I were at Brantwood one summer, not long after a visit to Oxford of Princess Alice of Hesse, for whom Ruskin had promised to paint a water-lily. One Sunday afternoon we drove with Ruskin up to a tarn, where water-lilies grew. But those within reach were poor flowers, while those out in the middle looked (and were) fine. Collingwood and I tossed which of us should strip and swim out to them. I won, jumped in, and brought back – I think, with their stalks in my mouth – some of the lilies, Collingwood's readiness and mine much delighting Ruskin.

Thanks to the index of Cook and Wedderburn's Library Edition we may take the clue further. Princess Alice was a daughter of Queen Victoria who by marriage became Princess Alice of Hesse-Darmstadt. She and her brother Prince Leopold shared a measure of their father Prince Albert's social and artistic conscience. In 1871 they consented to act as witnesses to the deed which made a legal reality of the Ruskin Drawing School at Oxford. 'Princess Alice on this occasion,' Wedderburn recalls, 'having examined some of the cabinets "eagerly asked me," wrote Ruskin. . . "to 'lend' her some drawings for her children. So of course I asked if I might make them for her and give them to her, and of course she was good enough to be pleased: and then I asked her to tell me what she would have, and she said 'a water-lily' and some tree stems. And I think I shall do one for her that she'll like. For she verily knows what drawing is."'[3]

Wedderburn had reason to remember this water-lily, for he gathered it. And in due course the Princess repaid Ruskin for his kindness. The indebtedness, and the repayment, were not of the crude and heartless kind proper to ordinary economics. And the outcome of the transaction was too indefinable to be catalogued under the ordinary historical heading of 'influence'. What the water-lily does is to provide a clue to a whole network of conscientious Victorians co-operating with each other in ways known and unknown to themselves.

Octavia Hill first met Ruskin in 1853. By 1864 he was an old and valued friend. With the death of his father in March Ruskin came into his substantial inheritance. He was now in a position to transform Octavia's efforts, on behalf of 'a few friends' among the wretchedly housed London poor, into a pilot housing scheme which would pay for itself and which, with suitable publicity, could become an example for State action. Octavia records that it was Ruskin who insisted on this more radical approach. He himself describes the scheme – envisaged in April 1864 – in *Time and Tide*:

> I bought, in the worst part of London, one freehold and one leasehold property, consisting of houses inhabited by the lowest poor: in order to try what change in their comfort and habits I could effect by taking only a just rent, but that firmly. The houses of the leasehold pay me five per cent.; the families that used to have one room in them have now two; and are more orderly and hopeful besides; and there is a surplus still on the rents they pay after I have taken my five per cent., with which, if all goes well, they will eventually be able to buy twelve years of the lease from me. The freehold pays three per cent., with similar results in the comfort of the tenant. This is merely an example of what might be done by firm State action in such matters.[4]

It was due to Ruskin's close connection with Octavia Hill and her work that Princess Alice came to know her, in 1866. This followed Octavia's first published work: an article for the *Fortnightly* that November. It was written with Ruskin's help, and stressing Ruskin's influence. Others whose imaginations were seized by the article were George Eliot and Thomas Hughes, now famous as author of *Tom Brown's Schooldays*, but then enjoying modest notoriety as the new advanced Liberal MP for Lambeth.

By 1875 Octavia Hill was a famous personality herself, and able to command wide attention. Her sister Emily takes up the story, and shows how Princess Alice repaid a hundredfold the gathering and drawing of a lakeland water-lily:

> *Homes of the London Poor*, by Octavia Hill, brought out in America in 1875, was afterwards translated into German by the Princess Alice of Hesse Darmstadt. General interest was awakened, and Octavia received frequent communications from social reformers in various countries – Austria, France, Germany, Holland, Ireland, Italy, Norway, Sweden, Switzerland; and housing improvements were set on foot

in many cases – notably in Holland.

In Amsterdam a town-planning scheme covering many acres was initiated on the outskirts of the city. In January 1928 no less than 28,648 dwellings had been built. The 'Octavia Hill System' has been adopted over the whole planned extension of the city. It is carried on by fifteen inspectors, of whom fourteen are women, with six assistants. Special attention is given to the cases of families who have been removed from condemned houses and cellar dwellings.[5]

'Condemned houses and cellar dwellings': these were all too frequent aspects of Victorian 'architecture': not least in an ugly boomtown like Bradford, one of the fastest growing and most chaotic centres of activity in the world during the mid-century. Engels was not alone in calling it a 'filthy hole'.[6] But it is because there were more intelligent forces also at work in Victorian Bradford that it deserves attention. It is these forces which make Bradford an irreducible factor in this story of the Princess and the water-lily. For how did Octavia herself become a Going Concern? How was she lifted out of the close côterie of literary eccentrics and artistic ladies? Her biographer and relative William Thomson Hill gives the answer in his chapter 'Rough Road to Fame':

Some signal mark of success can be noted in most careers. In Octavia's case there is no such dramatic moment as came, for example, to the author of *Pickwick*, or comes to a lonely adventurer returning from far-off places to a tumult of cheers. The date of her coming into the public eye can, however, be stated precisely. It was in the autumn of 1869.

Octavia was staying with friends in Bradford, where she was to see the new model village of Saltaire [actually in process of creation from the early 1850s]. A dinner party had been fixed for September 17. She found that several influential people had been asked to meet her; and in November she wrote to Maurice [Rev. F. D. Maurice, founder of the Working Men's College, and Octavia's chosen pastor] about 'the perils of success'. . .

. . . Among eager personalities and swift moments of the national life Octavia Hill attempted something which nobody else had yet tried to do. She succeeded; and recognition came early enough in life [she was still only 30 in September 1869] to enable her to make it serve wider purposes.[7]

Public 'recognition' – and all the necessary if ambiguous ballyhoo which went with it, was the gift to Octavia Hill of the same group of hard-headed, active and intelligent Bradfordians whom Ruskin had met in March 1859 and again in April 1864. These two dates were merely the high points of his contact with the Bradford middle-class, which was international in composition and cosmopolitan in outlook. He had tried to seize their imagination in favour of a new Design School on his first visit. His second Bradford lecture was on 'The relation of the architecture of public buildings to daily life'. On both occasions he told them they were not ambitious enough. Commanding as their international influence was at that time in textiles and in armaments, and in railway rolling stock, they had it in them to become 'more influential for all kinds of good than many lecturers on art, or many treatise-writers on morality'. Supreme votaries of the Goddess of Getting-on, they knew how to 'attract attention'. Their interests were commercial, but he was not there to deride them for that: 'one does not see why feeding the hungry and clothing the naked should ever become base businesses, even when engaged in on a large scale. . . Are not all forms of heroism conceivable in doing these serviceable deeds?'[8]

He was not preaching to an audience of ignorant philistines, but to one of the liveliest and most intelligent communities of the nineteenth century. His contact with Bradford was an essential part of his own education. Equally important, many Bradfordians were interested in allowing the influence of his lectures and books to make a contribution to their own ongoing debate, which was of the most alertly educated kind. Bradford's position and survival demanded intelligence and alertness. 'Think on' was the popular form of greeting in the place; and there were good reasons for the custom.

In this particular matter of the launching of Octavia Hill, a pattern emerges. It was made possible by an alliance between the Harris clan – conservative bankers of the Bradford Old Bank – and those middle-class Radical reformers, the Kell brothers, who were 'skilled manupulators of public opinion'.[9] Nor was the personal element lacking. The most active and intelligent of the Harrisses was Alfred Harris, known in Bradford as Alfred Harris junior, to distinguish him from his uncle Alfred. It was with his sister Mary Harris, resident in Dulwich and an active member of the Society of Friends, that Octavia Hill corresponded very regularly over a period of twenty years, from the early 1850s. To Mary Harris Octavia chronicled 'not merely the events in her life, but many of her deepest thoughts and serious questionings. . . [Miss Harris's] spiritual nature and complete sympathy were of untold help'.[10] Alfred's first wife, Harriet, also a Friend, died in December 1865. She had welcomed Ruskin into her Bradford home in April 1864. He found her character, and early death, deeply moving. One of her brothers was Alfred Tylor of Carshalton, the noted geologist, and one of Ruskin's most valued friends. Another brother, Louis Tylor, resident in Bradford, was quite close to Bradford's famous MP W. E. Forster. Forster, too, had been reared as a Friend, but was compelled by the rules of the Society to forego full membership on his marriage, in 1850, to Jane Arnold, the poet Matthew's favourite sister.

A web of connections and co-operations begins to emerge; and the commercial and intellectual life of Bradford is an essential part of it.[11]

Wedderburn's collaborator on the Library Edition of Ruskin's *Works* was E. T. Cook. He provided the introductions to the various volumes, and much of the editorial documentation. When Cook came to write his two-volume *Life* of Ruskin, in 1911, Bradford did not qualify for an entry in the index. Cook and Wedderburn's extensive notes and references for the Library Edition shed little more light on Bradford. Only the most careful scrutiny of the small print serves to unearth a fact which must have helped to motivate Ruskin's faith in Bradford. It is in a footnote to a page of Volume XXXVI, picturesquely headlined *Swiss October* by the editors. This footnote cites a letter of October 1859 from Ruskin's father, who cites a letter from his son. A gentleman (the name is suppressed) at Winnington – a charming spot in Cheshire where Ruskin had many friends – had given Ruskin news of the recent meeting of the National Association of Social Science. Ruskin's editors do not tell us, but this was held at Bradford. Ruskin writes:

> Mr —— told me last night that at the Social-Science meeting one of the principal Speakers said that if my recommendations as to the Employment of the workmen had been adopted, there would never have been any Strikes; and that this reference and statement were accepted as quite just and true by the members of the meeting. The whole discussion in which this occurs is omitted in the *Times*.

And Ruskin senior comments drily: 'Of course the *Times* omits what is regards as of minor importance.'[12]

Bradford remained 'of minor importance' in the eyes of the expensively educated. It could not be guessed from Cook and Wedderburn's Library Edition, for instance, that the very first intelligent appreciation and advocacy of Ruskin's social essays entitled *Unto This Last* was made, as they appeared in *The Cornhill* of 1860 to screams of execration from most other reviewers, in the pages of the *Bradford Observer*, edited by W. E. Forster's good friend William Byles. It was thanks to the growing influence on the *Leeds Mercury* of Forster's other journalist friend, T. Wemyss Reid, that Ruskin's articles *Time and Tide*, with their account of Octavia's housing work, appeared in that paper during 1867. *The Scotsman* had dropped them like a hot potato after two issues. The only other paper to take the series was the *Manchester Examiner and Times*, which had been foremost in denouncing *Unto This Last* in 1860, but had warmed a little to Ruskin after his lectures of 1864 in Manchester, published the same year as *Sesame and Lilies*. Ruskin was much blunter and kindlier in person than in print. He learnt something from the experience of delivering distinctive lectures in Manchester and Bradford; and his mainly middle-class audiences there thought him much less of a monster after experiencing the charm and humour of his living presence. This is why it is important not to rely on the published versions of the lectures as evidence of audience reaction.

W. G. Collingwood's biography of Ruskin barely mentions his Bradford appearance of 1859 or the fortunes of the Design School with which he and his audience were concerned. Yet W. E. Forster followed those fortunes with some anxiety and learnt much from them as to the limits of voluntary effort in education. They revealed some more of those gaps in the system which it would be the business of his Education Act to fill. They were made a test case at the International Exhibition of 1862. With the aid of his brother-in-law Alfred Harris and the Bradford artist James Lobley, Alfred Tylor wrote at length on the symptomatic problems of the Bradford Design School in his official report. At the insistence of his colleagues on the international jury, the details were translated for re-publication in their native languages, notably German and Swedish.

On Ruskin's Bradford lecture of 1864 Collingwood's 1911 edition has three sentences. This is the first. Most people interested in Ruskin have hitherto been content to derive their view of Bradford from it: 'He had been invited to lecture at Bradford, in the hope that he would give some useful advice towards the design of a new

Exchange which was to be built, in curious forgetfulness, it would appear, of his work during the last ten years or more.'[13]

This is extremely misleading; as are the extracts on the same topic quoted by the Library Edition editors from the *Bradford Observer* which had its own axe to grind in the matter. The *Bradford Review*, run by no less a man than James Hanson, founder of the country's first publicly maintained secondary school, has an account all the more vivid for being pedestrian in its accuracy. *The Bradford Advertiser*, whose editor was the Chartist sympathiser John Marshall Jowett, gives a report of the lecture so exultantly in agreement with Ruskin's message that even a short quotation from it in the Library Edition would have spared Bradford much opprobrium from Ruskin's biographers.[14]

Collingwood proceeds: 'Indeed, the picture he drew them of an ideal "Temple to the Goddess of Getting-on" was as daring a sermon as ever prophet preached.'

That view has been corroborated by J. D. Rosenberg, who calls the Bradford lecture of 1864 Ruskin's 'finest'. Andrew Saint, the biographer of R. Norman Shaw, calls the same performance, published in 1866 as *Traffic*, 'the most violent and thrilling of his whole career'. This may be true of the published text.[15] Looked at more closely, and with reference to the 'live' context, it becomes less surprising that Bradfordians should have been among the very earliest patrons and friends of R. Norman Shaw, and Rossetti and the Morris Firm. There were also a number of people in Ruskin's Bradford audiences who were among the first to take him seriously as a social thinker. Their very toughness made it possible for them to see his value, undeterred by the weaknesses which thrilled and enraged the more fashionable auditors.

And though not fashionable, neither was this Bradford audience quite out of the world. In 1859 their Unitarian minister Mr Ryland had the job of expressing the audience's thanks: in 1864 the task devolved on the vicar, Dr Burnet. Ryland had helped Mrs Gaskell with her biography of Charlotte Brontë, whose father was Dr Burnet's curate. Skilled orators addressing public-minded professional and business men, and aristocrats of labour – an audience of rhetoricians – they managed to speak extempore, briefly, and very much to the point. They were quite at home with genius. And when a Yorkshire audience has erupted into cheers, laughter, applause, open weeping and cries of 'Hear, hear!' – as they did for Ruskin –

they have probably had a good evening.

Collingwood ends his account of Bradford thus: 'But when he came to tell them that the employers of labour might be true captains and kings, the leaders and the helpers of their fellowmen, and that the function of commerce was not to prey upon society but to provide for it, there were many of his hearers whose hearts told them that he was right, and whose lives have shown, in some measure, that he did not speak in vain.'

That is a rather surprising statement in view of what Collingwood assumes to be Bradfordian ignorance. It becomes less surprising in view of Bradfordian intelligence. To examine the truth of Collingwood's statement will be quite a test of the value of Ruskin's Bradford audience. It might be said at once that the Bradford socialists Fred Jowett and Arthur and Alfred Priestman, alertly 'revisionist' admirers of Ruskin, would figure more prominently in such an enquiry than would Ruskin's mainly *nouveaux-riches* audiences of 1859 and 1864. Fred Jowett became one of the first Labour Cabinet ministers; but he began his working life as a mill-hand. The Priestmans were Quakers; and capitalists by inheritance rather than by effort or choice. Nevertheless, the more intelligent middle-class entrepreneurs of mid-Victorian Bradford were to some extent already implicating what *Traffic* in fact advocates – the gradual abdication of commercial 'kingship' in favour of 'commonwealth'. As many of them gloried in their descent from Cromwellian yeomen, they perhaps understood *Traffic* better than Collingwood seems to have done; whose account of it above has helped to lend credence to the view of Ruskin as a sort of water-colour Carlyle, keener on authority than justice. Jowett and the Priestmans, at least, could appreciate Ruskin's keen satire in *Traffic* on model villages like Saltaire, designed to keep the 'better' class of work people in their place. They could contrast this with Ruskin and Octavia's housing scheme, designed towards the raising of a whole submerged class – the proletariat of the proletariat – by 'firm State action'. It was in such a direction that Fred Jowett worked, in housing and other matters, on the Bradford Council and in the first Labour Cabinet of 1924. Another Bradford Ruskinian with an important job to do in the London of the twenties would be William Rothenstein, who presided over the most creative epoch in the history of the Royal College of Art.

The effects of the debate to which Ruskin contributed – by action as well as words – were not felt overnight. *Fraser's Magazine* of October 1859 had this comment to make on the West Riding, of which Bradford was such an important part: 'If indeed the people were bound together by some cementing tie. . . they might become very formidable in a political point of view'. To examine Ruskin's modest contribution to this development will be quite a test of his real significance. Ruskin's immediate audience – for books and lectures – was mainly middle-class, but came to include also many 'workmen' in his own definition of the term: 'people who must use their heads as well as their hands for what they do'. Most formidable among that body, and particularly in his thoughts while writing *Fors Clavigera*, were the 'Yorkshire operatives'. 'Let the Wakefield and Bradford people look after themselves' became his essential message to them. It was one some of them would be prepared to take; and it typifies the whole direction of his thinking.

With the West Riding in mind, Ruskin looked forward to the day 'when none but useful work is done, and when all classes are compelled to share in it'.[16] He had a great love of princesses when they were charitable and intelligent, and had work to do in the world: not otherwise.

As for his own work, he defined it in *Proserpina*. 'If we think honestly, our thoughts will not only live usefully, but even perish usefully – like the moss' whose task it is 'to form the earth out of which all other leaves are to grow. Not to cover the rocks with golden velvet only' – so much for the "finest writer living" – 'but to fill their crannies with dark earth, through which nobler creatures shall one day seek their being'.[17]

That was a glorious hope, as well as a modest one.

An epochal role in the pages of history would one day be taken by one of those 'children' for whom their mother Princess Alice had begged a Ruskin drawing of a water-lily. This was little Alex, who would become the last Tsarina. Ruskin has something to say even of this. There is 'the apparent. . . the only recognised world history. . . And yet the real history is underneath all this. . . wasting. . . wandering. . . slaying.'[18] For 'under all sorrow, there is the force of virtue; over all ruin, the restoring charity of God'. It was because he had that hope that Ruskin offered a water-lily to a princess and a pair of lectures to Bradford.

CHAPTER TWO

A CHILD OF GENIUS

> I mentioned to you a book which I had been reading in praise of J. M. Turner on landscape painting. I have read it all through with the greatest delight. . . The book is by Ruskin, a child of genius, certainly.
>
> —Benjamin Jowett
> letter of 23 December 1844 to B. C. Brodie,
> on reading the first volume of *Modern Painters*

Modern Painters was published in the first week of May 1843, when its author was twenty-four. It was to be the first of five volumes, of which the last did not appear till June 1860. 'If,' Ruskin had writen in his *Preface* of 1843, 'its real feeling and intention be understood, I shall shrink from no labour in the execution of a task which may tend, however feebly, to the advancement of the cause of real art in England.' He expressed it as his imperative duty 'to come fearlessly forward, regardless of such individual interests as are likely to be injured by the knowledge of what is good and right, to declare and demonstrate, wherever they exist, the essence and the authority of the Beautiful and the True'. These phrases were typical of the writer; and it was typical of Jowett, less than two years older than Ruskin, but already beginning to emerge as the greatest tutor of the Victorian age, to greet them with a blend of humour and tenderness: 'a child of genius, certainly'. There is speculation, as well as protectiveness, in his phrase.

Jowett's insight into Ruskin, and his care for him, are significant in themselves. The circumstances of his boyhood provide a contrast with Ruskin's upbringing which serves to illuminate the qualities of both men. Jowett's family background provides a clue to the historical significance of Ruskin's interventions in the life of

Bradford.

Benjamin Jowett's father may be seen from two points of view. In the light of contemporary political economy, he emerges as an unsuccessful furrier turned not very successful printer and publisher's reader. By 1829 he found it impossible to support his family, who removed to his wife's sister's house in Bath – all but young Benjamin, who remained alone in lodgings in the City of London, that he might continue to benefit from the academic discipline of St Paul's School. This period of independence and perseverance was the making of Jowett. Looking back after 1870, when he had become Master of Balliol College, and was moulding it into one of the greatest of all academic institutions, Jowett might justifiably confide to his notebook certain details on his ancestry, both distinguished and undistinguished, under the general heading *On rising in life*. 'My ancestors lived at Manningham, near Bradford,' he records, 'where they had land, part of which they sold in 1740. They were probably in the condition of yeomen. The Rev Dr Joseph Jowett Regius Professor of Civil Law in the University of Cambridge, who died in 1813, was my great-uncle. He had a brother, Henry Jowett, Rector of Little Dunham in Norfolk, and another brother, John Jowett, a wool-stapler, I believe, who had three sons, clergymen. . .'[1]

Benjamin's paternal grandfather had left the West Riding at the age of seventeen in 1771; but in 1785 he married his cousin Anne Jowett of York, like him two generations away from the Manningham farm: and it was from her family that Benjamin Jowett inherited an estate near Knaresborough and thus became, in 1870, as land was losing its value and prestige, a Yorkshire landowner. He sold it. But he never showed his ancestry more clearly than when as Vice-Chancellor of Oxford in 1882–6, he determined to bring to bear on the Clarendon Press the criteria of cheapness, availability and profit.

Jowett's rise to eminence had not been smooth. It is a moment of difficulty in his career that introduces the second, and stronger, aspect of his own father's life. In 1864 Jowett of Balliol was appointed Professor of Greek. The pietist lobby, outraged at his heterodoxy in the crucial area of New Testament Greek, made the mistake of soliciting the aid of that great Evangelical Lord Shaftesbury in the campaign to deprive Jowett of his salary. Shaftesbury's honour, and religion, were too genuine to make him their accessory. His championship of the Factory Reform movement had shown him to be more interested in good works than in quibbles about faith. Moreover, he had a deeply personal reason for refusing to help them. He regarded Bradford as the scene of his own earliest labours, the cradle of the Ten Hours Bill, and the home of his 'earliest and most efficient friends'.[2] None had been more efficient than Jowett of Balliol's father, Benjamin Jowett senior, who for years had been Shaftesbury's statistical secretary. The initiative belonged with John Wood, a Bradford Tory mill-owner, of Wood and Walker's mills. It was in 1830 that his partner Walker and the now more famous local Factory Reformers Richard Oastler and Rev. George Stringer Bull, all devout Anglicans, had rallied to Wood's call to seek a reduction in the hours of work for children employed in the textile trade throughout the kingdom.[3] It was John Wood who had recommended the failed printer Benjamin Jowett senior to Shaftesbury's attention. And now, in 1864, Shaftesbury could not be induced to betray the son of his old friend and 'matchless' secretary.

Benjamin Jowett senior had died in 1859; Richard Oastler in August 1861. One of the last of the old gentlemen-Chartists, Lieutenant-General Perronet Thompson, MP for Bradford, was not asked to stand again in the election of 1859. These events marked the passing of an era. Gone were the days of the Chartists, with their valiant efforts in aid of political justice for the working classes. Gone too the pioneering days of Tory Anglicans, whose work for social justice had been truly the complement of Chartist endeavours; though in the political arena the two sides had been opposed.

But the early sixties also saw the birth of something new. Fred Jowett of Manningham – who denied any relationship to the great Benjamin – was born in 1864. Margaret McMillan, of Scots parentage and education, was born in July 1860 in Westchester County, New York. For them and other socialist pioneers, Bradford would be the natural place for the foundation of the Independent Labour Party. This 'grew largely from spontaneous local movements in the West Riding', to quote Keir Hardie's biographer. In many ways it 'provided the lynch-pin of the Labour alliance that came into being after 1900'.[4] Like the Factory Reform movement, the ILP was a political group with political battles to fight. But each deserves to be remembered as far more than a political party. In Bradford particularly, Fred Jowett and Margaret McMillan, the pioneer of nursery schools, and the author of *Education through the Imagination*, were able to lead the country in the fundamental areas of child health and nourishment. They infringed Westminster law to do so. The Bradford Council, where socialists held the balance of power, paid the fines. Both as a Bradford Alderman and as an MP and Cabinet minister, Jowett pursued housing and financial reforms of some interest. And he prevailed on Westminster to change the law in such matters. As he himself said, Ruskin's *Unto This Last*, which Jowett first read in his dinner-break at the mill, had made him a 'socialist in all but name'.[5]

Ruskin, in the Bradford of the mid-Victorian period, was most obviously contributing to a debate dominated by middle-class liberals like Titus Salt. With his model village at Saltaire, and his support of the National Reform Union, Salt demonstrates how the twin battles, for social, and for political justice, were still going on in new forms, despite Gladstone's famous complaint of 1860 that these were ' anti-reforming times'; despite Richard Cobden's perception of 1862 that the upper classes were showing a 'reaction. . . against humanitarianism'.[6]

The Conservative Second Reform Act of 1867 would produce some new lessons. The more prosperous working men, who began to be able to vote as a result of this Act, were not in a hurry to unseat their 'betters'. At the same time the trade unions were gradually growing in strength and respectability. Both political and social justice seemed to be slowly on the increase without too much cause for alarm. It is in this light that one should view what at first seems one of Ruskin's more startling gifts to Victorian Bradford.

When Octavia Hill was dined and fêted by the Bradfordian publicists the Kell brothers, in 1869, she was also introduced to Dr J. H. Bridges, physician to the Bradford Infirmary. Before 1867 the Kells had been leading lights of the National Reform Union, pledged to the doctrine that political emancipation was the panacea for working-class ills, which trade unionism merely exacerbated. Bridges, on the other hand, a positivist and trade union supporter, had regarded political emancipation as a mere middle-class device for distracting workmen from their true interests: namely better wages and working conditions.[7] That Dr Bridges and Robert Kell should both rally to the cause of Octavia Hill was a promising sign of the times.

'The moment we find we can agree,' Ruskin urged in Dublin in 1868, 'as to anything that should be done, kind or good (and who but fools couldn't?) then do it; push at it together: you can't quarrel in a side by side push.' He had specified 'providing lodgment for people', which 'means a great deal of vigorous legislature and cutting down of vested interests that stand in the way'.[8] John Holmes, the West Riding Co-operator, would recall the essence of this messsage as part of Ruskin's Bradford lecture of 1864.[9] It was in Bradford in 1859 that Ruskin had first made clear how essential such social reforms would be to that 'advancement of the cause of real art in England' for which *Modern Painters* had been begun. Dr Bridges' predecessor at the Bradford Infirmary, Dr MacTurk, had been on the platform for that performance. Later, as chairman of the book-purchasing committee for the Bradford Subscription Library, the good Dr MacTurk, whose prestige was great among all classes, made sure that the book of *Unto This Last* was purchased the moment it appeared. At the time, this was a most eccentric choice.[10] MacTurk might well have echoed the words of the High Master of Manchester Grammar School introducing Mr Ruskin to the boys. He could understand Mr Ruskin's books much better after the short opportunity of hearing him in person.[11]

Ruskin 'has always been a deep digger,' wrote the *Bradford Observer* in April 1864, 'looking not merely to the surface of things. . . but to the springs of human action.' 'It is difficult for a Londoner to realise,' Will Rothenstein would recall of his own Bradford youth of the '80s 'how cut off we were from art and literature and how eventful a lecture was'. He remembered hearing Andrew Lang and H. M. Stanley. 'I was all ears at those lectures.'[12] Such, but magnified, was Ruskin's impact on his Bradford audiences.

Less obviously, he was helping to prepare the way for the socialists of the '90s: and in doing that, he was helping to keep alive, and to reconcile, the twin movements of the '30s: the Anglican crusade for social reform, and the Chartist fight for social justice. A double thread of continuity is visible, even in small things. The Anglican factory reform tradition is recalled by the fact that the younger Mr G.Wood, of Wood and Walker's mills, was among the committee welcoming Ruskin to Bradford in 1859. On the other hand, the most sympathetic report of Ruskin's Bradford lecture of 1864 appeared in the *Bradford Advertiser*, run by a third Manningham Jowett. This lent space to the old gentleman-Chartist Perronet Thompson, who in more radical days had been Bradford's MP. Though he was related to neither of them the terms of John Marshall Jowett's appreciation of Ruskin's lecture would have made sense to Benjamin Jowett senior and would make sense again to Fred Jowett: 'The lecture was a pleasing testimony to Mr Ruskin's belief in man's high destiny on earth as a "Son of God" so commonly ignored by the unbelievers (religious and otherwise) of our day.' Such practical and spiritual passion had been Richard Oastler's and Lord Shaftesbury's, and would also be shared by Margaret McMillan and Keir Hardie, head of the ILP. Hardie, Jowett and McMillan were all three of them inspired by Matthew, Mark, Luke and John no less then by their four modern gospels. Carlyle was particularly precious to the Scots McMillan and Hardie. Jowett valued Morris more highly than they did. All of them derived something from Marx. All of them, Jowett especially, felt the irresistible inspiration of Ruskin's real intervention in their own battles: his brilliant art teaching at the Working Men's College in London,[13] his critique of Bradford liberals made to their face in the days of their glory.

But for Benjamin Jowett of Balliol Ruskin's sheltered upbringing and isolated life meant that he had 'never rubbed his mind against others'. Ruskin, on the other hand, called Jowett's famous translation of Plato a 'disgrace'.[14] It does have the effect of blurring into Victorian rationalism those transcendental, and those naïvely practical, elements, which Ruskin was always eager to bring out in his own renderings of Plato. Ruskin's articulacy was always something less and more than Jowett's intellectual converse. He made a point of humbling himself to receive inspiration from a great range of people. Some of the more eminent were his friends Henry Acland, Regius Professor of Medicine at Oxford; John Simon, Medical Officer to the Privy Council; William Cowper (later Lord Mount-Temple), Vice-President of the Committee of Council on Education. For hours at a time Ruskin would give childlike attentiveness to his 'Master' Carlyle; or with nearly equal patience and politeness would interview an eleven year old apprentice,[15] a street sweeper or the Marchioness of Waterford. And he would digest such information in long meditative silences, afoot on Whernside or the Alps, or in contemplation informed by observation in the train from Ulverston to Oxford, King's Cross to Bradford, or Boulogne to Amiens. The Italian liberator, Mazzini, to whom Mrs Carlyle probably introduced him, called Ruskin 'the most analytic mind in Europe'.[16] The synthesis was a personal one, mystical, yet also practical. Thus, while engaged in 1868 on a study of Greek religion for the lecture series *The Queen of the Air*, he was also active on the Executive Sub-committee for the Unemployed. In the latter activity, he saw the truth, as Cook and Wedderburn put it, of 'Jowett's saying, that the way to get things done is not to mind who gets the credit of doing them' (XIX, xliv). But he could see no discrepency between such decently anonymous employment and the platform performances which Jowett, along with other academics, tended to find so distasteful. 'I have never given myself out for a philosopher'; Ruskin announced – in the *Revision* chapter of *Deucalion*, issued in May 1883 – 'nor spoken of the teaching attempted in connection with any subject of inquiry, as other than that of the village showman's "Look and you shall see".' That was the part of his mind into which Jowett could no more have followed him than he could have followed him onto the platform of Bradford Mechanics' Institute, with its vulgar string of turns, like the Celebrated Blind-Born Sardinian Minstrel and Musical Phenomenon on the Pastoral Tibia Signor Picco, or the Specimens of African Bosjeman Exhibiting their Superstitious Songs and Dances, etc. All that, in every one of its connotations, was for Jowett something to get away from. 'Very poor taste – very poor taste': such is the reaction of Dr Jenkinson to the showy sermon of Mr Herbert in Mallock's *The New Republic* (p. 251). These names are thin disguises for Benjamin Jowett and John Ruskin – and no doubt Mallock, who knew both men, was right in representing Jowett as equally fascinated and repelled by the showmanship that was part of Ruskin's character.

This showmanship was not a new departure of Ruskin's middle years. Nor was the essential message of his 'social' lectures a new discovery of his at that time. The origins of both are to the found among his earliest pieces of writing. These are the precocious notebooks of 1826–9, called the 'Red Books' from the colour of their covers. They include an original continuation of the pedagogical Maria Edgeworth's *Harry and Lucy*. This, and the fact that they mimic book printing, underline their self-consciousness, while their command of language – when the child is writing prose – enforces the feeling that perceptions and expression are already fused. The division that does exist lies between the two 'characters' who share their articulation: for 'Harry' tends to be pugnacious, 'Lucy' submissive. It is she who excels at drawing, Harry who delights in riddles. They unite in closest scrutiny of the world around them; but it is Lucy who insists such powers be devoted to geology, Harry who prefers 'running up and down'. While 'Lucy' tends to slide away into metaphor, 'Harry' with a cry of 'Nonsense' insists on particularity. He prefers working out projects in his head to Lucy's rapid verbal response. It is 'Harry', too, who creates already masterly little sentences descriptive of observed phenomena – the pattern that runs through all Ruskin's writings till it achieves its matured perfection in *Praeterita*. The Red Books deserve closer study; but one incident in partucular provides a significant clue to Ruskin's later lectures. It shows Harry and Lucy co-operating to wring laughter from their enlightened, but somewhat undemonstrative mother. She remains Lucy's mother, Lucy herself being startled into laughter by Harry' games:

> The first thing Harry and Lucy did when the morning came was to make some grand scheme It was settled thus Lucy was appointed to go into a bush by which her mother always passed while Harry made a cave. This cave had holes in the top and a chair in it.
>
> Chapter 5
>
> Now Lucy waited till her mother passed the bush and then suddenly darting out seized her and carried her away to Harry's cave where she sat quietly and read. But besides reading her mother had other amusements prepared for her. Harry had taken one of Lucy's rabbits, a parrot, canary, finch, bullfinch, sparrow and robin redbreast, and had put them into a little hole in the bottom of the cave and then opening it all of them marched out the rabbit munching, parrot talking, canary singing, bully cheeping, robin hopping, and went dancing and flying and eating and hopping and jumping all over the green.
>
> Lucy's mother laughed heartily at this and so did Lucy for Harry had kept it a secret even from her.[17]

The scheme is like a sprung trap for provoking an emotive response. Lucy is the decoy, but to Harry belongs the epiphany, with Lucy part of his audience. His embarrassed spontaneity erupts naughtily into an euphoria all the more hectic for being contrived, yet the contriving has its own verve. The essential character of that euphoria is expressed by the individualising of the various present participles, all dependent on the military finite verb 'marched'. Petty rules of grammar are discarded in favour of a vivid truth: for the logic of Ruskin's use of 'opening' is that Harry becomes the creatures he releases. Discipline, yet individuality; energy, yet continuity, are a single movement.

A feature of the incident would seem to be that Ruskin has transformed the earthquake that shatters the hero's cave in Robinson Crusoe into an explosion of creative and individuated energy. But the child's vision is no mere escapist fantasy. For economic reality is already a part of his lawful delight. That eruption from the 'cave' during his 'Cock-Robinson-Crusoe' existence may have been partly 'inspired' by John James's gift of the book. Margaret Ruskin writes on 25 May 1826 to send her husband 'Johns love and he is getting on finely with Robenson Crusoe his cave is almost finished and what can he do to made return for your spending two guineas on him.' What is more, *Robinson Crusoe* was approved for Sunday reading.[18]

It can be seen that the discoveries with which Ruskin confronted mid-Victorian England renewed the earliest articulation of his private life principle: 'My principles of Political Economy were all involved in a single phrase spoken. . . . at Manchester: "Soldiers of the Ploughshare as well as Soldiers of the Sword": and they were all summed in a single sentence in the last volume of *Modern Painters* – "Government and co-operation are in all things the Laws of Life; Anarchy and competition the Laws of Death"' (XVII, 74–5).

'Share' alone sums all those theoretical, legislative and active harmonies of order and allotment that the Greeks called *nomoi* ('laws') and dramatised as *Nemesis*. The stunning and embarrassing 'Tree-twigs' lecture of April 1861, in which the plants characteristically became little creatures, was perhaps the moment the strain of repayment began to be publicly evident in Ruskin's own case. Carlyle found the 'explosions' of that occasion 'manifold, curious, genial', but was not the only one to be alarmed. That same week Ruskin had increased his burden by adjudicating the work of the Bradford School of Design. It was typical of his prodigal expenditure of energy.[19]

In Oxford in 1884, at the very end of Ruskin's platform career, many of his friends became alarmed for his health. The Regius Professor of Medicine was touched to note that 'a very hard and stern man' of his acquaintance could be so moved by his friend the Slade Professor's lecture on art that 'he could not speak for near an hour afterwards'. But he was anxious about the strain such wonders imposed on their performer. Particularly as every applauded eccentricity was distorted at length in the popular press. When in December 1884, Ruskin's nerve and energy failed, it was Benjamin Jowett who nursed him back to life and reason with a 'tender courtesy' worthy of Jowett's own friend Florence Nightingale. He saved Ruskin the poet of nature, whom he knew and loved – 'the gentlest and most innocent of mankind' he called him – from Ruskin the Dionysian showman, whom as a Victorian Professor of Greek Jowett found distasteful, if fascinating. In doing so, the tutor of genius enabled Ruskin to complete his life's work with *Praeterita*.[20] Yet that the child Ruskin wrote so successfully as a Dionysian showman indicates that the man's lecturing style was inevitable, and right.

By 1829, before any 'scientific definitions' on sex or religion could inform his language, Ruskin was an already articulate, yet genuine, primitive who would outlive the possibility and perhaps outlast the unacceptability, of being so. 'Harry's' cave of beasts suggests analogies with the animals of palaeolithic cave-paintings implanted in the very womb of the earth, perhaps that she might bring them 'forth abundantly for the feeding of mankind'. There are fascinating parallels with those Greek legends in which Dionysus, rejected by the daughters of Minyas, appears to them first in the form of a girl to persuade them to join his band of maenads. As they persist in their refusal, the god appears in his own person, filling the room wth visions of wild beasts. But Ruskin's carnival is not only 'primitive'. It is also already articulated in terms of a 'delight' in 'law'. It celebrates the opening phrase of the first psalm, which sings of the blessed man whose 'delight is in the law of the Lord'. It anticipates that state of mind Plato has Socrates invoke as he is about to take up the argument for the divinity of the soul. Those who have attained philosophy are comparable to the true 'Bacchoi' – who have achieved union with the god. We must not abandon logic, but what matters supremely is to be in 'the right way'. Thus *The Two Paths* of 1859 'tried to hold that choice clearly out to [the reader], and to unveil for him to its farthest the issue of his turning to the right hand or the left'.[21]

For Ruskin, man is dust: but ethical dust. All depends on the discriminations of 'volition, which the philosophers may properly call merely a form or mode of force – but then to an artist, the form or mode is the gist of the business. . . It is the fact of the choice, not the equal degree of temperature in the fulfilment of it, which appears to us the more interesting circumstance – though the other is very interesting too.'[22]

The 'choice' might be delusion, and the 'degree of temperature' beget nightmare: but the inevitable cannot be dismissed or analysed in terms of disaster. As Aristotle put it, in a passage of the *Ethics* that drew Ruskin's undergraduate eye, the 'making' and 'faring' are different. There is an eternal distinction between the *poesis* and the *praxis*, the 'creativity' and the 'getting-on'. But he who makes has this comfort. The origin of possibilities lies with him who makes, however well or ill he fares.[23] Ruskin was trained early literally to 'number his days' under the conviction that 'three-score years and ten' are the allotted span of a man's life work. Meticulously, year after year, he counted those allotted days. With the aid of rescue operations by Benjamin Jowett and others, he was enabled to measure out his creative energy all the way to the final instalment of *Praeterita*, published a few months after his seventieth birthday in 1889.

Meanwhile the child's carnival of animals presents the intimate gathering and excited release into ordered jubilation of individual living things.

'His work essentially is this: it is the gathering of material by imagination so as to have in it at least the harmony or helpfulness of life, and the passion or emotion of life.' So in *Modern Painters* Volume 5 would Ruskin describe the human 'creator', choosing words with care: 'Harmony' – form first, and not that without the teleology – 'helpfulness'. From this ethical direction comes intensity of meaning – 'passion', and only then, the complex simplicity in which 'form' and 'meaning' are a single experience: 'the emotion of life'. From the plurality of defined material, through the singleness of indefinable emotion, which in a human creation surpasses, but can never bypass, either morality or economics, we are brought at last to a sense of life as a unity amid the multiplicity from which we started. It is so serious a function, Ruskin reminds us, that it was the last regret of the Socrates of the *Phaedo* that he had 'negligently listened to the divine voice within him', bidding him 'labour and make harmony'.[24] One might ask in what sense the term 'creator' might be used of Ruskin himself.

Harry's animals provide no analogy with a Pygmalion's image. Here is no 'artist' bringing into 'life' the discoveries of his fancy. Nor can we equate them with the puppets of Plato's cave which the philosopher must leave for the light of day. Here is no nascent 'philosopher' stretching his 'wonder' along the logical lines of dialectic till like Plato's it transposes itself consciously into figurative language, or like Aristotle's is set aside to be sought again at the end of the argument, when reason fails as yet to embrace the deity intimate to its own genesis.[25] Ruskin's subject matter will become such that he cannot abandon, or postulate, the wonder in the pursuit of principles; his intellect such as to compel him beyond mere delight in the particulars; the style of his personality such as to discipline and organise his own genius for metaphor. He must all his life run along the delicate edge of 'particular principles':[26] and the least he must be, to do that, is as George Eliot described him, literally 'the finest writer living'. One can analyse his diction, and gesture towards 'poetry', or his arguments and hint at 'philosophy'. Yet the statement that could be made about his uniqueness would be a claim rather than a definition: that he is a 'prophet', not in the cheaply arguable sense of 'foretelling the future' – the result of alert habits of language – so much as in the absurdly profound and costly sense of 'proclaiming God'; or to put it another way, of maintaining publicly the whole truth of the Self. Only such wholehearted 'making' could qualify him to become Aristotle's 'origin of possibilities'. Only such deep digging could unseal in a place like Bradford the 'springs of human action'.

In the words of Chapter Five of the second volume of *Modern Painters* Ruskin wishes the reader to begin the rediscovery of beauty 'as a little child', to return to his 'youngest and least learned days, as those of the most intense, superstitious, insatiable and beatific perceptions' (*Works*, IV, 77). To develop, expound, yet retain clear, this synthesising vision would be quite work enough for a lifetime.

CHAPTER THREE

A LABOURER IN THE VINEYARD

> But what think ye? A certain man had two sons; and he came to the first, and said, Son, go work today in my vineyard. He answered and said, I will not: but afterward he repented, and went. And he came to the second and said likewise. And he answered and said, I go, Sir: and went not. Whether of them twain did the will of his father?
>
> —*Matthew* 21.28–31

The water-lily that Ruskin drew for Princess Alice is a graceful enough symbol of his appeal to artistic ladies and earnest young Oxford idealists like Alec Wedderburn. It provides a clue to a whole network of conscientious Victorian individuals of the influential classes, making efforts by charity, by education, and by example, to 'demonstrate' in the wordsofthe *Preface*to *Modern Painters*, 'the authority of the Beautiful and the True'. Even in the case of the Princess and her water-lily, those vigorous mobilisers of public opinion the Bradford middle class were a necessary, though much less charming, part of the story of Ruskin's contribution to the life of his century. The case of Bejamin Jowett, with his Manningham background and his Balliol foreground, tenderly solicitous of Ruskin the child of genius, yet bemused and even disgusted by that genius's exhibitions of Dionysian showmanship, serves to demonstrate the danger, but also the value, of Ruskin's interventions into a community Jowett preferred to keep at a comfortable distance, as part of his past. Ruskin's lectures in Manchester in 1857 'must be stirring up young minds in a promising way,' George Eliot thought.[1] This, she realised, was an important motive for the man she called the 'finest writer living': and while not agreeing with everything he said, she respected him for the motive. An altogether more convulsive and committed style than anything usually favoured by a Professor of Greek would be necessary to bring to life in the Victorian age the Platonic values of the beautiful and the true.

Ruskin's performance in Bradford in 1864 produced in John Holmes, a listener who recorded his impressions, 'an elysium of pleasure approaching to enchantment'. Next day, he sent Mr Ruskin 'a few facts and publications' on the subject of Bradford's ruling Liberal elite, 'to show him how well he had hit the nail (on their heads)'.[2] This detail typifies Ruskin's appeal to the thoughtful new classes coming into existence with the onward march of education. After the passing of Forster's Education Act in 1870, there began to be more chance that Ruskin's message might reach people still lower down the social scale. Whereas the good Tory gentlemen of the Factory Reform movement for whom Benjamin Jowett senior performed his labours were partly concerned to stabilise society – and their own position[3] – the eager Bradford socialists among whom Fred Jowett worked were busy deploying literature in the interests of social change. Their politics bore a paradoxical relation to Ruskin's theory, in this and other respects. Ruskin had dreamed of a society in which all who wished might be able to 'devote some leisure to the attainment of liberal education and to the other objects of free life'. Because of that dream, he had insisted on durable editions of good books, and on the provision of great public reference libraries.[4] Paradoxically, but perhaps realistically, those working-class socialists fired by Ruskin's dream demanded cheap editions; partly because just like their betters they wanted to own books, and partly in the interests of providing pocket arsenals for invidual campaigners in what they saw as a dialectical struggle.

And below the respectable, and not so respectable, working classes, respectable Victorian society tolerated, and even required, a great reservoir of human misery and need.

There is a connection between Ruskin and the people commonly referred to by comfortable Victorians as the 'dregs of society'. The connection is a significant one. It was made manifest in the West Riding before Ruskin was born. Indeed, it was an instrument of his own begetting and conception.

'Typhus fever', in the words of a Victorian encyclopaedia, 'is a malady which is fatal in a large percentage of cases, and is liable to spring up wherever human beings are crowded together in circumstances of misery and destitution. It is the "gaol fever" of the middle ages, and the fever which follows after the ravages of famine or of war. . . Typhus seldom occurs except among the poorer classes in densely populated places, and only exceptionally affects those who are able to command moderate ease and competence of living'.[5] Though Victorian doctors were not always clear about the fact, the carrier of typhus is the louse.

Typhus was a major scourge of the slums of the industrial revolution, as of other slums of other times. As Barbara Thompson has shown, it was particularly virulent in Bradford in the terrible 1840s.[6] It throve there among other diseases associated with bad air, inadequate drains, and dirty water – none dirtier than Bradford's main water-course, the Bradford beck. This 'stinking stream' as Engels called it,[7] enters the River Aire at Shipley. Just upstream from Shipley is Salt's hygienic factory and model village of Saltaire; a little further upstream the little town of Bingley. In Victorian times Shipley, Saltaire and Bingley, constituting the north-western suburb of Bradford, made their own contribution to the pollution of the Aire: but the overwhelming initiation of the river into foulness was the contribution of Bradford beck, the drain of Bradford.

It is worth noting that a source of the Aire is at Malham, a favourite haunt of Ruskin's. Here, far above Bradford, is Malham Cove, an enchanted wilderness 'so lovely that scarce a branch could be gathered without injury,' he wrote. This hollow 'cove' or 'sweep of interior Coliseum wall' terminates 'a valley which runs up to it from the lowlands, just as a railway cutting enters the piece of high ground which leads to a tunnel; and at the foot of the cliff, where in the railway cutting the tunnel would be, wells out of a low horizontal cleft, not a foot above the water in any place, the innocent little River Aire'.[8]

Below Shipley, where Bradford beck enters the Aire, comes Kirkstall, with its weir and Abbey ruins, beloved of Turner; then the great industrial town of Leeds, Bradford's close neighbour. Below Leeds the Aire skirts Castleford, where one day Henry Moore would be born: then comes Fryston, the seat in Ruskin's day of Richard Monckton Milnes, Lord Houghton. Below Fryston, the River Aire is crossed by the Great North Road, at Ferrybridge: a place of importance in the Ruskin family annals, for it was there, in August 1813, that the hard-worked young businessman, wine merchant and commercial traveller John James Ruskin was, in his own words, 'seized with typhus-fever'.[9]

Typhus was the disease picked out by Thomas Carlyle in that great contemporary of the first volume of *Modern Painters*, *Past and Present*, as typifying most vividly the remorseless organic connection that subsists between persons, despite the machinery of the cash nexus which pretends to replace it. The point was made in one of Carlyle's most famous chapters, *The Gospel of Mammonism*. A *locus classicus* of Victorian social literature, it made a strong impression on Engels and W. E. Forster, to name but two of Ruskin's contemporaries. Of this book Ruskin himself wrote, 'it has become a part of myself. . . in my heart I mark it all'.[10]

> One of Dr Alison's Scotch facts strikes us much.[11] A poor Irish Widow, her husband having died in one of the Lanes of Edinburgh, went forth with her three children, bare of all resource, to solicit help from the Charitable Establishments of that City. At this Charitable Establishment and then at that she was refused; referred from one to the other, helped by none; – till she had exhausted them all; till her strength and heart failed her: she sank down in typhus-fever; died, and infected her Lane with fever, so that 'seventeen other persons' died of fever there in consequence. The humane Physician asks thereupon, as with a heart too full for speaking, 'Would it not have been *economy* to help this poor Widow? She took typhus-fever and killed seventeen of you! – Very curious. The forlorn Irish Widow applies to her fellow-creatures as if saying, 'Behold I am sinking bare of help: ye must help me! I am your sister, bone of your bone; one God made us: ye must help me!' They answer, 'No, impossible; thou art no sister of ours.' But she proves her sisterhood; her typhus-fever kills *them*: they actually were her brothers, though denying it! Had human creatures to go lower for a proof?

It is in the light of this passage from Carlyle that the final words of *Modern Painters* should be read, with their summary of the potential of all human arts to fulfil or maim the destiny of the whole natural world. 'So far. . . as your own prosperity seems to you to issue out of contest or rivalry, of any kind, with other men, or other nations. . . kindred of the earth shall you yourself become; saying to the grave, "Thou art my father," and to the worm, "Thou art my mother, and, my sister." The earth, resisted and elaborately denied, is terminated into a grave: accepted, and nurtured, it awakes as the real garden of resurrection, enabling 'you to claim another kindred than of the earth, and to hear another voice than that of the grave, saying, "My brother, and sister, and mother" '.

The typhus louse is not so comfortable a symbol as the water-lily, but it is just as relevant to an understanding of Ruskin's connection with his age. It might be said that it brought his parents together. There would be a 'ghastly ludicrousness' in such a claim, as well as a measure of truth. But this same element of 'ghastly ludicrousness' is itself important. It characterises a number of the choicer samples of Victoriana – such as the relation between the author of *The Stones of Venice* and Bradford Wool Exchange. It provides an insight into Ruskin's sense of absurdity and horror at the presence of famine and nakedness among the principal manufactures of the most prosperous and progressive society yet known. It is a central aspect of Ruskin's relation with himself. And it summarises the reaction of many twentieth-century readers to him – unable to see beyond the commonplace fiasco of his marriage. That actual phrase, 'ghastly ludicrousness' is Ruskin's own from the *War* lecture of *The Crown of Wild Olive*. He uses it to introduce some thoughts of Carlyle about the terrible farce that is modern war.[12]

The sense that things might not connect of themselves; that any connection which merely occurs may be in terms of 'ghastly ludicrousness': this awareness of Ruskin's may be seen as having to do with his own complex inner nature. But the awareness has little to do with feeble-mindedness. It is a perception of someone phenomenally intelligent and articulate from an early age. And quite as central to Ruskin's mentality is the equally absurd – but exultant – drive to make connections. This has its dangers, and even its own nemesis of ghastly ludicrousness. But Ruskin's feeling that connections are creative acts – that they have to be *made* – is a most valuable insight that takes him quite outside the normal run of Victorian thought. It makes him a little nearer to Newman than to Clough: two names which suggest themselves as his intellectual peers. But Ruskin's Newman-like self-dedication to the Catholic doctrine of free will, with its stress on the importance of works as the only true evidences of faith, was made – and constantly renewed – in the Clough-like suspicion that integrity is founded on nothing; that good works may never be rewarded; and that the end of all things may be darkness. To say that Ruskin himself was 'religious' would be an understatement rather than an exaggeration. Yet in the *Preface* to *The Crown of Wild Olive*, and elsewhere, he performs the profoundly useful task of liberating personal and social morality from the shackles of dogma.

'The "principle" of development through polar relations" is the thing that amazes me so, as found in higher organisms.' Ruskin wrote that in a note to his biologist acquaintance Richard Owen; and went on to characterise himself as a 'clothed sum of segments'. But in a letter to his physican friend Henry Acland, he expressed himself thus: 'I am forced by precisely the same instinct to the consideration of political questions, that urges me to examine the laws of architectural or mountain form. I cannot help doing so – the questions suggest themselves, and I am *compelled* to work them out.'[13]

After a pattern not uncommon in the case of only children, Ruskin was two sons of his father. He was the accepted son who stayed at home, and he was the prodigal. In *Praeterita* he records an incident that suggests quite a measure of his sympathy lay with the tribulations of the son who stayed at home.[14] The aphorism from St Matthew's gospel which stands at the head of this chapter gives a variation on a similar theme. It is notable that Ruskin was making a particularly close study of Matthew during 1859. The aphorism is certainly appropriate to his own case. There was the Ruskin who submitted himself to do his father's will, and the Ruskin who resisted. The first Ruskin would set aside childish plans to make a 'Punches Show' in order to 'labour' at a poem for his father's birthday.[15] He would offer to labour in the vineyard of his father's desire by developing those gifts of aesthetic concentration and biblical exegesis which make *Modern Painters* so extraordinary. But the other Ruskin – neither less nor more real than the former – refused to become a clergyman (his father dreamed of a bishopric for him) or a poet (his father felt he could have been a moral Byron). He vexed his father's love by adventuring into political economy. He made crazy schemes during the winter of 1862–63 – when *Unto This Last* had emerged as a book and the equally vexing *Munera Pulveris* was coming out in *Fraser's* – to abandon his parents' sururban home in favour of a lonely fastness in Savoy. One Ruskin said 'Yes' in daily letters of almost femine sweetness to the father he loved. The other said 'No' in occasional[16] letters of steady cruelty to the father he resented.

Yet it was the Ruskin who refused who really did go to labour in the same vineyard as his father.

The title of *Unto This Last* (1860) refers to the parable of the vineyard. All the labourers in the vineyard, whether they come early or late, must receive – even this last – such payment as is necessary to enable life. 'I will give unto this last,' says the master of the vineyard, 'even as unto thee' (*Matthew* XX, 14). Justice consists in such enabling of every individual and all corporate power. It is the exercise of law through the medium of delight.

It was in response to Social Darwinism that Ruskin, in 1877, clarified for his readers the 'Ideas of Power' of *Modern Painters* Volume 1. 'Plato threw out systems like the gleam on foam,' he said. 'Herbert Spencer throws them out like boys blowing bubbles full of dirty air. My system. . . was wrong too in denial of the delight in Ideas of power. Veneration, desire for exertion, and sympathy are all involved in "ideas of power", and are all legitimate elements of delight.'[17]

Ruskin's reminder that sympathy and delight properly form part of the 'IdeasofPower' of *Modern Painters* Voluem 1 (1843) more closely connects them with the 'Ideas of Relation' of Volume 5 (1860). Such ideas, for Ruskin, had the most pertinent consequences. Those 'labourers in the vineyard' were no spiritual allegory. Thanks to the new time-scale suggested by Darwinism, Christ's remarks about vineyards become contemporary. As Ruskin put it himself, 'Certain labourers in Spain. . . produced from the earth annually a certain number of bottles of wine. These productions were sold by my father and his partners, who kept nine-tenths, or thereabouts, of the price themselves, and gave one-tenth, or thereabouts, to the labourers. . . Then my good father gave all his money to me. . .'[18]

Spanish labourers supplied the Ruskin product. As far as England went, English labourers paid for it. 'You really ought,' Ruskin told his American friend C. E. Norton on Midsummer Day 1886, 'to look at our lovely England again – as a Manufacturing town.' His own first view thereof had been as a juvenile tourist amid the picturesque environs of commercial centres often visited by his father in pursuit of orders for wine. Such towns were where the new money was, and represented a rapidly expanding market that John James Ruskin had every compulsion to exploit. The compulsion – honourably enough – was for the sake of achieving the status of influential spender. It was a not uncommon English pattern, and one which may have revealed itself to Engels, the capitalist financer of Marx. Excellently educated at Edinburgh High School, but thwarted from entering a profession, and drained by years of careful acquisition, John James unhesitatingly placed the whole responsibility for achieving value out of all he cost upon the son.

The strain to his father's health was not only part of the son's cost; it was a cause of his genesis.

John James's own father, John Thomas, son of a prosperous London family, was himself a failed vintner and grocer. He had married Catherine Tweddale, a Scottish minister's daughter. Her mother was a gentlewoman of the Adair landowning family, in Galloway. Living with them as companion and help was John Thomas's niece, Margaret Cock, the dowerless daughter of his sister Margaret who had herself taken a step down by marrying a retired seaman, the landlord of the King's Head, Croydon. To a frustrated climber and bankrupt like John Thomas, his niece was a disgraceful object; but Margaret Cox – as she now styled herself – had his wife's love and respect, and his mother's opinion weighed most with John James. This alliance between the two women is significant. It was an alliance between a gentlewoman and a woman of the lower middle class against pretentiousness and 'getting on'.

In August 1813, worn out by nine years of labour in the wine trade, John James journeyed north to spend a holiday with his parents, and cousin, at Bowerswell in Perth. At Ferrybridge, thirteen miles south-east of Leeds, where the Great North Road crosses the River Aire, he was struck down by typhus fever. Described by nineteenth-century authorities as 'only exceptionally' affecting those 'able to command moderate ease and competence' the disease was the effect of the partly self-imposed hardship of a young man with his way to make in a competitive world. Cousin Margaret sped down to Yorkshire to nurse him, prevailing over the fever by her strong attentions, which included the compromising economy of sharing his room. It was in such an atmosphere that their love, stronger it seems on Margaret's side to begin with, first came into its own. When he was fit enough to move north, she went with him, and never left his side. Thanks to her, he was able in 1814 to return to the battle in London, and begin, as he put it, 'navigating on a plank saved from the wreck of several Large Vessels – and patched up at length into a little craft for my self.' This was the firm of Ruskin, Telford and Domecq, founded in 1815, and one day to be the financial raft of *Modern Painters* and *The Stones of Venice*.

In September 1817, Margaret's mother died at Croydon. She sped south to the funeral, and John James. On 13 October, the sudden death of John James's mother brought him back to Bowerswell, and Margaret's consoling love. This attachment promised nothing but disaster to the bankrupt and bereaved John Thomas, who on about 27 October cut his own throat. Margaret held the wound closed with her two hands as the doctor sewed it together: but on 30 October John Thomas died. The cousins' marriage, so prepared for by disease and death, was celebrated in London the following February. Their only child John was born a year later. His mother was ill for months afterwards and could never have another child. Their aspirations for him, as it turned out, led him away for a time from the origins of their own income, and union, to such romantic scenes as 'the Rhone, running with a million of Aire power, – all pure'. But while – as *Praeterita* acknowledges – such informative tourism helped to develop his genius, Ruskin's parents could not disinherit him from the legacy of their own virtues.[19]

'The Relation of the Architecture of Public Buildings to Daily Life', delivered in Bradford as Ruskin's first public venture after his father's death, became, as *Traffic*, his testament to his father's memory. From John James he inherited a sense of the spiritual opportunities of duty. By the 1880s, Ruskin was prepared to admit an affection for what he termed the healthily 'practical' heresy of Pelagianism, which was an extreme form of philosophic realism, with its emphasis on free will and the capacities of human merit. Ruskin much preferred this heresy to what he called the 'speculative' heresy of Luther, whose denial of free will, human merit and therefore of the spiritual value of duty was anathema to him.[20]

From Margaret Cox, Ruskin inherited something else besides an Evangelical upbringing. The extreme Protestant denial of human merit and hence of free will lead to the terrible doctrine of predestination: God had fore-willed every man or woman to heaven or hell. The glozing Romish doctrine of purgatory could have no room in such a theology, and was theoretically anathema to Mrs Ruskin and all of her party. But when Ruskin's nurse Annie died, on 31 March 1871, she changed her mind. Ruskin noted in his diary: 'My mother's epitaph upon her, "She always persecuted *me*. But one must hope there are intermediate kinds of places where people get better."' She would herself not outlast the year. Like his mother, Ruskin tended towards the absolute, but also possessed a willingness to demolish it in the face of experience. She may have been taught the Lutheran theory of nominalism – the belief that human merit was nominal, not real – but she behaved with all the fierce practical courage of her seafaring father. Immediately after his mother's death, Ruskin was asked to provide a topic for a prize essay at St Andrew's University. He suggested 'The Definition of Heroism'. It had been his mother's natural element – though never, perhaps, so clearly as in her late flash of inconsistency.

Ruskin's own 'definition of heroism' would include willed functions of duty, that effort after consistency which never blurred down into continuous habit for all the trying, in his father's case or his own; and also those vivid capacities for intervention, and inconsistency, which went with his mother's sharpness. The first he called 'honesty'. The second come together under the heading of 'Fors'. The surrealists would call it 'objective chance'. Whereas his father helped John, even to disablement, in becoming what he wanted to be, his mother, even to annihilation, saw what he was. Doubtless without his father's mental companionship the annihilation might have been complete. As it was, his parents possessed all the love – and money – he needed to fulfil their hopes as well as their fears. Most of all, they possessed intelligence. When the legacy of John James's economic acumen was revealed in the shocking *Unto This Last*, the father called it 'important', and immediately forwarded it to the publisher's. When Margaret's religious sense was strangely born anew in the interpretation of pagan myths, she wrote her son, 'I am reading your *Queen of the Air* with more and more deep sense of its merit.' Unintentionally, no doubt, she had stepped out of nominalism as definitely as he.[21]

Journeying, in 1859, to lecture in the industrial north, Ruskin was fulfilling himself by imitating the painstaking commercial tours of his father, and that passionate capacity for intervention which got his mother a husband.

The collection of lectures he was compiling – with its title *The Two Paths* – dramatised his own sense of being at a crossroads. He was finishing *Modern Painters* and preparing to write *Unto This Last*. To make clear his debt to Carlyle, and his own assumption of the Carlylean mantle of social criticism, he made 'Christmas and New Year's presents of "Past and Present" '.[22]

Ruskin's education in the commercial topography of England began as soon as he could comprehend his father's frequent letters. Writing to him at Manchester in February 1822 in reply to a letter from Kendal, 'Your boy. . . talks continually about you,' Margaret tells John James. In February 1831, she sends him at Sheffield the manuscript of *Iteriad*, John's versified chronicle of the family trip to the Lakes. John writes the same day by a later post to Rochdale, 'Oh it is a delightful sensation,' he says, to open a letter from his father, 'your very soul up at your eyes wondering what it's all about.' His father replies with an enthralling and circumstantial account of the new Manchester to Liverpool railway.

John James's commercial tours were extensive, though they took him not so far north as Newcastle, nor during his son's life, so far west as Bristol. There were a number of visits to such places as Lancaster, Kendal, Birmingham, Yarmouth. A regular winter tour took him to Leeds via Sheffield, then on to Manchester, and often Liverpool, via Halifax and Rochdale. *The Ruskin Family Letters* show him sending his observations from Leeds either shortly before or not long after John's birthday (8 February) in 1822, 1831, 1835, 1838, 1839 and 1840. He spent Christmas there in 1836. Leeds was his least favourite regular stopping-place; though by his own account Bradford was worse. He may only have visited the place once, shortly before John's third birthday, when he travelled from there to Kendal with two messengers of light hastening out of the benighted spot – the 'seriously disposed' Mr Wilson of Abbot Hall, Kendal, and a 'well informed Quakeress', one Miss Birkbeck.[23] They were not untypical visitors. Descriptions of Pennine scenery near Rochdale were vividly presented to John by his father's pen at least twenty years before he himself saw it: and the partly humorous, partly serious, comparison and contrast between Pennines and Appennies – between modern economics and medieval art – was a family talking-point long before John developed the theme in his first Bradford lecture.

For Ruskin to travel through this landscape and enter its industrial towns in his father's carriage at the same time of year as his father used to do was a means of dramatising and discovering his own economic and functional continuity with his father. His Yorkshire trips in 1837 and 1838 had been directed towards the picturesque and the geological – 'a Science and Art Education' as he remembered it, without much reference to books. By 1851, Turnerian fame, money, and a charming wife made him a welcome visitor at Farnley Hall, near Otley, in Wharfdale. It was the home of Francis Hawkesworth Fawkes, the son of Turner's friend and patron. Such journeys – and sojournings – were Ruskin's father's idea of the value wrung from his own efforts in less pleasant places. Nor was he wrong. But the son, just like his father, was interested in cost as well as value;

and in problems of spending as well as of acquisition.

Farnley Hall was the sort of place to visit in Effie's company, as he did in 1851 – but relations with the Fawkes family were broken off for some years afterwards. Without his host's permission, Ruskin had dedicated to Fawkes the pamphlet that the visit had inspired – in which Turner's works at Farnley were used to present an estimate of him as 'the first and greatest of the Pre-Raphaelites'.[24] This may have been meant as gratitude: but it looked like climbing. The Pre-Raphaelites were the taste of pushers from Leeds and Bradford, not of old landed families; of the Liverpool Academy, not the Royal Academy.

One Bradfordian who commissioned a Rossetti picture was the advanced Liberal, John Mitchell,[25] head of the Bradford branch of the huge international shipping and trading firm of A. & S. Henry. By the time the picture arrived, in 1869, Mitchell would have moved to Manchester, as principal manager of the A. & S. Henry empire. He was W. E. Forster's election agent, and one of the businessmen who had done much work behind the scenes on Cobden's Commercial Treaty with the French of 1860. He was full of new educational and social ideas of the advanced and efficient type; drawn to the radical ideas of *The Political Economy of Art* and the *Appendices* to *The Stones of Venice*. Ruskin, for him, was only one among a gallery of notable acquaintances, which included Louis Kossuth, the Hungarian liberator. Ruskin was booked to stay in Mr Mitchell's Parkfield House, and to lecture at the Mechanics' Institute. He did so on 1 March 1859. The hall held 700 people. It would be packed for him in 1864; but on Ruskin's first visit it seems only to have been respectably well filled. Louis Kossuth was booked for Parkfield House and St George's Hall. He spoke there on 28 May 1859, Mitchell beside him, before an ecstatic audience of three and a half thousand – the streets being crowded outside.

Effie would not have like Mr Mitchell. At Venice in 1851 while Kossuth was touring England to applause, she was offering pretty apologies for such radical British behaviour to the 'agreeable' Archduke Albrecht. He was the Austrian Governor of Hungary charged with annihilating the Kossuth rebellion. Since the Austrian colours of orange and black suited her so well, she was surprised Venetian friends, at this time, seemed to dislike her in them. As for her husband, he was, she teased, a 'great radical in Austria' only because 'there everyone is conservative.'

The central incompatability between John and Effie was theological and philosophic, not physiological. 'I am very glad that Mr Moore gave you that sermon,' Effie wrote to her intended on 9 February 1848. 'I think you are coming round by degrees to the point I want you to arrive [at] but as all great changes are – not sudden but the work of time and affected [sic] by slow degrees – I care not how long you are in coming to his way of thinking so that you *do* arrive at the desired end –.'[26] An exquisite introduction to the year of revolutions. Moore was the evangelical minister of Camden Chapel, Camberwell; a pleasant enough soul, but in theology one of those fundamentalists who adore their own trivial prejudices as revealed infallibly to themselves in bits of Holy Writ. By December 1861 Ruskin was calling Moore the principal of his spiritual 'perverters'.[27] And to a mind thoroughly responsive to the philosophic realism of Plato, of Thomas More, whose favourite poet was George Herbert, whose pet theological writer was Isaac Taylor, and whose *bête noire* was Bunyan's *Grace Abounding to the Chief of Sinners* – so must poor Mr Moore have seemed. That human virtue was a sham; that life was nothing but the muffled echo of eternity: such was Moore's philosophical position. Faith was everything, works less than nothing, free will illusory.

Isaac Taylor's *Natural History of Enthusiasm* deals very satisfactorily with this antinomian tendency – as fostered by Stoicism and quasi-Stoic versions of Christianity. These schools of thought are similar, 'not so much in the similiar abuse which is made in both systems of the doctrine of necessity; but in the leading intention of both, which is to enclose the human mind in a perfect envelope of abstractions, such as may effectively defend it from the importunate sense of responsibility, or obligation, and such as shall render him who wears it a passive spectator of his own destinies.'[28] Away with it, and Effie in its wake.

The worst part of Effie had seized on Ruskin as ambitious provincial girls have always seized their passport to the great world. The worst part of Ruskin grabbed Effie as the conceited and ignorant have always grabbed for the conventional beauties of their day. It is to both their credits that their better selves could not seal the bargain. The honeymoon was a disaster – Effie became ill; the groom left for eight months on the Continent without her. When they eventually journeyed to Venice together in 1850, Ruskin discovered Venetian Gothic and Effie discovered her real sexual nature thanks to the attentions of several Austrian cavalry officers. Letters of 1851 make it clear that any chance of happiness the marriage may have held were already dead. F. J. Furnivall first met the couple in the spring of 1849. 'There was no pretence of affection,' he would reminisce for Will Rotherstein half a century later, 'or of sympathy even, betwixt Ruskin and her.'[29]

When the break came, in 1854, both were relieved. Yet both would suffer. Ruskin's 'failure' would damage his reputation and influence in certain circles. It still does. Apart from his other attributes, Millais was a good catch: he became President of the Royal Academy and a baronet. But Effie, whose virtue had never been compromised, was never again received at Court. After the annulment, Lady Trevelyan – who could not bear Effie – became Ruskin's friend for life. Lady Eastlake – who could not endure Ruskin – became the champion of the new Mrs Millais. This was dangerous, for Lady Eastlake was an art critic and historian in her own right, and her husband was President of the Royal Academy. Her notoriously destructive review of *Modern Painters*, in the *Quarterly* for March 1856, was anonymous. 'No man with a heart. . . could have written' it, was the reaction of the Dean of Christ Church.[30] Ruskin was thrown more and more out of fashion – more and more dependent on provincials, eccentrics and the young. It was perhaps in the West Riding that his reputation suffered least. Richard Monckton Milnes of Fryston – whose capacity for friendship and innuendo was enormous – was the centre, or so Millais believed, of rumours in London society damaging to Effie. Certainly Milnes propagated Ruskinian ideas when engaged to speak at the Sheffield Art School in 1858.[31].

In February 1859 Ruskin travelled to Manchester via Northampton, Lichfield and Matlock. He intended for the first time to give Manchester something designed for the place: but he was baulked by the nature of his audience. His lectures of 1857 on *The Political Economy of Art* had been delivered at the Manchester Athenaeum in connection with the Art Treasures Exhibition. They had not, as he warned his audience, been originally intended for Manchester: but the Secretary of the Athenaeum had asked for a lecture and Ruskin had responded with material that he had long had on his mind. This was slightly disingenuous: but its essential truth points to the reality of his audience on that occasion. The Manchester Art Treasures Exhibition was visited by British aristocracy, royalty, and fashion; and by eminent foreigners like Prince Louis Napoleon. The exhibition itself was mounted at Trafford Park: not far from Manchester, but then still the home of the eminently aristocratic and artistic de Traffords. It was a particle of the old world surviving on the threshold of the new. It was not Manchester. It was what the Manchester middle class admired. Now, in 1859, Ruskin was addressing the Manchester Art School at the Royal Institution, Mosley Street, on *The Unity of Art*. As delivered, it was partly made up from material already used at South Kensington. It was – unfortunately – appropriate that this should be so. His words were suitable, indeed flattering, to Manchester, in their attempt to reconcile Cottonpolis to the metropolis, and the great masters to one another. Ruskin could speak in an extempore manner, and assume his audience had adequate acquaintance with the artists referred to, and the technical sense and taste to learn intelligently from them. So far, he was the Victorian cultivator propagating a little further, and digging in a little deeper. His meetings with the Bradford businessman John Mitchell in November, and with Charlotte Brontë's friend Mrs Gaskell after the Manchester lecture, may have warned him that very little of that would be suitable in Bradford. There were no Athenaeums or Royal Institutions there: no aristocracy; no likelihood of royal visitors. The word 'gentleman' had pejorative overtones, even in the respectable *Bradford Observer*. Elsewhere, it was a term of abuse. Ruskin had some notes ready for these people; but illness, partly nervous, partly diplomatic, as well as organic, led to the postponement of the Bradford lecture by one week, allowing a very thorough preparation for this new audience.

Ruskin wrote the new lecture in Wharfedale, at Bolton Abbey. The river scenery there was already showing the effects of the Bradford reservoir which had been built upstream to gather the waters of the Wharfe's tributary, the Dibb. Ruskin would travel south into Airedale in his father's carriage. There was a conscious symbolism in this movement away 'from those shores of Wharfe' which Ruskin believed Turner 'never could re-visit without tears; nay, which for all the latter part of his life, he never could speak of but his voice faltered.'[32]

The family coachman Mr Fudge was in the driving-seat, and Ruskin's valet Crawley was with him to dress him for his appearance in Bradford Mechanics' Institute. Ruskin's voice had best not falter, for this would be the toughest audience of his career. He was about to see men whose newspaper had declined to report Emerson's 'ephemeral' lecture to them of 1848; who in 1856 had made Thackeray so ill after one lecture that he had to postpone the second; whom in 1858 Dickens with his most poignant flights had 'failed to carry'; who would stay 'very cold' for Beerbohm Tree in 1880; and who in 1905 would kill off Henry Irving.

Ruskin advisedly faced them, like his first lecture audience in Edinburgh seven years before, with a complete script: though now he had more skill in extemporising at the beginning and the end, and in blending lighter touches, where required, with the various seriousnesses of the discourse. As he wrote to his father at the time, 'I think the Bradford will be a better address than the Manchester one.'[33]

CHAPTER FOUR

MR RUSKIN'S FIRST APPEARANCE

> Mr Ruskin's first appearance in Bradford was on March 1st 1859 when he came to deliver the inaugural lecture of the Bradford School of Design, an institution which had recently been established for the furtherance of art for its own sake, and also with a view to its technical bearing. Its active advocates were Mr Aldam Heaton, the Honorary Secretary, Mr Alfred Harris, the Vice-President, and Mr James Lobley, the Head Master. The text of this address, subsequently incorporated into *The Two Paths* was the practical principles of decorative art. His thesis led the seer to the position that the art must be conditioned by its soil and climate, and this in turn to some unflattering remarks about the habitat of his audience. —*The Bradford Daily Argus*, 22 January 1900

> I could as soon tell you how to make or manufacture an ear of wheat, as to make a good artist of any kind. . . And what I have to speak to you about, to-night, is mainly the ground and the weather, it being the first and quite most material question in this matter whether the ground and weather of Bradford, or the ground and weather of England in general – suit wheat. —*The Two Paths*, 86

Ruskin's eyes must have told him the ground and the weather of Bradford did not suit wheat. Located 'on the sharp bend of a Pennine stream isolated from the outer world by a crescentic rampart of bleak moorland',[1] its landscape was not friendly to the plough. Bradford, as William Byles of the *Observer* remarked in September 1866, would always have to be made and renewed by man, almost like another Holland. The building of a huge town in this craggy setting was an artificial process. To pay for that process, Bradford had to make herself the wool capital of the world. It was only after 1860, when she had become rich, that Bradford could finance large-scale development of her own local quarries, productive of excellent building stone for most purposes. She was soon exporting her stone across the world. At home, the town's inevitable plan was a tiny jumbled centre from which hilly access routes had to be carved like the spokes of a crazy upside-down umbrella. This meant that a Bradford building of any size was liable to occupy an extremely uneven site, and to be triangular or segmental in ground-plan.

The problem of water was as great as the problems of the site. Steam power was Bradford's life: a canal its first necessity: the railways its access to the world. The canal of 1774 made it possible to get at the limestone of the upper Aire valley, essential to the iron industry. The Bowling Iron Works were constructed; and for a time gained almost a monopoly in the production of armaments of truly pulverising quality. The Low Moor Iron works were constructed; and took the lead in railway and marine engineering. They provided part of the Atlantic Telegraph cable of 1858–66. The world's largest output of woolcombing, in velvet manufacture, in alpaca, in piece-dyeing of cloth of all kinds – raw materials for these examples of Bradford work had to be brought from South America, from Australia, from the continent of Europe, and to be sent back again at a profit. India and China and Russia must be open to Bradford, too. If Bradford was to make textile goods for the world, the world's communication system must be shaped and its wars influenced by Bradford's iron goods. And with her great stake both in textiles and their transport, Bradford would deal in the goods of other cities, other nations: become a great warehousing and shipping centre. And on these foundations she would begin to make money out of money and become (by 1900) the second financial centre of the United Kingdom with power in all lands and the most tempting interest rates and insurance schemes on the face of the earth.

And all this while, Bradford's main watercourse was the beck, a Pennine stream forcing its erratic way across the town centre towards the single natural outlet towards the north-west, Shipley and the River Aire. During the Ice Age the beck was dammed by a glacier. Fragments of glacial rock were the original Bradford building stone: and many old walls remain as testimony to this fact. Anyone with Ruskin's knowledge of geology would have read the meaning of the immediate terrain: the cavities between the hills, linked by great channels carved through the hills, spoke eloquently of Bradford's Ice Age status as a lake. During the Victorian age when the beck was choked with every species of refuse and effectively dammed at many of its twists by boundary walls and railings up the middle of its course, there were a number of unpleasant and expensive reminders of Bradford's geological status as a lake. Heavy spring rain melting the winter's snows; or summer thunderstorms bursting over the hilly town, would swell the beck and its host of tributaries; and the many natural cavities or man-made gravel or coal pits or quarries – exploited, and then abandoned – would overflow to contribute their water to the rain and streams flooding the centre of the town. The financial damage, in June 1859 for instance, was £30,000: just about the price of the Wool Exchange of 1864–7.

Large numbers of wells of pure soft water were essential to the wool trade. One of the oldest and purest, in the centre, was known from time immemorial as Jacob's Well. But there were never enough of these wells to meet the demands of the textile industry: not to mention the iron forges, among a host of other industries. And then there was drinking water to be found. An early Bradford waterworks was sited at Chellow Dene – a cavity created by Bradford's Ice Age lake. The Corporation gained control of this in 1855. At the same time more and more reservoirs began to be constructed: first, out in the Worth valley, near Haworth; then, as a result of an Act of Parliament of 1854, a whole series of large reservoirs in the valleys of the Aire and the Wharfe. Even then, many Bradfordians remained dependent for water on the dubious supplies to be purchased from itinerant water carts. As for drainage – the first main drain was begun only in 1863. By 1866 the Corporation were still looking for £120,000 to construct main sewers: and the borough surveyor was still talking of street sewers and house drains in almost mystical language: the former were for the most part 'yet to come' and the latter remained 'for the future'.

The stench of all this, the disease, the filth of Bradford beck and of the dead-end Bradford Canal – a navigable cut of the Leeds–Liverpool Canal – comprised 'associations' not very conducive to art. And to the harshness of the site and climate and the nightmare of the water 'system' must be added the aesthetic properties of the innumerable mills, dyeworks, iron foundries, chemical works, grease works, vitriol works, soap works, gas works and coal pits which made Bradford one of the world's great industrial towns; and – more significant and characteristic – the huge development of lofty warehousing packing the tiny town centre, which was an effect of Bradford's growing progress as the wool capital of the world: a progress both affirmed and accelerated by the French Commercial Treaty of 1860. The artistic problems of the site and of the drains were therefore exacerbated by the artistic problems of darkness and perpetual noise.

In the heart of all this, on an island site where the steep slope of Cheapside ran down into busy Kirkgate, was Victoria Buildings, partly occupied by Fattorini's the Jewellers. It was in an upper room of this structure that the new Bradford School of Design of 1859 prepared its display of work for the interested inspection of Mr Ruskin.

Dr Furnivall, friend of Ruskin and of Ruskin's West Riding admirer the Co-operator John Holmes, gives this sympathetic description of Bradford Design Schools's noted guest:

> Ruskin was a tall, slight fellow, whose piercing frank blue eye lookt through you and drew you to him. A fair man, with rough light hair and reddish whiskers, in a dark blue frock coat with velvet collar, bright Oxford blue stock, black trousers and patent slippers – how vivid he is to me still! The only blemish in his face was the lower lip, which protruded somewhat: he had been bitten there by a dog in his early youth. But you ceast to notice this as soon as he began to talk. I never met any man whose charm of manner at all approacht Ruskin's. Partly feminine it was, no doubt; but the delicacy, the sympathy, the gentleness and affectionateness of his way, the fresh and penetrating things he said, the boyish fun, the earnestness, the interest he showed in all deep matters, combined to make a whole which I have never seen equalled.[2]

Ruskin was in Bradford because the mayor Henry Brown had noticed that 'colour was not understood' in the town. Fancy fabrics from the continent or Scotland outsold local equivalents in his own emporium. The current rage was for cashmere shawls. Only wealthy women could afford the real thing from India: but thousands of local women preferred copies made at Paisley to the offerings of Bradford designers. And this was merely the tip of an iceberg. Alderman Mitchell, whose shipping firm A. & S. Henry supplied the homesteads and saloons of the American West with pretty ginghams and other 'fancy' goods, was certain that it was the 'fancy trade that tipped the scale' in the struggle for prosperity. In the hard winter just ending the scale had tipped the wrong way: with disastrous consequences to the Bradford poor. It is in this context that Ruskin's reaction to Bradford must be placed. He shared it with his audience. 'It is not a question of appreciation at all,' he would write in the *Appendix* to *Ariadne Florentina*: '*all* beautiful form and colour is physically invisible to them as human speech is inaudible during a steam whistle.' Was Bradford deaf to colour? Ruskin's aesthetic judgment of 1876 makes the identical point as a wry joke current in the Bradford streets at the time of his arrival in 1859: 'Why are Cashmere shawls like deaf persons?' went the grim riddle. There could be only one answer in Bradford: 'Because we cannot make them *here*'.[3]

The Bradford Design School of 1859 was only the most promising of a series of attempts made in the town during the Victorian period to further by voluntary association the cause of education in art and design. It professed large ideals as well as specific technical aims. Such education was vital to the prosperity of the wool capital, and the story of the school's very partial success casts curious light on this most ebullient period of Bradford's history. For in this powerhouse of liberalism and nonconformity, Tories – or what in Bradford at this time must be called crypto-Tories – and Anglicans, were curiously dominant in this important initiative. They would, however, need the assistance of the 'advanced liberal' John Mitchell in order to challenge, albeit modestly, the deadweight of the more illiberal *laissez-faire* 'Liberals'. Moreover, the English note of nationalism all too audible in this period becomes less vibrant with the discovery that the original school premises were over an Italian jewellers and that, in the event, German immigrants were to do much of the donkey-work. The political personality of 'Education Act' Forster, their MP from 1861 till his death in 1886, emerges the more interestingly by the fact that he was compelled, or chose, to adopt a somewhat guarded attitude to the enterprise. James Lobley, the original master, was brought over from the Mechanics' Institute: but in 1865, weary of battling with committees and with his own former pupils and patrons at the older institution, he resigned. The enterprise was saved only with help from the Germanic High School and its efficient friends. This was appropriate, because at this time the bulk of Bradford's export trade was to Germany. By 1867, Forster was able to tell the reconstituted Bradford School of Art Committee (nearly half of it German) that their experience provided useful guidelines for the establishment of Schools of Science.

The fourth Annual Meeting and Exhibition of this re-formed Bradford School of Art – the nearest natural heir to the 'Lobley' school of 1859 – was held in 1870, the year of the Education Act. The occasion provides an enlightening miniature of some problems generally current in English education. The scene is impressive enough. W. E. Forster himself, author of the Education Act and brother-in-law of the author of *Culture and Anarchy*, is an active Vice-President. The President is no less a person than Rt. Hon. the Earl de Grey and Ripon, Lord President of the Committee of Council on Education, in addition to being a member of Bradford Chamber of Commerce. Alfred Harris junior, a foremost northern banker and H. W. Ripley, the world's largest dyer, are active advocates. Between them, these two men control most of the land on which Bradford's warehouse district is built. They are landlords to the world's fabric trade, hard-headed businesmen: and they are not philistines. Their speeches suggest they have remembered with admiration a number at least of the sentiments of their old guest, the new Oxford Professor of Art. Another speaker, Louis Tylor, is still closer in spirit to his brother Alfred's friend Professor Ruskin. These men surely, if any group of men in Victorian England, should carry all before them. And what is the result? Frustration and dilemma, it seems. The millionaire dilettante Arthur Briggs points helplessly to the discrepancy between private wealth and public neglect. Bradford has many wealthy private collections but no public gallery. H. W. Ripley, one of Britain's most powerful capitalists, points helplessly to the impotence of wealth and influence of national dimensions in the face of local intransigence and jealousy. He is reduced to pleading with the hostile witnesses from the rival Mechanics' Institute School 'not to regard' the present enterprise 'as antagonistic to themselves'.

Bradford Mechanics' Institute is a power centre of the local Liberal caucus – the men who are threatening to abandon Forster over what they see as his betrayal of the Nonconformist cause in his Education Act of 1870. Their pet politician is Edward Miall, the other Bradford MP, editor of *The Nonconformist* and the 'political dissenter' of *Culture and Anarchy*. Collectively, they see art as an investment for personal financial gain, rather than as an investment in the country's capital of life and talent. Their pet art master, and adviser on artistic investment, is John Sowden, Lobley's pupil and rival.

The Bradford School of Art – natural heir of Lobley's School of 1859 – remained mostly at loggerheads with the Mechanics' Institute

School of Art, which continued to be dominated by the ever more affluent John Sowden. Sowden's autocracy in the Bradford art world was further consolidated by the founding of the Bradford Art Society in 1869, with himself as President. With the revival of Bradford Toryism in the 1870s – H. W. Ripley, in 1874, became Bradford's first Tory MP since 1847[4] – the feud was taken up by a new Church of England Art School. There were others.

The twin problems of technology and design – too often seen as separate – remained of immediate importance to the town's survival. The supporters of the Design School of 1859 had their various aesthetic interests but they were fundamentally far-sighted businessmen. Those who opposed the school from motives of confessed, even proudly proclaimed, 'jealousy', were preaching a very false economy. Till about 1875, their attitude seemed justifiable from the fact that, even in the 'fancy trade', huge stocks of the same pattern might be sure of a steady sale. After that time, women the world over were not content to dress alike, or to retain the same pattern for long. In addition, that old Bradford stand-by, the 'mixed fabric' – cotton warp, woollen weft – no longer counted as 'fashion material'. A much wider range of stuffs and patterns was needed. And in supplying them, Bradford was now competing with rapidly expanding local industries in America, Russia and Germany. 1873 was an *annus mirabilis* for Bradford – business was enormous, and they ventured to afford a Gothic Town Hall. The Franco-Prussian War, like the American Civil War before it, had given Bradford stuff merchants and iron-masters ample opportunity to exploit the needs, and weaknesses, of both sides. But in 1875 the German trade in piece goods collapsed. Energy and enterprise succeeded in finding ways out of the difficulty, but the farsightedness of the 'active advocates' of 1859 referred to in the quotation at the head of this chapter is indicated by the fact that not till 1878 – when there was talk of grass growing in the streets – would the Technical College be founded by subscription to place, for a time, technical and design teaching on a firmer basis. It never 'paid'. In 1899 it was handed over to the Corporation £14,000 in debt. The Corporation's first economy was to abolish design courses.

But the centralisation independent Bradfordians detested had by then begun to be effective. The Technical Instruction Act of 1889 and the Local Taxation Act of 1890 had enabled local authorities to raise money for technical education; and independent Bradford would seize the opportunity with outstanding energy. Before long Bradford's various feuding schools would mostly consent to be gathered into a new public Art College.[5]

Forster's Act of 1870 had enabled the Bradford School Board to become the most adventurous in the country, and the pattern of the 1859 Design School to become more largely visible. This time the 'advanced liberal' was James Hanson, and his unwilling but necessary partner was the Tory Henry Mitchell, the prime mover of the Technical College. He was no relation to John Mitchell but – interestingly enough – had succeeded him in 1868 as the managing partner of the Bradford branch of the huge international firm A. & S. Henry.

This small-scale enterprise, therefore, of 1859 was implicated in large political and economic forces. It could hardly avoid being so. Unfortunately issues dividing the world outside were also sufficient to disrupt the important alliance it represented between Bradford's handful of influential crypto-Tories and the advanced Liberal John Mitchell. Rossetti, who thought him 'the decentest of the lot', noted that Mitchell's colleagues tended to look down on him 'as a cad rather'. Such may well have been the view of Aldam Heaton, the decorative artist and Honorary Secretary of the 1859 School. He was quite close to Rossetti, and he was certainly a man fond of speaking his own mind. Conversely, 'Mr Mitchell is a middle-aged (rather young) manufacturer – very benevolent and modest,' Ruskin wrote to his father. Local evidence tends to confirm the outsiders' impression, though there is a tartness in Ruskin's description that permits shades of reservation.[6]

It was one of Ruskin's major strengths, as *The Bradford Observer* commented in 1864, that he was able to insinuate his notions into people of different party. His irrigation of the Bradford Design School may serve as a model for his general manner of influence, which may be summarised as encouraging people of good will to think and act for themselves – preferably together. As usual, his Bradford lectures were sharpened up for the reading public: but though he was sometimes blunter in delivery, he was also gentler, funnier and more agreeable. Heaton, the school's Secretary, Harris, its active Vice-President, and Lobley, its Master, seem to have taken to Ruskin immensely, and he undoubtedly influenced them. Mitchell, indispensable element though he was, seems to have been playing his own game. His radicalism lacked the deep philosophical conviction of James Hanson, and his 'benevolence', as Ruskin observed of British benevolence in general, was something that was intended to pay.[7]

No wonder Ruskin approached his audience of 1859 with apologies for remarks 'rather suggestive of difficulties than helpful in solving them'; and no wonder the *Bradford Observer*, in 1864, looked forward 'a generation or two' in the effort to get the visitor into perspective. Yet the same paper noted many a reader found *Modern Painters* 'an epoch in his intellectual life'. The adjective was promising. Charlotte Brontë had not been the only inhabitant of Bradford parish to read Ruskin and the local landscape together. And it was a landscape worth meditating. Not surprisingly, the three 'active advocates' of the school named by the *Argus* were all young men, ready to receive suggestions from Ruskin's 'particular principles', and to some extent agreeing with him on the nature of what he called the 'obstacles which stand at present in the way of our success in design'. Partly meant as an 'advanced' branch of the Mechanics' Institute School, the new Design School was also an attempt to grow away from the somewhat circumscribed 'establishment' liberalism of that institution. With it new vision of educational largeness and sense that art 'for its own sake' would in the end be of more practical benefit than rote-learned 'applied design', the enterprise was doomed to failure in the short term. At this distance, however, it looks rather promising.

John Aldam Heaton (1830–97), Honorary Secretary of the new school was no blood relation of Ellen Heaton of Leeds (1816-94), Ruskin's persistent correspondent: but the two families became allied when Aldam's sister married Ellen's brother, the distinguished Leeds physician, John Deakin Heaton (1817–80). Aldam and Ellen were both early patrons of Rossetti, and they were both enabled, with help from Ruskin, to form a bridge between local sense and metropolitan sensibility. They were neither of them 'self-made'. Ellen's father was Yorkshire's leading bookseller, and though, unlike her brilliant brother, this eccentric independent spinster was by no means the cream, even of Leeds 'society', she saw no need to moderate her accent, or her manner, while attending the Brownings' soirées in Rome and Florence. Aldam Heaton came from a family of stuff merchants with relations among the elite Quaker dynasties of Leeds.

As Dr Heaton recorded in his diary, by 1855 Aldam's father's business 'had been for some time declining; in part owing to the general tendency of the stuff trade to leave Leeds for Bradford.'[8] Aldam himself set up business in Bradford at about this time. Before long he had become a partner in the Beehive Mills on Thornton Road, where the Bradford beck disappeared underground as it entered the town centre. At first, by way of contrast, he leased the charming vernacular Manningham Old Hall as a residence. Medieval in origin, the fabric of this house dated mainly from 1639. It was under imminent threat from the new straight avenues and Italianate villas demanded by Bradford's expanding middle classes. Heaton moved out. He had acquired the means and leisure to renovate, adorn and landscape the enchanting seventeenth-century Woodbank, deep in the Harden Valley, near Bingly. Here in 1861 Rossetti spent a month – at his own suggestion – working on an oil portrait of Mrs Heaton: *Regina Cordium*. It turned out to be a replica – *mutatis mutandis* – of his own marriage portrait of Elizabeth Siddal, which he had sold to Ruskin. While at Bingley, Rossetti also designed a stained glass window of his hostess as the Lady of Woodbank, complete with halo and a model of the house in her hand. They had need of a retreat, for Mrs Heaton had been a governess, and the marriage was not popular with local advocates of 'getting-on'. Yet it was probably through this connection that Morris & Co. gained their earliest important commission for a stained-glass window: the east window of Bradford parish church of 1862–3. It included one of Rossetti's very best designs for stained glass – the central figure of Christ.

Heaton was actually leasing Woodbank from the Busfield-Ferrands, an ancient county family who were to some extent his own patrons. He exhibited a watercolour of their house – new St Ives – at the Royal Academy in 1867. Just as they had been Factory Reformers in the 1830s, so he would become a Christian Socialist in the 1880s, from a natural sense of decency. The Ferrands were of the class to entertain Disraeli and Lord John Manners – First Commissioner and Tory Gothicist. They provided a window for Bingley Parish Church, by Morris & Co. to Burne-Jones's design; but seem not to have been such wealthy or prolific purchasers of the arts as the manufacturer Walter Dunlop, whom Rossetti dubbed 'the Demon'. In 1859 the 'Demon' took on lease from the Ferrands the site of their original house – old St Ives – standing above Woodbank on a prominent knoll just below the road that runs along the valley.

The time had come for the original proprietors to retreat into spacious seclusion in the new St Ives, still higher up above the Harden Valley. In some senses it was a retreat into history, for new St Ives replaced old Harden Grange. Old St Ives, below the road, was gradually replaced, as Dunlop amassed capital and accrued to himself 'much of the environs of Bingley', by a solid new Harden Grange, commanding, at the head of its own pleasant bank of grass, a prospect up and down the valley. The traveller following the road that runs along the valley from Bingley to Harden – as Ruskin did in 1864 – would be given an eyeful of Harden Grange's grand stables for a moment, before they disappeared behind high walls, to be replaced in the line of vision by a huge textile mill that appeared to block the road as it swung sharply left towards Bradford or Haworth. In the mid-Victorian period, the gentry, and the artist, were in hiding above him, or below, and the Demon capitalist seemed quite capable of annexing either if they ventured into the open, or lingered on the road. Mercifully, amid so much social juggling and nominal reversibility, the modest Woodbank, built down by the stream in 1635 for a junior Ferrand, still survives, thanks largely to Heaton's sensitive and effective restoration, begun in 1860. It may be he was encouraged in this by Ruskin's magical evocation, made in Bradford the previous year, of the Caroline vernacular.[9]

Heaton may well have helped to get Morris, Rossetti and friends the commission for the stained-glass windows at Harden Grange, of 1862, with their scenes from the legend of Tristram and Isoude. He certainly composed letters for Rossetti which, with considerable admixture of his own pepper, Rossetti forwarded to the Demon, demanding advance payment for a proposed picture. The pepper probably lost him the commission – and, eventually, much of Heaton's affection. Not that the relationship with Heaton was apparently worth very much to Rossetti. When Murray Marks sold Heaton a Rossetti drawing too cheaply, the artist bought it back at cost, and resold elsewhere for a higher figure. Heaton himself showed a lifelong tendency for over-playing the part of injured innocent, sometimes to the point of self-righteous rudeness which Rossetti was justified in disliking. These tantrums among the 'artistic' were a source of amusement to their patrons.[10]

When Ruskin was composing *Traffic* for publication, it was such houses as Dunlop's that he had in mind when describing the 'banks' of Bradfordian aspiration: but the term also has a financial reference.

Alfred Harris, junior (1825–1901), Ruskin's host of 1864 and in 1859 Vice-President of the new Design School was the son of a prosperous London shipbroker, Edward Harris, of Quaker origins. In 1849 he joined the Bradford Old Bank, controlled by his two uncles, Henry and Alfred senior. Alfred senior was by this time an Anglican. When his first wife Harriet died, in 1865, Alfred junior too joined the Established Church, finding in the advanced Broad Church Party a congenial environment for his social and artistic conscience. He was good looking and athletic, given to lecturing the YMCA on the ruins and public buildings of Rome; but was also an extremely astute banker with pleasantly gentlemanly manners. He was himself an amateur artist. He served on the Committee of the Church Institute and as Treasurer to the Ragged School Bazaar. He would not have risen, as he did, to become one of the leading bankers in the North of England by exhibiting the grossness of Dickens' Bounderby or the sneering snobbery of Thackeray's Barnes Newcombe. Like most of the people Ruskin made a point of cultivating, and studying, he exhibited the strengths and weaknesses of the best of his kind. Meanwhile, the rawness of Bradford, and something of the pathos of the Harrises' efforts are perhaps best set in context by reference to the foundation by that more eminent banker William Roscoe of the Liverpool Society for the Encouragement of the Arts of Painting and Design, in 1773.

More encouragingly, Alfred Harris junior played the gentleman in supporting local talent like Ben Preston, the dialect 'poet of the poor', and Lobley himself – patronage for which he received very little credit – while his taste in architecture and financial good sense would be demonstrated in striking contrast to the behaviour of his colleagues in the Chamber of Commerce over the matter of choosing a design for the new Wool Exchange in 1864. Of contemporary artists, he would acquire Rosetti's *Tessa la Bionda* – which has since vanished – and Simeon Solomon's *Night*.

He would also acquire a share in a number of financial enterprises. He was for many years chairman of the Leeds and Liverpool Canal Company, a large shareholder and director of the British Steamship Investment Trust and of Ilkley Wells Hydropathic Company, the convalescent establishment in Turner's Wharfedale. He also drew revenue from the Leeds, Bradford and Wakefield railway. His family bank, the Bradford Old Bank Ltd, had been founded by a Mr Peckover in 1803. It was on land belonging to the Old Bank that most of Bradford's European export warehouses were built. The Bank epitomised respectability, and Harris worked hard for his uncles there, becoming chairman, however, only in 1882. Twice married, he failed twice to secure election as Tory candidate for Kendal, but he was rewarded by becoming, in 1885, High Sheriff of Westmorland.

Harris's patronage of Norman Shaw, of Burne-Jones and Rossetti, in the fine church of Holy Trinity at Bingley, marks him as a distinguished and perceptive member of Ruskin's wide circle of spiritual friends. There is a certain mystery, though, about the choice of subject matter for the east window he presented to Holy Trinity in 1873. It commemorated Henry Harris of nearby Longwood: Alfred's senior uncle, a devout Quaker, and head of the Bank. Burne-Jones provided a fine Crucifixion; and below this was Rossetti's superb Abraham and Isaac. As Uncle Henry had been the occupant of Longwood, Bingley, with its 'open prospect' towards the sacrificial stones of Bingley's Druid's Altar, this insistence on the Old Testament parallel may have had other than autobiographical pertinence for Alfred junior, but a sense of thwarting and constriction remains: and constriction of energy is certainly one of the effects of Rossetti's treatment of the subject.

The Old Bank's most evident bequest to Bradford proper was £3,800 in shares to found an isolation hosptial. Though Salt contributed £5,000 to the scheme, it was Alfred Harris senior who laid the foundation stone, with a silver trowel, on 10 September 1869. By that time, he had removed himself to a country house near Ripon.

From soon after that, Alfred junior spent most of his time at his new home near Kirkby Lonsdale. Ashfield, where Ruskin had stayed in 1864, was sold. James Lobley, the Bradford Design School taken out of his hands, would depend more and more for financial succour and moral support on Harris and his family at Kirkby Lonsdale. Here in an ambiance of high minded Christian reformism the Countess of Bective (a neighbour) would teach the young Harrises weaving, and James Lobley, the tanner's son from Hull, would teach them to draw. Here, far from Bradford and on Bradford money would be realised in miniature and for a time some of the social reconciliations and some of the 'simplicity and economy' of Ruskin's Bradford lecture of 1859.

Ashfield, like Mr Harris's Kirkby Lonsdale house, has been demolished: but out-buildings and service cottages in a Victorian-

Caroline style, not uncomely, may represent Harris's attempt to revive those decencies of a refined vernacular such as Heaton enjoyed at Woodbank. But Ashfield was not Woodbank. Situated, properly speaking, at Dubb, not far from Saltaire, it was socially at the 'wrong' end of Bingley, yet not quite in Cottingley: a little world of its own, constituting an industrial hamlet by the Leeds–Liverpool Canal, beyond which lies Primrose Hill and Gilstead Moor. On the hither side, Ashfield – consisting of a rocky outcrop above the canal, where the Harrises built Holy Trinity, and a more sheltered platform where the house was. The railway ran in a cutting between house and church. Stations were close by, offering rapid transit equally to Leeds and London (via Saltaire) or to Skipton and Kirkby Lonsdale. Mr Harris might well feel, in the words of *Traffic* 'king of a small part of the nation, and lord over its means of maintenance'. Indeed, with his canal at the bottom of his garden, laden with freight on its way to his steamships financed by his bank, he may have sensed that the adjective was intended – as it undoubtedly was – to stimulate him into some proof of a generous largeness. Nor did he, to continue the quotation, 'take all the produce of that piece of the foundation of national existence' for himself. He ran the Leeds–Liverpool Canal for years at a loss. From the viewpoint of conventional political science, this was mere foolishness, a betrayal of his own best interests.

Given his Ruskinian sympathies Harris himself may have seen it as a piece of Christian service in the public interest. There is no evidence that he was a fool. Private spending for public good was a theme and a practice of his: in the matter of the Bradford Design School, and later in his efforts on behalf of the crafts of Westmorland and the trades and agriculture of Ireland. It is sad that Harris's grand church has gone, replaced by a much more modest modern structure: but the handsome school and a comely terrace of houses are still in use: and some of his masonry of Gilstead sandstone has proved very useful in building an old people's home called Ashfield. As Ruskin reminded his audience, their reign would be short.

It would be unfair to call the Harris church an indulgence – though the spire perhaps was. But it exemplifies a difficulty. The Bradford 'kings' did much, in their various ways, with their patches of kingdom. All was not selfishness – though selfishness there was such as to make Ruskin's vituperation at its most flamboyant seem restrained. The difficulty arose in acting 'collectively'. That telling adverb is from *Traffic*, but the difficulty applied even more to the Design School. Marshalled under the brilliant and tireless German, Jacob Behrens, Bradford capitalists got the best postal service in the provinces, the best possible terms under the French treaty of 1860. To co-operate where they were rivals was another matter. Harris had an outlet for his artistic Christianity and gentlemanly social conscience – in Dubb; but, Conservative as he was, he stood at the outer corner of those ideas proliferating in the three Bradford newspapers. Nor, unfortunately, did he have the ruthlessness of personality necessary to overcome these disadvantages when it came to persuading *laissez-faire* liberals of the need to vitalise and co-ordinate the teaching of art and design.[11] Symptomatically, when it came to drawing up a list of patrons for the new institution, these were, with three exceptions, drawn from the board of the Old Bank. The three exceptions were Lord Rosse, Dr Burnet, and Titus Salt. Each was an unusual example of his class. Lord Rosse was titular head of a number of things in Bradford, including the Mechanics' Institute by virtue of his own scientific distinction and his marriage to Mary Wilmer-Field, a local heiress. The vicar, Dr Burnet, was a popular and fair-minded chairman of many local committees; and had published a sermon urging the harmonious distribution of the nutritive elements in the body politic.[12] Titus Salt was the most famous of all paternalistic capitalists. His generosity led him to give away a quarter of a million pounds during his lifetime, most of it unasked, and to run Saltaire on the 'ludicrously' low profit margin of four per cent. In art as in everything else he aimed at being up to date: and when Kis's *Amazon* won the gold medal for sculpture at the 1851 Exhibition, Salt naturally purchased one of the casts. Another, Ruskin noted, formed a 'good grotessque' for the museum steps in that hideous city, Berlin.[13]

The Old Bank patrons were five: F. S. Powell, of Horton Old Hall, the Tory MP for Cambridge; H. W. Wickham, MP, of Kirklees Priory, the most conservative of Liberals; Charles Hardy of Odsall House, iron magnate, Anglican Sunday School teacher and endower of churches; and Harris's two uncles: uncle Henry, at that time still resident in Heaton Hall, an enchanting Queen Anne house that had been the girlhood home of Lady Rosse; and uncle Alfred of Ryshworth Hall, an omnium gatherum of styles going back some centuries, complete with chapel. These were just the sort of houses which a progressive taste all over England would soon be demolishing in favour of sprawling and soaring neo-Gothic creations.

Meanwhile, the design School of 1859 sees the Bradford Tory tradition flickering into life and confidence. Since February 1858, Lord Derby had been Prime Minister. It was he who in 1834 deserted the Whigs for their attacks on the Established Church of Ireland – 'those d—m Whigs who would upset the Church of England' as William IV would call them in October 1836.[14] The occasion was C. T. Longley's doing homage as first Bishop of Ripon, the new diocese that included much of the industrial West Riding. William charged him as he would answer before Almighty God never to give the Whigs encouragement. They hardly needed it. There was plenty of ammunition available in the form of sectarian and party jealousy for those who chose to debunk the 'Church and King Tories', Richard Oastler and Parson Bull, the local Factory Reformers. These men, together with the elder Benjamin Jowett and his Bradford friend John Wood, of Wood and Walker's mill, were among the earliest and most valued friends of Shaftsbury, as he would acknowledge in October 1859 on the platform of St George's Hall. Their aims were, in the best sense, conservative; and when, in 1848, revolution swept Europe and hordes of Chartists were meeting on Bradford's hills, quite a number of people began to see sense in them. In the calm after the storm came the foundation of St Paul's Manningham, confessedly erected against the twin evils of Chartism and Dissent. According to the Orangeman Dr Burnet its restrained grandeur epitomised the stablility of the Church of England. It was entirely appropriate that one of the last public acts of William's dowager Queen Adelaide should have been to head the list of patrons to its building fund.

Alfred Harris senior, that zealot for sectarian privilege (so Hanson described him) would present himself to the Bradford electorate in 1859 as a supporter of Lord Derby, John James Ruskin's favourite politician. Alfred senior was President of St Paul's Sunday Schools. John Hollings, of Manningham House, and a principal support of St Paul's, is on the Design School Committee. So is John Taylor, Tory solicitor and – in Forster's words – 'thorough gentleman'.[15] Their Honorary Treasurer is George Wood, of Wood and Walker's mills. William Mossman, main support with the Harrises of the tottering Church Institute, is on the committee; as is H. W. Ripley, on the way to becoming, by 1874, Bradford's first Tory MP since 1847, and at last a Churchman. Another member is Moses Bottomley junior, whose Roman Classic warehouse was perhaps the finest of all Bradford warehouses. An Anglican with a 'pedigree' going back to 1326, he was the proud possessor of a copy of Delaroche's *The Imprisoned Laud blesses Strafford on his way to Execution*. Thomas Wentworth, of Wentworth Woodhouse in the West West Riding of Yorkshire, first Earl of Strafford, was locally regarded as the vilest betrayer of local values. Botomley's sympathies were contrary.[16]

Such a cluster would be unexceptional in Leeds or Manchester; in Bradford they amount to a minor revolution.

The advanced liberal among them, John Mitchell, had formed a strange but evidently necessary alliance. Pragmatic reform was his natural element as Bradford partner, from 1847, of the international firm of A. & S. Henry. Their grandiose Italianate warehouse in Leeds Road, at a time when most Bradford exports went to Germany, was filled with goods bound for America. Personalities and family traditions were less important to him then the needs and opportunities of the firm: a fact that makes Mitchell a more 'modern' phenomenon than the pedigree tracers and conservers of private chapels among whom he found himself. Something of a 'cad', in fact. His firm had been founded by an energetic Ulsterman, Alexander Henry (1766–1862), who made one fortune in Philadelphia, from 1783, and came to Manchester in 1804 to begin making another with his brother Samuel. As MP for South Lancashire in 1846, Alexander was a fervent supporter of Cobden and Bright: a tradition Mitchell would uphold as an efficient informant to Cobden over the negotiations for the French Treaty of 1860. Stability, and increased opportunities for trade: such were the benefits of the Second Empire in Mr Mitchell's eyes, a view close to John James Ruskin's. But another hero of Mitchell's was the radical J. Roebuck, whose censure motion on Sebastopol threw the Conservatives out of office in 1855. John Mitchell proposed to invite Roebuck to a Bradford Reform meeting in January 1858. The move was out-voted even by his Liberal allies: the 218 'Principal Inhabitants' whose names headed the reform petition. That list included even conservative Henry Mitchell. Needless to say all the above supporters of the Design School, Salt excepted, were conspicuous by their absence. Roebuck, it is worth noting, was no friend to *laissez-faire*: that Mitchell should admire him suggests a belief – shared by Ruskin – in economic planning at national and international level.

Mitchell's aspect of comparative youthfulness went with radical ideas and international interests. It is significant that his age would remain a secret to the writer of his obituary in the *Manchester Guardian* of 21 August 1884. He was in fact born in 1808. In 1861 he was offered the Bradford mayoralty, but refused it. He had been a natural supporter of Perronet Thompson, the old philosophic-radical and Chartist sympathiser of 1836, and rival candidate at Bradford in 1847 of Gathorne Hardy, of the Low Moor iron family. Thompson's triumph over Hardy seriously weakened the local prestige of that Tory dynasty, nor would there be another Tory MP for twenty-seven years. Not content with this, Mitchell was one of those English enthusiasts for Mazzini and Kossuth who drew Shaftesbury's amazed indignation. Indeed, he was locally regarded as one of Kossuth's 'most intimate friends and admirers', especially after 14 May 1856 when he had first entertained the Hungarian liberator at his Manningham Lane residence, Parkfield House. In April 1864 Parkfield was being prepared to receive Garabaldi: but Mitchell was disappointed. In 1868 he became managing partner of A. & S. Henry in Manchester.[17]

Such was the man, who thanks to his connection with Ruskin's great friend John Simon, would be enabled to draw the famous art critic to Bradford. In adding Ruskin to his list of famous visitors, Mitchell was entertaining another 'great radical in Austria' as Effie had disapprovingly described her husband, another political Protestant against the secular authority of the Pope. Appendix 7 of *The Stones of Venice* – on 'Modern Education' (1853) – would have stamped Ruskin as belonging to the 'advanced' camp in that department, and *The Elements of Drawing* of 1857 was sufficient indication that he knew his special subject. Certainly, Ruskin's connection with the Working Men's College was a promising sign. It was there in 1854 that F. J. Furnivall had introduced Ruskin to John Holmes, and it was probably on the same occasion that Ruskin found himself involved in a 'chat about Leeds'[18] where Holmes had his business. A trip to the industrial sector of that landscape which had meant so much to Turner seemed to be imminent, especially as Ellen Heaton of Leeds was pressing its claim. But in the event it was the enterprising John Mitchell who got hold of him.

The alliance between Mitchell, the advanced liberal, and Bradford's small clique of crypto-Tories was not in itself enough. A major enabling factor was the championship of the Mayor, Henry Brown, the town's leading draper. Along with many other influential Bradford Liberals, Brown worshipped at the Horton Lane Congregational Chapel, which was known as the Cathedral of Nonconformity. He owed as much as Ruskin himself to the influence of a mother formidable, rational and devout.

A more obvious essential to the Design School's existence, yet perhaps a more significant one, is the active consent of John Venimore Godwin, Vice-President of the Mechanics' Institute. He was the son of Dr Godwin, the revered Baptist pastor of Bradford's Zion chapel. In the 1820s Dr Godwin had been largely responsible for the success of the campaign against the 'atheist revolutionaries' who were the original founders of Bradford's Mechanics' Institute. Philosophic, humanist and democratic, this partly working-class group ('atheist revolutionaries' was Dr Godwin's phrase, not theirs) were for a short while one of the sources of Bradford liberal and middle-class anxiety. Henry Harris and Titus Salt revived the Mechanics' Institute on respectable lines in 1833. Another cause of anxiety was the National Regeneration Society, a grand-sounding body of Anglican Tories who, under Rev. George Stringer Bull, curate of Bierley, rallied in support of Oastler and the Factory Reform Movement. Whereas the 'atheist revolutionaries' were sure that Reason demanded drastic reform of working conditions and wages, Bull was certain that Almighty God demanded it too. The young John Venimore Godwin, in a long letter of March 1834 to the *Bradford Observer*, laid bare the miserable hypocrisy of this Anglican claim.

The co-operation of disparate elements of Bradford middle-class opinion in this matter of the 1859 Design School was an indication not of mutual satisfaction, but of discontent with the institution which was the setting for Ruskin's performance – the central showpiece of consensus liberalism, the Mechanics' Institute. Mitchell was not a very alarming radical. He was not, like the old 'atheist revolutionaries', in favour of a wholesale re-ordering of the educational and social system. Alfred Harris senior was no Richard Oastler: he did not tear the English language to tatters in his fury at middle-class exploitation of the poor. But both men were eccentric among contemporary Bradfordians in the ways that they offered to continue at least some of the implications of these two traditions. Mitchell's voice would be almost alone in the Chamber of Commerce in urging that at least some of their huge surplus be spent on education, in place of that elaborate Gothic showpiece, the Wool Exchange.

Alfred Harris senior, just like Mr Ruskin junior, was in favour of more direct taxation.[19] He proposed a higher income tax for the wealthier classes in order to ease taxation on the 'poor man's commodities'. He did not believe that a reduction of the malt tax would lead to unbridled drunkenness among the lower orders. On this issue, both Tory and radical were at odds with Bradford's straitlaced Liberals.

Bradford was most unlikely to welcome the neo-feudal fantasies of the High Tory Young England group, whose pet novel was Disraeli's *Sybil*. A Working Men's Banquet, sponsored by the local Operative Conservatice Association, presided over by Alfred Harris senior and Mr Busfield Ferrand, in 1866, would be a sufficient cause of derision in Liberal circles. This was the first time for many a long year that anything so quaintly feudal in the political line had been attempted in Bradford. Nor, on the other hand, was Bradford ready for the dreams of a proletarian culture, administered by disaffected middle-class intellectuals, such as inspired the pen of the young German poet Georg Weerth. From December 1843 to the summer of 1846 Georg was a Bradford company secretary and commercial agent. Thanks to the research work of Bradford woolcombers, he was able to expose some of the horrors of Bradford's slums to the readers of the *Rheinische Jahrbücher*. As a contrast, he supplied the same organ, in 1845, with a rhapsodic account of a working-class flower show, as an example of the proletarian future, in which man, nature and art would be at last reconcilied to each other. Georg went on to the climax of his own short life: the year 1848, when, along with Engels and others, under Marx's supervision, he helped to edit the *Neue Rheinische Zeitung*.

But the friend who had introduced Weerth to the traditional northern flower show was John Jackson, a woolcomber who became a gardener. In 1825 he had been one of the 'atheist revolutionaries' who attempted to found an independent Mechanics' Institute. Unfortunately for that enterprise, most Bradfordians were not at home with atheism and revolution. The way things were going is indicated by Jackson's subsequent career. In 1835 he became a founder member of the Bradford Reform Association, together with such eminently middle-class men as Titus Salt and Robert Milligan – who would be Bradford's first mayor. Matthew Thompson whose father owned the local gaslight company, was a driving force behind the peculiar efficiency of this

Association during the Palmerston years. He organised, and helped to finance, the purchase of Peel Park for the town during his mayoralty in 1863: and in due course organised the building of the Forth Bridge for the Midland Railway, of which he was chairman. Such men were formidable proponents of gradualism. Even by the time Weerth met him in 1843–4, Jackson – by then turned fifty – had already severed his connectons with the Chartists. Nor did he ever become a communist.[20]

'Getting-on' met with few dissenters in Bradford. A Roman Catholic canon might invoke the Greeks to belittle 'advancement' as an aim of education, and it was only in the Church of England Institute that in the year of the Great Exhibition the factory inspector Robert Baker could have compared 'conditions of labour under Elizabeth' with those obtaining 'with the introduction of machinery', when 'the master manufacturers kept no faith with the industrial property of the people, nor had any mercy on their powers of endurance'.

John Venimore Godwin, spokesman for the Mechanics' Institute Committee and its doctrine of getting-on, was able to harangue the National Association for the Advancement of Social Science in 1859 on his institutions's function as a self-supporting voluntary organisation designed to advance its members 'in the social scale'. There was even a financial inducement to employers to nominate their operatives. Alas, a look at the small print of the Annual Report reveals that in 1859 there were apparently only eighty-seven nominated members out of a total of 1,203 in a town whose population by 1861 would be 196,475. 'Unless an Institution becomes as far as possible self-supporting,' Godwin proclaimed, 'neither vigour of management can be expected nor a keen and active interest be felt in its operations.' Bradford's Institute was, however, unusual in having working men on its Committee – the result of James Hanson's agitation of 1848.

Not socialism and a proletarian culture. Not Toryism and neo-feudal culture. Liberalism and the Mechanics' Institute are the means of addressing Bradford's Victorian establishment. That year of 1848 which saw revolution in Europe and St Paul's Church built in Manningham also saw an interesting series of extra-curricular lectures at Bradford's Mechanics' Institute. They were by W. E. Forster, and their moderation and modernity were sufficiently demonstrated by the titles of the series: *Communusm* and *Competition* must alike yield to the golden mean of *Organisation of Labour*. Forster, for a year or two longer still tolerable to Carlyle, was happy to take the word 'organisation', and some of its meaning, from him. It was in any case almost the favourite Bradford word. The Committee withheld their official support, but hired him the hall – and the strait-laced temperance advocate Alderman Beaumont presented Forster to an intelligent, largely working-class, audience. Forster's notions were somewhat milder than those urged not long before on France's revolutionary republican government by the left-wing Louis Blanc: but they showed that grasp on new ideas which was a necessary feature of Bradford's survival.

A month before Ruskin's arrival on the same platform a lecture on the thought of Carlyle was given by special request of the Committee. This was at least appropriate. His own lecture was in some sense a sequel to Forster's series and to Carlylean modes of thought. The nature of Carlyle's influence is typified by Forster's response to a meeting with Carlyle in September 1847. Carlyle's voice was 'like the blast of a trumpet, stirring up all my powers to the battle of life'.[21] On the other hand, Ruskin's, in the words of his Bradford auditor John Holmes, was 'a thin, small voice' but a voice of 'enchantment'; and a voice which was an 'effectual awakener of the intellect in. . . relations and realities'.[22] It demanded co-operation, not mere assent, from the listener. In 1859 it teased away the migraine of Young England: 'We don't want the life or the decorations of the thirteenth century back again.' It demurred to any implications of atheist revolution: 'Let us have touching and thoughtful representations of human nature. . . rational, deeply-felt realisations of the events which are the subjects of our religious faith.' Ruskin spoke on the subject of *Manufacture and Design* in the only terms his audience would tolerate – capitalist, paternalist, liberal-conservative. But he hoped they might be induced to think. Salt, along with most of the more vocal Bradford liberals, favours Universal Manhood Suffrage; and yet Salt is no fool: he knows that to extend the vote is to affect, at the least, the modes of political power. Ruskin is in favour of universal culture (not the same thing as believing all may be equally cultured in the same way). He is no fool either. He knows that to extend culture – the nominal function of this very hall – is to affect, at the least, the mode of manufacture and design:

> Design is not the offspring of idle fancy: it is the studied result of

> accumulative observation and delightful habit. Without observation and experience, no design – without peace and pleasureableness in occupation, no design – and all the lecturings, and teachings, and prizes, and principles of art, in the world, are of no use, so long as you don't surround your men with happy influences and beautiful things. It is impossible for them to have right ideas about colour, unless they see the lovely colours of nature unspoiled; impossible for them to supply beautiful incident and action in their ornament, unless they see beautiful incident and action in the world about them. Inform their minds, refine their habits, and you form and refine their designs; but keep them illiterate, uncomfortable, and in the midst of unbeautiful things, and what ever they do will still be spurious, vulgar and valueless.[23]

Ruskin's lecture of 1859 was in another sense a sequel to Bradford events of 1848. The year of Forster's lectures also saw the first real attempt to establish a Design School in Bradford. Inevitably, it was set up in the Mechanics' Institute. Its master was Claude Lorraine Nursey, a pupil of David Wilkie. It was intended 'for designers connected with the manufactures of the district, for modellers, ornamental painters and sculptors'. There were a number of reasons why it was not very successful. There was never enough money; its Liberal champions were somewhat provincial and conservative in their artistic tastes; the dreary and narrow ethos (and rooms) of the Mechanics' Institute inspired little. It is significant that a revival of the school on more enlightened lines was attempted in 1852, under a Tory government. The prime mover was the Bradford Conservative William Rand. The Conservative swing at the election of February 1852 had been locally sufficient for radical Perronet Thompson to lose his seat to conservative-liberal H. W. Wickham, despite the efforts of Thompson's campaign chairman, John Mitchell. Perronet Thompson and his followers tended to despise fancy modern nonsense in the art line, and indeed their radicalism had become a little old-fashioned too. By 1853 a new 'higher drawing class' had been established under Mr Richardson. And then, in 1855, in an atmosphere of increasing adventurousness and reform contemporary with the outcry over the 'condition of the army before Sebastopol', James Lobley, protégé of the Harrises, became the new master of the drawing class, and was a great success. Lobley had roots in Lincolnshire, but was born in Hull, a hotbed of radicalism and republicanism. As the protégé of Tories Lobley was an oddly appropriate choice to bring a little culture to that merely Liberal watchtower, the Mechanics' Institute.

The Harrises' great allies were the Hardys of Low Moor Iron Works, which was at the time of Lobley's appointment 'almost solely employed in smelting iron for the making of monster guns, mortars and cannon-balls'. This patriotic activity – directed against the serf-empire of Russia – compensated for the Hardys' Church and monarchy politics in the eyes of all but a few liberals. And it helped to make Bradford a place to be reckoned with on the international scene.

It may appear disproportionate to allege the Crimean War as a cause of Mr Lobley's brief acceptability with Bradford Mechanics' Institute. But even a war may be good for something. Political, social and commercial jealousies were certainly a factor in his eventual migration thence to the new Design School of 1859. Since February 1858, the Conservatives, under Lord Derby, had again been in power. Of Bradford's two current MPs, H. W. Wickham was daily becoming more conservative; and the old radical Perronet Thompson had announced his wish to retire. Conservative reform bills were in the offing. All was buoyancy in those two strongholds of Bradford conservatism – the board rooms respectively of Low Moor Ironworks, kingdom of the Hardys, and of the Old Bank, the Harris domain. Wickham had large investments in both. Gathorne Hardy was Under-Secretary of State for the Home Department.

In the event, Derby's government was defeated by thirty-nine votes in March 1859 – the very month that began in sunshine both literal and metaphorical for Alfred junior, with Ruskin's inauguration of what jealous people were calling 'his' School of Design. It now seems amusing that Alfred senior should, in the following month, address himself to the Bradford electors as a 'Liberal' of curious cut: offering to gather Nonconformist sympathy for that 'safe leader' Lord Derby under the banner of No Sunday Opening for the British Museum. But others than the Bradford electorate were poised uncertain. Gladstone himself finally threw in his lot with the Liberals only in June 1859; while not till 1861 did W. E. Forster throw in his lot with Bradford. In April 1859 he was exhausting his energies as advanced Liberal candidate for Leeds – John Mitchell beside him at the hustings. At Bradford in 1861, Mitchell's organisational powers were hardly needed. They returned Forster unopposed. Meanwhile, the man who was brought forward in 1859 to maintain Liberal honour in Bradford and to keep Harris out was Titus Salt. He was not enthusiastic, and would gratefully take the Chiltern Hundreds in February 1861. As it was he beat Harris by only five votes.

English – and Bradfordian – Liberalism was saved. Palmerston could form a government with Gladstone at the Exchequer. Forster could pursue a career whose hightlight would be the Education Act of 1870. At the local level Mitchell could join the consensus Liberalism which, through all its shades, saw the prime necessity of an institution to be that it must pay for itself. The brief alliance between advanced Liberal and Conservative, so promising it its educational institutions, seemed in Bradford to be over; though the born-and-bred Tory Mr Gladstone was in Parliament doing great things with the help of reforming Liberals Cobden and Bright.

In the Bradford School of Design, the genuine talents of Aldam Heaton and James Lobley were by 1866 replaced by Lobley's much less interesting pupil John Sowden, or by temporary masters borrowed intermittently from Leeds, like Walter Smith. The architecturally 'advanced' Alfred Harris junior was replaced by the sentimental Baptist Arthur Briggs. Henry Brown (1803–78), the universally respected mayor who had been the school's first President, was replaced by J. V. Godwin. Tireless advocate of the self-supporing system, Godwin urged that gentlemen must withhold their subscriptions if they suspected that mere drawing and colouring for pleasure were practised in the school, divorced from sternest industrial application. Indeed, he perennially hoped that 'next year' the place could survive on the artisans' fees alone – though he would not spurn the grants awarded by the South Kensington Department for examination success. The sole survivor from the 1859 committee, Godwin, with Salt and Mitchell, had been the only one of its members to support parliamentary reform in January 1858. His clarion call of 'independence' would be answered, in the case of the Design School, by a cluster of German names: Behrens, George, Müller, Siltzer. Some local Tories – Sharp-Powell included – were liable to advocate central, or local, government grants. John Mitchell – the cad – had opposed either from the first. The determination to keep the enterprise 'purely local' lead directly to dependence on Germanic thoroughness and Leeds experience. Relations with the Mechanics' Institute school – liable to resolve itself into a school for technical drawing – were sometimes co-operative, sometimes antagonistic. They became almost impossible to follow. What do emerge are constant complaints by Godwin – he was involved with both – that despite healthy competition within and between these schools, with list of prizes and offers of treats, designs for fabrics continued to be 'disappointing'. Mr Foggo, erstwhile pupil of Cotman, and now headmaster of Bradford's Germanic High School, might in 1869 marshal plans for improved instruction in that artistic work which 'brings us some kind of consolation for the loss of Nature's sunshine'. Forster declares himself impressed. But the principal usefulness of Schools of Art, he tells his audience, is to provide a model for Schools of Science.

Lobley's own master, Claude Lorraine Nursey, had been a pupil of the genre painter David Wilkie. Nursey, who hied from Suffolk, contributed to exhibitions of the Royal Society of British Artists works with titles like *Devotion* (1844), *Asking a Blessing* (1856) and *The Tea Party* 1857). In 1844 he was at the Government School of Art, Norwich, from whence he removed to Leeds where in 1848, Lobley was his prize pupil, gaining the highest award for design. This success Lobley propagated as master at Bradford Mechanics' Institute, where, as Harris rejoiced to note, his pupils 'gained individual and average merit superior to anywhere' in the Society of Arts Examinations for 1857–8. Proud Liverpool came 'second'. By such measurable standards, the new Bradford School, with Lobley at its head, seemed poised to lead a national revival. Mr Ruskin, viewing their work, was moved to place their prospects above those of the metropolis: and, as *The Art Journal* noted, the semi-fashionable intelligentsia pouring into Bradford in the autumn for the Social Science Congress, found one more cause for optimism in the 'healthy and flourishing' condition of the new institution.

Alas, the disabling and reversible 'needs' of mammonism and dilettantism were written into the institution from the beginning, despite Lobley's efforts to break them down. By 'day' to the rooms above Fattorini's the jewellers at the bottom of Cheapside would come 'ladies' for 'Elementary' and 'Advanced' classes in 'Pictoral Art'. By 'night' would come 'artisans' for 'Elementary' and 'Advanced and Special' classes in 'Practical Art'. The former would be offered 'landscape, figures, fruit, flowers, still-life, etc.': the latter, 'elements of geometry, linear perspective, elementary colour' – and, if they proved themselves, 'shading model drawing; ornament; flowers' and, somehow, 'design in its general and specific application'. No sign for the artisans of Ruskin's 'animal and figure drawing'. Ruskin might affirm 'no great man ever minds stooping', but it would be unsuitable to ask the ladies to do so: and the 'men' are raising – themselves – as high as they can, to avoid ever having again to stoop, if possible. Angels descend, as well as ascend, so *Traffic* tells us, but 5*s*. and 7*s*.6*d*. a quarter is too large an outlay, compared with 2*s*. at the Mechanics' Institute, to suppose that many 'artisans' would invest it for the ultimate purpose of returning down the ladder.

The 'elementary' ladies paid one guinea, the 'advanced' two guineas, a quarter. Some had the pleasure of going 'a-sketching with Mr Lobley'. Opportunities for sketching 'from nature anything that comes in their way' seem remote near the school's actual premises – with the railway, foul 'beck' and dead-end canal converging in the immediate vicinity. 'The light is not Rembrandtesque on the current, or banks of a river; but it is on those of a drain,' Ruskin wrote in 1865. The murky 'possibilities' of his own age cannot have improved his view of the Rembrandtesque tendency. Rembrandt, according to Ruskin's *Cestus of Aglaia*, enables us to 'see, when another man would have seen or dreamed he saw, the flight of a divine Virgin – only the lamp-light upon the hair of a costermonger's ass.' Alas, for James Lobley and his students, the 'possibilities' of animal drawing, in the premises at the bottom of Cheapside, will be reduced precisely to such a market 'donkey craned up from street to studio much to the distress of the animal and the amusement of the crowd'.[24]

The pattern of 'reversibility' had become the more emphatic by 1865, when the projected day classes for 'gentlemen' – a term by 1859 at least tentatively available to describe certain Bradfordians – seem to have disappeared. There is doubt, also, as to how many real 'artisans' attended the school. At the outset, John Mitchell spoke of 'seventy pupils of whom forty one belong to the operative classes'. This, Alfred Harris thought, was about 130 pupils short of solvency. The *Bradford Antiquary* claims the School 'developed' as an 'academy' for the young and prosperous. Perhaps it was too expensive: or any 'artisans' felt more at home in the Mechanics' Institute, which in any case itself contained a high proportion of middle-class students. What 'artistic design' there was in the new school's Cheapside premises was provided not so much in the Design School itself as downstairs – in Fattorini's the jewellers. Their proudest achievement was the sturdy, reliable railway guard's watch. And perhaps, in a railway age, to have designed that, together with much of the necessary ironmongery and cloth for the uniforms, was a more commendable source of Bradfordian pride than such embellishments as Heaton's marquetry work for the dining-cars, derived from San Miniato, Florence.

The problem of advancing the claims of the 'phosphatous prop of flesh' in the coming age of steel runs through *The Cestus of Aglaia*, published 1865–6 in *The Art Journal*, the last instalment appearing in April. *The Crown of Wild Olive* came out in May, and it is not surprising to find close verbal and thematic links between the *Art Journal* articles and the two Bradford lectures. The best Ruskin could hope to do in the Bradford of 1859 was to open up vistas in both art and life. Genre painters of the Wilkie school painted from groups of figures, modelled in clay, and inserted into 'a small box. . . subjected to the light, introduced through a small opening in the side, in imitation of a window'. So Ruskin offers them the *Paradise* of Tintoretto. 'M. Angelo himself,' Ruskin had exclaimed in 1845, 'cannot hurl figures into space as he does, nor did M. Angelo ever paint space which would not look like a nutshell beside Tintoret's.' Wilkie himself had seen nothing but 'mere technicality' in Tintoretto, while confessing that 'nothing could more effectually correct the errors now going' than the Venetian's generous style.[25] When something of that generosity imploded into the lecture hall of Bradford Mechanics' Institute, a new criterion – and that the highest – was set for its thrusting opportunism. At Manchester the previous month, Ruskin had suggested particular models of study. He used the Bradford lecture to stretch the imagination, to demolish barriers to enjoyment, to bring a little of that expansiveness so natural to the Yorkshire landscape into this little mercenary hole which, as Engels had seen it in 1843 offered 'a superb picture when viewed from the surrounding heights'. Within, upon the banks of its 'small coal-black, foul-smelling stream' lay 'filth and debris in heaps'; the houses were 'ruinous, dirty, and miserable'.[26] So Ruskin offers also a vision of a new Bradford too large to have room for such 'ecomomy'. Let the banker Harrises' ambition pass all reasonable bounds. Let them dream of patronising another Raphael, in imitation of the Renaissance banker Agostino Chigi. Is there any grander model of decorative art then Raphael's Loggia at Rome, in which, to please a banker, Raphael immortalised a baker's daughter? The root of that grandest of all possible decorative schemes is just the same as anything worth patronising by Alfred Harris. Bread, and the healthy human body, were at the root of the arabesques of the Raphael Loggia. Is Bradford capable of wheat?[27]

To turn from Tintoretto or Raphael to James Lobley is an almost unimaginable leap. But there is something in him of that 'heroic' quality which, to Ruskin's regret, was so sadly lacking in Wilkie; and which, he hoped, the Pre-Raphaelites might resurrect. It had nothing to do with size of canvas or grandeur of theme. Wilkie was least heroic when essaying heroisms. Ruskin hoped to see a new art of contemporary life which would neither trivialise nor flatter its subject. It is to Lobley's credit that he attempted to do this. There is little in him of that Podsnappery which flourished in Bradford, as elsewhere. His best pictures have compassion without sentimentality, social intelligence without shrillness. They are worthy of the principles of the Bradford Design School as it might have been.

Ruskin's lecture soars. But it also gives its audience some touchstones in humour and commonsense. Any decent design, Ruskin urges, must be based on observation of healthy human forms engaged in healthy activity. Conventionalism in colour and shape – down to a zigzag on a plate – is only alive if it has access to those living shapes, those breathing colours. All of which, he and his audience know, is so far from being an immediate possibility in Bradford that, 'I can fancy your losing patience with me altogether just now. "We asked this fellow down to tell our workmen how to make shawls, and he is only trying to teach them how to caricature".' There is a realism in that which is both funny and very sad. The men of Tintoretto, the women of Raphael, were interpretations. They were the high points of great schools of applied design. But the persons they interpreted were alive.

Next to Mr Ruskin – his skinny form and ugly eager face highlighted by the concentration of gaslights on the daïs – sits the solid, unnervingly shrewd, but not altogether unkindly figure of Mr Henry Brown, the prosperous and conscientious draper, and Mayor of Bradford. At the School's preliminary meeting in December 1858, Brown had invisaged an institution open to all classes, in which drawing and colouring, and the benign influence of nature and art, might refine taste and improve design as part of a widespread educational process. Brown's 'radical' streak is shown by the abolition during his years of office (1856–9) of expensive mayoral banquets in favour of contributions to the relief of decayed tradesmen; and his generosity of spirit by his active involvement in 'good works' across the whole religious and political spectrum. He was a 'broad' Congregationalist where J. V. Godwin was a Baptist. He co-operated happily with the churchman Burnet, because they were both conservative liberals with a public conscience. He gave £32,000 to charity, including £6,000 for scholarships at the ancient grammar school, which opened the way to the universities for incomeless boys. With such a man liberalism might be said to work. His very virtues, like those of that other Congregationalist Titus Salt, offered opportunity of ascribing the virtues to liberalism, instead of the man. Brown was Bradford's largest draper, an Early Closing Advocate, and President of Bradford's Temperance Association, the oldest in the country. His support of wholesome educational activity – popular concerts, instructive dioramas, and the rest – was motivated partly by a wish to close the pubs. His business was inherited from a formidable, devout mother, and he retained her Puritanical values. But he also had reason to know that 'colouring was little understood in Bradford'. French, even Scots, lines in fancy fabrics did better in his shop than local ones. The Design School, in the words of Ruskin's lecture, provided a means of 'making his wares educational instruments'. There was an admixture, no doubt, of self-interest and partisanship in Brown's provincial career; just as self-will and showmanship were involved in Ruskin's own appearance at his side on the platform of the Mechanics' Institute. But the two men become more than the sum of their parts in a paragraph of the published lecture which, with the peroration that follows, may be said to put into glowing and memorable form Brown's own clumsily expressed, partly pragmatic, but nonetheless genuine idealism. The lecturer moves skilfully through a sequence of alienations, in which the 'I', and 'you', and the 'them' – touring celebrity, capitalist patrons, and those artisans for whom the school is intended – are carefully defined, and to that extent sundered. When he puts all together, 'we' see that there are indeed connections between that temperance that disciplines effectively designed curvature in *The Stones of Venice* and Henry Brown's variety. The decencies of nonconformity, the humanitarianism of the Early Closing Association, have something to offer to both art and life. 'And thus, between the picture of too laborious England, which we imagined as future, and the picture of too luxurious Italy, which we remember in the past, there may exist – there will exist, if we do our duty – an intermediate condition, neither oppressed by labour nor wasted in vanity – the condition of a peaceful and thoughtful temperance in aims, and acts, and arts'.[28]

It is the voice of co-operation and compromise. Yet it is also a little disturbing, reminiscent in some ways of that golden mean between capitalism and communism that Forster had advocated from the same platform eleven years before. Ruskin's means, like his subject matter, are more fundamental. Forster had named the great Bradford panacea – organisation. Ruskin, somehow, wants to foster the workman's vitality. He calls designing a 'power': 'And if you want to give him the power, you must give him the materials and put him in the circumstances for it'.

All this artificial – horror – outside the hall, which Ruskin parodies till his audience laugh out loud – isn't it supposed to be in pursuit of what Bradford *cannot* produce? Of what Bradford *needs*? And isn't *wheat* – which through all its darkness and noise and dirt Bradford is trying to produce – the end of all economics and the beginning of all art? Surely Bradfordians should know economics can have no other sane end; art no other credible beginning?

Such was the venture of a man 'bred a Tory' as he told his friend Acland in 1856, who had 'gradually developed' himself 'into an Indescribable thing – certainly *not* Tory'.[29] Certainly not in any party sense. Ruskin's philosophy of the organic life will win praise, in a few moments, from the Tory Alfred Harris junior. That eccentric Unitarian J. H. Ryland, Mrs Gaskell's adviser on the Yorkshire character, will take up the lecturer's theme of the need to improve the Yorkshire workman's environment. The immediate political implications of the School wll be noted, with approval, by that champion of self-help, J. V. Godwin. An Association of Designers has been formed. Godwin proposes to succour it with specimens of hot house plants. Such an Association had great implications for the future – since it prepared the way for some measure of independence from the manufacturers, who preferred at this time to treat designers as their private property. Too many rivals were ready, in Ruskin's words, 'to pilfer every idea of a successful neighbour's'.

On the surface, Ruskin's message is what Henry Brown, that is, the very best of the liberal capitalists in Ruskin's audience, wanted to hear and fulfil. But read with attention – as they would be able to do when it was published – the lecture demands the shaping of a new and fairer world. That the bill for this would somehow have to be met neither the wine-merchant's son nor his capitalist audience could for a moment forget. Ruskin is not quite sure where he is going – nor are they. But it is becoming clearer to him, and – to their honour – to those Bradford journalists Hanson of the *Review*, Byles of the *Observer* and that stay-at-home member of the Jowett clan who edited the *Advertiser* – that intellectual, moral and economic disturbance of some fundamental kind will be needed if that liberalism which at its kindest Brown represents is not to wither into complacency. Dickens will call it Podsnappery.

Mr Godwin is not quite Mr Podsnap. But he comes rather near. Opponent of interference in local affairs by central government, he is himself ceaselessly interfering in local affairs. This support of his for the Association of Designers is an example. The Association will be the most interesting feature of the new School. Because of the jealousy of the manufacturers it will also be a fatal feature. Mr Godwin is not the man to take the next logical step: to invoke central government in favour of giving a little more freedom of association to the designers and a little less freedom of competition to the manufacturers. That would mean revising the conventions of political economy. And Mr Godwin infinitely prefers to become Mayor – which he does in 1865 – and allow the Association of Designers, like Bradford beck, to be forced under ground.

It is quite necessary for Ruskin to make the bold assertion of irreducible necessities that constitutes *Unto This Last*. And fortunately, in the case of Bradford, another member of that 1859 Platform Party – Dr MacTurk – will take up the challenge by ensuring the purchase of the book of *Unto This Last* for the subscription Library at the earliest opportunity. While arty Londoners giggle, and Manchester economists tear their hair, the central organ of Bradford opinion – *The Observer* – will grasp the fact that if the golden dreams applauded by Ruskin's audience of 1859 are to become a financial reality, something fundamental will have to happen to the national economy.

Ruskin's positioning of local 'good works' in a national political and economic context, confronts a 'most material question'. In this instance, the final blow that drove Lobley away in 1865 was delivered by central government. Walter Smith, of the Leeds School, who would be called in to advise Bradford after Lobley's withdrawal, described the impending situation in letters to *The Builder* during March 1865. The new regulation of the Council of Education: abolishing payment for art pupil-teachers; requiring a 2nd grade drawing certificate for a mastership, yet offering no increase in grant for a 3rd grade; removing restriction as to size of fees: these 'improvements' spell disaster to Smith. He feels only a quarter of all grants will reach provincial schools, so that the able will 'sell their labour' elsewhere, leaving nonentities in 'pauper schools'. The separation of London from her provinces, of the practitioners from the teachers of art and of the well-to-do from the rest, has been thoroughly provided for, thinks Mr Smith. And in six years' time he will leave to become State Director of Art Education, Massachusetts.[30]

Centralised incompetence had an ally in local intransigence. In November 1858 the manufacturer Waud sets the tone for the many subsequent complaints in the Bradford Chamber of Commerce, with his contention that there is 'a good deal of jealousy' against Harris's proposed Design School. Waud is proud to share it. He wonders why he should contribute to the Design School committee's first option on 'good ideas'. He himself claims to spend £1,200 a year on designers – more than the School will ever command, it might be noted. What possible benefit could such a School bring? Any 'clever' design would be immediately pirated and sold 'cheaper'. The elaborate iron gates of Bradford's warehouse yards may have been an ornamental feature but their function was to frustrate prying eyes from spying on the latest lines as they were unloaded. It seems to Waud that the arty Tories are ganging up to grab a corner in available talent. The skilful Forster agrees whole heartedly with Mr Waud. But he feels that, with Brown's and Mitchell's influence, the Town Council will give the scheme its blessing.

CHAPTER FIVE

THE TWO PATHS

Reason also is choice. —*Paradise Lost*, III, 108

There is no tracing the real outcome of the Bradford Design School of 1859. Like the Crimean War, its story is not yet over. Something of its fortunes during Ruskin's lifetime will be told in due course. One immediate sequel of Ruskin's lecture at the Mechanics' Institute was that, after expenses, the sum of £23.6*s*. was netted for the school fund. Ruskin, like the Anglican clergy, and unlike those whose religion was political economy, gave his services *gratis*.[1]

The banker Alfred Harris junior warned against the excesses of extravagance and timidity; but extravagance would never be the lot of the Design School. Earlier figures are not available; but as late as 1868 the daughter school, in the premises of the German High School, would glean only £101 from subscriptions, only £88.11*s*. from fees. £173 *per annum* was needed to pay the Master. Lobley's departure, and the removal of Harris, Heaton and Mitchell from any real influence on the School's policy, enabled even Mr Waud, in 1865, to make a subscription of two guineas. His old 'jealousy' was no longer necessary: and he was *en route* to becoming Mayor. The School continued to glory in its independence, and to vie with the Mechanics' Institute School which, under Lobley's pupil John Sowden could claim, by 1873, a greater share in the favours of South Kensington.

An impartial observer in Bradford in 1859 might have noticed something of an anomaly between the charges of 'extravagance' levied against the Design School and the very grand parade of cultured expenditure which was the Bradford Triennial Music Festival of that year. Held in August, this four-day event, together with the National Association for Social Science Congress in October, helped to put Bradford on the cultural map of Great Britain. The Bradford Festival Choral Society was the showpiece of the town's vigorous and long-established musical life, and had sung in Buckingham Palace – and the Crystal Palace – in 1858. August 1859 sees the chorus extended to 300 performers, trained to the admiration of metropolitan music critics under Mr Jackson. Its powers are complemented by the whole of the Royal Italian Opera Orchestra, Covent Garden, under their eminent conductor Signor Costa. Mde Clara Novello, Mrs Sutherland, Mlle Titiens, Sims Reeves, Guiglini and Belleti, are among the chief singers. There is a fine and progressive programme. Visitors from far and wide are impressed by the crowds lining the streets to see the grand arrivals. Kept out of the way of the carriages by strategic barriers and a number of efficient police officers under the command of Chief Constable F. W. Graham, these examples of the Bradford working class appear very orderly, sober and respectable. They are a credit to the town; and the whole proceeding is worthy of the patronage – *in absentia* – of Her Majesty the Queen, the Prince Consort and the Prince of Wales. But the charges for admission range from one guinea to six shillings. These are not remotely within the range of most Bradfordians, respectable or otherwise. As with membership of the Mechanics' Institute, there is a discount available for employers willing to pay for their work people. As with membership of the Mechanics' Institute, very few employers avail themselves of the discount. And – as appears from close attention to the newspapers – some of the grand concerts in the newly redecorated St George's Hall, which holds 3,328 persons in comfort, fail to draw even half that number.

The Design School, and the Triennial Music Festival, may serve to introduce the cultural dilemma Ruskin discusses in *The Two Paths*. Which of the two tendencies in Victorian culture is to triumph? Are the efforts of the English to be in favour of small beginnings, or of grand finales? Is it foundations that are to be dug? The nurture and education of all the faculties of each of the inhabitants of every place – is this to be the programme? It isn't likely to 'pay' – just yet. Or is England to continue elaborating the cluttered structures that already deface the landscape? 'The defilement of our own Oxford,' Ruskin will say in extempore support of William Morris, in 1883, 'has been mostly due to the *plutocracy of learning*.'[2] That compressed and telling phrase sums up much of Ruskin's grievance, even against his own beloved Oxford. At Cambridge he implied the same thing. In an exquisitely lucid and carefully prepared reply to the University Orator's speech ceremoniously offering him an Hon. LlD, in 1867, Mr Ruskin provides an image for culture: it is like 'dung'.[3] It spoils the place where it is merely heaped. Dug in everywhere that it is needed, it provides a foundation for the finest flowers of civilisation and of art.

Whatever the audience, Ruskin the showman threw himself into his lecture work as though determined to 'convert' them on the spot. As his own editor, he was able to give each lecture final form and relation within a carefully planned volume. To each volume, he supplied a preface that drew his themes together. In the process, the pertinent and interesting became significant and abiding. Part of that process derived from the influence of Ruskin's audiences on him.

The Two Paths was published in May 1859. Each of the five lectures in the book makes its contribution to the total scheme. Thus, South Kensington was the place for *The Two Paths* to review the perils of *Conventional Art*; the Architectural Association the audience before whom to make a not very optimistic plea for *Imagination in Architecture*. On a more therapeutic note, the beautiful phenomenological sermon on *The Work of Iron* was appropriate to the spa atmosphere of Tunbridge Wells; and the 'exceedingly fashionable' amateurs of Manchester were well rewarded by a gracefully 'colloquial' review of *The Unity of Art*, which in its original delivery flattered their metropolitan pretensions by including the stated re-presentation of some of the South Kensington material and illustrations. It was only in the postponed and carefully written Bradford lecture, later placed at the centre of the book, and alone justifying its subtitle, that Ruskin assailed the shocking problem of *Modern Manufacture and Design*. Unlike the other lectures in the volume, it was considered worthy of notice in *The Working Men's College Magazine*, and of approving comments from *The Economist*.[4]

Thus, at Kensington we analyse, at Manchester consolidate, the past; among the Architectural Association, we allow imagination to speculate on the long secular future; finally, at Tunbridge Wells, with a characteristic glance back at Ruskin's own childhood, we voyage into an apocalyptic vision of this world as a moral organism. It is an impressive scheme: but it is through the contemporary dilemma of Bradford that we must pass to understand and, perhaps, to judge it.

The first lecture, in order of delivery, was *The Influence of Imagination in Architecture*. It was given on 23 January 1857, in the Hall of Lyon's Inn. The audience were the members of the Architectural Association.

As always, the ambiance of the setting provided Ruskin with a powerful silent witness to the relevance of his remarks. Originally one of the Inns of Chancery, where young lawyers had been trained to fulfil some of the highest functions in the realm, Lyon's Inn had faded into a mutual benefit club for solicitors, retaining corporate property but little very obviously significant public function. Chancery itself, of which this place was once a seminary, was now a much despised survival from Norman times from which some of the last shreds of dignity would be stripped by the Judicature Act of 1873.

It is, typically, an aspect of Ruskin's art in this lecture that he has no need to say any of these things. The walls themselves are left to say clearly enough to this Association of Architects: 'Achieve relevance to the world outside, or perish: neither privilege nor your professional rules can save you'.

Mr Ruskin had created a public for his ideas on architecture with the publication of *The Seven Lamps of Architecture* (1849) and *The Stones of Venice* (1851–3). More important though, for him if not his audience, was the question of Imagination. Readers of the chapter on 'Imagination Penetrative' from *Modern Painters* might have remembered a curious passage in which Ruskin had likened imagination to the tongue of a pholas. The pholas is a sea animal of the mollusc family that makes holes in stone. And human imagination at its deepest, Ruskin wrote, 'is a piercing pholas-like mind's tongue that works and tastes into the very rock heart.'[5] Profound and intimate knowledge of materials was likely to be a criterion for such a speaker in addressing architects. There could be no true revival of architecture till this knowledge was regained. 'Phidias, Michael Angelo, Orcagna, Pisano, Giotto – which of these men do you think, could not use his chisel?'[6] Despite all their superficial differences, Gropius and Frank Lloyd Wright and Gaudí and Le Corbusier would one day share this Ruskinian sense of the continuity between technique and art; the necessity for intimate knowledge of materials; the feeling that architecture and sculpture were profoundly one. Gropius would also share the social corollary of this feeling. His insistence on 'the common citizenship of all creative work' is a democratic summary of Ruskin's grand paternalist challenge to the Architectural Association: 'It rests with you either to repress what faculties your workmen have, into cunning subordination to your own; or to rejoice in discovering even the powers that may rival you and leading forth mind after mind into fellowship with your fancy, to association with your fame'.[7]

Such was the belief that lay behind Ruskin's refusal, in this lecture for the Architectural Association, to enter into the search for a new 'style'. As Gropius would acknowledge, 'Ruskin and Morris strove to find a means of reuniting the world of art with the world of work'. Ruskin, moreover, liked to be audacious, to thrust aside the claims of snobbery and affectation in the interests of enjoyment. For him, it was the gothic more than other historical styles which was 'entertaining'. The adjective was literally his last word on the The Nature of Gothic.[8] But here, in this *Two Paths* lecture, Ruskin the amateur made himself ruthless even with his own predilections. His analytical sense admitted Palladio as the main influence on English architecture of the recent past, with Paxton as its current master; for the future he envisaged an urban complex under a single weather-shield. It is one of the 'trenchant truths' of *The Two Paths* that there is no easy marriage to be looked for between this mechanistic 'asceticism', with its incapacity for the unpredictable, and the ineradicable 'intense, superstitious, insatiable' faculty of imagination, with its intolerance of the standard. That is one of his complex and far-seeing contributions. The 'sapling truth' of *The Two Paths* – the dependence of all noble design . . . on the sculpture or painting of organic form' – was only meant in its obvious and endlessly difficult sense, not in the controversial sense in which it has since been 'applied' to *art nouveau*. In the mid-Victorian context it led Ruskin into the sort of mere confrontation at which it was the cost of his value to be incompetent.

While acknowledging Ruskin as one of the intellectual pioneers of the new architecture, Gropius would also echo Ruskin's sense of the 'heart' of the matter. It is not new techniques or new styles that make architecture. Still less, for Ruskin or Gropius, would true architecture be a consequence of the rise of a new profession of 'architects', avid for status, ignorant of materials and technique, disdainful of their employees, contemptuous of the social setting and environmental responsibility of their work. Such are the inferences about one possible future for the Architectural Association which this *Two Paths* lecture permits Ruskin's readers to make. His tone is polite and humorous; and his contrary hopes are finely uttered: 'You alone are called by kindness – by necessity – by equity, to fraternity of toil'.[9] But on the whole the wry tone of the lecture anticipates the reaction of the *Athenaeum* review.

Lashing himself into a froth of snobbery and contempt, 'What does he propose,' rails Ruskin's critic, 'to enlist the greed and hopes of our. . . Art-tradesmen?' (So much for the social aspirations of the Architectural Association.) Mr Ruskin proposes nothing but 'niggling puerile trivialities'. What Ruskin had proposed was that only by the honest attempt to draw and colour could the eye learn to appreciate the form and colour of the natural world; only by effort with their own hands in shaping stone could architects designing stone buildings for an age that loved stone ornament gain any real comprehension of what they were doing. *The Athenaeum* summarises the challenge thus: Mr Ruskin proposes 'to make architects painters and sculptors also – a thing impossible in these busy times, when labour is subdivided, and useless if it were possible'. The 'also' is insultingly inattentive to Ruskin's whole argument. The remarks about subdivision of labour are well answered for sympathetic readers by the Nature of Gothic chapter in *The Stones of Venice*. For it is not only labour that is subdivided: it is men who are being subdivided, from each other and from themselves.[10] But the *Athenaeum*'s final judgment is Ruskin's best vindication: 'He wants healthy power and vigour. . . he never gives one a sentence that crushes an adversary at a blow'.[11] For Ruskin, profoundly serious and deliciously ironic, there is but one adversary: the Devil; and his crushing is to be achieved not by any display of 'power', but by the patient resurrection of all the divine powers latent in the world: 'You must love the creation you work in the midst of. . . keep yourselves, therefore, quiet, peaceful, with your eyes open. . . you must love the creatures to whom you minister, your fellow men. . . you will find that your work must be associative. . . you must surrender your pre-eminence in your love of building.' These gentle and profound insistences are the *Athenaeum*'s notion of 'puerile trivialities'. Gropius, who would assent to the meaning of them all, notwithstanding their Victorian 'style', would still find himself faced with the natural heirs of the *Athenaeum* mentality. For, 'worst of all, "modern" architecture became fashionable in several countries' – just as 'Classical' or

'Gothic' had once been fashionable – 'with the result that formalistic imitation and snobbery distorted the fundamental truth and simplicity on which this renascence was based.'[12]

The second lecture in order of delivery became the first in order of printing when *The Two Paths* was published. The lecture's title announces the broad challenge of the book: *The Deteriorative Power of Conventional Art over Nations*. It was delivered on 13 January 1858. The occasion was the removal of the headquarters of the Architectural Museum Society to the South Kensington Museum. Ruskin's personal involvement in this project, and its national character, combine to make a significant prologue to the collection of lectures. The occasion signalled a current tendency for informal voluntary groups to be drawn more and more closely into centralised national institutions.

Ruskin had vividly divided views on this tendency. On the whole, his views were more honestly expressed than many Victorian meliorists would have liked: but they were not in themselves eccentric. He was more challenging than most in hoping to see the State spend real money on housing, education, art patronage; but he was also shrewder than most in anticipating – and denouncing – tendencies towards mindless centralisation and the enforcement of mediocrity by bureaucracy. This vivid ambiguity of his is dramatised in the title *The Two Paths;* but it is one of the most constant and suggestive aspects of all his writing. As Elisabeth Helsinger has shown in the case of *Modern Painters*, Ruskin's style is also a 'canny bit of educational psychology'. It embodies not merely 'ideas' or 'description', but also and most importantly 'the kind of analysis he is trying to teach'.[13]

This aspect of his style is very much in evidence in this South Kensington lecture of 1858. It shares with other lectures in the volume a very wide range of tone. It has many shades of seriousness and humour. Because of its theme – the deadening effect of mere conventionalism – Ruskin also permits himself in this particular lecture, as printed, a somewhat fuller use of the easier and more colloquial manner which was now always a telling aspect of his lecture performances. It remains only necessary to add that Ruskin's use even of cliché was always fresh and individual, and that his style of delivery was concentrated on conveying his nuances of meaning, and the bewilderment of Victorian critics becomes understandable.The manly rant, the partisan argument, the mere indulgence of melodrama or sentiment: all these were easily recognised. Ruskin's failure to perform satisfactorily in any of these departments met with bewilderment and bad temper from the newspaper critics of his books. *The Illustrated Times* rather condescendingly opined that 'the colloquialism of the style strikes us as being here and there a little overdone'. More viciously, *The Illustrated London News* referred to 'nonsensical jargon'. A Ruskin lecture needed a Ruskin to perform it. What delighted auditors often enraged overworked reviewers. His books were accused of contradictoriness and dogmatism as often as his 'live' performances were praised for sincerity and disinterested intelligence.

Because Ruskin's style and meaning are always complexly one, it is worth glancing at part of the peroration of this lecture, if only to illuminate the difficulties of the journalists:

> All of you have the trial of yourselves in your own power; each may undergo at this instant, before his own judgment seat, the ordeal by fire. Ask yourselves what is the leading motive which actuates you while you are at work. I do not ask you what your leading motive is for working – that is a different thing; you may have families to support – parents to help – brides to win; you may have all these, or other such sacred or pre-eminent motives, to press the morning's labour and prompt the twilight thought. But when you are fairly *at* the work, what is the motive then which tells upon every touch of it? If it is the love of that which your work represents – if, being a landscape painter, it is love of hills and trees that moves you – if, being a figure painter, it is love of human beauty and human soul that moves you – if, being a flower or animal painter, it is love, and wonder, and delight in petal and in limb that move you, then the Spirit is upon you, and the earth is yours, and the fulness thereof. But if, on the other hand, it is petty self-complacency in your own skill, trust in precepts and laws, hope for academical or popular approbation, or avarice of wealth, – it is quite possible that by steady industry, or even by fortunate chance, you may win the applause, the position, the fortune, that you desire; but one touch of true art you will never lay on canvas or on stone as long as you live.[14]

The style commands a finely persuasive rhythm. It deploys powerful subtleties of tone and pressure which produce something too passionate for sentimentalism and too shrewd for cynicism. The skilful adaptation of conventional phrases is especially telling. We must be wooden-headed indeed to miss the delicious thrill of parody in that 'ordeal by fire' in the first sentence. Yet there is a pure fire of sincerity in the sentence, too. The tone relaxes into unbuttoned 'straight talk' in the next sentence or so, down to 'a different thing'; – then the mood is heightened or rather enlarged, in the following phrases. There is a cleansing mockery in the rhythm, and in the suggestion of cliché, here, which burns away the defence mechanisms of stolid sentimentality or contrived indifference. The phrases are etched and slanted in a way that makes them almost funny, and the more piercing: 'families to support – parents to help – brides to win'. And then Ruskin deliberately slides over, first into conventionalism: 'sacred and pre-eminent motives'; and then into the dainty mannerism of the dated aesthete. There is more than a hint of the late Augustan Mr Samuel Rogers[15] in the phrase 'and prompt the twilight thought'. The phrase is there to be thrust aside by Victorian realism: 'But when you are fairly *at* the work' . . . Yet the Rogers manner is echoed and given a new validity, by the true delicacy of 'which tells upon every touch of it?' The next sentence, 'If it is the love of that which your work represents', swells finely to convey some of Ruskin's true passion in the observation of the natural world. Nothing here is as obvious as it may seem. The order – 'love of hills and trees that moves you' – floats the mental eye far out to the standing hills, then draws its focus nearer to the branches of the trees in the foreground. The whole phrase dances in a way that makes the leaves move and the hills regress. The sequence 'human beauty and human soul' is an empirical progression; the sequence 'love, and wonder, and delight' is a whole ethical theorem. The climax of the sentence is on the first syllable of the word 'Spirit'. With 'the earth is yours' and more so, 'the fulness thereof' the style deliberately topples over into a tongue-in-cheek smugness: a murder of cliché by exposure. There is a hard irony just below the surface of 'the fulness thereof'. All this is to gain the audience's approval for the dismissal of 'petty self-complacency' which follows. That pair of bores, pedantry and commercialism, are – deliciously – allowed to assassinate each other in the phrase 'hope for academical or popular approbation'. There is a whiff both of Molière and Balzac – favourite authors of Ruskin – in the greedy ravings implied by 'avarice of wealth' (nor '*for* weath'; but a craving that grows by gain). There is cruelty and compassion finely blended in 'by steady industry, or even by fortunate chance, you may win'. The head of the artistic climber pops up visibly out of the prison of its striving at the climax to the sequel 'the applause, the position, the fortune, that you desire' ('fortune' betrays the expectation of another assonance on 'p': it is both astounding and deflating). Finally, there is the firm challenge of the closing phrases which include, it must be confessed, something of a Victorian showman's elicitation of applause.

The passage is no more than an average example of Ruskin's style in *The Two Paths*. He is an author who cannot be summarised or paraphrased. In analysing the 'Deteriorative Power of Conventional Art' he naturally deploys a manner that teases both *naïveté* and sophistication out of their shells. C. R. Cockerell, Professor of Architecture to the Royal Academy, is in the chair: and the lecture will be interrupted for Ruskin to present a joint prize for stone-carving to Mr Chapman and Mr O'Shea. The latter endeared himself to Ruskin – and enraged the conventions of Victorian Oxford – by his lively freehand carvings of cats and other animals on the front of the Gothic revival Oxford Museum. He and the other Irish masons had been employed for that project partly because Ruskin thought they were lively but mainly because the authorities knew they would be cheap. Cockerell was the last great talent of the neo-Classical school in England. His masterpieces include the academic but brilliant Taylorian Institution in Oxford (1839) and the superb Liverpool branch of the Bank of England.

In providing a discourse for both Cockerell and O'Shea, Ruskin is able to stress the importance of vitality and honesty in art, regardless of the prevailing style of the day. With wit and calculated effrontery he leaves the audience in no doubt that for him the Gothic tradition is the livelier one. But he is careful to found his chief artistic thesis on the greatest of Classical architects: 'Michael Angelo, exercised primarily in the drawing of body and limb, distributes in mightiest masses the order of his pillars, and in the loftiest shadows the hollows of his dome'.

The lecture is charming and well balanced, and it is pleasant to know that the theatre of the South Kensington Museum was 'crowded to excess' for the performance, and that Ruskin was 'welcomed with an outburst of loud and hearty cheering' when he appeared. Ruskin's father was in the audience, and was full of approval. He found it 'a goodly discourse, with all the sincerity of strong conviction'. All this must have been gratifying to Ruskin. But complacency was not something he often felt. In the lecture as originally delivered he made clear his own intimate sense of bewilderment.

Here was an occasion intended to encourage from the outside and by patronage something that truly grows only from within. Since 1855 Ruskin had been offering a prize for sculpture. There seemed to be fewer competitors each year: and this year 'he certainly did expect some better response than had taken place'. There were only two competitors and they must share the prize of £10. But what a pity that they had done the reverse of what he hoped. They had produced anxiously attentive samples of stone-cutting technique instead of the vigorously and thoughtfully expressive works he had hoped for. They had produced in other words – Ruskin was too polite quite to say this – examples of the deteriorative power of conventional art! Perhaps, Ruskin said, he should have insisted on a particular topic, and on the workmen's freedom to express it. Instead he had left the topics to them, and they had chosen conventional topics which they had turned merely into samples of careful workmanship – highly commendable, of course. The fault was entirely his own.[16]

This affair was something of a lesson to Ruskin. Not all the prizes in the world would induce originality; and artistic freedom could not be created merely by leaving the artist notionally free. Their chains lay too deep for that.

The Work of Iron, in Nature, Art and Policy, was delivered a month later – on 16 February 1858 – in the recuperative atmosphere of the Sussex Hotel, Tunbridge Wells. Ruskin's cousin, W. J. Richardson MD, had his practice at Tunbridge Wells, among the convalescent officers and retired clergymen, businessmen and civil servants and their wives and daughters. Ruskin shows great skill in addressing himself to each and every part of this audience. He commences from what might now fitly be called the 'Proustian' image of his own childhood memory of the 'welling forth of the spring' of Tunbridge Wells 'over the orange rim of its marble basin. The memory of the clear water, sparkling over its saffron stain, and of the power, in other ways and other functions, of the steely element to which so many here owe returning strength and life'. What follows are the most relaxed, and the most obviously masterly pages of prose in the whole volume. Placed as the fifth and final lecture, it is a gift from the author to his sympathetic readership. Underlying the prose is Ruskin's inimitable blend of compassion and clear-sightedness. For the 'weakness' of rusting iron is the very colour of the earth: the pledge of its renewal. The sister of Dr William Richardson had been Jessie, the little Perth cousin who had captured Ruskin's heart as a child, and who died in childhood. Her brothers – Ruskin's father's sister's children – would be described in *Praeterita*: 'The Perth boys were all partly weak in constitution, and curiously inconsistent in elements of character, having much of their mother's subtlety and sweetness mixed with a rather larger measure of their father's tannin'.[17] William was the best of them, though thought the foolishest. Below his faults lay a firm bed rock of resolution and perseverance.

The *Work of Iron* lecture is fitly a celebration not only of human strength but of human weakness. The compassion and clear-sightedness Ruskin directs to his audience may be partly a symptom of his own self-forgiveness and self-renewal. In the deep background is Jessie Richardson, who died aged seven in 1827. Her brother, William, who taught Ruskin to play chess, a great solace of his, is here in the room. Ruskin has had time to recuperate somewhat from the 'ghastly ludicrousness' of his false attraction and lying marriage to that other girl from Perth, Effie Gray. That had been a publicly acceptable alliance – but inwardly a lie, committed by himself and Effie, each acting on behalf of a blind and selfish 'need'. The better side of them had very soon repented, would never quite recover; would somehow contrive to survive nevertheless. And now, in the last week or so, Ruskin had come into contact with Maria La Touche. The evidence is not absolutely clear: but by February 1858 he had certainly corresponded with Maria La Touche and felt her fascination. He had, most probably, also met her daughter Rose that January; and felt Rosie's enchantment. *The Work of Iron* springs from a deep power for life in Ruskin's inner being. In its published form it may be said to be in part a response to his new relationship with Rose and her mother. Most probably, the feeling of new life had already begun in Ruskin himself before he met Rose. She quickened what had already begun in him.[18]

The Tunbridge Wells lecture is the necessary complement to the Bradford lecture in this volume. The Bradford piece is a lecture for sensible men: it advocates a measure of altruism and co-operation and social renewal from logical grounds of enlightened self-interest. Its tone is that of a fair-minded marriage contract, a new disposition of goods between the parts of society drawn up by a professional wordsmith of superlative powers. The *Work of Iron* is Ruskin's love letter to the world. It appeals to a capacity for passion and communion: it affirms the response of the heart to creative processes beyond the individual. An individual's common sense or happiness may or may not be compatible with these processes. For Ruskin, individual life is worthless – ultimately impossible – without them. The 'sensible' social vision of Bradford may never materialise. But vision or materialisation are alike impossible, to Ruskin's mind, without these primal spiritual convictions of Tunbridge Wells. These transcend the Bradford vision. They do not need the materialisation of that vision. They need to hope and work for it, however. Tunbridge Wells and Bradford are set together in the same volume because the vision permitted to the convalescent 'failures' of an industrial world is just the vision that world most needs if it is to achieve even those sensible, hard-headed and limited reforms which enlightened Bradford already wants.

The importance of the personal biography should not be overstressed: but whereas the Ruskin who snatched at Effie wanted marriage, this new Ruskin has recovered love. He is able to embark on a reappraisal of the social contract from the deep and sure certainty that fair contracts are *desirable*, not transcendent. Love, which seeks them, and needs them, and abolishes and renews them, is transcedent.

The Work of Iron marks a stage in Ruskin's movement at this time from Old Testament habits of thought – which are about a God who never betrays those who are in covenant with Him – towards a New Testament intelligence of feeling: which is about a God who is Himself betrayed by those who are in covenant with Him. Ruskin was becoming less and less capable of conventional religiosity and more and more profoundly and personally religious at this time. He was studying the gospels in his private notebooks, and would use them more fully than ever before in the final chapter of *Modern Painters* and in *Unto This Last*. *The Work of Iron* looks forward to the metaphysical ground of *Unto This Last* as surely as the Bradford lecture of 1859 looks forward to its political and economic contentions. Whereas at Bradford Mr Mitchell's guest is seen encouraging sensible Victorian tendences for improvement; at Tunbridge Wells Dr Richardson's cousin is seen in his response to what for him lie behind and beyond such encouragement: his own response to the idea of an incarnate and suffering godhead; to the meaning, not the ritual, of the Christian sacraments; and to the primitive, and perhaps future, communism of a true church.

Faith, hope and charity are the three theological virtues. Their symbolic colours are white, green and red. In *The Work of Iron* it is the green earth itself which is the ground for hope; it is the creative rust – the *weakness* of iron – which takes the part of charity. The white 'steely element', which is the *strength* of iron, provides Ruskin's message of faith. It is no soothing unguent, but a scalpel, a sharp sword.

Reports make clear this Tunbridge Wells audience was very sympathetic. It is for them that Ruskin is able to formulate in perfect clarity three articles of faith – as he sees them – not very easily acceptable to the liberal England of Lord Palmerston. One carries connotations of High Toryism: it is only by valour and preparedness for war that England will earn peace. Another smacks of philosophic radicalism: money must be spent, not in punishing criminals into further crime, but in training them to be capable of life and dignity without crime. This directly foreshadows the 1862 preface to *Unto This Last*. The third is the most alarming of all: it is a pronouncement of the labour theory of value, usually referred to nowadays as Marxist, but in fact derived from Ricardo. It is introduced in a paragraph that is deeply moving, deliciously funny and sharply challenging. And it gives even the feeblest of Ruskin's middle-class audience a responsibility and something to do: 'For, to take one instance only, remember [pillaging] is literally and simply what we do, whenever we buy, or try to buy, cheap goods – goods offered at a price which we know cannot be remunerative for the labour involved in them. Whenever we buy such goods, remember we are stealing somebody's labour. Don't let us mince the matter. I say, in plain Saxon, STEALING' . . .

The lecturer goes on to apply the same criterion to that prime dilemma of the genteel classes living politely on small fixed incomes – whether or not to taint one's hands with speculative investment in order to maintain a façade of respectability.

Placed as it is at the climax to the whole volume, this startling and 'heretical' revival of Ricardo's labour theory of value – ripped from its original *laissez-faire* context, and placed firmly within the Tory pattern of paternalist government – comes near to justifying Bernard Shaw's description of Ruskin as 'one of the prophets of the Bolshevist party'; which Shaw defined as a party of Tory communists.[19]

Much less startling was *The Unity of Art*, delivered for the Manchester School of Art on 22 February 1859. Ruskin wisely began by hailing a new concordance between art and manufacture. But he slyly proceeded to insist on the literal meaning of 'manufacture': 'hand-work'. Manufacture becomes art when the head is involved as well as the hand. Fine art exists only when 'the hand, the head, and the heart of man go together'. For those prepared to contemplate the lecturer's phrases there was a critique being offered here of the common Manchester use of the word 'hand' to mean 'a human being who minds a machine', but Ruskin did not press the point.

Not venturing as yet to question the advice of the Manchester school of economics – to buy in the cheapest, and sell in the dearest market – Ruskin nevertheless makes clear the moral struggle that an artist will undergo in the Manchester world. The higher delight without which art is impossible is liable, at present, to be often in conflict with that lesser delight which an artist is required to serve in order to pay the rent. Ruskin is most polite: he does not accuse Manchester of bad taste, or of the unjust commercial exploitation of the artist. It is enough to indicate that the artist is an explorer. He will wish to venture into speculations unlikely to pay – just yet. If he is not allowed to do so, the business of art will languish. If he is over-indulged as a kind of luxurious pet while he does so, art itself will become diseased. Quite a puzzle for the art-financier. Ruskin recommends a new kind of eclecticism for both patron and artist. This will be an 'eclecticism of temperance'. Art training should aim at rounding-out the general skills of an artist, without undue strain of nerve or effort. He will then proceed to develop his speciality from a secure base. The patron, too, should show an eclecticism of temperance. Let him invest what he honestly can in as wide a range of art as he feels able to enjoy. This is a safer method than wild spending on this season's much-publicised 'genius' who may be a dead letter in a few years.

Thus Ruskin fulfilled his brief from the dealer Gambart, who was with him as manager on this occasion. Ruskin was giving general encouragement to the art 'market'; was not that what Gambart required? It was not. Gambart, the Belgian art-impresario, made his millions out of a lifetime habit of trading on 'discoveries'. He bought their work cheap, puffed them into international fame, and sold while the going was good.

Once again, Ruskin had preserved a balance between his own

conscience and the expectations of the worldly-wise. When it came to offering a safe model for the instruction of the art-scholars, Ruskin was able – just – to advance them a living example. This was William Hunt, whose command of line and colour, and modest prices, made it advisable 'to put in the principal schools of England a little bit' of his work. His craftsmanship was secure; very little of his appeal was due merely to fashion; his subject-matter was homely and easily available. Students might learn much, and could come to no harm, by studying him. For this purpose, Ruskin now presented to the Manchester School of Art a watercolour drawing of Hunt's which he himself had commissioned. It depicted a snail shell with a spray of holly. It 'is still frequently used,' Ruskin's editor E. T. Cook was able to write in 1905, 'by the students for reference and study, being an admirable example of Hunt's painting and colour.'[20]

Cook has no such amiable reference to any work of Hunt's Ruskin may have commissioned for the new Bradford School of Design.

An exhibition of Hunt's work was held at the Fine Art Society's Galleries in New Bond Street, in 1879–80. Ruskin supplied the catalogue notes. When he came to describing No. 146, the 'Dead Chicken', a certain vagueness overcame his style. He remembered the drawing as one of a number of studies by Hunt 'done by the old man, in all kindness and care, at my own request, for me to give as types of work to country schools of art. Yet no kindness or care could altogether enable him to work rightly under the direction of another mind; and the project was ultimately given up by me, the chicken, finished as it is, having been one of my chief disappointments.'[21] The fact is that the 'Dead Chicken' had been Ruskin's intended gift for the Bradford School of Design. This is known from Ruskin's letter of September 1879 to Alfred Harris, acknowledging the sorry return of the 'little chick from the dispersed effects of the School'.[22] There had certainly been an appropriate touch of 'ghastly ludicrousness' in the choice of subject.

But between the Manchester lecture and the Bradford one, during the last week of February 1859, in the respite which Ruskin gained for his own private thoughts by a diplomatic illness which freed him from Gambart's company and ensured the postponement of his Bradford appearance, it finally became clear to him that an inner voice of despair he had been resisting was truly a hopeful voice.

In his Academy Notes for the previous May, Ruskin had talked bravely of 'experiments and early lessons'. The Pre-Raphaelite

School had begun well, and would advance with patience and time. But he also let slip one of his profounder insights: that 'in learning to work carefully from Nature, everybody has been obliged to paint what will stay to be painted; and the best of Nature will not wait'. Studying Hunt's drawing of a dead bird would never resurrect art. Hunt himself could not paint living animals. As Ruskin would put it in 1879, 'To a weakly, sensitive, nervous temperament the perpetual changes of position, and perpetual suggestion of new beauty in an animal, are entirely ruinous: in ten minutes they put one in a fever. Only the very greatest portrait-painters – Sir Joshua and Velasquez – can draw animals rightly.'[23]

At Manchester in 1859 Ruskin had offered Reynolds and Velasquez as studies. It was the very greatest geniuses who were always the most workmanlike craftsmen. But now, at Bradford, Ruskin could face with a certain relief a kind of cleansing despair. What makes animal painting possible is simply the following of the obvious commandment: 'never to pass a day without drawing some animal from the life, allowing. . . the fewest possible lines and colours to do it with, but resolving that whatever is characteristic of the animal shall in some way be shown'.[24]

So far from this Bradford statement being a new discovery of Ruskin's, it is simply and at last the clear pronouncement of his own childhood delight in living things, as recorded in the Red Books: 'rabbit munching, parrot talking, canary singing, bully cheaping, robin hopping'.[25] The despair lies in the fact that Ruskin's Bradfordian new commandment had become an impracticality in the 'practical-minded' mid-Victorian England of which Bradford was the embodiment and extreme example.

'You must love the creation you work in the midst of' had been Ruskin's commandment to the Architectural Association. But his prophecy about them had been of their capacity for the conquest of that creation: 'You shall put, if you will, all London under one blazing dome'. Bradford promised England a less brilliant future. 'I will suppose your success absolute,' Ruskin prophesies: 'that from shore to shore the whole of the island is to be set as thick with chimneys as the masts stand in the docks of Liverpool: that there shall be no meadows in it; no trees, no gardens; only a little corn grown upon the housetops, reaped and threshed by stream: that you do not leave even room for roads but travel either over the roofs of your mills, on viaducts; or under their floors in tunnels:

that the smoke having rendered the light of the sun unserviceable, you work always by the light of your own gas. . .'[26]

That vivid caricature of the Bradfordian tendency was drawn from what Ruskin had seen of Bradford. In his original lecture he had confined himself to making the same point in more generalised terms. The disdain of life Ruskin detected in metropolitan architects was merely a symptom of the industrial world's misuse of life. At Bradford the process had advanced to a state of 'ghastly ludicrousness'. Bradford had not achieved the annihilation of the animals; though there appeared to be no limitation to their powers in that direction. Their actual environment gave sufficient clues to the tendency.

Where was the delight in watching the sorry dray-horses and market donkeys, worked even harder than their drivers; in contemplating the backstreet piggeries, dirtier than pig-sties ought to be, and nearly as filthy as those dwellings of the Irish poor clustering round the parish church Ruskin was taken to admire? What charm could there be in the bedraggled sooty chickens, the mangy tethered goats, the rummaging curs with matted coats and wary eyes? Such things were visible amid the chaos of Bradford's streets. These still combined, even close to the centre, the double function and appearance, of urban thoroughfare and moorland track. The detritus of advanced industry and the droppings of animals were vividly commingled. Moreover, the local fauna was merely what it always was: the symptom of what had happened to the human beings.

'A good, stout, self-commanding, magnificent Animality is the make for poets and artists, it seems to me.' That had been Ruskin's conclusion, formed at Turin in the summer of 1858. Man is more than animal: not less. His highest spirituality is the crown of life: not an arrangement for the betrayal of life. Ruskin's own father – sensitive and intelligent merchant that he was – had been the recipient of this opinion.[27] Now, in Bradford, Ruskin must smuggle this opinion, and some of its implications, into the consciousness of other intelligent merchants. Because he had intended it for them, Ruskin gave Hunt's *Dead Chicken* into the safe-keeping of the officials of the Bradford Design School. But there was no 'presentation', no ceremony or vote of thanks in the matter; and no report of the gift in the papers. Still less was there a lecture designed to culminate in the revelation of William Hunt as a safe revivifier of art. Bradford did not need the *Dead Chicken*. It needed poultry. Its inhabitants needed feeding: 'try to conventionalise a butcher's or a greengrocer's with Saturday night customers buying cabbage and beef. That will tell you if you can design or not.'

Ruskin was fairly safe in assuming the subject would be difficult. It is unlikely he knew just how difficult. The local council was involved in perennial legal action with the absentee ladies of the manor – the Misses Rawson – over the uncleansed privy hard by the butcher's stall in the local market, from which the ladies derived revenue. Only the Misses Rawson had the legal privilege of cleaning their own lavatory. And they were not obliging.

Ruskin rightly assumed that his audience – the very backbone of respectable liberal England – were not in favour of a return to the wicked Middle Ages, when the 'pride of the so-called superior classes; a pride which supported itself by violence and robbery' was exercised to maintain the masses in a state of subserviency and dirt. The charming examples of the work of their school – not least the designs for embroidered fire-sceens by Mr Alfred Harris junior which Ruskin has just been admiring – surely suggest that 'beautiful art' is what they require. Well then: 'Beautiful art can only be produced by people who have beautiful things about them, and leisure to look at them; and unless you provide some elements of beauty for your workmen to be surrounded by, you will find that no elements of beauty can be invented by them.'[28]

The West Riding notables Ruskin was addressing had entered a little later, and perhaps more hesitantly, into the realm of fine art than their fellow capitalists in other districts of England. In applied art, they were required to 'come to the rescue' with inventive new designs at a time when a flaccid Bourbon-survival style, derived ultimately from Versailles, seemed at last to be dying. In that respect they were in a more than usually anomalous position, for their determination and efficiency had already made whatever 'taste' they displayed in their mechanically inventive products a widely visible aspect of the civilised world. From Ruskin's point of view, the natural process had been reversed. 'The fact is, that all good subordinate forms of ornamentation. . . *can* only be invented by men primarily exercised in drawing or carving the human figure,' he put it to Bradford in 1859. 'We have at present no good ornamental design: we can't have it yet, and we must be patient if we want to have it. Do not hope to feel the effect of your schools at once, but raise the men as high as you can, and then let them stoop as low as you need; no great man ever minds stooping. . .': which is as much as to say that the principles of good design ran counter to the values of their acquisitive and competitive 'society'.

Opportunities for 'figure study' in the immediate vicinity were thus reviewed by Bradford's poetical doctor, John Brereton:

> . . . the 'factory hands'.
> Women that never had been young, and girls
> Shrivelled to age, boys never to be men,
> Trooped by in thousands. . .[29]

The Social Science Association was regularly alarmed about the debility of army volunteers from the industrial south of the West Riding, as compared with those from its rural north.

Ruskin's 'particular principles' on design, offered in person in Bradford – the very heart of the British problem – necessarily related to the above phenomena. Their originality lies in their infinitely suggestive use of organic language. They may be described as the refinement of current ideas – the refinement being much of the point. Thus, while popular design wallowed in the solecism of three-dimensional floral 'effects', the 'advanced' Department of Practical Art at South Kensington urged the antagonistic principle of subordination of form to function and material. To help this doctrine along, they advocated stripes and lozenges rather than flowers and leaves. This was repellent to a public reared on associationism. They wanted design to remind them of 'things'. Too 'sharply and grossly', as Ruskin put it, Dickens in *Hard Times* had caricatured what he saw as the dreary abstraction of the department. The poor of the conurbations were to be denied all pleasant things by their improvers – even reminders of roses on carpets.[30]

It was left to Ruskin to insist both on the careful, but spontaneous observation of natural colour and of natural form – particularly the human form – and on the need to conventionalise from a sensibility so trained. There was no infallible formula that could be applied to produce such a lively process. One thing was certain: the modes of production and distribution of essential goods would have to be humanised before there were forms and colours to be seen or people capable of seeing them. Meanwhile – and this truth of his has provided plenty of 'contradictions' to keep his critics employed – 'taste' was not a prospectus of what people ought to like. It was an index to what they did like.

The title of Ruskin's book, *The Two Paths*, was readily recognised by Victorian reviewers as referring to the familiar moral tale of the choice of Hercules. A pair of female figures confront the hero at the outset of his career. They are Ease and Duty, or – much the same things – Vice and Virtue. Hercules, we are told, chose the latter lady, and after a lifetime of useful difficulty achieved immortality. Hercules, says a popular Victorian encyclopaedia, was 'a source of the most splendid tales of force and courage which have been produced. . . his myths have passed onwards to become part and parcel of our daily life'. Mr Gladstone, on his visit to the new iron town of Middlesbrough in 1862, readily drew applause for his definition of the place as 'an infant Hercules'.[31] Strength, efficiency and will-power were entirely acceptable virtues to the aggressive, materialist and dutiful, Victorian age.

Ruskin confronted this England, as exemplified in his five audiences, with a series of choices. Like Milton's God, he was enough of a Protestant to have a Ramist view of reason. 'Reason also is choice,' Milton's God pronounces, echoing the French Protestant philosopher Peter Ramus. Every step of life's journey confronts us with an active test of our powers of thought and feeling. Theory offers no escape from practice. Nowhere is there a safe refuge from politics or economics. No one can disdain responsibility.[32]

This pair of awesome themes: Herculean labours, and the conduct of the Christian soul, are subtilised, energised, made humorous, searing, tender, in the prose of *The Two Paths*.

Each audience is given a cunning mesh of choices: and in each case, those choices are compressed into a single, astute challenge.

The rising men of the Architectural Association are tempted with a pair of futures: as *artists*, or as *mechanics*? By a sly inversion of the expected, Ruskin suggests that the more associative their labour, the more practical their training, the broader their experience of all classes of human life, the nearer they shall be to artists. Internment in a London office, in a well-made suit, supervising other people's stereotyped drawings of elevations meant for Australia – such a future is that of a genteel mechanic; and mechanics can be turned off the moment their services become redundant.

At South Kensington, the members of The Architectural Museum Society are offered a choice between 'dead barbarism' and 'living barbarism'. Newly rich England can now amass examples of the world's finest architectural art. A raw, rich country eager for art must learn the difficult task of doing what it really likes. Pretentious imitation of the technically unparalleled treasures of old Europe and the ancient East would produce – has already produced in much of the work at the Great Exhibition – a 'dead barbarism'. The alternative is the way of 'living barbarism': encouraging and nurturing the crude vigour and undisciplined imaginations of our hand-carvers. Fortunately, these native gifts have for centuries been under-exploited. So that, whereas Britain shares the dead barbarism of the rest of Europe, it is possible she also yet retains some vestiges of a 'living barbarism', and some hope of a beginning. Finished high art – which is what most of Ruskin's audience fancy they can have – is impossible now, and would be a sign of national collapse if it were possible.

At Tunbridge Wells, the genteel retired persons and convalescents are given a vivid, almost melodramatic, shock to their nervous systems. The spinster student of the circulating library is handed a real romance: will she become a *labourer* or an *assassin?* There is no other alternative. The dreary round of making ends meet on a fixed income is given a revitalising tingle: every act of spending or investment has its part in a thrilling drama of influence. Officers without regiments, parsons who no longer have a parish, retired upper servants and civil servants with nothing much to do, are given a new lease of responsible life. It was perhaps this therapeutic element that made this lecture the most popular with its immediate audience. It was an extraordinary act of virtuosity on Ruskin's part to give the 'Marxist' labour-related theory of value to a bourgeois audience as a present from Tunbridge Wells.

The Manchester artists, and art lovers like the London Architectural Association, were asked to see their own hobby-horse in a new light. Their choice is between lapsing into *idealists*, or continuing to prosper as the Manchester *realists* Ruskin knows them to be.[33] Idealists pervert both art and life by imposing formal conditions on both: Realists foster life and art on the patient habit of producing 'some image of nature, or record of nature'. Their path is to give 'information about nature, but not necessarily imitate it'. That word 'information' is more than a nod towards the Mancunian motto: *Concilio et Labore*. It is in perfect accord with the moderately and powerfully presented social writing of those Manchester stalwarts Dr Kay and Canon Parkinson. They were both much used by Engels.[34] Canons Richson and Anson, who will invite Ruskin to Manchester again in 1864 to deliver *Sesame* and *Lilies*, continued the Parkinson tradition. On the morrow of this lecture of 1859 Ruskin will call on Mrs Gaskell – the Manchester novelist whose work is the supreme example of the art Ruskin is defining.

At Bradford the central challenge was no less precise. Bradfordians were offered a choice between their own glory and their own shame. Their wares may be one of two things: 'educational instruments, or mere drugs of the market'.

Ruskin's meeting with John Mitchell would most likely have introduced him to Mitchell's interest in technical education. It was a lifetime concern also of Alfred Harris junior, as of many of the middle-class men who formed W. E. Forster's power base. Many nonconformist churches had their northern or national colleges in the immediate vicinity; the newspapers were crowded with every kind of educational advertisement. Visitors never failed to comment on the passion for self-improvement manifested by all classes of Bradfordian; and in a boom-town where 85 per cent of the population were under forty-five, 40 per cent being under fifteen, the phrase 'educational instruments' was one designed to elicit an approving response. It was carefully noted by the educational pioneer James Hanson in his *Bradford Review*.

Liberal Bradfordians called 'hear, hear' to Ruskin's information of 1859 that the art of Pisa exhausted itself in subserving 'the pride of the so-called superior classes'. Having secured attention, he went on to say that a similar subordination of Bradford's manufacture would be an atrocity. Let them show true Bradford 'independence', he said. He seems to have spoken with especial bluntness and particularity at this point of the original lecture. Cheap and nasty imitation of modes whose very proliferation was designed to ensure they never could be successfully copied, represented the pseudo-need of one class to pass itself off as another equally determined to elude it. If manufacturers of 'fancy fabrics' could retard this vicious spiral by appealing to more decorous and 'substantial' taste, they would be opening a more certain road to prosperty.

Whether Ruskin realised it or not, these suggestions made especial sense in Bradford. However hard they tried, Bradfordians could not compete with Paris, or even Paisley, in the production of fine cashmeres. Nor were local silks or velvets – however suitable for upholstery – really of high fashion quality. Yet they might command the world with blends of silk and angora; even more democratically, their 'mixed fabrics' of cotton and wool were unsurpassed. And they would 'show an edge' when it came to suitings for both men and women. Sense, as well as sensibility, suggested the cultivation of decency and delight, rather than flamboyance. A ballroom crinoline of 1859, with four skirts, each trimmed with ruches, might require 1,100 yards of tulle. Such an obscene waste of material, and of human effort, disgusted local Puritans quite as much as Ruskin. Moreover, they were not serious contenders for the trade. The *Bradford Review* was still homely enough, in 1860, to regard 'the female form as far surpassing all other exemplifications of beauty', and to wonder what had happened to that criterion. Even more evidently, Ruskin's remarks applied to that Bradford speciality, children's dress material. As a disciple of Pestalozzi, Hanson naturally developed their pedagogical message. Children need strong cloth and 'colours such as will not suffer from use and exposure'. Heaton as naturally responded to their aesthetic implications.

In making his suggestions for the educational properties of manufactured goods, Ruskin was contributing to a local debate which had already had some impact on the national scene.

It had been a Bradfordian, Edward Hailstone, who suggested and helped to organise the Exhibition of Ancient and Mediaeval Art, held at Adelphi in 1850. Planned as an educational preliminary to the Great Exhibition, and designed to be of 'practical application to manufactures', the event was thoroughly to Bradfordian taste; and local papers relented a little of their contempt for the gentry in noting the crowds of rank and fashion who were good enough to turn up.[35] Principal contributors were the royal and noble houses and the various ancient colleges; and a theme of the show was the attempt to revive, in modern terms, Wedgwood's capacity to learn intelligently from ancient art. Ruskin was aware of the general, if not the particular, acceptability of the theme in reviving Wedgwood's good name for his Bradford audience of 1859. On the negative side, Hailstone's phrases about giving manufacturers 'patterns of the choicest works of art of ancient days to work from' are much in need of correction from Ruskin's discussion of 'living barbarism' *versus* 'dead barbarism': but it remains fair to speak of a partnership between Ruskin and his Bradford audience.

But partnership was not all that Ruskin offered them. They could have war – if they preferred. Their notion of 'educational instruments' was not so different from his own. That made them partners in his advocacy of 'Government and Co-operation' as the 'Laws of Life'. But their having allowed the production of 'drugs of the market' made them enemies: perpetrators of those 'Laws of Death', anarchy and competition. Which would they choose?

Haydn's Dictionary of Dates gives only one cross-reference under 'Bradford'. It is – 'Poison'. As elsewhere, the inclusion of plaster-of-Paris ('daff') in cheap lozenges was common; but a series of mishaps in October 1858 led to the substitution of arsenic for 'daff'. 225 people were poisoned, eighteen fatally. This dramatic illustration of the 'Laws of Death' received much attention in the national press, notably *The Times*, which the Ruskin family took.[36] The offending substance was ceremoniously consumed in Alderman Rand's furnaces in January 1859. The legal decision was: 'no case to answer'. Hanson's 'radical' *Bradford Review* regretted the notoriety of this case, and the defects of the law, and juxtaposed to its report a letter recording that: 'The Truck Act and Factory Act were passed in opposition. . . to the scribes of the old school of political economy'. Parliament may meddle, then, with the 'system of business'.

Ruskin's response involved the creation of literature. His first Bradford lecture came seven weeks after the ceremony at Rand's furnaces; John Rand himself forms part of Ruskin's platform party. The indignation of the lecturer's last two paragraphs is not only righteous, but pertinent. The solemnity of warning passes into the euphony of hope: but the transition poses a challenge. First, a smile in the voice to lower the temperature: then a sensible challenge given in an even, communicative tone: and then just before the opening of the dawn, one of the most tellingly placed phrases of the lecture with which the consciences of the audience are firmly pierced: '. . . you may literally become more influential for all kinds of good than many lecturers on art, or many treatise-writers on morality' – a smile, even if we know not the literal meaning of 'influential': now for something more straightforward: '. . . considering the materials dealt with, and the crude state of art knowledge at the time, I do not know that any more wide or effective influence in public taste was ever exercised than that of the Straffordshire manufacture of pottery under William Wedgwood' [sic]. Their pride of locality and generation is touched with that reference to an eighteen-century merchant from Staffordshire. That pride will be wounded: '. . . and it only rests with the manufacturer in every other business whether he will, in like manner, make his wares educational instruments, or mere drugs of the market. You all should be, in a certain sense, authors. . .'[37]

With his careful reading of the newspapers, it is unlikely Ruskin was unaware of what *The Times* was calling throughout November 1858 THE BRADFORD TRAGEDY. It is impossible he did not know the difference between the cliché 'drug on the market'; and the careful phrase 'drugs of the market'.

What matters is the superb modulation of the oratory for the delivery of an accurate shaft. The 'drugs' were sold, in a most 'literal' manner, from a stall in the Bradford 'Market'. The metaphor's reception is prepared for by the puzzle of 'literally. . . influential', abetted by the repetition 'influence'; and it finds its mark fledged by Bradford's particular source of pride – 'education'. It is a conscientious, flexible and delicate technique. And its precision shoots accurately beyond Ruskin's conscious knowledge.

In this single matter of adulteration, that 'efficiency' of Bradfordians Shaftesbury relied on would soon begin to achieve something. In their Report on the Adulteration of Food presented that October to the Social Science Congress, they defined the crime in exactly the same unemotionally useful way as Ruskin himself: it was, at least, equivalent to the use of false weights, and should be proceeded against accordingly.[38]

CHAPTER SIX

UNTO BRADFORD FIRST

> Mr Ruskin. . . remarked that. . . first to them did he propose a question. . . as the representative of the powerful manufacturing interests in this northern part of England. . . What did they want to bring the final condition of things to? —*Bradford Review* 23 April 1864

Bradford possessed in extreme form the characteristic tension of the moorland industrial towns. Its central concentration of horror was extreme; but it could be traversed in a few minutes. Given vigour, initiative and a fine Sunday, a working man could fortify his body and soul with glorious visibilities. Emily Brontë was a spinster of the parish. Ruskin himself, in March 1841, had turned away from sunset over the bay of Naples to confide to his diary the mere memory of 'some of our own Yorkshire hills – such as have made me happy, to intoxication, when first discerned blue and faint from some of our Yorkshire villages. . .'[1]

George Weerth, the Marxist poet who knew Bradford in the 1840s, described the town as 'Hell'; and its setting as 'Heaven'.[2] Frederick Delius, born in the centre of Bradford of German parents, would retain to the end his Bradford accent and his lust for ineffable skies and hills. William Rothenstein, another child of Bradford's German community, both loathed and loved the town which helped to form him. He was especially 'thankful. . . the open country was so near. Above Saltaire, a couple of miles from home, were the moors, and one could walk. . . as far as Scotland, without taking the road.'[3]

It was the getting across Bradford that required energy and determination. There was no escape from the constant need to descend to the centre before making the chosen ascent. That need made Bradford a centre of traffic – and suggested to Ruskin the image of a Jacob's ladder. It also for centuries provided daily lessons in patience and realism.

A small valley set in a crescent of precipitous hills, Bradford had known intermittent periods of prosperity, during which the large parish church was built, the grammar school founded; but it was never dominated by any ecclesiastical or aristocratic establishment. When lord of the manor, John O'Gaunt would stay there one night annually as he passed from Pontefract to Bowland. His father Edward III confirmed the town's right to hold a market, but it was soft water that had made Bradford a wool centre. Charles I, compelled to compound for his debauched father's debts to the Puritan City of London, made over to the London Corporation many of his crown lands and possessions, including this manor of Bradford. The place was solidly Cromwellian during the Civil War.

Many of the attitudes of Palmerston's England were not only compatible with such Bradford Puritanism, but had actually sprung from it. In the long intellectual and spiritual struggle of compiling his *Observations on Man* (1749), David Hartley had had constant need, as corresponsdent and confessor, of his Bradford schoolfriend, Rev John Lister of Shibden Hall, Halifax, who himself became headmaster of Bury Grammar School, across the Pennines. Hartley's book informed Wordsworth and appealed strongly to one half of the mind of Coleridge. The child of his father's *Frost at Midnight* was christened 'Hartley' with fervent hopefulness. Moreover, the *Observations* were fundamental to Joseph Priestley's educational mission, and meat and drink to the young John Stuart Mill. Hartley's attraction for Utilitarians lay in his propositions; for Romantics, perhaps in their pervasive tone. Hartley was a necessarian materialist with a belief in ultimately resolved antagonisms. He believed fervently in the Kingdom of God – on earth. It would not arrive automatically; men could only willingly work for it. Willingly; because, unlike his incompetent pupil Mr Gradgrind, Hartley had discovered divine justice and divine love as the central necessity and the fundamental fact. The achievement of that justice and the recognition of that love were the true aims of man's material and mortal being. God was love. There could be no question of his preparing an eternal hell for individuals. But God was also justice. Wickedness was apparently in the ascendant; and the human race might be due for a protracted period of suffering, or even absolute abolition. On the whole Hartley was inclined to hope for the best. What makes his special brand of Christianity different from the old individualistic faith of his Puritan forebears is his sense of the corporate responsibility of all humanity; and his conviction that the human destiny was a corporate one. Men would probably all be redeemed eventually, but might possibly all be annihilated and quite soon. God would make no favourites. This faith was an impression Hartley had come to feel after agonies of doubt. His sublimity was of that level-headed kind which soothes too little or too much.[4]

The other half of Coleridge's mind, mystical, ideal, uncertain, may have despaired of achieving Hartley's stability; he certainly rejected the Hartleyan machinery. So also, from similar motives, did a group of Anglican Tories working in Hartley's native region in the 1830s. Times were hard, and the inebriate Hartley Coleridge, sometimes to be seen at this time in the inns of Bradford's Market Street, grubbing up material and support for his books on northern worthies, was not the only spectre of disillusion. It was John Wood, a Bradford mill-owner, who inspired his friend and neighbour Richard Oastler and the local parson George Stringer Bull to launch a practical campaign against factory conditions – particularly the treatment of children. To Hartley, the material 'Duties towards Children' had been 'sufficiently obvious, and can scarce be neglected by those who are truly solicitous about the principal Point, a religious Education'.[5] The confidence behind that 'truly' may be a testimony to Mrs Brooksbank, who looked after him – his mother was dead by the time he was two – and kept him fed and clothed while he attended the grammar school of that little green market town – Bradford. 100 years or so later, hypocrisy had many more crevices in which to skulk, and duties, too, were less obvious. Oastler and Bull deployed enormous energies in the effort to make them so much as audible. They found a 'matchless' secretary in the elder Bejamin Jowett, and a great champion in Lord Ashley, later Shaftesbury. But it was under the chairmanship of Bradford's vicar Dr Burnet that to Oastler's 'inexpressible grief' the Yorkshire Committee of the Factory Movement decided to refuse further agitation for the restoration of the full Ten Hours Bill. That was in 1853. By 1863, we find Shaftesbury himself offering 'the happy issue of all our labour' earlier in the century as a consolation to the Lancashire operative during the Cotton Famine. Hartley's doctrine of necessary progress might seem to have ground to a halt. The Lister family of Shibden Hall preserved his energetic letters, but as Halifax grew daily filthier below them, universal happiness seemed further off. They did not give up. It was another John Lister of Shibden Hall who in January 1893 became treasurer of the first Independent Labour Party Conference. Before that new phase of Bradfordian and British history, and perhaps of progress, could be reached, there was a great deal of business to be done.

Dr Hartley's son David, carefully nurtured on his father's principles, had been returned by radical Hull to Parliament, where his Yorkshire worsted suit and his support for the American rebels, were equally notable. David's friend Benjamin Franklin was the American plentipotentiary at Paris in 1783: Hartley signed for England. David's invention for 'securing buildings and ships against fire', and his opposition to the African slave-trade, were part of the tradition which must have seemed triumphant by the late fifties of the new century, as Bradford's warehouse princes applauded Forster's announcement that the world's two advanced political centres were his future constituency and Maryland. The day before Ruskin's first Bradford appearance, John Rawson, who would be a member of the 1864 Ruskin reception committee, was giving a lecture on the life and times of Benjamin Franklin.

James Lobley, born in Hull, and for a time master of the new Design School, has a brother christened 'Washington'.[6] When the Wool Exchange is opened in 1867, the streets will be draped with the banner of the slave-liberating 'young Republic' and decked with caps of Liberty.

But that building rose partly by the eclipse of elements in Bradford life, which, as 'centralisation' proceeded, would again insist on their contribution.

Material and educational optimism, consensus Christianity whose practical doctrine was enlightened self-interest: radicalism in politics, and resource in commerce – these things were natural to Bradford but, as elsewhere, there were complexities. The Sharp family illustrates some of them.

From a strictly local viewpoint, the Sharps fell neatly enough into talented Dissenters on the one side, distinguished in theology, medicine, astronomy; and untalented Anglicans on the other. But there was also a collateral branch of Anglican Sharps, producing quite as much talent as their Nonconformist relations. Bradford, however, was not the place where it could ripen.

The Dissenting Sharps of Horton Hall were yeoman gentry and tradesmen. Some prospered in London. There was a Cromwellian incumbent of Adel – replaced in due course by a King's man – and a physician trained at Leyden. Abraham, who inherited Horton Hall in 1704, provided the drawings of constellations for the British Catalogue and was responsible also for many of Flamsteed's calculations. His neighbour Richardson, of Bierley Hall, botanist Fellow of the Royal Society, had been, like Abraham, educated at the Bradford grammar school. Abraham's father had been financial secretary to the head of Cromwell's army, General Fairfax. Such was the kind of history most Bradford liberals were content to dwell on – in moments of leisure – during the mid-Victorian period. It contrasted comfortably enough with the dozy pieties, or dotty impieties, associated with resident Anglican families, like the 'other' Sharps – of Horton Old Hall.

But the Anglican Sharps of the collateral branch included John, also educated at the local grammar school. His father had been Cromwellian like most influential Bradfordians of his day; but his mother was Royalist. Their son, as would the majority of Bradford Anglicans, became an Episcopalian Puritan who favoured constitutional monarchy. During the brief reign of the Catholic James II Sharp was intelligent and brave enough to combine denunciation of Popery with protestations of loyalty to the Crown. When Parliament declared for William III, so did John Sharp. William made Sharp Archbishop of York in 1691. His son John Sharp ran a humane lunatic asylum in Bamburgh Castle, made his library public, provided schools and an Infirmary, and delighted in architecture and pictures. Son Thomas, archdeacon of Durham, wrote father's biography: his son Granville obtained ten writs of *Habeas Corpus* against slave owners and colonised Sierra Leone, dying in 1813.

The family representative in the mid-Victorian era, Francis Sharp Powell, was the son of an Anglican clergyman at Wigan. He became Tory member for Cambridge, and an 'ardent advocate of the promotion of education, elementary, religious, and technical'. He inherited Horton Old Hall from an elderly bachelor uncle, eccentric and inactive representative of the resident Anglican Sharps. He purchased Horton Hall, ancient stronghold of their relatives and rivals, the resident Dissenting Sharps. The tradition he chose to emphasise was that of the third group – the expatriate Anglican Sharps.[7] The locality, and the island, were moving towards new arrangements. In Sharp Powell's case, legal inheritance, capitalistic purchase and a personally adopted tradition, were the positive, comparative and superlative forms of 'tenuous' as a predicate of 'relations'.

But Bradfordians in general cared little for Powell's Anglican reading of their history. At the election of 1837, the *Bradford Observer* saw the Tories losing far more voters by removal than the other side. By 1858, a Nonconformist minister noted that 'scarcely one representative' of the old families remained. He did not think they had done anything worthy of remembrance. One family he mentioned was 'Balme' – resident since the fourteenth century. Abraham Balme's educational work had gained him the commemoration of a monument by Flaxman in Bradford Parish Church. In 1858, G. B. Wheatly Balme's employment of test labourers for the removal of pit-hills won the unanimous disapproval of the Workhouse Guardians, who henceforth forbade such affronts to 'independence'.

'Gentleman' remained a term of disapproval in the *Bradford Observer* for twenty years. Richard Oastler and Rev. George Stringer Bull, the local factory reformers, were dismissed in that paper as the 'Church and King Tory' and the 'unhappy ecclesiastic'. It was easy to dismiss these Tory-radical gentlemen as hysterical sectarians: embarassing to discuss Oastler's charge that the Poor Law was 'unconstitutional', or Bull's arguments that a reduction in hours could rationally be demanded 'in the name of God and Mammon'. Meanwhile, the Haworth puritans were available for the demolition of Anglican pretentions – on theological grounds: and historical 'enlightenment' threw the bishops onto the same heap with the Druids and the Pope.

By 1859, Oastler and Bull themselves, while lending their voices in Huddersfield to the Early Closing Association, had become dismayed at working-class misuse of the 'time' already gained for them.

The non-radical 'Tory' element was represented by the Hardys. John was found to be 'less torified' in the House, except on 'religious questions' than the liberals had feared: but his son Gathorne failed to 'succeed' him in 1847. Charles and Gathorne continued to be directors of Harris' Old Bank – and to draw substantial revenue from Low Moor Iron Works – but Gathorne removed from the town. In 1865 he replaced Gladstone as MP for Oxford.

This political situation contributed to the difficulties of the Design School, nurtured by Alfred Harris junior, Conservative art dilettante and director of the Old Bank. The éclat of Ruskin's 1859 inauguration was impaired by the political failure of Harris's uncle, Alfred senior, in the same year. This latter was declared to be a Tory 'pure and simple' by the *Review*: to have done 'nothing for popular education on general principles'. Titus Salt stepped in to keep him out: but resigned in 1861 to allow Forster an uncontested seat. Miall, Arnold's 'political Dissenter', shared Bradford with Forster between 1869 and his resignation in 1873. His supporters, opined the *Observer*, 'learnt to love him as few representatives make themselves beloved'. It was Miall's own paper, the *Nonconformist* which in 1842 had first released to the world the fashionable doctrine of 'administrative nihilism' in Herbert Spencer's *The Proper Sphere of Government*.

Of the three Bradford papers, Hanson's *Review* somewhat favoured Miall; Forster's friend Byles ran the *Observer*; Jowett, the proprietor of the *Advertiser* had notions of Anglo-Saxon federalism: he lent space to the gentleman-Chartist Thomas Perronet Thompson, who had been one of the philosophical radicals as member for Hull in 1836. Disraeli drove Thompson from Maidstone in 1837: from 1847–52, and again from 1857 till his withdrawal in 1859, Thompson represented Bradford. He had been the first governor of Sierra Leone in 1808, and in 1820 had commanded sepoys against pirates in the Persian Gulf. His departure from Bradford may have been hastened by his hardihood in blaming the British for the sepoy revolt, but he continued a weekly letter in the *Advertiser*.

Amid complexities of opinion, it is appropriate that Bradford should also have been represented from 1852 till his death in 1867 by H. W. Wickham. A Bradford Grammar School boy of mixed gentle and bourgeois descent, and a large shareholder in Low Moor Iron Works, he was a 'respectable man, and a sort of liberal-conservative', as the *Review* commented. He was one of the 'wealthy, respectable, local, inactive' MPs the *Review* saw as the price of the 1832 Reform Bill.[8]

To turn to internal relations. In 1857, Alderman Rand introduced the temperance 'convert', Gough, to the 'immense assemblage' in St George's Hall with the announcement that henceforth it was the social and moral position of the working classes, rather than their political position that was the concern of reformers. An attitude as old as the 1832 Reform Act, and the watchword of the re-formed Bradford Mechanics' Institute, as of many others: 'Wisdom and knowledge are the stability of our times'. 'A Friend to Knowledge' had admonished Parson Bull in 1834 to replace 'enmity towards their employers' in the minds of his flock by the ability 'to read and write'. By 1850, the *Observer* considered: 'We have emancipated ourselves from the bad or doubtful conventional laws of man, and now we have to do with the perennial laws of nature'. Even the radical *Review*, though advocating manhood suffage, felt that its task was not to demand the vote for the working classes so much as to help them 'deserve' it. There was strain in maintaining such a position which seems locally to have reached a crisis by 1858. 'Philosophy' and 'Dissent' were parting company. In August 1858 the Mechanics' Institute, never Milton's Areopagus, in spite of assertions – its wide range of newspapers did not include the local *Advertiser* for example – decided under sectarian pressure to banish the 'sceptical' *Westminster Review*. The gap was made up by taking, for the first time, the more safely dilettante *Athenaeum*. In less 'metaphysical' days, Perronet Thompson had been the *Westminster*'s proprietor. His too vociferous attacks on the record of the East India Company, and his view of the working-classes as a 'better race. . . knocking at the doors of the constitution' seem to have increased the elective following of 'the more fully representative' Miall.

A 'political Dissenter' like Miall would not be popular with Bradford Anglicans, whose strongholds were the parish church and the grammar school. But affronted connections may sometimes be stronger than principles. The Chairman of the East India Company, Colonel William Henry Sykes, was an old boy of Bradford Grammar School and had family connections with James Sykes, one of Bradford's eighteenth-century vicars.[9]

If we take the years of Ruskin's visits as approximate termini, we shall find the town maintaining a short-lived balance between its local independence and its relation to national affairs. 1859 was the year the Social Science Association met in Bradford: 1864 saw Palmerston laying the foundation stone for the Exchange. It was an anxious period for liberals, yet one when they were ready to welcome outsiders no longer as missionaries, nor yet as national executives, but as 'visitors'. The temperance missioner of the early '50s who wondered how 'total abstinence' could be 'introduced into such a fiery atmosphere'[10] would not have been thanked for his anxiety amid the *arriviste* cultural activity that took the local choir to Buckingham Palace and brought Thackeray, Shaftesbury, Brougham, Joseph Paxton, Dickens, Ruskin and Palmerston to their 'platform': 'In these days, the royalty and aristocracy of intellect step down (if we may call it stepping down) to the broad, wide, platform where the skill and enterprise of capitalists, where the bone and sinew of manual labourers in necessary, if not always harmonious combination, are making their wealthy and beautiful England more wealthy and beautiful day after day.'

Such was Byles's welcome for Palmerston in 1864. But the radical *Morning Herald*, observing the antagonism and leaflets, described the occasion as a 'reform demonstration'. Hanson, quoting this with approval, claimed wide support in the Chamber of Commerce.

That Chamber was to refrain from inviting any 'outsiders' to the 1867 opening ceremony of the Wool Exchange, when even the conventional toast to the Lord Lieutenant of the West Riding was manoeuvred into a focus for local patriotism. 'So far as he knew, the present Lord Fitzwilliam possessed the good qualities of his father', was the limit of Mr Oddy's enthusiasm for 'aristocracy'. But as soon as he proposed a toast 'for his work's sake' to Mr Titus Salt, the whole company 'at once rose, and loudly and repeatedly cheered'. It was a hardening of exclusive local pride in the face of increasing 'centralisation'.[11]

Beyond that time, the local and national institutions became increasingly linked across the barriers of religion and party. Local pride rejoices in any son of fame; the Duke of Devonshire unveils Salt's statue before the new Town Hall in 1874; even Gathorne Hardy, soon to be 1st Earl of Cranbrook, returns briefly to inaugurate the new Mechanics' Institute. Harris's protégé Lobley symbolises the new reconciliations with his bronze plaque of a local Chartist quietly weaving at the foot of Lord Masham's statue in the park he sold cheap to the borough.

Meanwhile, the West Riding, which had helped to form the prosperity and some of the attitudes of the Palmerston era, was also in some ways its phenomenon. By national standards, all shades of Bradford political opinion could be fairly described as 'Liberal', and all shades of Bradford religious thought as 'Puritan'. Even the priests of Bradford's poor Catholic Irish of the inner town were temperance advocates: nor is it hard to see why these men should have been especially anxious to build up for their vulnerable people a reputation for respectability.

The *Athenaeum* called Bradford the 'youngest and rawest child of the industrial revolution': its population increase between 1801–51 was over six times the national average; and when 'opulent merchants from Manchester, Leeds, Germany, etc. . . . flocked to it' they helped to provide a lively forum which demanded national notice.

The *Westminster Review* thus stated the case for the economic importance of the area in 1859: 'It clothes one third of the human race in wool, and finds them in files and penknives. It furnishes our wardrobes, our dinners and our armouries. It feeds, wraps, shaves and stabs the greater part of humanity subject to these processes.'

In optimistic mood nine years earlier, the *Bradford Observer* had claimed a didactic mission for this commercial preponderance: 'We have to outfit the Sailor, to guide the helm on the Seas, to ply the hammer and wield the axe. . . We are the guardian angels of the world, and a great source of this year's happiness is to arise from our attention upon ignorance and indigence.'

To carry that vision across the Palmerston years among the 'Sleuth hounds after money' and amid the 'hideous abnegation of grace and feeling' also noted by the *Westminster* was the task of the men of principle – as various as the society to which they belonged. The *Westminster* had hopes: 'Individually. . . the victors in the great life-struggle for self are more sensible to the emotions of generosity. . . softened by success, there are no more liberal patrons of art and literature.'[12]

It was not individualism, but the spirit of 'combination' that Byles invoked as Palmerston 'stepped down' onto the Bradford 'platform'. This sorts oddly with the *Westminster*'s view of industrial Yorkshire society as locked in a 'life-struggle'. Was 'combination' to be the goal, or the condition, of 'struggle' – or was it only a word for 'occasions'? Certainly, 'antagonism' is a frequent liberal catchword.

Hartley had believed that, just as in the individual, Association had the tendency to transform a condition of mixed pleasure and pain into complex pleasure, so in society, undesirable differences would at last compensate one another to produce a state of equality and happiness. Most likely, man had no separable 'soul' to survive death. The gospel message of bodily resurrection was the only hope for a personal eternity. It was Priestley who set on one side Hartley's 'system of moral and religious knowledge', and underlined those contradictions both in scientific theory and in society from which any new synthesis must be made. Contradiction was perhaps even an attribute of the divinity – should there be such a personage.[13]

John Stuart Mill wrestled with his father's faith, derived directly from Hartley, in philosophic 'antagonism' – by which an individual collated all approaches to a question, and a society laid itself open to 'complete liberty of contradiction'. This did not, however, answer the question of how a government was to enforce a decision. Mill might denounce the cynically pragmatic view that: 'There are. . . certain beliefs so useful. . . that it is. . . the duty of governments to uphold those beliefs';[14] but the deadly fact is that it was precisely a 'belief' in *laissez-faire* that Mill's theory of 'antagonism' would prevent a government from repressing. That was the point at which Ruskin, who supported Mill as a politician, diverged sharply from Mill as a political theorist. In presenting his chapter *The Task of the Least*, in the last volume of *Modern Painters*, as a complement to Mill's one-sided theories, Ruskin was in effect re-asserting the spiritual and corporate half – the Coleridgean half – of the wholeness which was Hartley's original vision.

At a local level, newspapers helped to monitor the debate with prizes for acceptable essays on the law of wages. Hanson also published a confrontation between *Equitas* and *Humanitas*.

By whatever route, *Equitas* echoes Priestley's *Preface* to Harley: 'Antagonism is the order of all things. . . in physics, in astronomy, in chemistry. . . in the use of all medicines. . . combats produce. . . an exact balance.' Selfishness, he feels, is innate, but to be resisted by will.

The same issue of the *Observer* that saw Bradford liberals as 'the guardian angels of the world' had been equally emphatic that 'the condition of the national, as of the individual life is a condition of incessant conflict'. For the Bradford Nonconformist Chown, such conflict was the heroism of the saints: 'Christian martyrs battled with the lions' in his Colosseum.

If the law of supply and demand was not a 'bad' or 'conventional' law, but part of the 'order of all things', such ferocity of martyrdom was not called for. But if innate selfishness was the premise of that 'law', how was it to operate fairly? As *Humanitas* pointed out, it was the employer's 'will' that was the 'important factor'. One of Hanson's prize essayists decided Robert Owen's productive co-operation had failed, 'because he thought human nature was better than it really is'. Clearly the 'will' of those without the 'power' of capital must be devoted to what Brougham told them was the 'absolute necessity of provident and prudent conduct in every part of their lives', or as another prize essayist pathetically echoed: 'striving hard to keep up their independence in the battle of life.'

In 1834, the *Observer* challenged Bull's followers: 'never be ashamed of declaring your adherence, but always hold yourselves prepared to abandon an error'. Or, presumably, a job. By 1858, the same message had gained an anxious vigour. Lord Radstock told the 'hands' of Bradford to rely 'not upon others, not upon law, but upon themselves': much 'grappling' would be involved.

Hanson's *Humanitas*, considering the 'human misery which the action of this "beneficent principle" [of 'antagonism'] has hitherto left festering at the base of the social pyramid' – called for the 'strong arm of the law. . . to protect labour against capital'. The notion of 'mutual competition' was 'as if a naked, defenceless man should. . . contend for life against an armed and practised gladiator'.

At least in Bradford, what made the operation of any 'antagonism' of ideas incomplete was the fact that the middle classes had purchased the platform.

Hall Ings – near the old hall – had been the local Hyde Park Corner. Thus in 1834 'a meeting of operatives' had gathered there to discuss the sentences 'passed against the agricultural labourers at Dorchester' – the Tolpuddle Martyrs. But an adjacent site was purchased by shareholders and St George's Hall erected in 1854. That platform was managed and hired out by the appropriate committee. Anything else was a disturbance.

The ATTEMPTED REVIVAL OF CHARTISM made a headline for the *Review* in 1858, but it amounted only to a 'not numerous' gathering whose 'divided' leaders argued out on Bradford Moor. That afternoon a Protestant missioner addressed a 'packed assembly' in Peel Square.[15]

Such was the Bradford that would be satirised and challenged in *Traffic*. A degenerate Puritanism postponed salvation to another world. Its religious practice worked in complicity with a brutal materialism which made its own false heaven in the suburbs of Manningham and Bingley and created real hells for the very poor – many of them Irish Catholics – in the squalid cellars by the Bradford canal. Purgatory as a doctrine was confined to these same poor Irish: but existed practically in the many struggling families of respectable artisans and lower-middle-class tradesmen. In opposition to this religion of getting-on there was only, it might have seemed, a handful of godless eccentrics, ranting against the great English and supreme Yorkshire quality of respectability and all it stood for – that very quality which is most deeply cherished by those who have to work hardest to attain it.

It is against this polarised Bradford – the topical, 'contemporary' Bradford as an image of mid-Victorian England – that the published

Traffic scores its most splendid hits. But to turn to Ruskin's original 1864 lecture, as faithfully recorded by James Hanson's shorthand writer (or perhaps Hanson himself) is to discover a different Ruskin and a different Bradford. The criticism he has to offer is not less outspoken: it is more so. But the earnest, gentle and searching tone of it differs considerably from Ruskin's own literary version. It is clearly meant to appeal to the deeper qualities of his Yorkshire audience; which Ruskin would later define as 'Honesty and Piety'.[16] It speaks in an intimate tone to that tradition of true Puritanism which Hartley had represented. It addresses a Bradford character which had existed centuries before the steam-engine and would survive its passing:

> MR RUSKIN. . . was especially attached to this district of Yorkshire, and on the previous occasion, he had come down to address them, as the representative of the powerful manufacturing interests in this northern part of England, – to address to them a question which they did not answer at that time. He had now come to ask the plain question again. What were they going to make the architecture of the districts of which the manufacturers were the prevalent powers? What did they want to bring the final condition of things to?

This is no alienated Eminent Victorian haranguing provincial Victorian philistines. It is John Ruskin conversing with the Bradford character as he has learned to appreciate it in the persons of his 'good friend' the engraver John Cousen; of the 'excellent and zealous' Mr Lobley; of the 'modest and benevolent' Mr Mitchell; of the 'good and thoughtful' Alfred Harris.[17]

Ruskin's original peroration includes – as will *Traffic* – Plato's depiction of the good Puritans of Atlantis corrupted by sudden access of unjustly distributed wealth. Immediately beyond the villas of Manningham, a fifteen-minute walk from the lecture hall, is the ancestral farm of the yeoman Jowetts. Benjamin Jowett, the new Regius Professor of Greek, is already hard at work on his classic translation of Plato, which Ruskin will come to use, and abuse.[18] But tonight Ruskin is allowing the learning of Oxford and the Puritanism of Bradford to co-operate. The words of Plato are eloquently relevant to the Bradford of Palmerston's England. They co-operate with it: yet they go beyond it. They are not likely to be entirely misunderstood by men with sons at Bradford Grammar School, or at the new High School, with its classical masters imported from

Heidelberg. But Ruskin looks beyond even their advanced schemes for educational reform.

When W. E. Forster has personally supervised the reform of their Grammar School, as the first of the schools to be dealt with under the Endowed Schools Act of 1869, High School and Grammar School will merge into a single establishment. Once Jowett and other reformers have removed the last of the sectarian bars to Oxford entry, and thrown more scholarships open to free competition, Bradford Grammar School – already thriving in the reign of Edward III – will take its natural place as a provider of Oxford scholars. In science, particularly, it will do nearly as well as Manchester Grammar School; and their success will do much to restrain in the north of England the new fashion among the commercial classes for patronising the neo-medieval boarding schools grafted onto old endowments, such as that at Eton, now like its imitations a seminary of centralism and classical reaction, but remembered in Bradford as the showpiece charitable establishment of the parvenu Lancastrian dynasty, built partly with Bradford money by Bradford's most disastrous squire, King Henry VI.[19]

Ruskin appeals to the subjective, but factually accurate, view of history fostered by the Bradford middle class he addresses. Wickedly so. He gives inspiration to their sense of centuries of injustice and maladministration, now at last to be superseded by their own efficiency. In *Traffic*, Plato's words form part of an exquisitely complex, infinitely allusive piece of high literary art. The impression is that Ruskin is speaking beyond his audience to posterity; but that he has his audience and their jealousies well in train. But in the original lecture Ruskin's Platonic comparison was accompanied by extempore sentences of searching immediacy.

These sentences compelled the *Bradford Observer* to ask, 'How genuine is our education?' Not content with flattering the Bradford elite by quoting Plato to them, Ruskin was appealing to the deepest springs of their radical Puritanism. A favourite historical cameo with Victorians was the picture of Roger Ascham, the Yorkshire schoolmaster, reading Plato with the Protestant Lady Jane Grey. We have heard this story 'a hundred times over', as Ruskin himself will write in *Fors Clavigera*, ironically dubbing himself the Roger Ascham of his own day.[20] In Bradford he was asking for a Reformation so far-reaching that it would affect that vast majority of Bradfordians who would never see the inside of Bradford Grammar School, or find their way to the Mechanics' Institute. A great difference between the experience of reading *Traffic* and the experience of reading Hanson's original report in the *Bradford Review* is that Hanson's record conveys the strong impression that the audience are listening; and that Ruskin is pleading with them to listen to their own best selves.

A reading of the contemporary local newspapers gives an impression of an extraordinary amount and range of educational activity, most of it with a strong sectarian bias of one kind or another. It is with the hope of making up the gaps in this system that Forster, with the support of Ruskin's audience, is engaged in the battle which will result in the triumph of the Education Act of 1870. But Ruskin is already looking beyond that desired result. He is not in Bradford merely to join the chorus of protest against the failures of contemporary education. He is here to warn against the consequences of its success. He has seen Saltaire; that model of efficiency and segregation. And he feels bound to criticise his audience, not for having as yet failed to achieve an ideal Republic; but for having already laid the foundations of their ideal Republic on the backs of efficiently submissive neo-Platonic slaves:

> They were always wishing for their money's worth and what was that? That was just what political economy had not answered. No definition had been given of that which constituted true wealth. If they would have patience he would give them a definition. The perfect type of humanity involved the perfection of his body, affections and intelligence. It was the object of true political economy to accumulate for use those things which served to sustain the body, exercise the affections, or to form the intelligence. Whatever served any of these purposes was useful to man; whatever served none of those purposes, and much more what served to counteract them, was in like manner unlawful and unholy. Now, he came to tell them that their ideal line of life was a false one, for whilst to one family their goddess was the goddess of getting on, to thousands she was the goddess of stopping. In fact, whatever word they liked to use, she was the goddess of slavery. The subdued person came into the form and position of a slave. They were perpetually crying out, and sacrificing their strength to do away with slavery away from them, but they were forgetting the slavery at home.

James Hanson's own response of fervent affirmation to these remarks may be measured by the fact that it was he who in 1876, as Chairman of the Bradford School Board's Education Committee, would become the founder of England's first publicly-endowed secondary school.

The wholeness of Dr Hartley's vision had encompassed a scientific materialism informed by passionate convictions of justice and working by empirical means towards the fulfilment of man's whole being. This vision had never died; it had only been buried under the foundations of the temple of Britannia Agoraia.

That ferocious combination of spiritual and political impulses which – for better and worse – was so much a part of the English Revolution of the seventeenth century, and so particularly treasured by the stronger part of the Pennine tradition to which Dr Hartley belonged, had apparently been divided into Sunday superstition on the one hand and workday practice on the other. The English tradition of respectable revolution had apparently faded.

At the dawn of the Industrial Revolution in the late seventeenth century those new religious ideas and new political ideals for whose open discussion Milton had pleaded in his *Areopagitica* had been contained and tamed by the 'Glorious Revolution' of 1689. When Dr Hartley's father, a poor man from the Halifax region, was able to go up to Oxford as a servitor in 1691, he might have thought that a new age was beginning. It was an *annus mirabilis* for his home region. Sharp of Bradford became Archbishop of York in that year; and the Puritan Tillotson of Sowerby – a mile from the Hartley home – was made Archbishop of Canterbury in place of the still living but politically embarrassing William Sancroft. Yet there was no career open to the elder Hartley but that of Yorkshire curate. To have supplied the Established Church with both of its Archbishops in a single year must have seemed to many local Puritans a rather sorry substitute for the new heaven and earth for which their Cromwellian fathers had worked and died.

The political situation was eased, but not radically improved by the Reform Act of 1832. The condition of the people was hardly made less wretched by the New Poor Law of 1834. Yorkshire curates continued to suffer from intolerable frustrations and calamitous preoccupations. Charlotte Brontë, an expert witness, has described the 'reserved. . . abstracted. . . brooding nature' of these thwarted lives; their 'Calvinistic doctrines', their fatalism 'inexorable as death'.[21]

Healthier aspects of the Puritan tradition were still alive, not least among the Yorkshire curates who supported factory reform. But they were able to achieve very little, and were subject to bitter opposition from the degenerate heirs of the local Dissenting tradition, whose 'Scrupulosity' in religious matters Dr Hartley had already well defined as 'a Degeneration of the Moral Sense, resembling that by which the Fear of God passes into Superstition'. True to his own doctrine of Association, Hartley linked this craven piety with 'bodily Indisposition' and an 'erroneous Method of Reasoning'.[22]

Ruskin was reading De Quincey in 1860;[23] and it is De Quincey who provides the most telling critique of the strengths and weaknesses of the Yorkshire Puritan tradition. De Quincey's own brief sojourn in the grammar school at Manchester – where he had been born – was, in his editor's words 'the very crisis of his youthful life', and is described in the *Confessions* of De Quincey's characteristic pattern of revulsion and exaltation.

Manchester Grammar School, in De Quincey's day, was a lingering stronghold of that romantic Jacobitism in which Ruskin, too, was reared. There was 'ingenuity. . . and breed' in the balance of the Lancashire character, Ruskin thought. A flattering combination – tossed off in a *Fors Clavigera* paragraph of searchingly humorous invective against its dislocation.[24] Lancashire and Yorkshire have been traditonal rivals for centuries, and the Manchester and Bradford Grammar Schools regard themselves as the leading schools of northern England and natural antagonists of each other.

The Manchester school's ancient motto – *Sapere Aude* – De Quincey himself exemplifies with considerable emphasis on the audacity. If we are to believe his *Confessions*, others of his Upper School contemporaries were devastating exponents of the Horatian balance: 'Dare to have wit'. Samuel Bamford, who knew only the Lower School, records in his *Life of a Radical* the school's institutionalised rituals, encouraged by masters, which were designed to foster the entrepreneurial spirit, and the formation of power cliques. Before a boy could hope to be promoted from a lower class to a higher one, he had to obtain the personal invitation of the head boy of the superior class. Such was the education of many of the makers of modern entrepreneurial capitalism; the men who created the industrial Manchester that shocked and fascinated the world in the 1830s and 1840s.[25]

Ruskin had given his two Political Economy of Art lectures in Manchester in 1857. In 1859, under the management of the dealer

Gambart and the suave surveillance of Sir Elkanah Armitage, Ruskin had addressed the flourishing Manchester Art School, with no impolite references to political economy. In 1864 came Ruskin's fourth and fifth Manchester lectures, known as *Sesame* and *Lilies*. His dear friends the ladies of Winnington School were in the audience, and *Lilies*, especially, is pervaded by their atmosphere, and by Ruskin's dream-longings for the Queen of all his young girl friends, Rose La Touche.

Lancashire and Ireland have always been close, in trade and other matters: as close as Yorkshire has been to Germany and Scandinavia. David Digues La Touche, founder of the La Touche fortunes, had been a Huguenot refugee who became a Dublin poplin manufacturer and banker. His grandson and namesake was admitted to Manchester Grammar School in the new term of September 1781.[26]

One sees why Ruskin's sixth, unscheduled lecture in Manchester, which was given in this school on 7 December 1864, took the form of leaping onto a bench in the middle of the hall and urging the boys to tell their masters what they really think – not what they think they want them to say. Laughter, renewed cheering, and sustained applause.[27]

You could not say – or do – that in the Victorian Bradford Grammar School. The educational aspects of Hartley's vision were those which survived most strongly in Victorian Bradford. Hartley had believed that children are *tabulae rasae* who are made what they are by the associations of early education. He had received his at Bradford Grammar School, whose motto for some centuries had been the dour *Hoc Age*. Hartley deserves to be remembered as the father of physiological psychology; but despite his sympathetic character there was a grimness in the associations he bequeathed to his many Utilitarian disciples.

Hoc Age means 'Pay attention', or 'Get on with the matter in hand'. This was a master's reminder to maintain concentration and obedience, not an invitation to be 'clever', such as is implied by *Sapere Aude*.

De Quincey, in an article of 1850 reprinted by him in 1860, explains the meaning of *Hoc Age*; and in doing so helps to explain why it was the remorseless single-mindedness of Bradford, raising itself from Pennine market town to the wool capital of the world, which had replaced the anarchic opportunism of Manchester as the leading spirit of Victorian England:

> The Roman *formula* for summoning an earnest concentration of the faculties upon any object whatever that happened to be critically urgent was *Hoc Age* . . . In the stern peremptoriness of this Roman formula we read a picturesque expression of the Roman character both as to its strength and its weakness: of the energy which brooked no faltering. . . and also of the morbid craving for action which was intolerant of anything but the intensely practical. In modern times it is we of the Anglo-Saxon blood, that is, the British and Americans of the United States, who inherit the Roman temperament, with its vices and its fearful advantages of power.

De Quincey's article is called *Presence of Mind*. It remains – which is no surprise – 'A Fragment'.[28] But De Quincey adverts us to 'the celebrated John Foster', who became a professional exponent of *Decision of Character* – the title of the most popular of Foster's *Essays* of 1805. Foster was out of fashion with intellectuals by the mid-1850s, but remained a stirring example for the consumption of the readers of that sanctimonious periodical, heavily subsidised by Bradford capitalists, *The British Workman or Friend of the Sons of Toil*. He was the son of a farmer near Hebden Bridge – which is in a Pennine valley south of Haworth – and he 'would retire into a barn to read, then return to his work with fresh vigour'. Such was the model working man of the Palmerston years – the years of the 'pull together', of 'Work, Boys, work and Be Contented'. As Gladstone remarked in 1860, these were 'anti-reforming times'.[29]

In a review of November 1845 for *Tait's Magazine*, De Quincey's Lancastrian venom had already been at work on Foster. Decision of character, he suggests, may be an heroic code of conduct for a Pennine farmer. It makes a disingenuous pose for a comfortable Baptist minister in Bristol, which is what Foster decided to become. He degenerated, indeed, into a mincing piety reminiscent of that other Yorkshireman Lawrence Sterne. Worse, his 'jealousy' was 'inexhaustible', De Quincey adds.[30]

The 'Honesty and Piety' of the Yorkshire character – the description is Ruskin's – could degenerate into a religiosity rancid enough to turn any Lancastrian stomach. The patient strength of Yorkshire, so tersely defined in *Hoc Age*, could degenerate into the relentless simple-mindedness of 'Getting on'. Yorkshiremen have always hated, and rarely comprehended, the irrepressible vein of irony and the touch of craziness in their Lancashire neighbours. No wonder Ruskin in 1864 would entrain whimsy and repress giddy inattention in Manchester; but in Bradford plead to strong homely sentiment while robustly denouncing jealousy.

Moreover, on the platform of Bradford Mechanics Institute, Ruskin would allude to *Hoc Age*, of which his own father's motto *Age Quod Agis* was a less literate version: '. . . at Bradford they wished to get on. Well, that was his motto too; but what sort of getting on did they want?' That was just the question of the age. When Manchester came to choose a municipal motto, in 1838, *Concilio et Labore* ('By policy and labour') was selected. Bradford in 1847 chose an execrable bit of Latinity from a corrupt text of Vergil's *Bucolics* – perhaps because it was thus quoted in Bacon's *The Advancement of Learning*: *Labor Omnia Vincit* ('Labour conquers all'). That was Ruskin's opportunity. For Manchester, by the 1850s, was in a self-congratulatory mood. Their grandest building of the 1850s spoke for itself. It was the Free Trade Hall. The *concilium* had been vindicated – it was the Manchester School of political economy. *The Manchester Examiner and Times*, with an offensive lack of local irony, refers to it on a par with Holy Writ. But Bradford, plodding on with 'Labour conquers all' was by 1859, an *arriviste* community looking for a direction.[31] They had thick skins, but tender centres – with little of that adroit continuity of sophistication that characterised much of middle-class Manchester by that time. They were an indispensable audience; and they responded with feeling to Ruskin's onslaught on their degeneracy and to his challenge to their pride.

De Quincey sniped at West Riding degeneracy, as represented by John Foster's 'inexhaustible... jealousy' and sentimental euphemisms. Ruskin seized the opportunity to enlarge its vitality, of which, – though he may not have known it – the wise Dr Hartley's inexhaustible courage and belief in 'practical Religion' had been an intelligent example. 'Presence of Mind', that great quality Ruskin had attributed to the Venetians in *Modern Painters* and which De Quincey had allowed his pen to play with as the ambiguous quality of Pennine yeomen and preachers, played its part in Ruskin's own decision to return to Bradford in 1864, in his new role of capitalist after his father's death. That the Pennine tradition of 'practical Religion' was not really dead is most clearly demonstrated by the response of Bradford's most eccentric, traditional and radical paper, the *Advertiser*. The terms in which its editor defined Ruskin's message bear repetition: 'The lecture was a pleasing testimony to Mr Ruskin's belief in man's high destiny on earth as a "Son of God" so commonly ignored by the unbelievers (religious and otherwise) of our day'.[32] It was Ruskin's genius to entrain tradition and to give a direction to discontent. John Jowett's terms of reference would have made sense to Bradford's Tory Factory Reformer Richard Oastler, and would make sense again to Bradford's socialist educationalist Margaret McMillan. Their lives overlap by the twelve months which Ruskin began by sending the first article of *Unto This Last* to the printers. Every leading journal in the kingdom, except the *Bradford Observer*, would denounce him or consign him to oblivion.

The *Saturday Review* (10 November 1860) was particularly vicious; and Blanchard Jerrold, editor of *LLoyd's Weekly Newspaper*, was eccentric among metropolitan journalists in venturing to defend *Unto This Last*, as the 'fine outburst of a noble nature', from the *Saturday's* 'stale eggs' (18 November 1860). Jerrold aimed at lower-middle class popularity; and his criteria were non-intellectual. Provincial papers, with no axe to grind against the *Saturday*, were mostly incapable of joining Jerrold in his request for fairer play for Ruskin and a more philanthropic attutude to the poor.

The *Manchester Examiner and Times*, battering its head confidently against the bars of its locally manufactured cage, had offered to present *Unto This Last* to its readers as 'the incoherent babblings of an artist mildly mad'. Current political economy 'shares the taunt of partial failure with the highest truths ever known to man' and 'shallow sceptics, like Mr Ruskin' are flirting with infernal fire. The London papers offered various shades of abuse – the *Saturday Review* called Ruskin a 'mad governess' – though none perhaps gave the game away quite so robustly as *The Morning Star* of 5 November 1860: 'England is a very prosperous, progressive, and on the whole, happy nation,' it contended, 'at least we are in motion, and our activity so far has had very happy results.' The erosion into pettiness of the old-style radicalism he represented had been shown by Perronet Thompson's 'review' of *Unto This Last* of 21st September 1860, which wrangled for a column-length of this same *Morning Star* over the terms of the *Economist's* terminological disapproval of one of Mr Ruskin's instances. Long ago – in 1826 – Thompson had publicly crossed swords with T. B. Macaulay in defence of James Mill's 'self-interest maxim'. He seems scarcely to have noticed that Ruskin's essays might be an unstoppable sea-spout through that hoary bulwark of Utilitarianism. Only the failing and soon to be extinguished radical and coadjutive *Saturday Analyst and Leader* attempted a fair analysis of

Ruskin's *Cornhill* papers, and that was made very much in its own terms, which held little room for art.

In reviewing *Modern Painters, The Bradford Observer* had assigned Ruskin a 'place among the foremost teachers of the age', and expressed delight in his 'gorgeous descriptive eloquence'. More guardedly, 'on the "Political Economy of Art" we demur seriously to many of his conclusions' – nevertheless, 'he has lived to see many of his brilliant paradoxes take rank as admitted truths'; indeed, 'his strongest opponents. . . have often been fain to combat his conclusions with weapons furnished by himself'. Perhaps the writer had in mind the anonymous article on *Modern Painters* in the *Quarterly* for March 1856, which could only discredit Ruskin's supposed demand for 'moral worth' from a painting by the moral criterion that such a demand was part of a 'body of. . . criticism morbid and diseased'. Alluding to an ill-defined 'taste' which she was nevertheless educated to feel, Lady Eastlake, the article's author, could safely enunciate without troubling to be specific: 'the broad, false principles he has laid down may be easily refuted'. *The Bradford Observer*, lacking the prejudices of such education, confessed that for many a 'lover of nature' Ruskin's 'description of the clouds and mountains' had proved an 'era' in his 'intellectual life': moreover, 'that which is special and individual in Mr Ruskin's books may be regarded quite independently of the principles which form the essence of his teachings'. This is partly the consolidating liberal speaking, and yet in seeing that Ruskin's 'philosophy of art' was not dependent on his pronouncements about Turner, Gothic architecture or Pre-Raphaelitism, but was an attempt to establish 'in the artist's sphere. . . some reflex of all that is pure, great and noble', the consolidating liberal had admitted the disturbing factor of art into the amalgam of serious human activities.

The instructive comparison is with the 'old favourite' of Ruskin's father – Dr Hook, the Tory vicar of nearby Leeds. This same issue of the *Bradford Observer* had little time for Hook's politics or churchmanship, yet could not 'but do justice to his sagacity, uprightness and zeal'. Not for him 'the sentimental and nonsensical side of Tractarianism'. Similarly, Ruskin was eccentric, but 'On all the multifarious topics which he has touched, he is worthy of the attention of any thoughtful man'.[33] So far away from the metropolis, the *Observer* had no difficulty in separating Ruskin from the 'sickening. . . mauve-coloured angels' beloved of some young artists there. Eager for mental food, and sitting loose to fashion, Byles showed the value of his individualism, and an essential honesty behind his amalgamations, by taking *Unto This Last* as seriously as *Modern Painters*, and by drawing the attention of his readers to *Munera Pulveris*.

Cannier than some, and honester, perhaps, than others, another Bradford bourgeois journalist was able apparently to cope with the organic criticisms of *Unto This Last* only by clinging resolutely to an individualistic interpretation. The panic of the *Manchester Examiner and Times* had been too patent. Tying himself in knots to get away from Ruskin's economic points. '. . . his wild words,' gasps the reviewer, 'will touch the springs of action in some hearts. . . a moral floodgate may fly open and drown us all.' There was chicanery in the *Quarterly Review's* only reference to the work, made in 1861, which consisted of accusing its author of 'Euphuism' in a review of an edition of *The Dramatic Works of John Lilly* published three years before. Even then, we are hurried from Ruskin's 'bewilderments in political economy' in his 'affected. . . *Unto This Last*' to the safer 'extravagence' of the last volume of 'Modern Painters'. Then in August 1864 *The Cornhill* would cleanse its pages of the memory of *Unto This Last* by throwing the label of 'provinciality' at its more analytical sequel, *Munera Pulveris*, for giving 'that degree of prominence' of which a footnote is capable to the question of Shakespeare's symbolic use of names. This time, the writer was Matthew Arnold, who in December 1860 had informed his sister Jane Forster that it was time to demolish Ruskin's reputation.[34]

Like the *Quarterly*, *The Bradfordian* for August 1862 approaches *Unto This Last* deviously: by means of a commentary on T. S. Glennie's views about Thomas Buckle. But we are reminded that the latter was author of *Civilisation in England*, and this, together with the title of the article – *On Wealth* – sets Ruskin in a serious context. *The Bradfordian* has no time for the 'dreary and hopeless task' of evolving a 'deductive' science of political economy capable of universal application: and he commends Ruskin for 'noble utterances, too applicable to our times to be disputed'. The journalist's morality, however, is entirely individualistic, and he accepts the 'cash nexus' without much qualm. 'Money,' he is sure, 'is the lever of Archimedes that moves the world, and the pursuit and possession of it are not necessarily demoralising. A state of poverty is even more so.' Interestingly, it is Mrs Gaskell's *Life of Charlotte Brontë* which comes home to him, with its anecdote of a 'hard-headed Yorkshireman' who paused while dying to say: 'Then I shall *do* the Insurance Company'; and on this text he expatiates with some humour. As he does so, he reveals the positive side of his provincial Puritanism: a desire for the 'cultivation of those faculties that enrich mind and heart'; and a consequent anxiety lest accumulation beyond 'a competency for old age' should bring its own 'Nemesis' of exhausted faculties. He draws attention to the necessity for calling a halt to acquisition lest the 'infatuated individual' destroy himself. His 'touchstones' – to employ one of Arnold's more applicable labels – have a straightforward moral connotation. There is Cowper's: 'Absence of occupation is not rest. / A mind quite vacant is a mind distressed.'

And there is this from the *Book of Proverbs* – invoked by Ruskin himself in Appendix 10 of the second volume of *The Stones of Venice* against what he would tell Bradfordians was their particular idol of riches: 'Give me neither poverty nor riches; feed me with food convenient for me.'

Failing, therefore, to comprehend Ruskin's vision of society as an interdependent totality, the *Bradfordian* nevertheless offers at a personalised level fertile ground for Ruskin's 'principle of *pause* in business' which the *Work* lecture would uphold as 'one of the most important in economy'. Among the people of the 'forbidden deity', then, there yet survives a pietistic and humane tradition ready to collaborate with one of the principles of *The Crown of Wild Olive*.[35]

The book of *Unto The Last* was issued on 13 June 1862. Bradford's middle-class Subscription Library, which made a point of keeping up-to-date, ordered the book at the first opportunity: their monthly meeting of 15 July 1862. The chairman of the Committee at this time was Dr MacTurk. It included Jacob Behrens and Dr Lewis. There was perhaps some little discussion or disturbance involved, as the usually punctilious recording secretary, in numbering all other purchases (sixteenth, and last, was *Lectures on Language* by Max Müller), failed to number 'Unto This Last by J. Ruskin', which is slipped in between '2. The History of Parish Registers' and '3. The Channings'. But a neat tick at the side indicates that Ruskin's book was in fact purchased. Some little disturbance would certainly be comprehensible, as only 898 copies of *Unto This Last* were disposed of during its first nine years. A copy of the third edition was purchased by Bradford Subscription Library in 1882. Though not grubby, this second copy became very well worn all through – 'well-handled' would better describe Ruskin's art books in the library. The first edition copy remained in good order – having been neatly rebound in black like a Nonconformist hymn-book. But the edge of almost every page had to be reinforced, very many of them twice. This could hardly indicate anything other than attentive reading by a great many people during the remaining effective years of the library, whose decline was rapid after the Kaiser's war. Meanwhile, Bradford Mechanics' Institute Library, which acquired a number of copies of Ruskin's art books, including several copies of *Modern Painters*, Volume 5, does not seem to have extended itself to *Unto This Last* till 1892.[36] This fits very well the vision of its Vice-President, J. V. Godwin, who assured the Social Science Congress of 1859 that within its portals 'taste' could be 'harmlessly acquired'.

Dr MacTurk's personal influence may well have been crucial in acquiring the book of *Unto This Last* for the Subscription Library in 1862. At the Social Science Congress of 1859, John James, the local historian, had delivered himself of a paper on 'The Condition of Factory Operatives'. The factory system was 'not injurious to Health'. The workrooms James had seen were whitewashed; and troops of mill-girls, in respectable black, could be observed making their way to Sunday School on Sabbath afternoons. Dr MacTurk, the widely-respected physician of the local infirmary, spoke on 'Diseases'. He put 'the factory system itself foremost' among the 'malign agents' undermining local health. There must be 'more time and opportunity for recreation' and a more intelligent management of the economy to avoid 'sudden and severe depressions of trade'.[37]

In MacTurk's native Scotland, *The North British Review* of February 1862, while claiming to have been among the first to recognise the merits of *Modern Painters*, expressed a common reaction against 'The series of papers in the *Cornhill Magazine* throughout which' Ruskin 'laboured hard to destroy his reputation'. The *Glasgow Examiner* of 3 November 1860 had professed not to understand what Ruskin was about, with his 'curious jumble, the secular and the sacred – human and divine aphorisms, and political and economic principles'. The same paper had plenty of room for T. J. Dunning's offering at the Glasgow Social Science Meeting that same month, which argued perfectly clearly the case for man's carnivorous teeth, irrefutable evidence of man's predatory instinct, which should henceforth be recognised as a leading principle among 'the conditions of man's nature, and consequently of all arrangements of civilised society'.[38]

In Wales, *The Swansea and Glamorgan Herald* ignored *Unto This Last* altogether, preferring two columns on the spirit-rapping story also featured in the *Cornhill*, and this very anti-Ruskinian text from the same magazine, which it offered its readers on 7 November: 'All honest labour, be it the merest handwork, brainless and mechanical drudgery, dignifies human life' – which must have been consoling news in the local mines and quarries. Up in Birmingham that September, the *Gazette*, perhaps advisedly, had proferred another in its series of short extracts from *Modern Painters* where one might have been looking for something on *Unto This Last*. As for industrial Yorkshire, The *Wakefield Express and Barnsley Pontefract and Dewsbury Advertiser* offered nothing better than the judgment that Ruskin's discussion of wealth is 'fully as fanciful as the title'. In the same issue – 8 September – Samuel Jubb's *History of the Shoddy Trade* necessarily received much more space, and respect. The *Sheffield and Rotherham Independent* of 3 November was characteristically sporting, but little concerned: 'Poor Mr Ruskin in the hands of the Philistines. . . is thorough game, and strenuously fights against the odds'. The *Leeds Mercury*, which in 1867 would publish Ruskin's *Time and Tide*, had no particular comment for *Unto This Last* in 1860. The editor was too fearful of the repercussions of a 'gloomy harvest' to have breath for more than 'cheerful confidence in the future of England'. It was this draught from the *Cornhill* for September that assuaged his hiccup: 'there may be a few honest beggars; but given an opportunity the majority of them are thieves'. He was happy to quote that.[39]

Only the *Bradford Observer* showed the patience, and courage, to allow its response publicly to change and grow. Its tone is altogether removed from the whining and bullying rant that now reads so tediously in then more vaunted organs. In September the *Observer* expressed regret that 'a writer of Mr Ruskin's position and ability should have committed himself to statements so obviously fallacious'. But October brought the awareness that Ruskin 'enunciates great moral principles that ought to regulate the relations between employers and employed, and between traders and their customers, far more than they do'. November's notice warmed into advocacy: 'We recommend all political economists, and all dabblers in that science, to. . . find wholesome food for thought' in Ruskin's 'lay sermons'. Then, on 29 November, came a lengthy and reasoned apprecition – the first the work ever received – which, while pointing to 'fallacies', conveyed earnestly to its readers Ruskin's 'chief object' in writing the papers. No other journalist seems to have been capable of digesting Ruskin's double insistence, not only on the distinction between public and private wealth, but on the healthy modes of their interdependence. As he writes, the reviewer becomes almost carried away by the enthusiasm of this discovery, until he exults, rather like a lay preacher himself, over that enabling distinction: 'There is no Wealth but Life', and summons the Bradford capitalists to read 'without wincing' Mr Ruskin's concluding words – which, far from being a lachrymose effusion, are the perfected expression of realistic considerations about the 'higher economics of a nation' in relation to the world. Mr Ruskin has a deal of sound sense in him, none the less for 'curious illustrations and puzzling questions' that 'lead us beyond the familiar bounds'. Like many Bradford liberals, Ruskin was an international free trader. He has just conveyed to their leading organ the other – and nearer – half of that visionary struggle. Need is previous to freedom; and both begin at home. In his own schematic way, Byles sees what he calls Ruskin's 'Christianised humanity' as the nineteenth-century third term to the 'political freedom' of the seventeenth, the 'political economy' of the eighteenth, century.

This one review does as much honour to Bradford as to Ruskin, and one only hopes he was aware of its existence. Byles does valuable work in toning Ruskin down for local consumption, while insinuating that Bradfordians – if they are truly 'men' – are capable of responding to his intellectual and moral challenge. For Byles himself, it is like a gust of fresh air. His moral and economic intelligence are one again, as they had been, briefly, during the crisis years 1848–9,[40] but rarely since.

More immediately, there was a special compatibility between Ruskin, and Bradford, that November of 1860. November 1860 saw none other than Louis Blanc, radical minister of the short-lived Second Republic of 1848, addressing the Bradford Temperance Hall on 'Co-operation'. There was not much response in the middle-class press. That same day there was an inquest that grabbed far more attention. Margaret Sutton, common-law 'wife' of one J. G. Gowland, an attorney's clerk, had slit the throats of their two daughters, and – less forcibly – her own. She lingered long enough in the Infirmary to find salvation through the ministry of the Parish Church curate, Rev. John Wade. She had been the Bishop of Durham's cook – which may have eased Wade's task: the publicity ensured that Wade, not Charlotte's widower Mr Nicholls, would succeed Mr

Brontë in the Haworth parsonage. While the deed was doing, Gowland had been rioting on oysters in a house of ill-fame. On the day of the triple funeral, thousands lined the route; and many were the imprecations of respectable working women against Gowland who, while in receipt of a guinea a week, had kept his illicit family wretched and starved. In typical Bradford fashion, these events provided material for innumerable sermons, verses, newspaper leaders: a sustained crisis of soul-searching brought the community momentarily together.

Ruskin's wise old father, while forwarding *Unto This Last* to the *Cornhill's* publishers, had expressed the fear that his son might be confused with Louis Blanc.[41] Virilistic hacks would give vent to their own even deeper anxieties by defaming the essays as 'Effeminate'. Bradford knew better; for between Louis Blanc and Margaret Sutton, between political remedies and the inextinguishable hells of human passion and crime, there is much virtue in *Unto This Last*. Ruskin deploys analysis – and emotion. He has a savagely 'masculine' sardonic vein; an irresistibly 'feminine' capacity for teasing the tear-ducts. He makes fundamental political and economic demands without pretending that to meet them is to do away with human failings. He can spin the biblical and the revolutionary into a continuous thread and make strong sails of them for the political imagination.

Searching for a sufficient image to define the West Riding character, a Devonian writer in *Fraser's Magazine* for October 1859 compared it to the '*nil admirari* quality' of the North American Indian. 'Impatient of cant and intolerant of humbug, they are suspicious, reserved and inquisitive, nor is it till they have thoroughly gauged the characters of those with whom they have to deal that they will admit them into their friendship and confidence.'

Such primitive honesty and tough-mindedness could become bogus or perverse under the strains of salesmanship, but that they survived as criteria and points of reference is sufficiently indicated by the contrast between the *Athenaeum*'s dismissal of *Traffic* and the response of Byles's *Bradford Observer* to the original lecture on which *Traffic* was based. 'Mr Ruskin,' sneered the *Athenaeum*, 'is good at pictures: how can he expect the world to admit his merit in dealing with problems?' But 'John Ruskin,' thought the *Bradford Observer*, 'has always been a deep digger, looking not merely to the surface of things, the traditions of the schoolmen and the dilettanti, but to the springs of human action.'[42]

William Byles himself was the fourth son of a Congregationalist ship's chandler of Huguenot stock. He was born in Henley-on-Thames. It was in 1833, as his biographer records, that eighty-six 'public men' of Bradford, 'sturdy yeomen' who 'by dint of thrifty living and keen adventure in business found themselves established as manufacturers and merchants'[43] had summoned Byles from his job as printer on the *Athenaeum* to come and manage their new paper the *Bradford Observer*.

Dilettantism or anything smacking of it, thought the *Bradford Observer*, was something for the 'mental lumber room'. It was quite a triumph for Ruskin to gain regard as a 'deep digger' in a community where that mattered.

CHAPTER SEVEN

THE STONES OF BRADFORD

> . . . among all the new buildings which cover your once wild hills. . . if you can fix some conception of a true state of life to be striven for – life, good for all men, as for yourselves. . . You will know then how to build, well enough; you will build with stone well, but with flesh better. . .
> —John Ruskin (1819–1900), 1866

> Even when I was a boy at school, asked to write an essay on a 'beautiful view', I wrote a savage, ironical description of Bradford's reeking chimneys and dismal slums. . . I want to see Bradford the City Beautiful. . .
> —Fred Jowett (1864–1944), 1944[1]

When Ruskin first entered the town the great Bradford Stone Age was only just beginning. The locality was rich in prime building stone for all purposes – paving, walling, roofing.[2] From about 1860 new machinery and new wealth made it possible to exploit this local asset; and for the next decade or so Bradford, like Athena or Milton's Sin, rose entire out of itself. From about 1875 it became more economic to use Welsh slates for roofing and Scottish granite setts for paving; but Bradford enterprise exported Bradford walling-stone to the whole of the United Kingdom and the Empire. Manchester Town Hall was built of it; the new Catholic Church at York, its tower triumphantly interrupting the view of the Minster's limestone west front, was built of it.[3] Bradfordians knew well enough that London streets were paved, not with gold, but with their own good stone, which looks like gold only when newly cut.

The sight of fresh-cut Bradford sandstone, of an indefinable pale, strong gold against the kind of blue West Riding sky that sent Emily Brontë and Georg Weerth into poetic raptures: such would be

Ruskin's view of Bradfordian possibilities as he first passed Saltaire on his way into Bradford from Bolton Abbey. Here were materials fit for a New Jerusalem: a sharp contrast to the grim millstone grit of Halifax to the west, which rapidly turns black on exposure to air; a contrast also to the sooty brick of Leeds immediately to the east.

The people, too, seemed not unworthy of the place. W. E. Forster's character as an MP during the 1860s had much to do with the nature of Bradford. 'He is more radical that he would otherwise be,' opined the conservative *Pall Mall Gazette*, in October 1866, 'more confident of the fitness of the operative classes to be entrusted with the franchise and more sanguine as to the safety and good effect of a movement in a democratic direction, because he represents one of the very best constituencies in the kingdom, a town in which the working men are peculiarly shrewd, reasonable, intelligent and incorrupt.'

In 1859 Ruskin was enlisted on behalf of Bradford's new Design School; in 1864 he was called in to champion a new Bradford, better built and better planned, with the new Wool Exchange – Bradford's first public building in Bradford stone – as its centrepiece. By the very nature of these occasions the middle-class men Ruskin met were the pick of the public-spirited among rich Bradfordians. The artisans whose work he was summoned to admire were the very élite of the Bradford working-class, men who verily fulfilled what *Punch* in May 1865 would satirise as Forster's picture of the working-man, 'absorbed in the task of mental improvement. . . a very noble, benevolent and intellectual conception'.[4]

Ruskin's criticisms of Bradford, and his meditations on it, are thus an important contribution to Victorian social criticism; and one of a particular kind. In 1872 Ruskin would write, 'this London and Manchester life of yours shall. . . become a horrible, and but on evidence, incredible, romance of the past'. The 'horrible. . . romance' of early Victorian Manchester lives on in Engels's *The Condition of the Working Class in England*. Dickens's pictures of early Victorian London are even more ambivalently terrible and thrilling. But Ruskin in Bradford is an intensely sensitive but detached observer of the mid-Victorian efficiency which was building an 'enlightened' modern capitalism and an 'enlightened' modern educational system to serve its ends. 'The literary loss is infinite,' Ruskin wrote at the death of Dickens, acknowledging the novelist's 'entire superiority to me in every mental quality but one – the desire of truth without exaggeration'.[5] Bradford demanded nothing less: and would listen to nothing more.

The nature of the Bradford terrain made it quite different from the Manchester Engels had depicted, with its corridors of level shopping streets leading from bowery suburb to showpiece centre, with poverty hidden behind the neat façades. The rocky bowl of Bradford, with its fissured and jumbled centre, provided a clear rhetorical parable of 'getting on' – from the hells of Wapping down by the Bradford canal to the heavenly mansions up in Manningham and beyond; and the Bradford middle class frankly exulted in it. Troops of working men could be seen, as Weerth attests, trudging past the fronts of Bradford's wealthiest shops; the rich burghers of Claremont, where Delius was born, knew the maid would soon arrive with the morning tea from the noise of hundreds of clogged feet passing along the cobbles outside on the way to work.[6]

Bradford had blossomed more suddenly than most towns, and from more sternly Puritanical roots. Unlike Manchester, Leeds, Wakefield, Bolton, Halifax and other northern industrial towns, Bradford had no pretty eighteenth-century Anglican churches, with their attendant niceties of symmetrical terraces and squares for the modestly comfortable and conservative new genteel classes of eighteenth-century prosperity.[7] In the respectable streets of the Bradford Ruskin visited, buildings of stern and squat vernacular style were being shouldered aside by raw new edifices in the grand Italian manner.

It was not till April 1864 that Ruskin's chairman of that month, H. W. Ripley, began collecting subscriptions for the building of Bradford's first big hotel, the Victoria. The principal financial backing was provided by the Harris Old Bank. Once the hotel was built, and a grand new station provided behind it by Lockwood and Mawson, no visiting lecturer need stray outside the charmed enclosure of hotel, Mechanics' Institute, St George's Hall and the Court House. The same month – April 1864 – saw the completion of Bradford's first respectable theatre – the Theatre Royal.[8] Never again would a lecture be quite such a treat as Ruskin's were for his Bradford audiences: and never again need a lecturer have to negotiate, as Ruskin did, the central chaos of Bradford in order to reach the haven of the Mechanics' Institute platform.

Travelling by carriage from Bolton Abbey in 1859, Ruskin would gain a clear impression of Bradford's geographic position, a broken crucible above and to the south of the Aire valley, its beck and canal emptying their effluent into that river upstream from Turner's Kirkstall. Stepping out of the train from Leeds in 1864 on a Thursday afternoon, Bradford's market day, he would be pitched into the centre of Bradford at its busiest. 'In the crowded streets of Bradford, in walking,' the Municipal Year Book commanded, 'endeavour to keep on the right hand side, and instruct your friends to do the same.' Leland, in the sixteenth century, had found Leeds as large as Bradford, but 'not so quick'.[9] By mid-Victorian days that 'quickness' was efficient, triumphant and unashamed.

The evidence of newspapers and memoirs can provide only a very incomplete picture of how contemporary Bradfordians reacted to Ruskin. Ruskin's reaction to the physical impact of Bradford is even harder to determine. The volumes of his diary for 1864 are missing; the nature of his own writing style is constantly an allusive one, and allusion may easily be misread.

To confine the enquiry to those Bradford sights which Ruskin is known to have encountered is to leave the picture incomplete: but it is a picture crowded with suggestion, nonetheless.

Ruskin's own view of places was based on his profound knowledge of geology; it was informed by the full collection of Ordnance Survey maps which were his frequent study; and it was illustrated by his large collection of newspaper cuttings.[10] In particular, Ruskin's local admirer John Holmes 'sent Mr Ruskin a few facts and publications' after the 1864 lecture 'to show him how well he had hit the nail, (on their heads) and how the getting on at Bradford bore out to the full all the objectionables that he had so witheringly exposed'. This material was no doubt helpful in writing *Traffic*, but Holmes specifies no details.[11]

That Bradford was a rocky crucible liable to flooding and filled with the smoke and glare of foundries were fundamental things Ruskin noticed: inescapable, too, was Bradford's social order, with the rich living 'above', and the poor 'below'.

From its shape as shown in the Ordnance Survey map Ruskin drew a fanciful and suggestive analogy between the lecture hall of Bradford Mechanics' Institute and the head of a wasp. Was Bradford a wasp's nest?

His geology presented him with a less diverting puzzle. The Bradford Canal had been constructed to bring limestone from the Skipton region. The lime was necessary as flux in the process of making iron from the ironstone of Bowling and Low Moor. The rich local coal-measures provided the necessary fuel; and an extensive mineral tramway system scuttled back and forth across Bradford to bring together these three geological deposits. Human labour and ingenuity forged from them the armaments, railway rolling-stock and miracles of marine engineering for which Bradford was world famous.

But it was a little surprising that such prodigious industry had not yet found it economically worthwhile to pave its own thoroughfares. There was an abundance of easily split local sandstone flags. How was it that the most prosperous residential road in the world's economic boom-town – Manningham Lane, down which Ruskin travelled into Bradford – had to make do with deposits of this same Skipton lime to fill its ruts and slake its mud? In dry weather, as on Ruskin's first visit, the road was dusty 'with matter very prejudicial to the eyes', as locals commented.[12] Apart from a few old cobbled streets in the town centre, most of Bradford's better streets were slaked with lime. The majority were not made up at all.

And then the buildings. The splendid building material of Saltaire had clearly come from quarries in the hills close by. How was it that Bradford's grand buildings – St George's Hall, and the Italianate warehouses with their rusticated basements, which drew Ruskin's comment – had to be built of an alien sandstone much greyer than the local variety? This stone was the fine grey sandstone from the Park Spring quarry, near Leeds. It was favoured because it permitted the elaborate 'symbolical carving' the Victorians admired. *The Builder*, while admiring the carving, commented that these grand buildings were reared above a drainage system 'shockingly imperfect'. Ruskin's eyes and nostrils would have suggested to him obvious questions about such 'economics'.[13]

At the other end of the scale, the homes of the poor dating from the early Victorian period were often heaped together out of rubble, thinly coated with flags. This, too, was a curious form of 'economics'.[14]

There was a major discrepancy to be noted. The prevailing style for Bradford's commercial buildings, and for most of the merchant's houses, was a robust, unexaggerated Italianate. But the modern Anglican churches on Ruskin's route were inconsistent with the workaday world and with each other. St Paul's was 'Early English';

St Jude's of 1843 was in an indescribable paper-Normanesque; Christ Church was in a cardboardy 'Gothic' of 1815. Religion and business would seem to be at variance: and business clearly had the advantage.[15]

The Bradford Grammar School, also on Ruskin's route, with its Grecian doorway and Tuscan columns; and Harris's Old Bank with its modest bow-fronted windows, were examples of local gentility seemingly threatened by vulgarity and squalor. Both were likely to survive as institutions only by investing in Bradford's commercial future:[16] and what would that bring?

It was the Bradford Parish Church on its rocky eminence that suggested a hopeful answer. The sturdy commonsense of its early fourteenth-century arcading and its robust mid-fifteenth century windows; its broad, solid tower of millstone grit, still bearing the marks of Royalist cannon, spoke of a spirit surely not altogether dead, however remorseless in its 'getting on'. The 'getting on' was clear enough from the 'restored' south front of 1833. 'Worthy of a railway viaduct engineer', was Ruskin's comment. Below the church, 400 yards to the north-west, were the Bradford gas-works; which perhaps Ruskin was asked to admire, as he refers sarcastically to them in the 1859 lecture as published. It was not from the gas-works that Ruskin looked for light. Just to the east of the gas-works, between them and the slums and antediluvian warehousing below the parish graveyard, seeped 'the monster nuisance of Bradford' as it was locally known, the canal; whose 'water. . . when viewed from above, looks like a flood of ink'. Along its grimy shore were some of Bradford's worst slums.[17]

But clustering round the parish church, and also inside it, were some vestiges of hope. Inside was Flaxman's fine monument to the educationalist Abraham Balme. This was one of the Yorkshire sculptor's 'simple groups in marble, which were always good and interesting', in Ruskin's judgment. It showed Balme like an undisturbing Socrates teaching a boy and girl to read.[18]

Clustering round the outside of the church were a number of crumbling and decayed but still existing vernacular buildings – notably Paper Hall of 1648. Quite near – though Ruskin may not have known this – was the best surviving example of this Pennine vernacular style in the Bradford parish: Mira Shay, the birthplace of Ruskin's 'good friend' John Cousen. Ruskin evoked such a place in his lecture of 1859: 'cottage or mansion, I hardly know which to call it'. He was in Bradford to remind his audience of their own past, and to bid them revive in 'the circumstances. . . of happy modern English life' a state of society in which mansions were kept modest and cottages made commodious.

Bradford was at a turning-point at the beginning of the 1860s. The merchant's mansions were still relatively modest. Not till the late '60s did vulgar ostentation become the fashion in Bradford.[19] On the other hand, new building techniques were making possible, in the Bradford Ruskin saw, the construction of solid and decent rows of artisan dwellings, called, with pathetic conservatism 'cottages' by their fortunate new occupiers.[20] John Mitchell's mansion, where Ruskin spent the night, was of unostentatious neo-Classical style, and supplied with every modern convenience.[21] Domesticity, convenience, respectability: with unlimited building stone, a willing and ingenious work-force and thousands of breezy acres to build on, why on earth should Bradford not obtain its heart's desire?

The hope for the life of Bradford lay at the heart of Bradford; in Flaxman's truly Classical monument to the teacher Abraham Balme, perfectly conformable to the truly Gothic dignity of the church that housed it.

But Ruskin himself must preach from the Mechanics' Institute platform that had replaced the church pulpit as the authentic Bradford Areopagus. The Mechanics' Institute, despite its lantern-tower, was not a beacon of unmingled light. It was built in neo-Grecian style, with Doric pilasters, and its internal details bastardised Greek ornament in exactly the manner condemned by Ruskin's 1859 lecture. A little further up Leeds Road was the Temperance Hall; but across the road was one of Bradford's innumerable pubs; the Junction, lit with flaring gas. This area, even by Bradford standards, was particularly congested with smoke, Doric pilasters notwithstanding.[22]

Worse still. The Rifle Volunteer barracks, which Ruskin passed in 1864,[23] held suggestions of violent outbreak and repression which he would deploy in *Traffic*: and as he left Bradford for Knaresborough by the Otley Road in 1859 Ruskin could see the antagonism of the Bradford social order clearly enough in Garnett Hall at the top of the bank and Garnett's Mill at the bottom.[24] At the very top, above even Garnett Hall, was Bradford's private cemetery; with one great pallid obelisk in particular, glimmering over the town like the Angel of Death himself.[25]

There was hope for co-operation and life in Bradford: there was the threat of anarchy and death. But there were stones of Bradford set deeper even than the Bradford canal and higher even than the granite obelisk to Joseph Smith in the Bradford Cemetery.

Since the Bronze Age the Bradford wool trade has depended on its deep wells of pure soft water. The most precious was known as Jacob's Well. It is still commemorated by a pub of that name. The centre of the Bradford coat of arms, to which Ruskin refers,[26] was a 'well sable'. And above Bradford, over the Harden Valley where Ruskin went walking in 1864, is the Druid's Altar, immemoriably old, a place of ancient sacrifice and of pilgrimage for the Victorian tourist. This is the 'Druid's Bethel', as Ruskin would recall it in *The Bible of Amiens*. It is a single block of coarse millstone grit and stands 650 feet above the River Aire. Many of the nearby blocks were hauled to Liverpool in the early 1800s to provide foundations for the docks.[27] In 1859 Ruskin mocked Bradford with what he then supposed was their vision of the future, an England 'from shore to shore. . . set as thick with chimneys as the masts stand in the docks of Liverpool'.[28] Was it not in order that Bradford might get its goods to Liverpool that a whole new hell of iron and steam had been created?

But in 1864 Ruskin understood Bradford better; and on the platform of the Mechanics' Institute at the bottom of Well Street he evoked the image of a Yorkshire Jacob, laying the foundation of all architecture[29] with a single stone that was both resting-place and place of vision.

CHAPTER EIGHT

MR RUSKIN'S SECOND BRADFORD UTTERANCE

> Mr Ruskin's second Bradford utterance is better known, as it forms the second lecture in *The Crown of Wild Olive*.
>
> —*Bradford Daily Argus*, 22 January 1900

Bradford Wool Exchange stands like a toy monster in the heart of a modern city having no particular use for it. It is occasionally the scene of exhibitions by the Bradford School of Art, now partly housed more permanently in what used to be a chapel. Much of the labyrinth of blackened stone in which both were, within recent memory, enmeshed, has been ruthlessly cleaned or razed to the ground. Delius's birthplace at Claremont, for instance, was levelled just in time for his centenary celebrations, and the site used for a petrol station, since defunct. Many of the Victorian churches have perished likewise: though the parish church, now a cathedral, has a grand new apsidal window about which had been redistributed the first masterpiece of Morris's workshop. Rossetti's Christ in Glory, which Ruskin was taken to admire in 1864,[1] still occupies the centre. Less fortunate was the many windowed Italianate warehouse of A. & S. Henry's, demolished among many others during the 1960s. Among those reduced to rubble was the nearby masterpiece of Lockwood and Mawson: a marvel of planning, the best façade in Bradford, and the town's one building of unquestioned international distinction. Built in 1853 on land bought by Titus Salt as part of a scheme to put Bradford on the cultural map, it had helped to proclaim that the warehouse premises of the great merchants were designed not only to finance but also to complement in dignity the best features of civic life – symbolised and even realized in the adjacent and contemporary St George's Hall, whose choral concerts were the envy of metropolitan music critics. During most of its Victorian heyday, this warehouse was occupied by Moses Bottomley & Co. It was handsomer, if not grander, than any civic building, having tiers of arches derived ultimately from the Colosseum. H.-R. Hitchcock has called Bottomley's warehouse one of 'the two masterpieces of the genre at its best moment', the other being what he calls the admirably 'Ruskinian' Stokes Croft warehouse in Bristol, by E. W. Godwin.[2] Dating from nine years later, that building reflects the best taste of its own moment – an intelligent application, not of the inimitable detailing, but of the common sense structural principles of Venetian Gothic; and something of its proportional finesse. Unfortunately, Lockwood and Mawson's Wool Exchange would ape only the inessential among the stylistic aspects of this change of fashion; though in solidity of material and construction they might be called 'Ruskinian' themselves.

Even more ironically, their Roman Renaissance masterpiece for Messrs Bottomley had been more truly Ruskinian than they knew. For in the exactly contemporary Volume 3 of *The Stones of Venice*, Ruskin had given a detailed appreciation of the Casa Grimani, then recently rescued by the Austrian government from demoliton, and turned into the Venetian Post Office. 'It is composed of three stories of the Corinthian order,' Ruskin wrote, 'at once simple, delicate, and sublime. . . Nor is the finish of its details less notable than the grandeur of their scale. . . This palace is one of the best in Europe, of the central architecture of the Renaissance schools; that carefully studied and perfectly executed architecture to which those schools owe their principal claims to our respect. . . I have called it Roman Renaissance, because it is founded, both in its principles of superimposition and in the style of its ornament, upon the architecture of classic Rome at its best period.'[3] Bottomley's warehouse was thus in a grand tradition; a not unworthy successor, given its time and place, to the Casa Grimani, which Ruskin placed at the head of his third volume as a prime example of that restraint, solidity and unity which Renaissance architecture destroyed itself by abandoning. Delightfully, if impatiently, he charted the decline in the rest of the volume, entitled *The Fall*.

It is likely Ruskin saw Lockwood and Mawson's warehouse of 1853, since it was close to the Mechanics' Institute. It was the best example of that Bradfordian commercial style of which he could hardly avoid gaining a general impression – indeed it had little to lose by comparison with what Ruskin called 'the fair Roman composite' of the body of Leeds Town Hall.[4] No wonder, then, that when the designs of the new Gothic Bradford Wool Exchange were generally known, Ruskin was horrified. For Bradford, like Venice, had clearly fallen – but backwards and into a parody of Ruskin's own predilections. Not that he thought Venice the major centre of Gothic. Veronese, still more, Florentine, Gothic was nobler. And in structural power and majesty of conception the best French work was in a class by itself. But – he had communicated his love for Venetian Gothic, and the public had responded in their own fashion. It was relatively easy to parody the lily capital of St Mark's; merely impossible to reproduce it. More difficult – barely possible – to digest what lay behind Ruskin's love: the commonsense impatience of the sea-captain's grandson with architectural and social 'symmetry' and 'superimposition', and the desire to see windows – and people – positioned where they could most usefully transmit light. A later Slade Professor – Nikolaus Pevsner – would in July 1968 lament the passing of Bottomley's warehouse in the Bradford *Telegraph and Argus*. But Ruskin had more difficult work to do: the demolition of a society structured – like the Colosseum – too obsessively on the lines of grandeur and subordination, and the generation of a new world which – somewhat like the Gothic of Amiens – would require the alert co-operation of every participant.

The nobly storm-defying Sublime of *Modern Painters* Volume 1 must accommodate the 'affectionate watching of what is least' which is the Sublime of Volume 5. These were both as essential to Ruskin's own nature as they are to architecture; and in Bradford as elsewhere he needed to steel himself with the one while pleading for the resurrection of the other.[5]

Vast quantities of Bradford's back-to-back houses have been levelled since the Second World War. This would have pleased that majority of councillors who briefly outlawed them in 1860. The city has, to date, been less reckless than some places in proliferating the once modish alternative – skyscraper slums in neo-Bauhaus style. But purists resent the fact that the relatively compact flats along Otley Road are in brick, as are many of the houses with pocket handkerchief gardens on the new estates. With the influx of thousands of refugess from the Europe ravaged by the Second World War, and of British subjects from what used to be the Indian – and West Indian – Empire, Bradford is even more obviously cosmopolitan than it was under Palmerston. Yet from the top of the splendidly busy new Public Library can be seen green hills coming down again everywhere towards the town. That fresh air and grass are again possibilities in what Engels once called the 'filthy hole' of Bradford must comfort the nostalgic reader of that contemporary of *Traffic*, the *Continuation* of James's *History*. 'Where,' James wrote in 1866, 'within the memory of even the middle-aged native inhabitants, the noisy rooks made their nests, – where, in the clear brook, numerous trout disported, – buildings, warehouses, rivalling in size and splendour the palaces of Venice, rear their proud fronts' (p. 139). In terms then certainly unexpected, Bradford continues that emulation, with its International Print Biennale, unashamed counterpart of the Venice Art Biennale. In 1983 the National Museum of Photography, Film and Television was opened in Bradford; and to inform the cultured visitor the city has produced a series of admirable guide books to what remains of its Victorian splendour. The grandest warehouses naturally occupied the more central sites, and have accordingly vanished. The mercantile hub of Victorian Bradford, centred on Peel Place – at one time largely owned by H. W. Ripley – has been all but completely demolished. But much remains to console us of Little Germany: export warehouses built mainly between 1860 and 1874, on land controlled by Harris's Old Bank. The tourist is advised not to miss the earliest Temperance Hall in England, now transfigured into the Bradford Playhouse. Observe the boards trod in her school days by Samuel Beckett's favourite performer – Billie Whitelaw. About a century after Ruskin first took note of the local theology this building, among others, provided an 'authentic' setting in which to film that somewhat lengthier diagram of the cult *Room at the Top* – a book whose title explained itself.

Bradford University is splendidly getting on in many fields. As elsewhere, they know the value of their own social history. As nowhere else, they for long stood out against the Westminster parochialism which insisted on charging 'economic' fees to students from beyond the toll-bar of the European Economic Community. But time has removed the nearby Mechanics' Institute building which Ruskin visited, as well as its successor of 1873. Two small rooms now house what is left of the institution, including the catalogues of its magnificent scattered library. As for the Subscription Library in Darley Street, founded in 1774, the glass-fronted bookcases of its smoking room still held at Christmas 1979 some of its well-handled copies of Ruskin's books on art. *Unto This Last*, among hundreds of other volumes, had been auctioned off to members in the autumn of the previous year, in a perhaps final effort to conserve such life as the place retained. Taking down from those shelves at that time their copy of *Aratra Pentelici*, I found it fell open at Ruskin's plate of the Sicilian Apollo confronting the Self-made Man out of *Punch*; the latter looking for all the world like

> One of the low on whom assurance sits
> As a silk hat on a Bradford millionaire.

That justly commemorates Ruskin's effort to give Bradford a literary existence.[6] Neither *Traffic* nor *The Waste Land* is so uncunningly written, however, as to permit cheap exultation or a safe derision.

The Salt mansion of Milner Field would briefly join Kirkstall Abbey among the 'awful' Gothic ruins of Yorkshire, before being more thoroughly razed.[7] But under very different auspices, Saltaire is still in business. None of the problems of 'design' or 'organisation' has gone away. When, in the autumn of 1978, Bradford's Lord Mayor re-opened as a College of Higher Education the Italianate Ilkley Wells Hydro in which Alfred Harris had been so large a shareholder, the solidity of the building once sketched by Bottomley's warehouseman Henry Fearnside was more in evidence than the insolidity of its original final cause. Yet, with a little generosity, the heirs of the Victorians can accord a certain largeness and a sort of permanence even to that. The search for health is not ever likely to be outmoded.

Ruskin's intelligence – and his prose – co-operate more intimately than most both with the writers of assured greatness and with the minutiae of the perennially modern. Bradford of 1859 was the place, for instance, to sow again the seed of Aristotle's strong biological sense of necessity, nature, and possibility. Such worldly wisdom was then more than compatible with 'deeply-felt realisations of the events which are the subject of our religious faith' – in the 'materialist' Pre-Raphaelite manner. In art and all things, reason and belief might seem solidly one.

Ruskin's Bradford lecture of March 1859 fitted well enough the mood of optimism among the intellectual tourists who would crowd into the town that autumn, to applaud Lord Shaftesbury's charge to social science. As yet only at the 'alchemical stage' this new empirical science would nevertheless one day under Christian guidance and female influence emerge to 'save the millions from neglect'. Prolonged applause. The taste of the moment was on view at Mr Harland's Picture Repository, at 6*d* admission: Hunt's *The Light of the World*, with its empirically observed nettles and its head of Christ idealised from those of Lizzie Siddal and Christina Rossetti.

But by 1864, if we are to believe John Holmes, the atmosphere of the town had changed. New prosperity brought new divisions. People of all classes began to have more chance to cultivate, or acquire, such enjoyment as they could. The respectable classes flocked to 'artistic' revivals at their new Theatre Royal. The lower orders yelled approval to clever 'turns' in the new music halls and drinking houses. As Holmes summed it up in 1886, alluding to a catch phrase of the time – 'Shakespeare, taste and the musical glasses' – at Bradford 'Nothing was tolerated between Shakespeare and the musical glasses'. But if taste was a casualty, patronage flourished: 'Books, pictures, statues, and articles of vertu went up in the market, as did the styles of building all round'.[8] The merchant princes moved avidly into the art market, and began pulling down quiet comely houses – ancient, and early Victorian – in favour of operatic Italianate popping with Brummagem stained glass (1864); or the 'ornamented Elizabethan order' requiring a sixty-foot tower (1869); or 'domestic gothic' [sic] running to a 130-foot frontage (1866).[9] On the other hand, some at least of the working classes began to have a little more money available for their own brand of fun. The artification of the private was accompanied – gradually – by that of the public house. The earnest counselling of a shared Christian enlightenment in which Brougham, Shaftesbury and local journalists alike united in the Bradford of 1859 ascends and descends to acknowledgedly separate levels of 'culture'. By the early sixties, the great Foster of Black Dyke has vanished westward into Hornby Castle, in Lancashire, once the seat of the Marsdens, erstwhile lords of Bradford manor. Young Henry Fearnside catches a glimpse of the elusive idyll as the excursion train whisks him past on its way to Morecambe – the popular west coast resort soon to be known as 'Bradford-by-the Sea'. Once at Morecambe, Fearnside invests some hard-earned money in a steel engraving of Hornby Castle.[10]

Such local developments – gradual as they were – can be seen as symptomatic of larger trends. *The Origin of Species*, for instance, had not helped to rivet those consanguinities, faith and works. It was in 1862 that Cobden noted a general 'reaction against. . .

"humanitarianism"'.[11] All the more reason for Ruskin in the Bradford of 1864 to generate deeper, and sublimer, notions of function and fruition. Jacob's stone, the pillow that became a monument, expresses something more primitive than building and more transcendental than architecture. Jacob's intervening dream of an angelic ladder conveys a social reciprocity resting, like an individual's honesty as defined by *Time and Tide*, 'in vacant heaven'.[12] Any dogma more secure or less pervasive would have been disingenuous – a treacherous comfort. *Traffic* has its organic debt to Dante, and to Aristotle; but Ruskin is now cautious to move in further and nearer ways than the eccelsiastical or the sophisticated. *On the Morning of Christ's Nativity*, first masterpiece of Milton, the Puritan whom Ruskin called the only 'real poet who is vulgar', co-operates with the *Critias* – those 'last words' of Plato, the transcendental pagan whom Ruskin sometimes thought not vulgar enough. The book of *Daniel* serves as a necessary third term; and the masterpieces of prophecy, philosophy and poetry – Hebrew, Hellene and republican Anglo-Saxon – naturally co-operate with a significant view of history.

The lateral irrigations implicit in the 'influence' Ruskin and Bradford might be supposed to share were, in the lecture of 1859, almost obliterated in the present horror of the 'curdling stream', and the probable future abolition of 'ground and weather'.

Yet, though Bradford had endeavoured to make its own stream infernal the elements would not be denied. If not the newspapers, then Ruskin's own literal-mindedness and sense of geography would tell him the image of 'flood' was no idle metaphor in the rocky bowl of the 'Broad Ford'. An attempt to escape 'influence' provokes inundation. In December 1837 three persons perished in floods six feet deep;[13] and there was a ruinous flood disaster in 1859 and another in 1866: the imprisoned beck, forced underground as it shoots like an archer's bow across the town centre towards the Aire at Shipley, being only too ready to reassert the natural meaning of the place.

When Ruskin came a second time to Bradford, in 1864, he abandoned the idea of lateral 'influence' for the vertical judgment and inspiration of the stone and the sky; for the two Gods of the sky, Jehovah and Plato's Zeus; for his own reading of the Greek and Hebrew myths of the Deluge, and for the historical implications of Bradford's main building materials – stone and iron.

The apocalyptic view of history which characterised this 1864 lecture was fully in accord with Bradford Puritan tradition. 'The present Circumstances of the world,' wrote Doctor Hartley at the end of his *Observations*, 'are extraordinary and critical, beyond what has ever yet happened. If we refuse to let Christ reign over us, as our Redeemer and Saviour, we must be slain before his Face, as Enemies, at his Second Coming.' During April 1864, that Bradfordian apocalyptic tradition had a feast for its imaginings in the three huge canvases of John Martin on display at Harland's Picture Repository: *The Last Judgment; The Great Day of His Wrath* and *The Plains of Heaven*.[14] While Ruskin was asking his Mechanics' Institute audience whether they supposed their mills, unlike Yorkshire's monastic ruins, would 'go on for ever', he had a pair of bizarre but forceful witnesses to the pertinence of his question on the very walls of the Institute: *Abdallah's Last View of Granada* and *The Death of Montezuma*, canvases of a large size by Mr Senior, being presented by Mr W. H. Leatham as fitting illustrations of his own poems on those epoch-making subjects.

Since the showman in charge is Ruskin, there is an alert response to the exactly contemporary, also. The date is 21 April 1864, and current traffic between work and war is of immediate interest. The destruction of Plato's 'fabled isle of Atlantis', for example, as Ruskin will slily call it in *Traffic*, will soon be actualised in the fate of Atlanta, through whose territory the Northern liberator Sherman will burn a land-annihilating march to the sea. Union dollars – 'greenbacks' – Ruskin hints, will be the crop (for somebody). Reports suggest the connection was made explicit on the night – to be picked up by the *Advertiser*, whose adjacent column is busy with an intermeshed discussion of Darwinism, the Book of Wisdom, and the American war which reads almost like an overflow from Ruskin's lecture. But the modern reader needs to turn to the *War* lecture of Ruskin's volume to be quite clear about the message: 'the black seals on the parchment of your treaties of peace are the deserted hearth and the fruitless field. There is a ghastly ludicrousness in this, as there is mostly in these wide and universal crimes'. But April 1864 also presents us with Shakespeare's tercentenary; and the invasion of Danish Schleswig-Holstein by the forces of Prussia. Last January, *The Times*, in coyest allusion to the confinement of the Princess of Wales, Alexandra of Denmark, offered to set the tone for future treatment of the composite theme: 'Never was it a less easy task for Royal bride to forget her own people. . . the great dramatist himself in his

Story of the Dane has scarcely brought together so strange and rapid a variety of incidents.' Of which the moral, for England, is *laissez faire*. *Traffic* gets more meaning than that out of the end and the beginning of *Hamlet*, taken together, and out of the persistent nonsense of a nation eloquent and heroic in the sale of arms – celebrating Shakespeare and St George together in their own inimitable fashion. In his own acicular fashion, it is in the *Work* lecture that Ruskin makes quite clear his damning message 'respecting loans to foreign military governments'. Throughout the volume, indeed, the topical and the esoteric are perpetually interpenetrated; open-hearted challenge is stitched to what the author called his personal kind of 'occult mischief'. *The Crown of Wild Olive* was direct enough to be quoted at length and with delight by the *Bradford Advertiser*, needing something to replace the sinking powers of the gentleman-Chartist Perronet Thompson. It was written fine enough to slide into the interstices of *The Waste Land*.[15]

Within the limitations available to him, Ruskin endeavoured for most of his life to fulfil Plato's definition of music: 'the movement of sound, so as to reach the soul for the education of it in virtue'. He himself spoke – and the phrase might describe his prose style – of the Eternal Piano.[16] Thought, for Ruskin, is indeed 'motion' – as Coleridge once put it, hastily summarising David Hartley[17] – but to be worthy of the name, Ruskin thinks, with Dante and Plato, it must also be music: it must be 'moved' by Him who moves the sun and all the stars. Nothing less then the most consummate articulacy, replete with images pertinent to the day, yet in living communication with larger values, could hope to exploit such a 'moment' as the only apparently static decade of Palmerston. Below the surface calm of the 'Balance of Interests' – to use the phrases of Asa Briggs – were many rapid currents that made it also a 'Prelude to Change'. The age's own favoured image of a 'platform' needs clarifying into that of a 'railway platform'. For people, and groups of people, in Palmerston's England, were *en route* for unforeseeable destinations.[18]

Mobility is bewildering the values of many. Henry Fearnside saves up to visit the Second International Exhibition of 1862. He goes straight from King's Cross to Wesley's Chapel, and is soon copying the inscriptions on Wren's Great Fire monument. Tired with the 'bus-ride', and the 'all sorts of things nearly' that the Exhibition offers, he falls back into the railway carriage only to be kept awake all night by 'half a dozen rough men' who have evidently not used the 'London-trip train' for educational purposes.

Such 'motion' as that would not, for Ruskin, constitute thought. Yet thought cannot but move. Indeed, for him it became a rapid dance that progressed by fulfilling his own essential pattern. In any case, these Bradford 'wasps', with their 'tiresome way of inspecting one, too closely, sometimes'[19] were not likely to let him rest. From Berlin – where he has just been laughing at Rauch's fatuous monument to Frederick the Great[20] – we find him in June 1859 declining Alfred Harris junior's invitation to present the Bradford Design School prizes that year. He does not forget to send regards to Mr and Mrs Tylor. In the midst of compiling the 'Tree twigs' lecture for the Royal Institution, in April 1861, he makes time to adjudicate by post the 'prentice hands working under the 'excellent and zealous' Mr Lobley. In 1862, on the point of leaving England to write *Munera Pulveris*, he snatches a moment to excuse himself from joining Harris amid the 'bazaar business of the mob' at the Second International Exhibition. 'I can't be useful anyhow or anywhere – within hearing of the noise of them,' Ruskin writes, 'but am always faithfully yours.' Harris cherished the distinction, for in April 1864, despite John James's recent death and the son's plea that he was 'unfit for society', Harris prevailed upon him to return. He would stay at Ashfield for two nights. Mitchell's offer of Parkfield for that purpose having been gently refused, Aldam Heaton was asked to arrange 'a quiet Inn' in which to recover from the train journey and prepare for the evening's ordeal.[21] Immediately before the lecture, Ruskin writes his mother that he is 'four miles out of Bradford in a country house among wood anenomes'.[22] For her information, that is Harris's Ashfield. But it may well be an Ashfield made charming by recent memories of Heaton's Woodbank. With help from his 'good Yorkshire friends', Ruskin is deliberately steadying himself for the realisation of that second Bradford utterance which began to be generated under Whernside a few days after his first appearance.

Admission to Ruskin's 1859 lecture would have cost various levels of the community two shillings and sixpence each, or a shilling, or sixpence. After expenses, £23.6s. was raised for the new Design School. The 1864 lecture was advertised as an 'intellectual treat'; and no charge was made, quite as if it might be valuable in itself. The audience would still be ranged according to income, but they had in this one small respect at least already acted as Ruskin would encourage them to do – 'collectively'.[23] At Bradford, as nowhere else, Ruskin was addressing a small, relatively coherent, and powerful 'liberal' establishment – the word was stretched there to include virtual Tories and outright radicals – a body of opinion ranging from eminently wealthy men to thoughtful and vocal artisans gathered together not, indeed, as Ruskin misremembered it, putting the spirit for the letter, in Bradford Town Hall – Bradford had no town hall till 1873 – but in the Mechanics' Institute, which fulfilled many of the functions of such a building. A glance at nearby Leeds will show the value of the 'intellectual treat' which was as typical of this Bradford audience as of their chosen lecturer.

On 23 April 1864, cultural Leeds was divided. The choice lay between Mr Hincks's archaeological lecture at the Philosophic and Literary Society, with its detailed discussion as to whether or not, in Leeds, the Bronze Age preceded the Iron age; and the Leeds Shakespeare Tercentenary, at which Mr John Coleman recited an appropriate ode, and Miss Helen Walker appeared as the First Fairy in portions of *A Midsummer Night's Dream*. On 22 April, there was opportunity to hear the Bishop of Ripon, at his visitation, anathematising Ruskin's friend Bishop Colenso for casting 'suspicion on the claim of our adorable Redeemer', by applying science to the Bible.[24] Bradford had had to make do with Mr Ruskin on 21 April. Having not much time or taste for any of the several spheres of Leeds culture represented by Hincks, Miss Walker, or the Bishop, Bradford was still backward enough to get its history, art and metaphysics all in a single sitting – quite as if there might be connections between the three.

The choice of style for the new Exchange had precious little to do with Ruskin. Advance notices of the 1864 lecture – 'The relation of the architecture of public buildings to daily life' – look forward to moral and public enlightenment, and make no connection between the style of the proposed Exchange and these typical Bradford concerns. Unique among British liberal journalists, Byles had responded warmly to *Unto This Last*. His *Observer* had also noted that Ruskin's searching philosophy of art must be distinguished from his necessary partisanship in favour of certain contemporary manifestations. The best of Bradford could separate as well as Ruskin the medieval revival from the exciting irrigations of this 'deep digger' as Byles called Ruskin, this reacher after the 'springs of human action'.[25] That positive 'not caring' about the dress of the Wool Exchange should not be forgotten. It was very close to Ruskin's own state of mind.

Ripley, Ruskin's chairman, was also chairman of the Chamber of Commerce and he was in favour of Gothic. Behrens, another prime mover behind the Wool Exchange, was a German native of Danish Schleswig-Holstein. His dreamchild was realised in Italo-Flemish-Gothic by an architect with a Doncaster background making good in Bradford. The satire on 'taste' and 'independence' is extended by the architect's name, which – *Wuthering Heights* now almost seems to prophesy – was Mr Lockwood. He boasted – probably inaccurately, and certainly unwisely – of having knocked up the final design in a fortnight.[26] Perhaps the cream of the jest lay in the structure's rentable cellars – designed for traffickers in quality wines.

No wonder his posthumous editors suggest that, 'Publishing his lecture at a time when the design was well known, Ruskin was careful to dissociate himself from it'. In fact, he had denied on the night that he was there to influence their choice; though he did offer Alfred Waterhouse as a suitable authority, and briefly praised what he could of his Manchester Assize Courts. 'In general effect' the Manchester Assize building 'was as beautiful as could be,' Mr Ruskin said, 'but if they didn't like that kind of building, they needn't build one (laughter).'[27] Since that building's admirers included Charles Barry, who had given Halifax an Italianate town hall, Ruskin was hardly being controversial; but it may be he yielded to pressure from Heaton or the Harrises in doing this. And perhaps that was why, after their solicitor John Rawson had troubled Waterhouse for a professional opinion, the consensus of assessors chose the design Waterhouse liked least, ignoring potential masterpieces by William Burges and the young R. Norman Shaw – either of which, as Waterhouse was at pains to tell them, would have been cheaper. The consensus of directors had virtually excluded Street and Waterhouse himself from the competition by refusing time for the proper preparation of plans: and got rid of Brodrick and Webb by 'refusing a concession of even nine days'. The outsiders' endeavours were hampered by the effort of providing what was required inside the advertised £27,000, a sum known by those who knew to be too mean. Lockwood acted on the assumption – justified in the event – that the directors could be coaxed into going somewhat higher.

Byles lent space to the lengthy and informed disgust over this mode of proceeding penned scathingly by Aldam Heaton and wearily – he was attending his sick wife in convalescence at Ilkley Wells

– by Alfred Harris junior. When the twelve Exchange Directors met, in May, Harris had thrice urged his colleagues, without success, to study Waterhouse's 'careful and complete report'. Had he told them what they wanted to hear, doubtless they would have heeded Waterhouse: as he did not, they decided his advice was uncalled for. He was in fact acting in a typically Victorian semi-official capacity, which in this case, failed to do the trick. Without (officially) knowing names, Waterhouse had given commendation to the plans of Burges and Shaw; particularising the former as offering 'the maximum of accommodation with the minimum of expense'. Burges, it is to be noted, was currently describing himself, in Ruskinian terms, as an 'art-architect' with the human figure as the root of his design. The design standing 'highest in unproductive area' – and absolutely the costliest – was Mr Lockwood's. Necessarily it was selected, one director deciding in fifteen minutes. After all, Waterhouse was quite capable of taking over the job himself. Heaton and his supporters felt any 'well-educated' layman would agree with Waterhouse, with 'professional men' tipping the scale in favour of Shaw. Heaton declared that the decision in favour of Lockwood was achieved by one half of the directors' browbeating the rest, among whom only Harris was capable of articulating a resistance. Harris himself, wishing to combine 'profitable return' with 'credit to good taste' felt Burges's plan was specially suitable, and 'far in advance architecturally of any but' – the Shaw design: a joint acknowledgment by decorator and banker of Shaw's originality here with which Stefan Muthesius, writing a century later, would be in agreement.[28] Heaton, energetic as ever, offered to pay the cost of forwarding the six sets of plans to suitable referees – including Ruskin and his friend Acland – 'if any other than' Burges or Shaw 'were to be selected by them'. What makes Heaton's challenge a little hollow is the impact of all three newspaper reports of Ruskin's lecture. It is clear that he thought – like most of the directors – that Bradford must build for itself.

When it came to a choice of style for a particular building, it was perhaps the more obviously pragmatic criteria which governed the choice. Bradford had its own piece of medieval symbolism. Though 'scarcely thought of in Bradford' by 1859, Bishop Blaize, patron of woolcombers, was still honoured by a remnant of traditionalists dining in public houses on his day. He and Edward III, whose Queen was granted Bradford manor and who favoured its market with a new charter, were obvious choices to place by the entrance of the new Exchange: but such sculptures were hardly 'the entire masters of the architecture' – as Ruskin's formative sense demanded – and as a local 'Lover of Gothic' commented, there remained the absurdity of Italo-Flemish-Gothic 'loosly treated' by a firm whose 'practice was in Italian'. It is more likely the pinched nature of the site suggested going over to Gothic to Mr Lockwood and his patrons if any sort of dignity was to be attained. Moreover, this made possible a tall corner tower upon which to place a visible spire; and a visible public clock – something Bradford had been struggling to achieve since 1836. The new Flemetian tower, with clock, was a cheaper amenity, and decoration, than the massive Classical equivalent Cuthbert Brodrick had given to Leeds. A personal triumph for Mr Lockwood – for in earlier days when they were both at Hull, Brodrick had been articled to himself.

There was justifiable effrontery in Ruskin's opening remarks, as delivered and published. 'I do *not* care about this Exchange of yours,' he said ' – because *you* don't.' A letter to the local *Observer* made the same point: 'The great source of mischief is that so few people care two straws *what* sort of Exchange we get'.

Shaw's hunched and knobby design, which would have complemented the neighbouring hills, was judged by 'XYZ' to be 'deliberately ugly, designed on the notion that Bradford people are a rough and uncultivated lot, without taste'.[29] Without, that is, the 'taste' of Leeds, which, under Ellen Heaton's brother John Deakin Heaton had insisted on George Gilbert Scott for their new Infirmary. Lockwood's design, as imitation Scott, would perhaps appease Bradford 'jealousy'. Miss Heaton had asked Ruskin's advice on the matter of Leeds Infirmary, and got a tart reply: 'It does not matter what people build at Leeds nor anywhere else at present. The Gothic they build is essentially worse than the Greek'.[30]

Ruskin's sardonic streak would probably have approved Aldam Heaton's judgment on Lockwood's design: 'What they *want* is ignorance and darkness and they have got it'. But then, for Aldam, G. G. Scott and his Leeds patron – Aldam's brother-in-law John Deakin – were reprehensible old fogeys, whereas Shaw was a personal friend. Ruskin's sense of humour would have applauded local writers who likened Lockwood's News Room to the dungeons of Venice: 'Plenty of light comes in at the floor, but very little at the top of the windows,' grumbled one shareholder, and added: '"If Greece must perish, we thy will obey/But let us perish by the light of day",' Ruskin's commonsense, too, would have detected flaws in Burges's grandly Gothic design. Local jealousy suspected Burges of being a personal friend of Harris and Aldam Heaton. Even more damning was his 'contrivance for getting snow off the lead flats round the Exchange roof by means of a tunnel six yards long through which the snow would have to be pushed'. Shaw and Burges were acknowledged to be 'clever', but too 'ultra' for Bradford taste: though there was also disaffection in Nonconformist Bradford with the 'churchy' look of Lockwood's design; and fun was poked at his 'small turrets or large pinnacles' at the corners. The 'interior would make a capital swimming bath' was another popular jibe.[31]

Ruskin's humorous invective was addressed to people well able to appreciate it. But there seems to have been only one letter in wholehearted support of a Classical new Exchange, with a Classical new Market Street to set it off. It is interesting that the letter anticipates, and even partly answers, some of the puzzles which would occupy Geoffrey Scott in his *Architecture of Humanism* of 1914. Scott was too intelligent not to see a certain truth behind Ruskin's correlation between neo-Roman architecture and 'political tyranny'. A letter to the *Bradford Observer* of 5 November 1866 envisaged a literally 'fascist' architecture for Bradford Market Street. Streets like the 'bundles of sticks' – *fasces* – carried by the lictors of Rome come 'cheaper, better, grander,' declares the writer, 'by combining façades' into one continuous and grand design. In Lockwood's Wool Exchange Bradford produced a vulgarised Gothic. This might, to some imaginations, make it a more hopeful building than Joseph Poelaert's far more coherent, infinitely more vulgar, contemporary Palais de Justice, on its preposterous 'classical' podium above Brussels. If Lockwood looks forward, however absurdly, to what Geoffrey Scott would term the 'democratic ethics' of Morris,[32] Poelaert anticipates the acceleration of Pandemonian kitsch which accompanied the death dance of imperialism, and the witless prolongation of both by Hitler and Mussolini. It is pertinent to add that had the Axis powers prevailed, Great Britain would have been ruled, under Hitler – who clearly shared Lord Shaftesbury's faith in Bradfordian efficiency – by one Martin Böhle, a Bradford native of German mercantile extraction and the Führer's designated Gauleiter for his empire's off-shore island.[33] That would have resolved stylistic discussions about Market Street.

The Bradfordians of 1864 chose a design which declared their sense of unity with the 'freedom' of the north Italian cities; and their abhorrence of the 'tyranny' of Rome: and there was a deep, if muddled, truth in their instinct.

Against this, the letters from E. W. Godwin and W. Eden Nesfield which appeared in the Bradford press in June 1864, seem of less moment. Godwin revealed Mr Waterhouse's estimate of the real cost of Lockwood's monstrosity: £38,000! No wonder the attempts of outsiders to meet the declared estimate of £27,000 had met with failure. 'I refrain,' Godwin added, 'from entering on the fine art question. If Mr Ruskin fails to set the people of Bradford right; it is surely vain for me. . . to attempt anything of the kind.' Nesfield, more modestly, wished Mr Ruskin would 'deliver another lecture for the especial benefit of the directors, as they certainly have not profited by the last he was good enough to give'.[34]

But Ruskin's lecture had been too good to be ensnared by mere stylistic puzzles. Ruskin and his Bradford audience shared a sense of the ludicrousness of most neo-Gothic; and they shared something even more important: doubt about the validity of the oppressive system by which Bradford – but not many Bradfordians – had so richly profited.

The Harrises gave Waterhouse the commission for rebuilding the Old Bank in 1867: and had certainly influenced the choice of the same architect for Bingley Mechanics' Institute, of 1865. And, when opportunity at last arose, Norman Shaw gained his revenge by abstaining from it. His extension of 1904–9 to the Lockwood and Mawson Town Hall of 1869–73 would have a steel framework and concrete floors. The suavely Edwardian Gothic of his stone covering alleviates, without disparaging, his neighbours' too congested revivalisms. Nothing could make them entertaining. The original Town Hall's unflinching pretensions are only of slight architectural interest. The building is nevertheless an invaluable monument. Before the century was out, Margaret McMillan and her friend Dr Kerr were using a room in its basement as the country's first extempore school clinic.[35]

Meanwhile, what makes Lockwood and Mawson, as Gothic milliners, unforgivable, is the fact of their having pirated, and spoiled, the 'inspiration' for the Town Hall design – most evidently in the case of the tower – from William Burges's unsuccessful scheme for the London Law Courts, of 1866. Lockwood had been one of

Burges's rivals in that competition, too: offering the metropolis a vision of Bradford Wool Exchange run mad. The assessors, eventually, chose George E. Street, whose towers, which owed something to Ruskin's personal intervention on the side of variety, still stretch along the Strand.

Lockwood's Wool Exchange, with its redundancy of pinnacle, and spikily saurian tower, is not so morbid as his Town Hall. A vegetable analogy would be the Ypres Cloth Hall in a state of etiolation. It has justly been described as 'heavily influenced by Scott' and imitates his partly Italian, partly Flemish, and wholly mid-Victorian 'Gothic' style. It is neither so coherent, nor so smug as Scott's slightly earlier Preston Town Hall. There is a sort of humour in its offensiveness. As Holmes put it, whatever you call it, it is pre-eminently Bradfordian. And as Ruskin virtually prophesied, the interior ironwork of gallery and roof carries some conviction. All this, however – to use Ruskin's metaphor – was mere 'millinery'. The 'object of the architect', as *The Builder* informed its readers in August 1864, was 'to avoid any sacrifice of the expensive and valuable ground. . . and yet to prevent the extreme irregularity of the site from being internally visible'. Somewhat to which end, the external details – including busts of Great Men peering from roundels – were shaved back as close as possible, while the main hall nestled within a frame of Gothic shops and offices, denying the spectator much notion of what went on inside. The building method itself was dictated by this shortage of space. As usual in Bradford, all materials were raised internally by means of a horse-driven gin in the basement. The site was also the usual Bradford type – an irregular, slanting wedge.

Ten years later, in the warehouse they designed at 63 Vicar Lane, Lockwood and Mawson would resort to similar expedients, this time in a Classic mode. From the ground plan, 'almost in the form of a quarter circle',[36] there arose a handsomely plain seven-storey warehouse, adroitly linked at its narrow edge to a five-story portico in a sumptuous Corinthianesque, which housed the grand staircase. The triumphant practicality and superbly meticulous detail of this building put it altogether in a higher category than the Wool Exchange.

The Wool Exchange is basically a Bradford warehouse, but in Gothic; and with its portico crowned by a 150-foot spikily saurian tower. The accommodation is disposed around a light-well, as was usual with warehouses. But in this instance the light-well is aggrandised into the Gothic Exchange Hall, and the enclosing accommodation is reduced to rentable shops and offices. The masonry detail is once again under firm control – pathetically so, since this nullifies any enjoyment that might have been got out of the style employed. Its potential practical advantages were alike discarded. Rows of continuous fenstration, such as employed in many Venetian Gothic palaces, might have obviated the need for almost perpetual gaslight[37] which became incumbent on tenants trapped behind the prettified, but meanly spaced lancets of Mr Lockwood.

Only Norman Shaw, in Alfred Harris's now demolished Holy Trinity Bingley, was wise enough to design a Gothic building of handsome plainness, in which meticulous stonemasonry could assume its proper glory. As his Wool Exchange would have done, it suited the non-nonsense boldness of the adjacent landscape. The builders were J. and W. Foster, of Bingley. Ruskin may have seen and approved what he called the church's 'original design' in Harris's house in April 1864. The resulting 'simplicity and dignity' of the actual building won his personal commendation in 1881. He had quite likely seen the church in his drive through Bradford of September 1875. Ruskin probably spared himself, on that visit, any glance at the millinery of Shaw's rivals of 1864, though he knew enough at second hand to have a good idea of the building by the time he published *Traffic*. If the interior of the Mechanics' Institute suggested the head of a wasp, the tower of the Wool Exchange had a more subaqueous aspect: a crocodile perhaps, or an ichthyosaurus.[38]

Now Mr Lockwood's ichthyosaurus presents in curiously resolute form what John Summerson has called that 'recurring element which cannot be missed' by students of Victorian architecture. That 'element is – doubt'.[39] Fatuously pseudo-Gothic in a town otherwise Italianate, it is yet in materials and workmanship a testimony to the Yorkshire craving for 'solid quality'. The discrepancy has one promising connotation. There was honesty in the Puritan Bradfordian confusion over the need to manufacture and design dress materials fit for 't'harlots i' Paris'.[40] Similarly in this matter of the relation of public buildings to daily life, there is some hope for a society stolidly incapable of rearing a convincing monument to exploitation and oppression.[41] As a building the Bradford Wool Exchange represents a loss of nerve – a failure to continue building in Bradford's adequate neo-Roman style. But that loss of nerve represented a deeper and more hopeful failure: a failure to continue to regard as adequate the suppressions and subordinations of a neo-Roman society.

The Builder continues: 'The principal entrance to the Exchange is under the tower, and is combined with an open arcade, giving a picturesque effect to the approach, and affording also the advantage of a covered outer area during the hours of 'Change.' All this – and more – can be appreciated from the accompanying full-page engraving of the exterior. Inside, 'the Exchange itself is a lofty and spacious hall, containing on the floor upwards of 600 yards superficial. The inner parallelogram is surrounded by band shafts of red polished granite, from the capitals of which spring arches filled with tracery of mediaeval design, the gable ends being also filled in with spandrel windows of appropriate character. The roof will be of open timber work, with carved hammerbeams and wrought iron spandrels, the design throughout having a strong constructional character, to which principles the decoration has been made subservient.' The News Room was ready by October 1866. It had a compartmented ceiling with 'elaborate enriched cornices, and with centre flowers'. Two Caen stone chimney-pieces, with serpentine shafts and carved capitals, were supplied by Messrs Maewr and Ingle, of Leeds. The chandeliers of mediaeval design came from the metal workshops of Messrs Skidmore of Coventry – famous in this line since their work for Ruskin and his friend Acland in the Oxford Museum. The painted decorations were executed by Messrs Briggs and Mensforth, of Bradford, and fittings in oak, inlaid with ebony, were purveyed by Messrs Mills and Backhouse. The Exchange Room itself, readers were told, would have an encaustic tile floor, again by Messrs Maewr. It would take 'two months to lay'.

'No book of mine has had so much influence on contemporary art as *The Stones of Venice*,' wrote Ruskin in his new preface of 1874. It manifested itself in 'dark and slippery arrangements for the advertisement of cheap coloured glass and pantiles'. The 'comparatively unimportant part of the book, its exhibition of the transitional forms of Arabian and Byzantine architecture' as adapted in Venice, contemporary architects succeeded in parodying. That word 'exhibition' confessed Ruskin's own complicity. He further noted the pathetic integrity of certain craftsmen under such bogus conditions. But the book's two major themes were hardly understood. He might have added they were adequately exhibited in current practice. Both involved questions of relation.[42]

Ruskin's first major theme was the relation of art to 'moral temper'. This has perhaps been sufficiently exampled by the subserviences of *The Builder*. No chance here for the Ruskinian principle that 'sculpture and painting were the entire masters of the architecture',[43] respectfully leading material to its proper fulfilment in form and colour, obtaining and transcending the functions of commodiousness and visibility. Heaton described the building as a rocking-horse 'much adorned with green and scarlet paint and brave in brass-headed nails' – a sinister–comic comparison that foreshadows exactly the tone of Ruskin's Dublin lecture. There, too, the 'really practical and sensible' children of Darwinian capitalism would declare nothing 'of any real consequence, that afternoon, except to get plenty of brass-headed nails'. Ruskin and his Bradford admirer would seem to have the same sense of the fatuousness of the tragedy – lives exchanged for something to stick into upholstery and pull out again.[44] The Bradford Exchange contractors were the same as for All Souls' Halifax – J. and W. Beanland. Their other successes included Leeds Infirmary, York Barracks, and the 'restoration' of Bangor and Chichester Cathedrals. William Beanland, the senior partner, died of overwork in 1887 after completing Bradford's huge French-renaissance Post Office, a design of Sir Henry Tanner.

Ruskin's second relation, that of 'the life of the workman to his work' – in Bradford – became national news with the local building strike of 1865. 'Improvements' such as patent machinery for stone dressing and heavy carpentry work were naturally resented by the unions, as their object was not to lighten their labour, releasing them for more creative work – the visionary Mr Ruskin's notion of machinery – but simply to make as many of them as possible redundant.

In ostensibly avoiding a discussion of the proposed Bradford Wool Exchange, Ruskin naturally took the opportunity to castigate English prevarication on Schleswig-Holstein – more appropriately than some would have liked to the occasion and place; for Jacob Behrens, a driving force behind the building, was a native of the duchies, and one of the Bradford Germans who had joined those of Berlin in presenting their own address to Garibaldi a fornight before – with obvious nationalistic implications. Ruskin expounded for Bradford his belief that a creative discipline of peace would be preferable to a struggle for the profits of wars left otherwise to foreigners. The moment, and the place, were appropriate for both sides of the theory, for strikes were in progress 'at many of the large iron-works near Leeds and Bradford' – the men demanding some of the profits of the 'exceedingly prosperous' trade in armaments and other impedimenta.

The theology of such 'progress' – thanks to Ruskin we know the name of the deity – is enunciated clearly enough by *The Bradford Observer* with reference to this same iron strike of April 1864. As Ruskin's train took him into Bradford from Leeds he had opportunity to notice, to the north of the main track, the private rolling-stock of Bowling Iron Works, not rolling. Byles feels he must bear witness against defaulters whose protests necessitate improvements, and their own redundancy: 'Introduction of new machinery is a gain to the world, but an invincible rival to those whose refractory conduct led to its introduction'.[45]

'Gunpowder explosions' was how Carlyle rejoiced to characterise Ruskin's 'Tree twigs' lecture of 1861.[46] The explosions of *Traffic* are more controlled – or contrived – but they remain very necessary. Reports suggest the actual lecture was both blunter and kindlier: proper to a Yorkshire audience. As published, we miss some of the sense of the immediate reaction: which included laughter, tears, applause and cries of 'Hear, hear'. Some people even cheered. But, as Holmes testified, explosions were also a feature of the night's entertainment; and then and as published these shot both ways. Dined and fêted by those 'great guns' the liberal Mr and Mrs Robert Kell, 'I wish someone would explode me,' Ruskin's housing agent Octavia Hill writes home from Bradford on 17 September 1869.[47] Ruskin, too, was subject to a day's lunching and dining, and a general round of enforced amiability and admiration before select mobs of people, 'very trying to my constitution',[48] and very useful for consolidating the published awarenesses of *Traffic*. Octavia, at least, is toured round Saltaire that she might approve and advise. The newly-celebrated housing reformer is interrogated and flattered by Dr Bridges and other influential people. Doubtless they are interested in those schemes of Mr Ruskin's outlined in *Time and Tide* and published the other year in the *Leeds Mercury*. Miss Hill's efforts in leading slum dwellers to self respect and the purchase of their own homes form a beautiful picture, presided over as they are by the great art critic. And Miss Hill's hosts will make sure her efforts receive due publicity. All this can now be seen as a valuable footnote to social history. But the sincerity of Octavia provides a pause. It is so difficult 'to unhumbug oneself', she confides. It is in such a context that Ruskin's apparent 'whimsicality' must be set. In Bradford and elsewhere, he consistently exploded himself, teasing his audience out of humbug into fuller, fresh awareness, exploiting the very oddness of his presence and personality. 'How it tells home!' was the *Observer's* [49] comment, and that journal was not given to glib enthusiasms.

The Bradford historian Scruton provides a useful point of reference. On the rare occasions when the Brontë sisters had ventured into the town, 'on a Thursday or a Saturday, when throngs of people were about, they invariably clung to the wall fast hold of each other, as if afraid of being noticed'. And no wonder. The 'people of Bradford who gazed with such curiosity upon Patrick's Brontë's daughters' were responding, not to genius, but to eccentricity: 'the most timid and sensitive creatures it was possible to gaze upon' in their 'old fashioned gowns', an inhabitant remarked.[50] Ruskin, too, arrived in Bradford on a Thursday, market day, when the tiny centre was jammed with people.[51] His train was due in at 3.10 pm. For one reason or another, he 'had only time for' an 'absurd line' to his mother by 7 pm, after he reached Bingley. When he returned to address them – doors open at 7.30, lecture to begin at 8 puncutal – he quite deliberately gave his audience something to look at, with his old-fashioned clothes, his quietly insistent yet various delivery, his disturbing self-mockery, malicious puncturing of cherished hypocrisies: his bewildering *cortesia;* his carefully positioned moments of naked sincerity. It was the sort of performance he could neither bear not to give nor sustain for long. Yet, as we have seen in the case of Harry's cave the outwards explosion could only be called healthy. It was the celebration of what he was. The mere statement of it was a quicker personal relief, but not so generally beneficial.

In a letter of 1856 to Henry Acland Ruskin had defended his right to political as well as artistic opinion. The self-portrait admitted a single 'ugly-looking' disqualification, however. 'You live out of the world,' he imagined his friend saying, 'and cannot know *anything* about it.' Ruskin rebuts the charge with a self-mocking piece of sincerity which tenderly but urgently communicates – as he was often doing – the value of his own alienation. 'Who do you suppose knows most,' he asks, 'about the Lake of Geneva – I, or the fish in it? It is quite true the Fish know a thing or two I don't – certain matters about feeding places, deep holes, and various other characteristics of Bottom. Nevertheless as to the general nature of the lake of Geneva, future prospects of it, and probabilities of all said fish being entirely broiled by a volcanic explosion, or petrified in their beloved bottom by advance of delta, I know more than they.'[52]

The clever analogy contained a value: that some organic and enabling balance is necessary in society lest an unjust system that fails to indoctrinate its victims earn catastrophe or one that dupes them harden as the currents of life flow elsewhere. *Unto This Last* sees the problem not as a melodrama of class, but as its tragedy; 'for in this (as I believe in every other kind of slavery) the oppressor suffers at last more than the oppressed'.[53] The oppressors do not usually evolve religions, or conserve skills: their 'victory' can thus only be the beginning of their defeat. Even their 'good taste', by this time, is a too evidently despicable nostalgia for a slave economy. Yet to pretend to any final happy ending, or to affirm recurrence, would be disingenuous and annihilating. At the moment, pressure of competition realises the words of Shakespeare's Duke of Albany. Failing the intervention of 'visible spirits': 'Humanity must perforce prey on itself / Like monsters of the deep'.[54]

If the platform is busy with something very like *King Lear*, then Ruskin's part must perhaps be Cordelia with appropriate modifications. As he confessed to Acland shortly after his father's death, 'It is an exquisite piece of tragedy altogether – very much like Lear, in a ludicrous commercial way – Cordelia remaining unchanged and her friends writing to her afterwards'.[55] And Cordelia's antitype – the Fool – has his part to play, also. John James spent his life to recover the prosperity of his own grandfather, John Ruskin, Marylebone property owner with the honorific title of Parish Clerk of St Bartholomew-the-Great.[56] John's great-grandson and namesake desires to be even more fundamental. St Bartholomew's Priory and Hospital were founded in the twelfth century by Rahere, the retired Fool of Henry I. And innovatory foolishness, in an age of transition, is where we must begin again.

The date of Ruskin's second Bradford utterance was 21 April 1864. Can he have known – what the newspapers might have told him – that the £30,000 about to be spent on the new Exchange was just the sum exacted by their flood of 1859? It was egregious of him to mention this sum – as he did – to their faces; since the directors were busy trying to hide the building's likely real cost. But Heaton or Harris may have informed him. The Broad Ford was a sufficient indication of the occasional pertinence, here, of the subaqueous. Casting for a wider time-scale, Ruskin would know from Agassiz how rich the Yorkshire coalfields were in fossil fish. One of Agassiz's choicest specimens of Megalichthys, preserved in the Leeds Museum, was found at Eccleshill.[57] If Bradford had had a museum, it would have gone there. What Ruskin almost certainly knew about – *The Times* of that week was busy with headlines on the subject – was THE CALAMITY AT SHEFFIELD. An illustration of quite startling immediacy. The water of the Bradfield Reservoir there – 'maturing the elements of convulsions', in the choice phrase of *The Times* of 18 April – had broken down its banks, flooding the country for fourteen miles around, sweeping away property to the extent of £327,000 and terminating 250 lives. The embankment collapsed on 11 March – the day after John James's funeral – but national and local newspapers had been giving space ever since to poignant sketches of the event, peering into the picturesquenesses of the varied tales of rapid and lingering annihilation. 'The scene indeed for miles,' commented the *Bradford Advertiser* of 19 March, 'is one of utter annihilation, and reminds us of the magnificent descriptions of public calamities in the scriptures, where we are told that men did eat, drink, and were merry, and laid down to rest in unconscious ignorance; but the flood came and carried them away, and their places knew them no more.' In due course, Millais gave the world *A Flood* – a bonny babe afloat in his quaint wooden cradle, with rustic rescuers comfortably close.[58] Charitable aid was collected to applause, and photographers moved their views of ruined abbeys to one side of the window to make space for albums on the Yorkshire Devastation. And now – on 18 April, and not before time – we read, 'The reservoirs of Bradford are under Examination'.

Woodbank, the modest seventeenth-century house deep in the Harden valley, which Ruskin visited in April 1864, was no refuge from the contemporary phenomena of jealousy, ironmongery and flooding, which Ruskin would bring together in *Traffic*. The house's voluble occupant, John Aldam Heaton, was endeavouring to turn his portion of the valley bottom into a charming water-garden. His house was on a tributary of Harden Beck. Just below Woodbank this stream turned sharply south-east below the knoll of Harden Grange, to enter Harden Beck, the valley of which, with the moors beyond, formed a fine prospect for the Grange's occupant, the

'Demon' Dunlop. The paintings and stained glass of Rossetti inside both houses were no solution to the problems outside which engaged Heaton's energies and rhetoric. 'Manufacturers,' he would write in fury to the *Bradford Observer* after another Bradford flood of 1866, are 'polluting everything near us. . . a cottager can do as much damage as a millowner – relative to size – everybody. . . seems to make the beck his garbage ground – I have suffered severely from the way the beck has become loaded and dammed up by rubbish. . . astonishingly numerous varieties of crockery ware, the endless supply of tin cans with holes in the bottom. . . I wish my neighbours would come and look before calling out "Shy it int' t'beck hoyle".'[59] The Harden and Bradford becks, tributaries of the Aire, were traditional property boundaries: and many proprietors erected walls and railings in mid-stream to keep their neighbours at bay. Jealousy, ironmongery and the nemesis of flood: these themes of *Traffic* were the bane of Heaton's life and frequent topics of his garrulous conversation.

What the great Sheffield flood and its aftermath revealed was the dangers of shoddy building: not merely the embankment, but the houses in the path of the water were shown up to have been very inadequately constructed. It need hardly be said that, had Bradford suffered a similar tragedy, Ruskin would not have made the Flood of the *Critias* part of the 'occult mischief' of *Traffic*. As it was, the distance was exactly right. Moreover, in the original lecture he apparently 'insisted on good honest work and and no scamping'[60] – a colloquialism highly current at the time in reference to those rubble structures thinly coated with flagstone which the waters had liquidated.

At this distance, the Yorkshire Devastation relates to *Traffic* only as one more illustration of the pertinence of literature to life. But Fors ensured that the proper ludicrous–sublime relation of the lecture to the Shakespeare tercentenary was made in *The Bradford Review*. For juxtaposed to the heading *Lecture by John Ruskin, Esq.* came a note on that latest fund-raising effort of Mr Foggo, headmaster of the High School and organiser, in his own words, of artistic 'substitutes for Nature's sunshine'.[61] 'His subject on this occasion was "King Lear".'

Perhaps it was James Hanson, and not merely Fors, who put it there. The same page juxtaposes Ruskin's remarks on oppressive female labour to highly relevant news about female children in the

Bradford Workhouse, turned out to compete for employment at the age of ten. From Hanson, too, we learn how much more direct, in its original delivery, was the lecture's onslaught on that local symbol for gradualism, the 'bank'. Some masters – not in Bradford of course – were pushing their men off the bank altogether; for when they 'knew that they had saved a little money they turned them off'. Hanson's seriousness certainly guaranteed a more appropriate response to Ruskin than was common in the national press.

On the actual platform, H. W. Ripley was a chairman close to Ruskin in some superficial ways that mattered little; and in some less obvious ways that mattered a great deal. Becoming daily fonder of Toryism, the Church and Gothic architecture – or so John Holmes describes him – Ripley was thereby all the more certainly a symbol of Ruskin's alienation. But as a practical town planner grappling with an environment that presented difficulties almost too frightful to contemplate, Ripley was closer to Ruskin's heart than an artistical gentleman would have been. Between them, the dilettante banker Harrises and the hugely successful dyer and businessman H. W. Ripley controlled much of the real estate of central Bradford. The Harrises and their protégé Aldam Heaton were merchant-gentlemen of taste, eager to see the Wool Exchange take the form of a Gothic masterpiece by an architect of national distinction. Ripley was more concerned with the drains.

In the late fifties Ripley had offered to provide Bradford with a drainage system, but jealousy put paid to that 'job' – as it was called. It was a job that needed doing, nonetheless. He had, in 1861, supported with his enormous industry and efficiency a second Street Improvement Act for Bradford; and at the same time helped to prevent a Wool Exchange being erected at the bottom of Church Bank, where it would have blocked the view of the Parish Church – an achievement reserved, in the event, for the national government who chose in 1884 to put Tanner's impressive Post Office there. In April 1864, Bradford, with Ripley's help, was on the point of achieving a piped sewage system. On a Herculean scale, Mr Ripley was engaged in performing for a great conurbation what Ruskin himself was trying to achieve for his father's London properties. He and his father had often conversed about drains with John Simon, Medical Officer to the Privy Council: and now, with the aid of Octavia Hill's practical genius, Ruskin was embarking on a little street improvement of his own in a corner of Marylebone. In welcoming Ruskin to Bradford Ripley called for and received the 'loudest acclamations' as he invoked the visitor's world-wide reputation in aid of Bradford's struggle from a 'state of chaos'. This noisy vulgarity must have set on edge the teeth of the gentlemanly Harrises. But the *Bradford Observer*, in a boyishly enthusiastic style not dissimilar from Ripley's own, gives a clue to Ruskin's complex appeal. 'Eloquence,' claims its report on the lecture, 'not of the mere word-painting type' is Ruskin's *forte*, 'pregnant with reflections resulting from a deep-seated knowledge of human nature. . . unsullied by the hot breath of politics, or the spitting venom of sectarianism. . . as might have been expected from a deep digger, looking not merely to the surface of things, the traditions of the schoolmen and the dilettanti but to the springs of human action. . .'

Ripley was not so poor a judge of human nature himself, in getting the audience to cheer Ruskin at the beginning: and when he came to publish *Traffic* in 1866 there would be points at which Ruskin seems to be speaking to Ripley. Yet he must not alienate dilettanti like the Harrises; and he must keep on his side a Co-operator like John Holmes, who will for many years remain a devoted correspondent. And there are things about Ripley's world that are not acceptable. There is a practical virtue to be addressed, which concerns itself with drains. But there is a 'Gothic' sensibility to placate, a sensibility to which Ripley is belatedly subscribing. It is here that doubt begins to be desirable. Bowling, scene of Ripley's piece-dyeworks – the largest on earth – received from him a site for the church of St Bartholomew; he also brought the number of almshouses up to ten; and provided schools. In spite of which, Ripleyville, his adjacent 'model village' was a mistimed experiment which failed because its inhabitants could not afford the upkeep of the houses.[62]

Ripley's methods are not always truly economic. Bradford's most chronic problem is the control of the water supply; and Ripley's practical flair is engaged in keeping the balance between deep wells of soft water for the wool trade; reservoirs on the outskirts for drinking; and the hard surface water gathered in disused pits which he exploits for his own dyeing purposes. The whole scheme is a miracle of true economy. But it is marred by false economies – murderous ones. Mr Ripley economises on plate for his boiler: as do other 'capital friends' – to quote Ruskin's sly expression. Various persons expire horribly from time to time as a result of the possibly foreseeable explosions. The law, so far, can do nothing to impede Ripley's career in this respect. Due to the thinness of the plate, a boiler at Ripley's dyeworks exploded in June 1861, injuring a workman named Brook and killing another named Rouse, aged sixty-four. These things are frequently happening – much more often at works less efficient than Mr Ripley's. The coroner records the verdict that 'no criminal responsibility is attachable to any party'.[63] This is the context in which Ruskin's private exclamations about fish in Lake Geneva seem restrained. To convey their value from a platform shared by Mr Ripley he must be exquisitely restrained, with just a touch of tartness:

> Do you mean to gather always – never to spend? If so, I wish you joy of your goddess, for I am just as well off as you, without the trouble of worshipping her at all. But if you do not spend, somebody else will – somebody else must. And it is because of this (among many other such errors) that I have fearlessly declared your so-called science of Political Economy to be no science; because, namely, it has omitted the study of exactly the most important branch of the business – the study of *spending*. . .
>
> . . . I know that none of this wrong is done with deliberate purpose. I know, on the contrary, that you wish your workmen well; that you do much for them, and that you desire to do more for them, if you saw your way to such benevolence safely. I know that even all this wrong and misery are brought about by a warped sense of duty, each of you striving to do his best; but, unhappily, not knowing for whom this best should be done. And all our hearts have been betrayed by the plausible impiety of the modern economist, telling us that, 'To do the best for ourselves, is finally to do the best for others'. Friends, our great Master said not so; and most absolutely we shall find this world is not made so. Indeed, to do the best for others, is finally to do the best for ourselves; but it will not do to have our eyes fixed on that issue.[64]

Now this Bradford audience, if any in the kingdom, know their Bibles backwards. Many could quote chapter and verse from the Gospel of John. 'A new commandment I give unto you' were the Master's words at the Last Supper, 'That ye love one another; as I have loved you . . . I am the vine, ye are the branches.'[65] But that was all for Sunday. Workaday dogmas of political economy were 'Free Competition'; and 'Buy in the cheapest, sell in the dearest

Market'. In practice this meant that distillations of selfishness were not merely intoxicating draughts for the very rich. Cheaper brands of selfishness formed the vinegar of life that ran in the veins of those ideal Bradford 'workers, who never drink, never strike, always go to church on Sunday, and always express themselves in respectful language'.[66]

In June 1864, Mr Ripley, as Chairman of the Bradford Chamber of Commerce, will hasten to preserve the 'independence' of the warehouses from the Factory Acts. The new Bill, he feels, should be limited to 'Warehouses employing children under 13'. The very 'persons to be protected oppose every legislative interference of the kind', he informs the Home Secretary. He notes that '1,200 warehousemen and boys have signed a petition against it'. Doubtless a boy like Fearnside, his father's support from his early teens, would not wish to be protected out of a job; nor would older men wish to see another adult replace a cheap juvenile, and adult male earnings – such was the wages 'science' of the day – averaged downwards. An example of the pertinence, and apparent hopelessness of what Arnold called Ruskin's 'pugnacious political economy'. But the evidence Ripley brings forward for his own urgent complacency is even more interesting: 'the Mechanics' Institute is well-used,' he writes: employing a phrase he may well have picked out of the current Post Office Directory. Too fond a dream, Mr Ruskin, that angels might descend a scale or two – the institution that pretends to assist their irreversible ascension is now something to allude to in clipping their wings at the foot of the ladder.[67]

Contemporary behaviour attests the relevance of Ruskin's criticism to a degree surpassing parody.

Expressing in the new Bradford Wool Exchange of 1867 all the assurance of the Rich Fool, the Mayor of Leeds will proclaim the cult of obsolescence that is his own vision of popular Darwinism. For he 'sincerely wished. . . if he lived. . . for twenty years longer he might. . . be present at the inauguration of another hall three times as large as the present Exchange'.[68] How they cheered – unaware of Reiss's electric telephone, invented in Frankfurt six years before. That, not boundless prosperity, would end the usefulness of their Exchange. On the same occasion, Malcolm Ross steps forward. He is the new brand of self-styled workman-poet who has replaced the possibilities of John Nicholson, whose patron has been Richard Oastler, the Factory Reformer.[69] Malcolm is not here to declare war on Macbeth, but to proclaim the 'mutual forbearance and mutual toleration' of 'peace'. Ruskin proclaimed peace, too: Milton's and Plato's. He had recourse to some of 'St Paul's dodges' to do so – 'Never were more sharp ones in this world,' he confided to Miss Bell – '(I've some doubt about the propriety of all Joseph's)'.[70]

Not Joseph, but his hardworking father the shepherd Jacob was the patriarch to invoke in a wool landscape. Smooth and cunning, his wrestling match with the angel taught him a degree of humility and self-awareness and helped to turn him into Israel. His stone of Bethel makes for intensely fundamental thought about building and religion. Those in the audience who have read Cary's *Dante* can fill in for themselves highly pertinent allegories on the active and contemplative life as manifested in his wives Leah and Rachel.[71] And the vision of Jacob's Ladder offers an endless fund of spiritual, social and political meaning. *Traffic* is a piece of organic propriety offering co-operation with their own common muse: for a well of soft water in the centre of Bradford, a boon to the wool trade, has been known from time immemorial as 'Jacob's Well'. Indeed – and Ruskin may have known this since he refers to their civic seal – a 'Well Sable' was in 1847 selected as the centrepiece of the new borough's coat-of-arms. Like Paul on Mars Hill Ruskin at the bottom of Well Street reveals to his audience their Unknown God – is it really Britannia Agoraia? – and enlists certain also of their own poets to do so.

The real baby who provided Millais with the inspiration for *A Flood* – his touching picture of the Yorkshire Devastation – was indeed rescued. And taken to the Beckett St Workhouse in Leeds, in March 1864. Nuns were able to get him adopted. But first they gave him a Christian name, and a surname: Albert Ignotus – Albert the Unknown.[72] Ruskin's consciousness or otherwise of that living memorial is quite irrelevant: the nuns knew exactly what they were doing.

But Malcolm Ross is of Joseph's generation:[73] and he publicly prays at the opening of the new Wool Exchange that Bradford may be a second Goshen; leaving his audience to recall that the blessedness of that spot depended on the prevalence elsewhere of famine, and on Joseph's sublime 'dodge' whereby he could say to the subdued persons of Egypt: 'I have bought you this day'.[74] Ross can make his annihilations because cash – and corn – have lost their material reality for him. 'You have separated your religion from your life,' Ruskin told them. Unfortunately, such incompetent metaphorising can provoke literal famine, literal enslavement to money, for those outside the mutuality of 'somebody's getting on'. That, at least, would appear to be Ruskin's thesis.

Ruskin may have noticed, on his various visits to Yorkshire, how the word 'jealousy' was often used locally with approbation. They rejoiced to apply that attribute at least of Jehovah to themselves. 'Your great English vice – European vice – vice of all the world,' he calls it, lest they be too offended. He alludes specifically to Palmerston's elaborate fortification of the south coast of England, and the prosperous trade in armaments. All highly pertinent and thought-provoking elements in what the Bradford socialist Fred Jowett, born in the year of this lecture, will characterise as Ruskin's 'even-flowing, but deadly, destructive' rhetoric against injustice.[75]

But it is when he seems to stray into romance that Ruskin becomes more 'deadly'. This time the audience are rushed to the northern borders of England. Politics, and political economy, have realised 'what was once true only of the rough Border riders of your Cheviot hills –

> They carved at the meal
> With gloves of steel
> And they drank the red wine through the helmet bar'd.'[76]

That quotation from *The Lay of the Last Minstrel* is at least appropriate in a lecture that insists on endings and beginnings. More occultly, it was Sir Walter Scott whose boyhood fantasies linked Jacob's ladder with the hangman's ladder.[77] *Traffic* insists on an end to such deathful fantasy of inexhaustibility, played out with real lives, and on the initiation of a reality – a *res publica* – in which the eternal will be indeed realised in the reciprocal harmony of those finite lives. The sacrament, like the Border riders' debauch, will always consist of human flesh and blood. Yet there remains a distinction between the 'lively sacrifice'[78] of Christianity and the holocausts of Mammon. Such reflections are available to the reader of Ruskin's text, which transcends its historical context. But the refined organism of his discourse gives his language an accuracy within that context often more exact than the man could know. It transcends the historical context because it uniquely pierces it. Ruskin cannot crush man's 'Adversary' the Devil, 'at a blow' as The *Athenaeum* would almost desire; but he can mortalise with unerring needle the preference of some of his 'Yorkshire friends' for what he calls the 'taste of the devils'.[79]

Henry Fearnside's employer, Moses Bottomley junior, we have encountered on the Committee of Bradford's Design School. In 1860, shortly after his marriage, his employees, Henry Fearnside among them, indulged in an almost Elizabethan bit of tomfoolery with him in the back field of Bottomley's father's house at Shelf, taking his horse recklessly over fences, and rolling 'young master' in the hay – as befits a bridegroom. A year or two later, Moses entrusted an extra room in his warehouse to Henry Fearnside's oversight. The first and last question he asked his favoured employee on that occasion was 'Are you in attendance at a Night School?' Yes, he was, at the Mechanics' Institute. But such attendance, Henry confides in his diary, requires all his 'powers of endurance'.

Removed, from 1869, to Woodleigh Hall, Rawdon, a 'realisation' of the 'ornamented Elizabethan order', by Lockwood and Mawson, Moses becomes too grand even for that kind of contact. His preferred neighbour is a ruin: the ancestral seat of the Rawdons – whose lands have been 'developed' for the benefit of Bottomley, among others. The male Rawdon line, which went back to the Conqueror's time, fell extinct last November, when 'the Wicked Marquis' – fourth and last Marquis of Hastings, Baron Rawdon – died of his excesses, bankrupt, at the age of twenty-six. Which makes a perfectly satisfactory view. But in 1877 springs up quite a new kind of development that threatens to supersede even Bottomley. This is the Woodlands Convalescent Home, an investment of H. W. Ripley. That sort of thing spoils a neighbourhood. Invalids and their friends 'interfere objectionably with the privacy of the drives'. Moses leads the residential protest, but Ripley is unrelenting. Indoors, Bottomley can console himself with Edith Martineau's *Embarras des Richesses* in his ebony dining-room, from which the impurity of gaslight is excluded; and by bronzes from Moreau of Paris; stained-glass illustrative of Shakespeare scenes supplied by John Gilbert. And by Pettie's *Temple Gardens*, after Henry VI, Part 1, showing Yorkists and Lancastrians plucking their respective emblems off the same rose tree. This information, dating from 1885, is supplied by Edward Healey, prize medallist of Bradford Design School, who waxes most lyrical over the large canvas in Bottomley's library: *A Raid on Chipchase Castle, Northumberland*, by Jones Barker. 'A band of border raiders are. . . driving off their plunder. . . securely bound to the horses' backs are the captives to be held for ransom, whilst in the background appears the Castle which has been delivered to the flames by its pitiless destroyers.' Mr Healey finds this 'a powerful subject', and altogether a 'very pleasing and successful composition'.[80] The antics of feudalism, still just possible at a time when Bradford was – ironically – building Roman warehouses, have been replaced by pleased contemplation of its atrocities in a quasi-Gothic library.

Bottomley has eight years only to savour the exit of the barons before the onslaught of the bath-chairs. The ambiguous innovator is Ripley, Ruskin's chairman of 1864 and from 1880 – baronet – of Rawdon. Bottomley's preferred interior view, in this context, is the return of barbarism.

'Friends,' Ruskin has said in the midst of an analysis of such taste, 'I know not whether this thing be the more ludicrous or the more melancholy. It is quite unspeakably both.'[81] Ascending and descending, Ruskin's needle pierces himself as well as his audience. That was one of his chief ways of joining them.

CHAPTER NINE

MY GOOD YORKSHIRE FRIENDS

My good Yorkshire friends. . .—*Traffic*

More important than any choice of style for the Bradford Wool Exchange was the decision as to what site it should occupy; and who should lay its foundation-stone.

John James tells the story thus:

> So great of late years had been the growth of the trade of the town, and the influx of spinners, manufacturers and merchants to its markets, that the Exchange Buildings had become totally inadequate for their accommodation. A Company accordingly was formed for building a new Exchange, and they chose for its site the block of old buildings in Market Street, where the old Market House stood. . . When the ground had been cleared, a strong wish prevailed in the town that it should be left open, and another site chosen for the Exchange. A public meeting was even held to carry out this object; but the requisite funds could not be raised, and therefore it was determined to carry out the original project. . . To give *eclat* to the occasion of laying the foundation stone of this future ornament and centre of attraction in the town, Lord Palmerston accepted an invitation to perform the ceremony, which took place on Tuesday, the 9th of August, 1864, with such a display of pomp and circumstance as has rarely been witnessed in Bradford.[1]

Ruskin's 1859 lecture – 'Modern Manufacture and Design' – was naturally associated in people's minds with the new Design School, and with the Social Science congress held in Bradford later that year. All this came under the heading of 'progress'. Byles's *Observer* could hail without irony the Design School Exhibition of July 1859. There was 'no more decided proof that Bradford is not wholly given to the worship of Mammon, or utterly indifferent to the beauties of art'. At the Social Science congress that October, despite the anxiety about public health expressed by Ruskin's metropolitan friend William Cowper and Ruskin's Bradford sympathiser Dr MacTurk, the general tone was one of assurance among the middle class; with a message of reassurance to the working classes that their restraint and manly independence would somehow find their reward. The Ruskinian influence seemed to be assimilable, to the satisfaction of this progressive mutual admiration society. On 20 October 1859, after resounding to Sir James Kay Shuttleworth's tirade against the 'lawless rule of trade unions', St George's Hall was cleared and beautified for the evening's Art Conversazione and Promenade Concert. There was room for a small but enlightened crowd to stroll about the Hall, admiring the drawings by Mr Lobley's pupils and giving occasional ear to the music of Mr Jackson and his choir and orchestra. Here was a feast of congratulation for the Bradford elite: for Mr Ruskin had seen nothing in London equal to the work of Mr Lobley's pupils; and Mr Jackson had been personally complimented on his compositions by that other gifted amateur, Prince Albert.[2]

But by 1864 Bradford relations, both internal and external, had changed. Middle-class Bradfordians of old yeoman stock had grown prosperous by making hideous a town which they nonetheless loved. This was beginning to disturb them. Centuries of Puritanism and practical virtue were in their blood. Lord Palmerston was the last surviving specimen of the species 'Regency buck', whose fodder had to be wrung from the land by yeoman managers like their own fathers. They thoroughly agreed with *The Economist* that Palmerston 'was born before earnestness was thought to be a virtue'.

The working classes had experienced five more years of waiting for the vote, and not getting it; five more years of waiting in vain for trade unions to be put on a proper legal footing; five more years of hoping for an Education Act; five more years of foreign war profits, unfairly distributed, and of peace at home unfairly maintained; five more years of gun-boat diplomacy, *laissez-faire* economics and Lord Palmerston.

The debate on 'Modern Manufacture and Design' had been mainly a matter of nervous reassurance in the setting of an Art Conversazione. But in this matter of Ruskin's lecture of 1864, Bradford was presented with questions more obviously public than the founding of a Design School. In the words of Ruskin's preface to *The Stones of*

Venice, 'men may live without buying pictures or statues; but in architecture, all must in some way commit themselves'.[3] The debate on 'The Relation of Public Buildings to Daily Life' was conducted in public; and some Bradfordians were even prepared to commit themselves.

The rough triangular bottom of Bradford's rocky bowl was no more than 600–700 yards across either way. Prosperity crowded this centre with an ever-tightening web of blackening buildings. At the pinched corners of narrow streets, formerly open sites were bought up for shops, or warehouses, or banks. It was into one of these pinched corner sites, recently cleared by the demolition of Bradford's old Market House, that the Exchange company proposed to extrude a bigger new gothic exchange, with Lockwood's saurian tower capturing the corner. An older exchange already occupied the broader end of this wedge-shaped site; and when the ladies of the manor, the Misses Rawson, released the thin end of the wedge, with the old Market House, for new development, the Exchange directors, nominally headed by Alderman Wright, but actually dominated by Ripley and Behrens, arranged the national competition for a new building which the local Lockwood, to nobody's surprise, would win. As Andrew Saint has pointed out, the massive tower proposed in Norman Shaw's scheme for this building, far more impressive and 'advanced' than anything in the gothic line by Lockwood, would have blackened the neighbouring shadows even more emphatically than did Lockwood's winning design.[4] There was sense in rejecting Shaw, in the circumstances.

But the circumstances were dreadful enough for some Bradfordians to want improvements.

The site of the proposed new Exchange was a long narrow triangle. Across the base of this triangle ran Bank Street. The other two sides were formed by Market Street, and on the other side, Hustler Street, which ran into Old Market, which might be described as little more than a long narrow yard. It was the block of buildings between this 'Old Market' and Bradford's main street, Kirkgate, which now suggested possibilities to Bradford's many amateur town planners. This block had been partly occupied by the old Piece Hall, with a gabled frontage to Kirkgate, demolished in 1853; and by a number of 'low' public houses – never popular with Bradford's Puritan elite – of which the most respectable was the Talbot.[5] William Byles, in the *Observer* of 12 May 1864, claimed that 'plans have been made' for urban renewal; 'yet all need more open space than can be had'; and suggested that an 'improvement that commends itself to the eye of almost every person that passes along Market Street' would be to site the new Exchange where the 'Talbot and Hall of Commerce buildings' stood. Properly designed, and with the aid of a little tasteful demolition, the new Exchange would then have sufficient space around it and command, instead of occupying, the Market House triangle, which at all costs should be left open.

There was sense in this, as well as sensibility. The congested traffic of Bradford, which helped to suggest the title of Ruskin's lecture as published, was an increasing problem. 'Between the reception of raw wool in Bradford,' John S. Roberts writes, 'and its final despatch from the town as manufactured goods, it was carted through the Bradford streets up to eight times.'[6]

Byles's *Observer* of 5 May produced a leader article on the town's future. It was the paper's policy to support the new feeling that Bradford needed more open spaces; and that the demolition of the Old Market House provided an opportunity to improve Bradford's tortured street system. 'Not long ago Mr Ruskin reproached us with our slavish worship of the Goddess of Getting-on. His remarks were pointed and barbed by the ugliness which surrounded him. We would have fared indeed badly, if tried by his canon of taste being the measure of man's moral inclinations and habits of mind. As the Vicar aptly expressed it, we might appear to a man of Mr Ruskin's exquisite architectural taste to be "old cankered coins in an earthen pot".' This 'salient and witty corner-stone' to Ruskin's lecture, with its shrewd summary of Bradford's shape and motivation, had 'made the room ring with laughter' on the night. Byles now pleads that surely the 'taste of the Bradford people is not so depraved as to be satisfied with the ugliness of the town, concealed as it is in the kindly skirts of a perennial Shetland blanket of smoke. Improvements which would have been denounced as wild and extravagant not many years back have been sanctioned, amidst some groans from the economists, by the conscript Fathers of the borough.' As Bradford expands, Byles continues, it will become more and more necessary to mingle the *dulce* with the *utile*. 'Fifty years hence, open places and squares adorned with statuary and surrounded by stately buildings will, we trust, be deemed necessary at *any* cost.' But, he adds, 'let us consider the profits to ourselves' which will accrue from a town planned with health, durability and long-term usefulness, in mind. 'What is the repair or rebuilding of mansions, warehouses, or even cathedrals,' asks Byles, 'to the renovation and reformation of a town sustaining 120,000 inhabitants?' The new Exchange, especially if it is to be 'the nucleus of further renovation' should not merely occupy the most obviously available site.

Byles pursued the issue over the following weeks. He supported what James would call 'the strong wish' which 'prevailed in the town' to keep at least the triangular site of the old Market House, and preferably the whole of the site intended for the new Exchange, as open ground. Bradford would then have an accessible and handsomely sited building overlooking the open site which the Exchange directors now proposed to fill with Lockwood's building. Light might even penetrate to the interior. Such an arrangement could be the nucleus of a whole pattern of development, with well-constructed public buildings overlooking pleasant public squares. If 'the Exchange company would have their next meeting' on the old Market House site, Byles promised on 12 May 'and picture the fine Place that might exist there, we almost believe the economists themselves would risk the price'. A public-spirited gentleman has already offered £500 towards the redemption of the land, and there are promises of further subscriptions up to another £4,500, leaving £5,000 to be raised. A major argument against this scheme of improvement in some people's minds, is that it would unfairly raise the value of properties on Market Street! But jealousy should be repressed: 'If improvements are desirable and necessary on public grounds, the community must shut their eyes to the incidental effect respecting individuals'.

By 19 May Byles was fairly confident. 'Fortunately, there appears to be a desire to sacrifice a little to the goddess of beauty and system as well as to her ladyship of Getting-on.' Dwelling-houses and warehouses were being better built. 'The taste which supplies such evidences of creative power must be pretty generally diffused.' Public opinion is overwhelmingly in favour of retaining at least the triangular Market House site as a pleasant open space. 'The convenience of trade, though the chief, should not be the sole end of our street improvement schemes.' The mayor Joseph Farrar has called a public meeting on the matter in 'compliance with a requisition numerously and influentially signed'. Let Bradford men make their descendants 'proud of their fathers', urged Byles.

By 28 May Hanson had joined the campaign to review the future of the whole triangular central area between Darley Street and Tyrrell Street; bounded by Kirkgate, Market Street and Ivegate. The demolition of old buildings gave Bradford a chance to develop on more seemly lines. 'Could the marvellous and rapidly augmenting wealth of Bradford make a more graceful offering than by throwing open forever the space now cleared, which would be speedily surrounded by elegant buildings that would give a new aspect and promise a nobler future for Bradford?' Voluntary public subscription was the only hope of achieving space, for the Council's funds were wholly spoken for by the demands of the new sewerage system.

For the moment the dreams of Bradford's environmentalists were doomed to fail. Bradford conservatism retained the name of 'Piece Hall Yard', but Bradford opportunism pursued the modernisation of that part of Kirkgate with relentless zest. The Talbot Inn, home of the Bradford chess team and a useful hostelry for commercial travellers, not only survived, but achieved a grand rebuilding scheme of its own in 1878. The Old Market House triangle was filled by the new Exchange. No one acted on the compromise suggestion of a *Burgess*, whose letter in the *Observer* of 2 June urged that that part of Market Street opposite the Exchange should at least be widened to permit traffic and light. In Bradford, light, and even traffic, were hard to provide for because of what the *Burgess* called the 'dish-shaped' topography of the town.

Despair enters Byles's rhetoric on 16 June 1864. He is still hoping against hope to see a 'breathing space' in the centre of the town; a 'plaza' where people might meet.

Byles's leader of 16 June can now be seen as joining together Ruskin's two Bradford lectures. For Byles's 'plaza' might have provided opportunity for a little 'figure drawing', instead of drawing up of figures; some 'accumulative observation' and 'experience'; instead of accumulative acquisition: perhaps even a moment's 'peace and pleasurableness'. Such were the criteria for design Ruskin outlined in 1859.[7]

But the exchange shareholders wanted £25,000 for their land, not the £10,000 of Byles's first estimate. Public subscription raised less than half what was required. Cudworth supplies the information that the main subscribers were (as ever) Titus Salt; also M. W. Thompson; the Quaker John Priestman, who helped to run a Ragged School and evening classes; Thomas Firth; A. & S. Henry's via John

Mitchell; J. Wade & Sons and George Hodgson.[8]

'The people,' Byles's leader of 16 June continues, 'take a greater pride in the town than wealthier men who meditate retirement into rural bowers, when the golden fruit of commercial success is housed by them.' His metaphor of 'golden fruit' co-operates, however unconsciously, with Ruskin's disquisition in *Modern Painters* on the industrialised Garden of the Hesperides,[9] its golden accumulations guarded by the evil dragon of cynicism and superstition. Byles's dream-plaza was 'unnecessary luxury', said the Exchange shareholders. No more so, rejoined Byles, than public baths or a free library, neither of which Bradford yet possessed.

Alfred Harris, sufficiently vocal in defence of Burges and Shaw, was notably absent from the debate on Byles's dream-plaza. Till the early seventies, Old Bank and Exchange apart, Market Street remained 'a typical nondescript Bradford Street'; but from that time stringent corporation requirements for building were introduced. Henry Brown's old drapery store, by 1871 known as 'Brown Muff's' departmental store, was in that year handsomely rebuilt to meet these requirements. 'By 1875,' John S. Roberts writes, 'rigorously enforced Bradford bye-laws demanded twenty yard streets for cottage property, fully sewered, flagged and paved before building commenced.'[10] The town would create more open spaces, would build its public baths, its free library, its subsidised housing schemes. By such measures, and not by any brief fashion for Italo-Gothic would Bradford begin to catch up with the Ruskin of the 1851 preface to *The Stones of Venice*:

> In architecture, all must in some way commit themselves: they *must* do mischief and waste their money, if they do not know how to turn it to account. Churches, and shops, and warehouses, and cottages, and small row, and place, and terrace houses, must be built, however joyless or inconvenient. And it is assuredly intended that all of us should have knowledge, and act upon our knowledge, in matters with which we are daily concerned, and not be left to the caprice of architects, or mercy of contractors.

The view up Market Street, by 1873, was closed and crowned by the tower of Lockwood and Mawson's Town Hall. This had been built on land made available by the demolition of the Old Foundry. William Scruton describes the place as it was in 1860. The verbal echoes of Ruskin's lecture of 1859 are perhaps coincidental: 'no pleasanter objects met the eye than the roofless walls of old dismantled dwellings, like ruined cloisters blackened by age, chimney-stalks belching out perpetual clouds of dingy smoke, and blast furnaces with fire leaping from their summit and glowing at their base, keeping up one ceaseless, deafening roar by day and night'.[11] For Ruskin that sight, or something like it, was the necessary centre of the problems of English design. Replacing it with a Gothic Town Hall was not quite what he meant. As he would put it in 1866:

> There is no national virtue, small or great, which is not manifestly expressed in all the art which circumstances enable the people possessing that virtue to produce. Take, for instance, your great English virtue of enduring and patient courage. You have at present in England only one art of any consequence – that is iron-working. You know thoroughly well how to cast and hammer iron. Now, do you think, in those masses of lava which you build volcanic cones to melt, and which you forge at the mouths of the Infernos you have created; do you think, on those iron plates, your courage and endurance are not written for ever, – not merely with an iron pen, but on iron parchment?[12]

The same awareness that had related Turner's 'litter' to that of Covent Garden, and as such necessarily preferred the market to Belgravia, ventures in Bradford to affirm the irreducible factor in the new possibility. For when the time came for the West Riding to give the world a sculptor, it would be the 'slag heaps larger than the Pyramids' and the iron coal-hole covers in the street where he was born which provided the miner's son Henry Moore with his introduction to art.[13]

Ruskin's Yorkshire legacy is to be sought with the liberals who wanted 'knowledge'; with socialists like Jowett and Priestman who wished that 'all of us should have knowledge, and act upon our knowledge'; with that other Bradford Ruskinian William Rothenstein, the influential principal of Henry Moore and Barbara Hepworth at the Royal College of Art. The Gothic millinery of Lockwood and Mawson is not even a distraction.

Already in 1864, Ruskin had helped to awaken in Bradford a new consciousness of what he elsewhere called 'our debt to the future'[14] among middle-class environmentalists. He also helped to inform the rhetoric of working-class campaigners who were angry with Lord Palmerston.

In this matter of providing a space for Bradford, the muddled, idealistic efforts of voluntary subscription were no match for the bold individualism of H. W. Ripley. Ripley invited Palmerston to come and lay the foundation stone of the Exchange in the last week of April 1864. After some hesitation the premier accepted. There would be precious little time for such appointments between the end of the parliamentary session and the ritual ornithological slaughter of the glorious 12 August. 9 August was fixed as the date. The site of the Wool Exchange was connected with, if not determined by, Ripley's determination that Palmerston should lay its foundation stone. Cudworth discloses that the prospect of a Bradford plaza, with the Wool Exchange to one side of it, was 'brought to a final and sudden close by a decison of the Exchange Directors not to give up their site',[15] however much money was offered. Ripley wanted Palmerston; to advertise Bradford, and to promote his own career. There could not be time to 'secure and prepare' a new site. Let the Exchange be, and let Bradford accrete around it.

This high-handed dealing helped to lend respectability to the latent fury against Palmerston shared by many shades of Bradford opinion.

When he published *Traffic*, Ruskin chose to begin his final paragraph with the last words of Hamlet: 'The rest is silence'. For his Bradford readers, and perhaps for the author, there was a very particular significance in that silence.

As the day drew near for Lord Palmerston to lay the foundation stone of Bradford Wool Exchange, George Jacob Holyoake's *English Leader* made every effort to turn the occasion into a 'Reform Demonstration'. It was, however, the local working-class leaders who formed the more tasteful and compelling idea of greeting Palmerston 'not by hisses and groans. . . but by a dignified and significant abstinence from all cheering'. Georg Weerth's old friend John Jackson was still adding his voice of reason to this resolute concert. Genteel cheers there were, within St George's Hall, from the 'distinguished' and 'imposing' assembly therein who were admitted by ticket. But when Palmerston emerged, that 9 August 1864, he was confronted by 30,000 workmen who stood and looked at him in orderly and 'stony silence'. According to Holyoake, Palmerston confided to Forster that he had been '"touched and pained" at standing as it were alone in that vast and voiceless crowd'. Did Ruskin know of this? It was widely reported in the national press;

though not quite in such melodramatic terms as Holyoake uses. Within the hall, W. E. Forster and Francis Crossley, wasting no time in putting words into the mouths of potential constituents, had articulated the silence of the working-class crowds that prevailed throughout Palmerston's visit as a demand for the vote.[16] And so, at the least, it was.

The beginnings of Ruskin's co-operation with the public rhetoric of working-class assemblies can be read in the *Bradford Review*'s report of the Working Men's Meeting of July 1864, in the Temperance Hall, Leeds Road. The meeting had a single item on its agenda: 'to undeceive Lord Palmerston on the supposed apathy of the people on. . . Parliamentary Reform'. The Marxist Georg Weerth's old friend, who was also Titus Salt's old friend, John Jackson, was in the chair. Joseph Wilkinson proposed the only motion of the evening.

Victorian notables, from the Queen downwards, expected cheering from the masses as their due. To abstain from cheering was the only 'constitutional' way of showing working-class disapproval. This was Wilkinson's proposition. Let Bradford men abstain from all expressions of approval, especially cheering, when the premier showed himself. Let them be present in as great numbers as possible; but let them greet him with a resolute and united silence.

Wilkinson's speech showed that the improvement of living standards, the mission of the unions, was for him an aim inseparable from that of parliamentary reform:

> Lord Palmerston's education was received in rather unfavourable times. . . They could not do better than be peaceful, obliging, and keep their hats on when Lord Palmerston came (Laughter). He knew they had lungs, and so had a donkey – (renewed Laughter) – but don't use them so much. If they cheered, it might be fine fun for those his lordship was stroking down, but let them remember he was not stroking them down yet (Laugher).

Ruskin had denounced to their faces the local Liberals' idol of riches, Britannia Agoraia. Her 'ladyship of Getting-on' was a reference Liberal readers of the *Observer* for 5 and 19 May were expected to pick up, with their ears burning. The grandiloquence of *Traffic* would publish the notion more widely:

> The rest is silence. Last words of the chief wisdom of the heathen, spoken of this 'idol of riches', this idol of yours; this golden image, high by measureless cubits, set up where your green fields of England are furnace-burnt into the likeness of the plain of Dura: this idol, forbidden to us, first of all idols, by our own Master and faith, forbidden to us also by every human lip that has ever, in any age or people, been accounted of as able to speak according to the purposes of God. . .

'But the Bradford working men,' Joseph Wilkinson, perhaps consciously, answers, 'could not worship idols': 'It was their blood, their treasure, their groans, that they wasted [in India and China] and wilfully misspent. Let [working men] look to themselves again [a common middle-class message, this one]. When they got the franchise, let them mind how they used it, but let them never rest till they got it (loud applause).'

Wilkinson's motion, to greet Palmerston in silence, was carried, 'almost unanimously'.[17]

'There was no great thinker in the old days,' Holyoake exults, in his autobiography of 1893, 'like Mr Ruskin to teach the world that piety and progress were the same.' That equation requires any amount of refinement, but there is an essential restraint and passion in it which helps to explain how Ruskin could appeal not only to free-will Christians – Keir Hardie among them – but also to secularists such as Holyoake who had a natural penchant for philosophic realism. All were capable of the intention to 'make something of this world'. The phrase comes from a speech of Holyoake's made in August 1858 at Shipley, hard by Saltaire.[18] But its spirit is as eternally British as the free-will heresy of 'Pelagius'. The name is a translation of the heretic's British name, 'Morgan'. It means 'man of the open sea'.

The Pelagian heresy proclaims, Ruskin was glad to note, that for all practical purposes 'men can save themselves by the exertion of their own will'. It is 'like the staunchness of masts and trim of sail in a good ship', he added.[19] Thanks to their MP's Education Act, the Bradford people were soon in a position to choose their own charts to steer by. 'So that nearly every house had its little library now,' Margaret McMillan remembers, 'a library that was common to all, for the choice of books was often the same in most cases. More than a few began to read good poetry and the older classics; Ruskin and Whitman and Carlyle silently appeared on many, new-made shelves.' With 'seeing eyes and conscious choice', they were generating 'a new religion – a heresy'. Soon Bradford was flooded with it. 'The whole community,' she writes, 'had become to me like a sunny sea.'[20]

CHAPTER TEN

SEVEN LAMPS

> If the Seven Lamps of Architecture resemble their predecessor, *Modern Painters*, they will be no lamps at all, but a new constellation.
> —Charlotte Brontë
> to W S Williams, 16 April 1849

> Now I have always a great suspicion of the number seven; because when I wrote the *Seven Lamps of Architecture*, it required all the ingenuity I was master of to prevent them from becoming Eight, or even Nine, on my hands. —*Fors Clavigera* Letter 5, 1 May 1871[1]

A satiric memento of Ruskin's overnight stay with Mr Mitchell at classic Parkfield House in 1859 remains today in the villas that sprang up nearby, their fronts adorned with windows in the Italo-Gothic manner. His railway journeys of 1864 between Leeds and Bradford were contemporary with the construction, close to the line, of the Veronese chimney-campanile of Tower Works. This was joined in 1899 by a yet larger chimney, with dust-extraction plant, that remains today to parody the campanile of Giotto. It has recently been cleaned, and is an admired example of Victorian art, particularly the gilded panels of tiling behind the tracery of its fake 'bell-louvres'.[2]

A more sympathetic student of Victorian gothic might prefer to dwell on Ruskin's disciple G. E. Street. It was Francis Sharp Powell of Horton Hall who persuaded Street to lecture at Cambridge on 'The Fitness of Medieval Art for Us in Our Civic and Domestic Buildings'. That was in April 1865. The lecture was repeated, more or less, at Bradford a year later. Jacob Behrens was in the chair for this meeting of the Philosophical Society, which had recently been revived with the help of the ubiquitous H. W. Ripley. They met in the Mechanics' Institute. Mr Street disdained 'electicism', urging the use of twelth- or thirteenth-century models, with just a little introduction here and there of effective decorative elements from the fourteenth or fifteenth centuries. This would 'do great good in the community'. But, in his own words, Street 'spoke without any feeling, for he knew nothing of the architecture of Bradford'.[3]

It is in all these ways that Ruskin the amateur differs from Street. 'Feeling' was his forte and nemesis. Doubt about the viability of reviving Gothic was by 1859 one of those feelings. Examples of the style were part of the nemesis. He was conversant with something more fundamental than the architecture of Bradford: its geology. And it was the reconstuction of this exemplary mid-Victorian community that occupied his thoughts more than any 'truth of construction' in the vaulting of its neo- gothic buildings.

The Seven Lamps of Architecture had its ambiguous influence on many other Victorian Gothicists besides Street. But, as Ruskin's editors point out, and as Dr Burnet's curate's daughter Charlotte Brontë had anticipated, the book was also, like its predecessor *Modern Painters*, 'a new constellation' in the world of feeling and morals: a portent of things more fundamental than Ruskinian Gothic.

Tired, old and not a little disillusioned, Richard Norman Shaw looked back at his own career in 1910. His own favourite early design had been made for Bradford Wool Exchange. Its rejection helped him to learn the bitter truth that success would depend on pleasing rich clients, not all of them of the highest cultivation, with a suitably elastic repertoire of styles. 'It was always supposed that "Gothic" was to develop', he wrote, '. . . but it didn't do anything. It was like a cut flower – pretty enough to look at – but fading away before your eyes – and if we don't take care, the English Renaissance that we now have will do the same – so unlike the French – they went on all the last century doing work that was founded on their old work, and magnificent work it was – and this was the result of gentle development, new features and arrangements growing from the old stock. In fact their architecture was alive – ours dead – a mighty difference – and arising of course from their having a School – and we have none'.[4]

Shaw's retrospect of 1910 shares something with Ruskin's prospect of 1849: 'If there be any one condition which, in watching the progress of architecture, we see distinct and general. . . it is this; that the architecture of a nation is great only when it is as universal and established as its language; and when provincial differences of style are nothing more than so many dialects. Other necessities are matters of doubt. . . , but this one condition has been constant, this one requirement clear in all places and at all times, that the work shall be that of a *School*'.[5]

But Ruskin the amateur digs deeper. 'The art of a nation,' he wrote in 1867, 'much resembles the corolla of a flower; . . . and you can only command the hue, or modify the form of the blossom by medicine or nourishment applied patiently to the root, not by manipulation of the petals'. By 1884 Ruskin was even more pugnacious: 'I have especially to signalise the French contempt for the 'Art de Province'. . . All great art, in the great times of art, is *provincial*, showing its energy in the capital, but educated . . . in its own county town. . . Further, – the tendency to centralisation, which has been fatal to art in all times, is at *this* time, pernicious in totally unprecedented degree, because the capitals of Europe are full of monstrous and degraded architecture. . .'[6]

It is now possible to see, not only why Ruskin lamented the passing of the Pennine vernacular at Bradford, but why he went to Bradford at all. He saw art as a social, political and ultimately geological, organism. In his own view that organism had become diseased. *The Seven Lamps* of 1849 was mainly an optimistic challenge to his age. *The Cestus of Aglaia*, of 1865–6, has the marks of bitter experience upon it. What he openly called the 'Essay' of the *Seven Lamps* and what, by dark allusion, he defined as the ambiguously 'kind conference'[7] of *Cestus*, form a dialogue as though between a slightly nervous Hope and an unflinchingly ironic and convulted Despair. The writing and reception of *Unto This Last*, and the apparent failure of Ruskin's Bradford forays, are important contributions to the distinction between these two tones. For Ruskin the aloof theorist there could be no hope for the social organism until 'this last' person – what his socialist readers would call 'the bottom dog'[8] – had begun to be capable of hope and life. And there could be no hope for British art till Bradford – the physical centre of the chief British island and the abysmal boom-town of Britain's most 'prosperous' age – had begun to understand this truth. Ruskin the 'child of genius', on the other hand, was confronted by the absurd and hurtful discoveries that the 'bottom dog' might not want to be elevated,[9] and that Bradford's Puritan virtues and obdurate geology were at the root of the horror which it represented.

Thus, the 'Lamp of Memory' had offered this glowing insight: 'Every human action gains in honour, in grace, in all true magnificence, by its regard to things that are to come. It is the far sight, the quiet and confident patience, that. . . separate man from man, and near him to his Maker. . . Therefore, when we build, let us think that we build for ever.' *Cestus* answers from experience that '"getting on"' is what the age really wants. 'Most men's eyes are. . . fixed on the mere swirl of the wheel of their own fortunes. . . friends, if you would make a little less dust, perhaps we should all see our way better.' The 'Lamp of Obedience' had warned, in a slightly priggish and immature tone: 'It is not enough to find men absolute subsistence; we should think of the manner of life which demands necessitate; and endeavour. . . to. . . raise, as well as feed, the poor'. *Cestus* counters with a slightly weary mockery: 'I am about to ask. . . how far, among the lower classes, exercise in certain mechanical arts might become a part of their school life? – how far, in the adult life of this nation, the Fine Arts may advisably supersede or regulate the mechanical Arts? Plain questions. . . and, as clearly, boundless ones. . . – only to be mined into in a scrambling way by poor inquirers. . .'

The Seven Lamps was sure that 'beyond a certain point, and that a very low one, man cannot advance in the invention of beauty, without directly imitating natural form'. *Cestus* warns any suitor of beauty that 'ravelled briars of thought entangle our feet, even at our first step. We would teach a boy to draw. Well, what shall he draw? – Gods, or men, or beasts, or clouds, or leaves, or iron cylinders? Are there any gods to be drawn? any men or women worth drawing, or only worth caricaturing? What are the aesthetic laws respecting iron cylinders. . . ?'

'You cannot get the feeling back into art,' proclaimed the Ruskin of 1849, 'by paying for it – money will not buy life.' By 1865, a wiser, more bewildered Ruskin knows '*no* captivity so sorrowful as that of an artist doing, consciously, bad work for pay. It is the serfdom of the finest gifts. . . There is much serfdom, in Europe'. 'For there is a crust,' Ruskin answers himself from the fifth paragraph of 'The Lamp of Power', 'about the impressible part of men's minds, which must be pierced through before they can be touched to the quick; and though we may prick at it and scratch it in a thousand separate places, we might as well have left it alone if we do not come through somewhere with a deep thrust. . .' He himself would try some thrusts at the bowels of political economy. Carlyle hailed the *Unto This Last* essays as 'red-hot pincers' applied to 'bloated bellies', and exulted over *Munera Pulveris* as 'a dividing of joint and marrow'. But most of the world remained apparently untouched. In *Cestus* Ruskin, transposing the Carlylean tone, sees all the higher powers of Victorian man, including his own, as 'chained down to a rock. . . by the merciless Necessities or Fates, of present time; and so having his very heart torn piece by piece out of him by a vulturous hunger and sorrow, respecting things he cannot reach, nor prevent, nor achieve'.

That image of 1865 is a transposition of the myth of Prometheus, the light-bringer, who was punished for his illumination of the mortal clay by an angry Zeus. The Ruskin of 1849, on the other hand, had yet to experience the 'ghastly ludicrousness' of a life of sacrifice: 'Your gift may be given in an unpresuming way,' he assured his readers, '. . . but do not think the feeling itself a folly, or the act itself useless.' The very imperfections of man and of his work, added the 'Lamp of Truth', are a part of their 'admirableness'. The 'true delightfulness' of Gothic sculpture particularly, 'depends on our discovering in it the record of thoughts, and intents, and trials, and heartbreakings – of recoveries and joyfulnesses of success; . . . and in that is the worth of the thing, just as much as the worth of any thing we call precious'.

The Ruskin of *Cestus* had hardened. The work of the lives of innumerable gifted men is nowadays sacrificed to 'nothing but promotion of costly commerce'. And his own answer to this disgusting state of affairs is to revoke for the time the tender humanisation and complexity of 'The Lamp of Truth' in favour of an academic new beginning: 'May we. . . begin with the hard line?', he asks. 'It may be convicted at our leisure.'[10]

The most memorable, certainly the most frequently quoted, passage of *Cestus*, is that which presents us with Ruskin as an absurd Prometheus, a dabbler in light and colour, brought before the judgement seat of the age of steam and iron. Such must have been Ruskin's feeling on the morning of 21 April 1864. He had been looking out a photograph of his recently dead father to send to his cousin William at Croydon. 'Few people,' Ruskin tells William in his hasty covering note, 'are more misrepresented by it, than your old uncle but it is always nice to have it.'[11] By 10 am Ruskin was in the train at King's Cross on his way to Bradford, the great foundry town and centre of educational reform currently in the grip of an ironworks strike:

I cannot express the amazed awe, the crushed humility, with which I sometimes watch a locomotive take its breath at a railway station, and think what work there is in its bars and wheels, and what manner of men they must be who dig brown iron-stone out of the ground, and forge it into THAT! What assemblage of accurate and mighty faculties in them; more than fleshly power over melting crag and coiling fire, fettered, and finessed at last into the precision of watchmaking; Titanian hammer-strokes beating, out of lava, these glittering cylinders and timely-respondent valves, and fine ribbed rods, which touch each other as a serpent writhes, in noiseless gliding, and omnipotence of grasp; infinitely complex anatomy of active steel, compared with which the skeleton of a living creature would seem, to a careless observer, clumsy and vile – a mere morbid secretion and phosphatous prop of flesh! What would the men who thought out this – who beat it out, who touched it into its polished calm of power, who set it to its appointed task, and triumphantly saw it fulfil this task to the utmost of their will – feel or think about this weak hand of mine, timidly leading a little stain of water-colour, which I cannot manage, into an imperfect shadow of something else – mere failure in every motion, and endless disappointment; what, I repeat, would these Iron-dominant Genii think of me? and what ought I to think of them?

But, as I reach this point of reverence, the unreasonable thing is sure to give a shriek as of a thousand unanimous vultures, which leaves me shuddering in real physical pain for some half minute following; and assures me, during slow recovery, that a people which can endure such fluting and piping among them is not likely soon to have its modest ear pleased by aught of oaten stop, or pastoral song. Perhaps I am then led on into mediation respecting the spiritual nature of the Tenth Muse, who invented this gracious instrument, and guides its modulation by stokers' fingers; meditation, also, as to the influence of her invention amidst the other parts of the Parnassian melody of English education.[12]

Ruskin would spend 23 April 1864 in the arms of this 'Tenth Muse'. He had promised Miss Bell he would not be late; and the fast morning train would take him from Leeds to Manchester in two hours. The easiest way to catch it – if he could excuse himself from the Harrises at Ashfield – would be to take the 8.08 from Shipley Station. Half an hour to wait in Leeds. It was there, while waiting for another train long ago, he had received a letter from Miss Gray, signing herself for the first time 'Effie', and giving him the opportunity – even obligation – to propose. Over the Pennines now to Manchester, then on to Warrington; and by a quarter to three he would be at Hartford, ready to be whisked by carriage to Winnington and Miss Bell. Behind the shrubbery at Acacia, Rawdon, it was Mr Ripley's fifty-first birthday. But in England it was St George's day when by a quirk of the calendar Shakespeare's birth and death are commemorated. Wordsworth's death, too, and Turner's birth. And at Bradford on the 21st Ruskin had celebrated that wise economy of finite life close to common sense and genius. He had spoken modest, deadly truths, like Cordelia, and defended his father's honour against usurpers, like Hamlet. He had challenged the 'wise passiveness' of Wordsworthian nature lovers to be a little more alert,[13] he had hailed the Sun of Righteousness; and had invited his audience to promote themselves from cannibalistic brigands to a salaried chivalry of commerce.

'The book I called *The Seven Lamps*', runs this Bradford lecture, 'was to show that certain right states of temper and moral feeling were the magic powers by which all good architecture, without exception, had been produced'.

Taking Ruskin's own terms as guides, it may be worth identifying seven members of his public in order to enquire what imprint, if any, this Victorian Prometheus might have had on 'this clay that burns. . . this colour that changes'.[14]
When the lamps were burnished in the industrial cave, and their magic powers evoked, did the widow's son provoke anything more agreeable than Iron-Dominant Genii?

John Holmes, the Co-operator, whose memoir of Ruskin appeared in 1886 in *The Sheffield and Rotherham Gazette* may serve to represent Memory. Ellen Heaton, on whom Ruskin urged those rising artists Rossetti and Hughes, was more often than not 'ready to comply with his wishes'.[15] She may supply Obedience. Her brother-in-law John Aldam Heaton, multi-talented designer,Norman Shaw's lieutenant, and author of *Beauty and Art*, may kindle an ambiguous Lamp of Beauty. Alfred Harris, the great Bradford banker, with his two wives and family of fourteen, king of an eager community of amateur craftworkers at Kirkby Lonsdale, may stand for Life. For Power, there is John Mitchell, rising to the executive headship of the international business empire of A. & S. Henry's. He commissioned, under pressure from the painter, what Ruskin called Rossetti's 'wonderful...awful' *Venus Verticordia*, with its 'enormous power' and 'coarseness'. For Sacrifice there is poor James Lobley, Harris's protégé whose career as a genre painter, along with that of many others, received a disabling setback from the new policy of Leighton as President of the Royal Academy from 1878. For Truth there is the geologist Alfred Tylor, whose sister was Harris's first wife and whose brother was the Bradford businessman, Louis Tylor. Alfred Tylor was personally the closest of all to Ruskin; and he and his daughter Juliet were the recipients of some of Ruskin's most outspoken confidences.

Memory: John Holmes

John Holmes, the West Riding businessman and Co-operator, contributed two articles on Ruskin to the *Sheffield and Rotherham Independent* of 17 and 24 April 1886. He begins his memoir by describing Ruskin as the 'effectual awakener of the intellect' in the realm of 'relations and realities', and he ends by hailing him as 'MASTER'. But the discipleship was by no means lightly given.

Holmes's interest in art operated to begin with at a rather primitive level. Like the Brontë sisters, he was a painstaking amateur; and like them, he acknowledged no greater 'Masterpiece' in his early days than John Martin's *Belshazzar's Feast*. A more educated interest was awakened by the 'room full of Turners' loaned to Leeds in 1836 by 'Old Squire Fawkes', the artist's friend and patron. The curator of the exhibition, Mr Burrass, pointed out to Holmes a Turner drawing of sheep coming out of the Colosseum. 'Gods,' said Burrass, 'Turner must have *been* a sheep when he painted that lot.' Holmes was convinced, and began to 'collect pictures in a small way'.

Holmes's income was mainly derived from a business started 'in a very humble way' in Leeds in 1840. The business expanded greatly with the coming of railways, 'and would have been profitable by merely small gains and savings; if the body could have borne the strain of 16 hours work, for 7 days a week, in premises most wretchedly unhealthy, in a situation near to a filthy river, surrounded by an atmosphere clouded thick by smoke, and heavy with soot and stenches of works, chemicals, dyeing, etc. etc.' There was much speculation at the time in land, engines and iron: and Holmes seems to have taken a share in this. But his health broke down, and in order to 'live' he had to give up business altogether. From the vantage point of 1886 he comments: 'Manufacturers' fortunes were made as by magic, which was followed, *as inevitable*, by gluts, by trade-depression, surplus of "hands", reduction of wages, poverty, and discontent'.

On retiring from business, Holmes flung himself into the Co-operative movements of the time. The Co-operative Stores movement, begun by the Rochdale pioneers of 1843, became more than a great club for the sale of goods to their members, who divided the profits. Sick and burial insurance and land and building societies grew from the small beginnings at Rochdale: and from the beginning 'the social and intellectual advancement of its members' was the aim of the movement. Night classes, drama and discussion groups and dozens of similar activities, generated a broad front of respectable working-class power and awareness. The movement was non-sectarian and in a conservative but invincible fashion transformed the lives and status of its one million members (by 1891) and their families. Co-operation in productive industry was less successful. It was not till 1865 that Act of Parliament made it legally possible for employers of labour to form partnerships with their workers. Briggs's colliery at Wakefield was one of the first, and few successful, examples of this method of resolving some of the chronic labour-relations problems of Britain's divided society and divisive educational system.[16] Henry Mitchell (motto: *Dante Deo Reddam*), when he succeeded John Mitchell as head of the Yorkshire branch of A. & S. Henry's, would opt for the compromise of giving his workers first refusal on the purchase of share stock. Even this was regarded as eccentric and philanthropic, and only warranted by the firm's huge efficiency and profitability.

It was while propagandising and working for Co-operation in both these areas that Holmes became a friend of F. J. Furnivall, who stayed with him in Leeds, and went with him to Farnley to see the paintings 'arranged by Ruskin'. 'Betwixt Co-operation and art we had a "good time"', Holmes remembered.

In 1854 Furnivall introduced Holmes to Ruskin at the London Working Men's College. Holmes had brought the art critic two of his prized possessions to see: a Hogarth engraving of prostitutes and prisoners, and a water colour of the Roman Forum Holmes claimed was a Turner. Ruskin made a forceful extempore critique of the Hogarth that Holmes delighted in and remembered in detail thirty years later.[17] The watercolour showed ignorances that revealed it to Ruskin as merely 'Turneresque'. Holmes begged to differ, and remained unshaken. Ruskin's views on employment probably made more sense to him. Holmes was one of those who advocated them at the Bradford Social Science Congress of 1859. Holmes also thought long and hard about *The Political Economy of Art*. An enthusiast of *Unto This Last*, Holmes forwarded to the author a pastiche of *The House that Jack Built* on themes borrowed from it, with particular reference to public ownership of land. The reply delighted him: no platitudes but a sharp question: What mode of letting did Holmes envisage? In these and other ways, Holmes was indebted to Ruskin for suggestions that 'converted' him from a mere follower of contemporary 'movements' to a man thinking for himself.

To hear Ruskin speak in Bradford Mechanics' Institute in 1864 was for Holmes 'elysium'; and he forwarded to Ruskin some facts and publications, doubtless of use to *Traffic*, which demonstrated how well Ruskin 'had hit the nail (on their heads)'. He received a note of thanks from Ruskin, which included, to Holmes's delight, a side-swipe at the 'snobs' of Leeds who had insisted on Brodrick's crushing his 'fine Roman composite' Town Hall under a grandiose tower and cupola. But Ruskin had a more radical message, which Holmes also remembered:

> At Bradford they wished to get on; well, that was his motto too; but what sort of getting on did they want? . . . if they thought that the "hands" – who happened to have both bodies brains and hearts – should get on too, he was with them. . . In that way, he could tell them how factories, works and warehouses might be constructed with strength, utility, and even beauty in both outline and detail, and so on from college to mansion, from farm and forge to chapel and from factory to church. . . Some people confounded style with principles. . . the lecturer did not exactly accord with that idea – there might be Greek wise men. . . and Gothic fools. . . Proper style was, in a great measure, a question of fitness; and with a given material and means, how to evolve the greatest convenience and comfort along with the best ideas of the conscientious in life work, and the highest sense of beauty in life enjoyments. . .

Holmes was an eager reader of *Time and Tide* as it appeared in *The Leeds Mercury* during 1867.

In 1870 Holmes was on holiday at Lugano. He spotted Ruskin in the company of three ladies looking at the Luini frescoes in the chapel there. Rushing back to his hotel, Holmes brought the tidings to a pair of American Ruskinians – an 'exceptional' brother and sister – who scurried back with him to the Chapel and Ruskin. 'Mr Ruskin preferred to bring us out than to be evolved himself,' Holmes recalled. The Americans could 'see nothing' in Luini, but Holmes saw a discrepancy, and pointed it out to Ruskin. 'At times I thought that his eye lit up his smile, as I gave my [enthusiastic] impressions of the background; but he looked grave as I pointed out what appeared to me unequal or defective [in the figures]'. Was it *all* by Luini? Hadn't it been 'restored'? 'Sir,' Ruskin eventually said, 'Luini is an artist of such surpassing excellence that I have never yet ventured to criticise him in detail.' The Americans were amused, but Ruskin showed his own kindliness and good sense in assenting respectfully to the Yorkshireman's practical solution to the problem of the chapel's peculiar plan. The contact was vitalising: Holmes by no means sank into veneration. He had felt, throughout the discussion, that Ruskin was actually interested to find out what he thought.

Then, in 1873, the Turner engraving of the windmill and lock from the *Liber Studiorum* was exhibited in the new Bradford Mechanics' Institute. Holmes, after examining it with his practical intelligence, wrote to Ruskin asking how it was 'the lock was made to open the wrong way – that is *with* instead of *against* the course of the stream?' In *Modern Painters*, Volume 4,[18] Ruskin's interest had been in the stark grandeur of the windmill, not the lock, but he found time to reply to Holmes's workaday query in a whimsical and sympathetic note that ensured Holmes's respect:

> 13th December 1873
>
> My dear Sir –
> I have been long in reply to your letter, not having access to the Liber Studiorum, as being at Brantwood; and then I forgot the matter for some time.
>
> Turner is assuredly wrong, unless we can imagine the stream to run the other way (up the hill), and that would imply other wrongnesses. He simply has not been minding what he was about.
>
> Ever very truly yours,
> John Ruskin.

The note is one of innumerable examples of Ruskin's personal contact with his public. Such contact would become rarer under the twin pressures of illness and the increasing surveillance of Ruskin's cousin Joan, one of the 'three ladies' Holmes had seen hovering behind the MASTER at Lugano.[19] The contact kept alive a source of inspiration that only Ruskin in his own person was qualified to give. For Holmes, this inspiration was naturally marked by the quality he himself most admired. It was the quality Ruskin had attributed to his Yorkshire audience in *Traffic*. Holmes felt he recognised it as Ruskin's own distinguishing feature: COURAGE – thus he puts it in capitals. Mr Ruskin's courage had compelled him to venture from art into political economy. 'Lord bless us all – 'twas quite another thing,' Holmes recalls, to most Yorkshire businessmen, when the respected art critic assailed their 'one-sided economy. . . in expression as once forcible as it was true and telling. Ruskin became feared, if not hated by some – while he was loved, admired and almost adored by others.'

Obedience: Ellen Heaton

Ruskin was certainly 'almost adored' by Ellen Heaton. She absolutely adored Elizabeth Barrett, sending her long confidential letters and finally invading the invalid chamber in Wimpole Street on 6 May 1846. Miss Barrett found her 'an intelligent woman with large black eyes and a pleasant voice'; but the accent was provincial, and the voice went on endlessly about the petty social details of Leeds – probably a sign of Ellen's near hysteria at meeting her idol in the flesh. Robert Browning, who eloped with Elizabeth later that year, was at first angry with Miss Heaton, but later grew fond of her, despite what his wife called Ellen's 'ill-breeding and want of delicacy'. Miss Barrett had been delicately reared on her father's estate in Herefordshire on the profits of the West Indies. Robert, whose father had been a superior clerk to the Rothschilds, was perhaps more tolerant of Ellen's lack of breeding. She was certainly better behaved in his presence, even to the point of being 'extremely quiet', and they remained, in Browning's words, 'old friends' till the year of his death, 1889.[20]

Ellen Heaton's is partly the sad story of a frustrated provincial spinster of independent but limited income, gatecrashing into the Brownings' circle, at Rome and elsewhere. The frustration was intellectual and cultural. There is an odd irony in the image of Ellen, the Leeds bookseller's daughter, pursuing Miss Barrett to Wimpole Street. For Ellen was an exact contemporary of Charlotte Brontë; and her schooldays were spent at Mirfield, only a couple of miles from Roe Head, Heckmondwike, where Charlotte lived as pupil from 1831–2, and as governess from 1835–7. Emily Bronte endured Roe Head for three months from July 1835: sufficient to make it holy ground, nowadays, for literary pilgrims.[21] A couple of miles north-west of Mirfield, and about three miles south-east of Heckmondwike, is Kirklees Priory, the home, in his day, of H. W. Wickham, Bradford's MP. Robin Hood's Grave, as it is known, still brings the tourists to Kirklees.

Ellen had what polite Victorians would call a 'sentimental friendship', and what Mrs Browning called a 'matrimonial alliance', with Miss Fanny Haworth, a woman of slightly higher social standing, but poorer. Its terminal dates were 1853–62. The relationship was almost certainly without sexual expression; but to the gossips of the Roman Bohemia, it had sexual overtones. Ellen, in Mrs Browning's phrase, was 'monsieur le Mari'.

Contact with the Brownings helped to ease Ellen's relations with Ruskin. She would tell him when Elizabeth had a bad cough; or when, in Ellen's judgment, her poetess required a little public encouragement from his pen. But it seems to have been the portrait painter Thomas Richmond who introduced his patron to the author of *Modern Painters*. Ellen was godmother to Richmond's second daughter; Ruskin would be godfather to Richmond's second son. In 1853 Ruskin refused the joint invitation from Ellen and her brother to give a lecture at Leeds.[22] But from 1855–64 he was in regular correspondence with Ellen, advising her with great tact and patience, to which she did not always succumb, about artistic investments. Ruskin introduced Ellen to Rossetti by correspondence in February 1855, and continued to recommend these not always compatible people to each other. In praising her again by letter to Rossetti in April 1856 Ruskin said all that was necessary to keep Ellen's path smooth; while warning the artist to show forbearance of her social manner and status. He described her as 'truly a good and kind person'. Sir Robert Peel, second baronet, had done the same for John James Ruskin eleven years before, commending the wine merchant to Arbuthnot as 'a person of the highest character and respectability'.[23] Ruskin's manner with Ellen is half that of a superior art dealer (amateur in his case) treating a new type of client as though she were a lady, though he knows her to be no such thing, and half that of a member of a higher world negotiating decent treatment for a worthy 'person' from the ranks of trade. Beyond these polarised aspects of their relationship, however, is an unspoken dialogue between the sage of genius and the provincial admirer who are both shrewd enough to know that they need each other.

Ruskin's letters to Ellen have been published with ample commentary by Virginia Surtees in *Sublime and Instructive.* They begin with Ruskin's very properly worded, but enthusiastic and engaging, letter of 3 February 1855 (addressed 'My dear Madam'), meeting her request for advice about Turner vignettes. By the middle of the month he is calling her 'Dear Miss Heaton', by April 1856 he feels free to be 'entirely frank' with her, and by the end of January 1857 he is addressing her as 'My dear Ellen'. But there are no more 'dear Ellen' letters after May that year; and Ellen subsides into 'Dear Miss Heaton' for the remainder of the correspondence, which was reduced to a minimum by May 1864.

There may have been a certain lumbering provincial coyness – or crass opportunism – in her response to being called 'dear Ellen' which led to Ruskin's withdrawal. Her letters do not survive. There is certainly an amount of arch trepidation in the air whenever Ruskin approaches the 'dreadful' subject matter of Rossetti's *Paolo and Francesca*, which on advice from the benighted Thomas Richmond Ellen persisted in refusing to buy. She perhaps shared Ruskin's dislike of Ford Madox Brown. Despite Rossetti's counter-pleadings Ruskin had no difficulty in deflecting her from Brown; but despite all his own eloquence Ruskin failed to overcome Ellen's disgusted rejection of Burne-Jones's fancy portrait of the sorceress *Sidonia von Bork*. More robustly, Ellen was disappointed over the lack of fire and passion in Arthur Hughes's picture from *Aurora Leigh* which she commissioned, and she had Ruskin's support in her campaign to repress Rossetti's indulgence in 'melancholy'.

Ruskin helped her to get Turners and Rossettis at reasonable prices. He gave her valuable hints in art appreciation; and provided (under duress) kindly but pertinent criticism of her nature fables. In return, Ellen obeyed Ruskin's precise instructions for the treatment of Turner's fragile drawings. As Octavia Hill's housing schemes were to be a model for State action, so Ellen Heaton, curator in miniature, was to be a model for a properly conducted National Turner Gallery, whenever that might be achieved. She gave money for windows in the Oxford Museum; and in return was able to storm Ruskin's stronghold at Winnington; and to enlarge her pride of literary lions by playing hostess to Christina Rossetti in 1868. To her brother's disgust, Ruskin even prevailed on Ellen to patronise the work of her fellow-townsman, the landscapist J. W. Inchbold.

A pair of incidents shows how evenly matched were the author of *Modern Painters* and the shrewd provincial he called 'the most tolerant person. . . I know or ever hope to know'.[24] Ellen was determined to have Ruskin's drawing of Alpine roses, which was in his own eyes too precious to give away – for it had connotations of Rose La Touche – and too amateur to be worth selling. Ellen got her drawing, but Ruskin made her give forty guineas for it to the Cotton Districts Relief fund. Ellen thus became the first person to invest in a Ruskin drawing, and she did so despite the disapproval of her rival mentor, Thomas Richmond.

An equally sporting encounter ended with the honours going to Ruskin. Ellen fished for a presentation copy of *Modern Painters*, volume three. Ruskin countered with a plea for a subscription to help a struggling pupil of his at the Working Men's College, an artistic haberdasher's clerk. In the end Ellen bought her own copy of *Modern Painters*, volume three, but Ruskin graciously signed it, and gave the price to his haberdasher's clerk as a gift from Miss Heaton. It is not known whether Ellen had the grace to refrain from exhibiting her 'presentation copy' in Leeds society.

There are two incidents in Ruskin's relations with Ellen Heaton which call for more specific attention. They provide clues to the significance of Ruskin's general relations with the industrial West Riding.

Ruskin wrote his first Bradford lecture at Bolton Abbey; and came down into the grimy town from those shores of Wharfe Turner had so much loved and so often interpreted. Ruskin's second Bradford lecture has Jacob's Ladder for its central image. The theoretic connections between these things are spelled out in Ruskin's letters to Ellen Heaton of 1855–6.

Ruskin was writing the chapter 'Of Mediaeval Landscape' for *Modern Painters*, volume three, during November 1855. The chapter includes a commentary on Dante's vision of Jacob's two wives, from the garden of the Earthly Paradise in *Purgatorio*. For Ruskin, Leah and Rachel signify the selfish pre-Christian forms of the active, and contemplative, life. The higher forms of action, and of contemplation, are supplied by Dante's Matilda, and Beatrice. Their role is unselfish and divine. Of the four types, selfishly active Leah is the lowest, divinely contemplative Beatrice the highest. None appears less than fair.[25]

Ruskin's series of letters to Ellen Heaton during November–December 1855 performs two functions simultaneously. On the one hand, he offers educational commentary on Dante's four ladies, designed to elicit Ellen's intelligent appreciation and criticism of her new purchase, Rossetti's *Dante's Vision of Rachel and Leah*. On the other hand, Ruskin is organising a little practical work for Ellen. In order to obtain information for the forthcoming 'Precipices' chapter of *Modern Painters* volume four, he insists that she commission a Leeds photographer to take views of the woods and rocks near Bolton Abbey. It was Ellen herself whose 'note about Bolton woods' inspired this activity. In due course she was herself inspired to go to Bolton and hack off pieces of the Wharfedale rocks to send to Ruskin for his better information.[26]

The ironic complexities of Ruskin's critique of the West Riding now become visible. It might appear that the beautiful northern part of the West Riding – containing Bolton Abbey and Turner views – is the realm of contemplation; while the southern industrial part – containing Ellen Heaton and Bradford Mechanics' Institute – is the scene of activity. Ruskin's symbolic journey from Bolton Abbey to Bradford in March 1859 appears, on the surface, a journey from contemplation into action. But such a view would be too naive. It was partly because contemplation of Bradford was unbearable that Ruskin busied himself, after his first Bradford lecture, in rushing round the northern part of the West Riding in pursuit of river scenery for the proposed Part of *Modern Painters*, 'Of Water Beauty'. That Part was never written. *The Two Paths*, and *The Crown of Wild Olive*, whose centres are the tender, savage contemplation of Bradfordian possibilities, are what was written. To sketch at Bolton Abbey might be the selfish activity of an earthly Paradise: to enter Bradford might be to contemplate the heart of a divine mystery.

In all his making, Ruskin writes of Turner, it was to the memory of Yorkshire scenery that the great painter returned.[27] Turner's was a life of poetry – of 'making' – whose final poem was 'The Sun is God'. But for Ruskin 'Man is the sun of the world; more than the real sun. . . where he is are the tropics'. A continual concern of Turner, as it was an occasional terror for Scott, was the image of Jacob's Ladder. The latter associated it with the grisly accounts of the hangings at Carlisle which were read to him as a child. But Turner's *Vision of Jacob's Ladder* was a canvas worked on almost for the whole of his career: it embodies the full range of his technique, and before his death had become so much a part of him as to be used as an impromptu palette. Such persistency included qualities even Samuel Smiles could admire.[28] If Scott's memories of Jacob's Ladder provide a psychological 'explanation' of Ruskin's Bradford performances, Turner's *Vision of Jacob's Ladder* provides their theolo gical justification. On the one hand are the melodramatic annihilations of momentary intervention; but on the other hand is the absurd sublimity of the everlasting attempt to reconcile and redeem.

Ruskin's acuity permits no cheap contrast between divine contemplation in Wharfedale and selfish activity in Bradford. In *Traffic* all four of Dante's ladies have their place. Leah – the selfishly active – is sufficiently disposed of in the image of the Goddess of worldly Getting on. Rachel, the selfishly contemplative – whom Jacob first saw and loved by the well – is parodied in the Bradfordian 'ideal of human life', with its mansion above and its mill below. But Matilda's divine activity is a more hopeful inspiration, provided it is applied in contemporary terms. Bradford's angels, like Milton's angels of the Nativity, had best be 'serviceable'. Let them give up the neo-medievalism of 'crusades, to recover the tomb of a buried God' in favour of 'travels to fulfil the orders of a living God'. It is only then that Bradford, like Beatrice, will be able to contemplate the divine presence in a lively sacrament perfected in Bradford's own 'temples not made with hands, but riveted of hearts; and that kind of marble, crimson-veined, is indeed eternal'.

It should be noted that Victorians were more alert to this kind of allegory than modern readers. Dante, like the Bible, provided many points of common reference. William Cudworth (1830–1906) the Bradford antiquarian and journalist, might be said to have ascended and descended both practically and theoretically in his many studies of local life and history which include *Historical Notes on the Bradford Corporation* and *The Condition of the Industrial Classes of Bradford and District*. In the memorial to him it was written that 'Bradford was his Beatrice'.[29]

The second incident in Ruskin's relations with Ellen Heaton which calls for specific notice may be dealt with quite briefly. It is more significant, and more ironic, than the matter of Rachel and Leah.

In his Oxford lecture of 1883 on 'Realistic Schools of Painting', Ruskin insists that 'Rossetti's great poetical genius justified my claiming for him total, and I believe, earnest, originality in the sternly materialistic, though deeply reverent, veracity, with which alone, of all schools of painters, this brotherhood of Englishmen has conceived the circumstances of the life of Christ. And if I had to choose one picture which represented in purity and completeness this manner of their thought, it would be Rossetti's "Virgin in the House of St. John".' Ruskin explains in his next lecture, 'Mystic Schools of Painting', what he means by 'materialistic' as applied to the Pre-Raphaelite brotherhood. 'I used that expression to denote their peculiar tendency to feel and illustrate the relation of spiritual creatures to the substance and conditions of the visible world; more especially, the familiar, or in a sort humiliating, accidents and employments of their earthly life; – as, for instance, in the picture I referred to, Rossetti's Virgin in the House of St. John. . . .'[30]

Ironically, the story of Rossetti's 'Virgin in the House of St John' clarifies more bleakly than his apologist ever publicly admitted 'the relation of spiritual creatures to the substance and conditions of the visible world'. For the picture was a disappointment to Ruskin; as he admitted to Ellen in November 1859. 'I expected far more of this subject,' he wrote.[31] It had been Ellen who had picked out the subject from a number of topics suggested by Rossetti. Ruskin was delighted at the prospect, in April 1856. '*By all means,*' he wrote 'the Virgin in the House of St. John – it is one of his finest thoughts.' Rossetti completed a version in 1858, but sold it to Lady Trevelyan, who was better qualified to advertise Rossetti in the right circles. The Leeds bookseller's daughter 'had to content herself with an inferior replica', as Virginia Surtees remarks.

Ellen herself, not always with the approval of her brother the physician, acted out the 'relation of spiritual creatures to the substance and conditions of the visible world' by delivering papers on the 'Care of Health'; by subsidising working-class attendance at University Extension lectures; by giving public teas 'to all working men'. 'I fear I am as busy as Ellen,' John Deakin commented tartly, 'I hope with rather more advantage, and a good deal less craze.' It appears there had been a supportive kindness as well as an ironic confession in Ruskin's words to her: 'I. . . think you one of the most sensible people I ever met in my life – I suppose that is because you believe all I say'.[32]

Beauty: John Aldam Heaton

As the blunt northern expression has it, John Aldam Heaton 'killed his mother'. She did not survive his birth. His first Christian name he took from his father John Heaton, a stuff merchant by inheritance, but by choice a dilettante who dissipated his fortune on artistic improvements to his home, St John's Cottage, Leeds, which he occupied only on leasehold. This pattern the son would follow at Woodbank, Bingley, and the general yearning for domestic beautification which it indicated would provide John Aldam with a career as an all-purpose decorator and designer. The middle name 'Aldam' suggests a connection with the Aldam dynasty, who with other Quaker families – the Peases, the Birchalls – were leading lights of the bourgeois hierarchy of Leeds: properous, well-established families whose values were more conservative than those of the thrusting new capitalists of Leeds's ever more victorious rival, Bradford.

Two families of unrelated Heatons became allied in 1850 when John Deakin Heaton physician to Leeds infirmary, and brother of Ellen Heaton, married John Aldam Heaton's sister Fanny. John Aldam, at twenty, was best man; Ellen, at thirty-four, was bridesmaid. They partnered each other on this occasion. In due course she would provide his introduction to Rossetti and Ruskin.

John Heaton's lack of commercial flair, combined with the 'general tendency of the stuff trade to leave Leeds for Bradford',[33] led to the closure of his business in 1855. His son John Aldam, now twenty-five and a recently married man, was one of many who removed their talent and capital to Bradford. He took up an engagement there with Messrs Lucock and Lupton in 1855, and in 1857 became the partner of the spinner Charles Hastings. John Aldam had produced his first successful design in 1846, at the age of sixteen. It was based on the Italian Renaissance designs which were his father's favourites, and remained in request at a Halifax mill for forty years. It seems that John Heaton refused to finance the secession of his son's talent to a Bradford firm. Mr Hastings must have had faith in Aldam's flair for business and design.

Aldam's new wife Ellen was a further source of family friction. She had been a Miss Morley, or Morlaix,[34] and governess to the family of the rich self-made machine-maker Peter Fairbairn, John Heaton's neighbour. The Fairbairns were eminently respectable.

Peter Fairbairn as mayor of Leeds would be knighted by Queen Victoria at the opening of the Town Hall in 1858. Moreover, Miss Morley continued to be a guest of the Fairbairns after she had ceased to be an employee. John Deakin Heaton, in view of his marriage to Fanny and what he regarded as John Heaton's incompetence, had taken upon himself the thankless role of head of the whole Heaton tribe. He would be a powerful supporter of Fairbairn in the building of Leeds Town Hall and the foundation of the Yorkshire College (in 1874). He 'could see nothing degrading nor absolutely inadmissible' in Aldam's proposed match with Miss Morley: still, the marriage was 'undesirable', as the bride was 'several years older' than the groom and 'entirely without resources'. Aldam's mother, it might be noted, had been nine years older than his father; at her death her place in the household at St John's Cottage was taken by her sister Miss Rimington, an unhappy woman who functioned in terms of barely suppressed fury, to judge from John Deakin's diaries. Given her overwhelming presence in his home, and the fact that Aldam had a pair of elder sisters – Fanny, and Marianne – it is not surprising that John Heaton chose in 1844, after keeping him for a year at Leeds Grammer School, to send his son to board at Repton in Derbyshire, where the family had a protector in the shape of Mr Barrow, an ironmaster. Mr Barrow was a bachelor, and after 1855 John Heaton's employer. If John hoped his son would join him in this state of clientship to Barrow, he was disappointed. Repton, a somewhat spartan and pronouncedly Churchy school, seems to have fed by precept Aldam's ecclesiasticism but by negation his craving for art. A typical expresion of his later years would be the pronouncement that poor church embroidery was 'a national disaster'. His two sisters, Fanny especially, seem to have initiated him into the mysteries of needlework; and in a curious form of sibling rivalry he proposed to outdo them in their own field. Aldam supported Miss Heaton in her Ruskinian enthusiasms – which were not shared by his sister Fanny.[35] The bride of his choice, Miss Morley, was an accomplished needle woman; and they probably collaborated on designs: another source of irritation to Fanny. John Deakin, who had a measured respect for Ruskin's earnestness[36] but little taste for Pre-Raphaelitism, records with some misgiving Mrs J. A. Heaton's *perchant* for the High Church clergy. As Miss Morley she had presumably been encouraged to share the views of her employer Peter Fairbairn, an Anglican radical-constitutionalist who wished to see an alliance between the old aristocracy and Anglican capitalists against the pretensions of Nonconformist subversives, and class-warmongerers like Cobden and Bright.[37]

In a variety of ways, therefore, John Aldam Heaton was qualified for a career in the business of interior decoration and disqualified from pursuing that career in entrepreneurial- capitalist and Nonconformist-dominated Bradford. He was the Anglican scion of a Conservative Leeds family with a Churchy boarding-school background; a disposition to dilettantism, and a sense of deference to old gentry families like the Busfield- Ferrands. Every one of these attributes was against him in Bradford; and it says much for his personality – and the power of the Old Bank – that he and Harris were able to provide the occasion for Ruskin's first Bradford appearance: the new School of Design. An unfortunate aspect was Heaton's flair for self- dramatisation. This had been fully in evidence at the time of his engagement to Miss Morley, which he paraded as an act of romantic rebellion, thus making it difficult for Fanny and her husband John Deakin to meet him half way, as they wished and hoped to do. The same histrionic tendency helped to make inevitable his famous quarrel with Rossetti; and, perhaps, his eventual break with Norman Shaw. This characteristic can have done neither the Bradford School of Design nor Shaw's chances in the competition for the Wool Exchange much good; and it may have weighed in the scales against Ruskin's immediate influence in Bradford.

Rossetti's 'Joan of Arc' was delivered to Miss Ellen Heaton in October 1864. The childhood of Joan provided an examplar of juvenile female sensibility for Ruskin's *Lilies*, delivered in Manchester that December. It may be that the accompanying reproach to his audience on the poor treatment allotted to contemporary governesses[38] was in part an acknowledgement of Ruskin's visit to Woodbank that April. The Aldam Heatons' home was adorned with ikons of the former Miss Morley as 'Regina Cordium' – a portrait in oils by Rossetti – and as 'The Lady of Woodbank' – a stained glass portrait by the same artist, halo and all. That Mrs Aldam Heaton was a powerful influence on her young husband seems clear. Her character is not clear from John Deakin's diaries. He records only her clothes in his account of an evening party given in 1872 by the Shaws and the Aldam Heatons in Bloomsbury Square. He calls her ensemble 'fancy dress'. 'Her Chinese purple velvet dress' had slashed sleeves and a long train of 'maize coloured satin'. The outfit was

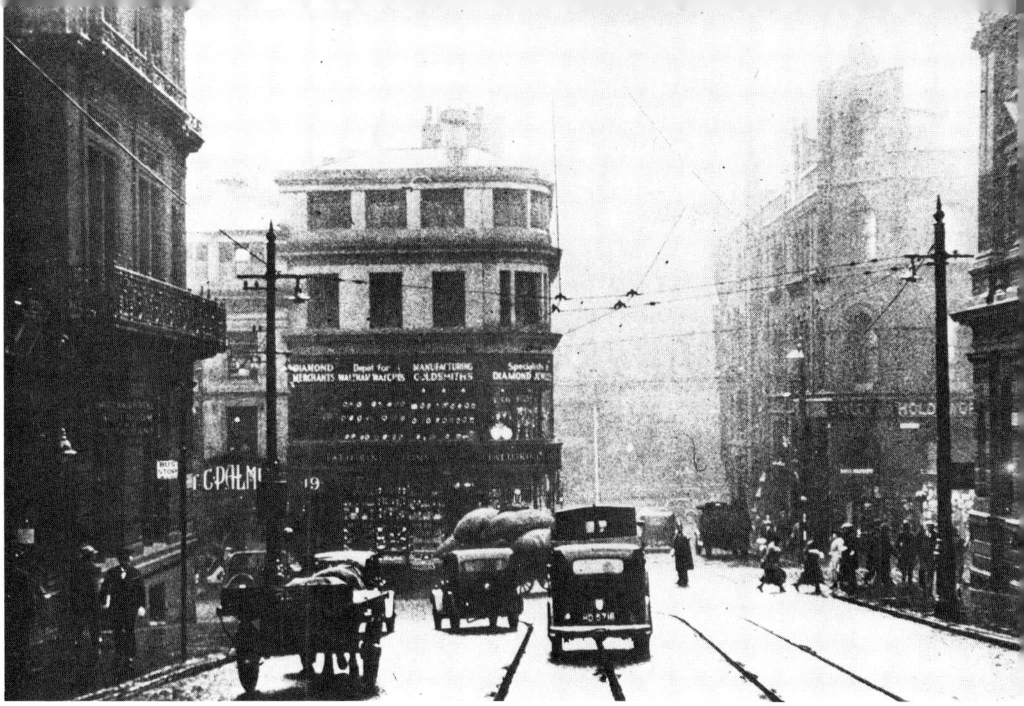

1
Bottom of Cheapside, Bradford – c. 1935. To the right, Beckett's Bank; to the left the Midland Hotel doorway where Irving collapsed and died after playing Becket (1905). Beyond, right: the Old Bank (Alfred Waterhouse, 1868); left of centre: Fattorini's the Goldsmith's, in the upper rooms of which Ruskin opened the Design School of 1859. Note the cart with woolbags

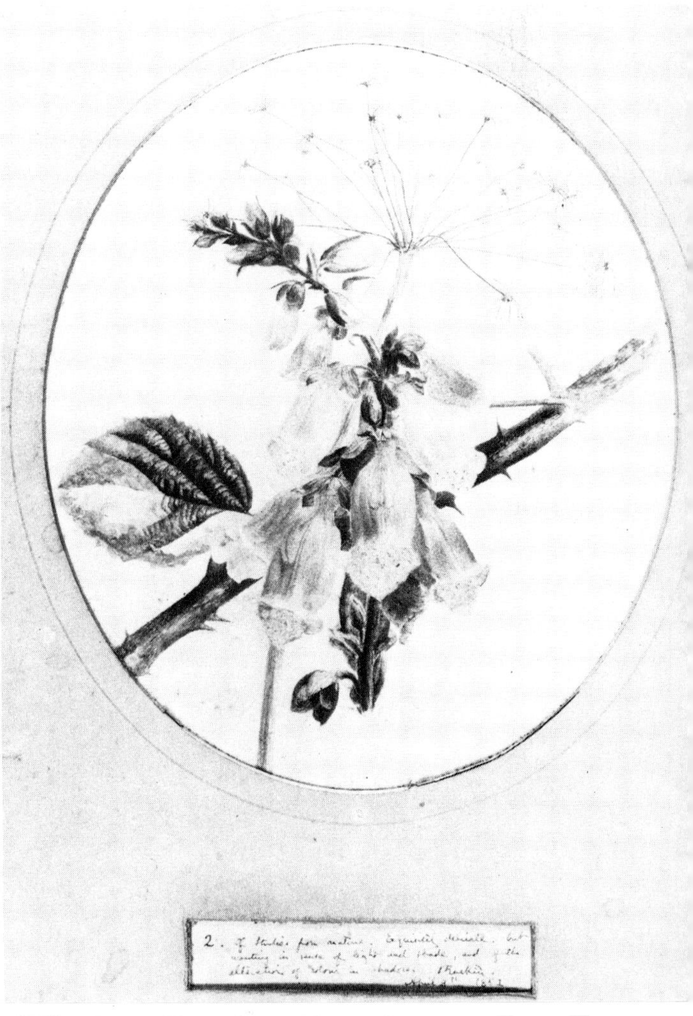

2
Watercolour study from nature by David Binns, pupil of Bradford Design School. Ruskin's MS comments: 'Exquisitely delicate; but wanting in sense of light and shade, and of the alteration of colour in shadow. J. Ruskin April 8th 1862'

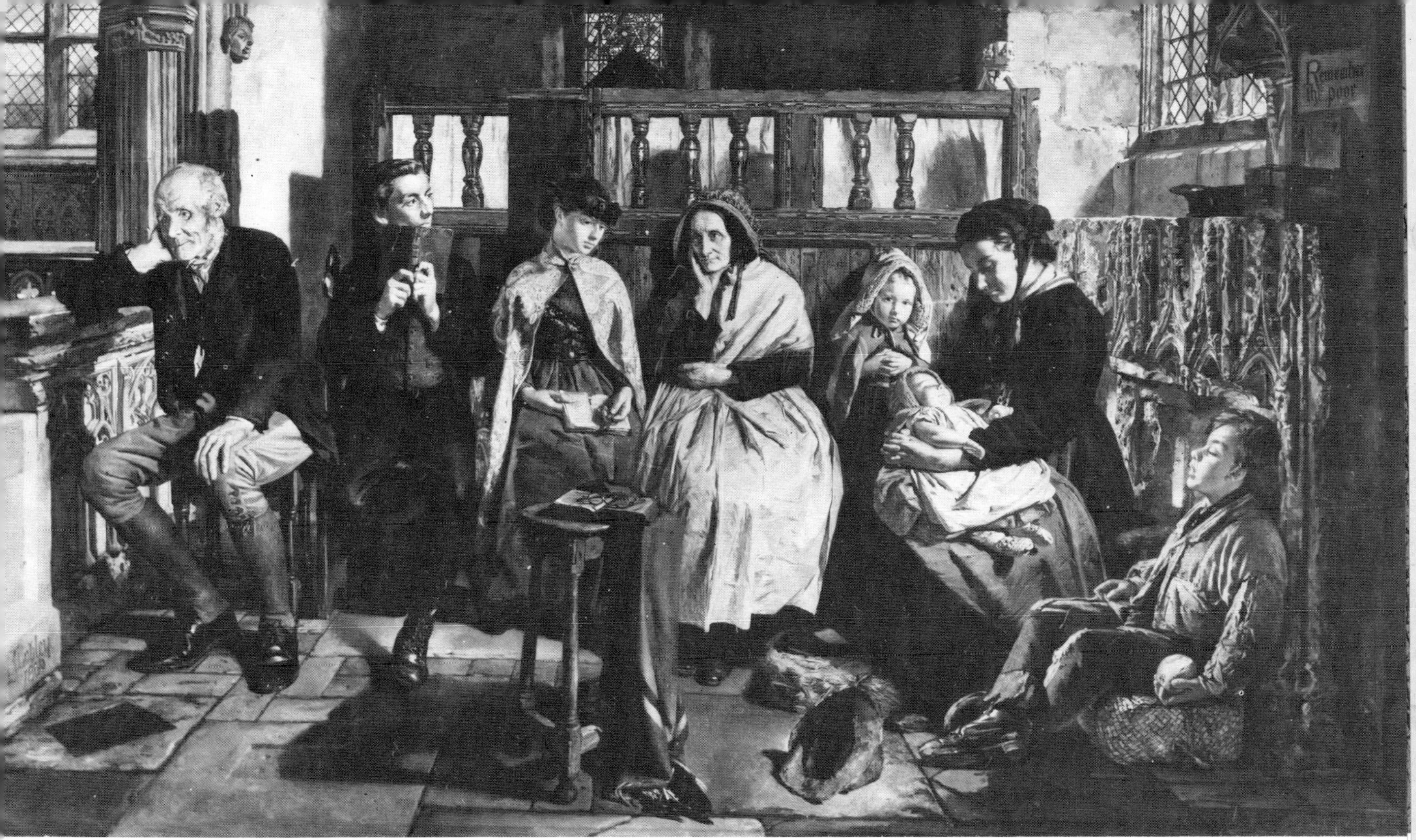

9 James Lobley, *The Free Seat*, oil on panel 21¾ x 33¼ inches (1869)

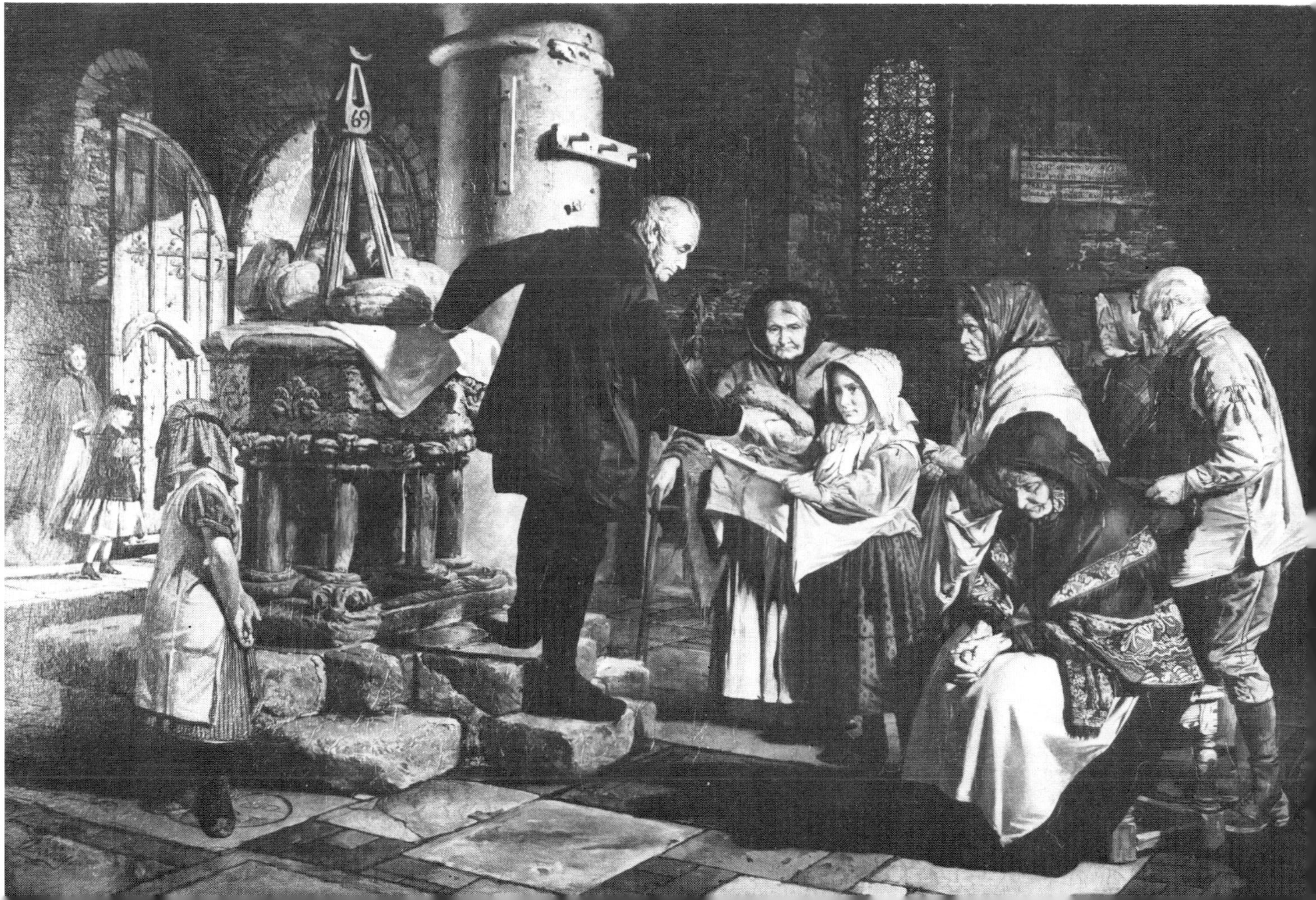

10 James Lobley, *The Dole*, Stow Church, oil on panel 19⅞ x 28 inches (1864–7)

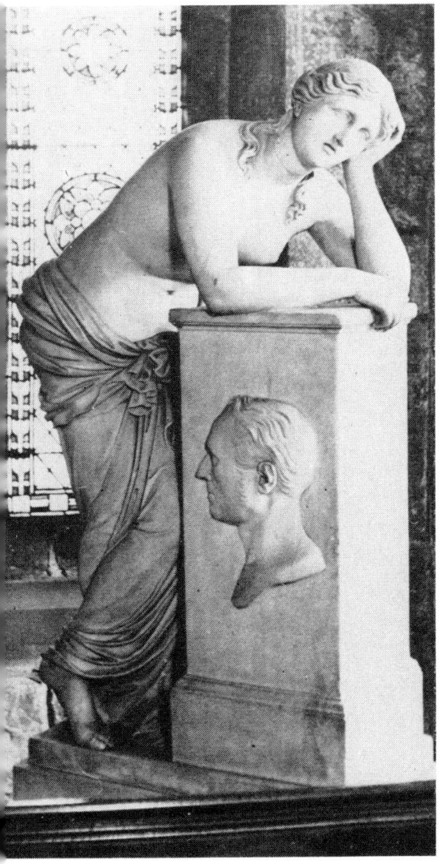

11
Bradford Classic: Joseph Gott, (1786-1860), memorial to William Sharp, surgeon (d. 1833). Formerly in St Peter's, Bradford

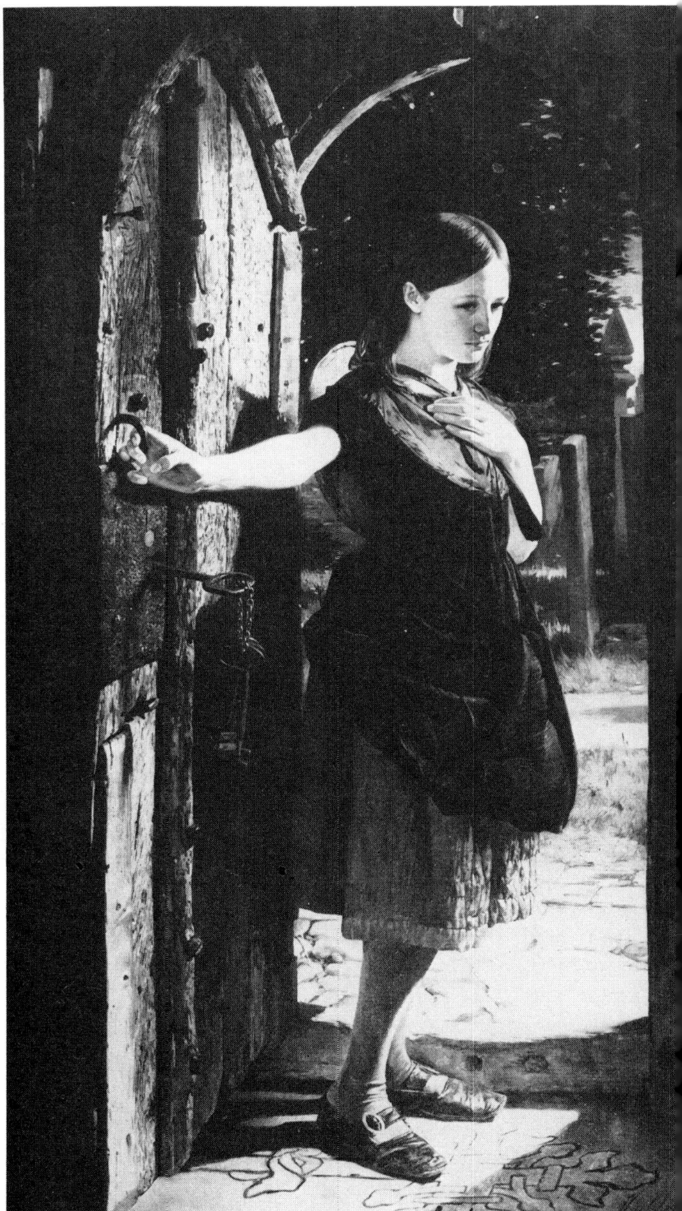

12
Bradford Pre-Raphaelite: James Lobley, *Little Nell leaving the Church*, oil on canvas 52¾ x 29½ inches (1867)

crowned by a 'beefeater's cap'. Only the most beautiful or the most brilliant woman could get away with that. Mrs Heaton, sweeping about with her 'stand up supper' in her hands amid bevies of 'High Church clergy', seemed less than satisfactory to the Leeds physician.

These two themes – High Church piety and romanticised domesticity – are apparent in the major Bradford commissions for stained glass which Aldam Heaton managed to win for William Morris and his circle. All were rare, eccentric victories.

As the local 'living barbarism' was crushed beneath the 'dead barbarism' which it imitated – the terms are Ruskin's – the acquiring of any genuine refinement was a painful process. Ruskin might tell Bradford a 'glowing mosaic of broken colour' was the proper 'gift and right' of stained glass, and deride the 'base vulgarism' of 'modern attempts to produce finished pictures on glass':[39] but the *Bradford Observer* of 16 June 1864 hailed the new Parish Church west window as a 'soothing and solemnising. . . memorial of piety and affection', rejoiced that 'two lights' had been 'thrown together. . . to make a picture', and respected the historicity of the 'sufficiently oriental' faces. One remembers Ellen Heaton's objection that Rossetti's Rachel and Leah were insufficiently 'oriental'. The designers of this window were Heaton, Butler and Bayne – a firm unconnected with Aldam Heaton. This was indeed 'a style for the age' and a proper refusal 'to imitate medieval patterns'. The *Observer*'s implied comparison is with the east window of 1862, the first sizeable commission of Morris and Company. Ruskin, 'though no admirer of this class of art as now practised,' James records,[40] gave Morris and Company 'his meed of praise' when shown their window in 1864. Made up, like Ruskin's Camberwell window of 1844,[41] from careful selection of existing glass, the east window's cobalt, silver and red, paint-green and gold mosaic of Christ, angels and saints, is a sufficient contrast to the beetroot plush within which the Magdalene of the west window writhes – twisted into impossibilities of genuflection before a thin-bearded Christ, oiled hair clinging to his scalp, who acknowledges her submission frailly amid the consternation of the onlookers.

It was not until 1868 that the 'glare' of the west window became embarrassing to the newly awakened sensibilities of the congregation, and it still stands, screened by Edward Maufe's organ chamber, as an expression of the taste of its own date. The 'soothing and solemnizing' effect achieved by its designers was part of the business acumen with which they 'promptly and successfully completed their engagement'.[42] When such was the efficiency of the supply, what need to question the quality of the demand?

'Sickliness and mawkish mediaevalism': the Tory *Leeds Intelligencer* thus dismissed the Pre-Raphaelites in February 1859. The phrase does less than justice to the Morris Firm window in Bradford Parish Church, but it was an esoteric art for that particular spot in 1862. Donated by Sarah Elizabeth Tolson of Baildon in memory of her husband Richard, the window represented the taste of a small cluster of 'advanced' Anglicans, some of whom had Puseyite tendencies which their Orangeman vicar Burnet would soon outlaw.

Mr Dunlop's windows of the same date at Harden Grange are more revealing. Designed by Arthur Hughes, Val Prinsep, Burne-Jones, Ford Madox Brown, Morris and Rossetti, they tell the story of Tristram and Isoude. One of the Burne-Jones panels, *The Recognition of Tristram by La Belle Isoude* is very charming. Tristram's dog, recognising him as he sleeps, is licking his face. Isoude and a handmaid look on. Isoude holds a red rose against her dress patterned very prettily with yellow swans – daisies speckle the grass. But there is something very private and chilling about Isoude's square, male head floating at the top of her dress. Ruskin's comment of January 1870 on Morris's *Earthly Paradise* springs to mind: 'There's such lovely, lovely misery in this Paradise. In fact, I think it's – the other place – made pretty'.[43]

Another of Dunlop's panels, made from one of Rossetti's designs, is more brilliant, and more disturbing. How much of its impact is due to Rossetti is hard to determine, as the drawing employed has not been found. Tristram and Isoude are shown drinking the love philtre. Cupid hovers above as a blood-red angel. A flame explodes in two hearts, tremulous gold and lethal, from the flask on the table. Even the platters are opulent with libidinous urgency. It is very accomplished design, but not quite, one imagines, what Ruskin envisaged for the domestic weal of Bradford.

Bradford Parish Church acquired another Morris Firm window in 1864. This was the south-east window. Albert Moore's contribution was Christ as Salvator Mundi. Burne-Jones provided a pelican, the emblem of Christ's sacrifice. Alfred Harris must have sympathised with this, for his crest was a pelican feeding its young with drops of blood.

It was from Denmark Hill, two days after his father's death, that

Ruskin had written to Edward Burne-Jones, at Winnington, begging him to 'put the black out of the box' and paint in jewel-like colours. It was at the bottom of Well Street, Bradford, that Ruskin denounced Britannia Agoraia that 21 April: and from Bingley that, on St George's Day, he had sped by train towards the Winnington haven. A memento of all this coming and going remains at Oakwood, Bingley, a dour gothic villa by local architects for Thomas Garnett, merchant, of Well Street. The Oakwood staircase window of *c.* 1865 has Morris images of the four seasons, with background quarries of flower patterns. Above, heads of Chaucer and five Chaucerian heroines; and in the centre St George, all by Burne-Jones. Burges, foiled of Bradford Wool Exchange, was allowed to design Mr Garnett's dining-room fireplace. This little victory, too, must have owed something to the tactics of Aldam Heaton.[44]

John Metcalfe Smith, the friend of Aldam Heaton's youth, was his principal support during his engagement to Miss Morley. The deaths of their fathers provided the pair with opportunities to fulfil long-cherished dreams; and in doing so, to upstage John Deakin Heaton.

Equal in charm and promise, though different in scale, as their income had been different, the memorials to John Heaton and to the banker John Smith were early examples of good work by Richard Norman Shaw.

To John Deakin's displeasure, Aldam caused to be set up in the Evangelical St George's Church, Leeds,[45] where all the Heatons worshipped, a 'brazen monument' to the late John Heaton, who had died in December 1864. The monument was in place by 1866. Recently rescued from the parish coal hole, it can now be admired for its stylised roundels of the four Evangelists, by Shaw, on the back of its outer leaves, which open to reveal the charming lettering by Eden Nesfield commemorating John Heaton and sundry other of Aldam's relatives. Below this is a very pretty flower border by Aldam himself. Nesfield's lettering splendidly fulfils Ruskin's insight that engraved letters should always show 'a certain quantity of organic variety' and look as though time has not been 'unworthily thrown away' to make them appear neat and 'unredeemably vulgar'. Aldam's flowers show some of that fresh conventionalisation from observed nature demanded in Ruskin's 1859 Bradford lecture. They certainly avoid the 'degradation' of attempted realism.[46] John Deakin considered the triptych a 'mediaeval affected design. . . chiefly characterised by the irregularity and bad formation of the letters, and one or two decided inaccuracies in the inscription'.[47] His own pet designer was George Gilbert Scott. He had been instrumental in getting Scott as architect to the Leeds Infirmary.

John Smith's memorial was the Cookridge Convalescent Home, Norman Shaw's only medical work of consequence. It was designed in 1867 and built 1868–9. 'The basis of the plan,' writes Andrew Saint, 'is an excerpt from Scott's Infirmary, a central emphasized service area flanked by long low wings for the wards and day rooms.' The style, by contrast with Scott's foreign and grim gothic, is a 'light and happy' Kentish vernacular, 'unashamedly transferred to Yorkshire to cheer the city convalescents up among the bracken and pure suburban air'.[48] John Deakin's comments are not recorded. He was a painstaking physician who won the recommendation of Professor Huxley to a Fellowship of the Royal Society – an honour of which he was cheated by death. Devoted to medical lecturing and the service of the poor in the heart of Leeds, he had few patients who could afford the luxury of convalescence. Aldam and his friend struck him as 'dreamers'.

John Aldam's mother lay buried in St John's Briggate, Leeds. This had been built for a Puritan congregation in 1634. It is partly thanks to Aldam's propaganda and the tactful restoration of Norman Shaw that this fine church survives today. Solidly vernacular in its happy blend of Gothic stonework with Renaissance plaster and wood work, the church was influential in reinforcing Shaw's sense of ' the continuity of Gothic and vernacular, if the latter were isolated from Ruskin's "foul torrent" of academic Renaissance'. But it was George Gilbert Scott who wrote the initial report that saved St John's from destruction. He had been approached to this end by his Leeds admirers; of whom the most vocal was John Deakin.[49]

Diversification was Aldam Heaton's strength and weakness. From the early '60s till 1874 he was building up his range of crafts, and at the same time retaining his business links with Hastings and branching into the art dealing business with the Bradfordian Brayshay and the Pre-Raphaelite go-between Charles Augustus Howell. Howell was taken up by Ruskin as private secretary for a few years from 1865, and was simultaneously working his way into Rossetti's confidence. A tricky line of procedure, for Ruskin and Rossetti had quarreled, the occasion, if not the cause, being Rossetti's 'Venus Verticordia' for John Mitchell of Bradford. In Rossetti's eyes, Aldam's usefulness was to advertise Rossetti among richer Yorkshire patrons than the modest Ellen Heaton. Between them, the commercial Brayshay and the devious Howell helped to exacerbate a now best-forgotten quarrel between the histrionic Heaton and the unforgiving Rossetti, which brought their relationship to an end in 1874. But Heaton was loyal to Rossetti's talent, if not to Rossetti, and if there was self-dramatisation in his decision to present himself at Rossetti's thinly-attended funeral at Birchington in 1882, there was also real regret. William Michael Rossetti records that the family 'were glad to make peace with Mr. Heaton over the open grave'.[50]

Heaton's own first big independent commission was for sanctuary hangings and other decorative work in the church at Hebden Bridge, which was extended by Norman Shaw in 1874–6. Heaton's sister Marianne was married to John William Atkinson, and Heaton was doubtless instrumental in getting Shaw the commission to build Atkinson's house, St John's Ilkley, of 1876–7. Shaw's commission for St Margaret's Ilkley may also have been eased by Heaton's influence.[51]

Heaton was an active pioneer in the launching of the School of Art Needlework in Sloane St (1872). A Higher School of Art was formed as part of the school in 1875, when it moved to Kensington and become Royal. Advice and instruction were given occasionally by Leighton, Val Prinsep and G. F. Bodley, with Heaton as an indispensable adjunct to the establishment. Heaton died at Frognal in 1897; and it was only then that design as well as practical needlework began to be taught at the RSAN.[52] Whether or not Heaton exerted any influence against letting the ladies loose on design must be a matter of speculation or further research. His ancient jealousy of his sister Fanny's proficiency raises some tantalising questions.

In 1876 Heaton moved finally to London; and there followed a decade of informal but close partnership with R. Norman Shaw. Shaw's 'ready-made clientele brought Heaton immediate success', Andrew Saint writes. Heaton had done something to build up that clientele. 'Within a few years he had worked at Adcote, Greenham, Flete, Dawpool, Frognal Priory and the Alliance Assurance Office, and was able to get Shaw to build him a large workshop in Bloomsbury.'[53] Heaton provided many designs in needlework, stamped leather, plasterwork, metalwork, marquetry; for furniture, plain and painted; stencils for wall decoration; and the occasional wallpaper design. A handful of these last are preserved in the Victoria and Albert Museum. At first glance they appear neither striking nor distinctive; but viewed at the proper distance they acquire a quiet allure which suggests they would be easier to live with than Morris's more demanding patterns.[54]

From about 1885 till the end Heaton was his own master, Shaw having tired of his designs, which he found too fussy for his own mature style. Heaton's personality was a little fussy too, beneath the volubility. His 'Flete' fireplace of white-painted deal of 1885,[55] which sold steadily, is charming, though a little frigid and a little forward, like a slightly too flirtatious parson's wife of the period. Bernard Shaw's Marchbanks might have warmed his toes at it while making up to Candida,[56] had her husband been able to afford her a private sitting room; and had she been indiscreet enough to entertain her poet in it.

Heaton began watercolour drawing 'from nature' at the age of four (in 1834), and continued to make at least one study of vegetable form every week of his adult life. Technical and business knowledge was instilled into him at his father's insistence from his early youth. He became a more efficient businessman than his father. He also became an attentive reader of Ruskin, and an admirer of William Morris. It was, however, the former's 'empiricism' that drew his respect; and while he had no doubt of the superiority to his own of the latter's powers of design, he had reservations about some of the uses to which they were put. Their 'influence' upon him was a function of his competence. It is impossible to tell how much of the 'Ruskinian' theory, or 'Morris' habits of design he had worked out for himself before he encountered either. In more comprehensible terms than usual, Ruskin's Bradford lecture of 1859 insisted on the need for constant observation of natural form, so that the applied designer might learn to conventionalise in a useful and lively way, and avoid the ludicrousness of attempted 'realism' on the one hand, and stultifying habits of copying stock patterns on the other. Heaton's practice was already in accord with this theory – a fact which at the time made him unusual in Bradford or anywhere else. Yet Heaton was glad to have heard Ruskin lecture. His experience was that the critic's 'books alone are quite beyond the average reader. . . full of an empiricism which ruffles a good many students. . . If you read them all through you arrive at the conclusion that their author knows eminently well what he is talking about.'[57]

Heaton got on with R. Norman Shaw much better than he ever did with William Morris. He contributed to many of the former's *bourgeois gentilhomme* interiors. But Heaton had a mildly socialist conscience which was not really happy in such work either. His own 'place' in social history most neatly focuses on the main room of the club in Norman Shaw's 'model village', Bedford Park, Chiswick (1880). Tapestry alternated with Japanese paper on the walls; there was furniture by Godwin, Morris and G. Jackson, tiles by De Morgan – and a large fireplace by Aldam Heaton.[58] But Heaton's real interest is less tangible. He was an admirable go-between: a boarding-schoolboy who married a governess, a capitalist who took to socialism, a northerner and a moderately High Anglican who could intercede between Rossetti and his 'employers', Shaw and his *nouveau riche* clientele; an intelligent eclectic for whom Ruskin's 'empirical' genius meant common sense – not 'the life or the decorations of the thirteenth century back again'. He encouraged his craftsmen to do what they wanted, provided his clients got what they wanted: an endeavour more valuable, perhaps, than some of the results.

In a series of articles on *Arts and Crafts Workers* in *The Artist* of 1897, Heaton finds his place between Walter Crane and Sir Thomas Wardle. The reviewer very fairly refers to the 'energy and vitality of his nature, and the earnestness of his artistic efforts'. These Yorkshire characteristics found a useful outlet in the organisation of the School of Art Needlework at South Kensington, whither for some time he travelled every week from his beloved Woodbank. In 1876 he had no choice but to move to London altogether: only there could he gather together a team of craftsmen of the quality he needed. He built up a comfortable practice in most forms of interior design, deploying, as so often happens, habits of 'Yorkshire' outspokenness for the entertainment and edification of the metropolis. 'In the higher branches of Decorative work, I try never to repeat myself', he was fond of saying; and he prefaced his *Records of Work* with celebratory obituaries on the enemies of taste – like 'the huge dinner-room mirror, round at the top like a mound of jelly'. Such an approach went some way towards enticing the very philistines who were repelled by the preciousness of Morris's Kelmscott. Just because he was competent rather than inspired, he represents a promising sign: the hope that, even without the genius of a Morris, seaworthy 'Ruskinian' ideas might change the cluttered aspect of the 'English room' so tellingly denounced in the 'Nature of Gothic' chapter into something resembling human habitation. Morris's superb products were only, as Heaton put it, 'a drop in the ocean'.

It would be interesting to know whether the energetic Heaton had anything to do with getting Morris designs onto the looms of the Heckmondwike Company, in the 'south-eastern suburb of Bradford'. The 'Lily' machine-woven ingrain carpeting that was there produced was made in relatively narrow widths, which could be sewn together if required. This was also Heaton's practice with the designs made for him by the Glasgow carpet firm of Templeton. In either event, West Riding ingenuity, contrary to Ruskin's worst fears, was able to supply some of the necessary links between his own reforming theories and industrial and commercial practice.

Bradford stone was shipped to Australia; and Aldam Heaton, equally expansive, shipped a house interior for assembly at Fullarton, near Adelaide.[59]

Bradford's traditional export market was in Protestant Germany. Both were provinces, as far as ladies' fashion went, of the gas-lit Empire of Napoleon and Eugénie. Already mill-girls in outlying villages were hankering after the 'newest fashions'. Unmarried girls, with money to spend for the first time, acquired showy outfits with an intemperance that was the female equivalent of taking to the bottle. While complacency glowed, or morality glowered, over such symptoms of affluence, uncertainty was the companion, even the motive, for such expenditure. Like drink, it promised enjoyment in the absence of security. The results were often garish, and local decorum could hardly reverse a trend having an external source. The Bradfordian-Scot Robert Milligan opposed the 'highly ornamented' to 'good taste' in his specification for zinc colouring on woollen fabrics of 1851. He preferred differences of intensity and shade to glaring colour contrasts.[60] Aldam Heaton, with a respectful glance at the Ruskinian maxim that 'colour begins where gradation begins', somewhat agreed with him. Unfortunately, Paris had other ideas. The French, when they chose, could outdo the English in subtlety. They could also wipe their eye with its opposite. As Octave Uzanne recorded in the nineties, the Second Empire had loved 'overwhelming violets, cruel pinks, glaring greens. . . blinding yellows'. Heaton, on his trip to Paris, noted an equal dislocation in materials: '"Effects" must be obtained by the use of straw, of feathers, of furs, of shells, of beads, of gold dust'. One reason, to their credit, that sober Bradfordians of the '60s failed to capture the French market was that some of the competition appalled them.

A chief enemy to colour was gaslight. One of the few technical 'advances' Ruskin welcomed was electricity, and Heaton agreed with him. In the '80s, when electric lighting became feasible for industrial premises, Bradford merchants like Henry Mitchell and Henry Mason would begin to be successful in selling fashion fabrics to the French. There may be a connection between these two developments. Electricity was no substitute for daylight, but it was incomparably better than gas, and Bradford, as usual, was a pioneer, The windows of 'Gothic' warehouses tended to be too narrow. Only two or three were ever built in Bradford, the most imposing being the 'Demon' Dunlop's mammoth essay in Scottish- Baronial. On the other hand, the usual Italianate style 'demanded' a heavy balustrade which seriously diminished the effectiveness of overhead daylighting. Often crowded into narrow alleys – and this was particularly true of the German export houses – these grim palazzi were the last places on earth for the work of colour-matching, nor did 'Nature's sunshine' as a rule illustrate the habitats of Bradford designers. In the short northern winter days the temptation to design or check, by gaslight, colours often intended to 'show up' by gaslight must have been hard to resist. In their efforts to 'contend in colour' – as Henry Brown put it – some Bradford businessmen resorted to the bright Mancunian idea of abolishing the winter dinner-hour.

In an essay clearly written under the triple influence of Ruskin's two Bradford lectures and a trip to Paris, Heaton amusingly evokes a fashionable gaslit boudoir in which the 'latest colours' scream out in cacophony from upholstery, dress fabrics and quilted silk walls.

From such a padded cell, Heaton suggests escape to the 'nearest hedgerow'. A return to the 'natural', a respect for the 'substantial', and a 'temperance', in its richest sense , in colour and design, become his watchwords. How he hates that arch-Victorian material, 'plush', which Bradford's own Lister produced by the mile for the upholsterer.[62] Though Heaton is thinking for himself, he is doing so along the lines of Ruskin's message to the Bradford Design School. Plain walls, plain curtains and floors of three-inch boards like the deck of a ship. No truck with the 'pestilence' of Japanese knick-knacks. Japanese prints, when good, are not good merely because they are Japanese. He dislikes 'miles of wall-paper, mechanically monotonous', even Morris's or Voysey's. Preferring, like Ruskin, proportion to mere symmetry and gradation to repetition, he advocates stencils which can be used by skilled workwomen to produce individually decorated and variously shaded walls, where required.

Heaton was an expert on eighteenth-century furniture,[63] and his general 'rule' was to base designs on the last healthy style available. His own designs for what would now be called 'reproduction Georgian' furniture are not over impressive, nor are they altogether symptomatic of healthy design practice. But one of his deserved successes was the 'Hampton Court' chair, a plain rush-seated affair selling at £2.10*s*.[64] Like the West Riding bourgeois he was, he knew the name would appeal to that shade of British snobbery offended by 'vernacular' connotations. He persuaded Templetons, the Glasgow carpet firm whose factory of 1889 would parody the Doge's Palace, to be more genuinely Ruskinian by employing those Persian designs which, while 'refusing the higher organisms of nature', as befits a floor, nevertheless 'take care to retain the magnificence of natural lines'. So Ruskin put it in 1859. 'Let us have adequate, fine designs, even if we have to stick to them for twenty years,' Heaton exclaims, putting the Conservative in him to practical use. The socialist in him co-operated with the Conservative. All engaged in business were fellow-workers. He had no time for the ordinary relations of employer and 'hand'. An inspiring friend who showed this useful largeness was Rev. Cary Shuttleworth, a moderate High Churchman, and a lecturer at King's College, London. He combined the widest cultural interests with championship of the Christian Socialist Movement. His Shuttleworth Club for men and women made some attempts to erode the existing divisions between sexes and classes, but he never aspired to the doctrinaire. Nor did Heaton. He designed marquetry work for railway dining-cars and steamship drawingrooms – a line of business in which his friendship with Alfred Harris, railway and steamship magnate, can have done him no harm. He also produced designs for churches where, he felt, 'false taste and blunders are a national disaster'. Like the Ruskin of the 1859 Bradford lecture, he wished to see an applied art that would 'make modern English life beautiful'. Nature's sunshine is his criterion. Colours which bear the admixture of a sunny yellow, fabrics which can stand the sunlight. 'Burnt Sienna, glazed transparent on white, is the most beautiful red in the world.' In his pamphlet for the Liverpool Architectural Association – written at their request – on *The Decoration of the House*; and his information sheet on *Fabrics* for the Architectural Institute of London,[65] Heaton shows the Yorkshire passion for 'education' at its best in relation to 'Modern Manufacture and Design'.

Life: Alfred Harris

Alfred Harris, junior, nephew to the Bradford bankers Henry Harris and Alfred Harris, senior, will hereafter be referred to simply as 'Alfred Harris'.[66]

Alfred's Quaker sister Mary was the close friend and mentor of Octavia Hill. His first wife, Harriet, also a Quaker, was the sister of Ruskin's geologist friend Alfred Tylor. His second wife, Anne, of Huguenot stock, was the daughter of Dr Edward Meryon; and a member of the artistic Meryon family which included Charles Meryon, the architectural engraver of fine and melancholy genius[67] whose father had been personal physician and companion to the eccentric Lady Hester Stanhope, niece of Pitt the Younger.

The Harris circle was thus Conservative, artistic, well able to cope tactfully with a nervous oddity of genius like Ruskin. Of all Ruskin's Bradford connections, Harris and his two wives seem to have been the ones with whom he achieved, for a period, a species of spiritual communion. Yet he was quite rude about Harris's new house at Kirkby Lonsdale in *Fors Clavigera*.[68] Perhaps it was the architect, Alfred Waterhouse, who had insisted on adding to the building that favourite motif of his: an eye-catching tower with open *porte-cochère* below. The rest of the house, though substantial, was modest and not uncomely. Harris's nemesis, it seems, was towers, at Kirkby Lonsdale, and in his church at Bingley. Neither building has survived the stringencies of modern insurance laws.

Harris's own tastes are perhaps indicated by the frieze in his billiard-room at Kirkby Lonsdale, which consisted of 'oil designs of football, wrestling and skittle-playing'. His first wife Harriet, who died in December 1865, after 'long-protracted suffering', was known in Bingley as 'the good lady'. Anne Meryon, who had helped to nurse her, was an artistic woman whose sympathies and powers of organisation found an outlet at Kirkby Lonsdale in the revival of local crafts. Like Ruskin's much grander friend the Marchioness of Waterford, these two ladies, though with less condescension, were fine examples of the Victorian lady as she still deserves to be admired: conscientious, public-spirited and unostentatiously charitable. Harris himself was an earnest and conscientious Conservative, who made efforts in later life to assist technical education in Ireland. A born Quaker who became a Broad Churchman, he was well aware that the British government, if it hoped to survive in

Ireland, must work in close co-operation with the Catholic Church.[69]

Ruskin found Harris, and both his wives, more admirable than any art they might cause to be produced. For him, there was a quite shocking discrepancy between their innate goodness and the opportunities for goodness available to a great Victorian banker and his family.

Alfred's Bradford aunt and uncles were Sarah, Henry and Alfred Harris. They were the children and heirs of Richard Harris, who had married the heiress to the Bradford Old Bank, Jane Peckover. Uncle Henry, a Quaker bachelor, was an art and curio collector. Uncle Alfred become an Anglican. His principal bequest to Bradford was £3,800 in shares for a fever hospital on Leeds Road. Aunt Sarah was a minister of the Society of Friends. Together with other Bradford Quakers, Benjamin Seebohm and John Priestman among them, she interested herself in a school for the sons of labourers and mechanics, founded in 1829, and run under the British and Foreign Bible Society system. This taught the three Rs, and Protestant doctrine. The fee was 2 pence per week. The school seems to have faded away by the 1860s.[70] Elementary working-class education was becoming polarised between the Church of England and other denominational schools, for respectable families in steady employment; and the Ragged Schools, of which a number grew up in Bradford, including one founded in 1853, of which Sarah's nephew Alfred Harris was treasurer. Many of the urban poor of inner Bradford were Irish Catholics. With the state provision of the Education Act of 1870, and the growth in prosperity of Bradford's Catholics, who acquired their own schools, the pioneering work of the Ragged Schools became less necessary; and the school closed in 1880. Alfred's contact with the poor Irish of inner Bradford was sufficient, however, to stir his conscience into action on behalf of technical education for Irish Catholics in Ireland, during the 1880s. Alfred's interest in art, and in Ragged Schools, came together in his encouraging and perhaps commissioning, of James Lobley's studies of Ragged School children. Both men were sympathetic to Ruskin's notion of the social obligations of art.

Harris, Aldam Heaton and James Lobley were responsible for arranging an 'advanced' art exhibition in Bradford Old Exchange during July 1860. It was intended to diffuse taste; but the *Bradford Observer* exhausted its rhetoric in vain in efforts to awaken working-class interest. Lobley, indeed, makes efforts to introduce Bradford to Millais, Madox Brown, Rossetti and Arthur Hughes; but, 'Be sure that you do not pass by,' the *Observer* critic urges his humbler readers, '*Hotspur and the Fop* [by Elmore] if you want to hate dandyism and love honest blunt manly soldierly strength a little more than you do.' How a Victorian factory worker might best imitate a medieval aristocrat he does not confide. Such a mind naturally finds William Shakespeare Burton's *Mary Mother* the disturbed product of 'ultraism', and turns with disgust from the 'green spots on the face' of Rossetti's *Saint Catherine*. Ruskin, too, had called that 'an absurdity'. There seemed to be less than usual significance in the ineptitude of its draughtsmanship. The Bradford critic admits a certain 'charm' in Madox Brown's *Cordelia at the Bedside of Lear*, but its 'hard, flat manner' is ultimately distasteful; and his 'sickening. . . utterly horrible' *Prisoner of Chillon*, lovingly studied from a none too fresh corpse, is something to hurry past. Arthur Hughes is more acceptable. The three angels at the top of his *Nativity* are 'exquisitely beautiful', but – despite Mr Ruskin's praise – the stable lantern seems to have no utility. His *Annunciation* is even sillier: 'the minor angels will not find it easy to extricate themselves from the lattice-work'; and comparison shows how inferior are the lilies and irises of Mr Hughes to similar studies by William Hunt. Millais's *Only a Lock of Hair* – a portrait of Effie – gets by as an 'accurate picture of a face and incident ordinary enough'. All the 'advanced' pictures are from Manchester or Leeds, and equally foreign to Bradford taste is a landscape by Corot, surely realised, 'if we judge of it by its dullness' from the suburban scenery of Manchester. Those old standbys, Frost and Etty, still have some attraction here; and the Bradford banker and iron master Charles Hardy is quite right to stick to such middlebrow men as W. F. Witherington, the rustic genre painter, or James Sant of portrait fame. He has some Thomas Creswicks too: 'all interesting and homely pictures possessing a pleasing charm in their simple subjects and their careful execution'. W. P. Frith's *Little Dorrit* is clearly a guinea-catcher; but a goat's head by Landseer has a proper 'smooth pink satin nose'. J. C. Herring's horses, T. S. Cooper's cows and G. C. Stanfield's ships repay attention. But local students are principally directed to William Hunt, Copley Fielding, David Cox, Thomas Girtin and, above all, Turner. Their united testimony assembled on the walls of the Old Exchange, proclaims that 'great results can be achieved only be earnest untiring study of nature'.

Lobley and his brighter pupils seem to have been stirred to greater efforts by this unusual feast of 1860; but the overwhelming indifference of local 'artisans' is undeniable. So is the 'backwardness' of most of Bradford's new bourgeois elite – if dismissal of Rossetti in favour of Turner can be so described.

Alfred Harris senior's 'principal contribution' to this exhibition was *The Apprehension of Alice Lisle* by E. M. Ward, RA (1816–79). Local critics found it more thrilling than the same painter's *Royal Family of France in the Prison of the Temple*, since that did 'not represent any momentary crisis'. A middlebrow painter of historical subjects, Ward's *Last Parting of Marie Antoinette and her Son* had been 'excepted from the progressive list' in Ruskin's *Academy Notes* of 1856. This, for a banker, might amount to a recommendation, especially as Ruskin added that the representation was 'not a bad one'. More positively for Bradford's external prestige, at least, Alfred junior's connection with the lady for whom they were executed served to bring two works by HRH the Princess of Prussia, the Princess Royal, to the walls of Bradford Old Exchange. Numbered 1 and 2 in the catalogue of 1860 and hung in a velvet-draped niche with gilded royal arms above, they might represent what painting meant for a conservative northern banker. It is unlikely that, in libertarian Bradford, they did the cause of art much good. But, unlike the Pre-Raphaelite works contributed by Mr Heugh of Manchester and Mr Plint of Leeds, which were of far more interest to Lobley, the Princess Royal's sketches earned a notice in *The Art Journal*.[71]

Bradford had the largest concentration of Irish in Yorkshire. Most of them were poor Catholics and lived near the Parish Church, which they never entered. The vicar, Dr Burnet, was chairman of the Yorkshire Orangemen; and seems to have used his influence in favour of peace. The Parish Church took on a more 'Catholic' look during the early '60s, when the ugly west gallery was removed; the magnificent medieval timber roof exposed to view, and the new Morris east window installed. But a handful of Church of Ireland stalwarts in the congregation, led by Squire Auty, dug themselves in against 'Puseyism' going any further than this; and Burnet was induced to close down the High Church St Peter's Guild that had formed itself among his flock.[72]

This entrenchment at the Parish Church of what they saw as the historically accidental Protestantism of the Church of England meant that Anglican modernists required a new church. They gloried in the largeness of the Anglican church, not its smallness, and in its unique retention among western sects of all three elements of early Christianity: an apostolic clergy; the scriptures in the common tongue, the Communion in both kinds to the laity. They were of the same mind as Octavia Hill's chosen pastor F. D. Maurice and Ruskin's Christ Church friend and rival Dean Stanley of Westminster. Their new church was to be Holy Trinity, Bingley, by Richard Norman Shaw. Aldam Heaton was people's warden; a Mr Lobley gave hangings and robes for the verger; and for Alfred Harris, the vicar's warden, its Broad Church policy was a spiritual meeting place for the two loves of his life: the Quaker Harriet Tylor and the Huguenot Anne Meryon. The church was also one of the finest examples anywhere of Victorian plain masonry, the mortar being everywhere kept back from the edge of the stone. But its building history reads like a parody of the story of the Tower of Babel.

Alfred Harris senior, of Ryshworth Hall and the Bradford Old Bank, had been a mainstay of St Paul's Manningham. He now gave a munificent £1,000 – a fifth of its cost – towards this new church at the Bradford end of Bingley. Anglican gentlefolk and manufacturers patronised All Saints', the ancient Parish Church – at the further end of Bingley. Many *nouveaux riches* were wedded to Nonconformity. Alfred Harris, nephew of Alfred senior, was anxious to break this pattern of patronage and passivity by canvassing less opulent parishioners. He and Rossetti's 'Demon', Mr Dunlop, together with the landed gentleman J. A. Busfield and the clergyman's son F. Sharp-Powell were among those who restrained their initial donations to £100 or £150. A similar 'advanced' spirit was shown by the new, young – and sadly short-lived – incumbent, Rev. Albert Hudson. He rejected pew rents, preferring to allocate seats on a democratic and catholic basis to Easter communicants.

Designed in 1864 in an 'Early French' style, and erected from 1866 under Alfred Harris's personal supervision on a craggy outcrop of land with canal on one side and railway on the other; the church's ministrations were impeded by the simple difficulty of getting to it. Most of its stone came from the Gilstead quarries hard at hand, but Norman Shaw added a reredos in alabaster (1869–70), and a font and pulpit (1868) employing Derbyshire marble. In 1881 Ruskin expressed a commendation of this church that contained a warning. He had 'the greatest admiration of the severe simplicity and dignity of the building in its original design'. The implied disjunctive alluded to the fact that the architect Norman Shaw – 'Corporal

Bullfoot' – and his patron Alfred Harris were between them determined to erect an enormous stone spire over the crossing. The scheme dated from 1869. At last it would be realised. Alas, the settlement caused by the weight of this fine piece of abstract sculpture – 3,300 tons of it – necessiated extensive repairs, and even so in January 1882 part of the clerestory window crashed onto the roof during service. The church wardens stood in the doorway gathering the collection from those who fled. There could never be enough. The means of maintaining such an expensive second church in Bingley were not available; it was financially impossible to ensure – or insure – the stability of the spire, and physically impossible to remove it without demolishing the church – which was the resolution taken shortly after its centenary.[73]

Alfred Harris's greatest single act of art-patronage was to commission the glass for the single lancet over the altar of this church. It was executed by the Morris Firm, in 1873, and combined a fine Crucifixion by Burne-Jones, with below it a superb strip of glass by Rossetti, showing Abraham, his hand stayed by the angel in the act of offering to sacrifice Isaac. Below them is the ram, caught in a stylised thicket.[74] Though it depicts a single point in the story, the work divides itself into three sections, and Rossetti makes use of this to set out a subjective drama in three scenes. The red stridency of the angel's robe in the upper third conveys violence both of terror and of rescue; the central ballet of stylised hands and faces conveys a drawn-out drama of will and resignation. In the lowest scene of all a green Keatsian netherworld of blessed relief around the slumberous ram pulls the beholder downwards and inwards into itself, away from the dangerous flame that threatens to set alight the kindling wood. The glass is worth a number of late Rossetti canvases, and would by itself vindicate Ruskin's Bradford plea of 1859 for the dignity of decorative art. Yet confinement of energy is one of the inescapable effects of its drama. And the implied sequel would be no scene of rejoicing for resolute father and resigned son. The implied sequel would be a folding away into some imaginary pastoral sleep.

In 1870 Harris put Ashfield on the Market and removed his family to Lunefield, Kirkby Lonsdale. He retained part of the grounds of Ashfield and continued his duties at Bradford Old Bank, becoming chairman in 1882. Harris was a conscientious JP and reached his social zenith in 1885, as High Sheriff of Westmorland, having twice failed to be elected as Conservative MP for Kendal. He moved south, to a house called Wharfenden, in Hampshire, in 1889.

Ruskin's stay at Ashfield contributed to the dialogue in *Traffic* between wistfulness and satire. For the house merited parody, but its mistress, the first Mrs Harris, deserved reverence. Similarly, Ruskin would loathe Lunefield, but be grateful for the sympathy of its mistress, the second Mrs Harris.

Ashfield was a monumental affront to Ruskin's 'Lamp of Beauty', being a showpiece for 'One of the worst enemies of modern Gothic architecture. . . the dripstone in the shape of the handle of a chest of drawers, which is used over the square-headed windows of what we call Elizabethan buildings'.[75] But inside was 'the good lady' of Bingley, Harriet Harris; and her personality and suffering moved Ruskin deeply. He wrote after his visit, expressing the hope 'that Mrs Harris is not suffering so much from the weather – though today indeed it is as bad as ever.'[76] When Mrs Harris died in December 1865, Ruskin wrote as follows:[77]

11th December 1865

My dear Sir,

I have received a Keighley paper this morning which brings me very sad news; sad, even to me, almost a stranger – as far as anyone who has ever received the hospitality of an English lady can feel himself a stranger any more, – and in calling myself one, I do not feel as if I said truth. I have past through too much various pain, and have seen too much pain ever to be able to *share* in any sorrow as other men might, and it is a great deal for me to say that anything is sad to me – on the contrary – events have long been to me as they must – one way or another. But I am sorry for this, fully feeling even from the little I knew and saw, and heard, the justice of all the praise given in the ~~slight~~ notice in the journal – and the extent to which the shadow of this loss of yours will be cast around you.

Forgive my hard and cold words,
and believe me always my dear Sir
Faithfully Yours,
J. Ruskin

Harris wrote expressing his thanks; and conveying especially the best wishes of his daughter Ellen. As was conventional in the opening stage of Victorian friendships, Harris forwarded photographs of himself and family. Ruskin found himself sadly at a loss when confronted with these handsome images: 'It makes me glad,' he wrote, 'to think my note could be of the least good to you. . . I am very grateful to you for sending me the photographs. . . If you insist on my sending you a carte of mine, I must – but please don't – I'm very – very ugly: and the little good that's in my eyes, or may be in them sometimes when I'm not half dead, the photograph wholly misses out – and makes a mere ape and horror of me. Please don't ask for it.' Instead of his picture, he preferred to send his new book, *Ethics of the Dust*, 'With sincere regards to Ellen. . . It's very dear and nice of her to recollect me, such a while: I'm very fond of girls – but I never expect them to recollect me beyond 3 days – and it's so pleasant, if they do. I've sent her my last book, today. I hope she may like it a little.'[78]

Ruskin's letter to Alfred Harris of 3 September 1879 is of special interest. Written in convalescence after Ruskin's mental breakdown, it offers solace for the apparent failure of the Bradford Design School; and provides a clue to the symbolic structure of the final chapters of *Modern Painters:*

Brantwood 3rd Sept '79

Dear Mr Harris,

It was very good and thoughtful of you to redeem my little chick from the dispersed effects of the Schools and indeed I was very happy to see it again and pleased still more by the sense of rightness and kindness in which you acted.

Mrs Severn said it might perhaps give you a little pleasure to have a drawing of mine – my book work so breaks the energy that ought to be given to my drawing that I am always too scornful of what I do, to give it to my friends – but I have sent you a little sketch of a Swiss village – Rheinfelden – which – you will see by the inscription on it – seems to me at least as good as I am likely ever to do, and it is not wholly unlike what it was meant for – I shall be very glad if you care to give it portfolio-room.

Joan and Arthur are eloquent of your kindness, and of the beauty of your house. Some day, I hope to have my part in their gratitude and admiration –

Believe me always, Dear
Mr Harris
Faithfully and heartily yours
J. Ruskin[79]

A chief point is that the letter records an exchange of drawings. Harris 'redeems' William Hunt's *Dead Chicken* from the 'dispersed effects' of the Bradford Design School. The new Technical College was coming into being, with its 'well-appointed' design courses. Perhaps this had been the final blow. So Harris sends the Hunt drawing back to Ruskin, who gave it, and in exchange Ruskin gives Harris one of his own drawings: a sketch of Rheinfelden.

In common with every other letter Ruskin wrote, this letter is a creative act. That it brings together the themes of his pair of Bradford lectures goes without saying. But it is more than a codicil to Ruskin's remarks about the Bradford Design School, and about the Bradford Exchange. It is intended as a clue to much more than that. In particular, the letter brings Bradford into a relation with Rheinfelden.

In the fifth volume of *Modern Painters*, Ruskin had chosen to present Kirkstall and Rheinfelden as the termini of Turner's adult consciousness. In so doing, Ruskin was offering his own interpretation of Turner's creative life in relation to the historical life of Europe. Ruskin's preoccupation with these places does not mean he was arguing any aesthetic case for the sketches Turner made there to be valued above any other invaluable evidences of Turner's genius. The Kirkstall sketch of 1797, the Rheinfelden sketches of 1844, are testimonies to the initial, and the ultimate, efflorescence of Turner's creativity: and for Ruskin, gateways into a whole world of contemplation.

In 1844 Turner had meant to cross the Alps; but had been foiled by rain. He withdrew to some small valleys of the Rhine, which he found more interesting than he had expected. The sketches he made there heralded the last and strangest, most transcendentally Turnerian flowering of Turner's style. Of the sketches, Ruskin's favourites were of empty fishing nets at Rheinfelden, with the town as background. He chose two to make plate 82 of *Modern Painters*.

Ruskin chose for the last two Plates of *Modern Painters* (83 and 84) two of his own drawings of Rheinfelden. The second of these – and the final chapter which it illustrates – he calls *Peace*. His footnote makes quite clear the fragile nature of such 'peace'. The drawing is there 'merely to show the kind of scene which modern ambition and folly are destroying throughout Switzerland'.

As Ruskin anticipated, Rheinfelden would join the progressive towns of modern Europe. His editors' footnote of 1905 leaves no room for illusion: 'The subject of Ruskin's drawing can no longer be seen. Rheinfelden has become the centre of salt works and breweries, and has outgrown its old boundaries. The old bridge, however, still stands (in company with a new iron one). The tower shown in the Plate also survives, but the town walls have for the most part been demolished, and the moat is filled up.'[80]

And so, also, in Yorkshire. The crypt of Kirkstall, the other terminus, with Rheinfelden, of Ruskin's imaginative account of Turner's genius, was a shelter from more than the rain. 'And at last fortune wills that the lad's true life shall begin,' Ruskin writes of Turner's first visit to Yorkshire. 'Beauty, and freedom, and peace; and yet another teacher graver than these. Sound preaching at last here, in Kirkstall Crypt, concerning fate and life.'[81]

Twenty years before Turner was born, Kirkstall was surrounded by collieries and quarries. By the mid-Victorian period it was engulfed by the pair of dirty Titans which flanked it; Leeds from the east, and Bradford from the west, ran into each other at Kirkstall. Since Bradford beck emptied itself into the River Aire upstream from Kirkstall, it was Bradford filth that formed the principal constituent of the Kirkstall Abbey weir. Since the prevailing wind thereabouts was the west wind, Bradford filth formed the principal constituent of the patina on the Kirkstall Abbey walls.

Turner died proclaiming that 'the Sun is God'. The Sun by which he worked was fading what he made, was itself collapsing. For nearly thirty years – since he first saw the Turner vignettes in Rogers's *Italy* – Ruskin had been approaching that dearest of all idols, 'the art of Turner'. And now he was ready to see the idol crumble, and to answer the man. 'The Sun is God,' said Turner. No, Ruskin answered, for Turner is more than the sun. His genius was born like Christ in a dark cavern among the cattle, at Kirkstall. Like Christ in the facility of resurrection he drew from the empy fish nets at Rheinfelden a miraculous draught.

By these symbols Ruskin hinted at his own meaning: and prepared to express, as he would do in *Unto This Last*, the sequel to that miraculous draught as its story is told in the last chapter of the Gospel of John. This sequel is Christ's command to Peter: 'Feed my Lambs. . . Feed my sheep'.[82] The God of the Sun, of shepherds and of art is the new Apollo; he is the light of the world. He is Christ, and Christ has told us He is ourselves:[83] 'Man is the sun of the world; more than the real sun. The fire of his wonderful heart is the only light and heat worth gauge or measure. Where he is, are the Tropics; where he is not, the ice-world.'[84]

The corollary is absurd, as well as captivating. It was to Farnley Hall that Turner had sent his account of the Swiss journey of 1844;

not long after, he at last thanked Ruskin for *Modern Painters*, and also praised his tyro sketch of the Falls of Schaffhausen.[85] Ruskin discovered Rheinfelden for himself in 1858. He was bound to make his own account of all it meant to him for the new audience who had replaced the Fawkses – in the hall of Bradford Mechanics' Institute.

Ruskin's letter to Henry Acland dated 'Rheinfelden, 25 May 1858' appeared under that head in their book *The Oxford Museum* of April 1859. It provides an introduction to themes linking 'Modern Manufacture and Design' and 'Traffic'. Ruskin desires 'to make art large and publicly beneficial . . . fixed instead of portable, associating it with local character and historical memory'. He wants 'informative' decoration instead of 'meaningless ornaments'. His analogy with a 'great chorus of music . . . all being ruled in harmony' shows him more kindly disposed than he often was towards the Victorian phenomenon of choral concerts.

Charles Semon, one of Ruskin's reception committee in April 1864, would later that year as Mayor inaugurate the first of the Bradford Subscription Concerts, in which the local choir – which had surprised and delighted London music critics during 1858 – would join with the Hallé orchestra of Manchester. Charles Hallé was in close touch with Ruskin at this time, and had undertaken – with some misgivings – to improve Ruskin's musical education. The Bradford Subscription Concerts, which are still in existence, would allow a wider audience to make better use of St George's Hall than had been possible under the more pretentious and expensive Triennial Music Festivals.

Fittingly, Ruskin's coda to *Traffic* would invite Bradfordians to leave their selfish little kingdoms behind in favour of a broader 'commonwealth' in which life and lives 'will join and increase into one magnificent harmony'. This may stand as tribute to the Bradford Subscription Concerts, and may even have been so intended.[86]

Harris was on the platform with Ruskin during the delivery of both Bradford lectures. His large household at Kirkby Lonsdale was a hive of Ruskinism. Such a clue from the Master's own hand would hardly be missed.

Hunt's *Dead Chicken* was exhibited that winter of 1879–80 at the Fine Art Society's Galleries, New Bond Street. 'Your Hunt drawing of chick,' Ruskin wrote to Harris, 'is I am glad to say much admired.'[87] The exhibition was formed of works by William Hunt and Samuel

Prout. Ruskin wrote the catalogue notes: and Harris's name appeared in the list of contributors. Harris's own William Hunt – a study of variegated plums – was graciously noted by Ruskin as among his 'own favourites' and preferable in his eyes to the William Hunt plums in his own possession. This must have made the catalogue interesting to Harris; and with Ruskin's recent present of a Rheinfelden drawing in his mind Harris would naturally see what Ruskin had to say elsewhere in the catalogue about the Prout drawings of the Rhine. No. 78 was 'An old Rhine Bridge at Rheinfelden'. Ruskin's description reads: 'A favourite Turner subject and drawn and engraved with great care in *Modern Painters*. As a Prout it is inferior. . .' The reader is deflected from Prout towards Turner and Ruskin's symbolic treatment of the Rheinfelden drawings, Turner's and his own, which form the last three plates of *Modern Painters*. If Harris needed any clue as to Ruskin's mood about the Rhine, the note to nos 76 and 77 in the Prout catalogue would put him right. These Prout drawings represent 'Two lovely Rhine realities, when the river was something better than a steam railway'.[88]

The intelligent Mr Harris could hardly help being reminded of the comparision between industrialised Yorkshire and industrialised Switzerland which Ruskin made extempore at the beginning of his original lecture of 1864. That same day, or the day after, Harris took Ruskin across the River Aire from his Bingley house to admire Shipley Glen. Here could be seen evidence for three stages of world history: the morainic deposits from the Airedale glacier, the intriguing mounds formed by the retreat of the lake which succeeded to the glacier,[89] and, bright in the new-quarried freshness of that local honey-coloured sandstone which was the creation of glacier and lake, Saltaire, Titus Salt's great model village with its commodious chapel and huge and efficient mill. Ruskin thanked Harris for the tour, and promised that 'if I ever travel north again I'll come and see you and your glens which I remember with intense pleasure, though I was very ill,' he adds, 'when I saw them with you.'[90] The illness was in part an attack of toothache, not unconnected with his lecture performance.[91] In part, perhaps, 'illness' was also induced by those meditations on Saltaire which would form the climax to *Traffic*. The model mill of *Traffic* with its model workers, is irresistibly evocative of Saltaire. There is no proof that Ruskin had Harris's own gracious neo-Elizabethan home at Bingley in mind in satirising the capitalist's 'beautiful mansion' which is the other half of the *Traffic* picture: but Harris's Ashfield certainly enjoyed many of the amenities of that imaginary paradise. Ruskin's amends were ample, however, for the closing words of *Traffic* involve a tender and moving allusion to a newspaper report of the death of the first Mrs Harris, Ruskin's hostess: and Ruskin made sure that Harris had a clue to this loving testimony. The satire spoke for itself.

Should Harris have mentioned to his guest the fact that Shipley Glen was – for obvious reasons – popularly known as a miniature 'Yorkshire Switzerland', then Ruskin's circle of reflection embracing Bradford and Rheinfelden would be complete. If, as courtesy demanded, Harris accompanied Ruskin to the railway station, and saw him on to the Leeds train which would take him under the walls of Kirkstall Abbey – where Turner had first learnt the lesson of 'fate and life' – then Harris's circle of reflection embracing *Modern Painters, The Oxford Museum, The Two Paths, Unto This Last* and *The Crown of Wild Olive* would be complete.

How far the banker Harris, devout, sensitive, but also a man of the world, would be willing to follow Ruskin's allusions may be questioned. His obituary in the *Kendal Mercury*[92] decribed him as a 'friend of Mr John Ruskin'. Of Harris's business operations it was recorded: 'In all commercial circles the deepest trust was placed in him, and it is not too much to say that it was never betrayed'. There may be good bankers. That Harris and Ruskin could understand each other, even in part, is a mark of the vitality of Victorian culture.

'It is a great pleasure to me to have any occasion to write to you,' Ruskin had told him, 'and to assure you how pleasant my memory of your kindness has always been. . . I am very happy to be of any use and to feel that I am so – being often apt to doubt.'[93]

In a poignant letter from Brantwood to Harris, with a postscript for his wife Anne, Ruskin laid bare the general strength and partial weakness of his own life of creativity and failure:

> Dear Mr Harris,
>
> I am very happy with your nice letter, and to know that I have not offended you.
>
> Of degree of wrong or right; I don't think we need reason, except judicially –
>
> Practically – how much or little does not matter – Gathering or scattering – Serving God or His Enemies, little or much, is the question.
>
> Ever affectionately yours
>
> John Ruskin

> More soon: I've been greatly helped by reading a letter of your wife's about Border ballads. Can she tell me which it is about a girl transforming her lover back[94]

Ruskin's interrogative breaks off too quietly to require a question mark.

Power: John Mitchell

James Burnley, the Bradford writer and journalist, opens his article on 'The Henrys of Manchester and Bradford' of 1887 with a resounding drumroll. Their 'operations', he records, 'extend over all parts of the civilised and uncivilised globe, and [their] well-known establishments at Manchester, Bradford, Huddersfield, Glasgow and Belfast, embrace every branch of our textile industries.'[95] The absolute head of this empire is Mr Mitchell Henry, MP, who resides at Kylemore Castle, Connemara. To the eyes of Alfred Harris who visited it in 1887, Kylemore Castle appears 'white as marble, with its chimneys, towers and battlements, rising above the dense masses of foliage and reflected in the calm waters of the lake'. Mr Henry has a gold medal for his turnips, and most of his thousands of acres take the form of smallholdings in the hands of tenants. On an awesome scale, Mr Henry has notions not dissimilar to those that lay behind Ruskin's Marylebone housing project and the Guild of St George. He wishes to assist his tenants towards independence and the purchase of their own land. He does not intend to lose too much money by his own original captial outlay for drainage, replanting, building and the provision of equipment, but the profit he looks for is a properous re-populated landscape, with Kylemore Castle and his own family, safely enshrined in popular esteem, at its heart. He urges government action along the same lines, if Westminster intends to retain any credibility in Ireland.[96]

In industrial Bradford, at the time of Burnley's article, the executive head of the Yorkshire branch is Henry Mitchell, a Conservative of local yeoman stock and a convert to Wesleyan (i.e. free-will) Methodism. He sells shares in the company to all employees who apply. He is a founding father of Bradford Technical College; he has been Mayor of Bradford and President of the Bradford Chamber of Commerce; and takes his artisans to Paris, in selected groups, to study French goods and training methods. 17,000 miles of textiles pass under his personal responsibility every year.

A powerful organisational brain who served this empire with exemplary distinction was John Mitchell. He was no relation either to Mitchell Henry or Henry Mitchell, nor were they relatives of each other. John Mitchell entered the firm in 1844, becoming a partner in 1847. Till 1868 he managed the Yorkshire branches from Bradford. He then transferred to Manchester as executive head of the whole concern. He died at Lytham St Anne's, the genteelest spot on the Lancashire coast, in 1884. He was a married man with a family, but his obituaries in the *Manchester Guardian* and the *Lytham Press* record no personal mourners at his graveside; only the Vice-President of the Manchester Chamber of Commerce and business connections in Lancashire and Yorkshire.[97]

Mitchell, in his day, had been a radical of the 'old school'. Benevolent and modest, as Ruskin knew him, he had declined the Bradford mayorality in 1861. He was a political supporter of the old gentleman-Chartist Perronet Thompson, and of W. E. Forster, in that politician's early stages of struggle. He would have preferred to see the Bradford Chamber of Commerce spend its money on technical education rather than on the Wool Exchange. There was no supporting voice for this at the time inside the Chamber, but doubtless Henry Mitchell had John Mitchell's approval for his support of the Technical College twenty years later – twenty years too late, some people were saying, casting envious eyes at France and Germany.

Alfred Harris's obituary assumes that the Design School he and Mitchell supported, and which Ruskin officially opened, was the natural precursor of the Bradford Technical College. In the light of complacent hindsight, so it might have been seen. It must have been some satisfaction to John Mitchell to see that Bradford had begun to listen to him, at last; but his health was broken at the end; and perhaps at seventy he had lost some of that fire and freshness which had made him seem 'middle-aged (rather young)' in Ruskin's eyes in 1859.

John Ruskin and John Mitchell first met at the house of Mr and Mrs John Simon, in Cumberland Street, Belgravia, on a Thursday evening of November 1858.[98] John Simon was Medical Officer to the Privy Council. All three men were members of the National Association for the Promotion of Social Science. This joint interest would most likely provide some of the terms of their conversation.

The *Times* and other newspapers were currently telling the story of the Bradford Tragedy. Perhaps this topic was touched on; and perhaps Mitchell chose to counter his town's reputation for mass poisoning by mentioning the acclaim its choral society, of which he was a patron, had won in the capital that summer.

Ruskin had asked his hostess to warn Mitchell in advance that 'I can't come to Sheffield. I must finish Modern Painters'. When he arrived in Cumberland Street Ruskin must have learnt quite quickly from Mitchell that Bradford, not Sheffield, was the town he represented. Mitchell's modesty, his interest in education and foreign affairs, and his evident highmindedness, must all have helped to persuade Ruskin to accept the invitation to come and speak in Bradford after all.

That summer in Turin, Ruskin had stood before Veronese's *Solomon and the Queen of Sheba* and achieved the shocking discovery 'that, positively, to be a first-rate *painter* – you *mustn't* be pious; but rather a little wicked, and entirely a man of the world. I had been inclining to this opinion for some years; but I clinched it at Turin.'[99]

Mitchell was no dilettante like Sir Elkanah Armitage, Ruskin's Manchester host. Advanced liberal John Mitchell seemed to think Ruskin's theories on art and education could have practical bearing on commerce. Only a man like Mitchell – who shared Ruskin's capacity for boyish enthusiasm, and who had a streak of idealism in his nature – could have had any such idea. Mitchell offered Ruskin an opportunity such as Armitage would be far too astute to offer. Thanks to Mitchell,the Venetian lesson of Veronese's *Solomon and the Queen of Sheba* could be taken forward into the life of commercial England.

The ocean-work of the Venetians had given them two great qualities, Ruskin thought. Bradford had one of those qualities in a pre-eminent degree. It needed the other very badly indeed. Mr Mitchell, as a sample of the active Bradford businessman, had one essential Venetian quality. He had pre-eminently 'Presence of Mind', that quality of Venice when she was alive. Antithesis to Venice in every other aspect but that, Bradford did have this quality as Ruskin would define it in the last volume of *Modern Painters*: 'Neither love, nor poetry, nor piety, must ever so take up our thoughts as to make us slow or unready. . . Vigilance, night and day, required of us, besides learning of many practical lessons in severe and humble dexterities.' But Venetians had something else besides presence of mind. They had what Bradford existed to destroy, while it needed it most: a 'great respect for the whole human body'.[100]

The form and needs of the whole human body must be unequivocally related to the art and business of modern manufacturing and design. Such a project presented an almost terrifying challenge. Mr Mitchell did not know what he was asking; but Ruskin, much involved at this time in meditating the life and writings of St Paul, might have found an analogy. Mr Mitchell was standing there in the Cumberland Street drawing-room – the comparison was absurd enough to be energising – like the vision in the night that had appeared to Paul: 'Come over into Macedonia, and help us,' the vision had demanded.[101] Mitchell may not have been much more articulate than that: but his mere asking was enough.

Another aspect of Mitchell's personality which was more ambiguous was a streak of asceticism. Asceticism was a trait Ruskin observed in dedicated and 'effective' men; and it was there to be observed in Mitchell.

Mitchell's asceticism would be revealed in a characteristic outburst over the proposal to treat Lord Palmerston to a banquet in St George's Hall, in 1864. 'Let the inhabitants of Bradford see Lord Palmerston in a full hall,' he said. The banquet would be an elite affair of visiting dignitaries. 'If they had a dinner there would be a lot of clumsy tables and dirty food, waiters running about making a great noise, and other objectionable things. Let us have a feast of reason and a flow of soul.'[102]

There was a great deal in such a man to make Ruskin think. Advanced Liberal, advocate of technical education and international good will, part efficient man of business, part boyish enthusiast, part tetchy old maid. Contrary to Ruskin's expectations, Mr Mitchell was already helping him to finish *Modern Painters*.

What a curiously diminished Bradfordian Mitchell was, in spite of his tremendous qualities, as compared with John Cousen, the engraver, who had worked for Turner, and since the early '40s for Ruskin himself. Cousen lived in Pawson's Road, Norwood, about five miles from the Ruskin house at Herne Hill; but he had been born and reared in Bradford. In his early twenties Cousen had been constrained to leave his old home, a typical West Riding farmhouse, a modest and comely building dating from the seventeenth century. This was in a pleasant spot called Mira Shay, still a leafy place in 1859, though it was less than a mile from Bradford Parish Church.

Cousen was only four years older than Mitchell; but whereas Mitchell represented the modern international world of Bradford business, Cousen was very much a pre-industrial native Bradfordian: modest, diligent, shrewd; retaining the manners and accent of the Bradford countryside.

Ruskin greatly admired John Cousen's work for Turner's *Rivers of France* of 1833–5; he employed Cousen for his own books, and in 1856 could refer to him publicly as 'my good friend'. Cousen was capable, in Ruskin's words, of producing 'perfect and beautiful interpretations' of Turner's work. Thanks to his sensitivity, and his upbringing at Mira Shay, Cousen's work in rendering leaves was particularly fine. In 1859 R. N. Wornum, Ruskin's friend at the National Gallery, would publish *The Turner Gallery*, including engravings by Cousen. It was perhaps while engaged in arranging the Turner drawings at the National Gallery that Ruskin had employed Cousen to make experiments in the fading of water-colours. Cousen conducted his experiments with typical Bradfordian thoroughness. Ruskin found their results conclusive; and decided that henceforth fine water-colours should be protected by screens from direct sunlight.[103]

John Cousen and John Mitchell, between them, most starkly demonstrated what Bradford had been; and what Bradford was becoming.

While Ruskin had been investigating the commercial and imperial history of dead Venice, formidable ascetics like John Mitchell had been making Cousen's Bradford one of the greatest commercial powerhouses of the British Empire. Most particularly they had made Bradford the commercial centre of that part of Yorkshire where, as Ruskin thought, Turner's 'true life' as an artist had begun. To the military ascetics of Austria, and the monastic asceticism of the St Bernard hospice, must be added these curious monetary ascetics of the industrial Pennines. With all their power, the single mindedness of monk, soldier, merchant, had generated the European death of the nineteenth century. They had provided Turner with a landscape.

When Turner's Kirkstall sketch of 1797 is evoked in *Modern Painters*, the same moment that culminates the exhilarations of Turner's youthful wonder also initiates 'sound preaching' about modern 'unsightliness' and the 'ruin' of patient handiwork. It seems very likely that Ruskin knew exactly what he was doing when he employed

John Cousen of Mira Shay to engrave Plate 60 of *Modern Painters*, with its samples of plant species which 'nearly all grow on ruins or neglected ground' (*Works*, VII.124).

No place was better qualified to express Ruskin's notion of the inter-dependence of all the stages, and levels, of a culture than Kirkstall as it had been for a century: a monastic ruin – of that Romanesque-into-Gothic style known as 'Transitional' – interpenetrated by a pastoral enclave barely surviving within an industrialised landscape. It is by a metaphor drawn from Mitchell's world that Ruskin seeks to dignify Turner's acceptance, and transfiguration, of the asceticism of his own vocation. Not beside the Romantic ruin, without the pastoral labour that surrounds it, neither by such labour alone without the implications of unpicturesque industry: but 'full of stern sorrow and fixed purpose the boy set himself to his labour silently and meekly, like a workman's child on its first day at the cotton-mill'.[104] For Turner, the vocation of 'art' was to imitate 'labour', even though their current reversibility denied hope to both.

Ruskin asked himself what should be thought about such things. Was such a society to be tolerated because it had produced its Turner? Should one consent to its continuance – even its worsening – for the sake of these crazy Pre-Raphaelites merely because in some technical aspects they were Turner's heirs? Where does the ghastliness end, and the ludicrousness begin?

When Ruskin arrived at Mitchell's Parkfield House in March 1859, he described it to his father as 'a nice home of the Bowers' Well type'.[105] At Bowerswell Ruskin had married Effie Gray. The word 'nice' has acid connotations; and indeed it describes Mitchell's house exactly. Of a commodious neo-Classic, it strikes one even today as slightly institutional: and not only because it is now part of a nunnery and boarding-school. It is what one would nowadays call 'a company house': designed to impress in a quiet and invincible fashion the solidity of the firm upon business acquaintances. 'The rooms are lofty and large and conveniently situated', run the particulars of sale of 1899. Henry Mitchell, who had taken over the job and house from John Mitchell in 1868–9, had greatly extended John's modest vinery; but doubtless the 'stables, situate at a convenient distance from the house' were there to be admired in 1859, along with the carriage house, harness room and coachman's cottage. The grounds 'tastefully laid out and suitably planted with well-grown shrubs' screened the house from Parkfield Road, a private road off Manningham Lane. The 'domestic offices being entirely cut off from the other part of the house. . . everything is conducive to convenience and comfort throughout.' On his way up to his room, where he hardly dared to stir for fear of activating some of the technological gadgetry that served this comfort and convenience, Ruskin had the pleasure of ascending 'a handsome staircase of easy ascent, lighted by a large Dome window'. A typical trick of neo-Classical decorators had already confronted him in the vestibule: a Corinthian pilaster, split neatly in two; its right half embedded in the left side of the doorway, and *vice versa*.[106]

Mitchell's sympathies lay with Roebuck, Chartist supporter and advocate of state education. As Asa Briggs records, it was foreign affairs rather than home policy which kept British radicalism alive in the 1850s. Mitchell was a friend and propagandist of the Hungarian liberator Kossuth; and one of the many who rushed to London to press the hand of Garibaldi in April 1864.[107]

It is permissible to imagine Mitchell's approval for Ruskin's charge, in *Modern Painters* Volume three, against a government, that of Lord Aberdeen, 'who did not know. . . what war was, or what blood was, or what life was, or truth' when they sent British men to perish in the Crimea. It was Roebuck's censure motion of 1855 'over the condition of the army before Sebastopol' that had toppled the Whig-Peelite administration of Aberdeen and put Palmerston into office. Yet Mitchell, like Ruskin, would also have seen some good in a war directed against the Russian tyrant. A die-hard radical helping to manage a world-wide business empire, Mitchell may have had cause, as Roebuck had, to be grateful for Palmerston's skill in balancing the contradictory British impulses for liberty and expansion, while keeping war at bay, or at least in check. Roebuck had praised Palmerston's foreign policy in 1850. He denounced Palmerston's aggression against China in 1857.[108] Still, it opened a new quarter of the world to A. & S. Henry's.

Keen on technical education, and a friend and election agent of Forster, Mitchell would warm to Ruskin's much-discussed Appendix 7 of the *Stones of Venice*, with its demand for state-subsidised scientific, technical and moral education for all capable of benefiting from it.[109] It is likely Mitchell shared Ruskin and Forster's dismay at the dominance of philology and the classics in the endowed schools. Forster's Endowed Schools Act of 1869, for the West Riding elite, meant getting the endowments of their grammar schools under middle-class supervision for the purpose of non-sectarian science teaching, something they had been impatient for since Lord Eldon's judgment of 1805, made against the governors of Leeds Grammar School, who were forbidden to use their ancient endowments to teach modern subjects. This disastrous precedent killed some schools; thus improving the boarding businesses of others. But till 1869 it was financially unwise for an endowed school to adventure much in science; and by then ignorance had become a habit and the initiative had passed to Germany and America.

It is quite possible that Ruskin's conversations with Mitchell helped to persuade the visitor to be more forthright about international politics. Ruskin wrote a letter from Berlin that June, published with his consent in the *Scotsman*, which hailed the army of the Risorgimento for their glorious protest against the secular tyranny of the Papacy; 'and not one jot of our precious Protestant blood gone to the signature'. Equally likely to appeal to Mitchell was Ruskin's letter in the *Liverpool Albion* of 2 November 1863, denouncing Russian tyranny in Poland and the English bombardment of Kagosima. If Mitchell chose to see Ruskin as a companion in arms – fiery radical in foreign politics; educational reformer; and a believer in universal suffrage – Ruskin had certainly committed himself, on paper, in a way that suggested support for all these causes.[110]

Ruskin got cries of 'Hear, Hear!' at Bradford in April 1864 for his denunciation of the 'black eagles' – the military tyrannies of Prussia, Russia and Austria. Perhaps his words were specifically meant to appeal to John Mitchell; just as his praise of Waterhouse was meant to entice Alfred Harris. Unfortunately, it seems that Mitchell was too busy with Garibaldi to attend Bradford Mechanics' Institute that night. He was not, apparently, on the platform, though he formed part of the reception committee. Two days before, 19 April, he was in London, presenting an address to Garibaldi.[111]

In the late 1850s Ruskin was passing through a period when his reputation was high; and his style, in public pamphlet and letter, somewhat dogmatic. Thus, in his letter of 1857, published 1858, and widely admired, on the Oxford Examinations for Associate in Arts – known to dons and journalists as the 'Middle-Class Examinations' – Ruskin was certain that, in history teaching, 'the class of manufactures produced by a given city at a given date should be made of more importance in a student's mind than the humours of the factions that governed it'.[112] To write thus was to gain a reputation for outspoken realism in the northern industrial towns. When it came to art, Ruskin's voice, in 1858, was at the service of the Pre-Raphaelites. The Royal Academy was not interested. But the Liverpool Academy, less provincial because nearer to the industrial power centres and to America, was. Ruskin, when he came to finish *Modern Painters*, could put the Pre-Raphaelites in their place; as admirable but limited interpreters of their day, which appeared to be passing. But to a busy man like Mitchell, Ruskin's message of 1858 to the Liverpool Academy, picked up in a newspaper report or at second hand, was all too memorable: 'Since Turner's death I consider that any average work from the hand of any of the four leaders of Pre-Raphaelitism (Rossetti, Millais, Hunt, John Lewis) is singly, worth, at least *three* of any other pictures whatever by living artists'.[113]

After his address to Garibaldi, Mr Mitchell turned his attention to art. On 28 April 1864 he knocked on the door of Rossetti's studio.

Rossetti was anxious lest the art market at Bradford had reached saturation point: the dealer Gambart having recently 'hauled in' a cool £5,000 in Bradford. Ruskin had his uses, but there were limits. As the editors of his letters record, Rossetti's relations with Bradfordians were characterised by the fact that they were 'astute commercials' who were wise to Rossetti's 'cleverness in bargaining', and to his habit of delaying 'everything but the question of payment'.[114]

Cash payment seems indeed the only nexus that joins Rossetti to his West Riding 'patrons'. In his labouredly boyish letters to Ford Madox Brown Rossetti tended to patronise John Mitchell, who purchased a watercolour and an oil from him: yet enjoyed haggling with him, and was prepared to write an obsequious explanation, in September 1865, of his delay in finishing the spectral fantasy *Venus Verticordia*. Mitchell, who had already paid, was constrained to wait four more years.[115] The artist's abusive letter to Dunlop of Bingley, forms an alarming contrast. The latter's 'dirty conduct' in not financing Rossetti's project for a picture on the Dantesque theme of the 'Boat of Love' received harsh treatment from the disappointed painter, who called him 'weakling' to his face, and 'Demon' behind his back. Rossetti even added the gratuitous fiction that the commission had involved him in a journey to Florence – a city he never visited out of his dreams.[116] Dunlop was the first purchaser of two of Rossetti's enticing earlier works: *The First Madness of Ophelia* of April 1864; and *Love's Greeting* of *c.* 1861. These Dunlop handed over in part exchange to Messrs Pilgeram and Lefevre, in 1872, in order to get his hands on the oppressive oil of that date: *The Bower Meadow*. He had the taste to regret his deal almost immediately.[117] But he seems to have leant rather to Bonington, Prout, David Roberts, de Wint, with a Millais – *Caller Herrin'* – a Holman Hunt, *The Young Lantern Maker of Cairo*, and a couple of William Hunts for good measure. He apparently acquired at least two Turner watercolours – of *Whitehaven*; and *Hatfield Castle*. [118] By the 1870s, his neighbour Henry Mason had taken up the vogue for Alma-Tadema, and would soon be heading the vogue for Cecil Lawson.[119]

Rossetti could ill afford abuse. In a review of Mitchell's 'not quite finished' *Venus* which appeared in the *Athenaeum* on 21 October 1865, F. G. Stephens saw her as a figure 'of the true Renaissance, that glorious Indian summer when art halted awhile before it fell completely'. Ambiguous praise from one founder member of the Pre-Raphaelite Brotherhood to another. Could there be malice lurking in the mind of 'Stephens chivalrous and bland' – as Christina had once dubbed him?[120] Speaking generally of his old friend, he added, 'Mr. Rossetti exhibits his pictures in his studio and on the walls of his employers – nowhere else'. A less chivalrous man might have spoken of a hireling privately advertising himself. Mitchell would have preferred an animal picture. Perhaps like Ruskin's other Manningham Lane acquaintance, Mr H. Jones of the Yorkshire Rifles, he would have been happy with a 'Landseer Dog'.[121] But there was little question of Mitchell's 'taste' – such as it was – affecting Rossetti. Arthur Symons saw the result – among others of its type – as 'lunar, spectral, an unintelligible menace'.[122] Protruding naked from a heap of roses, but fenced from us by honeysuckles of wire and wax, the Venus pouts with dully bloody mouth; its eyes slumber with no invitation. There is an unpleasant looking dart in the right hand, an apple in the left – neither of which is held with any conviction. At the side of the inescapable skull, with its long hanks of hair, a frantic blue bird pecks mulberries. Butterflies stick to the figure's halo of melted butter, to the dart, to the skin of the apple. Helen Maria Madox Rossetti suggests that the picture, which began well, was ruined by obsessive over-painting.[123] Ruskin's policy of rescuing Rossetti's works from the artist the moment they came literally 'up to scratch', appears to have been a useful one.[124]

Humbert Wolfe, minor poet and impressive Board of Trade expert on labour relations, himself originating from the Bradford commercial classes, thus recalled the genre in 1926, the year of the general strike:[125]

> Alas! the coward tried
> to make of the life he feared a secret bride.
> And this imposture wears the delicate shape
> of a Greek woman beside the business ape. . .
> She may have wings at her hair, her lips, maybe,
> fain the cold line of immortality. . .

She has turned his own generation into 'aching stone'.

In healthier times, as Ruskin saw them, Correggio, master of light and colour, had been able to give that mastery its fullest expression in the painting of human flesh. Titian, perhaps supremely, had bequeathed specific testimony of 'this clay that burns, this colour that changes'. He might paint a gentleman or a fisherman, but always the man. He had less need than Correggio to resort to 'mythology' – or undressing – as a means of rediscovering the essential beyond the contemporary. For Holbein, painting the town-bred merchant Georg Gisze, the contemporary and the essential had been one. It was a modester enterprise, but superbly valid nonetheless. Here was the merchant in his place, 'his common work laid out before him', with no posturing after assumed interest or dignity.[126] All three painters had known the difference between being alive and not being alive. No metaphor could escape that difference. For Ruskin, they were the true heirs of that Greek vitality and intelligence which was the true strength of the Renaissance. The nineteenth-century 'art' nude, on the other hand, typified the guilty indulgence of what was denied in a 'life' that shrank from an undraped leg, even when it belonged to a table. Human flesh, excluded from the acknowledged light of life, became material for an art of death which was the death of art; or, more properly, it was involved in that nineteenth-century vulgarity which, as Ruskin defined it, was 'death mingled with life'. Like the goddess of that vulgarity, Britannia Agoraia, such art was a 'Nonsense'.[127]

The older art took some time to die. The ineptitude and sensationalism of William Etty's nudes, for example, was offset for Ruskin so far as his flesh was not 'absolute clay'.[128] He had not quite cut off the living substance from the colours of nature's sunshine, and turned it into a metaphor of the grave.

When Etty was buried in St Olave's churchyard in his native York in 1847, tasteful demolition of intervening wall contrived to frame his neo-Classic tomb in a ruined arch of St Mary's Abbey. It was the very end of a certain taste. By 1859 George Gilbert Scott and his mercantile patron Akroyd would pretend to 'realise' St Mary's Abbey anew in Halifax, annihilating in the process all the vitalities that had once built it, and all those others who might have built otherwise. Almost necessarily, this parody of St Mary's Abbey was dedicated to All Souls, and its chief use, for Akroyd, was to be buried in.[129]

Rossetti would be equally eager to have done with 'a flesh and blood appearance'.[130] 'I really do not think the large picture chargeable with anything like Ettyism which I detest', is how he described John Mitchell's *Venus Verticordia*. 'Drapery of any kind I could not introduce without quite killing my own idea.'[131] The problem was to achieve an undressed Venus who should not, however, be naked. There is some doubt as to whether it was Mitchell who insisted on the cover-up, or Rossetti. His original design of Mary Magdalene for the window of Bradford Parish Church had certainly looked to local Puritans as though she had not yet repented, and they demanded a more sufficient costume, which Rossetti supplied.[132] But when it came to an easel painting, any asceticism of Mitchell's would have found an ally in Rossetti's confessed incompetence with the undraped form. In the event, he had recourse to a device common at the time for concealing the offensive garden goddesses of a less ambiguous age: honeysuckle.[133] Mitchell paid for quantities of the stuff, which Rossetti laboriously copied as it withered. In earlier versions the features were realised from those of a handsome cook. Titian might have immortalised her into herself, realising also in her something of the majesty of the mother of life. As it was, Rossetti's 'own idea' – realised, in the end, from the features of Alexa Wilding – merely served to fan the appetites of Mr Valpy, who found a naked arm indecent, and who in Rossetti's human menagerie occupied the cage labelled 'Vampire'.[134]

Negotiations between Mitchell and Rossetti had begun, ironically enough, in the latter's studio precisely one week after the delivery of Ruskin's second Bradford utterance. Mitchell, it seems, had wanted something 'effective as a room decoration' – quite as though he had attended to the Design School lecture of 1859. Ruskin detested the resulting picture, and told Rossetti so, in a series of letters of 1865 in which affectionate irony and cool criticism turned into cold contempt and calculated rage before ebbing away in elegiac hauteur. 'There are two methods of laying oil colour which can be proved right', he wrote, 'each for its purpose – Van Eyck's (or Holbein's) and Titian's (or Correggio's): one of them involving no display of power of hand, the other involving it *essentially* and as an element of its beauty. Which of these styles you adopt I do not care. . . you are, it seems, under the (at present) *fatal* mistake of thinking that you will ever learn to paint well by painting badly – i.e., coarsely. . . No great painter ever allowed himself. . . to paint ill. . . What he could not paint easily he would not paint at all. . . You knew exactly as much about Correggio as I knew in 1845. . . I purposely joined him with Titian to poke you up. I purposely used the word 'wonderfully' painted about those flowers. [Mitchell's honeysuckle] They were wonderful to me, in their realism; awful – I can use no other word – in their coarseness. . . I tell you the people you associate with are ruining you.'[135]

Ruskin specifically alludes to one of these 'people' as a 'mere blackguard'. This was the photographer William Downey, who had taken some photographs of Ruskin and Rossetti. One of these shows Ruskin seated in Rossetti's chair. This became what Ruskin called 'a visible libel upon me going about England'. To any mind not perfectly pure the picture must have provoked a good deal of sniggering and speculation. For it shows an unfortunate protuberance which suggests, at first glance, that Ruskin's wife had no grounds whatever for alleging congenital impotence against him. But – and here the fun brightens – on second glance it is revealed as only a Priapan fold in the thick material of Ruskin's trousers. Sadly, it is one of the best pictures of his earnest intellectual face. But it is a pity his hand is under his waistcoat, as though endeavouring to find his heart.[136]

Venus Verticordia – and Downey's photographs – brought on a rift between Ruskin and Rossetti which was never healed. The powers of capitalist, artist and photographer had conspired to declare Ruskin incapable.

Rossetti was currently taking up again *Beata Beatrix*, his famous evocation of Lizzie Siddal, who killed herself in 1862. He had begun it many years before her death. He was trying to interest Ellen Heaton with it during 1863; but would finish it – for Hon. Mrs William Cowper-Temple – only in 1869.[137] Love is as visible in it as obsession to the point of sickness is visible in *Venus Verticordia*. Mitchell's not-very-blessèd damozel leans over no 'gold bar of heaven'. At least, it may once have been gold, but those honeysuckles have covered it with quite a different effect – as though in pursuing and killing his own talent the erstwhile Pre-Raphaelite '. . . had made the emparadisèd spirits pewk'/from their jeweled terrace' (Pound, *Canto X*).

Rossetti could have little use for Ruskin after that – though he was amiable enough to plunder the white roses of Denmark Hill to set off that other Thyestean cracker – *Lady Lilith*, of 1868. Unconscionably repainted 1872–3, the picture now consists of a prettily patterned corner of white roses, and a large expanse of rather vapid female.[138]

Ruskin had helped Ellen Heaton to spend wisely. She acquired a number of Rossetti's magical early watercolours,[139] and commissioned two pictures from Arthur Hughes. '*That was a Piedmontese* . . .' expressed, if limply, her interest in Italian liberation. *The Dismissal of Romney* became in Hughes's hands one of the most poignant evocations of the Victorian difficulty. Miss Heaton was disappointed of course – she wanted something more animated. But as Ruskin reminded her, 'fiery depths' were not in Hughes's line. Based on a scene from *Aurora Leigh*, the picture became popularly, and on the whole appropriately, known as *The Tryst.* [140] John Mitchell, however, does not 'need' Ruskin's careful stewarding; and Rossetti no longer 'needs' a patron whose only qualifications were moderate funds and a liking for some of the things he could once do. Mitchell's purchase is 'free' from what Ruskin in *Traffic* called the 'only morality' – taste. Rossetti is by the same token free to sell a discoloured fantasy to a man not sure what he wants – being as much ashamed of his provincial taste for animal pictures as he is of the 'common work' that makes him the good man he is – but who has money enough for anything. Not for nothing did Rossetti give Ford Madox Brown this typical advice about a favourite model in April 1864: 'So just box her up, and don't let fellows see her, as I mean to have first shy at her, in the way of sitting'. His words mean the model is to be coffined as a rarity, and exhumed as an Aunt Sally. Mitchell's was set up in his new Manchester home in 1869; fourteen years after Courbet, whom Rossetti despised, had resurrected the art of figure-painting with *The Studio*.[141]

Rossetti's cockney recidivism is continuous with the provincial reaction it subserves. A life-size statue of a healthy naked woman, erected in Bradford Parish Church to commemorate William Sharp (died 1833), a local man who had been a distinguished gynaecologist at St Bartholomew's Hospital, London, was bundled into the vestry during the Gothic 'restoration' of the early '60s.[142] A year or two later, Ellen Heaton's doctor brother visited Rossetti's studio. What he found offended his medical, and artistic, sensibilities. 'He has only one style of female face which he continually repeats; the attitude is unnatural, the neck particularly distorted, the shoulders high. . .' John Deakin was old-fashioned enough to prefer Titian.[143]

It was appropriate, and fortunate, that Rossetti's real creative relation to the industrialised north of England should be made for him some years after his death – by L. S. Lowry. The Rossetti woman would provide a personally needed antithesis to Lowry's own very different form of artistic disingenuousness. His elegantly malicious canvases are sometimes painful, never morbid or trivial. They make beauty and tragedy out of the Coketown black and red. They evoke the vitality of that industrial world which craved Rossetti to minister to its disease. Thanks to such homoeopathy, the mature Lowry was able to fill his works with life.[144] They are often crowded with figures brilliantly conventionalised after the last – and first – of living conventions, that of a 'clever child's way of teaching itself to draw', as Ruskin put it in *Fors Infantiae*, the penultimate letter of *Fors Clavigera* (1884). He appended some drawings by a child of six, in case anyone should be interested.[145] Picasso, too, might have looked at them with love.

Sacrifice: James Lobley

James Lobley was born at Hull in 1828; and died in 1888 in his home at 4 Belle Vue, Manningham, after suffering a paralytic stroke in Darley Street.[146] It was perhaps his principal patron Alfred Harris who appended to Lobley's obituary in the *Bradford Observer* his 'regret that the possessor of such great talent should have passed away and have been so slightly recognised as he had been by the people of his adopted town'. Some amends have been made recently by the research of Yvonne Deane and Caroline Krzesinska, which enabled the mounting of a Lobley exhibition in the Cartwright Hall, Bradford, in the spring of 1983. Even so, knowledge of this interesting genre painter remains sketchy.[147]

Lobley's mother came from Lincolnshire, and he spent his adolescence and early manhood in Leeds, where he was the most promising pupil of the Art School master there, Claude Lorraine Nursey, himself a Suffolk man and a pupil of Wilkie.[148] But there is significance also in the fact of Lobley's birth and early upbringing in Daltry's Court, Dagger Lane, Hull; for Hull was the country's most consistently radical constituency; despite its official but rarely used nomenclature, 'Kingston-upon-Hull'. Andrew Marvell, John Wilkes and David Hartley junior were numbered among its MPs. That Lobley's father felt at home in this tradition is suggested by the fact that in 1839 James's new brother was christened 'Washington'.[149] Relations between England and the United States were not good at the time,[150] and there is a touch of home-grown defiance in the Hull coal-dealer and currier's choice of this name for his son. He was doubtless aware that Thomas Paine had dedicated his *Rights of Man* to Washington.

The support which the Harris banking family extended to Lobley was part of their extraordinarily broad-minded Conservatism: which ran not only to helping to maintain Ragged Schools and an Isolation Hospital; but to patronage of the Chartist sympathiser Ben Preston, 'poet of the poor', and of the blacks of the Southern States, faced with emancipation and starvation after the Civil War. Lobley himself had a fondness for church interiors, perhaps dating from his childhood near the grand perpendicular Holy Trinity Church, Hull. His painting *The Dole*, exhibited at the Royal Academy in 1867, and bought by Alfred Harris, shows an interior freely interpreted from that of Stow church Lincolnshire, his mother's county. The kindly, strong-faced parson who is handing bread to the poor is thought to be a portrait of Lobley's father. Affection for both his parents must have been part of Lobley's motive in painting the picture. Another motive must have been an affection for the past, for the painting shows certain details in the church which were being eradicated even as Lobley was making his studies; and the ceremony of the Dole, which he records with great compassion, had actually ceased a quarter of a century before, the funds of the charity having run dry. All of this suggests that a certain conservatism was intermingled with radicalism in the sympathies of the Lobley family. This would help to make Lobley an acceptable drawing-master and companion for the children of Alfred Harris. Besides Washington, James had a brother Robert. One of these brothers apparently became a naval captain. James also had three sisters: Emma, Sarah and Elizabeth. In 1853 James Lobley himself married a Pudsey widow, Mrs Ellen Whiteley, a shoemaker's daughter. They were both twenty-five. By 1859, they had four children: Ann, James Jennings, Arthur Lister and Helen Lister. Need as much as inclination may have inspired Lobley's acceptance of the post of Design Master at Bradford Mechanics' Institute, in 1856. He also took portrait commissions, and sculpture work with the Leeds firm of Bromley. He seems to have had a studio at this time close to the Parish Church at Kellett House on the Bradford High Stret,[151] amid a cluster of degraded but still picturesque vernacular buildings.

The great success of Lobley's pupils at the Mechanics' Institute school drew the attention and support of Alfred Harris and Louis Tylor, the brother-in-law and brother respectively of Ruskin's geological friend Alfred Tylor. Lobley was appointed Master of the new Design School, above Fattorini's in Victoria Buildings. He would most likely sympathise with the social concerns of Ruskin's inaugural lecture of March 1859 (delivered in fact a month or so after the school had begun work). It is to Lobley's credit that he attempted, from agreement or inspiration, an art of contemporary life which, as Ruskin desired, should neither trivialise nor flatter its subject.[152]

The years between 1859–65 were busy and important ones for Lobley. Though he never lost interest in Wilkie-like genre scenes, with small figures arranged in a stage-like space, he was at this time undergoing a partial conversion towards a more Pre-Raphaelite style of painting and subject matter. He would have the opportunity to study Hunt's *Light of the World* at its Bradford exhibition in 1859; and works by Millais, Rossetti, Hughes and Ford Madox Brown at the Bradford Old Exchange exhibition of 1860, which he helped to organise. He was also evolving a rational, step-by-step method of design teaching. At the International Exhibition of 1862, Lobley gave advice to the jury concerned with metalwork. Alfred Tylor was the Deputy Chairman and Reporter. He seized the opportunity to publish an appraisal of Lobley's teaching methods at the Bradford Design School, which provoked great interest among the foreign jurymen.[153]

Lobley's pupils, it seems, rivalled 'the pupils of the Royal Academy in excellence of drawing'. They worked for two and a half hours every evening, after a day's work; the 'progressive' tendency of their three-year course being 'explained at every stage' by the man Ruskin called 'an excellent and zealous master'. The subjects from which Lobley's principles were illustrated were 'selected as far as possible from such natural objects as are most likely in real or conventional shapes to constitute leading features in their after-practice'. Lobley was a great believer in 'success through knowledge', and would neither let his students endeavour subjects that were beyond them, nor let them tire by mechanical repetition of one subject. The youths studied the effects of various kinds of light on various surfaces, and learnt by experiment how these affected colours. The foundational work in drawing and shading led on to the study of construction, and the 'analysis of elements excitive of impressions of strength, richness, luxury, delicacy, sadness, frivolity, gaiety, grossness, weakness, purity, action and repose'. The 'delicacy, power and precision of the students' work have on more than one occasion, elicited the marked admiration of Mr. Ruskin'. Ruskin's description of Lobley as 'excellent and zealous'[154] shows why he admired him and why he feared for him. Excellence in art, in Ruskin's definition, is that quality admired by artists, where amateurs admire only beauty. Excellence, in particular, connotes the conquering of difficulty.[155] As for 'zealous', Lobley was a man subject to apoplexy who made great demands on himself, and perhaps on others.

A great boon to Lobley's new Design School was the participation of Bradford's new Designers' Art Association. These men employed a gardener, who distributed about the schoolroom at weekly meetings 'wild and other plants in bloom'. The established designers acted as informal tutors, taking tyros under their wing for special advice and encouragement. Lobley threw his heart into the venture, reading and illustrating papers on ornament and colour harmony. A study dating from his sojourn at the Harris home at Kirkby Lonsdale in the '70s gives some idea of the vitality of his work under speed. It was dashed off merely to show how to paint shadows thrown by corn-stooks.[156] It is a lively landscape sketch, sufficiently fresh and charming to make one wish to see more. While master of the Bradford Design School, Lobley also arranged competitions in applied design, and at first these met with a full and lively response.

What seems to have killed the school's early promise was the discouragement it incurred from the manufacturers, 'who, yielding to their jealousies of each other, were in constant fear lest processes each had found most profitable might be communicated to his disadvantage during conversation or discussion'. Harris and other gentlemanly patrons of the school appear to have been 'surprised' at this jealousy; and unable to understand why the principal material beneficiaries of improved design, the manufacturers, were anxious that a teaching arrangement which worked so well should be discontinued.[157] Harris, Louis Tylor and Lobley must have been in fierce agreement with Ruskin's denunciation of 'jealousy' in Bradford in 1864. Also against the school, in the eyes of most manufacturers, was Lobley's modest claim (very much in accord with Ruskin's lecture of 1859) that any benefits resulting to trade would be 'prospective rather than immediate'. His backers urged him to bring the influence of the institution to bear, and quickly, 'on the passing requirements of the trade'. In addition to the night classes for artisans, Lobley was expected to give day time lessons to lady amateurs.

Under all these pressures Lobley's health broke down. He withdrew 'south' for a year's convalescence during 1865–6 in the company and perhaps at the expense of a Mr Lister, a relative of Alfred Harris. By the standards of the *Bradford Antiquary*, which supplies this information, 'south' may not mean very far south. Lobley is known to have studied buildings in Lincolnshire, Derbyshire, Warwickshire, Leicestershire and Bedfordshire. A sketch book of 1873 suggests that Lobley may have accompanied the Harris family at that time on a trip to the continent: it includes drawings of foreign scenes, made for the second Mrs Harris, to demonstrate rules of composition and colour.[158] Another example of the ingenuity of the 'excellent and zealous' Mr Lobley was a leather sketching wallet which he designed to rest on a shooting stick. His talents were not wasted on the Harris family, who were well able to appreciate him, but it is lamentable that most middle-class Bradfordians were indifferent, or even hostile.

On returning to Yorkshire in 1866, Lobley set up a studio at Sycamore Cottage, Brighouse. Like Bradford's leading musician, Mr Jackson,[159] Lobley had added to his commitments of 1859–65 by teaching at Bradford's Germanic High School. It was to the resurrected Design School of 1866, set up in the premises of this school on Hallfield Road, that Alfred Harris, Louis Tylor and other Lobley supporters now transferred their patronage. Lobley may have continued a connection with this school and its pupils. This would explain the *Bradford Antiquary's* claim that Lobley's efforts to teach design to the working classes failed, and that his school became an academy for the young and prosperous. Lobley and Harris bombarded South Kensington with complaints against what they regarded as its stultifying official system, ensconced at Bradford in the Mechanics' Institute school run by Lobley's pupil and inferior rival, John Sowden. But it is doubtful whether Lobley ever ran a formal school after 1865. His purpose in moving to Sycamore Cottage was to become a full-time artist on his own account. 'Out of the 13 paintings exhibited by Lobley at the Royal Academy from this Brighouse address' only four can now be located: '*The Dole, Stow Church*, exhibited in 1867; *Little Nell Leaving the Church (The Old Curiosity Shop)* of 1867; *The Free Seat* of 1869 and *Ancient and Modern* of 1871. *The Passing Bell* exhibited in 1865 was rediscovered in the 1970s but has since disappeared, and *Fancies in the Fire*, exhibited in 1868 was last heard of in 1954.'[160] *Ancient and Modern* is a charming exercise in colour, showing a daughter of Alfred Harris and Anne Meryon in Huguenot dress besides a piece of tapestry. *The Dole* and *The Free Seat* combine the Wilkie fondness for groups of genre figures with an '"all over" treatment' of detail typical of the Pre-Raphaelite trend.[161] There is a dignified, even stern, compassion, about these pictures, however, which avoids the merely sentimental or anecdotal 'interest' of some of those technically more facile painters who had helped to form – or deform – popular expectations about genre painting by the time Lobley's work reached the Academy walls.[162] Now that the worship of 'sentiment' and the fetish of 'tactile values' which succeeded it have found their level, Lobley deserves to be remembered as a genre painter who repays attention. The most 'Pre-Raphaelite' picture of his which is known is *Little Nell*. Carefully studied and painted, without being 'morbid' – either technically or in expression – it raises Lobley altogether above the level of what is usually implied by the category 'provincial Victorian genre' painter. It is even better than that, for it dignifies each and every one of those mistreated expressions.

The Dole was exhibited at the Royal Academy in 1867. The setting is Stow Church, Lincolnshire: but Lobley took great liberties with the interior, providing a pillar and a coloured window to improve his composition.[163] The window, and some of the fabrics depicted, may reflect Lobley's interest in applied design. The row of wooden pegs fixed to the pillar and intended for sodden cloaks or overcoats helps the movement of the parson's extended arm. It also provides a slight but distinct barrier between the acquiescent poor to the right of the picture and the telling commentary to the left. There is an unemphatic suggestion of pathos, too, in its reminder of exterior weather conditions very different from the blue sky glimpsed through the door. There is a touch of Wilkie in the old men; and a memorable image is provided by an elderly woman, in blue scarf, spotted with white: grim face set, eyes closed, working hands clenched as she holds her apron ready for the bread. Resolute in dejection, she is a successful realisation of the kind Ruskin tried, and failed, to draw in Munich in 1859. He admitted himself defeated by the 'pose' of a peasant woman in prayer, still more by the face: 'I cannot make it more ugly and keep any expression,' he confided to his notebook.[164] It was a common failing. Lobley's capacity for conveying these elderly figures without a shadow of condescension or sentimentality is enough to make the picture distinctive.

To the left of Lobley's main scene, beyond coat-hanger, pillar, and the bread on the lid of the font, is depicted a confrontation of quite a different kind from the act of public charity on the right. A girl, her figure forming an extension to the mass of the old font, is shown with head turned away from us, observing, at a sufficient distance, a prim mother in striped skirt, grey cloak, carrying a prayer book, who ushers her daughter into the cloudless day. This second child wears a pork-pie hat, complete with feather, as in Ruskin's Camberwell lecture from *The Crown of Wild Olive*.[165] She has the statutory sweet profile, auburn hair and prayer book. She is thought to have been modelled either on Lobley's own daughter Ann, or on Amy, the daughter of Alfred Harris.

This memorable juxtaposition – the child waiting for bread turning to look after her more approved contemporary – echoes effectively Ruskin's unforgettable measuring in *Work*, of the tiny immensity between charity and justice. If Lobley regretted that the picturesquely charitable scene of the bread dole was no longer enacted in Stow Church, there is also a suggestion of a new plea for justice in the juxtaposition of these two little girls – the one leaving the church on her way to Sunday dinner; the other firmly anchored by the font, the 'single feature in the church accurately portrayed by Lobley'.[166] That charity will remain in abeyance till it is newly founded on the bedrock of justice, is Ruskin's theme in *Work*. For him, and for Lobley, this was a truth too important to be conveyed other than quietly. Alfred Harris, who bought the picture, was clearly not a man to be impressed by the sugary or the strident.

It was Louis Tylor who purchased Lobley's *The Free Seat*, which was exhibited at the Royal Academy in 1870.[167] It presents a telling frieze of figures in the 'free seat' set aside for the respectable poor in the days of rented pews. The abolition of pew rents was a favourite campaign of conservative reformers, such as those who sponsored the new Broad Church venture of Holy Trinity, Bingley. Lobley's poor are posed in a framework made up of crumbling medieval tombs, and the remnants of the wooden screen of a private pew of post-Reformation date. In one sense the people represent the present occupying the physical remnants of a vanished past; in another sense their stillness – and here is the strength of a limited painter who knows his own limitations – suggests that they have been there for ever. Over the poorbox to the extreme right is the pious motto in Gothic script: 'Remember the Poor'. There is a simple didacticism in that, but the thoughtful youth whose gaze in part directs us towards the lettering, also directs us beyond it, for he is partly in thought, partly gazing at the light coming through the window. 'For the poor always ye have with you'[168] is the text that would spring to the mind of any ordinarily educated Victorian. The boy seated immediately below the poor box on the downgraded hassock – obviously no longer fit for the knees of the more affluent members of the congregation – has his eyes closed in an expression that suggests his mind is at least partly on something fierce and juvenile like catapulting sparrows. And then there is the moral and physical effort of neither eating the apple nor letting it go. His dilemma would have given a Victorian reader of the bible and the classics some food for thought, also.

The art-school still life of the stool, with shawl, bible and spectacles is a frail barrier of privacy between the row of figures and any merely idle spectator. It also suggests the sermon is in progress. Has the preacher dipped into the Sermon on the Mount recently?

Despite a certain stiffness in the drawing, and the 'rich hot browns' of the colouring, there is real mastery of expression in the carefully and intelligently observed faces, with their suggested degrees and kinds of listening, nowhere quite free from the preoccupation with daily worries or concerns; nowhere quite free from a certain benumbed blankness which may hide little or much. They are – as Lobley's models must have been – people who have been sitting a long while under observation. Lobley's record of them imposes no contrived archness of whimsical story-telling; no tit-bits to feed moral superiority or to supply anecdotal intrigue. Lobley merely gives us the privilege of coming to the threshold of their collective presence. He is a Puritan and a provincial among 'artists broadly influenced by Pre-Raphaelite technique'[169]– and he gains much by all these qualifications. Beside this picture, even Ruskin's prose seems overly empurpled, when he writes: 'it is not in the high church pews, where the gay dresses are, but in the church free seats, where the widows' weeds are, that you may see the faces that will fit best between the angels' wings, in the church porch'. But then, those words had been crafted for the attention of the Members of the Architectural Association, in Lyon's Inn Hall, jaded with 'many merry parties' over Christmas.[170]

Lobley was clearly fond of children. They appear regularly in his water colour drawings of church interiors; and his drawings of cottage interiors, too, show a fondness for domestic life. A charming watercolour of 1877 shows a group of children as Lobley must have liked to see them and as they could not be seen in Bradford: happy, healthy and out of doors in the countryside, excitedly preparing for the celebration of *A Village Guy Fawkes*.[171] Three of his own sons, with less distinction, would follow in his footsteps: James Jennings Lobley (1855-1943) became a pianist and portraitist, Arthur Lister Lobley (1857-1927) a professional painter and art teacher, and Louis Tylor Lobley (1866-1945) an art teacher. The choice of 'Arthur Lister' as Christian names for his son suggests that Lobley's 'Mr. Lister' was Arthur Lister, the Bradford wool merchant whose brother was the great surgeon Joseph Lister.[172] One at least of Lobley's Bradford Design School students, A. Megson, achieved a place on the walls of the Royal Academy, in 1865, with a picture called *Autumn Gathering*.[173] Less is known of Lobley's three other children: Ann, Alfred Harris and Helen Lister. Alfred Harris Lobley was so christened not long after Alfred Harris had bought Lobley's *The Bellringer* of 1860, a highly finished watercolour in which the artist had indulged his love of old carved wood and stone and his fascination with the motif of a single preoccupied figure in a church interior.[174]

Helen was known in Lobley's family as 'Nellie', and it was she who posed for what is undoubtedly the best painting by Lobley which has come to light: *Little Nell Leaving the Church*.[175] This was exhibited with *The Dole* at the Royal Academy in 1867. Harris bought *The Dole*, and Louis Tylor bought *Little Nell*, for £300. It was possibly this second painting that Ruskin 'complimented', as the *Bradford Antiquary* records in its rambling and unspecific way, adding that *The Dole* aroused great interest. Ruskin visited the Academy Exhibition three times that year, but left no record of his impressions. His cousin Joan was with him on one of these visits; and she may later have conveyed any compliments to members of the Tylor or Harris families.[176]

Lobley was clearly attracted to Dickens's evocation of the old church and graveyard where little Nell makes her home, and meets her death, in *The Old Curiosity Shop*.[177] Ruskin's powers of analysis remain helpful to the modern reader who is trying to clear away the heaps of sentimentality and cynicism which stand between him and an appreciation of an intelligent Victorian's response to this theme. 'The temptation to weak writers of this order of subject is especially great, because the study of it from the living – or dying – model is so easy, and to many has been the most impressive part of their own personal experience.' There is astringency, as well as compassion, in that. Ruskin's own sentiment on this theme is rarely without its strong vein of common sense, despite his love for the early dead Rose La Touche. On Little Nell, he says, 'I could count the like among my best-loved friends, with a rosary of tears'. But he immediately goes on to add: 'It seems, therefore, that God takes care, under present circumstances, to prevent, or at least to check, the glut of that kind of girl'. He allows his readers neither to sneer at the reality nor to wallow in its fictional exploitation: 'Little Nell. . . was simply killed for the market', is Ruskin's most memorable judgment on the subject.[178]

Lobley, too, was a man of strong feelings, but also of intelligence, and with more than a touch of healthy Puritan restraint. These qualities help to give his little Nell an abiding interest and value beyond the demise of that more blatant Victorian sentimentality which Dickens shared and made use of. Lobley's Nell looks capable of the long tramp; and of the exertion of quiet moral influence over a tiresome and unhappy grandfather. Dickens's Nell never had such awkward, capable adolescent hands and feet, or such an expression of necessary stubbornness and veiled intelligence. Nor would Dickens ever have been content to put his main weight of pathos into a tired pair of feet in battered shoes. Lobley's girl is neither pretty nor picturesquely ragged. She assumes no intriguing pose. She is Lobley's daughter – a daughter of the lowest middle class – as she might be on the brink of social extinction; and its sequel. The door is painted as carefully as she is: and Lobley seems to have learnt something from his study of *The Light of the World*.[179] But the figure of Lobley's Nell, poised between the venerable wood and the living leaves, which will both survive her without meaning as much as she means; may today exert more spiritual power than Hunt's exquisitely upholstered, faintly sinister Redeemer. There is a gulf fixed between Lobley's technical powers and Hunt's, but in this case, Lobley has done enough.

A feature of Lobley's strength was his freedom from that quality Dickens mortalised as Podsnappery. There were Podsnaps in Bradford, as elsewhere, content with the faith 'that what Providence meant, was invariably what Mr. Podsnap meant'.[180] Dr Godwin, for instance, minister of Syon Baptist Chapel, had denounced the 'atheist revolutionaries' whose short-lived Mechanics' Institute was by 1832 replaced by a new foundation more acceptable to Nonconformist taste, under the Presidency of Dr Steadman, principal of Horton Baptist College. Dr Godwin's son had deployed his youthful rhetoric against the other half of the threat to *laissez-faire*: the polemics of Factory Reform Anglicans, notably Parson Bull. It is this spirit of reaction that seemed in the ascendant in Bradford during the late '50s and early '60s.

In 1860 and 1861 were published two editions of the *Memoirs of the Life and Gospel Labours of Stephen Grellet*. It was the Bradford Quaker publisher Benjamin Seebohm who was thus able to reveal to the world for the first time how the prince of 'atheist revolutionaries', Tom Paine, had expired with the words, 'Lord Jesus, have mercy upon me', on his lips. 'Tom Paine Silenced!' the *British Workman* exulted, only too sorry that 'Workhouses and prisons' were still 'full of religionless men'.[181] Why a Christian death should be damnable the journalist does not stop to explain; nor why the Son of Man should be an enemy to the *Rights of Man*. It was *Unto This Last* more than any other book which would erode this false alliance between respectability and repression: between the gospels and the witholding of the loaves and fishes.

Meanwhile in Bradford at this time, J. V. Godwin was esconced as Vice-President of the Mechanics' Institute under the merely notional presidency of Lord Rosse. Somewhat lower down the educational scale, the children of the Ragged Schools,[182] which had Seebohm among their supporters, were cheaply deployed in the interests of the ascendancy of this narrow liberal elite. How effective, for example, must have been the plea of Rev. J. P. Chown, a successor of Dr Godwin at the Syon Baptist Chapel, as he rose up on the platform of a packed St George's Hall, to save 'poor shivering hawkers of oranges and matches', not from their 'Saturday's mid-night' vending round the 'market steps', God forbid, but from 'pitch and toss, or something even worse', during the 'Sabbath hours'. For this was the Ragged School founded. And as he closes, the actual Ragged School Children rise from the choir seats where they face the audience, and sing: 'Hurrah for England'. That was in March 1858.[183]

It was for Alfred Harris and Louis Tylor that James Lobley executed a number of pencil and watercolour drawings of boys from such an institution. One at least is over-sentimental. Another has an excessively Holman-Huntish detail that suits neither Lobley nor his subject. But the others do convey some measure of 'truth and tenderness', as Ruskin had defined in Bradford the qualities at the root of good design; and these qualities were not over-flowing either from their exploiters of the market-place or their indoctrinators of the school room. Those privileged to attend Chown's pet Ragged School, at least, passed part of Sunday standing with toes touching a chalked semi-circle reading scripture, spelling the 'principal words' and tracing them, apparently, to their Latin roots. The best of the sketches is in a more open style than the others. It is refreshing not only because Lobley has caught one bit of 'life', but because the child has been mercifully distracted by another.[184] Even more engaging, while stopping short of the sugary, is a series of sketches of similar children dressed for a Mummers' Play.[185] Best of all, the *Village Guy Fawkes*, in which Lobley has imaginatively released his models into a piece of freshly observed Lincolnshire or East Riding landscape.

Lobley showed twelve of his genre pictures at the Royal Academy between 1865–78; from then till his death in 1888, only three: *A Foundation Scholar*, in 1880, *The Chapel, Haddon Hall*, in 1884, *A Village Choir*, in 1887.[186] Frederick Leighton's presidency, dating from 1878, might have had something to do with this. As Graham Reynolds tartly comments, 'By using his remarkable gifts of diplomacy and persuasion' Leighton 'sought to discourage the popular, small anecdotal painting, and encourage large canvases of classical scenes in their place': Poynter, Albert Moore, Alma-Tadema. Leighton was the son of a doctor from the fashionable Yorkshire resort of Scarborough. 'There was an ironic aspect of his success in imposing a foreign idiom in place of the national style. The affinities he encouraged in painting were with Bouguereau, von Marees, and the last of the Nazarenes at the very moment when a more radical Continental school was about to provide a far more potent challenge to the Academy's standards – the growth of plein-air painting and impressionism in France.'[187]

But if fate and Leighton made a sacrifice of Lobley, Lobley himself made a voluntary sacrifice which was more valuable.

The Victorians were not willing revolutionaries. Ruskin himself wrote *Unto This Last* only because he had to, and not because he wanted to. He had prepared letters on political economy for *The Times* in 1852, but had been 'quite as well pleased' to succumb to his father's advice not to publish them.[188] But he could no more escape the open quarrel with Victorian capitalism than he could avoid the implications of his own existence as a 'merchant's son'.

Similarly, James Hanson, editor of the *Bradford Review*, and by birth and breeding a Huddersfield liberal, had begun full-time work in his father's mill at the age of twelve, but was nevertheless long opposed to state education. In 1847 he reduced a Bradford meeting to a 'bear garden' with philosophic refinements on the theme. But once Forster's Act was passed Hanson threw himself into the work of the Bradford School Board. As the sole 'working-men's nominee' he was unofficial and supernumerary, and was nearly compelled to withdraw. But James Lobley, nominee for art education, was prepared to fulfil the notion of his admired Professor Ruskin that for art's sake we must sometimes seem to abandon art. He withdrew voluntarily in Hanson's favour.

Lobley was doubtless relieved to go. Louis Tylor, a close friend and supporter of W. E. Forster, was still in Bradford to back him up. The High School, which with help from F. Sharp Powell, MP, and H. W. Ripley, had stood out for the Lobley tradition against the rivalry of Sowden at the Mechanics' Institute, was about to be grafted onto the Grammar School and thus became a part of the Bradford conservative establishment which after thirty years of hibernation was again re-asserting itself. But Lobley's most valued friends, the Harrises, were moving their principal home to Kirkby Lonsdale.

Hanson went on to become Chairman of the Bradford School Board's Educational Committee in 1871, and of the Board itself in 1888. He died aged eighty, in June 1895, having received recognition at one national level – from the US Minister of Education. His career involved prolonged battles with Britain's Central Educational

Department over amenities, staffing and standards. Illegally, in 1876, he founded the country's first actually public secondary school – Feversham St Higher Board School, Bradford. By 1903 Bradford had six similar schools, out of a national total of sixty.[189]

Truth: Alfred Tylor

Alfred Tylor, FGS, was Ruskin's junior by some five years. On her husband's death at the end of 1884, Ruskin memorialised their friendship in a moving letter to Mrs Tylor: 'The little talks in the corner arm-chair at Herne Hill, when he used to come in at breakfast time and tell us wonderful things to think of all day! The first shake of the hand, always, at the London – the serenely bright, tenderly zealous face, distinct from all the wrinkled care and selfish formalism of common men. I am very thankful to have known him.'[190]

Tylor was on the Council of the London Institution, Finsbury Circus. He had business in Warwick Lane, Newgate Street; and would regularly call at Herne Hill on his way to the City from his house at Carshalton, in Surrey. Alfred's relations with Ruskin were not limited to these Herne Hill meetings, but Herne Hill meant 'home' for Ruskin; in both the tender and the bitter sense. The Ruskin ménage moved to Denmark Hill in 1842; but retained the Herne Hill freehold. Ruskin made over the lease to Joan and Arthur Severn in 1877, retaining his nursery there as a study. It was in that house that he began *Praeterita*.

Among Ruskin's male friends, Tylor was not so close as John Simon; and not of such long standing as Henry Acland. But Acland and Simon were poles apart.[191] It was Tylor who combined Simon's gift for emotional support with Acland's capacity for bracing intellectual challenge. He was a sympathetic scientist, whose literary memorial is Ruskin's charming lecture of November 1874 on the 'most purely and limitedly mathematic' genius of Ghiberti. This lecture was evolved after some days of conversation with Alfred Tylor at Oxford; and from it may be inferred the value of Ruskin's colloquy with him. For Ruskin numbers himself among 'the aesthetic or seeing people', and Tylor was surely among the 'mathematic or demonstrating people'. These types 'are contrary the one to the other. . . yet each necessary to the other'. The 'demonstrating' people tend to perish in 'dust', the 'seeing' people to perish in 'dream', Ruskin adds.[192] Alfred's patience, and his debating qualities, his sympathetic wife, and the slightly teasing charm of his three daughters, helped Ruskin to undertake those experimental works – *Ethics of the Dust*, *Prosperpina*, *Love's Meinie* and *Deucalion* – in which he points to a humanisation of the study of geology, of flowers and of bird life. They proclaim his perennial belief that both scientist and artist should remember that they are not machines. The best work of both deploys 'the intellectual lens and moral retina'.[193] Tylor, the noted geologist with an interest in art; and Ruskin, the Art Professor with a lifelong passion for geology; exemplified the belief they shared in the need for colloquy between the arts and sciences. For Ruskin, art was higher than science; but only because 'wise Art was the shadow, or visible reflection of wise Science'.[194]

Ruskin's St George's Guild was partly inspired by Alfred's researches into medieval guilds. This organisation, which is still in existence, was as open to mockery as the educational experiments of Ruskin's admirer Leo Tolstoy. Yet the determination of both writers, 'At least to try',[195] retains its value, however inaccessible to the academic or the mercenary. Ruskin's motive was the acquiring of the nation's land by voluntary subscription for the benefit of the whole nation. He advocated the use of machinery on a large scale, and the harnessing of the natural powers of sun, wind and water, and electricity, not to promote the redundancy of the human hand, but in order to release it for creative work and the human mind for recreative leisure. Meanwhile St George's Guild would foster in a few quiet places the traditional values and habits of conservation, in case an exploitative society remembered in time that these were useful. All this may once have seemed like an affront to progress. In today's small and threatened world it looks more like an alternative to extinction. And even at the time, Ruskin's seven-year legal battle to establish the right of voluntary secular bodies to the corporate ownership of land, was a bit of 'progress' worth the respect even of a sensible Victorian.[196]

Juliet Tylor, Alfred's daughter, became a member of St George's Guild. She and her two sisters appealed to Ruskin's sensibilities, without ever becoming so overpoweringly necessary and damaging to him as Rose La Touche. He could refer to them in self-mocking irony as a trio of Lady Jane Greys whose charms crushed 'into a mere Shamrock leaf' the heart of their occasional tutor, John Ruskin, a second Roger Ascham, as he styled himself. The image of the Irish shamrock leaf points to Rose La Touche, and Lady Jane perhaps shades into Effie Gray. But Ruskin could say of the Tylor girls, as he could not quite bear to say of Rose, and was too proud and angry to say publicly of Effie, that 'by very reason of their beauty and virtue, they have become the excuse for all the iniquities of our days'.[197] They were the excuse for the enslavement of their poorer sisters in the sweat-shops that purveyed their pretty luxuries.

In the booming Victorian art market, dealers like Gambart puffed their 'discoveries' as Hollywood studios would puff their sequence of 'stars'. Novelty and profit were the criteria; luxury and escapism set the tone. It was to Alfred Tylor that Ruskin set out his most radical views on this trend which would drive Lobley to the wall and Millais to *Bubbles*. 'As yet,' Ruskin wrote from Winnington in May 1864, 'the rise in prices has merely made the fortunes of a larger tribe of dealers. . . I have long intended to propose. . . that all sales of works of art should be under government control. . . that whatever was given by contention of purchasers' above the value set and obtained by the original artist 'should go to the government, to be employed in the form of art galleries for the nation, and support of schools. This would put an end to the dealer's trade. . . and to the purchases of art as an 'investment' by people who merely keep it out of sight and use.' Ruskin had wanted to say this in *The Political Economy of Art*, but his publisher had dissuaded him. It was good to have Mr and Mrs Tylor's sympathetic ear: 'I had a thoroughly happy afternoon, and hope to see you both often, and to help and be helped, by you both'.[198] As that last comma makes clear, the Tylors were to be delegate missionaries as well as comforters.

In April 1864, the 'very benevolent and modest' John Mitchell of Bradford had commissioned Rossetti's 'awful' *Venus Verticordia*. From about the same time, Gambart began directing public taste towards the neo-academic machines of Alma-Tadema.[199] The Pre-Raphaelite experiment, and Ruskin's influence on passing trends, were fading into history. Ruskin had never been beloved of the Royal Academy, and the native school of genre painters, of whom James Lobley was only one of the less cloying and more thoughtful, would be exiled from the Academy walls by 1878, when Leighton became President. Alfred Tylor had been impressed with the theory and practice of Lobley's Bradford Design School, and had taken up the cudgels on his behalf in his Jury Report at the International Exhibition of 1862. It was Alfred Tylor who undertook to approach Ruskin with a request for a testimonial to Mr Lobley, in November 1875. Lobley had exhibited at the Royal Academy in 1874, and would do so again in 1876, but had not been 'hung' at the exhibition of 1875. Tylor's letter does not survive. It may have contained only the modest request for Ruskin to put in a word that might improve Lobley's chances of being chosen another year. But Ruskin seems to have assumed that Lobley was petitioning for an Associateship. His reply to Tylor was certainly shattering: 'It is quite charmingly naive of you to think I could do anybody good in help to Academy appointments, a word of testimonial from me would ruin every chance Mr. Lobley had.'[200] Ruskin was right, to that extent. His *Academy Notes* of 1875 were the last he would write. They contained a withering account of Alma-Tadema's *The Sculpture Gallery* which made play of the fact that the artist's 'high degree' of 'skill and classic learning' had been expended on a 'tinted drawing', erroneous in colour, an advertisement for the 'sale of imitation-Greek articles of virtu'. Ruskin's ire was especially directed against a fan made of feathers 'like a peacock's, without the eyes'.[201] Tylor's approach for aid to Lobley certainly came at the worst possible moment, for on the very day Ruskin sent his reply the famous, but outmoded, critic was himself attempting to draw some peacock's feathers, not at all to his own satisfaction. He was simultaneously wrestling with the bible of the Royal Academy, Sir Joshua Reynold's *Discourses*, on which he was engaged in delivering a series of partly extempore, momentarily brilliant and wholly eccentric Oxford lectures.[202]

Seven weeks before, on 26 September 1875, Ruskin had 'enjoyed!' a 'drive through Leeds and Bradford', and a six-mile walk into Sheffield. This experience had probably not radically reversed his judgment made the previous February after a similar trip that 'a noxious lump of clay' would be the likely outcome of the region's wasp-nest strivings.[203]

Ruskin drew up the constitution of St George's Guild in 1875. Despite the ugly face of modern Yorkshire, he felt the Yorkshire qualities of 'Honesty and Piety' would survive, with a little irrigation from himself. And so, statedly instead of a church he inaugurated the Sheffield Museum, chief showpiece of the Guild of St George, in 1876.[204] And despite Ruskin's irascibility, Lobley and the Tylors continued to care for him. But Ruskin had to remind Juliet Tylor of his new order of priorities, in a letter of 19 August 1877. Asked to approve of her craft work, Ruskin wrote to Juliet: 'No, my dear, –

you cannot please me by painting plates for me, but only by doing something which will put food upon them for others. . . My kind regards to Mr. Lobley – please tell him there is not to be a single thing in the Museum from pebble to picture, Unexplained.' Mr Lobley's motto was 'success through knowledge'. It is to be hoped he was content.[205]

As Ruskin's hopes of having any immediate effect on the sense or sensibility of his own day faded, he turned more and more from immediate tactics to long-term strategy. He saw his work as being like that of moss, patiently filling the crannies of available rocks 'with dark earth through which nobler creatures shall one day seek their being'.[206] It was true that some of the more impressive church architects of these years – Street and Bodley among them – still acknowledged his influence. But in an age when ever accelerating machinery was throwing more people out of work and making work more anxious and exacting for those who remained in employment,[207] Ruskin considered luxurious church building to be blasphemy.[208] Webb, Nesfield, Shaw, Morris and other providers of luxurious houses and furnishing had their traces of Ruskinian influence, too. Ruskin was not impressed. Writing in October 1871, he gave this sort of life another 'forty or fifty winters'. The real architecture was being done by housing reformers like Octavia Hill, he thought.[209] Margaret McMillan, who from 1888–92 was 'companion' to Lady Meux of Park Lane and Theobalds, Waltham Cross, knew intimately this kind of world. She called it 'a cynical kind of Bohemia: backed by Mammon'. Lady Meux liked to arrange herself in front of her portrait by Whistler. Handing Rachel McMillan a copy of Ruskin's *Seven Lamps*, 'You may read it, my dear,' she said. 'Certainly I won't.'[210]

An advertisement for the disposal of a Wren building as a job lot, placed in *The Builder* of 17 March 1866 by Alfred Tylor's family firm, is enough in itself to suggest that Ruskin was in any case better employed to other ends than fuelling a fad for Gothic and a contempt for the Renaissance. 'To Architects,' it reads, 'TO BE SOLD, the Whole of the exterior stonework of the old College of Physicians, complete in a good state of preservation. . . would make a magnificent facade. . . apply J. Tylor & Sons Warwick Lane, Newgate Street, London.' Some elegant appreciations of Wren may be gleaned from Ruskin's pages, but his pervading tone of disapproval had done something to earn the ignominy into which *The Seven Lamps* would be cast by the Wren revival of the 1880s.

Ruskin's cousin tapped on his bedroom door after tea on the afternoon of 18 January 1900. She had brought him the latest Boer War news, and Edna Lyall's cavalier romance, *In the Golden Days*. His throat seemed irritable; and he admitted to feeling pain 'all over'. He died in his sleep the following Saturday afternoon.[212] The years since Ruskin's own final crisis have been so blackened by atrocities past even his imagining that there is now too little excuse for misunderstanding the images of siege and flood with which he sought to quicken the political intelligence of his age. And at this distance, it should not be too difficult even to forgive his streak of cavalier romance. His often fanciful imagery always has a cool analytical intelligence behind it. The geology of Bradford, seen early in March 1859, suggested to Ruskin the lesson of the Flood which he meditated at Ingleborough in the ensuing days, which would ripple under the surface of his Bradford lecture of 1864 with its allusion to the flood of Plato's *Critias*, and which he at last published openly as the first letter of *Fors Clavigera*.[213] Ruskin experienced at first hand the siege of Venice, and sat on the Lord Mayor's Committee 'for the victualling of Paris after her surrender' in January 1871. This double lesson of the siege is spelled out in the *Preface* to the new edition of *Munera Pulveris*, a copy of which Ruskin forwarded to Alfred Tylor in January 1872. 'I should be grateful to you if you would read the preface. . . you certainly ought not to read more than the preface' – Tylor was a busy man – 'but the book is occasionally referred to in the letters called *Fors Clavigera*, which I have ordered now to be sent to you regularly.'[214] The Flood is a geological memory, and a fantasy of the future. A fantasy, that is, on the assumption that the God of the rainbow has forbidden Flood as a metaphor for solution But siege is an event perennially in the news. Together, flood and siege teach the same lesson: that co-operation for survival is beneficial, and contest for supremacy is not. In the words of *Traffic*, 'There are always the elements to fight with, stronger than men; and nearly as merciless'.[215] Geology, like history, is always with us.

As a writer with a geological perspective, Ruskin deployed himself for the purpose of a long-term strategy which has the strengths and weaknesses of his own alienation. He knew that his St George's Guild, for instance, was a form of 'bitter play'; but then, how could he 'possibly help the nature of things, when *that* chances to be laughable?'[216] He encouraged his readers to learn to wrestle,[217] like Jacob.

It would have been odd to see Ruskin attempt that physically: but that theory must grapple with practice was essential to his theory. There were two main results of this long-term strategy and its odd contact with ordinary practicality. It tended to heighten Ruskin's optimism and deepen his pessimism: in both cases with transcendental connotations. Secondly, while it appealed to undergraduates,[218] it dismayed some of the practical tacticians of progress like Octavia Hill. Letter 10 of *Fors Clavigera* had praised her housing work: but had also contrasted it with the inanity of the upper classes to whom she looked for support and funds. Letter 45, with its devastating attack on the British squire, won Ruskin some friends among radicals, but made it difficult for Octavia to use the magic of his name in her efforts to conserve landscape and educate landlords.[219]

Letter 82, of October 1877, marks the catastrophe of their relationship. Academics would have been alienated by yet another swipe at Jowett's *Plato*, municipal busibodies by Ruskin's expressed preference to see Manchester brought to Thirlmere and drowned rather than Thirlmere brought to Manchester in pipes. And Octavia needed the help of enlightened classicists and educable municipal busibodies. There was an excitable footnote on 'the discovery made by another of my good and much-regarded friends, Mr. Alfred Tylor, who is always helping me, one way or other'. Tylor had done research on medieval guilds, and come up with the discovery that they preferred good work and daily bread to 'profit'. This cannot have seemed a useful discovery to a small landlord with ambitions for his children. Grand and good people like Alfred Harris could afford to lose money by running canals at a loss, out of conviction that they were necessary. But the tradition in the Harris family is that he was eccentric to do so, with so many children.

The mortal, or near mortal blow to Octavia's feelings was delivered by Ruskin in this same *Fors* letter 82, probably without his realising it. There was one person in the world whom Octavia revered even above Ruskin. That person was Mary Harris, who had laboured in Newgate prison, in the Quaker tradition of Elizabeth Fry, to bring comfort, alms and godly doctrine to the prisoners. Ruskin either never knew this; or had forgotten; or did not care. But he had published in *Fors* Letter 81 a letter from a Manchester correspondent who quoted with approval Thomas Hood's dismissive pun about Mrs Fry's 'nugatory teaching'. And now, in Letter 82, some imp of unreason – perhaps prompted by the flitting memory of Tylor's Newgate Street address – drove Ruskin to expand on the idiocy of the 'modern philanthropist of the Newgatory School', who tinkered with the souls of prisoners while outside the prison lay a world of social evil whose radical reform these tinkerings merely postponed.[220]

Had Octavia been made of iron, she might have seen this as merely a more vivid form of Ruskin's old words to her of January 1860. Octavia had expressed the hope of seeing 'great changes in individuals'. 'No!' Ruskin had answered. 'You can't change people.' He preferred to hope 'we may live to see some great changes in society'.[221] But Octavia was not made of iron, and moreover there were 'mutual friends' eager to make themselves important by setting Ruskin and Octavia at loggerheads. The two old friends dispatched letters to each other, of increasing stiffness, over the months October-November 1877. Octavia continued to assert her debt to Ruskin's personal inspiration and creative ideas, and to praise his insight into character. But he was unfit for directly practical affairs, and ruined himself by giving jobs to the wrong people, out of misguided kindness. Ruskin replied that she was determined, by a narrow insistence on false logic, to ruin his chances of ever again being of use in the world.

Ruskin had seen no illogicality in praising Millais the painter even after he had taken over his wife. Millais found this fair-mindedness sinister. So now, Ruskin could not see that by publishing this correspondence between himself and Octavia in *Fors Clavigera* he was destroying their friendship. That he wrote privately reassuring her of his personal regard was merely impossible of him. That he made their quarrel public showed that for better and worse Ruskin was no gentleman; nor had the instincts of one. He repented, and she forgave him, but their working relationship was ended, and his defence of his strategy for social change *versus* Octavia's tactics for helping people, had damaged his reputation.[222] Their controversy expressed a classic dilemma among social reformers, which in the case of Rachel and Margaret McMillan took the form of an enabling dialogue between Rachel's instinct for good works and her sister's crusade for social change.[223] But Ruskin and Octavia were not so close. The affair must have increased the doubts as to Ruskin's capabilities already engendered by *Fors* Letter 79 of July 1877, into which Ruskin had introduced his satire on Whistler. The rhythms of the offending sentence capture Whistler's painting style as perfectly as anything its author did for Turner. The paragraph from which it came provided Whistler with his own leading argument at the ensuing trial for libel.[224] Moreover Ruskin had half-consciously stage-managed a dialectical confrontation of some interest in art history. There is little to blame in all this; but there is something to notice. Ruskin had ceased to possess the ordinary man's instinct of self-preservation.

Ruskin's geological sense of time deepened his authorial pessimism and heightened his moments of authorial optimism. His own personal feelings, on the other hand, Ruskin viewed from above with an ironic arrogance that guarded him from private hurt;[225] though not always successfully.

The landscape around Ingleborough, whither Ruskin had sped after his Bradford lecture of 1859, was built up of the accumulated secretion of carbonate of lime from prehistoric and submarine animal bodies. The black Bradford canal provided for the exploitation of this lovely northern part of the West Riding: the landscape that had never been far from Turner's mind. The canal brought limestone to Bradford from Skipton and its hinterland to provide armaments and other hardware in conjunction with Bowling and Low Moor Ironstone. The dusty refuse of this co-operation was strewn as slag on Bradford streets as an 'economic' substitute for the abundant local sandstone flags. Giotto would have used it for fresco.

In his letter of February 1864 to the recently widowed Brown, Ruskin gives the gloomy side of the picture of flesh – 'that kind of marble, crimson-veined' – which he will unveil in Bradford: 'And now I'm going to see about some cracks in a vein of carbonate of lime, which I daresay I shall be soaked into some day myself, (if there are any phosphates in it), for it runs near my place that I'm going to die at. . . They're such pretty cracks you can't think. Just like people's veins with stone blood in them, quite as human as a great deal of human hearts' blood.[226]

But Ruskin's geological perspective allowed him a transcendent optimism as well as a transcendent pessimism. The 'good lady' of Bingley, Harris's wife and Alfred Tylor's sister, was one Bradfordian who helped Ruskin to feel this optimism. She died in December 1865. Another was Richard Thornton, the brilliant young geologist and African explorer, born and raised at Cottingley Hall. Ruskin would pass within a hundred yards of Cottingley Hall on his way to the Harris house, whose entrance was a mile further up the road from Bradford to Bingley. This was on 21 April 1864, the first anniversary of Thornton's death. Ruskin's letter of consolation to Harris makes it certain that Harriet Tylor is commemorated in *Traffic*, Ruskin's *In Memoriam* to his own father. Ruskin's footnote to his *Notes on Alpine Denudation*, published in February 1865 in the *Geological Magazine*, makes it almost certain that Richard Thornton has his part in *Traffic*, also.

When in April 1864 Ruskin investigated Shipley Glen and the Harden valley in the company of Alfred Harris, the conversation doubtless touched on geological topics. Perhaps they also touched on the low national 'estimate for scientific discovery', as recently displayed by the government's treatment of the geologist Richard Owen.[227] Harris's brother-in-law Alfred Tylor was a noted expert on the problems presented by these side valleys of the Aire and by the peculiar form of the Bradford basin. But Ruskin was even more interested in the geology of the heart as exhibited in the living virtues of Tylor's sister Harriet. When Mrs Harris died, in December 1865, Ruskin was sent a copy of *The Keighley News*, with its tribute to Harriet. An additional tribute took the form of extracts from a speech by Mr Newsome, taking the chair at a Literary and Musical Social Entertainment in the Bingley Mechanics' Institute, of which Harris was President. Harris was too grieved to attend. '"The loss he has sustained in the death of his beloved wife,' said Newsome, 'is incalculable. . . The late Mrs Harris was not very anxious about having her name emblazoned on monuments of marble. But by her pre-eminent goodness, by the weight of her moral character, by acts of mercy and benevolence to the poor and the afflicted she has left her name written on thankful but now sorrowful hearts, that will live to be remembered when the proudest monuments of human art are mouldered in the dust." At the close of the above remarks a deep sigh ran through the whole place.'

Ruskin's letter of consolation to Harris mentions that he had been sent this report by a third party. *Traffic*, when it was published in 1866, would transpose Mr Newsome's image into a geological parable. Ruskin relied on Bradford science and Bradford bible reading to point the lesson, and on the doctrine of the Incarnation to ratify its meaning. Science and religion were one, as body and spirit were one. A superstitious religion adhered like a mask to a wicked science that misused and killed the earth and its children. A true religion would be possible only when a wise science made a harmony of the great organism of which men were the thinking part. Ruskin now revealed which of the 'Two Paths' Bradford ought to follow. Not the Rochdale path of 'unctuous, sooty slime', but the Bingley road of honesty and simplicity. Let them remember that the veins from which they dug the ironstone to make their world-famous armaments and rolling-stock were as sacred as those human veins also coloured by iron. The stone, the bread, the flesh were half of the finite sacrifice of the earth. The iron, the wine, the blood made up the other half. The 'whole earth' was a finite sacrifice; but it was for Bradford to choose whether it would be a 'lively sacrifice', acceptable to God, or otherwise. 'For he that eateth and drinketh unworthily, eateth and drinketh damnation to himself, not discerning the Lord's body.' That text of Paul was no sectarian mumbo-jumbo for Ruskin; but a simple statement of the vulnerability of man in nature. A working audience of Protestants could add for themselves the corollary, 'if any would not work, neither should he eat'.[228]

A transcendent optimism is the theme with which Ruskin chooses to end. And among the innumerable allusions to scripture, the classics, and to English literature, which colour Ruskin's words, one of the clearest, for Harriet Tylor's sake, is to the commonplace sincerities of Mr Newsome: 'if you can determine some honest and simple order of existence; following those trodden paths of wisdom, which are pleasantness, and seeking her quiet and withdrawn paths, which are peace; – then, and so sanctifying wealth into 'commonwealth', all your art, your literature, your daily labours, your domestic affection, and citizen's duty, will join and increase into one magnificent harmony. You will know then how to build, well enough; you will build with stone well, but with flesh better; temples not made with hands, but riveted of hearts; and that kind of marble, crimson-veined, is indeed eternal.'

Ruskin's allusion is to the 'flammeate stains of haematite. . . characteristic of jasper. . . coloured with the same iron that colours the human blood'.[229]

For the magnates of Bowling and Low Moor Iron works, haematites are merely exploitable veins of traffic and death: railway rolling-stock carrying big guns. Huge profits assisted Henry Wickham Wickham, of Cottingley, Low Moor and Kirklees Priory (family motto:

Manners Makyth Man) into the House of Commons; and his co-shareholder of Low Moor, Gathorne Hardy, into the House of Lords.[230] Ruskin, in a moment of bad temper, in *Love's Meinie*, reads the heraldry of such arrangements as follows: 'Of the due and noble relations between man and his companion creatures, the horse, dog, and falcon, enough has been said in my former writings; unintelligible enough to a chivalry which passes six months of its annual life in Rotten Row, and spends the rents of its Cumberland Hills in building furnaces around Furness Abbey'.[231]

The geological investigations into the haematites of Furness, which laid the foundation for the development of the British iron industry, was done by John Sturdy, headmaster of Bradford Grammar School. In 1671 he reverted to Romanism, was duly cast off from Bradford, 'and became a Popish priest', pursuing his geology and his ministry in the more congenial atmosphere of north Lancashire, around Coniston and Furness.[232]

In 1887 Ruskin chose to demonstrate the continuity of Popish doctrines with iron-stains, as sympathetically understood, by donating a stained-glass window to the chapel of the Sacred Heart, at Coniston, where Sturdy's memory was revered as a torch-bearer in the dark days of Catholic exclusion. This was to demonstrate that Ruskin had become 'a Christian Catholic in the wide and eternal sense'.[233] The same intention of drawing the separate into the inseparable clearly motivated the coda of *Traffic*.

The geological vein in *Traffic* leads more securely to the Harrises' neighbour Richard Thornton of Cottingley and Kilimanjaro. In this case the internal evidence of the text is supported by Ruskin's footnote to his *Notes on Alpine Denudation* of 1865. This draws attention to the speech of Sir Roderick Murchison at the Anniversary Meeting of the Royal Geological Society, 23 May 1864, in which tribute was paid to Thornton's memory. Here was a Bradfordian whose 'getting on' took a rather different route from that of the ironmasters.

Thornton was a good example of his school's tradition of *Hoc Age*, which characteristically took the form of continuing into later life a flair for natural observation developed in the native landscape. Mr Thornton's short life as a geologist was begun by examining the local rocks as he went back and forth to school on his pony. He was of a class one degree less gentlemanly than the Wickhams, who were 'Esquires'.

Thornton's background is interesting, as it sheds light on his famous quarrel with Dr Livingstone. It also provides an instructive contrast with that of Henry Wickham Wickham (b. 1800), Bradford's MP from 1852 till his death in 1867. Wickham exemplified perfectly, and passively, the Victorian equation between his school motto – *Hoc Age* – and 'getting on'.

As Low Moor Iron works made the Wickhams too grand for Bradford, and Bradford too dirty for the Wickhams, they vacated Cottingley Hall, which was leased to Richard Thornton senior, the geologist's father, in 1835. There Richard was born in 1838. The family were prosperous; and now had a house that made them look almost like gentry: but Thornton senior also had a profession as clerk to the local Court of Requests. They were a cultivated family, if given to bluntness. When Charlotte Brontë applied for the post of governess, she had to be told that her musical attainments were inadequate.[234]

Henry Wickham Wickham removed to Kirklees Priory; where he could entertain Lord Shaftesbury or – with a brass band or two on the lawn – submissive crowds of Yorkshire operatives.[235] A feature of the estate was the grave of Robin Hood. Ruskin travelled through this part of the world occasionally, and his father knew it well. It is not surprising to note the theme of Robin Hood recurring in *Fors Clavigera* as a motif for open-hearted theft. The honourable alternative to Robin Hood is labour, Ruskin thinks. As Robin was betrayed to his death by the scheming Prioress of Kirklees, so is labour to its death by a church which will do anything but denounce the dishonourable alternative to Robin Hood: which is the 'occult theft' of the capitalists, the 'guilty thieves of Europe', who live on interest from the labours of others and who, by their arms profiteering, make unjust wars inevitable. In strictest fact, Bowling Ironworks was more the place for armaments than Low Moor. But both had made a handy killing in the Crimean War, and were ready to serve again. Ruskin's theme of Robin Hood, for excellent reasons, opened up a favourite vein of propaganda for Bradford socialists. The materials were so conveniently to hand.[236]

After Bradford Grammar School, Thornton studied at the Royal School of Mines, under Roderick Murchison, an acquaintance of Ruskin's since 1837, and the chairman for Ruskin's lecture on Tree Twigs at the Royal Institution in April 1861: a brilliant but erratic performance whose preparation was interrupted by the request of Alfred Harris, the Thorntons' neighbour, to please judge the drawings of Mr Lobley's pupils.[237]

The only hard evidence for Ruskin's knowledge of Thornton is his footnote of February 1865 in a paper on Alpine denudation which appeared in the *Geological Magazine*. This footnote draws attention to 'Sir Roderick Murchison's temperate and exhaustive statement' about the powers of glaciers in modifying the surface of the earth, made in his 'Address at Anniversary Meeting of Royal Geographical Society, 1864'.[238] That meeting was on 23 May, at a time when Ruskin was at Winnington, penning his letter about art dealers for Alfred Tylor. Ruskin's knowledge of the Address combines with internal verbal evidence to suggest that by the time he wrote *Traffic* Ruskin knew well enough that 'your great English virtue of enduring and patient courage' had had at least one outstanding Bradfordian examplar.[239]

In the light of Murchison's depiction of 'Richard Thornton of Bradford' amid the volcanic lava of Equatorial Africa, Ruskin's highly charged rhetoric in *Traffic* seems no longer exaggerated, but allusive. 'I am lost in admiration of his patient labours of registration when combined with his vivacity of description', Murchison recalled of Thornton. 'Those of us who are destined never to be able to penetrate into the southern part of Africa may quite realise to our mind's eye the true character of that grand continent. . . Through the devotion of the brothers and sisters of the deceased traveller, the whole of his voluminous notes have been carefully copied out and transmitted to us.'

Thornton left for Africa with Livingstone in 1858, at the age of twenty. Cast adrift by the missionary, Richard pursued his researches alone before joining Baron von der Decken on the slopes of Kilimanjaro, settling 'by his testimony the question of snowy mountains in Equatorial Africa.'[240] He met his death from fever in April 1863 after an eighty-mile trek across country to buy sh ep to feed the starving Universities' Mission.

Ruskin sought, in *Traffic*, which was originally delivered on the first anniversary of Thornton's death, to widen Bradfordian perspectives beyond their own local 'masses of lava which you build volcanic cones to melt', and to remind them, 'not that the Church is not sacred – but that the whole Earth is'. He invited them to consider 'why feeding the hungry and clothing the naked should ever become base businesses, even when engaged in on a large scale'.[241] All this would be very telling to Harris and other Bradfordians who knew of Thornton or read about him in the *Bradford Observer*.[242] To Thornton's family, recalling his geological work, his last mission and his grave by the cataracts of the Shire, so far from the little Mill Gill waterfall which was his mother's inheritance, sentences such as these would have been unbearably moving: 'It is stony ground, and boggy. . . your boy. . . cannot go one foot farther that night. Down he lies, to sleep, on Wharnside, where best he may, gathering a few stones together to put under his head: – so wild the place is, he cannot get anything but stones'. Had he lived, Thornton would have shared the Royal Geographical Society gold medal with von der Decken. But Jacob's pillow was his 'Crown of Wild Olive . . . "And indeed it should have been of gold, had not Jupiter been so poor".'[243]

This is sentiment; but of a fine order. And it is perfectly murderous against the industrialist's 'ideal of human life': the pretentious, deadly world of the new mansions that were thrusting into the background the Thorntons and their ways.[244]

Thornton was of that type of Saxon yeoman stock just too proud to call themselves gentlemen. Livingstone was the son of a Scots tea-pedlar with inflated ideas about his own remote ancestry.[245] He reduced Thornton to an insubordinate youth who ate and loafed and did not do his share of work. Thornton laughed openly at the Almighty's special intentions towards David Livingstone, and wept in rage[246] when his puerile hobby of stone-gathering had to be sacrificed to more important matters. From Thornton's side, Livingstone must have seemed a Scots tinker with religious mania: a creature whose holy mouthings turned to unmannerly abuse whenever his insane self-will was contradicted by a ray of Saxon honesty. Serve such a man? He would have turned the dogs on anything like him that ventured up the lane to Cottingley Hall.

Ruskin found Livingstone a displeasing object too, taken by himself. But he did not remit his efforts to see true science and religion as partners. Alfred Tylor's business address – Newgate Street – had prompted Ruskin to revive Hood's pun about 'Newgatory teaching'. But Alfred Tylor's kindness and sincerity helped Ruskin to a kinder pun. The Scots missionary and explorer was a 'living stone': distorted, unpleasant, but nonetheless part of a temple not made with hands, a structure of civilisation that had to be built from the means available. For the sake of his associates, and the associations of his name, Ruskin would forgive Livingstone his 'petulant courage' and his bible-bashing.

The last chapter of the first volume of *Deucalion* was issued after Ruskin's nervous breakdown of 1878. It records his debt to Alfred Tylor. The second chapter of the second volume of *Deucalion* is called Revision.[247] It is Ruskin's renewal of his difficult but useful claim that truth, though various, is one:

> Men do not sing themselves into love or faith; but they are incapable of true song, till they love, and believe.
>
> The lower conditions of intellect which are concerned in the pursuit of natural science, or the invention of mechanical structure, are similarly, and no less intimately, dependent for their perfection on the lower feelings of admiration and affection which can be attached to material things: these also – the curiosity and ingenuity of man – live by admiration and by love; but they differ from the imaginative powers in that they are concerned with things seen – not with the evidences of things unseen – and it would be well for them if the understanding of this restriction prevented them in the present day as severely from speculation as it does from devotion.
>
> Nevertheless, in the earlier and happier days of Linnaeus, de Saussure, von Humboldt, and the multitude of quiet workers on whose secure foundation the fantastic expatiations of modern science depend for whatever good or stability there is in them, natural religion was always a part of natural science; it becomes with Linnaeus a part of his definitions; it underlies, in serene modesty, the courage and enthusiasm of the great travellers and discoverers, from Columbus and Hudson to Livingstone; and it has saved the lives, or solaced the deaths, of myriads of men whose nobleness asked for no memorial but in the gradual enlargement of the realm of manhood, in habitation, and in social virtue.
>
> And it is perhaps, of all the tests of difference between the majestic science of those days, and the wild theories or foul curiosities of our own, the most strange and the most distinct, that the practical suggestions which are scattered through the writings of the older naturalists tend always directly to the benefit of the general body of mankind; while the discoverers of modern science have, almost without exception, provoked new furies of avarice, and new tyrannies of individual interest; or else have directly contributed to the means of violent and sudden destruction, always incalculably too potent in the hands of the idle and the wicked.

CHAPTER ELEVEN

THE CROWN OF WILD OLIVE

'And indeed it should have been of
gold, had not Jupiter been so poor'
Aristophanes (Plutus).
—From the title-Page to *The Crown of Wild Olive, Three Lectures on Work, Traffic, and War*, 1866

Ruskin revised the proofs of *The Crown of Wild Olive* on 24 March 1866; and a month later left England for Switzerland, leaving his old friend and publisher W. H. Harrison to see the book through the press.[1] The book's title is taken from the *Plutus* of Aristophanes. In this comedy the poor and honest Chremylus succeeds in creating havoc by restoring the eyesight of the blind god Plutus ('Wealth'). 'Poverty' attempts to dissuade him, but to no avail:

> Zeus is certainly poor [she says] and I'll make this clear to you directly.
> For if he were rich, how would he, in personally instituting the Olympian Contest,
> In which he gathers all the Greeks together every four years,
> Advertise the victors among the participants by crowning them
> With a crown of wild olive? And yet it ought rather to be with a gold one, if he were rich.[2]

Chremylus replies that such stinginess proves that Zeus must really be rich; and Poverty counters that to accuse Zeus of illiberality is more impious than to assume that he must, after all, be poor.

Poets, singers and orators, as well as athletes, took part in the ancient Olympic Games at which, as at their modern equivalent, provincial rivalries were sublimated in the name of civilisation. The word here translated 'participants' means 'practitioners' or, literally, 'ascetics': those men who have disciplined mind and body to be of service to the State. For the Greeks, these 'ascetics' were opposed to the 'idiots', or merely 'private men', who had no practised talent to bring to public service. By allusion, Ruskin indicates that his lectures on Work, Traffic and War are intended for those 'ascetics' whom he had admired and criticised in the last volume of *Modern Painters.*[3] In that volume, monks, merchants and soldiers made up the company of modern 'ascetics'. *Traffic* and *War* are intended for these last two groups. Monks were not a great feature of Victorian England. In their place, in *Work*, Ruskin addresses the hard-working, respectable artisans of Camberwell and their lower middle-class supporters, Protestant in the main,[4] and for the best of whom town trades and domestic bible-reading took the place of the pioneering work and worship of monasticism.

The Crown of Wild Olive is a reward for ascetics; and an encouragement to further endeavour in the virtues they already practise. It is for 'the deliberate reader',[5] and not for the 'idiot'. . . a person entirely occupied with his own concerns'.[6] The book is for an elite, self-elected from all classes. 'There is, then,' Ruskin writes in *Work*, 'no class distinction between idle and industrious people; and I am going to-night to speak only of the industrious. The idle people we will put out of our thoughts at once – they are mere nuisances – what ought to be done with *them*, we'll talk of at another time.'[7]

Ruskin ends *Work* with a plea for a return to the childlike mind. He can be seen to be looking forward to the revaluation of true monasticism which he would make in later works. A key passage comes from his lecture on Angelico of 1874, where he defines the 'Universal Monasticism. . . taught by St Francis and interpreted by Giotto, as required of all men, not of the monk only – the Renunciation of the world even by those who live in the midst of it – the Baptismal renunciation of it, and of its works and ways'.[8] It is worth noting that in Ruskin's Notebooks for 1858–9, commentary on the *Plutus* is interwoven with commentary on the gospel of St Matthew,[9] the apostle chosen from among the tax-gatherers.

Ruskin is aware of the ludicrousness, and danger, and necessity, of his proclamation of *Unto This Last*, that ' THERE IS NO WEALTH BUT LIFE'. It is printed like a headline, as though it were news: but it is the policy of the angels, and the economy of heaven. It sets its face for ever against the policy of the world father: '"Buy in the cheapest and sell in the dearest"' market.[10] Like Ruskin himself, St Francis was a merchant's son christened John. As he was dying, Giovanni Bernadone, nicknamed 'Francesco', asked to be laid on the bare ground. An affecting passage in hagiography. But what was the outcome when at last a poor Franciscan achieved the tiara? The ascetic Sixtus V is still remembered for his attempts at draining the marshes of the Campagna and for bringing fresh water to Rome. His pontificate is also memorable for a crowning moment in the history of art, for it was due to his despotic vigour that Michelangelo's dome of St Peter's was completed. But there are harsher things in the record. Sixtus revived the Roman economy, and enforced peace. Mass executions of banditti were a necessary step to this. He is still remembered at Venice as an over rigorous Inquisitor and burner of books. And he has a niche in English history as the Antichrist who gave his blessing to the Spanish Armada.[11] Like St Francis, Ruskin can find no other bride but Poverty.[12] The alliance may prove a mixed blessing, but his choice is limited. The banker's daughter Rose La Touche, for whom he has already waited three years, puts him off for another three in February 1866. He is still hoping for some arrangement with Rose: perhaps a little house in the country for useful work and charity, away from that fashionable world which brings out the worst in both of them.[13] But while she keeps him off, her suitor, like Jacob for Rachel, must – amid unbearable ironies – continue to work towards her. As a prime specimen among the young female salmon, Rosie is way upstream in the biological and sociological scheme of things. Ruskin, an odd male fish who is already getting on in years, is struggling somewhere at the tail end of the seasonal rush, and liable to be hooked and cooked long before he can reach her. But she keeps him going.

It was at the end of *Unto This Last* that Ruskin invited his wealthy readers to 'face the light; to Raise the veil boldly' on the world about them.[14] And now the wine-merchant's heir is pursuing the spelling out of some of the consequences of that endeavour to give Wealth eyes. The outcome, in Aristophanes, was hilarious and terrible: and Ruskin does not expect much improvement in his own plot.

At the end of the *Plutus*, once Wealth has been given his eyes by Asclepius, one honest man does indeed become rich; and he rewards the god, as a rich man would, with his worst old coat. An informer is ruined, a rich old woman loses her gigolo, Hermes, god of rogues, is outlawed from heaven and comes to earth looking for fresh mischief: and the priest of Zeus himself begins to die of hunger.

Unto This Last is Ruskin's text of radical Victorian meliorism; nor would he ever abrogate that desire for reconciliation on fair terms. The terms would be spelt out in *Fors Clavigera*; and many of them remain far in advance of anything yet achieved by Britain's Parliamentary Labour Party. But reconciliation is the motive behind them. *The Crown of Wild Olive* is a more disturbing, more Aristophanic, work. It is still full of Victorian hopes for progress: but it also represents a return to the Greek sense that many things never really change; that there is an irredeemable mercenary cowardice in some men; and an irredeemable love of fighting in others.

This reassertion of common sense may seem retrograde by the light of those popularisers of Darwin and Marx: Herbert Spencer and Friedrich Engels. The Hegelian pattern of hypothesis, antithesis and synthesis was deeply entrenched in nineteenth-century thought. Evolutionary change: inevitable progress or inevitable, but beneficial, revolution; such habits of thought would be affronted by the Ruskinian insight that underlying and limiting all growth and change were certain irreconcilable and inveterate differences that would not resolve themselves into the results one might look for.[15]

In *The Queen of the Air*, of 1869, Ruskin would praise Darwin's 'unwearied and unerring investigations'; but modestly advance his own observation that 'Species are not innumerable; neither are they now connected by consistent gradation. They touch at certain points only; and even then are connected, when we examine them deeply, in a kind of reticulated way, not in chains, but in chequers; also, however connected, it is but by a touch of the extremities, as it were, and the characteristic form of the species is entirely individual.'[16] When that was written, Mendel's work on genetics was virtually unknown, and quite unknown in England.[17]

There is much more than an artist's preference for form over process in Ruskin's dissatisfaction with Darwin's 'one-sided intensity'.[18] That there were ignorances invincible by education; and aggressions untameable by cricket; that the Divine Comedy of existence had an inescapable hell somewhere in it as well as an improving purgatory; that real classes of men were born, however the superficies of class were made; and that neither economics nor politics could afford to ignore these distinctions, however desirable it might be to mitigate – and in some points, abolish – class differences of the man-forged kind:[19] these insights lie behind much that seems wayward or unacceptable in *The Crown of Wild Olive*.

The basis of *Traffic* was the lecture delivered in Bradford Mechanics' Institute on 21 April 1864. Some of its sharpest felicities were not achieved till the final correction of the proofs. As published, the lecture's setting was described as 'the Town Hall, Bradford'. This may be a publisher's error, or an accurate piece of misremembering on Ruskin's part. Bradford had no Town Hall till 1873; and St George's Hall and the Mechanics' Institute served instead. The impression that Ruskin is addressing the whole town of Bradford, through its leading citizens, is accurate enough. To have depicted the piece as a Mechanics' Institute lecture, would have been either merely misleading or too deviously satirical for plain sense. The 'ascetics' who helped Ruskin to write it were the high-minded Bradfordians Ruskin had met: Harris, Mitchell, Lobley and the worthy artisans of the Design School, like the sensitive draughtsman and furniture carver, David Binns.[20]

Work, as published, was described as 'Delivered before the Working Men's Institute, at Camberwell'. The date was 24 January 1865. The 'at Camberwell' is accurate. This was not a body with official support, but a 'working Institute', as Ruskin put it, 'established in the district in which I have passed the greater part of my life'. Like 'our college in London, a "Working Men's College"',[21] the Institute at Camberwell was an effort to enlarge the scope of working-class education: a function the old Mechanics' Institutes had virtually ceased to perform. In its playfulness, and oddly childlike way of looking at things, the lecture is in part a tribute to W. H. Harrison, of Camberwell Green, Ruskin's publisher. It is characterised by the discourse of playful seriousness which they shared. 'Its very fine sneering at my business,' Ruskin had mocked Harrison, not long after John James's death. 'I've drawn two primrose petals this morning – and done a metaphor – for which I've had to go a great deal farther than you for your epigrams.' Another note, of the same time, is tongue in cheek, but earnest for all that. 'I never write – or utter a word now – but with the sight of an angel at the end of the table and a red devil below it.'

Ever since the first volume of *Modern Painters*, Harrison had been correcting Ruskin's grammar, and curbing his eccentricities. This helped to win a public for Ruskin, but the writer was not altogether grateful. Dealing with Harrison had helped to sharpen Ruskin's ironies, and enlarge their range. On 22 March 1864 he scolded 'dear Harrison' in the third person: 'whatever sorrowful consequence he

[Harrison] brought upon me by his wicked praise – you know it was very naughty – don't you now – you dear old thing? – as Caroline says – to make one write all that nonsense and see to having it printed too? But the wicked praise pleased and comforted the father – that's one little redemption of it now.'[22]

Appropriately, *Work*, the first lecture in the book, is superficially the easiest to read, and the most obviously engaging. But it also goes further than the others in directions which would have made John James tremble for his son.

London south of the river was a different world from the fashionable West End – and different again from the miseries of the East End. Only during a rare east wind could the West End smell its own refuse, on which, sometimes literally, the East-Enders lived, or died. South London was not so neatly polarised. There was great poverty; there was some prosperity; there was a great deal of respectable lower-middle-class and working class life. Persons of means, but no pretensions, might live there. The Ruskins lived on Denmark Hill; Alfred Harris's relatives Lydia Harris and Jane Harris, proprietors with him in the Leeds and Liverpool Canal, lived at Walworth.[23] But South London, to this day, has a place in the unwritten book of British clichés as *terra incognita*. Apart from the Archbishop of Canterbury in his Palace at Lambeth, London 'south of the river' is where 'nobody' lives. When, at the beginning of their friendship, Mrs La Touche 'asked what sort of road there was to Denmark Hill', she was merely subscribing to this common cliché.

Work revives some south London memories; and enforces a few connections. Ruskin's plea for a return to the child-like mind gains meaning from the fact that Blake, a Lambeth resident from 1790, published *The Songs of Experience* in 1794, with a frontespiece to show his meaning: a man walking carefully with a winged child poised lovingly on his head.[24] Ruskin's 'crazy' but telling view of the City of London, across the river, as a 'great city of play. . . a huge billiard table. . . with pockets as deep as the bottomless pit'[25] is a message read from the death of Turner's mother in the lunatic asylum of Bethlehem, or Bedlam Hospital, Lambeth. The 'character' of Justice whom Ruskin brings to life with a few subtle strokes, is a modest tribute to Shakespeare's Globe, on Bankside.

The plea which Justice makes for the child crossing-sweeper reflects contemporary problems; yet also goes deeper. One of the country's busiest and dirtiest roads, the Old Kent Road, was in the care of the dilatory, pettifogging and impecunious Roadworks Committee of the Camberwell Parish Council. Bombs have destroyed most of its records: but some minutes of the period survive to tell the tale of tinkering, postponement and general incapacity.[26] Ruskin's picking out of the crossing-sweeper puzzled and annoyed contemporary reviewers,[27] but the symbolism is clear enough. Chaucer's pilgrims passed this way once from Southwark on their way to Canterbury. The modern world, pressing on with its own relentless pilgrimage, is asked to spare a thought for the child who has to deal with its droppings.

Spurgeon, whose grand Italianate Metropolitan Temple was erected near the Elephant and Castle in 1861, had set Ruskin among the sceptics because he hoped to make something of this world.[28] Ruskin admired Spurgeon in some ways; but the Baptist preacher's Calvinism was detestable to him. Ruskin had been taught by Plato to know that courage was the first of the four rational virtues and justice the second, and by Dante to see that faith, hope and charity were founded on these virtues, not a substitute for them. Ruskin rears a temple in rivalry of Spurgeon's. Its foundation is justice for all men, whereas Spurgeon's is founded on appeals to pure funk. Its upper storey is charity as the social energy of a people who rejoice to nurture human powers as divine gifts. Spurgeon's upper storey is the selfish security of those who, having despaired of mankind, look to their own enthronement above. Such a 'faith', in Ruskin's eyes, reduces life to the level of an indecent card game with God as banker.

John La Touche, the failing banker and Irish landowner of Huguenot stock, Rose's father, came south of the river from Mayfair to be baptised by Spurgeon, probably in 1863. Mrs La Touche was glad to see her husband more spiritual, but would have preferred to see him converted by the Archbishop of Canterbury, or even Cardinal Manning.

Ruskin, the South Londoner, looks across the river at another bridge: the bridge of deathful exchange, passing through the City, which links the West End and the East End. In the West End gentlemen keep themselves in training for hunting, even in the London season, with canters along Rotten Row. They love killing things, and they love gambling. These 'needs' must be served at all costs; hence 'that beautiful arrangement of dwelling-house for man and beast, by which we have grouse and black-cock – so many brace to the acre, and men and women – so many brace to the garret'. Their ladies play at dressing, and their 'needs' must be met, with similar results. Mr La Touche held back on his hunting when he got religion, and Mrs La Touche, too, had her conscience tickled into writing a little pamphlet *About Dress*, with some Platonic glimmers in it: 'With our minds trained. . . our bodies will be rightly dressed'. Ruskin is not over confident as to the results of either conversion. He presents his audience with a bone-picker found dead of exposure and starvation, on a dung heap outside 'the recently-erected almshouses in Shadwell Gap' in the East End. Drawing up sustenance from that dung heap is the lowest tendril of root of his paradisal Rose. Love, which is so near hatred, lends a terrible clarity to Ruskin's vision.[29]

War, placed at the end of the first edition, is described as 'Delivered at the Royal Military Academy, Woolwich'. Army cadets and their mothers seem to have made up the audience. Ruskin's editors could find no contemporary report of the lecture. It was delivered in 1865. When *The Crown of Wild Olive* was published, contemporary reviewers found little to approve in the book other than the straightforward pep-talk against betting, which Ruskin made in *War*.[30] The published lecture discloses that Ruskin left a newspaper on the table for his audience to consult: which suggests that the occasion was a small-scale affair. *War* was printed off separately in 1866; and this also suggests that its impact as delivered was not great. Ruskin's eloquent scorn of two soldierly vices – betting, and playing around with women – would be regarded as worth promulgating by the more serious-minded officers who had time for Ruskin. Though it made little stir, this lecture at Woolwich can hardly have been a fiasco, for Ruskin was asked back to Woolwich a number of times. In 1870 he spoke at the distribution of prizes gained by students in the Woolwich branch of the Science and Art Department. His theme was Arachne – the spider-rival of Athene – and the lecture has many comparisons drawn from military exercises. In 1872, in deadly irony, Ruskin lectured the Woolwich 'cannon-making workmen' on the halcyon – 'The Bird of Calm'. He gave a talk on minerals, 'badly' as he thought, in April 1876, at the Woolwich Repository.[31]

His lecture, *The Future of England*, was given at the Royal Artillery Institution, Woolwich, in December 1869. This was a significant date for Woolwich, for the Woolwich Naval Dockyard closed for business that year; the human race's technological progress demanding bigger and deadlier ships than could be built at Woolwich, the old

Saxon 'village in the bay'. Ruskin's lecture is full of 'advanced Tory' ideals in favour of paternalist education: universal, gratis and compulsory. Such a plea would have emptied the hall in Liberal Bradford. But the Army authorities, badly shaken by the terrible fiascos of the Crimean War, were prepared to listen to Ruskin's persuasions in favour of an educated army drawn from an educated and more healthy population, and to the idea of the State's taking responsibility for this. Prussia was on the brink of annihilating the military power of France, and ever since the Schleswig-Holstein crisis of 1864 it had been clear to intelligent military men that the British army would need to pull its socks up if Britain were to maintain any semblance of authority.

A new electorate, swollen by voters freshly enfranchised from the respectable working class, had put the Etonian Gladstone in power, in December 1868. Gladstone had picked for Foreign Secretary an amusing and ruthless aristocrat, Lord Clarendon, who referred to Victoria as 'the Missus'.[32] The Chancellor of the Exchequer was Robert Lowe, Ruskin's old Oxford examiner, and his current *bête noire*. For Lowe's idea was that the function of universities was merely to *examine*.[33] In *The Future of England* Ruskin urged that the working classes still looked for guidance from the upper classes – which from the last election results appeared to be true – but that these upper classes must give the lower orders much more enlightened leadership. The accession to power of a minority of the working class was having the tendency to depress the unenfranchised majority. In *Fors Clavigera*[34] Ruskin would address himself to the larger party of 'Labourers' coming into being as the pressure for the far wider Reform Acts of 1884-5 gained momentum. For the moment, in 1869, he felt it more necessary than ever to revive the best Conservative traditions of responsibility for the whole people. 'You are to spend on National Education, and to be spent for it', Ruskin warned his audience of potential and actual officers, 'and to make by it, not more money, but better men.' This was much more Tory, and radical, than Forster's Education Act of the following year which merely offered to fill up the gaps in the current voluntary system. The poor physical condition of many recruits during the Boer War would back up the Education (Provision of Meals) Bill of 1906; but not till conscription was brought in in 1916 by Lord Derby would it become clear to government how far England lagged behind Germany in general standards of technical and physical education. Ruskin denounced conscription in *War*; but not in *The Future of England*. By including this lecture of 1869 in his new edition of *The Crown of Wild Olive* of 1873, Ruskin was seizing the opportunity to address himself to England's now more obviously threatened situation as a small commercial island dependent on imported grain for its population and imported steel ores for their protection, squeezed between the triumphant capitalist mobocracy of General Grant's United States and the regimented and efficient tyranny of the Kaiser's Germany.[36] The additional lecture destroys the artistic balance of the book; but Ruskin, like his father, wanted to give value for money in a constantly changing market.

The personality who stands behind the *War* lecture of 1865 is Ruskin's model soldier, Sir Herbert Edwardes. This humorous and brave ascetic was clearly born to be a soldier, just as the 'very modest and benevolent' ascetic John Mitchell was born to be a commercial leader. Ruskin met both men in 1858–9. Edwardes, said Ruskin, gave him 'the most grave lesson he ever received from friendship', by his reading and commentary on Wordsworth's *The Happy Warrior*. Edwardes was normally gentle and patient, and preferred to win without striking a blow, if possible. He was the same age as Ruskin. As a young lieutenant in 1847, Edwardes had pacified the tribes of Bunnoo, an Afghan district tributary to the Sikhs, without shedding blood. Edwardes was as tactless and outspoken with his dilatory and absentee commander-in-chief, Lord Gough, as he was tactful and courteous to the Afghans and Sikhs. Ruskin admired his 'combined audacity and subtlety', and his preference for efficiency and strategy over expenditure of human life.[37] But Edwardes, like Mitchell, made Ruskin wonder. Mitchell was a man who enjoyed commercial challenges from which Ruskin would have recoiled. Edwardes enjoyed fighting, when he had to. Any political or economic theory must have room for both types of man. A born artist is useless for anything else, Ruskin had said in *The Political Economy of Art*.[38] From 1859 he began to realise that, however disagreeable the fact may be to an artist, some men are born merchants, and others born soldiers. These distinctions could not be effaced; but an ignoble collusion need not be the only terms on which they could get on. In *Unto This Last*, Ruskin had referred to the capitalist as a main cause of war, and revived his message from *The Political Economy of Art* of the need for a discipline of peace: 'Soldiers of the Ploughshare, as well as Soldiers of the Sword'.[39] The Woolwich

Laboratory Department contained the largest workshop in the Workshop of the World. Bradford had shot to prosperity by feeding the Crimea with guns and blankets. The British State was fairly organised, if only for death. Would it be unfair to organise it for life?

The connections between violence and art which are touched upon in *War*; and the links between madness and inspiration which are hinted at in *Work*, are brought together and analysed in the virtuoso lecture *Traffic*.

Turner's first recorded visit to Farnley, the Wharfedale home of Walter Fawkes, was made in the late summer of 1810. It proved an enabling friendship, and the visit was repeated almost every year till 1824. Yet few people have heard of Walter Fawkes. The whole world has heard of Guy Fawkes, born at York, and in January 1606 condemned on account of supposed treasonous activities at Westminster to be hanged, castrated, his heart drawn and his entrails burnt before his face while still alive. Guy was only a distant collateral of the Farnley Fawkses, who were ancient (and respectable) even then. He showed breeding of some kind, however. Though weakened by torture he climbed the hangman's ladder so high that his neck was broken in the initial fall.[40] All that – to any writer but Ruskin – might seem irrelevant to art and economics. But in *Traffic* Ruskin forces the connections. He snatches the audience from the upholstery of their suburban homes into all the implications of the newspaper lying unregarded on the arm of the chair. At first, the 'man-milliner' gains entry to the textile and iron centre, traditionally Puritan and anxiously *arriviste*, in the guise of interior designer. Railings and armaments, velvet plush and military blankets, were staples of Bradford traffic. A dazzling interplay of images relates suburban pretensions to the machinery of modern warfare.

So far, the man-milliner employs enough irony to place his entertainers in the ears of an eavesdropper, and provides enough suggestion of language unfit for parlour use to remind the attentive reader of *Unto This Last*. But suddenly, like steel springs, something begins to emerge from the upholstery. The manic strategem for preserving their acquisitions is a 'highly comic state of life for two private gentlemen. But for two nations, it seems to me, not wholly comic? Bedlam would be comic, perhaps, if there were only one madman in it; and your Christmas pantomime is comic, when there is only one clown in it; but when the whole world turns clown, and paints itself red with its own heart's blood instead of vermillion, it is something else than comic, I think.'

Is he – with antiquarian literalness – making a 'Guy' of his audience? The Gunpowder Plot traitors, like the rest of their kind, would have had their hearts torn out in some such striking fashion. There are other hangings than of pictures; different topping-off ceremonies than that for the Wool Exchange.

To open all the meanings of 'private', the art critic allows himself a stroke of 'bad taste' – will the audience at last see how wholehearted a word 'taste' is? It is unfair of him to play on their novel-reading habit of identifying with 'one' picturesque madman, sobbing over 'one' broken-hearted clown – in order to show them the 'whole world' as 'one', with themselves inescapably enlisted in it – tactlessly integrating, in the process, the 'two nations' of *Sybil* with the sentimental clown and madman of *Pickwick Papers*. Again, the financial page, the theatrical advertisement and the war notes are too horridly confounded with the upholstery. More tasteless still, in the build up to the horror, followed by its quiet, unnerving supression, the art lecturer's prose rhythms imitate too nearly more up-to-date execution methods, as carried out over in Liverpool last Saturday, and recorded in *The Times* last Monday. 'Calcraft in adjusting the cap and rope' – not 'cap and bells'? – 'appeared to take unusual care. These being completed, the reverend gentleman withdrew' – ah! – 'the bolt was drawn, and the drop fell. The sufferings of the poor fellow were protracted and severe, but the screen fortunately hid them from the view of the crowd', which was not of a 'respectable class'.[41]

But the hangman's ladder becomes Jacob's, and while the ladies relax moistly over that, Ruskin informs the gentlemen with its political meaning. 'Your so-called science of Political Economy,' he tells them, 'has omitted the study of exactly the most important branch of the business – the study of spending.' His 'aesthetic' metaphor, as always, transcends without belittling, his 'economic' information. The gibbet is related to the tree of life by that same economy of love that is expounded in the heart of *The Divine Comedy*. For in Canto XVII of *Purgatorio*, the fantasy of the hangman's ladder, summoned into being by the rage to possess, is transformed into the ascent towards God, as Vergil expounds the soul's task of discrimination.

A reading of *The Crown of Wild Olive* demonstrates that Ruskin, like any man with a sense of values, was a Tory; but like any human being with a conscience, also a communist; and like any person of moderate intelligence, a Liberal. *Traffic* urges Bradford's Liberal elite to liberalise their petty kingships into a broader 'commonwealth'. *Work* agrees heartily with many of the socialist demands astir among the intelligent artisans in the audience, but states that they must choose their captains (which sounds Liberal); and obey them (which could be called Tory). *War* gives Tory class pride any amount of necessary flattery, but provides scalding agitation for the most radical pacifist, in its contempt for the 'proudly idle' who 'use the productive and labouring orders partly as their cattle, and partly as their puppets or pieces in the game of death'.[42]

H. D. Traill, in *The Daily Telegraph* of 22 January 1900, caught some of the magic of Ruskin's style, its Dionysian incandescences and its epic sweep. Searching for metaphors, Traill called Ruskin's language a 'rich vesture through which the movements of his thought were half concealed and half disclosed. . . his imitators tried in vain to draw the bow which only Ulysses could wield'.

Ruskin has unnumbered heirs, in thought; feeling and in language. He is still too large, and too near, to be properly visible. Approaching *The Crown of Wild Olive* by the first paragraph of its *Preface*, one is struck by its zooming rhythm and stinging particularity, its tones of exaltation, detachment, venom; its angelic scorn and aeroplane velocity. Its outer effect, the sheen on it, is more than the high gloss of a Victorian craftsmanship in language which marked the culmination of the great literate epoch that opens in England with Spenser and Sidney. It is of no use trying to read it quickly or easily as though it were modern journalism: or with a straight face, as though it were Wordsworth. Proust describes best these Ruskinian 'views': 'ces vues assez particulières à Ruskin. . . qui frappent aussitôt toute personne capable à la couleur particulière d'une idée de deviner, comme ferait un pêcheur pour les eaux, sa profondeur'.[43]

Even this one paragraph of Ruskin, to the modern reader, is almost invisible for the cloud of witnesses who attest his influence. Its adjectives are decorative in the deepest sense: 'pathetic. . . passionate. . . tragic'. Here is a mediator of the Dionysian knowledge of terror and renewal which informs the four great Greek dramatists and the four great Greek gospels. The Proustian technique of creative memory is foreshadowed in it. Here is a fusion of pagan and Christian nature imagery that will be a mine for Lawrence, and Yeats and Joyce; all of them touched by Ruskin's arrogance as well as his allegories. There is an insistence on exactness and intellectuality, which makes

Hopkins inconceivable without Ruskin; a bringing down of Dante's stricture of ethical thought to bear on the suburban desolations which will be handed on to Eliot; a perfection in the deployment of indecency which suggests Pound: a purity of rage and geological transcendency which Owen, who loved Ruskin second only to Keats, would transpose in some of his own greatest poems. The list could be lengthened.[44]

The theme of Ruskin's first paragraph is the pollution of the springs of Wandle. He remembered them in their purity, and will begin *Praeterita* with that memory. But by the beginning of his second paragraph, Ruskin's feet have touched ground, and there follows a passage in his strolling style, tender and sardonic, as he walks 'up slowly through the back streets of Croydon', to the High Street. His maternal grandfather, the herring fisher, he will recall in *Praeterita*, 'was killed at two-and-thirty, by trying to ride, instead of walk, into Croydon; he got his leg crushed by his horse against a wall; and died of the hurt's mortifying'.[45] The sailor's widow kept the King's Head, at Croydon. Her grandson walks gently past Croydon's new public house in this second paragraph, with his eyes about him.

The strolling style of the second paragraph steadies to the pausing, gently definite style of the third; to the 'deadly' analysis of the fourth (Fred Jowett's favourite brand of Ruskin prose). There is a measured escalation, with a current of controlled hysteria, in the fifth. We move on, trying to keep pace with our author in the sixth. He is moving more rapidly, and with more emphasis now. Some of his remarks are perhaps contentious. Aware of this, he stops dead in the street, and turns to us with a winning piece of humour. 'It is far better to spend four thousand pounds in making a good gun, and then blow it to pieces, than to pass life in idleness. Only do not let it be called "political economy".'

If we are still with him – and humour excludes those it does not include – we pass indoors, or join him on some public bench that has survived progress; to engage in some reflective chat, with suggestions of debate. By the end of the seventh paragraph, his eyes are looking straight into the reader's, on the repeated second person singular: 'So that, conclusively, in political as in household economy, the great question is, not so much what money you have in your pocket, as what you will buy with it, and do with it'.

Into the human world, 'like a body of light', flows the natural resource of living water. 'Where the land falls, the water flows,'

Ruskin wrote in *Unto This Last*. The 'popular economist' rightly sees 'the action of wealth' as a natural movement, like that of a river. But the popular economist, like all bullies, is 'sentimental'. He relies upon pretty 'nature' imagery, to further the degradation of human nature. He has never met the God of nature. Like Wordsworth, he is 'incurious to see in the hands the print of the nails'. The fact is that for 'centuries, great districts of the world, rich in soil and favoured in climate, have lain desert under the rage of their own rivers'. Agreed, 'no human laws can withstand' the flow of rivers or of wealth. 'They can only guide it. . . that it shall become water of life.' And that 'only' is our challenge, and our hope: unless we prefer, like Luther, to abrogate duty under a view of a man as 'a beast of burden'.[46]

At present, at Croydon, man has so low an estimate of himself, and such a romantic view of nature, that he submits to a system whereby 'the strength and life of the English operative' are 'spent in defiling ground instead of redeeming it'. Men work in mine and furnace, and at the drawing-desk, to produce ugly railings for fencing off 'two feet depth of freehold land' below the pub windows: 'a little piece of dead ground. . . unsweepable by ordinary methods'. This is the logic of capitalism, which has forgotten the point of capital; which is to be as a ploughshare, put to good use.[47] There is no 'profit', for the moment, in keeping clean the pools of Carshalton; there is 'profit', only for the moment, in producing cages for the exhibition of rubbish.

The Crown of Wild Olive was published in May 1866. It was on 9 July 1866 that there occurred the famous incident of the subversion of the Hyde Park railings, which would form a stimulus to Arnold's *Culture and Anarchy* of 1867–9. That work, as Arnold's admirer Lionel Trilling has pointed out, puts to one side the differences of class interest, and ignores almost entirely – makes a virtue of ignoring – the injustices of a system which made those differences so unacceptable in Victorian England. And so 'Arnold's whole problem is thrown into the field of epistemology'.[48] Ruskin, in paragraphs 2-7 of the *Preface* to *The Crown of Wild Olive*, makes clear what he suggested in the Work of Iron lecture of 1858: that the anarchy is the railings, and everything that makes them possible. To overturn them may be an act of secondary anarchy: it may also be the initiation of culture. 'All healthy men like fighting.' Thank God for that. There may be 'human herds' containable by railings, but Ruskin is not of their number.[49]

The remaining paragraphs of Ruskin's *Preface* are an analysis of the theology that skulks behind railings. It is, as might be expected, a curiously divided one. On the one hand, God is an oppressive tyrant who has condemned men to bestial toil, to no end. On the other, He is so obliging that, without help from us, He will maintain in perpetuity the finite planet we abuse: tidy up our little messes, somehow, and supply the pious capitalist, and the 'sentimental schoolboys' who want to be officers – which is to say, the capitalist's policemen – with an endless supply of human cattle, and a sufficiency of 'pleasant banks' over which to 'hunt tigers or savages', of which God will provide a fresh supply, somehow, whenever required, like manna in the desert.[50]

In *Unto This Last* Ruskin had attempted to suggest an honourable course, even for the merchant, and had insisted that the poor are not a different race from the rich.[51] The audiences of *Traffic* and *Work* have their humanity in common with the audience of *War*. Hopefully, all of them are capable of being something other than merely 'vulgar'. All of them should know the inseparability of life from death, and the distinction between the two. Language is a metaphor. It is a making of connections and distinctions. Men should be relieved of the onus of misconducting themselves under subservience to a mixed metaphor, which is the alchemic quintessence of vulgarity, for it is 'death, mingled with life'.[52] 'We usually believe in immortality, so far as to avoid preparation for death; and in mortality, so far as to avoid preparation for anything but death.' Belief has its truth, and so has unbelief. But the costly luxury of Victorian 'doubt' is the old Dragon of the Hesperides in a new guise: the symmetrical monster of cynicism and superstition, undying enemy both of reason and of faith.

Ruskin's *Preface* sets out to murder superstition and cynicism; and to leave the immortalists no refuge but in 'divine' works, the mortalists no bolt-hole but 'untormenting' self-possession.[53]

The earlier colloquy is over. Ruskin and the reader have met: and battle is drawn. Ruskin's strategy begins in paragraph 8 with a calculated retreat. 'I have been long accustomed. . . to hear my statements laughed at. . . it seems impossible to gain so much as a patient hearing. . .' By the commencement of the ninth paragraph, the reader has Ruskin 'checked', confessing diffidently his three pieces. Thought will be necessary to capture the author's position, though:

the pieces 'were not prepared without reference to each other'. And this author can deal in outrageous truth as ruthlessly as the next man. 'I chiefly desired. . . to question my hearers. . . as to. . . what they expected or intended their manufacture to come to, their selling to come to, and their killing to come to.'

In paragraph 10, with the devastating irony of the born chess player, Ruskin asks his reader to remind him of the rules of their cosmic game. Do we play as immortals or as mortals? In paragraph 11, Ruskin parodies his own commonsense style, and his own angelic style. Which would the reader prefer? Are we dealing merely with 'a certain quantity of red clay'? If so, are we always to be players, never pieces? Or is there some 'astonished condition of soul' provided for in the rules? If so, are we mere pieces, with no say in the game? While the reader hesitates, Ruskin gets round his defences with a little viperish humour. In 'addressing a body of men subject to considerable hardship, and having to find some way out of it' does one tell them, 'My friends – you have only to die, and all will be right'? Let us consult a possible book of rules. There is the bible. 'I have read that book. . . and. . . am thankful that, on those who trust it, I can press its pleadings.' That last word is deliberately weak. True, as Ruskin demonstrates in the remainder of paragraph 12 the feeble old Bible has enough in it to annihilate Victorian capitalism in the soul of the Victorian Christian. But let us assume (paragraph 13) the reader 'inaccessible to appeals founded on it'? There is always the Church (paragraph 14); but 'a brave belief in death' is felt to be inconsistent with 'purity of character, or energy of hand' only by a Church in its 'last depravity'. Capture of usurous bishops. Shall we settle for the 'more probable apprehension' that man is mortal?

Ruskin's fifteenth paragraph is fairly under way. His still small voice is speaking inside the reader's own head. More particularly, he is speaking to the innerness of the Victorian intelligence. Clough, in his *Easter Day: Naples, 1849* had been able to rescue the meaning of resurrection (and 'meaning' is what Ruskin is after) only by denying it as a fact. Tennyson, in *In Memoriam*, had not been able to construct any affirmation out of his magical rhythms except across a sickening chasm of despair. Must we hate ourselves as pious frauds, or detest ourselves as meaningless scum? Robbed of the toy of superstition, are we to snatch at 'toys' of dust?

'I think better of you, even of the most selfish,' says Ruskin, opening his last paragraph with a routing rescue of his eclipsed opponent, 'than that you would do this, well understood.' Advance your pawn right across the board, and see what crown the unseen enemy will give you. Do you fancy a 'jewelled circlet flaming through Heaven above the height of the unmerited throne'? If you have any sense of style, you will recoil from that: it is 'kindly peace, fruitful and free' that you want, for a few moments at the end of the game?

'The wreath was to be of *wild* olive, mark you', Ruskin adds: 'the tree that grows carelessly, tufting the rocks with no vivid bloom, no verdure of branch; only with soft snow of blossom, and scarcely fulfilled fruit, mixed with grey leaf and thornset stem; no fastening of diadem for you but with such sharp embroidery!'

The image is typical of Ruskin in its concentrated allusiveness. To insist on the metaphor of the chess game; and to limit exploration of allusions to the literary top drawer, would be to leave much unexplained; but might also provide something worthy of reflection. There is also the question of 'embroidery'.

First, the crown has a 'thornset stem', as well as 'soft snow of blossom'. The expression 'sharp embroidery' is an odd one; and more than a Ruskinian homage to the arts of the needle. It is as though the reader were confronted by the three Fates, daughters of Zeus and Themis, or Divine Law, who allot him his portion of life. Much is defined by these three ladies, and it is safe to take the image a little further.

Clotho has special regard to the textile and manufacturing capitalists of *Traffic*: for she holds the distaff and the thread. Lachesis, who draws off the thread, may be assimilated to the working audience of Camberwell. Atropos, who cuts the thread short, relates more clearly to the audience of *War*. Ruskin's three pieces have grown to the size of the Fates from Athens, in the museum at Bloomsbury. Their functions are inseparable, and to some extent determining. But they do not weave the pattern of individual life; still less do they determine what Ruskin elsewhere calls 'the art of life', the particular beauty which the individual may stitch into, and out of, his own existence.

There is an obscure terror and absurdity in the phrase 'no fastening of diadem for you but with such sharp embroidery!' Our honours are in some sense attached to us; yet we, and they, are part of a larger pattern. In Ruskin's phrase, the diadem is realised for us from off the web of existence just at the moment when our own status as figures on that same web is realised. We pick out the crown in the tapestry just as we feel ourselves finally fastened into the tapestry beneath the crown; and there is a surreal glimpse for a moment of the whole fabric of human history as a Bayeux tapestry on the knees of enormous chess pieces.

The usual meaning of 'crowning' in chess is when a pawn reaches the end of the board, and is exchanged for a 'taken' queen. All this effort is in order to 'save' the king, who moves very little. It is here that the 'craftsmen – salesmen – swordsmen' of Ruskin's audiences are meant to say 'Wait!' It was Jessie Richardson whose brother taught Ruskin chess. Jessie was Ruskin's cousin and child-love; and she died as a child.[54] While completing *The Crown of Wild Olive* Ruskin had been endeavouring to find a substitute for her in the shape of Rose La Touche. But there is an indecency, a vulgarity, in this false resurrection, a 'death, mingled with life'. To impose the role of new-born Redeemer on another human being is to crown Christ with thorns all over again. Nor can God provide us with substitutes for those we have lost. The crown of wild olive is an adornment one is perpetually in the process of making for oneself: something to own up to, rather than to boast of. It is not transferable. One must wear it all by oneself, if at all, not seek salvation by pushing it onto another head.

Moments of high crisis from *Paradise Lost* and *The Divine Comedy* come to Ruskin's aid to tell his meaning. While Eve is succumbing to the serpent, Adam – her appointed guardian – is whiling away her absence by wreathing a crown of flowers for her head. As she returns with her terrible news, he drops the crown: and only then do we see what name and meaning the flowers have. They were roses; we see them 'faded': we, and Adam, first sense that these brightest of all flowers have thorns. Adam reasons with himself 'Should God create another Eve. . . yet loss of thee would never from my heart'.[55] God, like Zeus, is poor. He is an artist; not a manufacturer. He cannot repeat himself. Eve, ambitious ninny, is the inventor of Divine Wisdom, in her longing to be divine. Adam, moral weakling, is the inventor of Divine Love, as he determines to leave Paradise with Eve, whom he has in a deep sense lost for ever, rather than look piously round for some admissible substitute.

At the end of Canto 27 of *Purgatorio*, the hero is again alone. 'No longer expect word or sign from me,' his guide Vergil warns him, 'Free, upright and whole is thy will. . . therefore over thyself I crown and mitre thee.'[56] Dante must become himself before he is fit to meet Beatrice again, in her celestial being, crowned with cultivated olive.

If life were a game, it could be played by substitutes. If death were only 'loss', resurrection would only be a matter of strategy. It was from a thicket of wild olive that Odysseus woke to find Nausicaa. But she was not for him. In his own emotional crisis of 1865–6, Ruskin could allow himself to love Rose only by forbidding himself to need her. This odd pair left each other free.[57]

How much of his own crown Ruskin can forsee is suggested by his description: 'Free-heartedness, and graciousness, and undisturbed trust, and requited love, and the sight of the pleasure of others, and the ministry to their pain'. The inner pair of blessings, into which the first two, and out of which the final two, are fastened; may never be granted; and the whole wreath come to nothing for Ruskin himself. In the drama of life, it is a little late for him to play the juvenile lead. But when some Prospero draws back the curtain to disclose, where we saw Romeo and Juliet dead, 'Ferdinand and Miranda playing at chess', Ruskin hopes that at least in some unflattering role as an honest old counsellor, he may be able to exclaim: 'Look down, you gods / And on this couple drop a happy crown!'[58] He will have missed love but not the power of loving.

Meanwhile, on the cue 'pain', Ruskin the artist drives himself to tantalise his readers with a little sentiment, just as Ariel teases the shipwrecked invaders of his master's island with their own desires: 'the blue sky above you, and the sweet waters and flowers of the earth beneath'? The reader holds most of the pieces, and has advanced to the heart of his opponent's refuge:

> Go release them, Ariel:
> My charms I'll break, their senses I'll restore
> And they shall be themeselves[59]

Behind the sentimental view is 'the mystery of clearness. . . the deep infinity of the thing itself'. Ruskin's prose, like Turner's painting style, works 'like the most subtle moves of a game of chess'.[60] At the end of the *Preface* to *The Crown of Wild Olive*, the reader has won; for Ruskin bequeathes him the universe: the 'mysteries and presences, innumerable, of living things'. Here is material 'serviceable for the life that now is', if the right rational victor can use it. As for Ruskin, he vanishes, in the final exhalation, like Ariel set free: 'nor, it maybe, without promise of that which is to come'. For the pious, there is a holy joke under this. We have advanced right out of the gospel of John. God is gone up from Olivet, the mount of cultivated olives. 'Ye men of Galilee, why stand ye gazing up into heaven?'[61] The *Acts* of the Apostles has already started; and each man has a fair chance of becoming the new twelfth.

CHAPTER TWELVE

KINDLY NOTICE

> John Ruskin has recently sent his subscribers the fourth letter of the new series of *Fors Clavigera*. . . We know numbers in our small circle of friends, who look upon him in the light which he would value most, that of a man who loves truth for its own sake, and is a sincere lover of his fellow men. . .
>
> —Review of *Fors Clavigera* Letter 88 (March 1880)
> *Bingley Telephone & Airedale Courant*, 23 April 1880

> . . . a kindly notice. . . — Acknowledgement of the above review
> *Ford Clavigera* Letter 89 (September 1880)

It was only when he first took office that W. E. Forster's Bradford supporters detected in him the erosion of political innocence. That was in 1865, when he had the thankless task, as Under-Secretary for the Colonies, of dealing with the crisis caused by Edward Eyre's violent suppression of black insurgents in Jamaica. Forster followed Cabinet policy, and the advice of lawyers, in stopping short of officially prosecuting the wretched Eyre, who had gained a humanitarian reputation as a magistrate in Australia. The real culprit was the vagueness of colonial law, which would later be clarified and reformed in time to save Jamaica from the perpetual revolutions, insurgencies and tyrannies that bedevilled Haiti. Meanwhile opinion was violently divided. Dickens defended Eyre as a protest against the telescopic Jellyby philanthropy of a *laissez-faire* 'system' of which the Jamaica trouble was merely a symptom. Similar motives activated Ruskin, who felt obliged, as did Tennyson, to offer some support in this matter to the known views of Carlyle. Charles Kingsley was more wholehearted for Eyre. Mill, Huxley and Herbert Spencer were on the other side. After delivering himself of a speech in his defence, Ruskin, who had had meanwhile the opportunity to encounter the uncertain cavalier beneath Eyre's humanitarian public image, slithered out of the controversy as best he might. Forster remained the victim of his position.[1]

Radicals up and down the country were furious, notably the Huddersfield Liberals, among whom James Hanson had his roots. He could only agree with *The Morning Star* that 'officialism. . . places the whole man on a lower platform'. Not even Byles could consent altogether to acquit Forster on this occasion. On the other hand, Carlyle, who had enjoyed meeting and impressing Forster in London in 1845, in Yorkshire in 1847 and in Ireland in 1849, when he was still 'an enthusiastic young Wet-Quaker', now dismissed him as a 'nigger emancipator, Radical patriot'. *The Times* thought Forster had acted with admirable discretion.

The Crown of Wild Olive was published in May 1866. Ruskin had written to the *Daily Telegraph* in December 1865, denouncing the hypocrisy of the Huddersfield Liberals who wanted Eyre impeached, but were themselves supporters of an economic system that meant slavery and death for the inhabitants of the British Isles. In September 1866 Ruskin would deliver a flamboyant speech to save from 'ruin the man who had dared to strike down one seditious leader, and rescue the lives of a population'. This was at a meeting of the Eyre Defence and Aid Fund, with Carlyle in the chair.[2] While Carlyle seems to have supported Eyre's actions unequivocally, Ruskin seems to have been motivated by a sense of injustice at the Liberals' choice of Eyre as a scapegoat. Not everyone was in a position to see this distinction at the time, and Ruskin's involvement with the Eyre business made the maintenance of his good name, in Bradford as elsewhere, rather difficult among Liberals.

A reading of the *Observer* reveals that Charles Kingsley was thrown willingly to the dogs of liberalism; and Tennyson was not treated much better. The fact that the popular novelist Charles Dickens was also on Eyre's side seems to have been too delicate to mention, though sorrowful allusion was made to 'the most popular authors of the day'. Carlyle is dealt with by a somewhat disingenuous allusion to Alexander and Joseph Dacre Carlyle, the Divine, and Arabic scholar, respectively. In *Jamaican Echoes*, the leader article for 29 November 1866, comes this dark sentence: 'We look back for a parallel to the time, not a century ago, when the literary caste in Scotland, the Robertsons, and Blairs, and Carlyles,[3] broke off from the sympathies and impulses of the national life, and were in consequence stranded and left behind. . . it is with humiliation and pity that we bid adieu to Court poets and Court chaplains. . . if they will make themselves recluses and fossils, the world cannot therefore stand still. . .' These allusions to Carlyle, Tennyson and Kingsley, are typical of the tone taken by the *Observer*.

Ruskin required subtler treatment. In the *Observer* this treatment is meted out by two means: the one honourable and even sympathetic, the other much less so.

The strongest point in Ruskin's speech of 7 September in Eyre's defence was its contrast between English proprietorial anarchy and English righteous indignation. An English jury has just acquitted a fellow member of the middle class for shooting dead a drunken workman who staggered at night into his suburban garden. Why all the fuss about governor Eyre? The righteous English people 'for the sake of filling its pockets would pour mortal venom into all its air and all its streams; would shorten the lives of its labourers by thirty years a life, that it might get its needle-packets twopence each cheaper'. That Byles shared some of this irony is suggested by a juxtaposition in the *Observer* of 9 August 1866. A piece on Forster's very proper plea for a reform of colonial law is juxtaposed to a leader on 'The Ethics of Cholera'. To save themselves twopence a week, Bradford landlords neglect to connect their tenements with the public water supply. Their tenants must buy water from barrels in the street and hoard it in buckets till 'it becomes stale and deleterious'.

Byle's *Observer* deals honourably and tellingly with Ruskin on the matter of Governor Eyre, simply by selecting for quotation, on 13 September, the most profound phrase of Ruskin's own speech of 7 September. The threat of prosecuting Eyre 'was the cry of a nation blinded by its avarice to all true valour and virtue, and haunted, therefore, by phantoms of both'. Even in mid-rant Ruskin's genius could not help producing the occasional gem, and this the *Observer* selects for quotation, leaving its readers to come to their own conclusions.

The *Observer* dealt delicately with Ruskin in more senses than one. Like the *Review*, the *Observer* quoted the *Spectator* on Kingsley's 'flunkeyism' and Carlyle's worship of brutal despots. The *Observer* did not quote, as the *Review* did,[4] with approval, Edward Miall's *The Nonconformist* on 'our Carlyles, Kingsleys, Ruskins – who are found to be champions of brute force without regard to the claims of justice and humanity'. Byles bided his time till after Ruskin's speech, which began with the expression of 'the simple desire of obtaining justice, not for black men only, nor for white, but for men of every race and colour'. But, on the other hand, neither did Byles, in reviewing *The Crown of Wild Olive*, offer any quotations from *Traffic*. The *Bradford Advertiser* gleefully quoted in full Ruskin's satire on the Temple of Britannia Agoraia.[5] The *Observer* trod more softly, yet to more effective end. For Byles quotes, from *Work*, Ruskin's most scathing paragraph on the English games of making money, hunting and fine dressing. He gives in full Ruskin's judgment on 'these Fiend's servants, who have it principally for the object of their lives to make money. . . That is the modern Judas's way of "carrying the bag".' From *War* Byles quotes Ruskin's warning against the thoughtlessness of youth, and his final paragraph against religious hypocrisy: 'If you choose to obey your Bibles, you will never care who attacks them. . . the Bible tells you to have pity on the poor, – and you crush them under your carriage wheels. . .'[6] Thus the two areas where Ruskin himself had trod softly in Nonconformist capitalist Bradford – the separation of religion from life, and the destructiveness of reducing everything to the profit motive – are set clearly before Bradford Liberals by Byles, from other lectures, without any embarrassing reference to Bradford Wool Exchange.

But if Byles dealt honourably with Ruskin by skilful deployment of quotation, the *Observer* did Ruskin less than justice on one of his themes which became quite embarrassingly apposite during November 1866. A special convention of the Rivers Commission, meeting in St George's Hall, revealed the appalling condition of the Bradford water-courses, the foulness and inadequacy of its drains and salient details such as the fact that the lower rooms of the comparatively genteel Hanover Square were unusable because of the stench of what passed for sewers. Bradford took seven million gallons a day from the Wharfe and three million a day from the Aire – and discharged what remained of this after use back into the Aire in a murderously toxic condition. The Aire cattle – once a pastoral subject for Turner – knew better than to drink the water. The commissioners had barely packed their bags when Bradford was visited by yet another *Great Flood*: 'cascades from the hill-sides, swollen turbid torrents in the river-beds, the lake-like expansions in flats and river valleys, inundations of houses, factories, workshops and warehouses'. Four lives were lost in Bradford; with another twenty-one fatal accidents round about. 'To the town [the flood] has administered an irretortible rebuke. . . we must really treat Bradford beck with more respect', writes Byles. The water at the botton of Well Street rose to a height of two feet, with resultant dampness to the interior of Bradford Mechanics' Institute.[7]

Here, surely, was an opportunity to offer a little comment on Ruskin's invocation of the divine flood of Plato's *Critias*. And just such comment is promised by a headline on the literary page for 6 December: *The Gods, The Flood, and the Banquet*. But, alas, it is an amusing piece, and below the *Observer's* usual standard at that. Bored after dinner on Olympus, the gods descend to 'Blackford'. What they find there provokes their rage, and storms. What do they find? The absurd and appalling spectacle of a 'Tory Banquet' at which 'Around the board sat guests in grim attire on havoc bent'. This is easily to be identified as the Conservative Operative Banquet of November last, at which those antediluvian dignitaries the Church of England priesthood and squirearchy – notably Mr Busfield-Ferrand – had made a bid for a return to power, with banners proclaiming such names as Richard Oastler, and Lord Shaftesbury. Busfield-Ferrand, the old Factory Reformer, is also, to judge from an *Observer* leader of 15 November, personally guilty for much of the filth of Bradford. Has he not refused to permit the use of his streams at Harden and Cullingworth for the purification of the Bradford Canal?

And so, despite his positive response to *Unto This Last*, Byles, under the threat of a Tory revival at Bradford, allows an anonymous hack to deflect Ruskin's divine flood into the sewers of political controversy.

Forster had majority Bradford Liberal approval for his Ballot Bill of 1871 as for his Education Bill of 1870; though the latter motivated an alarming temporary revolt among local Independents (religious and other) when its terms were known. When 'Buckshot Forster' was deployed against troublous Ireland, there was far less disturbance – among Bradford Liberals. It was a sad sign of the times to see *The Bradford Observer* thus lending itself in support of his Irish Protection Bill: 'This government, of all governments, will not misuse the absolute despotic authority conferred upon it. Is not this an irresistible case?' Presumably only Liberals were equipped to play Governor Eyre.

Ruskin 'began' his distinctly social and economic work in 1859, in response, it seems, to the Bradford Mass Poisoning Tragedy.[8] His middle-class audience had not been altogether unresponsive. But in January 1871 he made a new beginning as Europe began 'another group of ten years, not in happy circumstances'. Paris was in process of being starved into surrender by the 'Red Prince', Frederick Charles of Prussia. The Bishop of London, the Baptist Dr Brock, the Roman Catholic Cardinal Manning, the Jewish Alfred de Rothschild, the indefinable Mr Ruskin, sank their differences in working for the Paris Relief Fund Committee.[9] The *Fors Clavigera* letters are addressed to the 'Workmen and Labourers of Great Britain'; yet the flood theme of Ruskin's first letter, of January 1871 – *Looking Down from Ingleborough* – was one which he saw on a European scale. He had lectured at the Royal Institution in February 1870 on *Verona, and its Rivers*, instancing the work of Can Grande della Scala in defending Verona against inundation as a most wholesome achievement of that not in every respect admirable Prince, protector though he was of Dante. In January 1871 Ruskin was writing to the press about the inundations of the Tiber, which had wrought such havoc in the new kingdom of Italy. 'The first thing the King of any country has to do is to manage the streams of it,' he wrote. 'If he can manage the streams, he can also the people; for the people also form alternately torrent and maremma, in pestilential fury or pestilential idleness. They also will change into living streams of men' by schemes of literal irrigation. Let the 'Red Prince' take note, adds Ruskin. The 'red inundation' of the Commune is, like other inundations, a natural result of unnatural wrong.[10]

It must not be supposed that Ruskin, in commencing *Fors Clavigera*, imagined himself to be a medieval prince or a modern king. He was merely taking a leaf out of Carlyle's *Heroes and Hero-Worship*. 'Burke said there were Three Estates in Parliament; but in the Reporters' Gallery yonder, there sat a *Fourth Estate* more important far than they all.'[11] Ruskin's irrigations are those of a freelance reporter, addressed to men who are for the most part on the outer fringe of the British constitution: for many of them have as yet no vote. Ruskin's tone is going to be subtler than Carlyle's. 'You cannot evoke any form of government by beat of drum.' What he hopes for is 'the considerate acceptance of a code of laws, and the appointment of means for their execution, neither of which can be done in an instant'.[12]

The Old Testament God had taught mankind sense in a very heavy-handed way; by drowning everybody but Noah and his family. In *Verona and its Rivers* Ruskin notes than Can Grande's trench through the limestone of Verona revealed 'fossil-creatures, still so like the living creatures they were once, that there it first occurred to the human brain. . . that the buried shapes. . . had indeed once lived and died. . . Under those white banks. . . was born. . . the Modern Science of Geology.'[13] That science has deprived the *Genesis* story of universal flood of any claim to be historical 'fact'. We can no longer comfort ourselves, from *Genesis*, with notions of cataclysm, designed by a primitive deity for the drowning of our neighbours and the salvation of ourselves. We must arm ourselves, from *Genesis*, with the spiritual meaning of the rainbow of reconciliation. The creation of such a covenant will be harder than lapsing into the old competitive mentality. It will require far more courage and intelligence than any military campaign.

'Suppose, for the present,' Ruskin writes, 'that France, and every other country but your own, were – what I suppose you would, if you had your way, like them to be – sunk under water, and that England were the only country in the world. Then, how would you live in it most comfortably? Find out that, and you will easily find how two countries can exist together; or more, not only without need for fighting, but to eath other's advantage.'

> '. . . the essential character of the war between Germany and France may be best understood by supposing it a dispute between Lancaster and Yorkshire for the line of the Ribble. . . Lancashire with its Cumbrian and Cheshire contingents invades Yorkshire, and meeting with much Divine assistance, ravages the West Riding, and besieges York on Christmas day. That is the actual gist of the whole business; and in the same manner you may see the downright common sense – if any is to be seen – of other human proceedings, by taking them first under narrow and homely conditions. So, for the present, we will fancy ourselves, what you tell me you all want to be, independent: we will take no account of any other country but Britain; and on that condition I will begin to show you in my next paper how we ought to live. . .'[14]

Ruskin's next paper certainly makes clear how Britain ought not to live, is indeed, not living. Ruskin lampoons no villains; he merely juxtaposes three extracts from the Press. One describes the rags and starvation of Wapping. Another gives an account of the successful trial of the largest gun yet made: the 'Woolwich Infant'. The third is taken from a party-political speech by Ruskin's good friend Mr Cowper-Temple, 'one of the best and kindest of our public men'.

As an amateur associate of the Fourth Estate, Ruskin merely sets the three extracts together.

On the one hand come the 'performances of the 35-ton gun called the "Woolich Infant", which is fed with 700-pound shot, 130 pounds of gunpowder at one mouthful'. On the other side, 'the Wapping infants, starving on a half-chance meal a day'. How does Mr Cowper-Temple defend this state of affairs? 'Mr Cowper-Temple. . . informs the Liberals of Portsmouth, that in consequence of our amiable neutrality "we must contemplate the contingency of a combined fleet coming from the ports of Prussia, Russia, and America, and making an attack on England".'

Ruskin gives judgment in terms of a terse summary of the Preface to *The Crown of Wild Olive*: 'Contemplating myself these relations of Russia, Prussia, Woolwich, and Wapping, it seems to my uncommercial mind merely like another case of iron railings – thieves outside, and nothing to steal within'.[15] Nothing, that is, for the Wapping infant to lose. Nothing for anyone remotely resembling either an officer or a gentleman to defend.

The first two letters of *Fors Clavigera*, taken together, provide the foundation on which the rest of the series is built. They are initiations into Ruskin's 'elementary principles of Human Economy'. These principles are basically simple, but infinitely various in application. The common sense of them is that natural and military disasters are best averted by our being prepared for them. What could be simpler? The organisation required after a flood or during a siege cannot be summoned into existence without preparation. The landscape, and the economy, need to be so organised that the whole population is always as physically fit as may be, and enjoying the best obtainable level of education and morale. These are the conditions under which disasters, when they come, may best be met. There is a superstition in men's minds – particularly in the English Liberal mind – that to prepare for disaster is to invite it. On the contrary, for Ruskin, the conditions of preparedness are the best guarantees against disaster. Crisis requires loyalty. The proper work of the legislature is to see that loyalty is available. Only fairness offers the possibility of that. Fairness cannot protect men altogether from war or natural disaster. But conditions of fairness make these calamities less likely; as well as offering the best protection when they come. Ruskin really means all of these things, which is why he cannot be appropriated by any political party.

As distinct from his 'Master' Carlyle, however, Ruskin has a strong streak of liberalism in him. His liberalism helps to make sense of the 'Tory' and 'Communist' strands in him. Carlyle was a great believer in work, and in leadership. Ruskin believes in effective leadership, too, and also in work. But the 'liberal' refinements by which he adjusts Carlyle's vision of work and leadership transform Carlyle's doctrines into something very different.

The man George Eliot called the 'finest writer living' cannot be summarised. But a point on work, and a passage on leadership, deserve to be noticed.

First, it was in 1871 that Ruskin revived Sir Thomas More's notion of a six hour working day: a suggestion so insanely Utopian that it was not till 1917 that it was first publicly and strenuously advocated by one of the most intelligent and efficient capitalists Britain has ever produced: W. H. Lever, the first Viscount Leverhulme.[16]

There is no excuse for an image of Ruskin as a watercolour Carlyle, palely following Carlylean thunders such as this: 'Not "I can't eat!" but "I can't work!" that was the burden of all wise complaining among men'. Poor Carlyle. 'What in my own personal way I chiefly regret and wonder at in him,' Ruskin wrote in confidence to C. E. Norton, 'is the perception in all nature of nothing between the stars and his stomach, his going, for instance, into North Wales for two months, and noting absolutely no Cambrian thing or event, but only increase of Carlylean bile.' Carlyle was lacking in sympathy, in the tenderness which concerns itself with the limitations of other human minds and bodies. A chat with his tenantry reassured the Yorkshire landowner Charles Woodd that his fellows were happier lying on their sides in coal-seams during the winter months than lounging by the fire. 'All I can say is, tastes differ,' Ruskin replies: 'but I have not myself tried the degree of comfort which may be attained in winter by lying on one's side in a coal-seam.'

Carlyle's great chapter on *Captains of Industry*, in *Past and Present*, was one Ruskin much admired. But, in one of its grandest paragraphs, there is too much of that worship of strong leaders, too much of that element which Ruskin referred to as 'howlings. . . about Cromwell':

> Look around you. Your world-hosts are all in mutiny, in confusion, destitution; on the eve of fiery wreck and madness! They will not march farther for you, on the sixpence a day and supply-and-demand

> principle: they will not; nor ought they, nor can they. Ye shall reduce them to order, begin reducing them. To order, to just subordination; noble loyalty in return for noble guidance. . . Work, the grandest of human interests, does now require it.[17]

In his *Fors* letter for the citizens of Sheffield, of January 1877, Ruskin calls for effective leaders. But their effectiveness is necessarily based on fairness, and exists for the sake of fairness. Ruskin is very particular in his details. The Carlylean doctrine is humanised out of recognition.

The Devonshire contributor to *Fraser's* for October 1859 had come away from the West Riding with the conviction that if its 'people were bound together by some cementing tie. . . they might become very formidable in a political point of view'. Ruskin shared that conviction, and also the implication that such a movement, though it would need direction, could not be directed from above. 'Let the Wakefield and Bradford people look after themselves,' he wrote in 1877. The Sheffielders also. Those landlords of Winnington, the Stanleys of Alderley, have a nominal link with the place. Indeed, the 4th Baron Stanley of Alderley will also one day inherit the 'Barony of Sheffield'. Facts for Debrett. Ruskin's imagination takes quite a different course. In his own whimsical and profound way, he offers the extreme localism of the West Riding a universally valuable direction. Today Sheffield, tomorrow the world:

> You must register every man, woman and child, in your Sheffield district. . . Then the next thing is to establish a commissariat. Knowing how many mouths you have to feed, you know how much food is wanted daily. To get that quantity good; and to distribute it without letting middlemen steal the half of it. . .
> . . . there are two laws to be carried into effect, as you gain intelligence and unity, very different from anything yet conceived in your co-operative stores (which are a good and wise beginning, no less). Of which laws the first is that, till all the mouths in the Sheffield district are fed no food must be sold to strangers. . . Then the second law is, that as long as any one remains unfed, or barebacked, the wages fund must be in common. . . for actual beginning of organisation of this Sheffield commissariat. . . you must elect a duke of Sheffield, for yourselves. . . honest doge he must be, with an active and kind duchess. If you can't find a copule of honest and well-meaning married souls in all Sheffield to trust the matter to, I have nothing more to say. . .
>
> Once found, you are to give them fixed salary, and fixed

authority. . .[18]

What does this flight portend? These leaders clearly have a very different face from the heroes of Carlyle. And splendours unconnected with coronets. A 'poetical temperament'[19] might see an Athenian democracy electing a neo-medieval Doge and Dogess of Venice to revive as a first step to social renewal the communism of the apostles. A 'common sense'[20] interpretation would see an informed electorate choosing responsible, stipendiary, leaders of limited powers to set in motion an economy based on welfare. Local needs are to be given due weight, and the leaders would combine traditionally 'male' and 'female' functions. The State would have begun to evolve into a community.

In the *Future of England* lecture of 1869 Ruskin addressed the military section of England's ruling class. As Oxford Professor of Fine Art, from 1869, he is consciously addressing the future ruling class. Ruskin's correspondence with the Marchioness of Waterford and his campaign against the Bishop of Manchester's toleration of usury are notable examples of his brushes with aristocracy and the established church hierarchy. Prince Leopold, the youngest son of Queen Victoria, was among Ruskin's friends; and spoke warmly and in public of the Professor's work at Sheffield. Ruskin's father would have been in ecstasy, and Ruskin himself was touched and encouraged.[21]

Otherwise, three main stages in the development of Ruskin's social rhetoric can be seen, and a sequence of three different concepts as to the nature of his audience. Each stage was connected in his mind with his meditations about Bradford, the boom-town of mid-Victorian England.

First, it can be seen that Ruskin's appeal to England through the social conscience of the middle classes – always present in his writing – becomes inescapable in the *Nature of Gothic* chapter of *The Stones of Venice*, and even more evident in *The Political Economy of Art* of 1857. Yet, as he recalled in 1874, it seems to have been the Bradford Mass Poisoning Tragedy of November 1858 which set him irreversibly on a campaign of social criticism.

The second stage began as Ruskin left Bradford for Whernside and Ingleborough in March 1859. It would be expressed in the opening letter of *Fors Clavigera*, *Looking Down from Ingleborough*, and its successors. In these, he addressed the conscience of Great Britain through its 'Workmen and Labourers'.

The third stage opens with the 'kindly notice' taken of *Fors* Letter 88 in the *Bingley Telephone and Airedale Courant*. Ruskin's response was contained in Letter 89, of September 1880, of which he had several extra copies printed for distribution among trade union leaders. He called these pamphlets 'dainty packets of dynamite'.[22]

The door at which Hunt's *Light of the World* prepared to knock was carefully studied from a hut abandoned by gunpowder workers.[23] As early as 1859 Ruskin had taken special notice of the tenth chapter of St Matthew's gospel, with Christ's promise, not of 'peace', but a 'sword'. This had reminded him of *Luke* Chapter 12. 'Nothing about *sentiments* here,' he commented: only 'Sell that ye have and give alms.'[24] Spiritual truth was buried somewhere in Hunt's *Light of the World*; but it was not to be discovered by contemplating a bejewelled redeemer knocking at the weed-tangled door of – somebody else's – soul. Now, in September 1880, Ruskin was ready to proclaim a theology of dynamite.

The significance of this development lies in two related facts. First, Unionism was a distinctly class-conscious movement. Ruskin, for whom innovation was 'against the grain',[25] was compelled more and more to deploy what he often still insisted on calling Tory values on the side of the poorer classes of society in their opposition to the richer classes. Secondly, Ruskin was more and more conscious that he could no longer pose as a paternalist educator of the lower orders. He was more consciously conversing with aristocrats of labour: men like Thomas Dixon,[26] who had been the recipient of *Time and Tide*. In short, Ruskin was drawn willy-nilly into the class struggle, and because of the intellectual nature of his discourse his place in that struggle would be as an energiser of the more idealistic, sensitive, and intelligent of the working-class leaders. 'When once the poorer classes began to read Ruskin they understood him,' reflected J. H. Whitehouse in 1919. 'His magic eloquence was to them like the discovery of a new Holy Scripture. Their material demands for better conditions of life were now given a spiritual significance. The demand for reform became part of the eternal conflict between right and wrong.'[27] There is truth in this. But only a minority of the poorer classes read so much as *Merrie England*, [28] Robert Blatchford's popularisation of Ruskin, Morris and other 'advanced' thinkers. Ruskin himself was read only by a minority of that minority. Marchionesses are rarer than miners: but Keir Hardies are no commoner than Lady Waterfords. From about 1880 Ruskin became the taste of a new kind of elite.

The qualities which had won him special favour among women readers remained. Towards the end, in the penultimate letter of *Fors Clavigera*, the writer who had said some hard things about Americans and denounced female interference in theology finally capitulated to the superior wisdom of two American women, and shook off altogether the dismal mantle of Carlyle. No one learns anything by force, Francesca Alexander and her mother had assured him. This was 'contrary to much that I have both believed and thought,' Ruskin confessed, accepting 'correction of what I may have myself too servilely thought respecting the need of compulsion.'[29] He was ready to embark on *Praeterita*, his last masterpiece and perhaps his greatest: an idiosyncratic piece of organisational wizardry informed by what Ruskin had called the 'naïvete of Dante. . . the instinct of a mind sanctified by Love into eternal youth'.[30]

In the pages of the *Bradford Observer* of 1866 can be read evidence for Ruskin's need to move away from a merely middle-class readership. In Ruskin's own writings of the '70s can be traced his recoil from merely paternalist preachment; till, in September 1880, he would seize with relief and apprehension on the 'kindly notice' of the working-class elite of Bingley.

CHAPTER THIRTEEN

MY DEAR FRIENDS

John Ruskin appears to run away with the idea that he is not appreciated by working people. We can assure him that he is mistaken in this. . . We have seen a letter which he once sent to a woolsorter in Cottingley, and he says in it that his correspondent was the first working man who had ever written to him. But John Ruskin must be told that humble working men look upon him as such a great man that it would be presumptuous on their part to do such a thing.

—*Bingley Telephone and Airedale Courant*, 23 April 1880
Review of *Fors Clavigera* Letter 88

MY DEAR FRIENDS. . . —*Fors Clavigera* Letter 89 (September 1880)

Ruskin is his own best critic. At the very end of his writing life he looked back with a shudder at his night in Manningham with the Mitchells, at his two nights in Bingley with the Harrises and at his lectures at the Bradford Mechanics' Institute: 'contemptuous audit',[1] he remembered was all he got for his pains. But, as the above quotations show, Ruskin had also known, while writing *Fors Clavigera*, of a very different reception from his 'good Yorkshire friends'. A 'kindly notice' might be one outcome of what seemed 'contemptuous audit'. *Traffic* provides a key to the understanding of how Ruskin's two judgments on himself and Bradford might co-exist.

Ruskin defines two kinds of knowledge. 'Athena. . . daughter of the Intellect' stands for 'perfect knowledge. . . in sign of which she is crowned with the olive spray, and bears the resistless spear.' But guarding this inner 'strength and peace' of Athena is the Gorgon Medusa graven 'on her shield, . . . representative mainly of the chilling horror and sadness (turning men to stone, as it were) of the outermost and superficial spheres of knowledge – that knowledge which separates, in bitterness, hardness, and sorrow, the heart of the full-grown man from the heart of the child.'[2]

In a passage of the *Inferno* frequently cited by Ruskin, Medusa is invoked by the angel from heaven who descends to open the gates of the inner City of Hell – the City of Evil Wealth. The Greek name for this dead wealth is Pluto. Dante calls him Dis. In *Unto This Last* Ruskin coins the term 'illth' to define his operations.[3] For Vergil and his pupil Dante the gates of Dis are opened, and they pass inside. But the damned souls without, avid with curiosity to penetrate the yet horrider mysteries within, are kept at bay by the angel's invocation of the Gorgon: '*Venga, Medusa!*'

One of the many levels on which *Traffic* may be read is as a sardonic repetition of this awesome scene. How easily, especially with reference to Cary's translation which Ruskin usually read, might one apply *Inferno* Canto 9 to Ruskin's descent upon Bradford. One can almost see him, like Dante's angel, 'full of noble anger' as he alights momentarily on the 'horrid grounsel', disdainfully 'from his face removing the gross air'.[4] Inhabitants of hell's suburbs are kept at bay – given only a glimpse of the inner Temple of Britannia Agoraia, which they are forbidden to penetrate. But third parties not truly at home in this spot of hell might pass lower to fuller knowledge, and – who knows? – eventually bring back to their faces that 'colour'[5] which Vergil restores to Dante on the windy seashore at the opening of *Purgatorio*.

The first edition of *The Crown of Wild Olive* was Ruskin's testament to the memory of his father, John James. It celebrates John, the apostle of love, and James the apostle of free-will. It sketches some of the tensions between these two concepts.

Ruskin's mother Margaret died on 5 December 1871. 'I am much more surprised,' he wrote to W. H. Harrison, 'at the new look of things in the twilight than I was after the sun had set for my father,' and added, for Acland's benefit, 'She reminds me altogether of what she was when she taught me the Sermon on the Mount. . . the sinking of all back to the bleak Mechanism was difficult to bear the sight of.' With Alfred Tylor's help, Ruskin hoped to honour her memory by cleansing the springs of Carshalton; and by erecting 'a low arch of marble, slightly sculptured in the manner of Pisan-Gothic, over the larger of the two springs'. Some cleaning was done, and a tablet erected, but the springs were quickly fouled again and the tablet disappeared.[6]

Ruskin spelt out the meaning of what might have been for his Oxford students in 1884. 'St. Margaret of Antioch was a shepherdess. . . Traditions of the resurrection of Acestis perhaps mingle in those of her contest with the dragon.' She expresses 'the soul's victory over temptation or affliction, by Christ's miraculous help, and without any special power of its own. She is the saint of the meek and of the poor. . . no other name. . . seems so gifted with a baptismal fairy power of giving grace and peace.'[7]

But the 'human herds' of Carshalton apparently wanted none of Margaret's grace and peace. When a new edition of *The Crown of Wild Olive* appeared in 1873, Ruskin would wreck the book's artistic structure by adding the radical-Tory lecture, the *Future of England*. Ruskin also ruined the *Preface* by importing into it phrases redolent of his mother's *contemptus mundi*. They abrogate the original motive of the *Preface*, while alluding to it. Persuasion was Ruskin's original motive; and it is the goddess Persuasion who is invoked as a reconciler at the end of Aeschylus's *Eumenides*. But the manner of Ruskin's allusion invokes temporal disdain, and the transcendant pain of one crying in the wilderness. It is a mood Margaret McMillan, too, would know. 'Not only one of the best women of her time,' as George Bernard Shaw would call her, '. . . but also one of the most cantankerous.'[8]

In the fifteenth paragraph of his original *Preface*, Ruskin turned to the men without faith, in these words: 'I would fain, if I might offencelessly, have spoken to them as if none others heard; and said thus'. In the 1873 edition these powerful and delicate phrases are replaced by a morsel of self-parody: 'Might not a preacher, in comfortless, but faithful, zeal – from the poor height of a grave-hillock for his Hill of Mars, and with the Cave of the Eumenides at his side – say to them thus'.[9] The tone of alienation is unmistakable. The allusions are easier to miss. But with the aid of *Modern Painters*, *Fors Clavigera*, Dante, a Victorian encyclopaedia and a map of Bradford, they may be made out.

'Eumenides', or 'Kindly Ones', was the Greek propitiatory name for the Furies, avengers of crime against kindred. At Athens their shrine was close to the 'Areopagus' or 'Hill of Mars', the meeting place for the Athenian Council and also for less formal assemblies; such as that at which Paul proclaimed to the Athenians their 'Unknown God'. Paul made use of local piety and poetry to do so. By Athenian custom, any unidentifiable fragment of shrine or temple that was unearthed by progress was set up and dedicated to the

'Unknown God' it had once honoured. Paul identifies this 'Unknown God': he is the one god of universal justice towards whom the greatest Athenian poets have aspired.[10]

So far, so good. 'The eyes of Persuasion please me', says Athena at the end of the *Eumenides*, resolving in reconciliation Orestes's trial before the Council of the Areopagus.[11] Paul was astute enough to give Athenians what they might accept. When Athens was converted she would not need to desecrate her Parthenon. The Turks would do that. Nor smash it into ruin. The Venetians would do that.[12] The Athenians merely changed their queen's name to Mary.

Intransigence has got on since the days of Athens. Revising the final proofs of *Traffic* in 1866, Ruskin has improved Plato's *Critias* by importing the ominous phrase 'blind hearts' into the naïve Greek's description of fallen man. This is Ruskin's historical gorgon-wisdom: refusing to imagine the 'eyes of Persuasion'. And now, in 1873, he reinforces that less cheerful view by reminding the reader, in the phrase 'Hill of Mars', of his own grim vision of the industrialised Garden of the Hesperides, from the fifth volume of *Modern Painters*. '"Mammon, the least erected spirit that fell"' is the evil dragon that holds that garden in thrall. 'That power,' writes Ruskin, '. . . is our British Madonna: . . . or, perhaps, more accurately still, our unknown god, sea-born, with the cliffs. . . of England for his altar; and no chance of any Mars' Hill proclamation concerning him, "whom therefore ye ignorantly worship". This is no irony. The fact is verily so.' The dragon's attendant slaves are the sad muses of such art as may exist in such a garden. These are the Hesperids, of whom Aegle, or 'Brightness', is the chief. Turner the painter who works in this 'paradise of smoke', is forever confined to portraits of the Hesperid Aegle: the crimson of sunset. Ruskin gives her picture, as painted by Giorgione. He has already compared the boyhoods of Giorgione, brought to fulfilment at Venice, and of Turner, stung into despair at Kirkstall.[13]

In bitter retrospective irony in the new phrases of 1873, Ruskin places himself as a new preacher on a new Hill of Mars. It comes to no more than 'the poor height of a grave hillock'. In universal terms, that might be any battlefield. It is indeed an image, sufficiently prophetic, of the whole world as empty battlefield. But in particular and literal terms, it is Church Bank, the grave-hillock of St Peter's Church, Bradford: from which Ruskin surveyed the Bradford paradise of smoke, its Stygian stream, the foul slums of Wapping and Bradford's 'own gas'.[14]

Why Bradford in particular? A first clue is poignant and unsatisfactory. In visiting Bradford Parish Church in 1859, Ruskin would probably have seen the memorial to Dr William Sharp, the obstetrician, by Joseph Gott, the Leeds sculptor. Leaning in mournful attitude over a plinth was a life-sized statue, of some provincial merit, of a woman naked to the waist and with hair dressed in braided Grecian style. Allowing for the Yorkshire preference for length and strength of feature, as compared with Venetian roundedness, she was sufficiently like Giorgione's Hesperid Aegle to provide a little reflection. Gott died in 1860. His Hesperid was bundled out of sight, as Ruskin may have noticed in 1864, during the puritanical 'restoration' of the early 1860s. Some busybody may even have been at hand, in 1859, to say what churchwardens have said since: that the monument was 'unsuitable for a church'. Which is one reason why Gott's figure has not been permitted to survive. 'Men say these Hesperids are sensual goddesses,' Ruskin writes in his analysis of the 'paradise of smoke' in *Modern Painters*. 'Crimson is impure and vile; let us paint in black if we would be virtuous.'[15]

A second clue is ludicrous and insufficient. Ruskin may have seen advertisements for Bradford's Full Dress Grand Concert of 2 March 1859; or read reports of it in looking at reports of his own lecture. There would be a certain irresistibly ironic irritation in seeing that his own appearance in Bradford was succeeded, the day after, by that of Signor Dragone, basso of La Scala Milan, doing battle with choice arias in St George's Hall.

Though insufficient, the clue is worth following: to Canto 23 of *Purgatorio*. Dante allegorises the corruption of the Church, drawing on images from *Jeremiah* and *Revelation*. The grieving voice of St Peter himself is heard from heaven. The chariot of the Church is turned into a bandwagon of cynicism and corruption by the treacherous sting of the dragon of covetousness: 'then it seemed to me the earth opened between the two wheels, and I saw a dragon come forth that drove its tail up through the car, and, as a wasp withdraws its sting, so, drawing back the malignant tail, it dragged out part of the bottom and made off on its wandering way'.[16]

Dante likens his dragon to a monstrous wasp. This points to an explanation for Ruskin's second image of 1873. The preacher has 'the Cave of the Eumenides at his side'. To quote the Victorian *National Encyclopaedia*, under Wasps: 'The solitary wasps form a group,

Eumenides. . . They are generally smaller that the social wasps, consist only of males and perfect females'. They construct 'small globular cells of mud. . . furnished with a store of small green insect larvae for the sustenance of the young of the wasp'. A perfect model of the political economy of the beautiful British family, whose cave is the Bradford basin, a paradise of smoke, and whose favourite hidey-hole, Bradford Mechanics' Institute, is even shaped like a wasp. These are the 'gentlemen of the jury', drawn not from the cast of the *Eumenides*, but from that of Arostophanes's *Wasps*: jurors who are the slaves of a corrupt regime, diverting to improper uses the revenue that should go to feed the hungry people. Homer had a word for such 'kings' as these. He called them 'people-eaters'.[17]

Ruskin would remember the wasp again in wickedly defining Bradford in *Fors Clavigera*, in 1875. Contrasting the lovely architecture of bees to the energetic mess of Bradford's suburbs, he designated the latter as a 'wasps' nest': 'I cannot but more and more reverence the fierce courage and industry, the gloomy endurance, and the infinite mechanical ingenuity of the great centres, as one reverences the fervid labour of a wasp's nest, though the end of all is only a noxious lump of clay'. But Ruskin's own private contact with Mitchell, Holmes, Ellen and Aldam Heaton, Alfred Harris, Lobley and others may well underlie the private confession, made at the same time to his Coniston friend Susan Beever, the naturalist. 'Wasps. . . are really much more amiable than bees', Ruskin writes, 'and never get angry without cause. All the same, they have a tiresome way of inspecting one, too closely, sometimes, I think.' Furthermore, 'they are our chief protector against flies'.[18] Every part of the natural pattern has the same right to exist. Soot, like wasps, is excellent for killing greenfly from off the roses of this world. And loving Rose as he did, Ruskin could never quite despair of a brighter future, even for a paradise of smoke with crazy roses in it.

In the 'Readings in *Modern Painters*' lectures of 1877, Ruskin would assail the wasp's nest creed; the creed of Bradford, England, and the modern world. Humour is a test of sincerity, and Ruskin gave his audience both:

> Plato threw out systems like the gleam on foam; Herbert Spencer throws them out like boys blowing bubbles full of dirty air. My system of 'Ideas of Power, Truth, Beauty, and Relation' was wrong too in denial of the delight in 'ideas of power'. Veneration, desire for exer-

> tion, and sympathy are all involved in 'ideas of power', and are all legitimate elements of delight. . .
>
> The food of Art is the ocular and passionate study of Nature. . . But nowadays sight has become mechanical. Ideas of power have become mechanical too. . . In Ealing cemetery I hear a tolling machine has been set up at the cost of £80, and the sexton, like a miller at his dam, turns on the lamentation. . . Well, next of course you will soon have steam organs and singers, and turn on your cathedral service. . . But of one thing I am sure, that you are trying with all your might to find out that you can turn on God. To take the idea of personal power out of creation; to destroy all art, from lowest to highest, and to substitute not merely mechanism – for there is ingenuity in mechanism – but blind force; nay, scarcely force, but the sticking of protoplasms to itself as of not merely ashes to ashes, but mud to mud.

All this does not make Ruskin despair. A lecture course on *Modern Painters* is necessary 'because *Modern Painters* itself is a lecture with no conclusion, and I have now to put the conclusion upon it. . . There were many things that puzzled me in Turner's life, and more that puzzled me in my own. . . and I was forced to finish the book while I was in this mess of thought, to please my father, and very lucky it was that I *did* please him.' 'Lucky' it might be interpolated, because Ruskin's father, pleased with *Modern Painters*, had sent its sequel to the press; and called it 'important'. The sequel to *Modern Painters*, Ruskin adds, was *Unto This Last*, which began the 'days of reprobation'. He invites his Oxford audience to undergo the same reprobation. They must refuse to be deprived of their 'intellectual lens and moral retina'.

At the end of his course, the Professor dismisses them with his blessing:

> First cultivate all your personal powers, not competitively, but patiently and usefully. . . Take Christ at His literal word, and, so sure as His word is true, He will be known of you in breaking of bread. Refuse that servant's duty because it is plain, – seek either to serve God, or know Him, in any other way: your service will become mockery of Him, and your knowledge darkness. Every day your virtues will be used by the evil spirits to conceal, or to make respectable, national crime. . . But obey the word in its simplicity. . . 'and the peace of God, which passeth all understanding, shall keep your hearts and minds through Christ Jesus.[19]

The Labour Church never heard so fine a sermon as that. But

dozens of preachers and lecturers were deploying the New Testament to the same ends by the early '90s. Margaret McMillan describes the first time she took her sister Rachel to a Bradford Labour Church meeting.

> The place of central interest for us was the Labour Institute in Peckover Street. It is approached. . . by a steep hill. . . on whose side the Parish Church stands like a dark sentinel. The institute was an abandoned Chapel. . . There was a crowd. . . on the first Sunday that we were here together. . . The Social Democratic Federationers were in force, and nearly all the newly formed Independent Labour Party; Swedenborgians from Bingley and the valleys near, old Chartists, Secularists and also inquirers and sympathisers.

Among the crowd were two of those who would stand by Ruskin's open grave at Coniston:

> . . . Arthur Priestman, dark-eyed, serene, a member of the Society of Friends [and] F. W. Jowett, and half a dozen women, hearty and hot from the preparation of the cellars as tea-rooms: this was the company that welcomed us. . . They were as kindred, not friends only. . . In spite of their differences, they did form one real party, united by a single hope. . . Rachel made many friends. . . 'Bradford is wonderful,' she said, drinking strong tea.
>
> The plans already made were very definite. . . I was to run for the School Board. . . and meantime I must join the propagandists and speak not only at various pitches in the town, but must tour the country as other young women were doing. . . And in November 1894 I was run for election for the Bradford School Board, and was elected. . .
>
> The movement grew rapidly. We, the members of the Independent Labour Party, had nuclei of friends all over the country. Chapel people joined us and local preachers. . . The sturdy life in the new party overcame the intolerances. . . and bore all this along as a river in spate. . . The leader, as far as platform work was concerned, was Keir Hardie, though there were others – such as Bruce Glazier. . . his. . . *Merrie England* . . . ran into a circulation of a million. He fed the growing appetite of a new public for good literature.[20]

Ruskin played a small but essential part in all this. He was not the builder to erect a nonsense-tower of atheism in opposition to the decayed castle of theism, to wheel up a naturalism-machine against the machine of idealism; or to found a petulant Protestantism across the street from the Roman Church. He merely unlocked for thousands such monuments of culture as Plato, the Bible, Dante: and revealed that they were granaries.

In 1873, Ruskin, the self-mocking preacher, placed himself in retrospect on the 'poor height of a grave-hillock' overlooking the Bradford Canal, the Bradford 'paradise of smoke', the slums of Bradford's Wapping. He may now be replaced there, even without irony. To Bradford's disgrace, the children of Wapping would not get their own bath for another quarter century. To the disgrace of England, the school bath at Wapping, opened in 1898 after intense effort by Margaret McMillan and her friends, would be the first in the country. 'The condition was indescribable,' Margaret said. 'At the first bathing centre the children had to stand on large sheets of paper while they were being undressed.' From Ruskin's viewpoint, the history of English education really begins in this last – and first – place. For education, he quaintly thought, 'begins. . . in washing,' and its 'final result' is 'to know what it is to see the sky.'[21]

Ruskin's Oxford lectures of 1877 ended where his *Fors Clavigera* letters of the same year, 'intended' for 'the Yorkshire operatives', had begun: in calling for honourable leaders whose work and policy should be the provision and distribution of bread. 'The first seven years' letters of *Fors Clavigera*', Ruskin wrote at the end of the seventh volume of that collection, 'were ended in Corpus Christi College, Oxford, 21st November 1877.' On 22 November he was delivering his eighth lecture in the series 'Readings in *Modern Painters*', with its message that 'great men feel themselves. . . less instead of greater than other people'.[22] His statement of 21 November, placed where it is, performs two functions. It brings Oxford undergraduates and Yorkshire operatives into a single focus: and it suggests that, in his next series of *Fors* letters, Ruskin would operate under a new policy. Hitherto, he had seen himself in a pair of comfortably vulnerable positions: as the Master of that eccentric coterie, St George's Guild; and as an Honorary Student of Christ Church and Fellow of Corpus Christi, creating the part of Oxford Professor of Art.[23]

His eighth and final series of *Fors* letters opens with the statement of his new policy, in letter 85 for January 1878:

> . . . in my former letters, I. . . allowed myself to write on each subject, whatever came into my mind, wishing the reader, like a friend, to know exactly what my mind was. But as no candour will explain this to persons who have no feelings in common with me. . . hencefor-

> ward, I shall endeavour to write, so far as I can judge, what may be serviceable to the reader, or acceptable by him; and only in some occasional or minor way, what may explain, or indulge, my own feelings.
>
> Such change in my method of address is further rendered necessary, because I perceive the address must be made to a wider circle of readers.
>
> The book was begun with the limited effort to gather a society together for the cultivation of ground in a special way; – a society having this special business, and no concern with the other work of the world. But the book has now become a call to all whom it can reach, to choose between being honest or dishonest; and if they choose to be honest to join together in a brotherhood separated, visibly and distinctly, from cheats and liars.

This new effort to unite all the Georges against all the Dragons is accompanied by a new determination to deploy 'the Book which our fathers believed to be divine, not as in former times, only to enforce, on those who still believed it, obedience to its orders; but indeed for help and guidance to the whole body of our society'. Ruskin intends to use the Bible – and will in practice also use other texts, Plato and Dante among them – not in their narrowness, as the sacred books of any cult, but in their largeness, as collections of wise information, won through experience and hardship by many people over a great period of time.

Another Ruskin text of January 1878 needs to be set beside *Fors Clavigera* Letter 85. It is a piece called *The Place of Dragons*, Ruskin's *Preface* to a chapter of *St Mark's Rest* written by his young collaborator J. R. Anderson. Ruskin's theme is the legend of St George. His message is a confession:

> I have never applied myself to discover anything, being content to praise what had already been discovered; and the only doctrine or system peculiar to me is the abhorrence of all that is doctrinal instead of demonstrable, and of all that is systematic instead of useful: so that *no true* disciple of mine will ever be a 'Ruskinian'! – he will follow, not me, but the instincts of his own soul, and the guidance of its Creator. Which, though not a sorrowful subject of contemplation in itself, leaves me none of the common props and crutches of halting pride. I know myself to be a true master, because my pupils are well on the way to do better than I have done; but there is not always a sense of extreme pleasure in watching their advance, where one has no more

strength, though more than ever the will, to companion them.[24]

St George's Guild would not be legally incorporated till October 1878. Yet Ruskin, its 'Master' – with a capital 'M' – is already abdicating, with reluctance and delight. God, 'the Master I hoped to Serve', dismisses him 'with a – "That's all I want of you, sir"'. Ruskin has been only a poor pupil-teacher, after all; a little 'master' whose glory it will be to see his pupils supersede him. 'It was like coming to the brow of some healthy[25] moorland, where here and there one had watched, or helped, the reaper of some patch of thinly scattered corn; and seeing suddenly a great plain white to the harvest, far as the horizon.' This is the Ruskin his enthusiasts loved. 'Justice was his Pole-Star', a Bolton admirer would exult. 'In the texture of his teaching. . . is a spiritual breeziness. . . which tones the mind and clarifies the mental vision.'[26] Textiles and breezes were the stuff of Bolton-le-Moors, and the writer's mixed metaphor conveys one sort of the personal and local loyalty Ruskin could inspire. Another sort was demonstrated by Thomas Barclay of Leicester, who compiled a brisk digest of *Unto This Last* under the heading 'The Rights of Labour'; and sold it by the thousand at the price of one penny. Ruskin expressed himself 'entirely grateful'. 'What working man is there,' Barclay demanded, 'that will not reverence these far-seeing and noble utterances. . . showing the truth and demanding justice?'[27]

Margaret McMillan would recall 'the Whitmanites at Bolton' and the 'Secularists at Leicester' among the most valiant friends of the new Independent Labour Party.[28] Thanks to Bradford organisation – and Ruskin's reconciliatory cunning – the Whitmanites could deploy their rhapsodies to solid purpose, and the Secularists could cease squabbling with believers long enough to implement some of the demands of the gospel.

Keir Hardie, the Scottish Miners' leader and first Chairman of the ILP was one of many socialists who consented to co-operate with Ruskin, the abdicatory 'master'. Raised in agnosticism, Hardie's own voluntary contact with formal Christianity was limited to the Morisonian Movement – a thorough-going reaction against the predestinationist traditions of the Presbyterian Kirk. 'In his politics, as in his religion,' his biographer writes, Hardie 'was a Revisionist, a "Morisonian among socialists". He argued that doctrinal rigidity was appropriate only for a sect – Calvinist or Marxist as the case might be. . . For Hardie, as for Ruskin the quality of living was to be the ultimate touchstone for any creed and any society.'[29]

Ruskin's bequest had its cost. February 1878 saw his first serious breakdown. He had suffered acute nervous exhaustion in 1840 and again in 1861, and would succumb again in 1884. To read his little notebooks of 1826–8 is indeed to marvel that a mind so crowded with complex ideas, and so articulate, should have managed, as he did, to number his days as his mother had taught him, and with the sense of duty which was his father's guiding principle, all the way to the biblical point of rest of three score years and ten. But the breakdown of 1878 spelt the inglorious failure of his resolution of that January: to write as 'to persons who have no feelings in common with me'.

Fors Clavigera was broken off, after Letter 87, published March 1878. Ruskin's letter of 3 September 1879 to Alfred Harris may be seen as a compressed and private equivalent of a *Fors* letter.[30] The public series begins again with a letter begun on 8 February 1880, Ruskin's sixty-first birthday. Ruskin's first acknowledgement is to the sympathy of Dr Parsons of Hawkshead, 'who really carried me through, and who never lost hope'.

Ruskin reaffirms the importance of his chosen subject matter: the 'arts, – which the vulgar economists are wholly incapable of weighing', and 'the spiritual affections, – which materialist thinkers are alike incapable of imagining'. The study of such topics has naturally led Ruskin to make a number of insane statements in an age that knows better. Here is his latest. It summarises all his teaching: 'Whether there be one God or three, – no God or ten thousand, – children should have enough to eat, and their skins should be washed clean. It is not I who say that. Every mother's heart under the sun says that, if she has one.'

There is a corollary: 'And the fishmongers who destroy their fish by cartloads that they may make the poor pay dear for what is left, ought to be flogged round Billingsgate, and out of it. It is not I who say that. Every man's heart on sea and shore says that – if he isn't at heart a rascal.'

Ruskin then goes on to explain that his private whimsicalities about St Ursula which have puzzled so many readers are only 'play, of personal imagination'. But nevertheless the play has been of real help and comfort to him. From what do his readers expect to derive comfort?

There follows one of the most moving passages in the whole

series of letters; in which John James Ruskin the dilettante tradesman, and his wife the invincible transcendentalist are set together. 'The father is to teach the boy's reason; and the mother, his will,' Ruskin had announced in the last *Fors* written before his breakdown. Thanks to Dr Parsons of Hawkshead, he is now able to give sympathy and *contemptus mundi* their true direction, at Sheffield:

> Here, for instance (Sheffield, 12th February), I am lodging at an honest and hospitable grocer's, who has lent me his own bedroom, of which the principal ornament is a card printed in black and gold, sacred to the memory of his infant son, who died aged fourteen months, and whose tomb is represented under the figure of a broken Corinthian column, with two graceful-winged ladies putting garlands on it. He is comforted by this conception, and, in that degree, believes and feels with me: the merely palpable fact is probably, that his child's body is lying between two tall chimneys which are covering it gradually with cinders. I am quite as clearly aware of that fact as the most scientific of my friends. But if they can see nothing in Heaven above the chimney tops, nor conceive of anything in spirit greater than themselves, it is not because they have more knowledge than I, but because they have less sense.
>
> Less *common* sense, – observe: less practical insight into the things which are of instant and constant need to man.

Ruskin goes on to dissociate himself from the judgment of his friend J. A. Froude on the middle ages, '"differing both outwardly and inwardly from that *into which a happier fortune has introduced ourselves*"'. A 'monk's cell, in the Dark Ages' compares unfavourably with Froude's own residence in Onslow Gardens, no doubt. For the enlightenment of Froude, Ruskin places 'beside his picture of the monk's cell, in the Dark Ages, two or three pictures by eye-witnesses. . . of the manufacturer's cell, in the happier times "to which Fortune has introduced ourselves"'. There follow extracts, translated by Ruskin, from Jules Simon's *L'Ouvrière*, giving descriptions of the horrible cellar dwellings inhabited by female wool-workers in Lille. Ruskin does not add – what his Bradford readers know – that these women are at the botton of a pyramid of capitalism of which Bradford Wool Exchange is the pinnacle.

Contrary to his resolution of January 1878, Ruskin put the whole of himself into this *Fors* letter for March 1880.[31] His reward was the 'kindly notice' of the *Bingley Telephone* on St George's Day. Ruskin's inglorious failure was turned into a glorious failure. His failure to write without 'friends' was rewarded by the discovery that he had many. The 'great illnesses which, for some time after 1878, forbade my accustomed literary labour'. Ruskin would write in the final *Fors* for Christmas 1884, were an 'initiation' into the knowledge that 'on many hills which I had thought left desolate, the hosts of heaven still moved in chariots of fire'.[32] He is writing expressly of close personal friends, and makes no reference to Bingley. He is writing, indeed, under a recurrence of his old nervous exaltation; a condition from which Benjamin Jowett, tutor of genius, is in process of rescuing him.[33] But the reader who peruses *Fors Clavigera* from end to end, can see that Ruskin makes sufficiently clear his debt to the working class of the West Riding, and also his hopes for them.

From the beginning, every letter of the series begins with the expression 'Friends', or 'My Friends'. But Letter 24, of November 1872, puts an end to that. 'MY FRIENDS,' Ruskin writes, 'I shall not call you so any more, after this Christmas. . . not one of you has sent me a friendly word of answer.' Every subsequent letter plunges *in media res*, often with the capital letter 'I'. But, uniquely, the letter for September 1880 begins 'MY DEAR FRIENDS'. Ruskin is at present no longer teaching at Oxford; and has already gathered enough sense to despair of St George's Guild. The future is not with sexagenarian Masters and Professors. *Sub specie aeternitatis*, or in the eyes of Yorkshire operatives, there is precious little difference between Ruskin's Guild and his University. The Guild is merely incomprehensible; in practice exclusive; probably useless. Oxford is quite comprehensible. It exists to exclude, and to shore up institutions which, like itself, are worse than useless. Ruskin cannot have talked with the thoughtful working men of Sheffield without discovering that open secret.[34] In writing to such men, Ruskin can afford to discard the lesser vanity with the greater. Reinstated as Professor, Ruskin will denounce Oxford's 'Plutocracy of learning' to the backs of his retreating colleagues and the applause of undergraduates. That will be in 1883.[35] Meanwhile, the attention of youthful intellectuals being denied him, he writes from Beauvais – with its famous fragment of a cathedral, dedicated to St Peter, and built in 'jealousy and determination to beat the people of Amiens. . . a most amiable weakness'[36] – to 'The Trades Unions of England'. A letter from Beauvais must pay respect to rivalries:

MY DEAR FRIENDS, – This is the first letter in *Fors Clavigera* which has been addressed to you as a body of workers separate from the other Englishmen who are doing their best, with heart and hand, to serve their country in any sphere of its business, and in any rank of its people. I have never before acknowledged the division. . . between you, and the mass of society to which you look for employment. But I recognise the distinction today, moved, for one thing, by a kindly notice of last *Fors*, which appeared in the *Bingley Telephone* of April 23rd of this year; saying, 'that it was to be wished I would write more to and for the workmen and work-women of these realms,' and influenced by the fact of your having expressed by your delegates at Sheffield your sympathy with what endeavours I had made for the founding a Museum there, different in principle from any yet arranged for working men. . . as a separate class, I know scarcely anything of you but your usefulness, and your distress; and. . . I never say a word about a single thing that I don't know. . . Now I know many things that are and many that must be, hereafter, concerning my own class: but I know nothing yet, practically, of yours, and could give you no serviceable advice. . . So that nearly everything hitherto said in *Fors* has been addressed, in main thought, to your existing Masters, Pastors, and Princes, – not to you, – though these all I class with you, if they knew it, as 'workmen and labourers', and you with them, if *you* knew it, as capable of the same joys as they, tempted by the same passions. . .

But there was another. . . reason for my never, until now, addressing you as a distinct class; – namely, that certain things which I knew positively must be soon openly debated – and what is more, determined – in a manner very astonishing to some people, in the natural issue of the transference of power out of the hands of the upper classes, so called, into yours, . . . these certain things, I say, coming now first into fully questionable shape, could not be openly announced as subjects of debate by any man in my then official position as one of a recognised body of University teachers, without rendering him suspected and disliked by a large body of the persons with whom he had to act. . .

. . . And now I turn to you. . . Now I write to you, observe, without knowing, except in the vaguest way who you *are!* – what trades you belong to, what arts or crafts you practise – or what ranks of workmen you include, and what manner of idlers you exclude. . . Whose is the Wealth of the world but yours? Whose is the Virtue? Do you mean to go on for ever, leaving your wealth to be consumed by the idle, and your virtue to be mocked by the vile?

The wealth of the world is yours; even your common rant and rabble of economists tell you that – 'no wealth without industry'. Who robs you of it, then, or beguiles you? Whose fault is it, you clothmakers, that any English child is in rags? Whose fault is it, you shoemakers, that the street harlots mince in high-heeled shoes, while your own babes paddle barefoot in the street slime? Whose fault is it, you bronzed husbandmen, that through all your furrowed England, children are dying of famine? Primarily, of course it is your clergymen's and masters' fault: but also it is your own, that you never educate any of your children with the earnest object of enabling them to see their way out of this, not by rising above their father's business, but by setting in order what was amiss in it: also in this your own, that none of you who do rise above your business, ever seem to keep the memory of what wrong they have known, or suffered; nor, as masters, set a better example than others.

Your own fault, at all events, it will be now, seeing that you have got Parliamentary power in your hands, if you cannot use it better than the moribund Parliamentary body has done hitherto.

To which end, I beg you first to take these following truths into your good consideration.

First. Men don't and can't live by exchanging articles, but by producing them. They don't live by trade, but by work. Give up that foolish and vain title of Trades' Unions; and take that of Labourers' Unions. . . remember there are essential. . . divisions of the Labour of Man, into which you *must* practically fall. . . and these eternal classifications it would be infinitely better if you at once acknowledged in thought, name, and harmonious action. . . Get these. . . each thoroughly organised, proud of their work, and doing it under masters, if any, of their own rank, chosen for their sagacity and vigour, and the world is yours, and all the pleasures of it, that are true; while all false pleasures in such a life fall transparent and the hooks are seen through the baits of them. But for the organisation of these classes, you see there must be a certain quantity of land available to them proportioned to their multitude; and without the possession of that, nothing can be done ultimately. . .

. . . And this, therefore, is practically the first thing you have to bring in by your new Parliaments – a system of land tenure, namely, by which your organised masses of labouring men may possess their land as corporate bodies, and add to it – as the monks once did, and as every single landlord can now; but I find that my St George's Guild cannot, except through complications or legal equivocations almost endless, and hitherto indeed paralysing me in quite unexpectedly mean and miserable ways. . .

Ruskin politely declines to claim knowledge of the working classes. Who is he to tell them what to do? In fact, his letter was perfectly timed to help inspire the growth, during the '80s, of large new unions of the 'unskilled'. Henry Pelling attributes much of the growth of the Independent Labour Party to the foundational work of these new unions. 'The I.L.P., in which Keir Hardie rapidly became the leading personality, had the bastion of its strength in the woollen area of the West Riding, which had hardly been unionised at all before the "new unionism". Its local branches set about the task of influencing trade-union branches and trades councils in the direction of Socialism, and sending delegates to Congress pledged to Socialist aims: their success was evident in the voting at Congress.'

Frederick Rogers of the Bookbinders', 'one of the ablest union leaders of the period', would express the aspirations of many reformers in 1894: 'We shall enlarge the frontiers of the State, and control, so far as Government can control, the power of the capitalist over the labourer more and more. But there must be an independent life within the state to prevent Government becoming tyranny, and the Trade Unions will be chief among those who shall call that independent life into being.'[37] Roger's words may stand as an acceptable summary of Ruskin's thinking about the State; and about the relations of unions to the State.

In Glasgow, George Mitchell, whose nickname was 'Geordie', was manager of the trading concern which first produced the socialist *Labour Leader*. Geordie was 'associated with the passing of resolutions by the Corporation in favour of Taxation of Land Values, Municipal Fire Insurance, and Municipal Banking'. David Lowe, who knew Hardie and Mitchell well, provides the best evidence for the personal quality of the response of these pioneers to Ruskin. 'John Ruskin would go a long way to see and know Geordie', was Hardie's idea of a compliment to his colleague. When Ruskin died, Hardie wrote: 'Thus disappears from earthly view last of the giants who made the modern British Socialist movement possible. We may not always agree with Ruskin's words, but the innermost thought of the man was sound, and his influence ever pure and wholesome. He has our gratitude.'[38]

It was Ruskin's genius to be able to relate his thinking to similar conditions wherever they occurred; and to be able to offer policies of reconciliation which would be truly such: for they would be founded on radical principles of justice. What he observed at Bradford and Manchester during the mid-Victorian years, would be reinforced and subtilised by what he observed at Amiens and Lucca during the early '80s.[39] In the *Fors* Letter for October 1872, Ruskin, with just a touch of malicious glee, proposed to reconcile the propositions of the Workers' International of 1864 with some of the statements of their antagonist the Cambridge Professor of Political Economy: for, occasionally, both sides were right and in agreement with each other.[40] The letter is called *The Mount of Compassion*. From what other vantage-point is truth visible?

The child of genius began with praise of Turner. In November 1887 he ended his career as art critic by meditating on the 'wonderful displays of etchings and engravings and photographs', these last especially suited to the 'living character of our big towns'.[41]

Ruskin's final work was called *Praeterita*. This title is an alternative Latin title to the Book of Chronicles. It means 'those things omitted' from the Book of Kings. Ruskin had sufficiently defined what he meant by 'Kings'. Subtilising Carlyle's hero worship, and broadening Plato's desire to see the rule of a few wise men, Ruskin, in *Munera Pulveris*, had looked to 'one vital necessity of policy – *that the wise and kind, few or many, should govern the unwise and unkind*'. Opening *Praeterita* with memories of his 'maternal grandmother. . . landlady of the Old King's Head. . . Croydon,' Ruskin recalls that 'it has become the main purpose of my life to grow pippins, and its chief hope, to see Kings'. His footnote stitches the private story of these 'things omitted' to his public volumes of criticism which are all of them, taken together, a Book of Kings: 'my only hope of prosperity for England, or any other country, in whatever life they lead, is in their discovering and obeying men capable of Kinghood'.[42] When his coffin came out of Coniston Church, the graveyard would be full of them – Ruskin's heirs, standing bareheaded in the rain. Mr Heighton, and Alderman Jowett, the Quaker businessmen and socialists Alfred and Arthur Priestman, were among the Bradford contingent. For Ruskin's memorial service, Westminster Abbey was not quite full. Journalists were surprised to note 'not a few manifestly drawn from the humbler ranks. Persons of note, indeed, were very few'.[43]

In the West Riding, there is more enthusiasm. Councillor J. H. Whitley, JP, delivers a laudatory address on Ruskin at Northgate End Chapel, Halifax. Liberal MP for his native town, Speaker of the House of Commons, Chairman of the BBC: Mr Whitley will get on to all these things. The Whitley Committee of 1917–19 will unionise white-collar workers in the public sector. A similar development in the private sector will not be seen till the 1960s.[44] Next to Councillor Whitley, in the pulpit of Northgate End Chapel, stands Rev. S. Whitehead, chairman of Halifax and Bradford Wesleyans. He links Ruskin's teaching with the coming cry of the twentieth century for 'righteousness, conscience, and equal rights'. John Mitchell, chairman of Halifax School Board, reminds the local Friendly and Trades Club, in transcendent language which would have raised eyebrows in Mayfair, that Ruskin's bequest is the certainty that 'we are not born for ourselves alone, and for our own narrow and selfish purposes, but rather. . . in the Divine image, and for Divine purposes'.[45]

Ruskin, in April 1883, dissociated himself from the West Riding in its narrow contemporaneity by refusing to become President of the Saltaire Schools.[46] In March 1883, at Oxford, he had allied himself to the West Riding in its largeness, by stressing the significance of the Rossetti work Ellen Heaton had commissioned: *Mary in the House of St John*. The picture heralded an inclusive 'materialism': a materialism which, as Ruskin explained in his lecture the following May, insisted on 'the relation of spiritual creatures to the substance and conditions of the visible world'. In the March lecture Ruskin had – perhaps unconsciously – reaffirmed both sides of the earnest Puritan materialism of Dr Hartley, born near Halifax, and educated at Bradford.

The Utilitarians had responded to Hartley's doctrine of association only as a political and educational instrument. The Romantic poets had read in it their own aspirations after transcendency. Ruskin demands both:

> I saw it lately given [!] as one of the incontrovertible discoveries of modern science that all our present enjoyments were only the outcome of an infinite series of pain. . . If such a doctrine is indeed abroad among you, let me comfort some at least, with its absolute denial. That in past aeons the pain suffered throughout the living universe passes calculation, is true; that it is infinite is untrue; and that all our enjoyments are based on it, contemptibly untrue. . . For all human loss and pain, there is no comfort, no interpretation worth a thought, except only in the doctrine of the Resurrection. . . all the beautiful work, and all the happy existence of mankind, hitherto, has depended on, or consisted in, the hope of it.[47]

Hartley's theory of the antagonism of pleasure and pain, and his necessarianism which saw all pleasure as evolving from series of such antagonisms, had had no meaning for the good doctor without the hope of resurrection. His book denounced what his divided legatees would pillage from him: *laissez-faire* politics and escapist individualism. No theory of survivable individual souls – disappearing elsewhere to find peace – could satisfy the corporate and material Puritanism of Hartley's upbringing: 'we ought to depend upon Him who first breathed into Man the Breath of the present Life, for our Resurrection to a better. *All live unto Him*. And if we depend upon anything else besides Him, for any Blessing, we may be said so far to renounce our Allegiance to Him, and to idolize that upon which we depend.'[48]

That hope may be fallacious; but it is a worthy one. It looks to the survival and ennoblement of humanity in its whole material being. It is an excellent prescription against superstition and tyranny. Hartley and Ruskin and Mr Mitchell of Halifax saw the same vision as Emily Brontë, and on the same hills:

> Thou – Thou art Being and Breath
> And what Thou art may never be destroyed.[49]

So far the wisdom of Athena. But for the formation of a political party, there is needed also the gorgon wisdom of *Venga, Medusa!* Before the fervour of what Margaret McMillan would call 'a new religion – a heresy' could be drawn into the focus of Peckover Street Institute, there was need for some painful antagonism and the throwing of a few stones.

The early career of Samuel Cunliffe Lister supplies evidence for the continuity of English society. His later career supplies an example of the disruptions of the 1890s.

Scion of an ancient county family, Lister was bequeathed the rectory of Addingham by his grandmother. His father was Bradford's first MP. Preferring trade to church or Parliament, he rose to be the world's wool-comber king and then with the help of a Spanish family of engineers the world's king of velvet, entertaining himself at various times with a thousand-acre tea plantation in Assam and model industrial villages in France and Germany, as well as large estates in the Punjab and Dehra. Eventually, he could afford to withdraw to Fairfield Hall, Addingham, the home of his Cunliffe ancestors.

Lister suffered a setback in 1871, when a great fire did £70,000 worth of damage at his Manningham Mill. 'Two lives,' adds *Fortunes*

Made in Business, 'were sacrificed.' Britannia Agoraia was propitiated, for Lister's Mill rose grander than ever; and with a splendid new chimney. 'The tower of St Mark at Venice would appear to have suggested the idea of the Shaft,' admits *Fortunes Made in Business*. 'But the immense double cornice which gives the crowning solidity to the chimney shows a boldness of design that is more imposing than the tapering belfrey which surmounts the campanile of the Adriatic.'

In December 1890, Lister suggested his 600 velvet weavers take a 12½ to 30 per cent cut in earnings to bring them into line with his hands in Germany in time for Christmas. They demurred to international worker solidarity in quite that form. His remaining 4,000 employees at Manningham agreed with them. Insensitive to chimneys that outshone the belfries of the Adriatic, they seem to have harboured notions that their lives were worth something better than sacrifice. During a four-month strike their self-effacing leader, W. H. Drew, never wavered in his moderate persistence. But by April 1891 hunger, frustration and the adventitious eloquence of Ben Tillett, the London dockers' leader, in St George's Hall, turned organisation into three days of drama: complete with police, the Riot Act and the Durham Light Infantry. A crowd of 20,000, Lister's hard-pressed employees at its core, surged into the Town Hall square and began prising up some of the stones of Bradford for use against troops and the police. A number of tasteful street lamps were smashed. The Italo-Gothic carillon tower was enhanced by a searchlight for the better control of mobs, baton charges were practised, and the strikers resumed work on their master's terms. Samuel Lister, the new Baron Masham, breathed more freely on his 34,000 acres.[50]

The immediate denouement for Drew's unionists was unconditional defeat. Moreover, they had been denied even national publicity. The O'Shea divorce case, the downfall of Parnell and the collapse of British credibility in Ireland had taken all the headlines. But Mr Drew was quite unshaken: he knew what were the real *propaganda*, for his abiding passion was the cultivation of his own garden, at Bingley. The Bradford Labour Union was formed in May 1891. The failure of the strike had only strengthened Drew's patience. In November 1891 he was elected to the Bradford School Board. A wider and wider span of doctrinal shades was drawn into the bright new focus of the nation's growing labour alliance. This soon had its powerhouse in a converted Bradford chapel in Peckover Street.

An army of matrons occupied the place with mops and brushes for several days of January 1893 to make it fit for a respectable revolution. They were not about to give the service of their lives in any combination less compelling than that.[51] Next year, Ben Tillett lost his bid to become Bradford's first socialist MP, but Fred Jowett the Manningham co-operator was installed as one of the country's first socialist councillors.

Samuel Cunliffe Lister got on, too, in his own way. A strike at his Ackton Colliery in 1893 led to the destruction of part of the works. The military fired on the strikers, causing loss of life. All this did not prevent Lister's twelvefold multiplication of his coal output, or his acquiring a new title. He became Baron Lister in 1897. He died in 1906; and his Lister barony became extinct in 1912.

Meanwhile, John Lister of Shibden – the descendant of Dr Hartley's schoolfriend and lifelong correspondent – showed a different model of continuity and disruption from Lord Lister's. John's family motto was *Propositi Tenax*. In 1893 he became the ILP's first Treasurer. The foundation of this party marked the freeing of the Labour movement from Liberal patronage; but for some time to come it would need to foster an alliance with 'advanced' Liberals. 'The Labour Representation Committee, dating from 1900, put up fifty-one candidates in the general elections of 1906 and twenty-nine of them got in.' One of these was Fred Jowett, the new MP for Bradford West. 'After this victory it changed its name to the Labour Party, and from that time onwards there has always been a Labour Party in Parliament. . . The Liberal Party, influenced more and more by Lloyd George, launched its programme of social reform most of which it achieved, with the help of the Labour Party.'[52]

In 1911 Ruskin's biographer W. G. Collingwood felt able to pay tribute to Bradford's part in this pattern. When Ruskin came to tell his Bradford audience of 1864 'that the function of commerce was not to prey upon society but to provide for it, there were many of his hearers whose hearts told them that he was right, and whose lives have shown, in some measure, that he did not speak in vain'.[53]

Keith Laybourn's essay of 1982, 'The Defence of the Bottom Dog', gives a more down to earth review of the Bradford ILP in local politics.

> Only Ruskin, perhaps, of all Radical and socialist writers, appears to have provided a clear lead, and even his strictures against Victorian

> society were focussed at the national, rather than the local, level. Fred Jowett, the leading ILP figure in Bradford, was most inspired by John Ruskin. . . *Unto This Last* was seminal to Jowett's thinking and in it he was attracted by the vision of government training schools for youth, government manufactories and workshops, the establishment of the right to work, the provision of a basic living wage and other provisions which Ruskin saw the state making. This national vision did not deter Jowett from applying Ruskin's aspirations to Bradford alone, with all the endemic weaknesses of local-government administration that entailed. He took up his 'new crusade' in 1892.

Collingwood's claim that Ruskin won over 'many' of Bradford's 'captains of industry' can hardly be sustained. But he did capture two: the cousins Alfred and Arthur Priestman. Alfred was an architect and businessman. Arthur was co-heir with his brother H. B. Priestman of a substantial woollen and worsted firm. While H. B. Priestman was a leading 'moneybags Liberal', Arthur and his wife Edith 'were amongst the chief representatives of municipal socialism' in the provinces. This polarisation within one family reflected a wider conflict. 'Although the "New Liberals", who wished to work with the I.L.P., did emerge under W. P. Byles, sometime editor and owner of the *Bradford Observer*, the majority of the Liberal "moneybags". . . remained unprepared to entertain working-class political ambitions. . .'

The municipal socialism of Jowett and the Priestmans had very wide ambitions: but its practical achievements were for the moment severely limited. Jowett's lecture of 1897 on the 'Bradford Land Question' owed much to the thought of that self-defined 'Tory of the old school', Professor Ruskin. It became the bible for the ILP's approach to the problem: but meanwhile provoked a backlash among property owners, who helped to return a Conservative majority to the Council in 1899. But in 1901 Jowett achieved a modest success in the matter of municipal housing. Otherwise, the effectiveness of Bradford socialism was virtually confined to the related areas of medical inspection and feeding of schoolchildren.[54]

The unparalleled pioneering work of Margaret McMillan was a vital local factor in the first area. Catholic opposition to her battle on behalf of the slum child – none more wretched that the Catholic Irish child – was a main obstacle at first; but it yielded to her wit and her faith.[55] Ruskin and Octavia Hill had had a similar difficulty in Marylebone, where the local priests had banned their flock from using the playground administered for their benefit by two such notorious Protestants.[56] As Ruskin knew, the Irish – which is terrible, but fortunate, – don't consent to be governed 'on scientific principles by heartless persons'.[57]

In the area of school meals, Bradford Liberal toleration of Socialist demands was assisted by the work of Dr Crowley, Medical Superintendent of the Bradford Education Board. Crowley estimated that 21,000 of Bradford's children were under nourished; and gave lectures on the theme during 1906–7. In January 1907, Bradford's Liberal leader Alfred Illingworth died. He was succeeded by H. B. Priestman, the socialist's brother. Dr Crowley was H. B. Priestman's son-in-law. By October 1907, Jonathan Priestley, headmaster of Green Lane School and father of the future writer and broadcaster J. B. Priestley, was serving school meals at the White Abbey Dining Room, one of five simultaneously opened by the local Education Authority. 'Feed My Lambs' was the text emblazoned on the wall. In 1908, the first official school clinic was opened in Bradford.

These local successes put Bradford in the vanguard: but they had not been achieved without the storming of Westminster. In 1906, writes Margaret McMillan, 'Mr. Augustine Birrell was Minister of Education. His secretary was Mr Percy Illingworth, who had been for years my colleague on the Bradford School Board. In him we had a friend. Nor were we quite friendless in the House, for in 1906 certain Labour men had been returned and among these were Mr Fred Jowett, Keir Hardie and others. We could count on some support for any proposal that was brought forward.' The successful proposals were the enabling Acts of 1906-7, which allowed local councils to spend money on the provision of meals for school children and on medical inspection. Dr Kerr, Medical Officer to the LCC, had begun his school medical work with Margaret McMillan in Bradford. In 1910 the Bradfordian Mr Norman became one of her teachers in the experimental school at Deptford. In 1911 the Exchequer granted funds for dental treatment of schoolchildren. Mr North of Bradford became the first full-time London County Council dentist. Another Bradfordian champion of the McMillan sisters was T. P. Sykes, President of the National Union of Teachers.[58]

These achievements in feeding and health might have been gained without the Liberal need for Labour support in the Commons, without Bradford and without Ruskin, but all three elements were in fact involved. Bradford's journal of municipal socialism was *The*

Bottom Dog. In its final issue for September–October 1923, tribute was paid to Ruskin, and *Traffic* was remembered as the movement's Book of Genesis. 'The Bradford I.L.P. was, indeed, the "educating party" its early supporters had anticipated, "entering upon a new crusade not", in Ruskin's words "to recover the tomb of a buried god, but to fulfil the orders of a living one".'[59]

It was Fred Jowett who in 1911 successfully urged that the conditions of the Provision of Meals Act be extended to allow councils to feed schoolchildren out of term. In his speech on the Education (Provision of Meals) Bill of 2 March 1906, he had said: 'It was only by setting the people free from material necessities that they were able to keep their attention on those matters which really concerned them more than material necessities.'[60] There was no possibility of excluding art from such a polity.

January 1924 saw the first Labour Government in office. The new Chancellor of the Exchequer was Philip Snowden, the former pupil-teacher of Cowling, an industrial village across the moors from Haworth. Fred Jowett was appointed First Commissioner of Works by Ramsay MacDonald, who insisted it be a Cabinet post. Jowett it was, newly in office, who insisted on adding to the already 'approved' monument for Nurse Cavell the woman's own words: 'Patriotism is not enough. I must have no hatred or bitterness for anyone'. The lettering quite fusses the brutal 'aesthetics' of that redundant structure, but as James Bone commented, Jowett had provided 'the best piece of art criticism ever given official utterance'. It was the only official apology for all the war memorials.

Peace proved more controversial. Jabob Epstein's scheme for a memorial to the naturalist W. H. Hudson had been rejected by Jowett's Conservative predecessor in June 1923. Jowett approved 'a large model of the Panel' in February 1924. Britain's first 'modernist' sculptor had secured his first public commission. The Labour government fell in November 1924. The Conservative Stanley Baldwin had the job of unveiling Epstein's completed work in May 1925. 'It caused high explosives of rage and hate in controversy,' Epstein remembered, adding that he argued the need for vigourous definition if such a small work were to retain in the London climate the vitality of Hudson's nature-spirit 'Rima'. The common sense of Ruskin's first Bradford lecture is pertinent: 'When work is to be seen. . . in some. . . imperfect way, it constantly becomes necessary to treat it coarsely or severely, in order to make it effective'.[61]

Jowett was 'entirely unrepentant' over his lack of 'good taste'. His native landscape had given birth to Heathcliff and Catherine Earnshaw. He argued that a wild spirit of nature would hardly present the 'ideal' appearance neo-Grecians demanded. Theirs was a view of 'nature', Ruskin might have added, which involved 'the irreverent habit of judgement instead of admiration. It is generally expressed under the justly degrading term "good taste".' Ruskin praised the Pre-Raphaelites in their day; and by the time of his death could be derided as an outmoded apostle of 'finish'. It is well to remember that he regarded Turner's sketches 'as in some respects more valuable than his finished drawings. . . they are. . . as true to the character of the places they represent as they are admirable in composition; while in his elaborate drawings. . . he too frequently suffered his mind to be warped from its first impression by attempts at idealism'.[62] The unamalgamated Ruskin had never been very acceptable to the 'British public'.

'I remembered as a young student,' Henry Moore recalls 'a sculpture called "Rima" by Epstein. At the time the work caused a tremendous fuss. I demonstrated with a crowd of students against the general Philistine public, who hated it. . . We of the generation that succeeded [Epstein] were spared a great deal. . . he had borne the brunt of the Philistine attitude to sculpture'.[63] Epstein bought some of Moore's work before it was ever publicly exhibited. But Moore's first sale had been to William Rothenstein's brother Charles.

Charles Rutherston – he preferred an anglicised form of the family name – remained in business in Bradford all his life. He formed one of the most important collections of modern English art in the country. True to the spirit of *The Political Economy of Art* and *The Two Paths*, he felt that 'works of art ought to be accessible to all who desire to enjoy them. . . a possessor of works of art is a trustee to the public'. He lent his possessions on a long-term basis to local institutions, and the success of his scheme was such that he was soon lending to Birmingham, Leicester, Oxford and Sheffield. Before his death, which came in 1927, he gave his collection to Platt Hall, Manchester, which ever since has been a centre for art-loan schemes throughout the north of England. Albert Rutherston, brother to Charles and Will, was a standard-bearer for the New English Art Club, which showed the work of 'rebels' like Augustus John and Wilson Steer. In 1930, Albert opened the Ruskin Galleries at Bembridge, and added one of his own Ruskin watercolours to the collection.[64]

Moore's 'instinct' began to lead him away from formal 'symmetry' (the terms are his, and Ruskin's) when he used to rub his mother's back 'as a boy when she was suffering from rheumatism'. Thus began Moore's life of observation, under narrow and homely conditions. A scholarship to Castleford Grammar School, whose art teacher Miss Gostick gave him invaluable encouragement; teaching experience, and the first world war, and then, at Leeds School of Art Moore insisted on studying sculpture, which 'created a bit of a difficulty, since there wasn't a sculpture-school'. But Mr Cotterill was appointed: '. . . he looked after me like a child. . . I got through the two year course in one year, as well as winning a Royal Exhibition, which was at that time the only way of getting into the Royal College of Art'.

Moore had prised open the door which Walter Smith of Leeds had reason, in 1865, to believe effectively sealed. But Moore's time in London might have been disheartening were it not for his Principal, William Rothenstein. 'Rothenstein brought an entirely new outlook to the College. He'd known Degas and he'd known Rodin, and he didn't regard the College primarily as a teacher's training college. Not only that, but he would ask one or two of us students when he kept open house. . . Rothenstein gave me the feeling that there was no barrier, no limit to what a young provincial student could get to be and do.'[65]

The vital international dimension that 'foreigners' like Moritz Rothenstein[66] had brought to the Bradford wool trade his son was able to offer the Royal College of Art. William had some years at the Bradford Grammar School, where he was alllowed to produce drawings, maps, and lantern slides in lieu of essays; and had some formal training, including life drawing, at the local Technical College under Durham, a pupil of Alphonse Legros. That training would have been unavailable a few years earlier, or later. Will Rothenstein 'also had the advantage of frequenting the studio of Ernest Sichel, the gifted son of a wealthy Bradford merchant'. In 1888, at the age of sixteen, Will joined his Bradford friend Bertram Priestman at the Slade School in London. He was offered portrait work by Ruskin's oldest Oxford friend, Henry Acland, in 1893, by which time many of Will's old schoolmates were in their third year as undergraduates. In 1899 he married Alice Knewstub, whose father had been one of

Ruskin's pupils.[67] Their son John would become Director of the Tate Gallery.

Henry Moore was not alone in benefitting from the use of Rothstein's private studio at the RCA. These privileged students were enabled and encouraged to draw and model from life, instead of duplicating models by the pointing-machine, as current doctrine then prevailing elsewhere within the College still dictated. Rothenstein was an unusual Principal. He connived at Moore's unauthorised trip to Paris to see an exhibition of Cézanne, and provided a sympathetic correspondent when Moore travelled to Italy under the Rome Scholarship in 1924. Moore's first exhibition was in 1931. Epstein wrote the foreword to the catalogue. 'Some of the criticisms in the press upset' Moore, and in a different way his Professor at the Royal College, where he was then teaching. This Professor showed press cuttings to Rothenstein 'as a reason for having me removed'. Rothenstein declined: 'Moore. . . stays,' he said.

Continuing where Ruskin had begun, Rothenstein urged in 1917 from the Chair in Civic Art at Sheffield the migration of art from the museum to the house and street, advising that patronage was not a matter of 'showing borrowed specimens. . . in a gallery', but of transforming public buildings, domestic crockery and metal-work. Speaking, in 1931, in more 'Victorian' tones than had been characteristic of Ruskin, Rothenstein nevertheless paid appropriate tribute to the unusual Victorian: 'Ruskin asked from those who used pencil or brush, whether amateur or professional, a scrupulous, a religious devotion to the grandest aspects of nature'.[68]

In the fifth volume of *Modern Painters*, Ruskin had placed at Kirkstall the beginning of Turner's 'true life' as an artist. He was inaccurate if he supposed that new possibilities for English art must begin again from there. But a very great possibility began to stir into life three miles up the hill, at Adel. 'Perhaps what influenced me most,' Moore recalled, 'over wanting to do sculpture in the open air and to relate my sculpture to landscape comes from my youth in Yorkshire, seeing the Yorkshire moors, seeing, I remember, a huge natural outcrop of stone at a place near Leeds. . . The whole of Nature is an endless demonstration of shape and form, and it surprises me when artists try to escape from this.'[69]

Moore first heard the name of Michelangelo at Sunday School. It was in the church at nearby Methley that he learned what Ruskin learned at Lucca: 'what a "Master" is. Here was one man at least who knew his business. . . "look! I know what a brute is. . . Also, what a woman is. . .".' For Moore, 'Methley Church, about two miles from Castleford. . . contains the first real sculptures that I remember. I was very impressed by these recumbent effigy figures, particularly by the simplicity of the woman's head. The female figure is always more simple than the male. . . Monumentality has always been important to me. . . It's almost impossible to define.' Ruskin, at Lucca, had attempted definition: 'The statue should be felt to be a statue. . . should be distinctly marble, severe and monumental. . . Not unnatural:. . . but lines so few and grand as to appeal to the imagination only.'

Well might Ruskin say that after meditation on the tomb of Ilaria at Lucca the search for general principles was abated; and he turned to the particular principles of 'individual character, provincial feeling'.

On a grander scale, stone and light spoke to Moore at Rievaulx Abbey. 'In its present state it is more sculpture than architecture. . .' He later experienced a similar impact from the Parthenon: 'Now that the light passes through it, it is far more sculptural'. A letter of Ruskin's from Sicily conveys this experience as fitly as mere words can: '. . . a Greek building standing up against the light, and the Apolline beams piercing it with Apollo's own presence'.[70]

But Moore's love of nature and of art has been, like Ruskin's, an inclusive one: 'I can't cut my sculpture off from living'. And so, to Methley and Adel, must be added the impact of Roundhill Road.

'Now, do you think,' Ruskin wrote in *Traffic*, 'in those masses of lava which you build volcanic cones to melt, and which you forge at the mouths of the Infernos you have created; do you think, on those iron plates, your courage and endurance are not written for ever. . .?'

Turner's encomiast was also the prophet of Moore. 'As a small boy. . . the slag heaps of the Yorkshire mining villages. . . were for me like mountains. . . these slag heaps seemed much larger than the Pyramids. . . I mean they had as big a monumentality as any mountain, in fact perhaps more.'

The medieval effigies of Methley, the rocky outcrop at Adel, but also the slag heaps and iron coalhole covers of Roundhill Road, Castleford 'where I was born': these, together, were Moore's introduction to nature and art.

In 1934, Herbert Read, who began his own higher education at

Leeds University, published *Unit One*, which included this manifesto from Moore:

> Between beauty of expression and power of expression there is a difference of function. The first aims at pleasing the senses, the second has a spiritual vitality. . . Because a work does not aim at reproducing natural appearances it is not therefore an escape from life – but may be a penetration into reality. . . an expression of the significance of life, a stimulus to greater effort in living.[71]

To what Ruskin said in Bradford in 1864 must be added this of 1849:

> It was stated. . . that the value of architecture depended on two distinct characteristics: the one, the impression it received from human power, the other, the image it bears of the natural creation. I have endeavoured to show in what manner its majesty was attributable to a sympathy with the effort and trouble of human life. I desire now to trace that happier element. . . of Beauty, derived chiefly from the external appearances of organic nature.[72]

The industrialised island of the 1930s was not the place or epoch for 'that happier element' heedlessly to flower. 'The people look just the same as they always did', Moore said of Castleford, even in 1968: 'that wide stance on a solid base, very firm on the earth.' Inappropriate to complain, with the art critic of the *Morning Post*, of the 'Waning Influence of the Elgin Marbles'. They themselves were never less than a possibility.[73]

Disputations of 'influence' are less interesting than evident quality. It is enough to echo William Rothenstein's judgment, also made in 1934: 'I still contend. . . that Ruskin said the wisest things about sculpture of any critic of his or our own age'.[74] Neither Rothenstein's Jewish, nor his West Riding liberal inheritance would wish to empty such an important statement of its 'ethical' implications.

Inclusive and creative: a critic needs to be both: '. . . very few art critics are practising artists. . . An artist should not be controlled by the opinion of critics. With friends it may be different.' Moore cites his wife, and Kenneth Clark and Herbert Read as the 'friends' whose opinion he respects.[75] The latter two have been happy to acknowledge the inspiration of Ruskin,[76] but there can be no question of polishing a system: only of 'friends' sharing an experience. And Ruskin's enabling and challenging influence, both permeating and direct, is part of the experience. No legislation can provoke the nature of a Henry Moore, or of a Miss Gostick, a William Rothenstein or Mr Cotterill. But it is the least duty of an art critic, if only for art's sake, to agitate for such legislation as might enable those necessities indispensable to the proper growth and contact of lives and minds. Since the world is continuous, it is there at least where it seems least likely, that one must look for new possibilities in art. Exquisite articulation must direct its powers to consider the 'most frightful' thing that there is – even 'the south east suburb of Bradford (six miles long)' – all the way to 'Wakefield Bridge by the chapel'.[77]

Equal in genius, though more consciously abstract and intellectual than Moore as her background was more traditionally privileged than his, Barbara Hepworth was another of the provincial students who came under Rothenstein's influence at the Royal College of Art. Educated at Wakefield High School, and introduced to formal beauty in Wakefield Cathedral, Hepworth, too, owed something to the propaganda on her behalf by Herbert Read. Read wrote the foreword of 1932 to the catalogue of an exhibition of work by Hepworth and the painter Ben Nicholson: 'It is now clearly recognised that the decadence of European sculpture during the last three or four centuries has been due above all to an increasing separation between the artist and his material'. Ruskin's 'puerile trivialities', as reviewers called them, of 1859, have become Read's permissible wisdom of 1932: 'The revival of the art of our own time is due to nothing so much as to the re-assertion of this vital connection between the artist and his material. . . art is a servant (and a redeeming sanction) in any sphere of the human spirit. . .'[78]

Read's phrase 'redeeming sanction' may be transposed into 'white witchcraft'. In Hepworth the most sophisticated, the most atavistic, requirements are answered. In her hollowed and pierced forms in marble or alabaster is realised that 'piercing pholas-like mind's tongue, that works and tastes into the very rock heart'. Ruskin calls it 'imagination penetrative'. It is the 'highest intellectual power of man'. The moral magic of Hepworth's greatest forms is not describable, but Ruskin comes nearest to anticipating their 'repose of magnificent energy and being. . . the consciousness of duty accomplished and of victory won. . .'[79]

Rivers achieve majesty in the great trading posts at their mouths, but a river's source is quite as significant.

The Aire flows into the Ouse; the Ouse, with the Trent, is a main tributary of the Humber, on whose nothern shore stands the great port of Kingston-upon-Hull. Half of the Aire's source is the trickle that comes from Malham Cove, Ruskin's Yorkshire paradise. But the other half is a stream that comes out of Gordale, to join the Malham rivulet below Malham village.

Ruskin's peregrinations of March 1859 took him among 'the sources of nearly all the Yorkshire rivers, in wild moors'. Here was no separable 'scene', but a vantage-ground from which to be aware of the bones and veins and breath of the island. Nor was there escape here from the problems of the age. To the north – as Ruskin knew – lay the native landscape of Adam Sedgwick. Sedgwick was reared and first educated at Dent, a village north-west of Whernside. Before going up to Cambridge, Sedgwick had read with John Dawson, a poor shepherd of Gordale who had taught himself mathematics out of an old textbook. Dawson invalidated – by mathematics – Priestley's semi-Hartleyan doctrine of philosophic necessity. Of the fourteen Senior Wranglers between 1781–94, eight were his pupils. Sedgwick did not do so well, but he became Professor of Geology at Cambridge. Sedgwick's geological studies pointed to conclusions which Darwin would investigate and extend. That Sedgwick refused these conclusions made him, ironically, an independent corroborator of Darwinism. Yet even this, for Ruskin, was less interesting than Sedgwick's kindness and nobility.[80]

To minds enamoured of Smiles's *Self-Help*, and degraded by myths of the self-made man and of 'getting-on', the one-way traffic from province to capital made an admirable show; and the relentless progress of evolution an enthralling panorama. For Ruskin, the traffic must flow both ways; angels must descend as well as ascend; and the dogma of the survival of the fittest requires information from man's intellectual lens and moral retina if mankind is to be fit to survive. Joseph Wright (1855–1930), the Bradford donkey-boy who rose to become Professor of Comparative Philology at Oxford has since been heroised as Gandalf in his pupil's popular epic, *The Lord of the Rings*. Ruskin's critique of culture concerns itself with all the other donkey-boys.[81]

'The art of a nation much resembles the corolla of a flower; its brightness of colour is dependent on the general health of the plant and you can only command the hue, or modify the form of the blossom, by medicine or nourishment applied patiently to the root, not by manipulation of the petals.' Great art blossoms in the great centres, but its root is likely to be elsewhere. When Charles Woodd, the Yorkshire moorland landowner, wrote to his friend John Ruskin with news of young Master Woodd's burgeoning interest in the 'pretty things' of nature, Ruskin tartly replied: 'How far might the hill peasant's child recognise them also?' Both root and flower, province and capital, have their part in the organic pattern. The root nourishes the flower, the blossom achieves its glory in beauty, but its function by running to seed. Irony and common sense are inseparable from Ruskin's finest flourishes and most radical interventions. As he wrote to a Yorkshire friend and correspondent in May 1867, 'I do not in the least propose any onslaught on public opinion or custom in any violent way; but only observation of certain laws which may be seen to be exemplary in their working'. His St George's Guild and his Marylebone housing scheme, his Sheffield Museum and his Oxford Drawing School, were mere botanical experiments which greater gardeners than he might care to extend.[82]

In the *Branch* chapter of *Modern Painters* volume 5, Ruskin sets out most clearly this organic thinking of which the image of Jacob's Ladder is a symbol. His botanical observation becomes for him also a political and economic law; and a cultural imperative:

> It is evident that the more leaves the stalk has to sustain, the more strength it requires. It might appear, therefore, not unadvisable that every leaf should, as it grew, pay a small tax to the stalk for its sustenance. . . Which, accordingly, is just what the leaves do. Each, from the moment of his complete majority, pays a stated tax to the stalk; that is to say, collects for it a certain quantity of wood, or materials for wood, and sends this. . . *down* the stalk to add to its thickness.
>
> 'Down the stalk?' Yes, and down a great way farther. . . from every leaf. . . one slender fibre, or at least fibre's thickness of wood, descends through shoot, through spray, through branch, and through stem; and having thus added, in its due proportion, to form the strength of the tree, labours yet farther and more painfully to provide for its security; and thrusting forward into the root, loses nothing of its mighty energy until, mining through the darkness, it has taken hold in cleft of rock or depth of earth. .[83]

Unto This Last had a small, but invaluable, contribution to make to the life and work of Fred Jowett. But it was only after Fred had got into Parliament and helped to change the statute book that some few of the fundamental ideas of *Unto This Last* filtered back, in the shape of publicly maintained school dining-rooms and clinics, to the Bradford which had helped to inspire those ideas. In a similar pattern – though by a process too complex to be traced – *The Two Paths* gave a stimulus to new ideas about the relation between an artist and his materials, and about the need to meet radical necessities before any true art could flower. And it is to be observed that it was only in the early 1930s when Moore and Hepworth – a miner's son, and a woman! – had begun to establish themselves as artists of international eminence that the message of *The Two Paths* became publicly acceptable even to a West Riding Professor of Textiles.

If we turn to the textbooks of Bradford design it seems, for a long time, as though Ruskin had never been born. Ashenhurst, in 1883, is local and muddled. His 'ornament' is an optional accretion, not an inevitable synthesis. All the 'conditions of structure' having been secured, 'we may proceed to ornament the structure as we please, always taking care that the ornamentation does not detract from the utility'. He is still thinking in reversibilities, not in organisms begotten of Ruskin's triple consistency of 'Material. . . Place and. . . Office'. Stephenson and Suddards of 1897 have become eclectic and, in the wrong sense, provincial. Wordsworth, vaguely amalgamated to Hartley, struggles with a desperate pragmatism: 'Advantage [may be] gained by using natural forms. . . but it is rather one of association than of artistic necessity. . . forms neither copied nor adapted from nature can be used with equal advantage after a plan of [one's] own.' Detailed comparison of both books with *Modern Manufacture and Design* reveals Ruskin's insights to be as pertinent as unheeded.

By 1903, eclecticism and flight from annihilated 'nature' have become competitive anxiety. Aldred Farrer Barker of Bradford Technical College requires, necessarily, a 'mental capacity' in terms of which 'trade changes' can be 'satisfactorily faced and made the basis of success rather than of failure'. He hopes he 'may assist. . . towards that state of efficiency in which life in these industries may become a pleasure rather than a burden'.

But by 1930 – among wider changes – Barker has become Professor of Textiles at Leeds. His new book opens with the three necessities Ruskin set into focus on his northern journey of 1859: 'The three fundamental activities of life – the provision of Food, Shelter, and Clothing'. The popularisation of Ruskin's biology has arrived to co-operate with that of Darwin's. Barker mentions Ruskin only at second-hand: via Roger Fry, and W. G. Rafee. The first has taught him, from *The Two Paths*, the need for 'natural forms severely conventionalised'. Barker has also taken up Ruskin's moral and social idea. 'A rampant industrialism', he writes, 'has imposed an enervating 'mechanism of design' which up to the present time [the English] have not had the spirit to combat. . . sternly repressing mechanism.' The old 'combat' mentality of the West Riding has recognised its real enemy as last. Barker shares Ruskin's admiration for children's art, and evidences natural, and gothic, form from photographs. His first pattern is by William Morris.

'Beautiful art can only be produced by people who have beautiful things about them and leisure to look at them,' Ruskin had told Bradford in 1859. Or, as Barker puts it; 'There is no such thing as good technique without soul', which should function 'irrespective of fashion'. He is still concerned, as in 1903, for 'efficiency and interest' as a 'reversible pair'. But he has imbibed Ruskin's sense of priorities. The 'enjoyment' must come first; cannot be earned by 'efficiency' in grappling. Accuracy he does not abandon, but the third-person preachment of 'smartness and application' of 1903 has, by 1930, been set aside for this: 'whoever you may be, take a pencil or a brush, or both, and working upon any form which specially appeals to you, try what you can do with it – how can you express your growing feeling for form and pattern by attempting to put form into design.'[84]

The 'woods decay' – literally: but Professor Barker, at least, after many a summer, has taken up the thyrsus.

The writer of an article in the *Westminster* for April 1859 noted with pain that the 'great manufacturing towns' of the West Riding 'lie in the midst of the most beautiful and romantic scenery, with which they are singularly dissociated'. Ruskin, in Bradford in 1859, was indeed crying in the wilderness when he urged the hopeful youth of Yorkshire 'never to pass a day without drawing some animal from the life. . . resolving that whatever is characteristic of the animal shall in some way or other be shown'. Ruskin's critical insight found no relevance worthy of the interest of a cultural historian till Ted Hughes's memoir of 1967: 'My interest in animals began when I began. . . I had a gift for modelling and drawing, so when I discovered plasticine, my zoo became infinite. . . At that time we lived in a valley in the Pennines. . . at about 15. . . I began to look at them. . . from their own point of view. And about the same time I began to write poems. . . It was years before I wrote what you could call an animal poem, and several more years before it occurred to me that my writing poems might be partly a continuation of my earlier pursuit. Now I have no doubt.' Who would venture to trace the relations between the child Ruskin's carnival of cave birds and Ted Hughes' *Cave Birds: An Alchemical Cave Drama*, of 1975-8?[85]

Still more fundamental than animal drawing, for Ruskin, was the human figure. The designer should be perpetually aware of 'so much of the nude body as in the daily life of the nation may be shown with modesty and seen with reverence and delight'. If shown at all, the nude should be 'shown fearlessly, and seen constantly'.[86] As Rothenstein commented in 1934, 'Ruskin practically said all the right things that needed saying, and one has to regard him, as all thinkers, in relation to his own age'.[87] By the Edwardian era, even Puritan Bradford had a life school in its art college. Mortimer Wheeler, and others of the fast set of Bradford Grammar School, would escape thither to study the female form divine on Tuesday or Thursday afternoons, when they should have been playing games. One of their masters, a Newdigate prizeman, was always talking about Picasso.[88] This was the Bradford J. B. Priestly remembered. He knew no millionaries; but 'quite a lot of people who were lively, intelligent, responsive to the arts'.[89]

It may be worth a footnote in art history that swimmers in the Bradford Grammar School baths have never been incommoded by costumes. David Hockney's observations there, and his application to life drawing, all day and every day, in the Bradford Art College, have helped to make him one of the few students actually capable, in the words of Ruskin's inaugural message of 1859, of 'sketching accurately and continually from nature anything that comes in their way. . . above all, figures'. The Rothenstein policy of drawing from life, still practised at Bradford in Hockney's day, had been – to his bewilderment – temporarily outmoded at the RCA by the time he attained its portals. His fascination with the male figure was regarded as provincial, or worse.

Hockney has got on to produce designs, notably for the stage; which suggests that Ruskin's emphasis on figure-drawing for designers may not have been so impertinent as most contemporary reviewers of *The Two Paths* chose to believe.

By the time of Hockney's adolescence, the Ruskinian influence of which Rothenstein was conscious has become dispersed; but hardly dissipated. The boy draws an icon of his two personal heroes:

Whitman, whose 'deadly true' vitality Ruskin was among the first Englishmen to champion publicly, and that great political disciple of *Unto This Last*: Mahatma Gandhi. The Ruskinian and Bradfordian streams commingle most appropriately in Hockney's chosen form of 'mental improvement' as a young man: making himself read Proust out of a cultural duty that grew into delight. He does this while serving as a pacifist National Serviceman; emptying bed-pans in St Luke's Hospital, the former Bradford Workhouse and his own birthplace.[90]

Ruskin's editor and biographer E. T. Cook placed Ruskin's contribution in its large organic setting: 'In an old and complex society, the growth of new ideas and the operation of fresh motive-forces require the combined efforts, from many different directions, of many thinkers and many workers. Before the fruit ripens upon the tree much digging and ditching is necessary: the rain must fall and the sun shine; and the procession of times and seasons be fulfilled. Nothing is more ridiculous that the scramble which sometimes sets in, on the part of competing claimants, for the whole credit and the sole credit of the ripe fruit of politics. No such exclusive claim will anywhere be found in Ruskin's writings.'[91]

Henry Pelling, in the Introduction to his anthology *The Challenge of Socialism* of 1954, places Ruskin in the context of the political debate. While 'all the main ideas of Marxist economics are to be found in the work' of the Ricardian socialists, 'none of them. . . in any way approached Marx as a master of economic analysis and constructive thought'. Pelling reminds us that Marx's *Capital* was not translated into English until 1887: and that since J. S. Mill chose to ignore the Ricardian socialists in his *Principles of Political Economy* – 'the textbook of economics in this country' during his lifetime – they 'passed into oblivion'. At which point Pelling introduces Ruskin: 'There was no question of Ruskin's views ever being forgotten in the same way' as the Ricardian socialists; though he 'followed them in accepting Ricardo's dictum that "labour determines value", and using it as a stick to beat the rest of classical economics'. It must be added that Ruskin's view of labour and value was far more humanistic that Ricardo's. He 'was no theoretical economist, but his commonsense contributions to the definition of terms such as "wealth" and "value", and his scorn for the conception of "over-production" in a world of almost universal poverty and scarcity, had a profound influence in the later nineteenth century: perhaps most notably on

J. A. Hobson, the "economic heretic" who, in his turn, propounded ideas which have been of primary importance in shaping recent Socialist thought.' More particularly, it was along the lines of Hobson's underconsumption theory (highly compatible with Ruskin, and to an extent influenced by him) that 'in 1936 J. M. Keynes formulated his General Theory'.

But Pelling adduces another Ruskin 'influence': partly a corroboration of the 'welfare economics' with which he is justly associated; partly amounting to a contradiction. It is the idea of an independent and dignified Unionism.

For the political idealist – and in this one respect at least, Ruskin might be called a political idealist – the desire is for the maximum of co-operation as the means to the maximum possible self-realisation of the individual. But, as the observer of society discovers, any 'progress' towards such an ideal must – paradoxically – pass through those medial forms of participation and amalgamation which, in practice, provoke antagonism, disruption, and the sacrifice of the individual to 'party issues'. It is just because these tensions are explored in their many nuances in his work that Ruskin's 'contradictory' contribution has been so valuable. The contradiction is a real one. Pelling indicates a general guideline: 'The issue between these two points of view' – the planned totality and the energies of voluntary co-operation – 'stimulated some of the ablest propagandist writing of the present century. This was largely because it raised questions of morals and aesthetics as well as of politics and economics. What are the relative advantages of centralisation and decentralisation? Which is more desirable, the satisfaction of the consumer or the freedom of the craftsman? What are the real incentives to the production of wealth? And what in any case is wealth? The debate outstepped the boundaries of Marxian and Jevonian economics and brought a new generation back to Carlyle, Ruskin and Morris.'

Ruskin's startling views of September 1880, addressed to his 'Dear Friends' in the trade union movement, remain to this day very much a matter of 'debate'. J. H. Whitley praised Ruskin from the pulpit of a Methodist Chapel in Halifax in 1900. In 1917 his Whitley Committee established the principle of 'self-government in industry'. But the principle has yet to be implemented. Alan Bullock, of Bradford Grammar School, Wadham and St Catherine's Colleges Oxford, and the House of Lords, made a further contribution to the debate in

1977–8, with a report which led to a White Paper on industrial democracy. This recommended that employees in private firms having more than 500 workers should have the right to representation at board level.[92] This modest proposal seems quite in accord with the views of Ruskin, 'Tory of the old school'; but the whole question of the relation between workers and employers, and between unions and the State, has so far proved insoluble by Labour or Conservative governments.

A classic confrontation occured in 1969. Two eminent Bradfordians, the British nation divided behind them, faced each other over the Labour Government White Paper *In Place of Strife* of January 1969. Barbara Castle of Manningham Lane, Bradford Girl's Grammar School and St Hugh's Oxford, First Secretary of State and Secretary of State for Employment and Productivity, proposed to solve Britain's labour problems by deploying penal sanctions against unofficial strikers. Vic Feather of Ripon Street, Hanson Board School and the Girlington Co-op., General Secretary of the Trade Union Congress, knew his members wouldn't stand for it. Harold Wilson, of Royds Hall School, Huddersfield and Jesus College Oxford, Chancellor of Bradford University, and Prime Minister, was in no position to disagree with Feather.[93]

Officials of the Labour Party retain their affection for the epic early days when *Unto This Last* pointed to the hope, as George Holyoake saw it, 'that piety and progress were the same'. On 10 April 1978, Denis Healey of Bradford Grammar School and Balliol, Chancellor of the Exchequer, delivered himself of the opinion that socialism goes back 'at least to the beginnings of the Christian religion'.[94]

But the debate between the transcendental aspirations Margaret Ruskin bequeathed her son; and the practical sympathies and duties which Ruskin took from his father, is not ever likely to be resolved. The minor poet Humbert Wolfe, of Bradford Grammar School, Wadham College and the Ministry of Labour, could glimpse the transcendental message of the flood which formed the theme of *Traffic* and *Looking Down from Ingleborough*: 'not drowning, but releasing, soul by soul,/ division in the undivided whole'.

But hard experience also made Wolfe share Ruskin's reservations about partial unions, liable to degenerate into 'co-operation among rascals', who: 'would make love a wholly different thing / by methods of collective bargaining'.

Opposing them, for Wolfe, as for Ruskin, is the Bradford

millionaire who has been mortalised by T. S. Eliot:

> He does not willingly abandon his
> inherited susceptibilities
> but recognising that the weak must suffer,
> when others cut up rough, he cuts up rougher.[95]

Yet there were intelligent capitalists, too. B. Seebohm Rowntree was not unworthy of his Bradford Quaker inheritance. 'A. . . growing number of employers,' he wrote in 1921, 'are trying to provide. . . the conditions which are demanded by the more thoughtful Labour leaders.'[96] *The Human Factor in Business* meets *Unto This Last* at least half way.

But below the capitalists and the union leaders; below Wolfe writing about both, there is always Albert Ignotus – Albert the Unknown – the baby who seized popular imagination in March 1864 when he was rescued from the Yorkshire Devastation. He inspired Millais's *A Flood*. He may have inspired Ruskin's imaginative re-working of Paul's sermon on the Unknown God. But he had to grow up. In 1932, at the age of seventy he would reminisce for researchers on his years of employment with William Walker Ltd, a firm of dyers, in their mill at Kirkstall. No, he never knew who his parents were. He had come from Sheffield on the flood tide.[97]

It as well to end by quoting the Sage of Bradford, if only in order to beg to differ from him – for surely Ruskin the Sage is inseparable from Ruskin the art critic? 'We could do with a splendid revival of John Ruskin,' wrote J. B. Priestley in 1972,[98] 'not the art critic but the Sage, the man who saw that the real test of a society is not the wealth it produces but the kind of people it creates.'

Notes

Abbreviations

BA – Bradford Advertiser
BO – Bradford Observer
BR – Bradford Review

Diaries: The Diaries of John Ruskin, selected and edited by Joan Evans and John Howard Whitehouse, 3 volumes, Oxford University Press, 1956–9.

Ruskin family letters: V. A. Burd, ed. *The Ruskin Family Letters*, 2 volumes, Ithaca and London, 1973.

Winnington Letters: V. A. Burd, ed. *The Winnington Letters of John Ruskin*, London 1969.

Victorian newspapers are dated briefly: e.g. BO 13.10.59 (*Bradford Observer* 13 October 1859)

The Works of John Ruskin, ed. E. T. Cook and A Wedderburn, 39 volumes, London 1903–12: references to volumes of this edition take the form of capitalised Roman numeral, followed by page number. As the edition is not generally available, Ruskin's titles and chapter and paragraph numbers are also given, as appropriate.

N.B. The place of publication, unless otherwise stated, is London.

Chapter One

1 XXXV.425 & n. *Praeterita* II.195

2 *George Eliot Letters*, ed. Gordon B. Haight, 1954, II.25

3 XXXI.xxiv

4 XVII.437 *Time and Tide* 148. E. S. Maurice, *Octavia Hill: Early Ideals*, 1928, pp. 161–5; C. E. Maurice, *The Life of Octavia Hill from her Letters*, 1913, pp. 212–22

5 E. S. Maurice, pp. 10–11

6 F. Engels, *Selected Writings*, ed. W. O. Henderson, Harmondsworth 1967, p. 392.

7 W. T. Hill, *Octavia Hill*, 1956, pp. 77–9.

8 XVI.344; XVIII.449 *The Two Paths*, 97; *Crown of Wild Olive*, 74

9 David Wright, 'The Second Reform Agitation 1857–67', *Victorian Bradford*, 1982, p. 176. C. E. Maurice, p. 255.

10 E. S. Maurice, p. 9

11 Details from M. Le Blanc Smith, Esq., grandson of Alfred and Harriet Harris.

12 J. J. Ruskin to E. S. Dallas, 31 October 1859. XXXVI.319, n. Compare XVI.26

13 W. G. Collingwood, *The Life of John Ruskin*, 1911, pp. 146, 174–5.

14 E.g. Q. Bell, *Ruskin*, reprinted Edinburgh 1963, pp. 45, 58.

15 J. D. Rosenberg, *The Darkening Glass*, 1963, p. 160. A. Saint, *Richard Norman Shaw*, New Haven and London 1976, p. 55.

16 XXVII.187; XXVIII.450–1; XXIX.13–14, 398 & n. *Fors Clavigera* 11.7; 59.11; 73.1; 89.1.

17 XXV.212–13 *Proserpina* 11–12.

18 XXXIII.38–9, 59 *Bible of Amiens* I.13, 19.

Chapter Two

1 E. Abbott & L. Campbell, *Life and Letters of Benjamin Jowett*, 1897, I.1.

2 BO 13.10.59.

3 E. Hodder, *Life and Work of the Seventh Earl of Shaftesbury*, 1886, I.143. E. Abbott & L. Campbell, I.17.

4 K. O. Morgan, *Keir Hardie*, 1975, p. 65

5 A. Fenner Brockway, *Socialism over Sixty Years: The Life of Fred Jowett of Bradford*, 1946, p. 29.

6 Gladstone to Graham 27 November 1860, quoted D. Beales, *England and Italy 1859–60*, 1961, p. 13. Cobden to M. D. Hill 1862, quoted W. L. Burn, *The Age of Equipoise*, 1968, p. 69.

7 David Wright, *Victorian Bradford*, p. 181.

8 XVIII.183, 185. *Sesame and Lilies*, 138, 140.

9 *Sheffield and Rotherham Independent* 24.4.86.

10 The book of *Unto This Last* appeared 13 June 1862. Bradford Subscription Library approved its purchase July 1862.

11 *Manchester Examiner and Times* 8.12.64.

12 W. Rothenstein, *Men and Memories*, 1931, I.10.

13 M. McMillan, *The Child and the State*, Manchester 1911, p. 147.

14 XXXVI.xcii; XXXVII.292. *Diaries*, p. 879.

15 *Diaries*, p. 538 (1858).

16 XXVIII.350. *Fors Clavigera* 54.14.

17 Original notebooks in Beinecke Library, Yale (unedited). Present extract from transcript at Bembridge, from notebook of 1827–9, pp. 34–6. See M. Hardman, 'The prose and ideas of John Ruskin', unpublished PhD thesis, Cambridge 1975, pp. 133–213.

18 XXXV.37. *Praeterita* I.40. *Ruskin Family Letters*, pp. 148–50.

19 T. Carlyle to John Carlyle, 23 April 1861 (VII.1ix). J. Ruskin to Alfred Harris 'Monday 15th April [1861]'. St George's Guild Collection, Ruskin Gallery, Sheffield. The 'Tree Twigs' lecture was delivered 19 April 1861 (VII.467–78).

20 XVIII.1x; XXXIII.1iv.

21 XVI.253–4. *The Two Paths*, Preface. W. K. C. Guthrie, *The Greeks and Their Gods*, 1950, pp. 5–8, 59.

22 XVIII.342. *Ethics of the Dust*, 107.

23 Aristotle, *Ethica Nicomachea*, ed. J. Brewer (1836); MS Notes & Drawings by Ruskin. British Library. The passage is *Ethica* VI.4 (1140a); Brewer, p. 228.

24 VII.215. *Modern Painters* Pt.VIII.I.20. *Phaedo* 60e.

25 Plato *Republic* 514, 614; Aristotle, *Metaphysics* 983a. W. K. C. Guthrie, pp. 355, 366–7.

26 BO 3.3.59. Report of Ruskin's lecture: 'I do not like general principles. I would much rather give particular principles.'

Chapter Three

1 George Eliot to S. S. Hennell 17 January 1858 (*Letters*, ed. G. B. Haight, 1954, II.422).

2 *Sheffield and Rotherham Independent* 24.4.86.

3 John Nicholson (1790–1843), protégé of Oastler, 'The Vale of Ilkley', *Collected Poems*, 1859, p. 140: 'Priest, lord and king, and ye ungrateful poor – Let reformation enter ev'ry door!'

4 XVII.316–17; XVIII.104. *Time and Tide*, 2; *Sesame and Lilies*, 49.

5 National Encyclopaedia V.458.

6 B. Thompson, 'Public provision and private neglect: public health', *Victorian Bradford*, p. 156.

7 *Condition of the Working Class in England in 1844*, translated F. K. Wischnewetzky, 1892, reprinted George Allen & Unwin, Ltd, 1952, p. 40.

8 XXV.293–4; XXVI.369. *Proserpina*, 5. *Deucalion* Notes for Intended Continuation, 3.

9 J. J. Ruskin to George Gray 1 September 1848, quoted M. Lutyens, *The Ruskins and the Grays*, 1972, p. 149. See also: *Ruskin Family Letters, p.* 64, n; H. G. Viljoen, *Ruskin's Scottish Heritage*, Urbana 1956, p. 128.

10 T. Carlyle, *Past and Present*, 1843, with MS notes and presentation letter to Alfred Magee, 10 January 1887, by Ruskin. British Library.

11 Carlyle's footnote: '*Observations on the Management of the Poor in Scotland*, by William Pulteney Alison, MD (Edinburgh 1840)', *Past and Present*, III.ii, 'Gospel of Mammonism'.

12 XVIII.468–9, quoting *Sartor Resartus* II.viii. *Crown of Wild Olive*, 99.

13 Ruskin to Richard Owen, 16 December 1865. Bembridge MS Collection BXV: 'The "principle of development through polar relations" is the thing that amazes me so, as found in higher organisms. I'm *delighted* with the definition of myself too – as a "clothed sum of segments". I feel so exactly *that*.' Compare J. Ruskin to Henry Acland 27 April 1856, and to C. E. Norton 11 January 1866 (XXXVI.237–40, 501).

14 XXXV.488–90. *Praeterita* III.16.

15 Notebook for 1858–9, p. 149/ 171 (double numbering system), Bembridge. Red Book for 1828. Transcript at Bembridge.

16 J. Ruskin to J. J. Ruskin, 16 December 1863: 'you thwarted me in all the earnest fire and passion of life' (XXXVI.461).

17 XXII.509.

18 J. Ruskin, letter in *Pall Mall Gazette* 31.1.73 (XVII.555).

19 XXXV.321. *Praeterita* II.84. The corn mill at Malham, head of the Aire, became a cotton mill in the early 1850s: L. Cooper, *Yorkshire: West Riding*, 1950, pp. 241–6.

20 XXXIII.210, & n. *Valle Crucis*. 8–10.

21 XVII.xxvii; XXXVI.xxiii.

22 Ruskin to Carlyle late December 1859. National Library of Scotland MS 555.7.

23 *Ruskin Family Letters*, p. 110. J. J. Ruskin wrote home from Bradford 30 January 1822; but the letter is missing.

24 XII.159. The Pre-Raphaelites followed Turner's practice in using tiny strokes of brilliant colour in watercolours.

25 *Winnington Letters*, p. 101. Alderman John Mitchell (1808– 84), Ruskin's host, should be distinguished from John Harper Mitchell (1828–93), who was no relation.

26 M. Lutyens, *Effie in Venice*, 1965, p. 220; *The Ruskins and the Grays*, pp. 86–7.

27 J. Ruskin to J. J. Ruskin, Lucerne 13 December 1861. XXXVI.396.

28 I. Taylor, *Natural History of Enthusiasm*, 1834, p. 88.

29 W. Rothenstein, *Men and Memories*, I.367.

30 XXXVIII.175.

31 T. Wemyss Reid, *The Life, Letters and Friendships of Richard Monckton Milnes, first Lord Houghton*, 1890, II.25. M. Lutyens, *Millais and the Ruskins*, 1967, pp. 19–20.

32 XII.1iv. John James, *Continuations to the History and Topography of Bradford*, Bradford 1866, pp. 118–23.

33 J. Ruskin to J. J. Ruskin, Bolton Abbey 27 Fenruary 1859. XVI.xxx.1xiv.

Chapter Four

1 J. S. Roberts, *Little Germany*, Bradford 1977, p. 3.

2 VIII.xxxiv, & edd's n.

3 XXII.473. *Ariadne Florentina*, Appendix 1. *Diaries*, p. 863. BO 10.11.59.

4 In November 1868 Forster and Ripley were returned over Miall, but Ripley was unseated for electoral corruption and Miall returned, in 1869. Forster and Ripley were returned February 1874, over J. V. Godwin.

5 J. Reynolds, 'History of education in Bradford 1870–1970: Bulletin 2', p. 33, cyclostyle pamphlet, Bradford City Libraries.

6 *Winnington Letters*, p. 101. See above, Chapter 3, n. 25.

7 XXIX.245. *Fors Clavigera*, 82.

8 Brian and Dorothy Payne, 'Extracts from the journals of John Deakin Heaton, M.D., of Claremont Leeds', *Publications of the Thoresby Society* LIII, pt. 2, no. 117, Leeds 1973.

9 XVI.338–9; XVIII.453. *The Two Paths*, 91; *Crown of Wild Olive*, 79. Of the 'two wings' of Dunlop's house, one is Scottish baronial, the other 'Saxon', with triangular window-heads. The grand 'stables, and coach houses' appear to predate his rebuilding of the property.

10 H. M. M. Rossetti, *Pre-Raphaelite Twilight*, 1954, pp. 73–4, 87, 101–3.

11 Details from Harris's grandson, M. Le Blanc Smith.

12 Rev. John Burnet, LlD, *Church Pastoral Aid Society Annual Sermon*, St Dunstan Fleet St, London, 1848.

13 XVIII.544.

14 A. E. McKilliam, *A Chronicle of the Archbishops of Canterbury*, 1913, p. 405.
15 T. Wemyss Reid, *Life of the Rt. Hon. W. E. Forster*, 1888, II.52.
16 E. Healey, 'Woodleigh Hall, Rawdon', in *Picturesque Views of Castles and Country Houses in Yorkshire*, Bradford 1885.
17 [James Burnley], 'A. & S. Henry', *Fortunes Made in Business*, 1887, III.201, seq.
18 Ruskin's note to F. J. Furnivall [1854] about the Working Men's College mentions an 'appointment to chat about Leeds'. British Library MSS Ashley A3917.
19 J. L. Bradley, editor, *Ruskin's Letters from Venice 1851–2*, New Haven 1955, p. 593.
20 G. Weerth, *Vergessene Texte*, Köln 1975, I.263–4, 266– 74.
21 T. Wemyss Reid, *Life of the Rt. Hon. W. E. Forster*, I.212.
22 *Sheffield and Rotherham Independent*, 17.4.86.
23 XVI.341. *The Two Paths*, 92. J. L. Bradley, p. 600 & seq.
24 XIX.108–9. *Cestus of Aglaia*, 60–1. *Bradford Antiquary* III (1912).255, seq.
25 John Burnet, *Practical Essays on Various Branches of the Fine Arts*, 1848, pp. 115–16, 121–2.
26 F. Engels, *The Condition of the Working Class in England in 1844*, 1892, pp. 40–1.
27 Alfred Harris, junior, lecturer on the art of Rome, should have been capable of drawing some of these inferences.
28 XVI.342. *The Two Paths*, 94.
29 XXXVI.239.
30 A. Callen, *Angel in the Studio*, 1979, p. 44.

Chapter Five

1 Bradford Mechanics' Institute charges for the Ruskin lecture of 1 March 1859 (2*s*. 6*d*., 1*s*., 6*d*.) may be compared with those of 7–12 February for the 'Farewell Levees of the Original & Celebrated American General Tom Thumb (Day: 1s; Evening: 6d.)'.
2 XXXIII.390, edd's n. *The Art of England*, 187. Morris's address in the hall of University College, Oxford, November 1883, and Ruskin's extempore quelling of donnish rage, is recorded Michael E. Sadler, Introduction to E. Hope Scott, *Ruskin's Guild of St. George*, n.d.
3 XIX.168, 185. *On the Relation of National Ethics to National Arts*, 6, 27.
4 'Modern Manufacture and Design', the third lecture in *The Two Paths: Being Lectures on Art and its Application to Decoration and Manufacture*, reported *The Working Men's College Magazine*, May 1859, pp. 90–2; *The Economist*, 15.10.59.
5 IV.251. *Modern Painters* Pt. III, Sect. II.iii.
6 XVI.361. *Two Paths*, 123.
7 W. Gropius, *The New Architecture and the Bauhaus*, trans. P. Morton Shand, 1965, p. 85. Compare: XVI.373. *Two Paths*, 138.
8 X.269. *Stones of Venice*, II.vi.114.
9 XVI.374. *Two Paths*, 139.
10 X.196. *Stones of Venice*, II.vi.16.
11 *Athenaeum*, 28.5.59, p. 703.

12 W. Gropius, pp. 20–1, 62.

13 E. K. Helsinger, *Ruskin and the Art of the Beholder*, Cambridge Mass. & London, 1982, pp. 20–1.

14 XVI.291–2. *Two Paths*, 49.

15 Samuel Rogers, *Italy* (1830) and *Poems* (1834), with engravings by Turner and Stothard. Ruskin dubbed Rogers 'the polished minstrel of St James's Place. . . a mere dilettante' (XXXV.93, 151).

16 XVI.lv–lx. Mr Chapman carved a scene in the Crimea: 'General Windham leading his men to the attack of the Great Redan'; O'Shea: 'The Queen presenting the Victoria Medal to her Soldiers'.

17 XXXV.410.

18 V. A. Burd, *John Ruskin and Rose La Touche*, Oxford 1979, p. 24.

19 A. Chappelow, *Shaw – 'The Chucker-Out'*, 1969, pp. 239– 42.

20 XVI.lxi.

21 XIV.441.

22 J. Ruskin to Alfred Harris 'Brantwood 3rd Sept '79', St George's Guild Collection, Ruskin Gallery, Sheffield.

23 XIV.152.

24 XVI.330. *Two Paths*, 83.

25 Above, Chapter 2, nn. 17 & 18.

26 XVI.337. *Two Paths*, 89.

27 VII.xxxix–xli; XXXV.494–6. *Praeterita*, III.i.23

28 XVI.338. *Two Paths*, 90.

29 *Athenaeum* 10.2.58, review of John Le Gay Brereton, *The Travels of Prince Legion and other poems*: 'pleasantly written and may be read without weariness'.

30 XVII.31, n. *Unto This Last*, 10, n. *Hard Times*, Chapter 2, 'Murdering the Innocents'.

31 A. Briggs, *Victorian Cities*, Harmondsworth 1963, p. 241.

32 Ancient sources for 'the choice of Hercules': Hesiod, *Erga*. 287; Xenophon, *Memorabilia* II.i.21. Ruskin would know the painting of this subject by Pompeo Batoni (1708–87) in the Turin Gallery. *The Spectator* 28.5.59 presented Ruskin as Virtue addressing 'the student Hercules'. Victorian approval for Herakles and Peter Ramus: *National Encyclopaedia* VII.130– 2; XI.359.

33 XVI.370, 275, 406, 304. *Two Paths*, 135, 30, 189, 61.

34 James P. Kay, MD, *The Moral and Physical Condition of the Working-Classes Employed in the Cotton Manufacture in Manchester*, 2nd ed., 1832, cited Engels, *Condition of the Working Class*, p. 49. Rev. Richard Parkinson, *On the Present Condition of the Labouring Poor in Manchester*, 3rd ed., 1841, cited Engels, p. 125. *Concilio et Labore*, in Manchester Latin, means 'by discussion and hard work', 'by policy and labour', 'by the Town Council and the workforce'.

35 BO 7.2.50, 28.3.50.

36 Reports of the Bradford poisoning tragedy appeared daily in *The Times*, November 1858, while Ruskin was at home. *The Times* 13.1.59 recorded the liturgical burning of the 'arsenical compound' in John Rand's furnaces.

37 XVI.345. *Two Paths*, 97.

38 Dr W. MacTurk, Titus Salt, and others, 'Report on the adulteration of food', *Transactions of the National Association for the Promotion of Social Science for 1859*,

1860, p. xxx. Compare: XXVIII 16–18. *Fors Clavigera* 37.4–5. Ruskin to Mr & Mrs Browning 15 January 1859 describes his mood as 'miserably benevolent. . . I hope to get just one more howl executed'. He sends 'kind regards to Miss Heaton [of Leeds]'. XXXVI.302–4.

Chapter Six

1 Diaries, p. 163.

2 B. Thompson, 'Public provision and private neglect', *Victorian Bradford* p. 137 & n: 'Georg Weerth. . . compared his first entry into Bradford with a descent into Hell'. Compare Georg Weerth to his brother Wilhelm, Bradford 23 May 1844: 'das Land Yorkshire ist jetzt voller Blüten, der Himmel meistens prächtig blau' (*Vergessene Texte*, Köln 1971, I. 58). For the extraordinarily mild and clear weather prevailing throughout England in early March 1859: *The Times* 3, 4, 7.3.59.

3 W. Rothenstein, *Men and Memories* I, 15.

4 W. R. Sorley, *A History of British Philosophy to 1900*, Cambridge 1965, pp. 195–7, 199, 238, 262, 350. Coleridge, *Bibliographica Literaria* (1817), Chapters 5–7, are devoted to his revision and rejection of his own interpretation of Hartley.

5 David Hartley, *Observations on Man* (1749), Scholar's Facsimiles and Reprints, Gainesville 1966, II.303.

6 Biographical material on James Lobley, Cartwright Hall Museum and Art Gallery, Bradford.

7 W. Cudworth, *Rambles round Horton*, 1886, pp. 119, seq. S. Smiles, *Self-Help* (1859), Popular Edition, 1897, pp. 250– 8: 'the chief merit belongs unquestionably to Granville Sharp' for the abolition of slavery.

8 For Bradford pedigrees, see John James, *Continuations to the History of Bradford*, Appendix.

9 John James, *Continuations*, pp. 318–19. Colonel William Henry Sykes, FRS, MP (1790–1872), of Frizinghall, entered the Bombay Army in 1804, became in 1810 interpreter in 'the Hindostanee and Mahratee Languages. . . commanded his Regiment at the battle of Poona [1817]. . . gained the appointment of Statistical Reporter to the Government [1824–31]. . . living among the natives, and prosecuting laborious inquiries into the resources of the country. . . in April, 1856. . . chosen chairman of the East India Company; in March 1857, he was elected MP for the City of Aberdeen, and in May, 1858, president of the Royal Asiatic Society'. In 1863 Sykes became founder-President of the Statistical Society. Wilkie Collins, *The Moonstone* (1868), is set in a perhaps meaningfully named but otherwise imaginary 'Frizinghall'.

10 Rev. Alex Wallace, recording an earlier visit to Bradford, in *The British Workman*, 28.1.56.

11 *BO* 9.8.64; *BR* 13.8.64, 16.3.67.

12 *Athenaeum* 20.3.58; *Post Office Directory for Yorkshire* 1857; BO 4.1.50; *Westminster Review*, April 1859.

13 David Hartley, *Observations* II.82. Compare: Joseph Priestley, *Hartley's Theory of the Human Mind*, 1775, *Preface*.

14 J. S. Mill, *On Liberty*, 1859, pp. 37–45.

15 *BO* 4.1.50, 20.10.59, 20.3.34, 21.4.34; *BR* 19.6.60, 1.1.59, 8.1.59, 8.8.58, 6.1.58.

16 XXX.52

17 *BR* 23.4.64. Cousen: V.163, R's n.

18 Among the 'few translations' of classics in Ruskin's Brantwood library was 'Jowett's *Plato*' (XXXIV.698). Jowett tends to reduce the earthiness and transcendentalism of Plato's Greek to Victorian rationalism. For Ruskin's censure of this, see: XXIX.228 *Fors Clavigera*, 8.

19 John James, *Continuations*, pp. 199, 239. The Bradford church was the ecclesiastical centre of an area of 33,373 acres, which became a separate parish shortly after the Norman Conquest. As was usual, the grammar school existed from early times to teach clerks their Latin. In 1553 the school recovered certain properties which had 'anciently belonged' to it. Henry VI, who held Bradford manor as Duke of Lancaster, devoted for some years the whole of the Duchy's revenues to the building of Eton and King's Colleges, an act of piety which crippled his finances and helped make the Wars of the Roses inevitable (Bertram Wolffe, *Henry VI*, 1981, pp. 135–45, 245, 297). Like Eton Chapel, Whitehall Palace, dream of James I, mortgagee of Bradford Manor, was permanently interrupted by royal bankruptcy and civil war. Ruskin's description of true Gothic as the achievement of 'free citizens and soldier Kings' accords well with Bradford memories of their squire Edward III, under whom their sturdy Parish Church was rebuilt, their market re-established and their Grammar School revived (for Edward III as squire, see XXVII.385). Ruskin's disdain for the 'perverted war' under which 'Gothic rose. . . to its most foolish dreams' is a pocket memoir of Henry VI for his Bradford tenants; and in the original lecture Ruskin apparently associated Whitehall with 'lust and pleasure and pride' (*BO* 28.4.64 and XVIII 440, 444). That none of this is coincidence is suggested by a comparison with the Manchester lectures of 1864. Building on Manchester Collegiate Church began in 1422, the year Henry VI was crowned in Paris. The church's founder was the vicar of Manchester, Thomas, last Baron de la Warre. It was dedicated to the Virgin, and to the patron saints of France and England, St Denys and St George. A cathedral since 1847, the church contains some of the most delicate medieval woodwork in England. In this context, Ruskin's use of the Mancunian De Quincey's biography of Joan of Arc, brought up near the woods of Domrémy (and burned at Rouen in 1431), and his wish to see the 'fairies. . . of the wood' triumph over the evil 'fairies of the furnace' (XVIII.133–4) assume their proper status as educative allusion, not wayward whimsy.

20 XXVIII.353–7 *Fors Clavigera* 54.21–5. Roger Ascham (1515–68), born Kirby Wiske, Yorkshire, tutor to Lady Jane Grey and the Lady Elizabeth (Elizabeth I), wrote the *Scholemaster*, published 1571. John Calcott Horsley, *Lady Jane Grey and Roger Ascham*, exhib. RA 1853.

21 *Jane Eyre*, Chapter 31 (St John Rivers).

22 Hartley, *Observations*, I.498.

23 XVII.83, edd's n., quoting Ruskin's discussion from an unpublished draft for part of *Unto This Last* of De Quincey, *Dialogues of Three Templars on Political Economy* (1824, revised and republished 1854: see De Quincey, *Collected Writings*, edited

by David Masson, 14 vols, Edinburgh 1889–90, 1X.36, n.).

24 XXVIII.40 *Fors Clavigera* 38.14.

25 Thomas De Quincey, *Autobiography*, Chapter 16; *Confessions of an English Opium-Eater*, Part 1 (*Collected Writings*, I.378–99, III.269, etc.) Compare: Samuel Bamford, *Life of a Radical* (1848–9) from *Autobiography*, edited by W. H. Chaloner, 2 volumes, 1967, I.83–92. For the contrasting memoir of Thomas Wright of Bradford Grammar School, see: J. James, *Continuations*, p.202.

26 *The Admission Register of the Manchester School*, edited by J. F. Smith, Chetham Society, Manchester 1866–74, II.99–100: 'Sept 7 1781, David La Touche grandson of David Digues La Touche Esq., Dublin, Ireland'.

27 *Manchester Examiner and Times* 8.12.64.

28 De Quincey, *Collected Writings*, XIV.335–44.

29 Gladstone to Graham 27 November 1860, quoted D. Beales, *England and Italy 1859–60*, 1961, p. 13. Shaftesbury's 'Address to the Working Classes of Lancashire' ('pull together') was republished e.g. *British Workman* May Day issue, 1863. Harry Clifton's 'motto songs' of the period included 'Work, Boys, Work and Be Contented' and 'Paddle Your Own Canoe'.

30 De Quincey, review of G. Gilfillan, 'John Foster [1770– 1843]', from *A Gallery of Literary Portraits* (1845) in *Tait's Magazine*, November 1845, reprinted De Quincey, *Collected Writings* XI.335–41.

31 In Manchester and Bradford, the grammar schools were strongholds of Anglicanism, the new Councils, to begin with, of Dissent. Nevertheless, *Concilio et Labore* accords well enough with *Sapere Aude* and *Labor Omnia Vincit* with *Hoc Age*. Francis Bacon, *Of the Advancement of Learning* 2.XIII.2, quotes Vergil *Bucolics* i.145: 'Labor omnia vincit/Improbus, et duris urgens in rebus egestas'. The now universally accepted reading 'vicit' is not only possible Latin but enforces the Vergilian poignancy as to the 'harsh circumstances' and 'urgent poverty' of the context. The Horatian line which inspired Manchester GS is: 'Dimidium facti qui coepit habet: sapere aude' (*Epistles* ii.40). An unsympathetic Bradfordian might infer that Manchester was good at seizing initiatives, at least.

32 *BA* 23.4.64.

33 *BO* 24.2.59.

34 *Quarterly Review* Volume 109 (1861) no. 218. *Manchester Examiner and Times* 2.10.60. Matthew Arnold, *Complete Prose Works*, ed. R. H. Super, Michigan 1962, III.252 & n.

35 *The Bradfordian Magazine* 1.8.62. This short-lived periodical was edited by Abraham Holroyd, an early publisher of poems by the Brontë sisters. His 'touchstones' are Cowper, *Retirement*. 623 and *Proverbs* XXX.8, 9. Compare: X.451; XVIII.415.

36 Accession Books and Minutes, Bradford Subscription Library, Darley Street. Catalogues, Bradford Mechanics' Institute Library. Both libraries are dispersed. The Mechanics' Institute, like the Subscription Library, took *Fors Clavigera* 'new', as it appeared in volumes. The Subscription Library placed *Fors* in a section by itself in their catalogues, not too far from the Hulsean Lectures on Theology.

37 *BO* 13.10.59.

38 See: XVII.xxvii–viii; and for Ruskin's attack on Dunning: XXVIII. 102–3,

158–9 *Fors Clavigera* 42, 45.

39 *Leeds Mercury* 6.9.60, 20.10.60. Edward Baines, the current editor, was notorious for his 'courtship of aristocracy' (E. D. Steele, 'Imperialism and Leeds politics', *A History of Modern Leeds*, Derek Fraser, Manchester 1980, p. 331). When the *Leeds Mercury* published *Time and Tide* in 1867, Baines's influence was already waning before that of his imminent successor, T. Wemyss Reid.

40 *Bradford Observer* 2 August 1849, quoting a temperance advocate: 'Bradford was the vilest sink in England – the seat of the devil himself', 9 August 1849, quoting *Chamber's Journal* on contemporary capitalism 'It is a system favourable to clever people and good people. . . but deadly to all others'. During December 1849 Byles also published lengthy and horrendous extracts from the *Morning Chronicle's* 'Impressions of Bradford'. A decade later, anything of this kind must be looked for in the *Advertiser* or the *Review*, not the *Observer*.

41 John James Ruskin to Mrs John Simon, Tunbridge Wells, 21 August 1860. XVII.xxvii.

42 *Athenaeum* 2.6.66 BO 24.4.64.

43 Henry Nathaniel Byles, *William Byles: by His Youngest Son*, Weymouth 1932, p. 24, quoted David James, 'William Byles and the *Bradford Observer*', *Victorian Bradford*, p. 118.

Chapter Seven

1 XVIII.440, 458. *Crown of Wild Olive*, 61, 84. A. Fenner Brockway. *Socialism over Sixty Years: The Life of Fred Jowett of Bradford 1864–1944*, 1946, pp. 9–10, 403.

2 See: Jane and John Ayers, *Bradford Old and New*, Wakefield 1976; John Ayers, *Architecture in Bradford*, Bradford 1972; Derek Linstrum, *West Yorkshire: Architects and Architecture*, 1978; John S. Roberts, *Little Germany*, Bradford 1977; *Chartered Surveyor*, December 1979, Cover.

3 Manchester Town Hall by Alfred Waterhouse, opened 1877. St Wilfred's York by Goldie, consecrated 1864.

4 The reality behind *Punch's* satire can be read in the warehouseman Henry Fearnside's diary: 'On Sunday May 4 1862 I got out of bed at 5.45 a.m., washed myself all over, walked up and down the Old Park, and at the same time reading 'Paradise Regained' I read aloud, the people in the neighbouring houses being, most likely, in bed, so early in the morning, and I found it very profitable in several ways a) In loosening my lips, and in removing all unpleasant sounds and stiffness in delivery. b) In giving exercise in reading long sentences which require much wind. c) Nobody is at all disturbed. . . After I closed the book I went round by Bradford Moor home. After getting a good basin of Cocoa into me I went to School. I stopped at Home in the Evening and read a good book written to young men on the importance of Mental Improvement'. For the Bradford Design School artisans, see: Alfred Tylor, *Education and Manufactures. Science and art education in relation to progress in manufactures.* The Second Part of the Jury Report Class XXXI, International Exhibition 1862. Reprinted 1863, p. 96: 'very few. . . persevere like the lads from the warehouses and mills of Bradford, who rival the pupils of the Royal Academy in excellence of drawing'.

5 XXVII, 255. *Fors Clavigera*, 14 (February 1872). Ruskin to C. E. Norton 8 July 1870 (XXXVII.10).

6 Georg Weerth, *Vergessene Texte*, Köln 1971, I.266–7. Clare Delius, *Memories of my Brother*, 1935, p. 19.

7 John S. Roberts, *Little Germany*, pp. 3, 7: 'Bradford began to eclipse Halifax as the key worsted town when steam power was introduced into a worsted spinning mill in 1798. . . The first important secular building in Bradford was the Piece Hall (1773), a down-to-earth structure [as compared with] the magnificent Halifax Piece Hall (1779). . . The raw uncouthness of eighteenth century Bradford is clearly displayed in the bizarre Market House (1783).'

8 Victoria Hotel, 1865–7, by Lockwood and Mawson, in the Italian medieval style Ruskin had warned Bradford not to attempt to revive in 1859. Mechanics' Institute, 1839–40, by Perkins and Backhouse, with rounded corner to Well Street. Two stories with giant Doric pilasters (demolished). Court House, Greek Revivàl, Hall Ings 1832–4 (demolished). St George's Hall, 1851–3, by Lockwood and Mawson. Theatre Royal, Manningham Lane, 1864, by Andrews and Pepper, with interior 'in white and gold in the Italian style' (*The Builder* 12.3.64). Scene of Irving's last performance.

9 Leland *Itinerary* of journeys made 1536–42, quoted John James, *History and Topography of Bradford*, 1841, p. 107.

10 XXXIV.698, 700. A cutting Ruskin probably saw was the report of his 1859 lecture in the *Bradford Review* (see *Winnington Letters*, p. 99). On the reverse is a review of the novel *Getting On*, by the author of *Behind the Scenes*. Reference is made to the 'mean creed' of 'Dagon Respectability'. Compare: *Crown of Wild Olive*, 73.

11 *Sheffield and Rotherham Independent*, 24.4.86.

12 Letter from 'Pedestrian', BO 3.1.61, decrying the 'scraping, rolling watering tinkering, everlastingly going on' along Manningham Lane, and demanding 'paving stones for pedestrians'. The editor advised that the Council had decided against 'a new footway for the present'.

13 *The Builder* 18.10.62. Compare: VIII.115; IX.350; XIV.386. Bradford's plain warehouses became less so with greater prosperity; and St George's Hall has rather a lot of rather ignorant 'Classical' adornment. A letter in the *Bradford Observer* of 19 May 1864 pleaded for the avoidance of the growing trend for 'overloaded and improperly placed ornament' in Italian style, but referred somewhat ambiguously to 'the quality of its rustic work to which Mr Ruskin adverted the other week'. This makes clear Ruskin noticed Bradford warehouses with their rusticated basements. The glory of Bradford sandstone was in plain walling, and this glory was displayed to great advantage in Norman Shaw's Holy Trinity, Bingley, of 1864–8; which had rough-hewn blocks with recessed bonding.

14 The inadequacies of this type of building were shown up by the Sheffield flood disaster of March–April 1864. The embankment of the Bradfield Reservoir above Sheffield – not, apparently, as soundly built as it should have been – gave way, and many of the houses in the water's path, being of rubble construction, were destroyed, to the great increase of fatalities (*The Times* 18.4.64). Ruskin's words to Bradford of 21 April 1864 were recorded by Holmes (*Sheffield &*

Rotherham Independent, 24.4.86): 'whatever the style, he insisted upon good honest work, and no scamping. If contract could not get this, then let it be done by open day work and wages'.

15 St Paul's Manningham, 1847–8, by Mallinson and Healey; with Early English Plate tracery and spire, at the head of a straight vista of 'Classical' villas nearly opposite the driveway down to Mitchell's house, where Ruskin stayed in 1859. Not all this work was completed by Ruskin's day; but quite sufficient was visible to justify Ruskin's judgment that in building styles Bradford had separated its religion from its life (XVIII.440). St Jude's clumsy and dumpy spire was visible among neat classic houses a little further down Manningham Lane to the right. Dr MacTurk was a main promoter of its building fund. The County Court, built from 1859 on Manor Row on the site of MacTurk's former residence, was in a Barryesque Italianate style. Christ Church, on Darley Street, behind Manor Row, reared its paltry Gothicisms above neat and solidly constructed Classical early Victorian houses and warehouses. St Jude's and Christ Church have since been destroyed.

16 Ruskin's natural route down into Bradford would be by way of Manningham Lane, Manor Row and Cheapside, at the botton of which was Harris's Old Bank with, on Lower Cheapside, the gloomy cheap-looking island called Victoria Buildings, housing, among more profitable ventures such as Fattorini's the jewellers, the new Bradford School of Design. At the junction of Manningham Lane with Manor Row, on the left, was the grammar school of 1820, in open grounds. The visitor might note how the ground to his left swooped steeply down towards canal, beck, and railway, and surged steeply up again. Canyons, half street, half moorland sheep track, plunged downward to reveal and hide an impression of lime kilns, saw pits, gas works, worsted mills, an industrial reservoir and all the charm of North Brook Vitriol Works: the background of the Grammar School and the future of its alumni. The school was demolished and the site covered with a gloomy German Gothic structure in 1873, a building that would cause acute depression to artistic pupils such as Frederick Delius and William Rothenstein. In 1868 the Old Bank moved to a new site near the Wool Exchange and into a new building (since demolished) by Alfred Waterhouse, in a phase of his personal Gothic style. Ruskin's ironic play on the word 'bank' in *Traffic* may have been influenced by a glimpse of the grandiose Venetian Renaissance Bradford Banking Co. premises of 1858 by Andrews & Delauney, at the junction of Kirkgate and Darley Street, a few yards 'up the bank' from Victoria Buildings. The contrast between the two structures, and their relative geographic position, were certainly suggestive of Bradford values.

17 XVI.338 *BO* 20.4.65. George Nicholson, of York St, Bradford thus described the canal-side slums of Bradford's Wapping in the *Bradford Review* 24 December 1858: 'those most wretched quarters filled with dirt and smoke, whose streets are ill-lighted, unpaved, and many of them only half built, looking more like the ruins of some plague-striken or war-desolated city than unfinished portions of a wealthy, thriving, manufacturing town'.

18 XV.225, n. (commendation for Flaxman's 'si nple groups in marble'); XII.153 (condemnation for Flaxman's more ambitious projects). The monu-

ments to Abraham Balme, died 1796, by John Flaxman (b. York 1755, d. London 1826) is now in the north aisle of Bradford Cathedral (former Parish Church, the arcades of which were rebuilt shortly after a fire in 1327; and the Perpendicular west tower of which dates from 1493–1508). Wm Scruton, *Pen and Pencil Sketches of Old Bradford*, Bradford 1889, p. 27: 'the choice piece of sculpture by Flaxman. . . was regarded by the great sculptor himself as one of his finest conceptions, and it has called forth the admiration of that severest of critics – John Ruskin'.

19 One outstanding example: Sir Titus Salt died in 1876, having spent the last few years of his life at the relatively modest eighteenth-century house, Crow Nest. But in 1872, Titus junior had demolished a seventeenth-century house in favour of the huge neo-Gothic Milner Field. Meanwhile, the heir to the baronetcy, William Henry, had established his 'family' far away – in Leicestershire.

20 By the mid '60s the respectable working class were moving largely into back-to-back houses. Machinery for cutting stone and timber, efficient drains and the availability of large new sites on breezy slopes could make back-to-backs an immense improvement on the old shoddily-built piecemeal development in lightless courts and alleys lower down in the Bradford basin. But as happened a century later with the high-rise system, the new technology was no guarantee against stupidity and greed. And since building systems are more easily distinguished than right and wrong, it was the system of back-to-back building that was outlawed by a Bradford bye-law of 1860. This was at least partly a reflection of the humanitarian mood that allowed the *Bradford Observer* to distinguish itself by lending public advocacy to *Unto This Last*. The mood changed however. Speculative builders created a rumpus in 1862, and when the matter was made a test question in the municipal elections of 1864-5, back-to-backs resumed legality.

21 John Ruskin to John James Ruskin, Knaresborough, 2 March 1859, published *Winnington Letters*, p. 101: 'Mr. Mitchell is a middle-aged (rather young) manufacturer – very benevolent and modest – has a nice home of the Bowers' Well type – everything of the best. New inventions – gas – and cocks and plugs and iron blinds and every conceivable convenience – so that I dared not stir a foot in my room for fear of setting something going and not being able to stop it.' It had been at New Bowerswell House (built 1842–4) that Ruskin had married Effie in 1848. Ruskin describes Mitchell's Parkfield House now the Convent and Boarding School of the Sisters of the Cross and Passion – rather as though it were Mr Gradgrind's Stone Lodge (*Hard Times*, Ch. 3: 'Gas and ventilation, drainage and water service, all of the primest quality. Iron clamps and girders, fireproof from top to bottom; mechanical lifts for the housemaids. . .'). Ruskin would not, however, make the mistake of confusing Mitchell with Mr Gradgrind or Alfred Harris with the fictional banker Mr Bounderby. The excitability of his description, and its humour, makes Ruskin sound like a second Gulliver encapsulated in his model home in apprehension of being released for the entertainment of Brobdignag.

22 A Bradford poet of 1858 tellingly described Bradford as hidden in smoke 'like a snail in its shell', and the New Leeds area (which began some 300 yards

away from the Mechanics' Institute) was, by reason of the prevailing west wind, frequently cited as the smokiest of the smoky. See: C. Richardson, 'The Irish in Victorian Bradford', *Bradford Antiquary*, New Series, IX.309. Any light in the moonless sky of 1 March 1859 would come from the glare of foundries such as Croslands Foundry or the Waterloo Foundry.

23 Rifle Volunteer Barracks and Drill Ground, on the left hand side of Manningham Lane, as one goes towards Bingley, as Ruskin did after leaving the Great Northern Station in 1864. Rifle Volunteer Clubs sprang up all over Britain in the early 1860s in hysterical fear of French invasion. As so often, Ruskin at first sympathised with the popular reaction, then on reflection diverged sharply from it. He commended Rifle Clubs in a letter to Ellen Heaton of Leeds, 9 March 1860 (quoted, XVIII.xxiv, n.) but by 1864 he saw the clubs more as increasing propensities to violence than as offering England protection, and in *Traffic* he satirises the relations between England and France as like that of two 'capital friends', their villa grounds divided only by a fruit-wall; but each fenced about with a maniacal panolpy of 'steel-traps' and 'spring-guns'. The gist of this message was delivered in April 1864, when the Bradford iron-workers were on strike, demanding a fairer share in the profits of armament sales. From his room (presumably the 'best bedroom', over the drawing-room) at Parkfield House, in 1859, Ruskin could have observed Mitchell's close proximity to his neighbour, political antagonist and 'capital friend', in Ruskin's pun, John Taylor, the Tory resident of Bolton Royd.

24 It would be most natural and convenient for Ruskin's coachman to turn up High Street, Barkerend, after leaving the Parish Church, and thence via the Otley Road to Knaresborough. To the right of Otley Road, towards the top of the bank, were the grounds of Undercliffe House (known as Garnett Hall, from its proprietor); at the bottom of the bank, on Barkerend Road, was Garnett's Mill. This was a typical relationship, and though it is not certain that Ruskin took this road, it is evidence of his ability to 'hit the nail', that Jack and Peggy Davies, who had known the area all their lives, exclaimed 'Garnett Hall' and 'Garnett's Mill' on being read the passage from *Traffic* (XVIII.453). This was in 1969: and Mr and Mrs Davies remembered their old friend Mrs Dennitt, a nurse at Garnett Hall in the late '80s, who treasured into the 1950s portraits of the 'beautiful family', to quote her own phrase and Ruskin's. Miss A. Midgeley, a mill-girl at Garnett's in the '90s remembered seeing the family drive 'through the shrubberies' in an open carriage, and was once privileged as a church-going teetotaller to carry letters up to 'the house'. James Garnett began business as a woolcomber with a dozen 'hands' in the late eighteenth century in nearby Paper Hall (b. 1648). The model mill presided over by his grandson William Garnett formed an admirable illustration of getting on to the readers of the *Bradford Weekly Telegraph* of 19 December 1885. William Garnett remained in possession of Undercliffe House, bought in 1854 from the Hustler family, till his death in 1887. But from about 1877 he was also in possession of a country house near Ripon. William Cudworth, *The Bradford Budget* 19 May 1906, notes that Messrs Wm Garnett & Co. retired from the worsted business about 1896, but that the extensive Barkerend premises remained (1906) in the possession of the Garnett family, and that great-grandsons of old James Garnett, a founder

(1781) of Horton Lane Congregational Chapel, still used portions of the works for spinning and other operations.

25 Obelisk to Joseph Smith, obit. 22 April 1858, land agent to the managers, Bradford Cemetery, Undercliffe. Under certain weather conditions this obelisk is also strikingly visible from the lower end of Manningham Lane. This joint-stock necropolis, a veritable Pandemonium of High Victorian funeral art, with hardly a Christian symbol to be found in it, has recently (1983) been sold off to a private speculator, and much despoiled. There are hopes of saving what remains.

26 XVI.321 *Two Paths*, 74: 'the wild boar of silver which you use for a seal'. The official description of the Common Seal of the Borough of Bradford describes this as 'a Boar's Head (without tongue) erased Or'. In *Traffic*, 76 (XVIII.451) Ruskin maliciously depicts Britannia Agoraia as having on her shield 'the Milanese boar, semi-fleeced, with the town of Gennesaret proper, in the field'. This is quite possibly a mockery of the official 'escroll entwined with a branch of Palm, and another of Olive, and pendant therefrom a Golden Fleece. . . In the compartment on the left of the Shield a representation of Justice with Scales and Sword and Seated upon a Woolpack, and at her feet an Alpaca – In the background a Mill.' (*Year Book* of the Bradford Corporation). But while Ruskin mocked the periphery of the Bradford crest, he was also drawing on the 'Well Sable' at its centre.

27 Harry Speight, *Bingley and District*, p. 13; *Chronicles and Stories of Old Bingley*, London 1898, p. 358. Ruskin was a guest at Woodbank, Aldam Heaton's house in the Harden valley and apparently 'paced the woodland walks', on 22 April 1864. The Druid's Altar, 650 feet above the Aire, is by far the most spectacular feature of the landscape, and Henry Harris, head of the Old Bank and an art dilettante, had his house Longwood, Bingley, positioned to capture the 'open prospect towards the altar crags'.

28 XVI.338 *Two Paths*, 89.

29 *Traffic*, like the original 1864 lecture, transfers to a Yorkshire context the story of Jacob's Dream: 'And he called the name of that place Beth-el' (*Genesis*, xxviii, 17–19). Compare: *The Bible of Amiens* IV.10 (XXXIII.131): 'From the unhewn block set on end in the Druid's Bethel, to *this* Lord's House and blue-vitrailed gate of Heaven, you have the entire course and consummation of the Northern Religious Builder's passion and art'.

Chapter Eight

1 John James, *Continuations to the History and Topography of Bradford*, 1866, pp. 155–6. 'Another great addition to the appearance of the chancel, results from the insertion of the new east window, presented by Mrs Tolson, in memory of her late husband, Richard Tolson, Esq., of Bolton House. . . executed by the celebrated firm of Morris, Marshall, Falkener and Co. . . . The large figure of the Saviour is, both in beauty of design and colour, a choice specimen of art. . . Mr. Ruskin the eminent art-critic, when lately at Bradford, gave it his meed of praise. . .' See also: A. Charles Sewter, *The Stained Glass of William Morris and His*

Circle, New Haven and London 1974, Illustrs. 177–180, and p. 67, where the Christ in Majesty is described as 'Rossetti's most effective composition of several figures', and the Bradford window as one of the earliest (1862–3) really big designs executed by the Morris 'Firm'.

2 H.-R. Hitchcock, *Architecture: Nineteenth and Twentieth Centuries*, Harmondsworth, 1963, p. 237. John S. Roberts, *Little Germany*, Bradford 1977, correctly dates the Lockwood and Mawson warehouse '1853', and in a letter to the author adds that it possessed 'a heptagonal entrance hall with an arched opening or mahogany door in each of its seven sides'. Godwin's Stokes Croft warehouse dates from 1862.

3 XI.44–5. *Stones of Venice* III.ii.2. For Ruskin's frequent extempore appreciations of Renaissance architecture, see: XXXIII.188.

4 John Holmes, *Sheffield and Rotherham Independent* 24.4.86, makes clear that Ruskin's remarks about the 'snobs' of Leeds who had burdened Brodrick's 'fair Roman composite' Town Hall with a gigantic cupola were made in private in 1864, not in public in 1859, as his editors (XXXIV.725) suggest.

5 *The Bradford Telegraph and Argus*, Centenary Supplement, 16 July 1968. Compare: X.333–4; III.129; VII.230.

6 John Ruskin, *Aratra Pentelici*, 1872, p. 131: 'The Apollo of Syracuse and the Self-made Man'. The 'Self-made Man' was taken from a *Punch* cartoon by Charles Keene (1823–91). Bradford's literary existence is *Traffic*, with its image of Jacob's Ladder. T. S. Eliot was lecturing on Ruskin in April 1917, and toured the provincial banking centres in 1919. Beckett's Bank, Bradford, was across Cheapside from the Midland Hotel. Henry Irving collapsed and died in the doorway of this hotel after an attack of syncope on stage while playing Tennyson's *Becket*. Irving's tour manager was Bram Stoker, and among Irving's impersonators besides Count Dracula is George and Weedon Grossmith's Mr Burwin-Fossleton (*Diary of a Nobody*, Ch. 11: '*Revenons a nos moutons* . . . I may crawl, I may slip, I may even falter, but *reach the top of the ladder I will!!!*'). *Diary* first appeared in *Punch*, and George Grossmith was leading comedian at the *Gaiety*, where the ex-Bradford mill-girl Gertie Millar was the reigning 'Gaiety Girl'. Lupin Pooter's successful rival for the love of Daisy Mutlar is Mr Posh of Posh's three-shilling-hats. Irving, who began his working life as a clerk, and was the first player to be knighted, wore a silk hat only when in benevolent mood. After hearing of his death, Ellen Terry, whom Lewis Carroll had crowned 'Empress of Art' after her Ophelia, broke down on stage during a performance of Barry's *Alice-sit-by-the-fire*. See: V. Eliot, *The Waste Land: A Facsimile and Transcript* 1971, pp. 6, 11–17; M. Hardman, 'The prose and ideas of John Ruskin', unpublished PhD thesis, Cambridge 1975, pp. 383–5; and NB: VI.85 (Turner's style 'a game of chess'), VII.435 ('the rape of Europa') 473–5 (the Persephone myth), IX.137, n., 386 (the symbolism of the Corinthian capital; the Corinthian capitals of Grosvenor Square in cages of wire), X.82–3 (the pieces of Eliot's chess-game with Ruskin's St Mark's: the piece Eliot removes is the queen, Cleopatra), XXXIII.15 (Avarice of wool merchants in England and Amiens), XXXIV.341 (the 'violet. . . evening' in a discussion of Byron), XXXVII.81, 303, 539 (Ruskin to Charles Eliot Norton on his chess games with the Automaton, with a quotation from Henry VIII V.1; Ruskin and Oscar Wilde share a box to see Irving's Shylock at the Lyceum;

Ruskin's works the prize in the British Chess Association Tournament).

7 Milner Field, designed for Titus Salt, junior, 1872, by Thomas Harris. Its ruins 'awful in the gothic sense': N. Pevsner, *The Buildings of England: Yorkshire, The West Riding*, Harmondsworth 1959, p. 103. Since demolished.

8 John Holmes, *Sheffield and Rotherham Independent* 24.4.86, alluding to the catch-phrase of John Hollingshead, manager of the *Gaiety* till 1885. (Ronald Pearson, *Edwardian Popular Music*, 1975, pp. 18–19).

9 Heaton Mount (for Robert Kell, 1864); Woodleigh Hall (for Moses Bottomley, 1869); Woodlands (for Angus Holden, 1866).

10 Henry Fearnside, MS diary entry Saturday 6 June 1863. In 1795 John Marsden of Hornby Castle conveyed the Bradford Manor to the Bolton merchant Benjamin Rawson (1758–1844).

11 *The Origin of Species* was published 24 November 1859. Cobden's remark: above, Ch. 2, n.6.

12 XVII.348 *Time and Tide*, 33.

13 J. James, *History and Topography of Bradford*, 1841, p. 183.

14 John Martin (1789–1854). The three large canvases, painted 1851–3, are in the Tate Gallery.

15 *The Times* 11.1.64. XVIII.452, 468, 416. *Hamlet* V.ii.37, I.ii.65. Compare: *Crown of Wild Olive*, 84, & R's n. ('The rest is silence. . . that kind of marble. . . fanciful kind). *BA* 23.4.64 suggests Ruskin alluded clearly to Atlanta on the night: 'Idols were forbidden, and he warned the worshippers that catastrophe would come to us, as it had to our brethren beyond the seas'.

16 XXIX.261 | *Fors Claviger*, 83.4 (translation of *Laws* ii.562.17) XXXVI.158 (the 'Eternal Piano').

17 S. T. Coleridge to Robert Southey, 11 December 1794: 'I go farther than Hartley and believe the corporeality of *Thought* – namely, that it is motion'. (*The Collected Letters of Samuel Taylor Coleridge*, ed. E. L. Griggs, Oxford 1956, I.137.)

18 Asa Briggs, *The Age of Improvement*, 1959, pp. 394, 489. Max Müller, *Auld Lang Syne*, 1878, pp. 127–8: Ruskin 'was one of the few Englishmen I knew who, instead of tumbling out their sentences like so many portmanteaux. . . from an open railway-van, seemed. . . even in familiar conversation. . . to make each deliverance a work of art'.

19 XXVIII.267 *Fors Clavigera* 50.16. Compare XXXVII.156, 159 and *Winnington Letters*, p. 489.

20 *Diaries*, pp. 542–3 (May 1859) sculpture of Frederick the Great in apotheosis, with four equestrian figures, by Christian Daniel Rauch (1777–1857): 'if you look the least above the apotheosis, you have a full view of the horse's posterior: and if it were alive, there is no saying what might happen at any moment to Frederick the Great in Apotheosis'.

21 John Ruskin to Alfred Harris, 'Berlin 12th June [1859]':

> My dear sir,
>
> I have been out of the way of all letters from home among the towns of North Germany for some weeks past. I regret not having been able to answer you sooner. I am never at home, nor in England if I can help it, in summer, and cannot therefore have the pleasure of attending the Brad-

ford meeting. With sincere regards to Mr & Mrs. Tylor believe me
faithfully yours
J. Ruskin.

The new Bradford Design School had an exhibition and prize-giving, 6 July 1859. First prize for drawing went to David Binns, for a chalk drawing of a cast of the Venus de Milo.

John Ruskin to Alfred Harris, 'Denmark Hill Monday 15th April [1861]':
My dear sir,
I delayed writing respecting the drawings of the students in your School of art, because I wished to say a few words about the system they are following – however, I shall not be able to say what I wished till I've got some business off my hands this week and therefore – lest I should cause inconvenience by delay I will only say that I had great pleasure in seeing *all* the drawings: and very heartily congratulate the students on their general success. It was a matter of difficulty to decide on the relative merit of the chalk drawings, but I think the students will feel that the first prize is justly due to the draughtsman who executed the study from the Venus of Milo: I think the second should be the mask of St Jerome, and the third, the boldest acanthus leaf; of the two coloured studies in oil the lobster is certainly the best.
You have an excellent and zealous Master.
Believe me, my dear Sir,
[signature cut off]

Ruskin's 'business' that week was the Tree Twigs lecture of Friday 19 April 1861 at the Royal Institution (VII.467). The 'excellent and zealous Master' was James Lobley.

John Ruskin to Alfred Harris, [Denmark Hill, late April–early May 1862]:
My dear Sir,
I am on the point of leaving England to pass the whole year on the continent – out of the way of the bazaar business of the mob – here. So I can't be useful anyhow or anywhere – within hearing of the noise of them but am always faithfully yours
J. Ruskin

A. Harris Junr, Esq.,
Ashfield Bingley
Yorks.

Ruskin left for the continent on 15 May 1862, and did not return to England till May 1863 (*Diaries*, pp. 560, 574). The 'bazaar business of the mob – here' would presumably be the International Exhibition of 1862.

John Ruskin to Alfred Harris, 'Denmark Hill 9th April [1864]'. On mourning paper:

My dear Sir,
I have left your kind letter thus long unanswered owing to a sharp attack of illness which rendered me at first doubtful if I should be able to come at all. I trust now I may, but the late death of my father leaves me unfit for society. I hope I may not be thought other than grateful for your kindness, for it will be with much sincere regret that I refuse your kind invitation & that of Mr. Mitchell – but indeed it will be wisest in me to go to a quiet Inn on the day appointed for the lecture – which I have asked Mr. Heaton to arrange. Believe me, my dear Sir,
Gratefully yours,
J. Ruskin

A. Harris, Esq.

John Ruskin to Alfred Harris, '18th April [1864]'. On mourning paper:

My dear Sir,
I hope to come by the Great Northern – 10 to 3.10 – as specified in your kind letter, on Thursday.

It does not tire me to travel. The brain is wrong, much more than the body. I should be quite fresh for lecturing after travelling all day if need were – but if I were to go and see anything that interested in me [sic] – or read for a couple of hours – or get into a talk on any subject requiring thought, I should probably be quite down in the evening.

This is why I like better to be with you the day after than day before. Most truly & gratefully yours, J. Ruskin

A. Harris, Esq. Jun.
Old Bank
Bradford
Yorkshire.

The above five letters, hitherto unpublished, are in the St George's Guild Collection, Sheffield. *Bradshaw's Railway Guide* for 1864 shows a 10 am express from King's Cross to Bradford via Leeds without changing, arriving in Bradford at 3.10 pm. The Great Northern Station, Bradford, at this time, was awkwardly placed off the Wakefield Road, on the south-east side of Bradford. Bingley, where Ruskin went before the lecture, is at the opposite edge of the Bradford basin, to the north-west.

22 John Ruskin to Margaret Ruskin, Bradford, Yorkshire, 21 April 1864 (*Winnington Letters*, p. 490):

Bradford,
7 o'clock

My dearest Mother
I got down quite comfortably in every way but the way of Teeth – which ached sadly, but am better now and hope to give a fair lecture. I am four miles out of Bradford at a country house among wood anenome's – and have only time for this absurd line. Ever your affectionate Son
J. Ruskin

23 XVII.434 *Crown of Wild Olive*, 53: 'You are going to spend £30,000 which to you, collectively, is nothing'.

24 *Leeds Intelligencer* April 1864.

25 Above, Ch. 6, n.42.

26 Henry F. Lockwood, letter in *The Bradford Observer* 2 June 1864.

27 XVIII.lxxv. *BR* 23.4.64.

28 Stefan Muthesius, *The High Victorian Movement in Architecture*, 1972, pp. 129–32, 157–9.

29 *BO* 2, 9.6.64. Another writer called Shaw's a design 'suited to a town of mud and wood'.

30 John Ruskin to Ellen Heaton [latter half of March 1860], published Virginia Surtees, *Sublime and Instructive*, 1972, p. 224.

31 *BO* 2.6.64, 18.10.66.

32 Geoffrey Scott, *The Architecture of Humanism* (1914, with epilogue 1924), ed. 1961, pp. 77, n., 163.

33 Michael Pratt, 'The influence of the Germans on Bradford', unpublished third-year history dissertation, Margaret McMillan College, Bradford: copy in Bradford Central Library, p. 69. Ernst Wilhelm Böhle b. 14 Bertram Rd, Manningham, 28 July 1908, was described in 1940 by Nazi sources as 'leader of all Germans not living in the Fatherland'; and was Hitler's choice as Gauleiter of Great Britain.

34 E. W. Godwin, letter to *The Builder* 18 June 1864, reprinted *BO* 23.6.64. W. Eden Nesfield, letter to [Heaton or Harris?] printed *BO* 2.6.64.

35 Bradford's first 'legal' school clinic opened in 1908 (Albert Mansbridge, *Margaret McMillan*, 1932, p. xxi.)

36 Law, Russell's Warehouse, 63 Vicar Lane, Bradford, by Lockwood and Mawson 1874. See: John S. Roberts, *Little Germany*, Bradford 1977, pp. 28–9.

37 *Little Germany*, p. 9.

38 Ruskin gives a clue to this comparison. 'The book I called *The Seven Lamps*', he writes in *Traffic*, 'was to show that certain right states of temper and moral feeling were the magic powers by which all good architecture, without exception, had been produced.' *Traffic* ends with a plea to 'build with stone well, but with flesh better: temples not made with hands, but riveted of hearts; and that kind of marble, crimson-veined, is indeed eternal' (XVIII.443, 458).

Opening *The Seven Lamps*, and turning to 'The Lamp of Truth', the reader finds: 'But the architecture of animals *here* is appointed by God to be a marble architecture, not a flint nor adamant architecture; and all manner of expedients are adopted to attain the utmost degree of strength and size under that great limitation'. The 'jaw of the ichthyosaurus is pieced and riveted' (VIII 71–2). Ruskin's editors' n.: 'The MS adds, "and that of the whale infinitely divided into elastic threads".' Looking further, to Chapter VII of Charles Darwin, *The Origin of Species* (ed. 1855, pp. 182–3), the reader notes 'The Greenland whale is one of the most wonderful animals in the world, and the baleen, or whale-bone, one of its greatest peculiarities. The baleen consists of a row, on each side, of the upper jaw, of about 300 plates or laminae. . . the middle lamina being, in one species, according to Scoresby, four feet, in another three, in another eighteen inches. . .' Dr William Scoresby, DD (1789– 1857) Dr Burnet's predecessor as

Vicar of Bradford, was the greatest British authority of the day on whales and on terrestrial magnetism.

39 John Summerson, *Victorian Architecture: Four Studies in Evaluation*, New York and London, 1970, p. 5.

40 Ben Preston, Bradford's 'poet of the poor' and protégé of the Harrisses and of H. S. Baring-Gould, verses of 1849, 'Just nah, when poor France regged on' tattered on' bare is / We're weyvin' silk lustres for t'harlots i'Paris'. Ben Preston, *Dialect and Other Poems* London and Bradford 1881, p. 17.

41 Ruskin's remarks on the ichthyosaurus ('The Lamp of Truth', 13: see above, n. 38) conclude thus: 'in the cumbrous movement of these unwieldiest of His creatures, we are reminded, even in His divine essence, of that attribute of uprightness in the human creature; "that sweareth to his own hurt, and changeth not"'(VIII.72, quoting *Psalm* XV.4). By binding together in 'acicular fashion' (XXXIV.261) this passage with the end of *Traffic*, Ruskin permits his readers to sympathise just a little with the fatuous self-revelation of Bradford which is the Wool Exchange.

42 *The Builder*, Vol. XXII, No. 1123 (13 August 1864), with full-page engraving by W. E. Hodgkin. Compare: IX.11.

43 VIII.10 *The Seven Lamps*, preface to second edition (1855).

44 *BO* 26.5.64. XVIII.165.

45 *Manchester Courier*, 18.4.64; *BO* 28.4.64.

46 Thomas to John Carlyle 23 April 1861 (quoted, VII.lix).

47 Octavia to Emily Hill, 6 Clifton Villas, Bradford, 17 September 1869, published C. E. Maurice, *Letters of Octavia Hill*, 1913, p. 255.

48 John to Margaret Ruskin, Bradford, Friday 22 April 1864. Published, *Winnington Letters*, pp. 490–1:

> My dearest Mother
>
> I got well enough through my lecture – an hour and 25 minutes – and had no pain in mouth during the evening – but nevertheless slept very little and am tired this morning – but I am now resting and hope to come all right soon. They bore with it very patiently, applauding in most places, and remaining politely silent when they did not approve. There will probably be two or three reports – of which I will send you the best.
>
> Will you please tell Lucy to make up all my letters into a packet, and send it to Miss Bells,
>
> Winnington Hall
> Northwich
>
> I will not write more to-day, for there are people coming to dinner, and I've got to go out to lunch & be amiable, which is horribly trying to my constitution. Love to the young ladies –
> Ever my dearest Mother
> Your most affe Son,
> J. Ruskin

49 *BO* 28.4.64. The reviewer also writes: 'The lecture. . . to any one but Mr Ruskin, would have formed subject enough for a course of six. . . The room

was filled to its utmost corner, and the lot of most of the audience was that of having expected much and having got more.'

50 W. Scruton, *Pen and Pencil Sketches of Old Bradford*, Bradford 1889, p. 237.

51 James Burnley, *Phases of Bradford Life* (reprinted from the *Bradford Observer*), London and Bradford 1860, pp. 66–7, on Thursday Market Day: 'The noise is unceasing, and ever and anon its effect is heightened by the melodious bray of a "Coster's" donkey. . . women-keepers of small shops. . . carry their purchases in their arms. . . I doubt whether Hope in its most flattering moments ever deluded them into the belief that they would some day arrive at the dignity of a donkey and cart. . .' German paper-hanging sellers cry "paper fit for ze Prince o'Vales's drawing room" at "tuppence for ze lot".'

52 John Ruskin to Henry Acland 27 April 1856. XXXVI.237–40.

53 XVII.73. Compare XVIII.458: 'Continue to make that forbidden deity your principal one, and. . . Catastrophe must come; or worse than catastrophe, slow mouldering and withering into Hades.'

54 *King Lear* IV.ii.49–50.

55 John Ruskin to Henry Acland. 8 March 1864. XXXVI.470–1.

56 Mary Lutyens, *The Ruskins and the Grays*, 1972, p. 1.

57 For Ruskin's study of Louis Agassiz, *Poissons Fossiles*, see: XXXV. 301, 306. John James, *History and Topography of Bradford*, 1841, p. 12, also mentions that in the Bradford coal measures, 'plants resembling the tree ferns and bamboos of the tropics are often met with; thus showing that they have either been wafted hither in some diluvial wreck, or that the climate of this country has at one time been tropical'.

58 J. E. Millais, *A Flood* Oil on canvas $39\frac{1}{8}$ x $57\frac{1}{6}$ inches, 1870. Manchester City Art Galleries.

59 John Aldam Heaton, letter of 19 November 1866, *BO* 29.11.66, with Byles's editorial note 'Let this be a warning'. Heaton may also have been the writer of a letter from 'A Ratepayer', *BO* 1.6.65, advocating pallisading screened by shrubs and forest trees to mark the boundary of Peel Park, instead of the 'nine foot wall' in machine-cut stone, adorned with 'an ugly square pillar. . . surmounted with what looks like either a huge Scotch cap or an enormous mushroom. . . How would Mr Ruskin sigh were he to see this evidence of the refined taste of our Corporation and their designer.'

60 *Sheffield and Rotherham Independent* 24.4.86.

61 *Bradford School of Art* Annual Report, 1869.

62 The Bradford Philosophical Society was briefly resuscitated in 1864, Ripley, Harris, Hanson and the Mayor Charles Semon being among the subscribers. But when in 1866 Ripley offered money towards a new building for the institution, he met with 'no response'.

63 *BR* 27.6.61.

64 XVIII.451–2, 455–6 *Crown of Wild Olive* 77, 82.

65 *John* XIII, 13 ('Ye call me Master and Lord. . .), 34 ('a new commandment'). 1,5 ('I am the true vine. . . I am the vine, ye are the branches').

66 XVIII.453 *Crown of Wild Olive*, 79.

67 H. W. Ripley to Sir George Grey, Home Secretary, 23 June 1864, published Bradford Chamber of Commerce *Report* for 1864. For Arnold's phrase, see above,

Ch. 6, n. 34.

68 BO 14.3.67. Lord Frederick Cavendish, MP, announced that the returns for the Bradford wool trade in 1866 had been 13 million; and that the American Civil War (blankets, overcoats, etc.) had caused a huge development of trade. M. W. Thompson subjoined that 'we should for many years to come occupy the very first place in the world'. For the Rich Fool, see Luke XII, 20.

69 John Nicholson, the Airedale Poet (1790–1843), *Poetical Works*, 4th ed. May 1859, by W. Dearden, with introduction by John James. Nicholson was retained as a woolsorter by Titus Salt 1833–43, despite his drunkenness and inefficiency. One of his most famous poems was on factory children, written in 1836 for Richard Oastler, with a ling stalk gathered on Rombald's Moor, where under the tutelage of a besom-maker who used a shooting-lodge for a school, Nicholson had learnt to read. James rejoices that Dearden has revised Nicholson's poems 'where practicable' to accord with 'ideas more intelligent and agreeable to readers of refined taste', and trusts that Nicholson's widow will continue to be able to finance her son's education at Bradford Grammar School from the proceeds of the edition.

70 John Ruskin to Margaret Bell 5 April 1859, *Winnington Letters*, p. 154.

71 V.274–81. Compare: *Genesis xxvii–xxxiii. Purgatorio* xxvii 91–108.

72 *The Dalesman* July 1979, pp. 296–7.

73 Malcolm Ross, woolsorter, lithographic printer and poet, was one of James Hanson's prize essayists in the *Review*, which on 12 March 1859 reported favourably on Ross's lecture 'The Character and Genius of Robert Burns, as tested by the Principles of Total Abstinence'. Ross elsewhere advocated closed-shop unionism and *laissez-faire* economics. David Wright, 'The second reform agitation 1857–67', *Victorian Bradford* p. 182, notes that Ross as 'political lapdog of the Non-conformist radical leaders' urged Bradford working-men not to upset Lord Palmerston when he came to lay the foundation stone of the Wool Exchange in August 1864. Ross's speech at the opening: *BR* 16.3.67.

74 *Genesis* xlvi.10, xlvii.23.

75 A. Fenner Brockway, *Socialism over Sixty Years*, 1946, p. 111.

76 XVIII.438 *Crown of Wild Olive*, 58, quoting *The Lay of the Last Minstrel* i.4. The popularity of this poem is attested by this report on Fattorini's Showcase at the Royal Jubilee Exhibition Saltaire, in *Bradford Illustrated Weekly Telegraph* 27.8.87: 'A very fine silver clock (£175) is noticeable from the modelled figures on it to represent the characters in Sir Walter Scott's "Lay of the Last Minstrel".'

77 XXXIV.280, R's n: 'Then came. . . the stories continually told [Scott] of the executions at Carlisle, his aunt's husband having seen them; issuing. . . in the unaccountable terror that came upon him at the sight of statuary – especially Jacob's Ladder'. Ruskin's Jacob, in *Traffic*, is on his was to see 'an uncle at Carlisle' (XVIII.441).

78 The post-Communion prayer, *The Book of Common Prayer*.

79 XVIII.436.

80 Edward Healey, 'Woodleigh Hall, Rawdon' in *Picturesque Views*, Bradford 1885. For the last Marquis of Hastings, see H. Blyth, *The Pocket Venus*, 1966.

81 XVIII.438. *Crown of Wild Olive*, 59.

Chapter Nine

1 John James, *Continuations*, 1866, p. 136.

2 *BO* 7.7.59, 20.10.59; *BR* 3.7.58; *Leeds Mercury* 3.3.59.

3 IX.10.

4 A. Saint, *Richard Norman Shaw*, New Haven and London, 1976, p. 57.

5 Ordnance Survey map, published Southampton 1852, but surveyed in the late '40s; Hart's block plan of the Town of Bradford, 1861. The Ordnance map shows, in the relevant area to the right of Kirkgate proceeding towards Lower Cheapside: the former drapery shop of Robert Milligan (modernised with plate glass windows in 1817), the Talbot, the Piece Hall, the Nag's Head, the Savings Bank, the White Lion, the White Horse. On the Piece Hall, see N. Pevsner, *The Buildings of England, Yorkshire: The West Riding*, Harmondsworth 1967, p. 126: 'the Bradford Piece Hall built in 1773 and pulled down in 1853. It was 144 ft. by 36 ft. in size.' Temperance was strong among the rulers of Bradford, and Byles's plea for the 'reformation' of this area may have been aimed at councillors and others who wished to close the pubs.

6 J. S. Roberts, *Little Germany*, Bradford 1977, p. 14.

7 XVI.330, 341.

8 W. Cudworth, *Historical Notes on the Bradford Corporation*, Bradford 1881, p. 155.

9 VII.389-408 *Modern Painters*, Pt. IX.x.

10 J. S. Roberts, *Little Germany*, pp. 10, 22.

11 W. Scruton, *Pen and Pencil Sketches of Old Bradford*, Bradford 1889, p. 230. Compare: XVI.338-9.

12 XVIII.437.

13 VII.375-7; XVI.440. *Henry Moore*, 1968, pp. 11-12; *Henry Moore on Sculpture*, 1966, p. 51.

14 XIX.164 (Cambridge, 1867).

15 W. Cudworth, *Historical Notes on the Bradford Corporation*, pp. 150-5.

16 G. J. Holyoake, *Sixty Years of an Agitator's Life*, 1893, II.79-80, 126. *BR* 13.8.64; *BO* 18.8.64. David Wright, *Victorian Bradford*, pp. 180-3.

17 *BR* 30.7.64. XVIII.457-8.

18 *BR* 13.8.58.

19 XXXIII.210

20 M. McMillan, *The Life of Rachel McMillan*, pp. 83, 89, 99.

Chapter Ten

1 Clement Shorter, ed. *The Brontës: Life and Letters*, 1908, II.44. Compare: XXVII, 82.

2 Derek Linstrum, *Historic Architecture of Leeds*, Newcastle 1969, p. 53. The tower of San Girolamo, Venice, became a chimney in 1842. See: IX.415, and J. Clegg, *Ruskin and Venice*, 1981, Pl. 5 and caption.

3 *Builder* 8.4.65; *BO* 26.4.66.

4 R. Norman Shaw to M. and C. H. B. Quennell, 1910, published in their

History of Everyday Things in England, 1933, III.152–4.
5 VIII.251–2 *Seven Lamps* Obedience, 3.
6 XIX.197–8; XXXIII.397.
7 VIII.3; XIX.49 *Cestus of Aglaia*, init., quoting *Iliad* xiv.220–1. Venus describes her Cestus (*Iliad* xiv.183, Chapman's translation) as bringing 'Kind conference, fair speech, whose pow'r the wisest doth inflame'.
8 Keith Laybourn, 'The defence of the bottom dog', *Victorian Bradford*, pp. 223–44.
9 e.g. XVIII.437 *Crown of Wild Olive*, 57.
10 VIII.233, 264, 139, 218, 105, 40, 82; XIX.96, 60, 62–3, 104, 66, 145, 67 *Seven Lamps* Memory, 10, Obedience, 9, Beauty, 2, Life, 24, Power, 5, Sacrifice, 8, Truth, 19; *Cestus of Aglaia*, 45, 8, 11, 56, 13, 100, 14. Carlyle: XVII, xxxiii, lxx.
11 Ruskin to his cousin William Richardson of Red Hill, letter dated 21 April 1864, postmarked London Ap 21, 64. Bembridge.
12 XIX.60–2.
13 Compare e.g. Wordsworth's *Expostulation and Reply* with XVIII.441. Effie: M. Lutyens, *The Ruskins and the Grays*, pp. 62–5.
14 XIX.7 Aladdin: XXVIII.736.
15 V. Surtees, *Sublime and Instructive*, 1972, pp. xi–xii.
16 Thomas Hughes and Mr Briggs addressed a Partnership in Industry Meeting, Robert Kell in the chair, Bradford Mechanics' Institute, 28 December 1865.
17 XXXIV.724. Holmes was sold it as a version of *Morning* from *Four Times of Day*, 'not published, as too indelicate'. Ruskin's analysis would fit *A Harlot's Progress*, 4. *The Bridewell*.
18 VI 16–20 and Plate 19.
19 Ruskin, Mrs Hilliard and her daughter and Joan Agnew were at Lugano 6 July 1870 (*Diaries*, pp. 692, 698).
20 V. Surtees, *Sublime and Instructive*, pp. 146, 258–61.
21 *Sublime and Instructive*, p. 142; E. C. Gaskell, *Life of Charlotte Brontë* (1857) Chapters 4, 6, 8.
22 *Sublime and Instructive*, pp. 261, 158–9, 155–6, 146.
23 Ruskin to D. G. Rossetti 14 April 1856: *Sublime and Instructive*, p. 185. Robert Peel to 'My dear Arbuthnot', note marked '*Private*', October 1844. Peel Papers, British Library. J. J. Ruskin had embarrassed the merchant's son Peel by presenting him with wines valued by the donor at £635.
24 Ruskin to Ellen Heaton 11 January 1857. *Sublime and Instructive*, p. 196.
25 V.269–93.
26 *Sublime and Instructive*, pp. 178–9.
27 VI.300–13 *Modern Painters*, Pt. V.xvi.25–38.
28 VII. 262. Samuel Smiles, *Self-Help*, Chapter 6. M. Butlin and A. Wilton, *Turner* 1775–1851, Tate Gallery 1974, p. 134.
29 *Bradford Antiquary* II (1912), 1.
30 XXXIII.270, 287.
31 *Sublime and Instructive*, pp. 186, 220–1.
32 *Sublime and Instructive*, pp. 150, 160.
33 John Heaton (1802–64) and Sarah Rimington (1793/4–1830) had three children: Marianne (b. 1827) later Mrs John William Atkinson, Fanny (b. 1828)

later Mrs John Deakin Heaton, and John Aldam (1830–97).

34 Both spellings occur in John Deakin Heaton's Journals.

35 J. D. Heaton, Letterbook entry 12 July 1857: 'I think Ruskin does not seem to have elicited any enthusiastic raptures from you; how different would have been Ellen's description. Instead of the stiff white cholar and the Scotch accent, and the lecture of not much practical utility in a hot dirty room, not crowded, everything would have been most fascinating and distinguished and rapturous.' Compare *Manchester Examiner and Times* 11.7.57, report of *Political Economy of Art* Lecture I at the Manchester Athenaeum: 'a very large and fashionable audience. . . repeatedly expressed their approbation with applause'.

36 J. D. Heaton Diary (1849) on *The Seven Lamps*: 'a great enthusiast, and runs to extremes. . . very earnest throughout'.

37 E. D. Steele, 'Imperialism and Leeds politics', *A History of Modern Leeds*, ed. D. Fraser, Manchester 1980, pp. 329–31.

38 XVIII.132–3 *Sesame and Lilies*, 81–2.

39 XVI.275, 324.

40 John James, *Continuations*, 1866, p. 156.

41 XII.435–47 and Plate.

42 BO 16.6.64.

43 Ruskin to Joan Agnew 21 January 1870. XXXVII.3.

44 Ruskin to Edward Burne-Jones 5 March 1864 (XXXVI.467–8). Morris, Marshall Faulkner & Co. glass for Harden Grange (1862) in Bradford City Art Galleries. Harris: A. C. Fox-Davies, *Armorial Families*, 1929, p. 884. Oakwood: N. Revsner, *Yorkshire: The West Riding*, second ed. revised by Enid Radcliffe, Harmondsworth 1967, p. 618. The Oakwood Garnetts seem not to have been related to those of Garnett Hall (above, Ch. 9, n. 24).

45 St George's, Leeds, was an evangelical stronghold, much approved of by the *Leeds Intelligencer*, contemner (26.2.59) of the 'sickliness and mawkish mediaevalism' of the Pre-Raphaelites.

46 VII.356, n; XVI.323.

47 J. D. Heaton, diary entry, 1866.

48 A. Saint, *Richard Norman Shaw*, New Haven and London, 1976, pp. 65–7.

49 A. Saint, pp. 63–5. G. C. F. Forster, 'The Foundations', *A History of Modern Leeds*, p. 16.

50 W. M. Rossetti, *Dante Gabriel Rossetti: His Family Letters*, 1895, I.401. H. M. M. Rossetti, *Pre-Raphaelite Twilight*, 1954, pp. 73–4, 87, 101, 122–3.

51 A. Saint, pp. 417, 422–3.

52 A. Callen, *Angel in the Studio*, 1979, p. 99.

53 A. Saint, p. 176.

54 Seven wallpaper designs by J. A. Heaton, presented by Messrs. Heaton, Tabb & Co. Ltd., the Print Room. Victoria and Albert Museum. MS marginalia by J. A. Heaton.

55 A. Saint, pp. 255–6 and Plate 195.

56 *Candida* (1895).

57 *The Artist*, March 1897, p. 121, seq. J. A. Heaton, *Beauty and Art*, 1897.

58 A. Saint, p. 206.

59 Urrbrae, Fullarton, near Adelaide. A. Saint, p. 457.

60 Robert Milligan, *Specification for Ornamenting Woollen Fabrics*, entered at Chancery 17 September 1851.

61 Octave Uzanne, *Fashion in Paris 1797–1897*, trans. Lady Mary Lloyd, 1898. J. A. Heaton, *Beauty and Art*, p. 31.

62 *Beauty and Art*, pp. 31, 144.

63 J. A. Heaton, *Furniture and Decoration in England During the Eighteenth Century*, 1892. The Introduction (p. 11) denounces Chippendale as a 'commonplace and vulgar hawker'.

64 J. A. Heaton, *A Record of Work*, 1894.

65 Both reprinted in *Beauty and Art*.

66 Alfred Harris (1825–1901) was the son of Edward Harris, shipbroker, of London. Alfred Harris married Harriet Tylor in 1849. Harriet's brother Sir Edward Burnett Tylor (b. 1832) was Professor of Anthropology, Oxford, 1894–1910. Ruskin availed himself of E. B. Tylor's 'rare and valuable research' (XXVIII.614 *Fors Clavigera*, 66.3).

67 Charles Meryon b. Paris 1821 d. Charenton asylum 1868. His father Dr Charles Lewis Meryon published 1845–6 the *Memoirs* and *Travels* of Lady Hester Lucy Stanhope (1776– 1839). Alfred Harris married Anne Meryon in 1868.

68 XXVIII.298–304 *Fors Clavigera* 52, 'Vale of Lune' (April 1875). Ruskin castigates the ugly railings and seats on the rubbish-strewn banks of the Lune. The local young ladies care nothing for the 'Pollution of rivers', provided they have 'their church curate and his altar-cloths to their fancy', and 'the real motive of it all is that the fashionable manufacturer may live in a palace'. The iron-framed seats which provoke all this ire are placed 'Just at the dividing of the two paths'. The literary context is clearly the Bradford lecture from *The Two Paths*, the filthy Rochdale path that figured in it; the embroidered altar-cloths which were Heaton's forte; and the 'palace' at Lunefield which Waterhouse built for Harris. How much is Ruskin's malicious allusion, and how much his mischievous guess work?

69 Lunefield: *Bradford Illustrated Weekly Telegraph* 28.3.85. Obituary of Harriet Harris: *Keighley News* 9.12.65. See also: Alfred Harris. 'An Untried Remedy for Irish Grievances', *National Review*, January 1884; *The Revival of Industries in Ireland*, Kirkby Lonsdale 1888.

70 Henry Harris (1789–1872); Alfred Harris senior (1801–82) whose marriage to Edward Peckover's daughter gave the Harris family controlling interest in the Old Bank; Sarah Harris (1785–1887). Benjamin Seebohm (1798–1871), edited *Lives of* William Forster (W. E. Forster's father) and Stephen Grellet, the Quaker missionaries.

71 BO 12, 19, 26.7.60. The Princess Royal's sketches were of a royal infant and 'The Good Knight Bayard' (canine). Ward: XIV.52 Hughes: XIV.162–3 Rossetti: XXXVI.272.

72 J. T. Ward, 'Squire Auty, Tory Churchman', *Bradford Antiquary* IX (new series) 1976, pp. 104–19. *Auty's Orange and Protestant Melodist* was published 1863.

73 Alfred Harris senior of Ryshworth Hall laid the foundation stone 21 May 1866. He then left Ryshworth for a country house near Ripon. The church was consecrated 23 October 1868 by Bishop Bickersteth of Ripon, and became a district chapelry 17 March 1869. The builders were J. & W. Foster of Bingley

(*Ripon Diocesan Calendar*, 1869, pp. 163–5). School opened 1871, extended 1879; Drill Hall 1867; a small chapel at Cottingley 1876, vicarage 1873–4: all by Norman Shaw. The church had a thriving cricket club and efficient choir trained by a 'Mr Harris of Bradford'. The dates of the incumbency of Rev. Albert Hudson, MA Trinity College Cambridge: 20 August 1868 – death at the age of thirty-five, 11 April 1877. (Harry Speight, *Chronicles and Stories of Old Bingley*, 1898, p. 174.) Alfred Harris junior was apparently vicar's warden 1868– 71. He put Ashfield on the market in 1870, having embarked on Lunefield, Kirkby Lonsdale from 1869. He retained part of the Ashfield estate, however, with some buildings (sale plan and photographs of Ashfield, Cowgill, Knight & Cowgill, 1870, in Bradford Central Library). The scheme of windows proposed by Hudson, but not carried out, shows the emphasis on 'practical Christianity': (1) The Good Shepherd (2) The good Samaritan (3) The Light of the World (4) Visiting the sick (5) The Resurrection (6) Dorcas providing raiment for the poor. The remark attributed to Ruskin, with the date 1881, sounds authentic; but that it was made 'while staying at Ashfield as the guest of Mr. Harris' (*Centenary Year, Holy Trinity Church, Bingley* 1968) seems most unlikely. A likelier explanation is that Ruskin saw the 'original design' at Ashfield in 1864, and in 1881 communicated, perhaps obliquely, his misgivings about the impending spire, completed 1882. See: A. Saint, *Richard Norman Shaw*, pp. 403–4.

74 *Abraham and Isaac* (1873) 76 x 52¾ inches. Designed by Rossetti for Morris, Marshall Faulkner & Co. Since 1977 on long loan to Bradford Art Galleries and Museums from the Vicar and Churchwardens, Holy Trinity Bingley. Burne-Jones's companion piece, the *Crucifixion* is now in the new, and much modester, Holy Trinity Church.

75 VIII.153 *Seven Lamps* Beauty, 14.

76 John Ruskin to Alfred Harris [April–May 1864] Letter on mourning paper St George's Guild Collection, Sheffield:

> Dear Mr Harris,
>
> I have been intending every day to congratulate you on your drawing. It is a quite superb and faultless one. Sadly faded – as you know – but very precious in any state – the wickedness of the treatment Turner's drawings have all received – in his early time is unspeakable.
>
> It was lucky for you that I couldn't *afford* it – or indeed to buy any drawings now – at their present prices –
>
> I hope you are better, and that Mrs Harris is not suffering so much from the weather – though to-day indeed it is as bad as ever.
>
> I am very truly Yours
> J. Ruskin

A Turner drawing of Luxemburg, the property of Alfred Harris junior, was exhibited Bradford Mechanics' Institute 1873.

77 John Ruskin to Alfred Harris 11 December 1865. St George's Guild Collection, Sheffield. Mrs Harris died at the Ilkley Wells Hydro, of which her husband was a large shareholder. Harriet was buried at Morton, a moorland churchyard south-west of Ilkley. In his letter of consolation, Ruskin calls himself

a 'stranger' in the northern sense of 'not a relative or close friend'. The word is used in this sense in the memorial to Harriet, *Keighley News*, 9.12.65, to which Ruskin refers. 'Strangers may be permitted,' it reads, 'to express the hope that. . . the memory of such a mother will remain a mighty influence for good. . . and that the general appreciation of her. . . character will. . . solace her surviving partner.'

78 John Ruskin to Alfred Harris Denmark Hill 11 January [1866 by postmark]. St. George's Guild Collection.

79 Ruskin to Alfred Harris, Brantwood, 3 September 1879. St George's Guild Collection, Sheffield. For the drawing of Rheinfelden Ruskin sent to Harris (not published in *Modern Painters*) see: J. H. Whitehouse, *Ruskin the Painter and his work at Bembridge* 1938, p. 58.

80 VII.437, n.

81 VII.384

82 *John* xxi. 15–17.

83 *Matthew* v.14: 'Ye are the light of the world': cited, and footnoted, by Ruskin, VII.263, & n.

84 VII.262

85 III.529, n.

86 XVI.215; XVIII.458. *Winnington Letters*, p. 531, n.

87 Ruskin to Alfred Harris [1879]. Ruskin's reply to Harris's acknowledgement of his of 3 September (above, n. 79). St George's Guild Collection, Sheffield:

> My dear Sir,
> Sincere thanks for your interesting letter and enclosure. I am very happy to be of any use & to feel that I am so – being often apt to doubt.
> Your Hunt drawing of chick is I am glad to say much admired in the exhibition. With kind regards to Mr Lobley
> Most sincerely yours
> J Ruskin

88 XIV.453, 445, 431.

89 W. P. Winter, BSc, *Shipley Glen*. Reprinted from the *Bradford Scientific Journal*, n.d.

90 Ruskin to Alfred Harris, 11 January [1866]. St George's Guild Collection. Compare report of Ruskin's lecture, *BR* 23.4.64: 'In Switzerland they had taken up manufacture, and there was not a town in that country that remained as it did ten years ago, in the slightest portion of its grand aspects. Now the spirit of Switzerland was not the spirit of England; it had caught the infection of money-making, but it had not caught that English earnestness, honesty and benevolence, that splendid spirit which even where the contest was vain, made the contest magnificent. It had become in Switzerland, nothing but a low money-making passion, which had slowly trampled down all that was heavenly and holy, and substituted – he came to ask them what? He wanted to know what they were going to bring this world to, if they had it all their own way?'

91 John Ruskin to Margaret Ruskin, Bradford 21 April 1864: 'I got down

comfortably in every way but the way of Teeth – which ached sadly, but I am better now and hope to give a fair lecture' *Winnington Letters*, p. 490.

92 Alfred Harris died, 14 November 1901. His obituary also appeared in *The Times* 18 November 1901.

93 John Ruskin to Alfred Harris [1879]. See above, n. 87. John Ruskin to Alfred Harris, Brantwood Coniston Lancashire (red embossed address) [1879?] St George's Guild Collection:

> Dear Mr. Harris,
> It is a great pleasure to me to have any occasion to write to you and assure you how pleasant my memory of your kindness has always been to me: ~~These~~ Your feathered tokens from the Highlands that you think of me have been promotion of festivity among a party of young people whose thanks I am to convey with my own – and remain always
> Dear Mr Harris
> most truly yours
> J Ruskin

94 John Ruskin to Alfred Harris, Brantwood Coniston Lancashire (red embossed address). St George's Guild Collection. The 'ballad' Ruskin enquires after may be *Tam Lin*, published A. Quiller-Couch, editor, *The Oxford Book of English Verse*, new edition 1939, No. 380 ('O I forbid you, maidens a',' etc.).

95 [James Burnley], 'The Henrys of Manchester and Bradford', *Fortunes Made in Business* [1887], III.201, seq.

96 Alfred Harris, 'Kylemore Castle and Reclamation of Waste Lands', *The Revival of Industries in Ireland: Notes made during a tour in October 1887*, Kirkby Lonsdale 1888, pp. 20, 23.

97 W. Cudworth, *Historical Notes on the Bradford Corporation*, p. 203. Mitchell died 19 August 1884 'at Lytham, where he had gone for the benefit of his health' (*Manchester Guardian* 21.8.84). *The Lytham Press*, 22.8.84, records his funeral and his age: seventy-six.

98 John Ruskin to Mrs John Simon, November 1858. Published *Winnington Letters*, p. 101: 'I shall be delighted to meet Mr Mitchell on Thursday in Cumberland St. but please tell him before hand I can't come to Sheffield. I must finish Modern Painters.'

99 Ruskin to C. E. Norton 24 October 1858. XXXVI.293.

100 VII.281–2.

101 Acts xvi.7. *Winnington Letters*, p. 154.

102 *BR* 30.7.64. Mitchell is quoting Pope's *To Mr Fortescue*, 127.

103 Butler Wood, 'Some Old Bradford Artists', *Bradford Antiquary* II (1892), 198. John Cousen's obituary: *The Times* 29.12.80. See also: XIII.53; XXXVIII.360, etc.

104 VII.389, 424 & Pl. 60.

105 *Winnington Letters*, pp. 100–1, n. 3. See above, Chapter 7, n. 21.

106 Sale plan, photographs, and particulars of Parkfield House, Manningham, 1899. The conditions of sale mention an indenture between John Mitchell and Henry Mitchell, 1 October 1869, presumably when the sale or transfer

of the house was settled. Parkfield House is now part of the Convent and Boarding School of the Sisters of the Cross and Passion.

107 *BO* 15.5.56; *BR* 23.4.64. Asa Briggs, *The Age of Improvement 1783–1867*, 1960, pp. 305, 336, 430.

108 V.414. Asa Briggs, *The Age of Improvement*, pp. 375, 381, 384, 421.

109 XI.258–63. An early election agent for Forster, Mitchell may have shared his dismay that the British commercial classes were handing technical hegemony to Prussia as the price of their sons' education in the polite languages and the barbarian code (Bradford School of Art, Bradford High School, *Report* of Annual Meeting and *Prospectus*, Bradford 1867).

110 XVIII.537, 546 (republished from *The Scotsman* 20.7.59); *The Liverpool Albion*, 2.11.63. John Lewis Bradley, editor, *Ruskin's Letters from Venice 1851–2*, New Haven 1955, p. 232 (John Ruskin to John James Ruskin, 29 March 1852): 'I hold it a gratuitous and useless insult to make any man incapable of giving an opinion' on political matters; but Ruskin would wish to see voting by number, not by name, to guarantee a degree of anonymity, and would also weight votes in favour of income and education. Ruskin's editors (XII.lxxx) justly refer to these opinions as a 'very Radical pill. . . with some Tory gilding'. XVII.253 *Munera Pulveris*. 129 makes similar points, with the minimal proviso of a vote for 'every man upwards of twenty, who had been convicted of no legal crime'.

111 *BR* 23.4.64. *Leeds Mercury* 27.4.64 *Manchester Courier* 23.4.64.

112 'The Arts as a Branch of Education': A letter to the Rev. F. Temple (25 September 1857), published T. D. Acland, *Some Account of the Origin and Objects of the New Oxford Examinations*, Oxford 1858, pp. 54–60; reprinted 1858, and again in *Arrows of the Chace*, 1880, I.37–49. See XVI.452.

113 *Liverpool Albion* 11.1.58. XIV.327.

114 D. G. Rossetti to E. Gambart, Cheyne Walk Chelsea, 28 April 1864 ('Mr. Mitchell, of Bradford, was here this morning'): Oswald Doughty & John Robert Wahl, eds, *Letters of Dante Gabriel Rossetti*, Oxford 1965, p. 504. Other references: pp. 131, 516, 519.

115 *Letters of Dante Gabriel Rossetti*, p. 570, 512. Mitchell bought the watercolour *Brimfull* of 1863 and the original oil version of *Venus Verticordia* (Surtees, Nos. 167, 173). *Brimfull* has disappeared.

116 *Letters of Dante Gabriel Rossetti*, p. 569. Virginia Surtees writes: 'About *The Boat of Love*. I see no reason to think that the subject is not the one submitted to Dunlop. In fact it almost certainly is. I only didn't mention it in my catal: [No. 239] as though the subject is the one he eventually made for Graham, no stroke of the pen or pencil or brush (so far as I know) was ever put on canvas/paper in the 1860s'.

117 Virginia Surtees *The Paintings and Drawings of Dante Gabriel Rossetti (1828–1882): a Catalogue Raisonné*, Oxford 1971: No. 169, *The First Madness of Ophelia* w/c 15½ x 11½ inches, April 1864. No. 126, *Love's Greeting*, oil on panel 22¼ x 24 inches, c. 1861. Also: No. 170A, *Morning Music* w/c 16¼ x 13½ inches, a variation made 1867 for Walter Dunlop of a drawing of 1864 of the same name. No. 131, *The Bower Meadow* oil 33¼ x 26½ inches, signed and dated lower left corner 1872. Acquired by Dunlop September 1872; No. 84, Christie Manson & Woods

Catalogue of the Dunlop sale, 8 March 1904. Now in the Manchester Art Galleries.

118 Christie Manson & Woods Catalogue of Dunlop sale, 8 March 1904. No. 78 (*Caller Herrin'* 43 x 31 inches, under *Pictures*). No. 31 (*The Young Lantern Maker of Cairo* 11 x 7 inches, under *Water Colour Drawings*), also ten drawings by R. Bonington, and two by W. Hunt. The Catalogue of the *Art Treasures and Industrial Exhibition*, the new Bradford Mechanics' Institute, 1873, and Edward Healey, 'The Grange, Harden', (Dunlop's house) in the album *Sketches for Picturesque Views*, Bradford 1885, are the sources for the other attributions.

119 Edward Healey, 'Bankfield, Bingley' (Henry Mason's house), in *Sketches for Picturesque Views*, 1885.

120 Frederic George Stephens, 'Mr. Rossetti's New Pictures', *Athenaeum* 21.10.65, pp. 545–6. F. G. Stephens was one of the original PRB (see Christina Rossetti, *Poetical Works* ed. William Michael Rossetti, 1904, p. 424):

121 Ruskin's Notebook, marked '24', at Bembridge. Entry under 1884 (p. 45): 'Landseer Dog, Mr. H. Jones, 3rd West Riding, Yorkshire Barracks Rifles, Manningham Lane, Bradford'. Mitchell, too, had wanted an animal picture, and shown great interest in Ford Madox Brown's *The Infant's Repast* (1848–9), in which 'doggie is jealous' (*Letters of Dante Gabriel Rossetti*, p. 131). See also; Ford M. Hueffer, *Ford Madox Brown: A Record of His Life and Work*, 1896, p. 57.

122 Arthur Symons, *Dante Gabriel Rossetti*, n.d., p. 31.

123 Elena Rossetti Angeli (Helen Maria Modox Rossetti), *Dante Gabriel Rossetti*, Bergamo 1906, p. 31.

124 e.g. John Ruskin to Ellen Heaton 8 November 1855 (*Sublime and Instructive*, p. 168). Ruskin laments Rossetti's habit of 'changing & scratching' and appoints himself 'general recipient of his spoiled goods'.

125 Humbert Wolfe (author, *Labour Supply and Regulation*, Oxford, 1923), *News of the Devil – a Poem*, 1926, p. 25. Wolfe (1885–1940), like William Rothenstein (1872–1945) a Bradford Grammar School boy of German Jewish descent, is best remembered for the *Twelve Songs*, set by Gustav Holst (1874– 1934).

126 XIX.7, 10–11.

127 'Nonsense' was Harry's dismissal of Lucy's fanciful metaphorising (see above, Ch. 2, n. 17). For Ruskin, vulgarity lay in the murderousness of mixed metaphors, most particularly the playing with other people's death or pain as a metaphor for one's own self-indulgent emotions (VII.362). An expert on sexual shyness, Ruskin's intellect nevertheless prevented him from the prurient Victorian confusion between 'bodies' and 'corpses'. An overdressed society thrilling to the 'mincing sensuality' of the salon nude is no substitute for 'that daring frankness' of the Greeks. On the other hand, coy drapery of Grecian allusion merely 'perverts taste in dress'. The designer should be aware of 'so much of the nude body as in the daily life of the nation may be shown with modesty and seen with reverence and delight'. If shown at all the nude 'should be shown fearlessly, and seen constantly' (quotations from: IV.198; XXII.234–5).

128 IV.197, & R's n. of 1883.

129 *BO* 3.11.59. Akroyd advertised his surrender of 'all private interest' in All Souls except for the Founders' Chapel, announced that his 'working people should feel it their duty to attend' and confessed himself a reformed prostitute

by likening his 'temple' to Mary's 'costly ointment'. Compare: *Crown of Wild Olive*, 61.

130 James Hanson, who with Fanny Hertz, the friend of Frederic Harrison and translator of Comte, and Mrs Delius, the composer's mother, ran the Bradford Female Educational Institute, spoke of Etty's figures as having 'little to recommend them beyond a flesh and blood appearance'; while at least retaining the rational interest, abandoned by the 'ultra' school of Pre-Raphaelites, in 'the female form as far surpassing all other exemplifications of beauty' (Review of the Art Treasures Exhibition, Bradford Old Exchange, *BR* 14.7.60).

131 Dante Gabriel Rossetti, quoted H. C. Marillier, *Dante Gabriel Rossetti*, 1901, p. 100. Marillier identifies Rossetti's 'Mr. Mitchell of Bradford' as 'J. Mitchell'; adds that Rossetti felt himself unequal to the undraped form, though there was the prudishness of clients to consider: and that Rossetti at his client's expense commandeered honeysuckle and other blossoms with 'a sort of Neronian magnificence'.

132 Charles A. Sewter, *The Stained Glass of William Morris and his Circle*, New Haven and London, 1974, p. 67.

133 Margaret Lane, *The Tale of Beatrix Potter*, 1946, p. 38. John Bright and Mrs Gaskell, among other guests of the Potters, in Scotland, would walk over to the old house at Stewartfield where there were garden statues 'with very little on'. The Presbyterian gardener 'trained and clipped honeysuckle to encage their nakedness. . . one goddess used to have a fly-catcher's nest in her bosom every summer, under the honeysuckle flowers'.

134 Elena Rossetti Angeli, *Dante Gabriel Rossetti*, p. 31, and Illustr. p. 117.

135 John Ruskin to D. G. Rossetti, 6 letters [1865], published XXXVI.488–495.

136 'Photograph by William Downey probably taken on 29 June 1863 in the garden of Dante Gabriel Rossetti' (Van Akin Burd, editor, *The Winnington Letters*, p. 15, & Illustr. opp. p. 144). Virginia Surtees, *Sublime and Instructive*, pp. 252–3, n. suggests that a prime, if innocent, perpetrator of this 'visible libel' was the tactless Ellen Heaton who demanded, obtained and doubtless displayed, this photograph of her hero.

137 *Beata Beatrix*, oil, 34 x 26 inches, begun 'many years' before 1862; completed 1869. Surtees, *Catalogue Raisonné*, No. 168. D.G.R. wrote to Ellen Heaton 19 May 1863 and 22 December 1863 urging her to finance the project, but it was finally bought by Hon. Mrs Cowper-Temple in 1870.

138 *Lady Lilith* oil 37½ and 32 inches. Signature and date 1868 on table in background, but the figure repainted 1872–3. Bancroft Collection, Wilmington Society of Fine Arts, Delaware. Surtees, Catalogue No. 205 ('vapid and lifeless').

139 William Michael Rossetti recalled that Dante Gabriel himself regarded his early drawings as the best (W. Rothenstein, *Men and Memories* I.230).

140 *Sublime and Instructive* , pp. 244–5, 227–8, 229.

141 D. G. Rossetti to his mother, Paris 12 November 1864: 'Manet. . . mere scrawls. . . Courbet. . . not much better' (*Letters*, ed. Doughty & Wahl, p. 527). W. M. Rossetti, *Rossetti Papers 1862–1870*, 1903, p. 407, citing D.G.R.'s diary for 18 September 1869: 'Gabriel's pictures of Lilith and Venus are now sent off to their owners'.

142 A. E. Simpson, *A Short History of Bradford Cathedral*, Bradford 1964, p. 22:

'a statue of a semi-naked female. . . most unsuitable for a church. . . in the old Bolling Chapel; the congregation thought it too conspicuous so it was put in a vestry [1860s, later replaced, but in the 1960s]. . . removed [and destroyed]. . . the tablet and bas-relief placed [on the west wall of the transept]'.

143 J. D. Heaton, Diary, June 1865. See: *Sublime and Instructive*, p. 207, n.

144 *L. S. Lowry R.A.* 1887–1976, Catalogue of Royal Academy Exhibition, 1976, with Preface by Hugh Casson and Introduction by Mervyn Levy.

145 XXXIX.508, Plate 7.

146 James Lobley, baptised Holy Trinity Church, Hull, 5 December 1828, died 4 Belle Vue, Manningham, 1888. Lobley's large plain first-floor balcony at Belle Vue, for open-air work, has recently been removed.

147 *James Lobley 1828–1888: Paintings and Watercolours*, Bradford City Art Galleries and Museums, 1983. Foreword by Robert Hopper, City Arts and Museums Officer; Introduction and Catalogue by Caroline Krzesinska, Assistant Keeper, Fine Art.

148 Claude Lorraine Nursey (1820–73), Landscape, genre and marine painter, b. Woodbridge, Suffolk, trained Central School of Design, Somerset House. From 1846 Art Master at Leeds, helped found Bradford Mechanics' Institute Design School, 1849, later at Belfast, and from 1855 at Norwich. Exhibited RSBA *Devotion* (1844), *Asking a Blessing* (1856), *The Tea Party* (1857), BI *Smugglers* (1844).

149 Lobley papers, Cartwright Hall Huseum, Bradford.

150 From 1837 till 1842, when the Washington Treaty settled the boundaries between US and British territories in N. America, Britain and the US were in a condition of undeclared war.

151 Butler Wood and W. E. Preston, 'James Lobley: a Bradford artist', *Bradford Antiquary* II (Bradford, 1912), 255, seq.

152 XVI.197–8, 415. *Cambridge Inaugural*, 22, *Two Paths* Appendix 1. Ruskin praised Wilkie's *Chelsea Pensioners* at Cambridge in 1858 for its attempt to convey 'some useful principle or impression', but in 1859 regretted having overrated Wilkie 'as an expressional draughtsman, not having then studied the figure long enough to be able to detect superficial sentiment'.

153 Alfred Tylor, *Education and Manufactures*, the Second Part of the Jury Report Class XXXI, International Exhibition 1862, reprinted 1863, p. 96, enters into detail about Lobley's 'drawing-school, which I believe is considered the best in England. . . at the express wish of my foreign colleagues, who have signified their intention of translating this Report for the benefit of their respective countries'.

154 Ruskin to Alfred Harris 15 April 1861. Above, Ch. 8, n. 21. A flower-drawing by David Binns (1840/1–76) in the possession of his descendants is accompanied by the following MS note in Ruskin's hand: '2: Of Studies from nature. Exquisitely delicate: but wanting in sense of light and shade, and of the alteration of colour in shadow. J. Ruskin April 9th 1861.' David Binns, a professional wood-carver, had a family furniture business which failed, and he became an employee of the Bradford furniture firm of Christopher Pratt. David's father John Binns wrote poetry, and John's sister-in-law, Martha Brown, sister to the famous Tabitha, was employed by the Brontës. Details from Christopher Binns.

155 III.96, & n.

156 *Landscape with Corn-Stooks* watercolour and pencil 9½ x 13⅜ inches (1870s) *James Lobley*, 1983, No. 22.

157 Alfred Tylor, *Education and Manufactures*, p. 101, quoting Alfred Harris's statement of 14 October 1862.

158 *James Lobley*, 1983, No. 23.

159 William Jackson (b. Masham 1815, d. Bradford 1866). Mainly self-taught; organist, tallow-chandler, music dealer and chorus master. Composed oratorio *The Deliverance of Israel from Babylon*, services, anthems, part-songs, etc.

160 *James Lobley*, 1983, p. 7.

161 Caroline Krzesinska, *James Lobley*, 1983, p. 8.

162 E.g. John Phillip, RA (1817–1867), whose *A Huff* (RA 1859) Ruskin put down as 'slightly vulgar' (XIV.216); or Abraham Solomon (1824–62) whose *Waiting for the Verdict*, c. 1857, now at Tunbridge Wells, Ruskin described as 'too painful to be invested with the charm of colour' (XIV.114) and as 'rubbish', when compared with Millais's *The Blind Girl* of 1857 (XIV.327).

163 *James Lobley*, 1983, No. 1.

164 *Diaries*, p. 547 (Sunday 17 July 1859).

165 XVIII.421

166 *James Lobley*, p. 12.

167 *James Lobley*, No. 3.

168 John xii.8.

169 *James Lobley*, p. 8.

170 XVI.372, 351.

171 *James Lobley*, No. 40. Now in Bradford City Art Galleries.

172 *James Lobley*, p. 9. Butler and Wood (above, n. 151) refer to Lobley's Mr. Lister as a 'brother-in-law of Mr. Harris'. Joseph Jackson Lister, the microscope pioneer, and Isabella Harris, Quakers, were the parents of the surgeon Joseph Lister and the Bradford wool merchant Arthur Lister.

173 Algernon Graves, *Royal Academy of Art: Dictionary of Contributors*, 1906, under 1865, gives Megson's address as '59, Market Street, Bradford'. *BO* 25.5.65 carried a letter from George Muller, Hon. Sec., Bradford Design School, praising Megson and the 'care and instruction of Mr James Lobley, the Headmaster of the late School', whose traditions Muller and others, many of them German, vowed to keep alive under the aegis of the High School, despite Mechanics' Institute jealousy.

174 *James Lobley*, No. 10.

175 *James Lobley*, No. 2. Prior to purchase by the Bradford City Galleries, the painting suffered a little over-zealous cleaning.

176 *Diaries* pp. 618, 620. Above, n. 151.

177 *Old Curiosity Shop*, Chapters 46, 53, 71.

178 XXIX.425; XXXIV.274–5, & n.

179 Exhibited Harland's, Picture dealers, Bradford, November 1859. J. R. J. Binns, *BR* 10.12.59, versed the picture's allegories. A 'simplified design of *The Light of the World* was used as an image to publicise the exhibition in the Old Exchange, July 1860'. (*James Lobley*, p. 8).

180 *Our Mutual Friend*, Chapter 11: 'Podsnappery'.

181 *Memoirs of the Life and Gospel Labours of Stephen Grellet*, second edition by Benjamin Seebohm, Bradford 1861, I.125, quoted *The British Workman* 1.1.62.

182 *BR* 26.6.58 notes a Ragged School opened 4 July 1854, with seven scholars. During June 1858 the Turkish Baths, Lumb Lane, were opened to the enlarged membership free for two days in the hope that this might give the Ragged Scholars 'a lasting impression of the advantages and comforts of cleanliness'. Alfred Harris, junior, was Hon. Treasurer at the Ragged Schools' Bazaar May 1858, at which Mrs Holloway of Eden Place presented each child with 'a savoury and substantial bun'.

183 *BR* 20.3.58. Rev. Joseph Parberry Chown (1821–86), from 1883 President of the Baptist Union of Great Britain and Ireland.

184 *James Lobley*, No. 19.

185 *James Lobley*, No. 20. John Preston (1822–88), brother of the dialect poet Ben Preston, was an 'old boy' of the Quaker School run by Sarah Harris and others, and went on from there to Bradford Grammar School. He was a chemist and photographer (an interest shared by Lobley) and keen on amateur theatricals. He was perhaps an organiser of these Mummers' Plays. John Preston, *Sermons by an Artist*, with a memoir by Ben Preston, the New Church Society, Saltaire 1888.

186 Lobley's *Searching for the Register* was offered at £52.10s. at the RSBA show of 1878–9 (Jane Johnson, *Works Exhibited at the Royal Society of British Artists 1824–1893*, London 1975). The following list of Lobley's contributions at the Royal Academy gives present location of pictures, where known: 1865: *The Passing Bell*; 1867: *The Dole, Little Nell Leaving the Church* (both Bradford City Art Gallery); 1868: *Fancies in the Fire*, 1870: *The Free Seat* (Birmingham City Art Galleries); 1871: *Ancient and Modern* (Collection of Mrs A. R. Potts); 1872: *Member of an Old Church*; 1873: *A Demurrer*;* 1874: *The First of the Congregation*; 1876: *The Oratory, Beauchamp Chapel, Warwick*; 1877: *'I believe'*; 1878: Itinerant Airs;** 1880: *A Foundation Scholar*; 1884: *The Chapel, Haddon Hall*;*** 1887: *A Village Choir*.****

* Possibly to be identified with *The Squire and the Gamekeeper* (*collection of Lady Scott: See James Lobley*, Catal. No. 5). Caroline Krzesinska doubts whether the flesh-painting in *The Squire and the Gamekeeper* could be attributed to Lobley, and the gamekeeper's pose is exceptionally wooden.

** Possibly to be identified with *The Pedlar* (Kirklees Metropolitan Council). See *James Lobley* No. 7.

*** There is a watercolour of this subject in the Bradford City Art Galleries. *James Lobley*, No. 44.

**** *Church Interior with Three Children*, watercolour (Collection of M. Le Blanc Smith, Esq.) may be a study for this. *James Lobley*, No. 46.

187 Lord Leighton (1839–96) was PRA from 1878 to his death, see: Graham Reynolds, Royal Academy of Arts Bicentenary Exhibition (14 Dec. 1968–2 Mar. 1969), *Catalogue*, Introduction, pp. 21–2.

188 J. L. Bradley, editor, *Ruskin's Letters from Venice 1851–2*, New Haven and London 1955, p. 240.

189 Information from: A. J. Evans, 'A history of education in Bradford during the period of the Bradford School Board (1870–1904)', thesis presented Leeds University for the degree of MA, 1947. Typescript in Bradford Central Library.

190 Alfred Tylor, FGS (1824–84). See: John Ruskin to Mrs Alfred Tylor, Brantwood 3 January 1885. XXXVII.506.

191 *Diaries*, p. 964. Entry for 5 July 1877: 'Long chat with Mr. Simon, and loving sense of his deep friendship. *How* is it that Acland and he can't get on??'

192 *Diaries*, pp. 825–6 (23–7 November 1874). What Ruskin calls his 'very satisfactory lecture. . . on Ghiberti' was given 27 November 1874. See XXIII.237–48.

193 IV.36, n. (1846), reaffirmed 1877 in 'Readings in "*Modern Painters*"' (XXII.513).

194 XXII.178, *Eagle's Nest*, 76.

195 Milton, *Paradise Regained* I.224.

196 XVII.543; XXVII.95, 199, 327–8; XXX.xxiv-v, 12.

197 XXVIII.353, n. 1, 354; XXIX.176, n. 1.

198 John Ruskin to Mr and Mrs Alfred Tylor Winnington, May 1864. *Winnington Letters*, pp. 505–6.

199 J. Maas, *Gambart*, 1975, p. 171.

200 John Ruskin to Alfred Tylor, Corpus Christi, Oxford, 14 November [1875]. Bodleian Eng. lett. c. 40. Ruskin was wise to abstain. In its obituary of Alfred Hunt, Ruskin's friend and protégé, *The Illustrated London News* 16.5.96 commented: 'The treatment of his pictures by the Academy called forth the animadversion of the great art critic in terms which unfavourably affected Mr. Hunt's chances of recognition by that body' (R. Secor, *John Ruskin and Alfred Hunt*, Victoria 1982, p. 19).

201 XIV, 271–3.

202 *Diaries*, p. 872. XXII.496.

203 *Diaries*, p. 863. XXVIII.267.

204 XXX.52.

205 John Ruskin to Juliet Tylor 19 August 1877. St George's Guild Collection, Sheffield. See also above, n. 153.

206 XXV.211–12.

207 Much information and passion in Charles Allen Clarke, *The Effects of the Factory System*, 1899, e.g. p. 91. The Russian edition of this book carried a preface by Tolstoy. See also: John Johnston, *Wastage of Child Life*, Fabian Series No. 7, 1908.

208 XXIX.120; XXXVI.460.

209 XXVII.175–6 *Fors Clavigera*, 10.15.

210 Margaret McMillan, *Life of Rachel McMillan*, pp. 47, 50–2, 66.

211 Andrew Saint, *Richard Norman Shaw*, p. 321.

212 XXXV.xliv-v.

213 VII.x1ix; XVIII.456–7; *Fors Clavigera* Letter 1, 'Looking Down from Ingleborough', 10 (XXVII.22).

214 John Ruskin to Alfred Tylor, 4 January 1872. (XXXVII.47– 8). See also: XVII.131–46; XXVII.623.

215 XVIII.450.

216 XXVII.373; XXIX.197.

217 XXIX.250.

218 Ruskin's suggestion of 1874 for an experiment in road- digging was taken up with more enthusiasm than skill by undergraduates (XX.xxix, xlii).

In a lecture of 1884, Ruskin challenged Oxford to revive the open-sea rowing of the Venetians. Apparently thus inspired, W. H. Grenfell formed a crew which rowed from Dover to Calais, 25 July 1885 (XXXIII.508).

219 XXVII.175–6; XXVIII.145–166.

220 XXIX.214, 223.

221 Octavia Hill to Miss Baumgartner 29 January 1860 (C. E. Maurice, p. 176). See also: Octavia Hill to Mary Harris (1816– 94) 7 November 1856: 'Why do I never hear anything of your work among the prisoners in Newgate?' – a rhapsody on the theme follows. (E. S. Maurice, pp. 24–5 ed's n.: 'this work had to be given up when Miss Harris went to live in Cumberland to take care of her five little nieces who had lost their mother'.) This mother was Mary and Alfred Harris's sister Ellen, Mrs Bassett. Because of their relation to her 'best friend', two of the orphaned girls became Octavia's charges in London during the early '60s. She discussed their education with Ruskin (E. S. Maurice, pp. 121–2, 148; C. E. Maurice, pp. 199–200).

222 XXIX.xxi, 354–60; XXXV.xlv, n.

223 Margaret McMillan, *The Life of Rachel McMillan*, p. 108.

224 XXIX.xxii–xxiv, 160.

225 Compare: *Fors Clavigera* 82.14: 'Plato declaring out of the very deep of his heart. that. . . man is a poor little puppet. . . and the virtue of him is to play merrily in the little raree-show of his life, so as to please the Gods' (XXIX.233–4).

226 XXXVI.465.

227 'In the national purchase of a rare geological collection, by Professor Owen, who having only £500 allowed, had himself to give £200, to secure the valuable purchase, he instanced the scrubbiness of our taste, and the low estimate for scientific discovery' (*BA* 23.4.64, report of Ruskin's lecture). Compare: XVIII.87–8.

228 I *Corinthians* ii, 29; II *Thessalonians* iii, 10. Ruskin to Rev. W. L. Brown, end of 1860: 'what [the rich man] calls Political Economy is the foulest form of Not discovering the Lord's Body' (XVII.xxxv).

229 XXVI.184. Compare: XXVI.501.

230 Low Moor Ironworks, first blast engine 1791. Rev. Joseph Dawson, Nonconformist, founder. Partners: John Jarratt, draper, Richard Hird, woolstapler, John Hardy, solicitor. Gathorne Gathorne-Hardy, né Gathorne Hardy (1814–1906), MP for Oxford 1865, Viscount Cranbrook 1878, Earl of Cranbrook 1892. H. W. Wickham, né H. W. Hird (1800–67), MP for Bradford 1852–67. See J. James, *Continuations*, pp. xi-xiii.

231 XXV.130.

232 J. James, *History*, 1841, p. 244; *Continuations*, 1866, pp. 200–1.

233 XXIX.92.

234 Harry Speight, *Chronicles and Stories of Old Bingley*, 1898, pp. 344–9.

235 *BR* 23.10.58; *BO* 31.5.49.

236 XVIII.103, n. (capitalism and war); XXVII.16, 127 ('Occult theft'), 243, 385; XXVIII.673 (Robin Hood). Fred Jowett, for many years Chairman of the Parliamentary Public Accounts Committee, relished these passages (A. Fenner Brockway, p. 380). Robin Hood: *The Bradford Antiquary* III (1912) p. 92. Low Moor Ironworks: J. Fieldhouse, *Bradford*, 1972, p. 86.

237 VII.lix, 467, 476. Above, Ch. 2, n. 19.
238 XXVI.23, & R's n.
239 XVIII.437. See also above, n. 198.
240 Report and President's Address, Anniversary Meeting, 23 May 1864, *Proceedings of the Royal Geographical Society* VIII (1863–4), 1864, pp. 184–6.
241 XVIII. 437, 442, 449.
242 *BO* 29.12.64.
243 *Crown of Wild Olive* (1866) 74, 62, and title page.
244 The baronial Bankfield, 1848, for Henry Murgatroyd, three times Mayor of Bradford, affronts the gaze as one enters the Bradford-Bingley road from the lane to Cottingley Hall. Ruskin would pass between the two houses in April 1864. The Yorke boys, in *Shirley*, are the Bradford Grammar School type. A literary image of Thornton's career is to be found in that of Roger, in *Wives and Daughters*.
245 O. Ransford, *David Livingstone: The Dark Interior*, 1978, pp. 6–7: 'The family claimed descent from a physician companion to St. Columba. . . Neil Livingstone [father of David] became a tea-pedlar'.
246 O. Ransford, p. 151. Rev. H. Rowley, Parson to the Universities Mission, was in Livingstone's words, 'perpetually writing to *MacMillan's Magazine* and the *Times*,' praising Thornton at Livingstone's expense (p. 180).
247 XXVI.338–9. Compare: XXXV.91.

Chapter Eleven

1 XVIII.xxxvi. *Diaries*, p.586. Proofs of *The Crown of Wild Olive*, with Ruskin's MS emendations, Bodleian Library Arch AA.e.29, with label: 'Messrs. Smith Elder & Co. Author's Proof 24/3/66'.
2 *Plutus* 582–6. The word here translated 'advertise' means literally 'cry up', like an auctioneer, something between 'proclaim' and 'sell'.
3 VII.424.
4 *Crown of Wild Olive*, 41 (1866): 'some day, assuredly, more pence will be paid to Peter the Fisherman, and fewer to Peter the Pope' suggests Ruskin suspected there were Irish Catholics among the workmen in his audience.
5 XVIII.393 *Crown of Wild Olive*, 12.
6 XVII.88 *Unto This Last*, 63.
7 *Crown of Wild Olive*, 21.
8 XXIII.256.
9 Notebook at Bembridge, pp. 75/98; 90/113 (double numbering system).
10 *Unto This Last*, 38, 77.
11 Felice Peretti of Montalto (1521–90): Pope Sixtus V from 14 April 1585, a Renaissance example of getting on. Son of a labourer, he taught himself to read, became a Franciscan at twelve; as Inquisitor to Venice burned 10,000 books in 1559, made General of the Franciscans and Cardinal by Pius V (1566–72), as Pope hurried on the work of St Peter's and blessed the last stone of the dome, re-erected the ancient obelisk in front of St Peter's, where it still stands, constructed the Fiume Sisto to drain the Pontine marshes, brought the Aqua

Martia to Rome, reconstructed the Quirinal, including the Aqua Felice, built the Piazza di Spagna, excommunicated Elizabeth I. Lived personally in Franciscan poverty, but by draconian measures enriched the Papacy.

12 VI.430 'The Mountain Glory', 15: 'the "Lady Poverty" of St. Francis may share the influence of the hills in the formation of character,' but Poverty does not 'produce the same effects' in the 'lowland. . . religious character'. *Crown of Wild Olive*, 1, laments the brutalisation of 'sweet human character' amid polluted 'lowland scenery'.

13 V. A. Burd, *John Ruskin and Rose La Touche*, pp. 95–8.

14 *Unto This Last*, 85.

15 Engels: 'The socialist appropriation of the means of production does away. . . with the positive waste and devastation of productive forces. . . The extraneous objective forces that have hitherto governed history, pass under the control of man himself. Only from that time will man himself, more and more consciously, make his own history. . .' (*Herrn Eugen Dührings Umwälzung der Wissenschaft* (1878), extracts translated E. Aveling as *Socialism, Utopian and Scientific* (1892), reprinted W. O. Henderson, *Engels: Selected Writings*, Harmondsworth 1967, pp. 222–3). Ruskin: 'in a science dealing with so subtle elements as those of human nature, it is only possible to answer for the final truth of principles, not for the direct success of plans. . . in the best of these last, what can be immediately accomplished is always questionable, and what can be finally accomplished, inconceivable' (*Unto This Last*, 1862, *Preface*, fin.).

16 XIX.358–9, & R's n.

17 (Gregor) Johann Mendel (1822–84), the first to demonstrate the system of particulate heredity by units ('genes') published his findings in the *Transactions* of the Brünn (now Brno) Society for the Study of Natural Science, in 1866, but was not recognised as the father of genetics till 1900, when other scientists were able to realise the significance of his work.

18 XXV.263.

19 *Crown of Wild Olive*, 23–4, 60, 100.

20 Above, Ch. 10, n. 154.

21 *Crown of Wild Olive*, 17–18.

22 John Ruskin, three notes to W. H. Harrison [1864] on mourning paper. Bembridge. The third one quoted is dated 22 March.

23 List of proprietors of the Leeds and Liverpool Canal, Bradford Central Library.

24 Kathleen Raine, *William Blake*, 1970, p. 57. Ruskin's purchase of Blake drawings, XXXVI.32.

25 *Crown of Wild Olive*, 24.

26 Minutes of Camberwell Roadworks Committee for the early 1860s, Walworth Public Library.

27 e.g. Anthony Trollope, Review of *Crown of Wild Olive*, *Fortnightly Review* 15 June 1866, reprinted J. L. Bradley, *Ruskin: The Critical Heritage*, 1984, p. 312: 'the gist of Mr Ruskin's teaching [of justice for the crossing-sweeper] is simply a denunciation of all property whatsoever'. Pictures that made Ruskin's point with more acceptable sweetness were W. P. Frith's *The Crossing Sweeper* (1865) and S. Faed's *Remember the Sweeper* (1868).

28 XXXIV.660–1 (March 1864). Spurgeon's Tabernacle cost £31,332.4*s.* 6*d.* and was opened in March 1861. On Monday 25 March 1861 Rev. G. Rogers addressed 'the assembly on "The House of God the Gate of Heaven"'. That evening Spurgeon's first sermon expanded on the need to preach Christ 'daily in the temple'. (Spurgeon: *The People's Preacher*, Walter Scott Publishing Co., n.d., p. 94). For Ruskin's comments on 'conversion', 'little Bethels' and the mis-use of both the above biblical texts (*Genesis XXVIII*, 17, *Acts* V, 42) see: *The Crown of Wild Olive* 51, 120, 62–3.

29 V. A. Burd, *John Ruskin and Rose La Touche*, pp. 31, 35, 95, 101. Compare: *Crown of Wild Olive*, 26, 27, 30.

30 *Crown of Wild Olive*, 127. Approved: *The Saturday Review* 2.6.66. (*Ruskin: The Critical Heritage*, p. 305).

31 XVIII.485, R's n., 376–7, 489; XX.371; XXII.239; XXVI.563; XXVIII.591; XXXVII.45. *Diaries*, p. 893.

32 Philip Magnus, *Gladstone*, 1963, p. 195.

33 XXXVI.15; XXII.206.

34 XXIX.409 *Fors Clavigera*, 89.

35 XVIII.503.

36 William I of Prussia was proclaimed Kaiser at Versailles 18 January 1871. On 23 October 1872 he 'awarded' the island of San Juan to the United States.

37 XXXI.x1, 383–510 (*A Knight's Faith*, Ruskin's edition of Edwardes's memoirs). n.b., p. 509, Ruskin's description of the plain of Bunnoo as 'a rubbish hole or pit among the mountains' and compare *The Waste Land*, 385: 'In this decayed hole among the mountains'.

38 XVI.29–30.

39 *Unto This Last*, 17–25, 54.

40 Guy Fawkes b. York 1570, executed London 1606. The official account: *A True and Perfect Relation of the Whole Proceedings against the late Most Barbarous Traitors*, pamphlet London 1606. William Hazlitt, the *Examiner* 12–20 November 1821, attempted a justification of Fawkes.

41 *Crown of Wild Olive*, 59. *Sybil*, Bk. ii. Ch. 5; ('Two nations. . . THE RICH AND THE POOR') Bk. iv. Ch. 8. *Pickwick Papers* Ch. 3 ('the clown's shrill laugh, blending with the low murmurings of the dying man'), Ch. 11 ('THE MADMAN'S MANUSCRIPT'). *The Times* 18 April 1864 (execution of James Clitheroe).

42 *Crown of Wild Olive*, 96–7, also 77, 80, 23–9.

43 John Ruskin, *La Bible d'Amiens, Traduction, Notes et Préface par M. Marcel Proust*, Paris 1947 (1st ed. 1903), p. 339, n.

44 *Lawrence:* Ruskin's Ursula, like Lawrence's, is 'the Bud of flowers, enclosed in its rough or hairy calyx, and her husband Aether – the air of Spring' (XXVIII.733 Fors, 71). Ruskin, too, uses the symbolism of Etruscan tomb sculpture to convey her meaning (XXVIII.744–5). *The Rainbow* Ch. 11 shows Ursula in the swing-boat with her lover: 'her face like a flower. . . they rushed through the bright air. . .'. She turns away to seek 'comfort' in a church, only to find 'fallen stones and rubbish' and the 'blows of the hammer'. The connection with *Fors*, 71, in which Ruskin adverts his readers back to *Fors*, 20, is inescapable. *Fors*, 71 presents 'The modern intellectual teacher' who 'erects swings upon the beach. There the suspended population oscillate between sea and

sky, and are amused' (XXVIII.734–5). *Fors*, 20, to which Ruskin adverts by footnote: 'it was some comfort to me. . . at Pisa, to watch the workman's ashamed face as he struck the marble cross to pieces. . . ashamed' (XXVII.348). Both Ruskin's and Lawrence's churches are being 'restored'.

Yeats: see W. B. Yeats, *Essays*, 1924, p. 307; Joseph Hone, *W. B. Yeats 1865–1939*, 1942, p. 64. It is Ruskin's complex influence, more than that of any other writer, which marries the Pre-Raphaelite Yeats to the intellectual and political Yeats.

Joyce: Compare *Ulysses*, Harmondsworth 1971, pp. 30–2 with VII.396, 408; XXXIII.54 ('Under the Drachenfels'). For Ruskin Genevieve is 'not the troubled and troubling Aphrodite, but the Leucothea of Ulysses, the guiding wave of deliverance'; the Dragon, her enemy, is youngest child of Nereus and the earth-volcanic, scaly and conveying 'instant destruction'. The modern artist can produce no 'Assumption of the Virgin' only 'Assumption of the Dragon': for 'this child [Turner] can only make manifest the dragon, not slay him' (VII.408). Stephen's smashing of the chandelier in the brothel (*Ulysses*, p. 517) is linked to the 'dragon scaly folds' of Stephen's mind, vainly 'sheltered from the sin of Paris' in the 'library of Saint Genevieve' (*Ulysses*, pp. 31–2) by the calculated repetition of the epic phrase: 'ruin of all space, shattered glass and toppling masonry' (pp. 30, 517). His chandelier-smashing is an Assumption of the Dragon: and in this respect he fulfils the modern artist's function as defined in *Modern Painters*.

Hopkins: See P. M. Ball, *The Science of Aspects: the changing role of fact in the work of Coleridge, Ruskin and Hopkins*, 1971.

Eliot: See above, Ch. 8, n. 6. *Crown of Wild Olive*, 1 alludes to *Purgatorio* V.133: 'Siena mi fe', disfecemi Maremma', which Eliot offers as footnote to l. 293 of *The Waste Land*. *Marina* is full of Ruskinian incandescences, of which the most inescapable occurs at l. 20: 'Whispers and small laughter between leaves and hurrying feet'; a co-operation with Ruskin's epic of the pine: 'those trees never heard human voice. . . No foot ever stirred fallen leaf of theirs' (VII.106).

Pound: *Yeux Glauques*: but also much else, e.g. *E. P.: Ode pour l'Election de son Sepulchre* is homage to, and therefore rescue from, Ruskin's critique of American culture: 'It is the new skill they have found there; – this skill of degradation. . . this is their speciality' (XXVII.216).

Owen: e.g. *Futility* l. 12: 'Was it for this the clay grew tall?' Compare *Crown of Wild Olive*, 11, 'discharge of artillery would merely knead down a certain quantity of red clay'. Also, *Strange Meeting* with its imagery of granite; and its 'sweet wells. . . too deep for taint' (35–6). To realise that Ruskin's context of 1866 is also Owen's context, is to realise that Ruskin's pure ferocity is not hysteria but prophecy: 'the welling of stainless water, trembling and pure, like a body of light. . . heaps of dust and slime, and broken shreds of old metal, and rags of putrid clothes' (*Crown of Wild Olive*, 1).

45 XXXV.18

46 XVII.60–1, 110; XXXIII.210; XXXIV.320. Luther defined man as a beast of burden to be ridden by God or the Devil in his *De Servo Arbitrio* (1525). He also perpetrated 'Away in a Manger'.

47 *Unto This Last*, 73.

48 Lionel Trilling, *Matthew Arnold*, 1949, p. 253.

49 *Two Paths*, 163; *Crown of Wild Olive*, 1, 100.
50 *Crown of Wild Olive*, 79, 118–19.
51 *Unto This Last*, 22–5, 79.
52 VII.361–2.
53 *Crown of Wild Olive*, 13, 16.
54 Derrick Leon, *Ruskin The Great Victorian*, 1949, p. 15.
55 *Paradise Lost* ix.838–42, 892–3, 911–13.
56 *The Divine Comedy of Dante Alighieri*, Italian text with translation and comment by John D. Sinclair, Oxford UP, 1971, II.357.
57 V. A. Burd, *John Ruskin and Rose La Touche*, pp. 96–8.
58 *The Tempest* V.i.201–2 (Gonzalo speaking). If 'this couple' requires identification, in Ruskin's life, they may be seen as his cousin Joan Agnew (later Severn) and Rose's brother Percy, who were for a time (till September 1867) engaged. Percy had four interests that came before Joan: fox hunting, salmon fishing, shooting and cricket (V. A. Burd, *John Ruskin and Rose La Touche*, p. 105). Joan was a rather distant cousin, but Ruskin eventually adopted her as his daughter. On 4 March 1868 Ruskin gave Joan a chess set, and invited her to 'reflect. . . That the worthiest person on the field is a woman' (XXXVI.548).
59 *The Tempest* V.i.30–2.
60 VI.85, 103 ('Of Turnerian Mystery').
61 *Acts* i.11. 'Joseph called Barsabas, who was surnamed Justus, and Matthias' are appointed as two possible successors to Judas, the final result to be determined by lot. The 'lot fell upon Matthias' – who is never heard of again. (*Acts* i, 23–6).

Chapter Twelve

1 Bernard Semmell, *The Governor Eyre Controversy*, 1962, pp. 25–7, 108–16, 169. Edward John Eyre, b. Whipsnade, Bedfordshire 1815. Shortly afterwards, Eyre's father became Vicar of Hornsea, Yorkshire. Eyre's grandfather, Anthony Fountayne Eyre was a canon of York. All this lent a local venom to the attack by Yorkshire Nonconformists on Eyre, who died 30 November 1901. Geoffrey Dutton, *The Hero as Murderer: The Life of Edward John Eyre*, 1967, p. 398.
2 John Ruskin, Letter to the *Daily Telegraph* 19 December 1865 (printed 20 December 1865) in response to 'the memorial you publish to-day from Huddersfield respecting the Jamaica Insurrection'. This memorial against Eyre was signed by 273 persons resident in and near Huddersfield, a town nine miles south of Bradford. James Hanson of the *Bradford Review* was born and brought up there. Ruskin's speech for the Eyre Defence and Aid Fund was delivered 7 September 1866, and reported *Daily Telegraph* 8.9.66. See: XVIII.550–4.
3 Presumably Alexander Carlyle DD (1772–1805), the Scottish divine and anecdotal writer; and Joseph Dacre Carlyle (1759–1804) the Arabic scholar and minor poet.
4 *BR* 25.8.66, 1.9.66; BO 16, 30.8.66, 13.9.66.
5 *Crown of Wild Olive* (published 14 May 1866), 76: 'But I can only at present suggest decorating its frieze with pendant purses. . . And I doubt not but that

people would come to see your exchange, and its goddess, with applause'. This appears *BA* 9.6.66 as 'A design by Mr. Ruskin for the Bradford Exchange'; but the editor, John Marshall Jowett, improves Ruskin by making the beginning into 'I suggest decorating. . . etc.'.

6 *Crown of Wild Olive*, 24–7, 33, 125, 131, printed as 'Leaves from *The Crown of Wild Olive*', *BO* 31.5.66. The adjacent column has a poem by 'William Matthews, New Leeds' (the slum half a mile further up Leeds Rd from Bradford Mechanics' Institute) on *Bolton Abbey: Past and Present*, with some wry and whimsical comments on progress and 'Modern Saints' who despise nature and the past. Byles demands no sympathy for *Traffic*; but Ruskin's question 'Shall Bolton priory [be in ruins] in its meadow, but these mills of yours. . . go on for ever?' (81) is brought a little nearer home to any Bradford reader who has access to the book. There would not be many. The Subscription Library Accession book notes that a copy of *The Crown of Wild Olive* was ordered 3 July 1866; but the book is not entered in the 1887 catalogue, which was intended to be complete. A new copy was not bought till 1898. This may be slip, sabotage or borrower's misbehaviour. It is not evidence for enthusiasm. The Mechanics' Institute Library also bought the book, or was presented with it (its price is not mentioned in their catalogue) in 1866, as far as can be judged. Borrowers were allowed seven days to read it.

7 *BO* 15, 22.11.66.

8 XXVIII.16 *Fors* 37. 3–4. See also above, Chapter 5, nn. 36–8.

9 XXVII.11, 623.

10 XIX.429–48; XVII.547–8.

11 *Heroes and Hero-Worship*, (1840–1) Lecture V.16.

12 *Fors Clavigera* 1.5.

13 XIX.429–30.

14 *Fors Clavigera* 1.10–11.

15 *Fors Clavigera* 2.19–21. William Francis Cowper (1811– 88) assumed the name 'Cowper-Temple' on inheriting the estates of his stepfather Lord Palmerston (1869), cr. Baron Mount-Temple 1880. In September 1871 he consented to become a trustee of Ruskin's St George's Fund (XXVII.159).

16 *Fors Clavigera*, 7.6 (July 1871). The Parisian Commune, proclaimed 28 March, had been put down 28 May 1871. Ruskin proclaims himself a 'communist of the old school' with a new political motto 'laissez *re-faire*' (2–3). At the Royal National Eisteddfod of Wales, Birkenhead 1917, Lever made 'an early public reference to the Six-Hour Day which was an industrial reform he would have dearly liked to bring about' (W. P. Jolly, *Lord Leverhulme*, 1976, p. 168).

17 Thomas Carlyle, *Past and Present* (1843) IV.iv.8. Compare *Past and Present* III.iv.8 ('Not "I can't eat!". . .) III.ii.4 ('There is endless hope in work, were it even work at making money'). Ruskin's strictures on Carlyle: letter to Charles Eliot Norton 10 March 1883. XXXVII.440–1.

18 *Fors Clavigera*, 73.8–11. Dated Venice 20 November 1876, published January 1877, as the first of a new volume in which Ruskin intends 'speaking directly, in every letter, to the Yorkshire operatives, and answering every question they choose to put to me, – being very sure that they will omit few relevant ones'.

19 'I was out early this morning taking a walk which a person of your poetical temperament would have been delighted with, the only thing that particularly interested *me*, was the dew upon a cabbage' (John Ruskin to W. H. Harrison, 'Fribourg 31st August [1854]', John Rylands Library, Manchester Eng. MSS.1250.

20 'The sea has such a harsh-practical body of rebuke – and massy commonsense about it – I cannot conceive anything more adverse to Gothic pinnacles than its wild rough-level unity' (John Ruskin to W. H. Harrison 30 October [1851]. Source as for letter above. Published M. Hardman, 'Ruskin's "Massy Commonsense"', *British Journal of Aesthetics*, spring 1976, p. 138).

21 Lady Waterford: Virginia Surtees, *Sublime and Instructive*, pp. 1–77. The Bishop of Manchester (Dr. James Fraser): XXVIII.243; XXIX.95; XXXIV.xxxvi. Prince Leopold: XX.xxxvi; XXXVII.273, 393.

22 XXIX.398, edd's n.

23 Timothy Hilton, *The Pre-Raphaelites*, 1970, p. 89.

24 *Matthew* X.34, XVIII.4, *Luke* XII.29. Ruskin's notes on the Greek text in his 1859 Notebook at Bembridge, p. 149/171 (double numbering system). Fuller discussion: M. Hardman, 'The prose and ideas of John Ruskin', unpublished Cambridge PhD dissertation, 1975, pp. 180–3.

25 John Ruskin to Henry Acland 27 April 1856. XXXVI.239.

26 *Fors Clavigera*, 78.1 (June 1877): '"Was the leisure of the Greeks not owing to the hard work of the helots and slaves they had?" asked my old friend, Thomas Dixon, in his letter given last month. Yes, truly, good labourer. . .'

27 J. H. Whitehouse, *Ruskin Centenary Addresses*, Oxford 1919, p. 65.

28 Robert Blatchford, *Merrie England*, 1894; *Dismal England* 1899. Blatchford, Morris, Ruskin and Carlyle were often cited in radical papers of the turn-of-the-century, such as the *Bradford Socialist Vanguard*.

29 XXIX.511–12 (October 1884). Compare XVIII.35–6.

30 XXXIV.533; XIX.173 (the Rede Lecture, Cambridge 1867).

Chapter Thirteen

1 XXXV.642.

2 *Crown of Wild Olive*, 69.

3 *Unto This Last*, 64.

4 *The Vision of Dante Alighieri*, translated (1819), H. F. Cary, *Inferno* ix. 76–111 (1908, p. 37).

5 '. . . mi fece discoperto / Quel color che l'inferno mi nascose' (*Purgatorio* I.128–9). Compare: 'the selling of clothes, old, or new, has never taken any colour of magnanimity. Yet one does not see why. . .' (*Crown of Wild Olive*, 74). The phrase 'colour of magnanimity' brings together Dante's 'colour', as above and at *Paradiso*, XXXIII.130; and the 'magnanimity' of Aristote's *Ethics* (1107.b.17, etc.). 'Colour' and 'magnanimity' can be speciously forced together 'when the whole world turns clown, and paints itself red with its own heart's blood' (*Crown of Wild Olive*, 59), but Bradford is invited to look deeper than the specious, into 'that kind of marble, crimson-veined' (84). The phrase 'colour of magnanimity' was not achieved till the final proof correction from 'heroic colour'.

6 XXII.xxiii-iv; XXXVII.48.
7 XXXIII.488 *Pleasures of England*, 98.
8 Mansbridge, p. 131.
9 XVIII.396.
10 *Acts*. 17.xxii-xxxiv.
11 *Eumenides*. 970.
12 The Parthenon became a Christian church; but after the fifteenth century Turkish conquest a mosque and later a powder magazine, which was detonated by the Venetian Morosini in 1687.
13 VII.402, 408; 384–5.
14 Above, Ch. 7, n.17.
15 VII.413. The monument to William Sharp (obit. 1833) by Joseph Gott (1786–1860) was dismantled and scrapped, all but the medallion of Sharp and the inscription, during the restoration of the early 1960s. Information from S. J. K. Baker, Esq., of Bradford. See above, Ch. 10, n. 142.
16 *The Divine Comedy of Dante Alighieri, Purgatorio* xxxiii.130–5, translated J. D. Sinclair, 1948. Compare: *Jeremiah* 9.xi; *Revelation* 12.
17 *Wasps*. 666–724, 1114–19. For Ruskin's acquaintance with this play, see: IV.114, ed's n. Ruskin cites Achilles' 'indignant epithet of base kings, "people-eating"', *Sesame and Lilies*. 48, and elsewhere. Ruskin noted Homer's epithet (*Iliad* i.231) in his 1863 notebook at about the same time (February–April) as he was translating the passage from the end of the *Critias* which he would use in *Traffic*.
18 John Ruskin to Susan Beever Bolton Bridge 23 January 1875; Castleton, 26 January 1875. Compare: *Fors Clavigera* 50.16, dated 'Castleton 27th January [1875]'.
19 XXII.509–11, 537–8.
20 Margaret McMillan, *The Life of Rachel McMillan*, pp. 75– 83.
21 Mansbridge, p. 34. XXVII.164; XXIX.23 *Fors* 9.19. 73.23.
22 XXIX.304; XXII.528.
23 E. T. Cook, *Manchester Guardian* 22.1.00: 'Mr. Ruskin accepted a call to "create" the part of Art Professor.'
24 XXIV.371–2 *St. Mark's Rest*, 209-10.
25 So the editions. But 'heathy' would have point, and Ruskin never writes without point.
26 'John Ruskin: Social Reformer' BY AN ADMIRER, *Bolton Journal and Guardian*, 27.1.00.
27 XVII.9.
28 Margaret McMillan, The Life of Rachel McMillan, p. 82.
29 K. O. Morgan, *Keir Hardie*, pp. 7, 211.
30 Above, Ch. 10, n. 79.
31 XXIX.380, seq.
32 XXIX.528.
33 Above, Ch. 2, n. 20.
34 *Sheffield Daily Telegraph* 28.4.76: 'Last evening about twenty persons assembled at the New Museum. . . for the purpose of hearing Mr. Ruskin's opinions. . . and of giving their own. . . Primarily the subject of Communism came up, and its most extreme principles were freely and enthusiastically advocated

by one or two of those present' (quoted XXX.306, n.).

35 Above, Ch. 5, n. 2.

36 XII.38–9, *Lectures on Architecture and Painting* (1854) 19.

37 Henry Pelling, *A History of British Trade Unionism*, Harmondsworth 1963, pp. 108, 258.

38 David Lowe, *From Pit to Parliament: The Story of the Early Life of James Keir Hardie*, 1923, pp. 50–1.

39 The chimneys, railway-sidings and 'works', with their 'portholes numberless of black square window', at Amiens: *The Bible of Amiens*, 4 (XXXIII.28). 'The Tanneries and cotton mills' of Lucca: *Diaries*, p. 1033 (15 October 1882). In medieval times, there was a certain volume of trade between Bradford and Lucca; and Bradford had a bridge-chapel to 'St Sitha', a local amalgamation of Sta Zita of Lucca, patroness of servants, and the Saxon St Ositha, patroness of lost things. See: B. C. Tempest, 'The Chapel of St Ositha', *Bradford Antiquary* III.251–5. The St Sitha chapel is mentioned by Leland, Henry VIII's Antiquary; but seems to have disappeared with the Reformation (see: J. Fieldhouse, *Bradford*, 1972, p. 44). Given Ruskin's devotion to Sta Zita (XXXII.67, seq) it would be amusing to imagine his reaction to this connection.

40 XXVII.381 & edd's n.

41 XIV.358–9 *The Black Arts*, 1.

42 XVII.248 (quoting Carlyle's *Latter-Day Pamphlets*, VI; and alluding to *Republic* 590.c); XXXV.17, & R's. n.

43 BO 26.1.00.

44 Arthur Marsh, *Trade Union Handbook*, Teakfield, Hants, 1979, p. 39.

45 *Halifax Guardian* 27.1.00. The chairman of Halifax School Board had no connection with the John Mitchell who was Ruskin's host in 1859.

46 Ruskin was 'sincerely grateful for the honour' and 'declined. . . with. . . regret'. Letter published *The Times* 16.4.83; reprinted *Ruskiniana*, 1890 (XXXIV.563).

47 XXXIII.275–7, 287 *The Art of England*, 14–15, 31.

48 David Hartley, *Observations on Man* (1749), reprinted Gainesville 1966, I.512. Hartley's letters to his schoolfriend Rev. John Lister of Shibden Hall are now in Halifax Public Library. The above quotation from the *Observations* comes from the end of the first volume. As he embarked on his second volume, Hartley wrote (1748) to Lister: 'The Resurrection of the Body seems an equivalent expression to a future state in the new Testament'.

49 This extract from the Gondal Poems is No. 747 in A. Quiller-Couch, *Oxford Book of English Verse*, 1957.

50 *Fortunes Made in Business* (1884–7) by Various Writers. The first two memoirs are of Isaac Holden, Lister's partner, who added a handsome Wesleyan Chapel to the architectural glories of Rheims, and of Lister himself. See also: *Dictionary of National Biography*; J. Fieldhouse, *Bradford*, pp. 148–51.

51 *Telegraph and Argus Centenary Supplement* 16 July 1968. The Parnell scandal 'ran' from late November 1890 till June 1891, when, politically ruined, he married his mistress Mrs Kitty O'Shea.

52 David Thomson, *England in the Nineteenth Century*, Harmondsworth 1950, pp. 187, 193. Old age pensions, labour exchanges and national health insurance

were among the reforms.

53 Above, Ch. 1, n. 13.

54 Keith Laybourn, 'The defence of the bottom dog: The Independent Labour Party in local politics', *Victorian Bradford*, Bradford 1982, pp. 223–40.

55 Margaret McMillan, *The Life of Rachel McMillan*, pp. 86– 90, A. Mansbridge, *Margaret McMillan*, p. 35.

56 S. E. De Morgan, 'Playgrounds for Poor Children', *Good Words*, 1 November 1867, p. 727.

57 John Ruskin to *Pall Mall Gazette*, 4.1.86 (XXXIV.582).

58 Margaret McMillan, *The Life of Rachel McMillan*, pp. 114–16, 130. Mansbridge, pp. 35–6, 75, 90.

59 Keith Laybourn, *Victorian Bradford*, p. 241, quoting *The Last Issue of the Bottom Dog*, (Sept–Oct 1923), quoting *Crown of Wild Olive*, 75.

60 Henry Pelling, ed. *The Challenge of Socialism*, 1954, pp. 310–11.

61 *The Two Paths*, 79. Compare: Jacob Epstein, *Epstein: an Autobiography*, 1963, pp. 107–11, 263–9; A. Fenner Brockway, *Socialism over Sixty Years*, pp. 213–23. James Bone's approval of Jowett's rescue of Nurse Cavell from her idolators: *Glasgow Herald* 5 February 1924.

62 VII.316 *Modern Painters*, Pt. IX.v.3. Catalogue of the Turner Sketches in the National Gallery (1857) (XIII.189–90). James Charles's letter on 'Ruskin and the Painters of Today' (BO 26.1.00) is quite as garbled on Ruskin's notions of 'finish' as anything exhaled from Bloomsbury, but Charles did praise Ruskin's life 'so regulated as to leave vivid and living memories behind him'.

63 *Henry Moore*: photographed and edited by John Hedgecoe, words by Henry Moore, 1968, pp. 37, 81, 481. Philip James, ed., *Henry Moore on Sculpture*, 1966, p. 194.

64 William Rothenstein, *Men and memories*, III (1939), 147– 52. J. H. Whitehouse, *Ruskin the Painter and his Works at Bembridge*, Oxford 1938, p. 140.

65 *Henry Moore*, pp. 17, 31–2, 81, 329. *Henry Moore on Sculpture*, p. 34. Compare: *Henry Moore*, p. 121: 'Art tends to arrive at a true result through instinct', with XVIII.167: 'in the doers of the best, there is an inner and voluntary power which approximates literally to the instinct of an animal'; and *Henry Moore*, p. 56: 'And as I began to find out that, in Nature, living things. . . are never perfectly symmetrical this principle became fundamental to my work', with XVI.330 (Bradford 1859): 'One great good arises from the first step in figure drawing, that it gets the student quit at once of the notion of formal symmetry'.

66 Moritz Rothenstein's letter to William Foster of Black Dyke Mills, written from 10 Howard St, Bradford, 26 July 1859, offering his services as foreign correspondent, is preserved in the Foster Collection, Brotherton Library, Leeds.

67 William Rothenstein, *Men and Memories*, I (1931), 20–1, 139–41, 229–231. In 1900 Rothenstein painted Ruskin's friend F. J. Furnivall (pp. 367–8).

68 *Henry Moore*, p. 81. *Henry Moore on Sculpture*, p. 190. R. Speaight, *William Rothenstein*, 1962, p. 379.

69 *Henry Moore*, pp. 8–9. For the rocky outcrop at Adel and '2-piece Reclining Figure Nos. 1 & 2 (1959, 1960),' see: *Henry Moore on Sculpture*, pp. 51, 241, Illustrs. pp. 266–71.

70 *Henry Moore*, pp. 12, 27, IV.122; XXXV.350. John Ruskin to Mrs Severn, Messina 28 April 1874: XXXVII.95.

71 Quoted, Herbert Read, *A Concise History of Modern Sculpture*, 1964, pp. 163, 272–4 (the book leaves the last word to Ruskin).

72 VIII.138 *Seven Lamps*, Beauty, 1.

73 *Henry Moore*, pp. 14, 80, 292–5. *The Morning Post*, 11 April 1931 (unfavourable critique of Moore).

74 William Rothenstein, in *To The Memory of Ruskin*, edited J. H. Whitehouse, Cambridge 1934, p. 18.

75 *Henry Moore*, pp. 159, 352.

76 Herbert Read, *The Tenth Muse*, 1957, p. 322, also p. 17: 'I would place Ruskin's achievement above all other criticism of whatever kind written in the English language'. Kenneth Clark, Introduction to Catalogue, Arts Council Exhibition, *Drawings of Ruskin*, 1960: 'I believe that [Ruskin] ranks high among the English water-colourists of the nineteenth century, and considerably higher than many of those artists who have dismissed him as a mere critic'. John Rothenstein, *Autobiography* III (1970) 48, writes that Kenneth Clark's 'urge to share his knowledge and experience with a very wide public has increased. This change owes much, perhaps, to the influence of Ruskin, to whose writings he has devoted sustained and intensive study and whose social preoccupations have affected his outlook.'

77 *Fors Clavigera* 50.16.

78 Barbara Hepworth, *A Pictorial Autobiography*, Bath 1970, pp. 7–21, and Illustr. 49. Compare above, Ch. 5, n. 11.

79 IV.77, 173, 251 *Modern Painters* Pt. III, Sect I.v.2, xiii.12; Sect II.iii.4.

80 *Winnington Letters*. p. 102 National Dictionary of Biography under Dawson and Sedgwick. Charles Darwin, *Origin of Species*, 1885 edition, p. 282. Adam Sedgwick (1785–1873) Ruskin first met at Oxford in 1847, and warmly commemorated before the Kendal Literary and Scientific Institution, 1 October 1877 (XXVI.243).

81 Wright began work at six as a donkey-boy in a Bradford quarry. In 1862, at seven, he became a half-timer at Salt's Mill, attending the Saltaire Schools in the afternoons. He attended evening classes at Bradford Mechanics' Institute and the Yorkshire College, Leeds; and in 1876 having saved £40 spent a short time at Heidelberg. He became an external London University student in 1878, gained a PhD at Heidelberg in Comparitive Philology (1885), and in 1891 was appointed Deputy Professor, and in 1901, Professor, of Comparitive Philology at Oxford. His *English Dialect Dictionary* appeared 1896–1905. For a letter from J. R. R. Tolkien to his old Professor, see E. M. Wright, *The Life of Joseph Wright*, 1932, II.651.

82 XIX.xxvi.

83 VII.59–60.

84 T. R. Ashenhurst, Headmaster, Textile Dept., Bradford Technical College, *Design in Textile Fabrics*, 1883, p. 1. C. Stephenson, Bradford Technical College, & F. Suddards, Yorkshire College Leeds, *A Text Book Dealing with Ornamental Design for Woven Fabrics*, 1897, pp. 100, 162, 170. A. F. Barker, Head of Textile Industries, Bradford Technical College, *Textile Design*, 1903, pp. xi, xvi, 22, 193. A. F. Barker,

Professor of Textiles, University of Leeds, *Ornamentation and Texile Design*, 1930, ab init., and pp. xv-xvi, 20, 31. Alfred Tennyson, *Tithonus*, init. Euripides, *Bacchae*, 174–6.

85 Ted Hughes, *Poetry in the Making*, 1967, pp. 15–17. *The Two Paths*, 83. See also above, Ch. 2, n. 17.

86 Above, Ch. 10, n. 127.

87 As above, n. 74.

88 Mortimer Wheeler, *Still Digging*, p. 20. The date was 1905, and the master was J. F. Barton.

89 *Bradford Telegraph and Argus Centenary Supplement* 16 July 1968.

90 *David Hockney by David Hockney*, ed. Nikos Stangos, 1976. David Hockney, individual contribution to *All Bull: The National Servicemen*, ed. B. S. Johnson, 1973, pp. 243–7. See also XXXIV.727. (Whitman); Chandra Kumar & Mohinder Puri, *Mahatma Gandhi*, 1982, p. 53.

91 XVII.cxi-ii.

92 Arthur Marsh, *Trade Union Handbook*, 1979, pp. 3–4, 9, 39.

93 Eric Silver, *Vic Feather, T.U.C.: the biography of Lord Feather*, 1973, pp. 129–63.

94 BBC Radio 4 broadcast 10 April 1978, 10.30 pm.

95 Humbert Wolfe, *News of the Devil*, 1926, pp. 16, 25, 37. Compare: XXIX.415, n.

96 B. Seebohm Rowntree, *The Human Factor in Business*, 1921, p. viii. See also above, Chapter 10. n. 181.

97 *The Dalesman*, July 1979, pp. 296–7.

98 J. B. Priestley, *Victoria's Heyday*, 1972, p. 181.

SELECT SOURCES

The following is not intended to be exhaustive. Works of very general application, and specifically local monographs and pamphlets, etc., while mentioned where appropriate in the notes, are for the most part not also included here. Apart from the *Bradford Advertiser*, which is at the British Newspaper Library, Colindale, the bulk of the local Bradford material derives from the *Local Studies Collection, Bradford City Libraries.*

Manuscript and Rare Book Collections

Bembridge School, Isle of Wight. Ruskin Galleries

MS letter John Ruskin to William Richardson, 21 April 1864.

MS note John Ruskin to Richard Owen, 16 December [1865].

Ruskin's Notebooks:

Volume xi: a vellum-covered book 8 by 6½ inches, with entries for 1856-9; and a note dated '21st. Dec. 1865'.

Volume xii: a vellum-covered book 8½ by 6½ inches, with entries for 1861-3, and some few notes March-June 1864.

Typewritten transcripts of three Ruskin juvenile note books ('The Red Books'):

(1) Ruled notebook (1826-7) containing 'Harry and Lucy' and six poems by Ruskin.

(2) Home-made plain paper book (1828) containing poems, letters, sermon notes, and part of 'Harry and Lucy'.

(3) Ruled notebook (1827-9), with title-page in Ruskin's hand: 'harry going across the sea in a steamboat', with pencil drawing of steamboat. Contains several Ruskin poems and the continuation of 'Harry and Lucy'.

The originals of the above are all in the Beinecke Rare Book and Manuscript Library, Yale University Library.

Bodleian Library, Oxford.

Typewritten transcript of Ruskin's note of November 1858 to Mrs John Simon. MS in Cornell University Library.

John Ruskin to Mrs John Simon, Winnington, 11 March 1859.

Bradford Art Galleries and Museums, Cartwright Hall, Bradford.

Biographical material on James Lobley.

Bradford City Hall

Nineteenth-century Minute Books of Bradford Watch Committee.

Bradford Mechanics' Institute Library
Minuted catalogues, covering the Victorian period.
Bradford Subscription Library, Darley St, Bradford.
Catalogues, Minute Books, Accession Books, covering the Victorian period.
British Library, Bloomsbury, London.
Aristotle, *Ethica Nicomachea*, edited by John Brewer, London 1836, with Ruskin drawings and MS marginalia.
Thomas Carlyle, *Past and Present*, London 1843, with MS notes by Ruskin and presentation letter, in Ruskin's hand, to Alfred Magee, dated Brantwood 10 January 1887.
Letters from Ruskin to F. J. Furnivall, in the Ashley Collection.
Letters from John James Ruskin to Sir Robert Peel, and of Peel to Arbuthnot, 1844, in the Peel Papers.
Brotherton Library, University of Leeds.
Letter Books of John Foster, of Black Dyke Mills, Queensbury.
Halifax Public Library: Archive of Dr Hartley's letters to Rev. John Lister.
Nineteenth-century Letter Books of Clay's of Rastrick.
London School of Economics: Letters of Fanny Hertz, the Bradford Positivist, to Frederick Harrison.
Sheffield: St George's Guild Collection, Ruskin Gallery, Sheffield.
Twelve letters in Ruskin's hand to Alfred Harris.
John Ruskin to Juliet Tylor, St Alban's, 20 April 1876, in the Tylor Collection of letters.
Walworth Public Library, London.
Minutes of the Camberwell Roadworks Committee for the early 1860s.

Picture, Pattern, and Stained-glass Collections

Ashridge Repository
HM Patent Office: Victorian carpet designs of John Crossley and Sons and Robert Crossley, Halifax.
Bembridge School, Isle of Wight, Ruskin Galleries
J. Ruskin, *Rheinfelden* ink, watercolour and pencil, 1858. Inscribed in Ruskin's hand 'Rheinfelden 1858. I never did nor shall do better. I think its violet carmine faded. J. Ruskin, Brantwood 1879'.
Birmingham City Museums and Art Gallery
J. Lobley, *The Free Seat* oil on panel 21¾ x 33¼ inches.
D. G. Rossetti, *Morning Music* watercolour 16¼ x 13½ inches. 1867.
Provenance: Walter Dunlop, Bingley.
D. G. Rossetti, Pencil Study for *Regina Cordium* (1861), the oil portrait of Mrs J. A. Heaton, now the property of her great-granddaughter Mrs L. D. Jackson. Pencil 8¾ x 8¾ inches. 1861.
Boston: Isabella Stewart Gardner Museum.
D. G. Rossetti, *Love's Greeting* oil on panel 22¼ x 24 inches. 1861.
Provenance: Walter Dunlop, Bingley.
Bournemouth: The Russell Cotes Gallery.

D. G. Rossetti, *Venus Verticordia* oil 32 x 27 inches. 1864–9. Provenance: John Mitchell.

Bradford City Art Galleries and Museums

J. Lobley, *The Dole, Stow Church* oil on panel 19⅞ x 28 inches. Signed: J. Lobley. Exhibited Royal Academy 1867.

J. Lobley, *Little Nell Leaving the Church (The Old Curiosity Shop)*

Oil on canvas 52¾ x 29½ inches. Signed and dated: J. Lobley 1867.

Exhibited Royal Academy 1867.

J. Lobley, 6 *Ragged School Studies* pencil and watercolour. Exhibited Bradford Mechanics' Institute 1873.

J. Lobley, *The Village Guy Fawkes* watercolour 5½ x 10½ inches. Signed and dated: J. Lobley 1877.

Morris, Marshall, Faulkner & Co., *The Story of Tristram and Isoude* (1862), a series of thirteen stained-glass panels made for Walter Dunlop, Harden Grange, Bingley. Between 26¾ – 30¼ x 23¾ – 28¼ inches.

(1) Arthur Hughes. (2) and (4) D. G. Rossetti. (3) Val Prinsep. (5)–(8) & (11) E. Burne-Jones. (9), (12), (13) W. Morris. (10) F. Madox Brown.

Abraham and Isaac Designed by D. G. Rossetti, 1873, 76 x 52¾ inches.

The above panel on long loan from the Vicar and Churchwardens, Holy Trinity, Bingley.

British Museum Print Room:

J. M. W. Turner, Sketchbook 1797, 14⅝ x 10½ inches. Inscribed on cover 'Yorkshire Tweed Lakes of Cumberland-Westmoreland Lancashire York'. Contains the sketch of Kirkstall Abbey Crypt, the basis of Plate XXXIX of Liber Studiorum.

Brooklyn Museum, New York.

D. G. Rossetti, *Silence* black and red chalk 41½ x 31½ inches. 1870.

Provenance: Sold by Murray Marks to J. A. Heaton without Rossetti's knowledge; bought back by Rossetti and re-sold to Charles Rowley, 1876.

Halifax Public Library

Victorian pattern-books of Clay's of Rastrick

Manchester City Art Galleries

J. E. Millais, *A Flood* oil on canvas 39⅛ x 57⅙ inches. 1870.

D. G. Rossetti, *The Bower Meadow* oil 33½ x 26½ inches. 1872. Provenance: Walter Dunlop of Bingley.

Michigan University Museum of Art, Ann Arbor.

D. G. Rossetti, *Winifred Heaton* pencil 19¼ x 14⅛ inches. 1861. Provenance: J. A. Heaton.

Oldham Art Gallery and Museum

D. G. Rossetti. *The First Madness of Ophelia* watercolour 15½ x 11½ inches. Monogram and date: 'April 1864'. Provenance: Walter Dunlop, Bingley.

Saltaire

Titus Salt's 1853 Album of Patterns.

Tate Gallery, London

D. G. Rossetti, *Dante's Vision of Rachel and Leah* watercolour 14 x 12½ inches. 1855.

Dante's Dream at the Time of the Death of Beatrice watercolour 18½ x 25¾ inches. 1856.

Mary in the House of St John watercolour 18 x 14 inches, 1859.

St George and the Princess Sabra watercolour. 20⅝ x 12⅛ inches, 1862.

Bethlehem Gate oil 17 x 14½ inches 1863.
Woman in Yellow watercolour and pencil 16¼ x 12¾ inches, 1863.
How Sir Galahad, Sir Bors and Sir Percival were Fed with Sanc Grael; But Sir Percival's Sister Died by the Way watercolour 20¼ x 21¾ inches 1864.
Joan of Arc watercolour 20¼ x 21¾ inches, 1864.
A. Hughes, *The Dismissal of Romney* oil on panel 11¾ x 15¼ inches, 1860.
That was a Piedmontese. . . oil on mahogany 16 x 12 inches, 1862.
All the above bequeathed by Ellen Heaton's nephew, B. R. Heaton, 1940.
Victoria and Albert Museum, London.
Seven wallpaper designs by J. Aldam Heaton.

Published Sources

Ayers, Jane and John, *Bradford Old and New*, Wakefield 1976.
Ayers, John, *Architecture in Bradford*, Bradford 1972.
Ball, P. M., *The Science of Aspects*, London 1971.
Baker, A. F., *Ornamentation and Textile Design*, London 1930.
Bower, J. S., *Hartley and James Mill*, London 1881.
Bradford Antiquary
Bradford Corporation, *Education in Bradford since 1870, Bradford* 1970.
Bradford in the Nineteenth Century: shown in maps. City of Bradford Metropolitan Council; Libraries Division, Local Studies Department, 1975.
Bradford Studies: An Annotated Bibliography, edited by G. F. Nowell and C. Richardson, Bradford 1969.
Bradley, J. L., ed. *Ruskin's Letters from Venice* 1851-2, New Haven 1955.
Bradley, J. L., ed. *Ruskin: The Critical Heritage*, London 1984.
Briggs, Asa, *Victorian Cities*, Harmondsworth 1963.
Brockway, A. Fenner, *Socialism over Sixty Years; the Life of Fred Jowett of Bradford*, London 1946.
Burd, V. A., ed. *John Ruskin and Rose La Touche, Her Unpublished Diaries of 1861 and* 1867, Oxford 1979.
Burd, V. A., ed. *The Ruskin Family Letters*, 2 volumes, Ithaca and London 1973.
Burd, V. A., ed. *The Winnington Letters of John Ruskin*, London 1969.
Burnley, J. *Phases of Bradford Life*, London and Bradford 1860.
Byles, H. N., *William Byles: by His Youngest Son*, Weymouth 1932.
Callen, A. *Angel in the Studio*, London 1979.
Collingwood, W. G., *The Life of John Ruskin*, 7th edition, London 1911.
Cudworth, William, *Historical Notes on the Bradford Corporation*, Bradford 1881.
Doughty, O., and Wahl, J. R., eds. *Letters of Dante Gabriel Rossetti*, 4 volumes, Oxford 1965–7.
Fieldhouse, J., *Bradford*, London 1972.
Finberg, A. J., *The Life of J. M. W. Turner, R.A.*, ed. Hilda F. Finberg, second edition, Oxford 1961.
Fortunes Made in Business, by Various Authors, 3 volumes, London 1884–7.
Fraser, Derek, ed. *A History of Modern Leeds*, Manchester 1980.
Fraser, Derek, *Urban Politics in Victorian England*, Leicester 1976.

Gropius, Walter, *The New Architecture and the Bauhaus*, trans. P. Morton Shand, London, 1965.
Harris, Alfred, *The Revival of Industries in Ireland*, Kirkby Lonsdale 1888.
Hartley, David, *Observations on Man* (1749) reprinted, two volumes in one, with an introduction by Theodore L. Huguelet, Gainesville 1966.
Healey, E., *Picturesque Views of Castles and Country Houses in Yorkshire*, Bradford 1885.
Heaton, J. Aldam, *Beauty and Art*, London 1897.
Helsinger, E. K., *Ruskin and the Art of the Beholder*, Cambridge, Mass. and London 1982.
Hepworth, Barbara, *A Pictorial Autobiography*, Bath 1970.
Hilton, Timothy, *John Ruskin: the Early Years*, London 1985.
Hilton, Timothy, *The Pre-Raphaelites*, London 1970.
Hockney, David, *David Hockney by David Hockney*, ed. Nikos Stangos, London 1976.
Hughes, Ted. *Poetry in the Making*, London 1967.
James, John, *Continuations to the History and Topography of Bradford*, Bradford 1866, republished Manchester 1973.
James, John, *The History and Topography of Bradford*, London and Bradford 1841.
Linstrum, Derek, *Historic Architecture of Leeds*, Newcastle 1969.
Linstrum, Derek, *West Yorkshire: Architects and Architecture*, London 1978.
Lobley, James 1828–1888: Paintings and Watercolours, Bradford Art Galleries and Museums, 26 February–24 April 1983, catalogue and introduction by Caroline Krzesinska, foreword by Robert Hopper.
Lutyens, Mary, ed. *The Ruskins and the Grays*, London 1972.
McMillan, Margaret, *The Life of Rachel McMillan*, London 1927.
Maidment, Brian, 'Ruskin, *Fors Clavigera* and Ruskinism 1870–1900', in *New Approaches to Ruskin* edited by Robert Hewison, London 1981.
Maidment, Brian, 'Interpreting Ruskin 1870–1914', in *The Ruskin Polygon*, ed. J. D. Hunt and F. M. Holland, Manchester 1982.
Mansbridge, A., *Margaret McMillan*, London 1932.
Maurice, C. E., *The Life of Octavia Hill from her Letters*, London 1913.
Maurice, E. S., editor, *Octavia Hill: Early Ideals*, London 1928.
Moore, Henry, *Henry Moore on Sculpture*, edited by Philip James, London 1966.
Moore, Henry, *Henry Moore*: photographed and edited by John Hedgecoe, words by Henry Moore, London 1968.
Morgan, K. O., *Keir Hardie*, London 1975.
Payne, Brian and Dorothy, 'Extracts from the Journals of John Deakin Heaton, M.D.', *Publications of the Thoresby Society*, LIII, Pt. 2, No. 117, Leeds 1973.
Pelling, Henry, *A History of British Trade Unionism*, Harmondsworth 1963.
Pelling, Henry, ed. *The Challenge of Socialism*, London 1954.
Pevsner, N., *The Buildings of England: Yorkshire, The West Riding*, Harmondsworth 1959, second edition 1967.
Priestley, J. B. *Victoria's Heyday*, London 1972.
Ransford, O., *David Livingstone: The Dark Interior*, London 1978.
Read, Herbert, *A Concise History of Modern Sculpture*, London 1964.
Reid, T. Wemyss, *Life of the Rt. Hon. William Edward Forster*, 2 volumes, London 1888.
Roberts, J. S., *Little Germany*, Bradford 1977.
Rosenberg, J. D., *The Darkening Glass*, London 1963.

Rossetti, Helen Maria Madox, *Pre-Raphaelite Twilight*, London 1954.
Rothenstein, W., *Men and Memories*, 3 volumes, London 1931–9.
Ruskin, J., *The Diaries of John Ruskin*, selected and edited by Joan Evans and John Howard Whitehouse, 3 volumes, Oxford UP 1956–9.
Ruskin, J. *The Works of John Ruskin*, edited by E. T. Cook and A. Wedderburn, 39 volumes, London 1903–12.
Saint, Andrew, *Richard Norman Shaw*, New Haven and London 1976.
Scruton, William, *Pen and Pencil Sketches of Old Bradford*, Bradford 1889.
Semmell, B., *The Governor Eyre Controversy*, London 1962.
Sewter, A. Charles, *The Stained Glass of William Morris and his Circle*, New Haven and London 1974.
Silver, Eric, *Vic Feather, T.U.C.*, London 1973.
Speight, Harry, *Chronicles and Stories of Old Bingley*, London 1898.
Surtees, Virginia, *The Paintings and Drawings of Dante Gabriel Rossetti (1828–1882): A Catalogue Raisonné*, Oxford UP 1971.
Surtees, Virginia, ed. *Sublime and Instructive: Letters from John Ruskin to Lousia, Marchioness of Waterford, Anna Blunden and Ellen Heaton*, London 1972.
Transactions of the National Association for the Promotion of Social Science for 1859, London 1860.
Tylor, Alfred, *Education and Manufactures*, London 1863.
Weerth, Georg, *Vergessene Texte*, in zwei Bänden, C. W. Leske, Köln 1975.
Whitehouse, J. H., ed. *Ruskin Centenary Addresses*, Oxford 1919.
Whitehouse, J. H., ed. *To the Memory of Ruskin*, Cambridge 1934.
Wolfe, Humbert, *News of the Devil*, London 1926.
Wright, D. G. and Jowitt, J. A., eds, *Victorian Bradford*, Bradford 1982.

INDEX